WESTERN HEMISPHERE

AUTHORS

Dr. Gary S. Elbow
Professor of Geography
Texas Tech University
Lubbock, TX

Dr. Gerald Michael Greenfield
Professor and Director, Center for
International Studies
University of Wisconsin – Parkside
Kenosha, WI

SERIES CONSULTANTS

Dr. James F. Baumann
Professor of Reading Education
Associate Director, National Reading Research Center
The University of Georgia
Athens, GA

Dr. Theodore Kaltsounis
Professor of Social Studies Education
University of Washington
Seattle, WA

LITERATURE CONSULTANTS

Dr. Ben A. Smith
Assistant Professor of Social Studies Education
Kansas State University
Manhattan, KS

Dr. John C. Davis
Professor of Elementary Education
University of Southern Mississippi
Hattiesburg, MS

Dr. Jesse Palmer
Assistant Professor, Department of Curriculum and Instruction
University of Southern Mississippi
Hattiesburg, MS

COVER PHOTOGRAPH
Temple of the Warrior Chac Mool, Chichén Itzá, Yucatán, Mexico

SILVER BURDETT GINN

MORRISTOWN, NJ • NEEDHAM, MA
Atlanta, GA • Deerfield, IL • Irving, TX • San Jose, CA

SERIES AUTHORS

Dr. W. Frank Ainsley, Professor of Geography, University of North Carolina, Wilmington, NC

Dr. Herbert J. Bass, Professor of History, Temple University, Philadelphia, PA

Dr. Kenneth S. Cooper, Professor of History, Emeritus, George Peabody College for Teachers, Vanderbilt University, Nashville, TN

Dr. Claudia Crump, Professor of Elementary Social Studies Education, Indiana University Southeast, New Albany, IN

Dr. Gary S. Elbow, Professor of Geography, Texas Tech University, Lubbock, TX

Roy Erickson, Program Specialist, K12 Social Studies and Multicultural Education San Juan Unified School District, Carmichael, CA

Dr. Daniel B. Fleming, Professor of Social Studies Education, Virginia Polytechnic Institute and State University, Blacksburg, VA

Dr. Gerald Michael Greenfield, Professor and Director, Center for International Studies, University of Wisconsin — Parkside, Kenosha, WI

Dr. Linda Greenow, Associate Professor of Geography, SUNY — The College at New Paltz, New Paltz, NY

Dr. William W. Joyce, Professor of Education, Michigan State University, East Lansing, MI

Dr. Gail S. Ludwig, Former Geographer-in-Residence, National Geographic Society, Geography Education Program, Washington, D.C.

Dr. Michael B. Petrovich, Professor Emeritus of History, University of Wisconsin, Madison, WI

Dr. Norman J. G. Pounds, Former University Professor of History and Geography, Indiana University, Bloomington, IN

Dr. Arthur Roberts, Professor of Education, University of Connecticut, Storrs, CT

Dr. Christine L. Roberts, Professor of Education, University of Connecticut, Storrs, CT

Parke Rouse, Jr., Virginia Historian and Retired Executive Director of the Jamestown-Yorktown Foundation, Williamsburg, VA

Dr. Paul C. Slayton, Jr., Distinguished Professor of Education, Mary Washington College, Fredericksburg, VA

Dr. Edgar A. Toppin, Professor of History and Dean of the Graduate School, Virginia State University, Petersburg, VA

GRADE LEVEL WRITERS/CONSULTANTS

Pamela Argo, Seventh Grade Teacher, Mountain Brook Middle School, Birmingham, AL

Carol Gemmell, Sixth Grade Teacher, North Side Elementary School, Harrisburg, PA

Gail Finger, Principal, Thorpes Elementary School Warren Consolidated Schools, Warren, MI

Linda Lucas, Sixth Grade Teacher, Gilmore School, Racine, WI

ACKNOWLEDGMENTS

Page 84: "The City Is So Big" by Richard García. From SELECTED POETRY by Richard García. Published by Ginn & Co.

Page 98: Excerpt from INVITATION TO ARCHAEOLOGY by Philip Rahtz. © 1985 Philip Rahtz. Used courtesy of the publisher Basil Blackwell Ltd.

Page 132: Excerpt from LOST CITY OF THE INCAS by Hiram Bingham. © 1948 by Hiram Bingham. Copyright renewed 1976 by Alfred M. Bingham.

Page 256: Text excerpt and photograph from MY HEART LIES SOUTH by Elizabeth Borton de Treviño. Copyright 1953 by Elizabeth Borton de Treviño. Reprinted by permission of Harper & Row, Publishers, Inc.

Page 273: "Evening" by Rubén Darío. Reprinted from SELECTED POEMS OF RUBEN DARIO by permission of the University of Texas Press.

Page 324: Text of "The Haitians in the Dominican Republic (Adapted). From THE KING OF THE MOUNTAINS: A TREASURY OF LATIN AMERICAN FOLK STORIES by M.A. Jagendorf and R.S. Boggs. Copyright © 1960 by M.A. Jagendorf and R.S. Boggs. Copyright renewed 1988 by Andre Jagendorf, Merna Alpert & R.S. Boggs. Reprinted by permission of Vanguard Press, a division of Random House, Inc.

Page 364: Excerpt from ANGELS FOUR by David Nott. © 1972 by David Nott. Used by permission of the publisher, Prentice-Hall, Inc. Englewood Cliffs, NJ.

Page 439: "Fear" by Gabriela Mistral. From SELECTED POEMS OF GABRIELA MISTRAL translated by Langston Hughes. Printed by Indiana University Press © 1957, copyright renewed. Used by permission of Joan Daves.

Page 519: From ANOTHER SHORE by Nancy Bond. Reprinted with permission of Margaret K. McElderry Books, an imprint of Macmillan Publishing Company. © 1988 by Nancy Bond.

ISBN 0-382-32182-0

CONTENTS

MAP SKILLS HANDBOOK   **2–37**
Using Latitude and Longitude
Scale and Elevation
Maps for Many Purposes
Projections
Time and Time Lines
MAP SKILLS HANDBOOK REVIEW   **36**
Countries of the Western Hemisphere   **38–41**

CHAPTER **1** EXPLORING LATIN AMERICA
                 AND CANADA   **44–65**
This New World
The Americas and the Americans
A View from Above
Seasons and Climates in the Americas
CHAPTER REVIEW: PUTTING IT ALL TOGETHER

CHAPTER **2** THE PEOPLES OF
                 THE AMERICAS   **66–88**
Foreign Things
Our Interdependent Hemisphere

        CITIZENSHIP AND AMERICAN VALUES
        Learning to Appreciate
        All Americans   **76–77**
Latin Americans and Canadians
Where People Live
CHAPTER REVIEW: PUTTING IT ALL TOGETHER

UNIT 1 REVIEW: COOPERATIVE LEARNING **89**

Understanding Graphs   **90–91**
Using SQR: Survey, Question, Read   **92–93**

Unit **1**

WHY STUDY
LATIN AMERICA
AND CANADA?

Unit

THE PEOPLES OF THE WESTERN HEMISPHERE

CHAPTER **3** THE FIRST
AMERICANS   **96–117**
Searching the Distant Past
 CITIZENSHIP AND AMERICAN VALUES
You Decide: Should Some
Animals Be Allowed to
Become Extinct?   **104–105**
Different Ways of Living
Indian Groups in 1492
CHAPTER REVIEW: PUTTING IT ALL TOGETHER

CHAPTER **4** THE GREAT INDIAN
CIVILIZATIONS   **118–138**
The Rise of Empires
The Aztec Empire
 USING SOURCE MATERIAL
The Great City of Tenochtitlán   **125**
The Maya of Central America
The Inca Empire
 LITERATURE *Lost City of the Incas*
by Hiram Bingham   **132**
CHAPTER REVIEW: PUTTING IT ALL TOGETHER

UNIT **2** REVIEW: COOPERATIVE LEARNING **139**

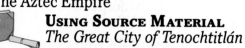

Identifying Primary and Secondary
    Sources   **140–141**
Actualizing Strategies   **142–143**

CHAPTER **5** THE CONQUEST OF LATIN AMERICA **146–167**

An Age of Discovery
Early Exploration
The Conquest of Mexico
The Conquest of the Incas
Spanish Exploration Continues
CHAPTER REVIEW: PUTTING IT ALL TOGETHER

CHAPTER **6** COLONIZING LATIN AMERICA **168–189**

Governing the Colonies
The Colonial Trade

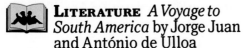 **LITERATURE** *A Voyage to South America* by Jorge Juan and António de Ulloa **176**

Living in Colonial Latin America
Brazil: A Portuguese Colony
CHAPTER REVIEW: PUTTING IT ALL TOGETHER

CHAPTER **7** INDEPENDENCE COMES TO LATIN AMERICA **190–210**

The Latin American Struggle
Independence for Mexico
Independence for South America

CITIZENSHIP AND AMERICAN VALUES What Makes a Person Great? **202–203**

USING SOURCE MATERIAL A Message from Bolívar **207**

CHAPTER REVIEW: PUTTING IT ALL TOGETHER

UNIT 3 REVIEW: COOPERATIVE LEARNING **211**

Analyzing Historical Maps **212–213**
Understanding an Author's Viewpoint **214–215**

Unit 4

MIDDLE AMERICA FROM INDEPENDENCE TO TODAY

CHAPTER **8**   MEXICO   218–237

Mexico's Land and Climate
Mexico in the Nineteenth Century
Mexico in the Twentieth Century
CHAPTER REVIEW: PUTTING IT ALL TOGETHER

CHAPTER **9**   MEXICO TODAY   238–259

Making a Living in Mexico
The People of Mexico
A Visit to Mexico City
Government and Politics

 LITERATURE *My Heart Lies South*
by Elizabeth Borton de Treviño   **256**

CHAPTER REVIEW: PUTTING IT ALL TOGETHER

CHAPTER **10**   CENTRAL AMERICA   260–281

Land Between the Seas
Central America's Troubled History
Nicaragua

 LITERATURE "Evening"
by Rubén Darío   **273**

Panama and the Canal
CHAPTER REVIEW: PUTTING IT ALL TOGETHER

CHAPTER **11**   CENTRAL AMERICA TODAY 282–305

A Diverse Population
Central American Economy
Living in Central America
A Search for Lasting Peace

 CITIZENSHIP AND AMERICAN VALUES
You Decide: Does a Country Need
an Army?   **302–303**

CHAPTER REVIEW: PUTTING IT ALL TOGETHER

CHAPTER **12**   THE CARIBBEAN   306–329

An Area of Differences
Island Nations and Colonies
Cuba: Delayed Independence

USING SOURCE MATERIAL
Early Impressions of Cuba   **316**
Puerto Rico: A Blend of Cultures
Haiti and the Dominican Republic

 **LITERATURE** *The Haitians in the Dominican Republic* by M.A. Jagendorf and R.S. Boggs   **324**

CHAPTER REVIEW: PUTTING IT ALL TOGETHER

 **CHAPTER 13** THE CARIBBEAN TODAY   **330–350**
Many Different Islands and Peoples
Growing Sugar: Then and Now
Making a Living in the West Indies
A Closer Look at Puerto Rico

CHAPTER REVIEW: PUTTING IT ALL TOGETHER

UNIT 4 REVIEW: COOPERATIVE LEARNING 351

 SKILLBUILDER

Reading a Mileage Chart   **352–353**
Understanding Comparisons   **354–355**

 CHAPTER 14 THE NORTHERN AND
ANDEAN COUNTRIES   **358–381**
Land and Climate: Colombia,
Venezuela, and the Guianas

 LITERATURE *Angels Four*
by David Nott   **364**
Land and Climate: Ecuador, Peru, and Bolivia
Since Bolívar
Three Indian Lands

CHAPTER REVIEW: PUTTING IT ALL TOGETHER

 **CHAPTER 15** NORTHERN AND ANDEAN
COUNTRIES TODAY   **382–403**
Wealth from Agriculture
Earning a Living from Land and Sea
Peoples and Cities of the Andes

CHAPTER REVIEW: PUTTING IT ALL TOGETHER

Unit 5 SOUTH AMERICA FROM INDEPENDENCE TO TODAY

 **CHAPTER 16** THE SOUTHERN CONE   **404–425**

Land and Climate
Argentina: In Search of Unity
Chile: Government for the Upper Class
Paraguay and Uruguay
CHAPTER REVIEW: PUTTING IT ALL TOGETHER

 **CHAPTER 17** THE SOUTHERN CONE
TODAY   **426–447**

The Economy of the Southern Cone
Peoples of the Southern Cone
Cities of the Southern Cone

 **LITERATURE** "Fear" by
Gabriela Mistral Translated
by Langston Hughes   **439**

The Return of Democracy
CHAPTER REVIEW: PUTTING IT ALL TOGETHER

 CHAPTER 18 BRAZIL   **448–469**

Land and Climate

 CITIZENSHIP AND AMERICAN VALUES
You Decide: Should the Amazon Rain
Forest Be Saved?   **454–455**

Imperial Brazil
The Brazilian Republic
The Brazilian Economy
CHAPTER REVIEW: PUTTING IT ALL TOGETHER

 CHAPTER 19 BRAZIL TODAY   **470–488**

Many Brazils
The Brazilian People
Urban Brazil

CHAPTER REVIEW: PUTTING IT ALL TOGETHER

UNIT 5 REVIEW: COOPERATIVE LEARNING **489**

Understanding Sequence   **490–491**
Skimming and Scanning   **492–493**

Unit
6
CANADA

CHAPTER **20** CANADIAN BEGINNINGS **496–515**
Native Americans
Early Explorations and Settlements
 USING SOURCE MATERIAL
First Days in Quebec **504**
The Challenged French Colonies
CHAPTER REVIEW: PUTTING IT ALL TOGETHER

CHAPTER **21** CANADA FROM
1710 TO TODAY **516–539**
A Great War Develops
LITERATURE *Another Shore*
by Nancy Bond **519**
Reactions to the Quebec Act
Toward Union and Independence
The Canadian West
Building a Nation
CHAPTER REVIEW: PUTTING IT ALL TOGETHER

CHAPTER **22** THE RICH CANADIAN
LAND **540–563**
Location and Climate
Physical Features of Canada
Natural Resources
Abundant Energy
The Canadian Economy
CHAPTER REVIEW: PUTTING IT ALL TOGETHER

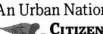
CHAPTER **23** CANADA TODAY **564–586**
Canada's Regions
An Urban Nation
CITIZENSHIP AND AMERICAN VALUES
Advantages and Disadvantages
of a Multicultural Society **576–577**
The Canadian Government
National Issues
CHAPTER REVIEW: PUTTING IT ALL TOGETHER
*UNIT **6** REVIEW: COOPERATIVE LEARNING* **587**

SKILLBUILDER

Interpreting Resource Maps **588–589**
Writing a Summary **590–591**

Resource Section

Atlas   **592–602**   Glossary   **611–619**
Gazetteer   **603–610**   Index   **620–629**

Maps

Latitude Lines	5
Northern and Southern Hemispheres	6
Eastern and Western Hemispheres	6
Longitude Lines	7
Using Latitude and Longitude	8
The World: Average Annual Temperatures	9
Mexico	11
Mexico City: Central Section	11
Puerto Rico: Contour Map	12
Understanding Contour Lines	13
From Photograph to Map	14
Ecuador	16
South America: Political	17
Canada: Physical	19
The Americas: Coffee and Bananas	20
The Americas: Wheat and Corn	20
Canada's Wonderland	21
Pizarro's Route	22
From Globe to Map	23
Mercator Projection	25
An Equal-Area Projection	26
An Interrupted Projection	27
The World: Time Zones	32
Ptolemy's Map	47
The Americas: Political	50
The Western Hemisphere	51
A Flight Over the Americas	53
Latin America: Major Regions	55
The World: Temperature Zones	61
Routes of the First Americans	99
Indian Ways of Living in the 1500s	119
Tenochtitlán	122
The Inca Empire	134
Four Voyages of Columbus	151
Further Exploration of America	164
Conquests in South America	165
Viceroyalties About 1650	169
Early Spanish Trade Routes	174
Quito, Ecuador	182
Latin America About 1700	183
Independence for Spanish Viceroyalties	204
Early Explorers in America	213
Mexico: Physical	220
How Mexico's Borders Changed	227
Mexico: Petroleum Industry	240
Mexico: Political	246
Central America: Physical	262
The Panama Canal	277
Central America: Coffee Production	289
Central America: Political	296
Caribbean: Physical	308
Federation of the West Indies 1958	312
The Caribbean: Political	332
The Caribbean: Crops and Natural Resources	340
Northern and Andean Countries: Physical	360
South America: Gold Production	390
Northern and Andean Countries: Political	397
Chile: Its Shape and Size	405
The Southern Cone: Physical	406
The Southern Cone: Cattle	429
The Southern Cone: Sheep	429
The Southern Cone: Political	437
Brazil: Its Shape and Size	449
Brazil: Physical	450
Brazil: Regions	471
Brazil: Crops and Natural Resources	474
Brasilia	482
Brazil: Political	484
New France and Acadia to 1672	509
North America in 1713	517
North America in 1763	517
The Battle of Quebec	520
Quebec in 1763 and 1774	521
The Provinces in 1818	527
Oregon Country and the Fur Trade	530
A Strategic Location	542
Canada: Climate Regions	543
Canada: Natural Plant Growth	543
The World: Ocean Currents	544
Canada: Physical	545
St. Lawrence Seaway	551
Canada: Oil Fields and Tar Fields	556
Canada: Coal Fields and Hydroelectric Projects	556
Canada: Physical Regions	565
Canada: Political	570
The Americas: Oil and Coal	588
The Americas: Iron Ore and Other Minerals	589

Atlas

The World (Political)	592–593
The United States (Political)	594
The United States (Physical)	595
North America (Physical)	596
South America (Physical)	597
Eurasia (Physical)	598–599
Africa (Physical)	600
Australia and New Zealand (Political and Physical)	601
The World: Climate Regions	602
The World: Forests	602

Time Lines

Spanish Exploration and Conquest	35
Aztec Civilization: 900–1521	123
Maya Civilization: 500 B.C.–A.D. 1697	129
Inca Civilization: 1100–1572	131
Exploration and Conquest: 1492–1541	152
Revolutionary Events: 1775–1821	192
Mexico: 1823–1934	225
Central America: 1823–1979	266
Puerto Rico and Cuba: 1898–1959	320
Haiti and the Dominican Republic: 1915–1986	323
Northern and Andean Countries: 1824–1884	373
Argentina: 1862–1983	410
Chile: 1924–1990	416
Paraguay and Uruguay: 1865–1952	419
Dictatorship and Democracy in the Southern Cone: 1954–1990	444
Brazil: 1822–1889	460
Canadian Beginnings: 1497–1755	498
Canada: 1774–1931	522

GRAPHS

The Largest Countries in the Americas	81
The 10 Most Populous American Countries	82
Population Growth in Anglo-America and Latin America: 1650–2000	83
Total Land Area of the World	90
Population of the Five Largest States in the United States	90
World Population by Continent	91
Climograph: La Paz, Baja California	223
Climograph: Mérida, Yucatán	223
Corn Production by Selected Countries	241
Population Growth in Mexico	245
Mexico: Urban and Rural Population	245
Climograph: Belize Lowlands	265
Climograph: Guatemala Highlands	265
Climograph: Ciudad Bolívar, Venezuela	365
Climograph: Georgetown, Guyana	365
Annual Inflation Rates: Selected South American Countries	377
Rural and Urban Populations	386
The Southern Cone: Largest Cities	440
Brazil: Longest Rivers	451
Population of New France: 1608–1760	508
Climograph: Calgary	546
Climograph: Dawson	546
Climograph: Toronto	546
Climograph: Vancouver	546
GNP: Selected Nations of the Western Hemisphere	558

TABLES

Length of Longest and Shortest Days	30
Using the SQR Strategy	93
Types of Literature	142
Strategies to Help Yourself Actualize	143
Battles for Independence	204
Understanding an Author's Viewpoint	215
Foreign Debt of Selected Nations	255
Central America: Area and Population	283
Independence in the Caribbean	313
Controlling Powers in the Caribbean	314
Literacy Today: South America	420
Immigration to Brazil: 1884–1913	458
Brazilian Regions: Area and Population	477
Skimming and Scanning for Information	493
When They Joined the Dominion	536
Minerals Mined in Canada	554

CHARTS

Countries of the Western Hemisphere	38–41
Guatemala and El Salvador: Selected Exports	288
Independence in the Caribbean	313
From Sugarcane to Refined Sugar	335
Highway Mileage Chart	353
Chart: Understanding Comparison	355
Coffee: From Farm to Factory	384
Early Reforms in Uruguay	423
The Southern Cone: Crops and Natural Resources	427
From Plant to Cloth	491
Canada: Provinces and Territories	573

DIAGRAMS

Silva Compass	4
Scale and Elevation	10
Contour Lines	13
Three Perspectives	18
Canada: A Cross Section	19
The Seasons	28
The Earth's Rotation	29
The International Date Line	34
Temperature Zones: Latin America	62
The Bering Strait	100
Size of Ships: 1492 and Today	150
Encomienda Layout	172
A Typical Hacienda Layout	180
West Indies: Trade Winds	310
Altitudes of Selected Cities	395
Rain Shadow	409
St. Lawrence Locks: A Cross Section	551
A Summary Ladder	591

SPECIAL FEATURES

USING SOURCE MATERIAL

The Great City of Tenochtitlán	125
A Message from Bolívar	207
Early Impressions of Cuba	316
First Days in Quebec	504

LITERATURE

Lost City of the Incas	132
A Voyage to South America	176
My Heart Lies South	256
"Evening"	273
The Haitians in the Dominican Republic	324
Angels Four	364
"Fear"	439
Another Shore	519

CITIZENSHIP AND AMERICAN VALUES

Learning to Appreciate All Americans	76–77
You Decide: Should some animals be allowed to become extinct?	104–105
What makes a person great?	202–203
You Decide: Does a country need an army?	302–303
You Decide: Should the Amazon rain forest be saved?	454–455
Advantages and Disadvantages of a Multicultural Society	576–577

SKILLBUILDERS

SOCIAL STUDIES

Understanding Graphs	90–91
Identifying Primary and Secondary Sources	140–141
Analyzing Historical Maps	212–213
Reading a Mileage Chart	352–353
Understanding Sequence	490–491
Interpreting Resource Maps	588–589

LANGUAGE ARTS

Using SQR: Survey, Question, Read	92–93
Actualizing Strategies	142–143
Understanding an Author's Viewpoint	214–215
Understanding Comparisons	354–355
Skimming and Scanning	492–493
Writing a Summary	590–591

MAP SKILLS HANDBOOK

Maps are useful because they can help people find the exact location of anything on the earth. For example, a map of the area where you live can show the location of streets, hospitals, airports, parks, and other points of interest. Maps can help tourists find a motel, pilots locate an airport, and your family find a certain beach you want to visit.

Maps are also helpful in showing the relationship between things on the earth. For example, a map can show the highways and rivers near a city, helping to explain why the city grew where it did. Maps can show the natural resources or the climate of a specific region.

Maps are important tools for students, too. They help you to see the similarities and differences among areas or regions on the earth. The maps in this book will help you understand the parts of the world you will study. All the map skills you will need appear in this Map Skills Handbook. Read the lesson titles and study the illustrations on pages 2 and 3 to preview the material.

LESSON 1
Using Latitude and Longitude
page 4

LESSON 2
Scale and Elevation   page 10

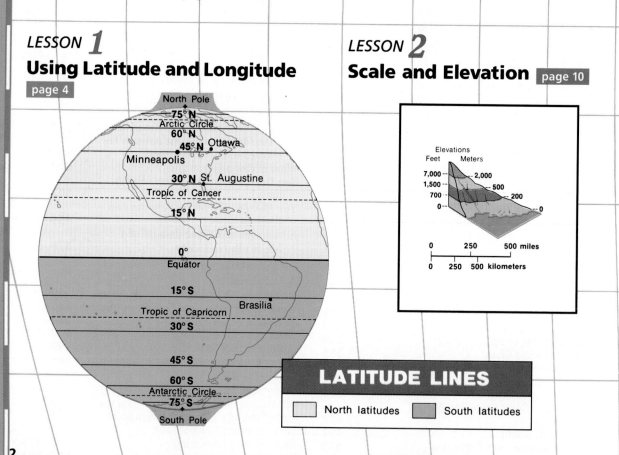

LATITUDE LINES

North latitudes   South latitudes

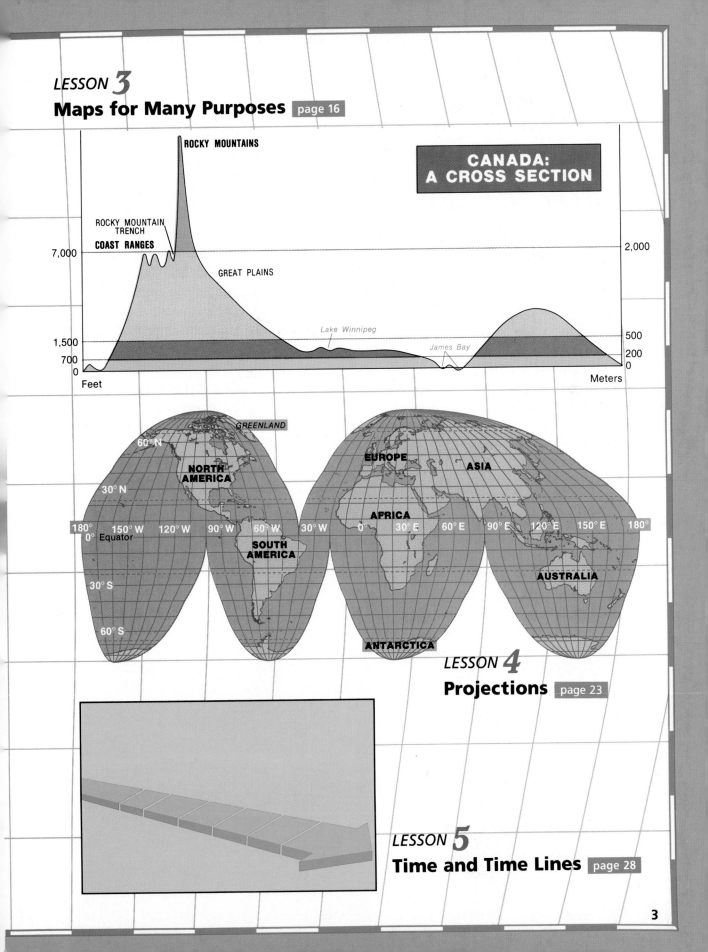

LESSON 3
Maps for Many Purposes page 16

CANADA: A CROSS SECTION

ROCKY MOUNTAINS

ROCKY MOUNTAIN TRENCH

COAST RANGES

GREAT PLAINS

7,000

Lake Winnipeg

2,000

James Bay

1,500
700
0

500
200
0

Feet

Meters

GREENLAND

60° N

NORTH AMERICA

EUROPE

ASIA

30° N

AFRICA

180°
0° Equator

150° W   120° W   90° W   60° W   30° W   0°   30° E   60° E   90° E   120° E   150° E   180°

SOUTH AMERICA

AUSTRALIA

30° S

60° S

ANTARCTICA

LESSON 4
Projections page 23

LESSON 5
Time and Time Lines page 28

Using Latitude and Longitude

THINK ABOUT WHAT YOU KNOW

Imagine that you have just received an invitation to a birthday party that will include a treasure hunt in a park. What might help you find the treasure?

STUDY THE VOCABULARY

orientation	longitude
parallel	meridian
latitude	geographic coordinates
hemisphere	key

FOCUS YOUR READING

How are lines of longitude and latitude used on a map?

A. Orientation

Orienteering is a sport that uses maps. In orienteering the participants form teams and use maps and compasses to find their way between points marked on the maps. Orienteering is similar to a treasure hunt because the contestants must find markers placed along the course. Sometimes the markers are hard to find.

Orienteering is also like a race. The winner is the one who first finds all the markers and completes the course. In orienteering, being able to use a compass and read a map are more important than fast hiking. That is because being able to find the shortest way around the course while locating all the markers saves time.

The maps used in orienteering are detailed maps of small areas. The compasses

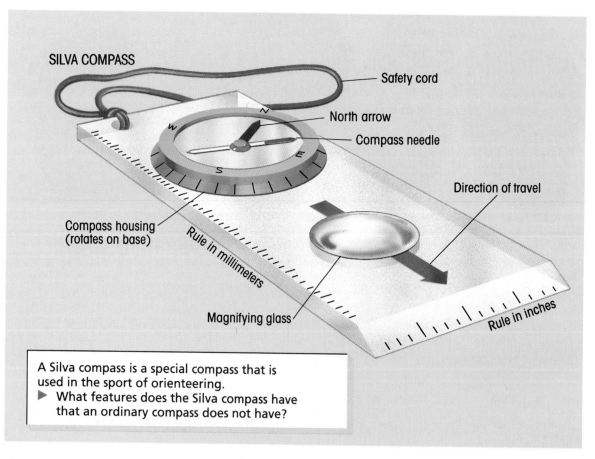

SILVA COMPASS

Safety cord

North arrow

Compass needle

Direction of travel

Compass housing (rotates on base)

Rule in millimeters

Magnifying glass

Rule in inches

A Silva compass is a special compass that is used in the sport of orienteering.
► What features does the Silva compass have that an ordinary compass does not have?

are specially designed for the sport of orienteering. They have markings along the side in inches and in millimeters for use along with the map. The direction-of-travel arrow is used in following and in laying out a course. The special orienteering compasses are called Silva compasses. Notice the diagram on page 4.

Orienteering was invented in Sweden in the late 1800s. It was not introduced in the United States until 1946. Orienteering has gained popularity in the United States. It is good practice for campers, hikers, Scouts, and hunters. It is even used in training soldiers in the army.

There may be an orienteering club in your community that you may wish to join. Orienteering is a good way to learn to read maps — and have fun and exercise at the same time.

The word *orienteering* comes from the base word *orient*, which is sometimes used for countries on the continent of Asia, especially the Far East. The Far East includes Japan, China, Korea, and Taiwan. The word *orient* comes from a Latin word meaning "east." (Latin was the language of the ancient Romans.)

At one time, maps were commonly drawn with east at the top. The word **orientation** came to be used for the location of directions on maps drawn with east at the top. It meant "finding the east." However, after the compass came into use in Europe in about the fifteenth century, most maps were drawn with north at the top. North is the direction in which a compass needle points. The word *orientation* remained and is still used today. Orientation is an element that every proper map should have. It shows where places are in relation to other places.

B. A Grid System

The main way that orientation is done on a map is with a grid, or pattern of evenly spaced horizontal and vertical lines. One set of lines is called **parallels**.

Parallels are lines across a map that are parallel to, or run in the same direction as, the Equator. They follow an east-west direction around the earth. They are numbered from 0 at the Equator to 90 at both the North Pole and the South Pole. Distances that are north or south of the Equator may be shown by parallels, also called lines of **latitude**. The unit of measure is the degree, shown by the sign °. Find the lines of latitude on the map.

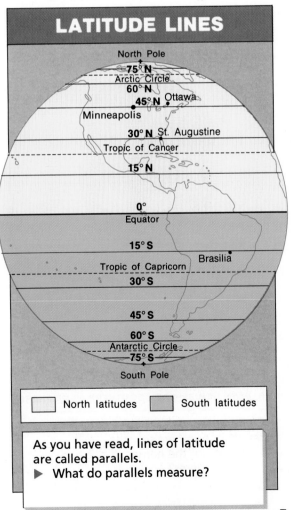

LATITUDE LINES

North Pole
75° N
Arctic Circle
60° N
45° N Ottawa
Minneapolis
30° N St. Augustine
Tropic of Cancer
15° N

0°
Equator

15° S
Brasília
Tropic of Capricorn
30° S

45° S
60° S
Antarctic Circle
75° S
South Pole

☐ North latitudes   ☐ South latitudes

As you have read, lines of latitude are called parallels.
▶ What do parallels measure?

A place that is exactly halfway between the Equator and the North Pole has a latitude of 45°. A place exactly halfway between the Equator and the South Pole also has a latitude of 45°. This is because the Equator divides the earth into equal halves, or **hemispheres**.

The half of the earth that is north of the Equator is called the Northern Hemisphere. The half that is south of the Equator is called the Southern Hemisphere. To tell whether a place is in the Northern or Southern Hemisphere, the letter *N* or *S* is added by mapmakers. If you wanted to describe a place in the Northern Hemisphere that is shown at 45°N, you

would say it is at "forty-five degrees north." If you wanted to describe a place that is shown at 45°S, you would say it is at "forty-five degrees south."

Measuring Distances The vertical lines on a map, which run in a north-south direction, are usually called lines of **longitude.** They can also be called **meridians**. Meridians are numbered from 0° to 180°. The meridian of 0° is called the *Prime Meridian*. This imaginary line passes through Greenwich (GREN ihch), England, which was once the site of the Royal Observatory. The meridian of 180° lies on the op-

NORTHERN AND SOUTHERN HEMISPHERES

North Pole

Equator

NORTHERN HEMISPHERE   SOUTHERN HEMISPHERE

North Pole

South Pole

Dividing the earth at the Equator results in two hemispheres.
▶ What are the names of the two hemispheres?

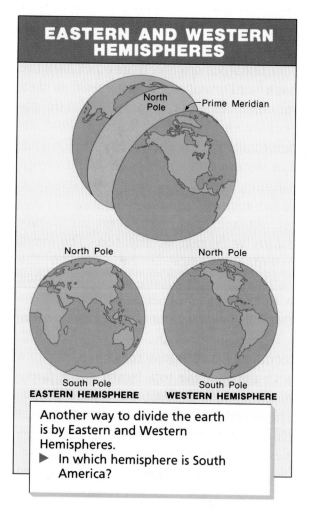

EASTERN AND WESTERN HEMISPHERES

North Pole

Prime Meridian

North Pole

North Pole

South Pole
EASTERN HEMISPHERE

South Pole
WESTERN HEMISPHERE

Another way to divide the earth is by Eastern and Western Hemispheres.
▶ In which hemisphere is South America?

posite side of the earth from the Prime Meridian, and it passes through the Pacific Ocean. There are 360 degrees all the way around the earth.

The line made by the Prime Meridian and the 180° meridian divides the earth. The half of the earth lying west of the Prime Meridian is called the Western Hemisphere. The half of the earth east of the Prime Meridian is called the Eastern Hemisphere.

A place that is exactly halfway between the Prime Meridian and the 180° meridian in the Western Hemisphere has a longitude of 90°. A similar location in the Eastern Hemisphere also has a longitude of 90°. Places in the Western Hemisphere are shown on a map by a *W* after the degree sign, and those in the Eastern Hemisphere have a letter *E*.

Exact locations on the earth are given by a pair of numbers, one for the latitude of the place and the other for the longitude. The place exactly in the middle of the Northern and Eastern Hemispheres, is shown as 45°N/90°E. There is no other place on earth with that exact location. The numbers are called the **geographic coordinates** of the location. If you know both the latitude and the longitude of a certain place, you can find its location. Try it. Use the map on page 8 to find the place indicated by the geographic coordinates 16°S/48°W. In what country is it found? If you do not know, check the world map in the Atlas, on pages 592 and 593.

Geographic coordinates are used in the Gazetteer at the back of this book. Find the city of Quito on the map on page 8. What are its coordinates? Now check your answer by locating Quito in the Gazetteer at the back of the book. The coordinates

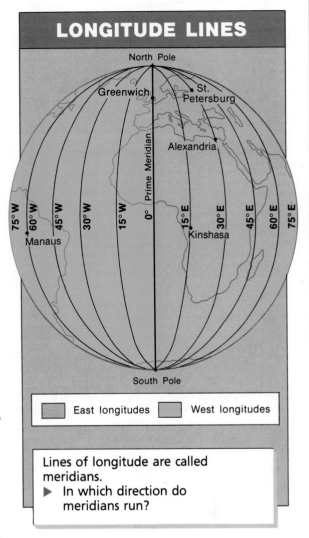

LONGITUDE LINES

Lines of longitude are called meridians.
▶ In which direction do meridians run?

given in the Gazetteer should be the same as those you named.

Some maps do not have a grid printed on them. Instead, a compass rose may show the orientation.

C. The Map Legend

The **key**, or map legend, is an important element on most maps. It tells what the symbols stand for on the map. The key contains all the symbols used on the map. It may also contain any other information that will help the user of the map understand the information on it.

USING LATITUDE AND LONGITUDE

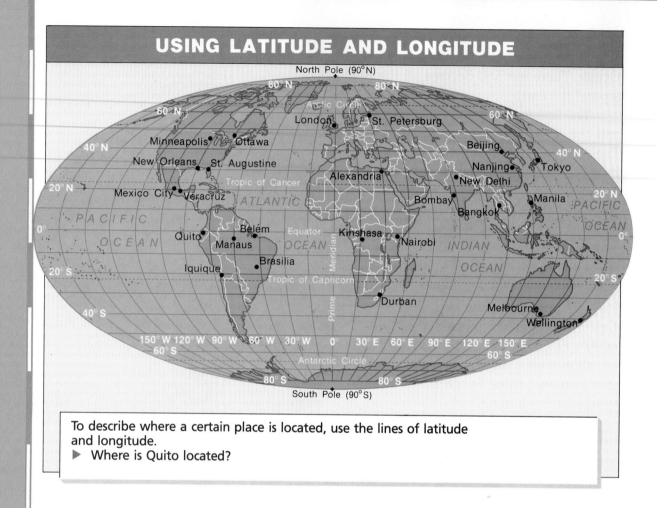

To describe where a certain place is located, use the lines of latitude and longitude.
▶ Where is Quito located?

THE METRIC SYSTEM OF MEASUREMENT

Kilometers and miles are both units of measure used to express distance or length. A kilometer is a unit of measure in the metric system. The system is called metric because it uses the meter in measuring.

The metric system can be used for measuring things other than distance. It can be used for measuring such things as weight and capacity, as well as temperature. The metric system is in use or is being introduced in the world's major countries except the United States.

In this book both customary measurements that are in general use in the United States and the metric measurements are used. When a customary measurement appears, it is followed in parentheses ( ) by the metric measurement that is about equal to it. Inches are changed to centimeters (cm), feet and yards to meters (m), miles to kilometers (km), and acres to hectares (ha). Pounds are changed to kilograms (kg), and quarts to liters (L). Degrees Fahrenheit (°F) are changed to degrees Celsius (°C).

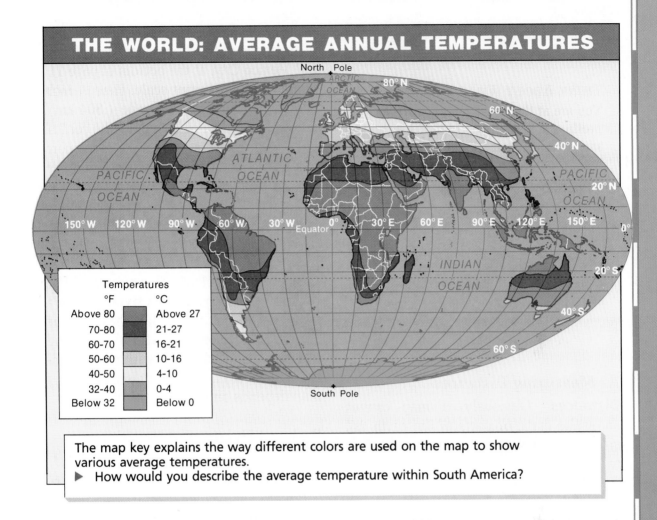

THE WORLD: AVERAGE ANNUAL TEMPERATURES

North Pole

ARCTIC OCEAN

80° N

60° N

40° N

PACIFIC OCEAN

ATLANTIC OCEAN

PACIFIC OCEAN

20° N

150° W   120° W   90° W   60° W   30° W   0°   30° E   60° E   90° E   120° E   150° E   0°

Equator

INDIAN OCEAN

20° S

40° S

60° S

South Pole

Temperatures

°F	°C
Above 80	Above 27
70-80	21-27
60-70	16-21
50-60	10-16
40-50	4-10
32-40	0-4
Below 32	Below 0

The map key explains the way different colors are used on the map to show various average temperatures.
► How would you describe the average temperature within South America?

The first thing you should look for on a map is its title. The title will tell you the subject of the map. Glance over the map. Does it have lines of latitude and longitude? What else does it show? Then examine the map key. On the map above, the key shows how colors can be used for different temperatures. It also shows degrees Fahrenheit (°F) and degrees Celsius (°C) and indicates different degrees. Read the explanation on page 8 about the metric system before you study the map more carefully.

LESSON 1 REVIEW

THINK AND WRITE

A. What does orientation show?
B. Why are both latitude and longitude lines used on many maps?
C. How is a map key helpful?

SKILLS CHECK

MAP SKILL

Look at the map on this page. Find the place that is 15° south and 45° west. What is the average temperature there?

LESSON 2

Scale and Elevation

THINK ABOUT WHAT YOU KNOW

You are at the beach, and your little brother has asked you to help him build a sand castle. What should you consider before you begin to build it?

STUDY THE VOCABULARY

scale	contour lines
elevation	cartographer

FOCUS YOUR READING

How are scale and elevation shown on maps?

A. Measuring Distances

Distances Obviously, a map cannot show the earth or parts of the earth full size. A measurement must be established to show the proportion that a map bears to the place it represents. This measurement is called **scale**. A person using a map would have no way of finding the real distances if there wasn't a map scale.

Using Scale The simplest way to show scale is to use a graphic (drawn or written) scale. The map at the top of page 11 has such a scale. It shows that a certain distance on the map stands for some other distance on the earth. If you measure 1 inch (2.5 cm) on the graphic scale shown on the top map on page 11, you find that it stands for 400 miles (644 km). If you could actually drive in a straight line between two cities that are shown 1 inch apart on the map, you would have to travel 400 miles. Use your ruler to find at least one city that is shown on the map to be 200 miles (322 km) from Mexico City.

You will find graphic scales on most of the maps in this book. The map of central Mexico City, at the bottom of page 11, is drawn to a different scale. Here, 1 inch stands for only about ½ mile (.804 km). Only a small area of Mexico — the central part of Mexico City — is shown, so more details are included. The Mexico City map can show individual buildings and streets, but it can cover only a few blocks of the city. On the other hand, Mexico City appears as only a small symbol on the top map. There are no details to show the way the city really looks. Such a map would be of no use at all to a tourist trying to find a motel in Mexico City! It could, however, be very helpful to someone who wants to find out where Mexico City is within the country of Mexico. The scale that is chosen for a map depends on the purpose of the map.

B. Land Height and Contours

Height On maps, the height of the land, called **elevation,** can also be shown. Elevation is usually given as the height of the land above sea level, which is considered to be 0 elevation. For example, if a mountain is 10,000 feet (3,048 m) high, the top of the mountain is 10,000 feet (3,048 m) above sea level.

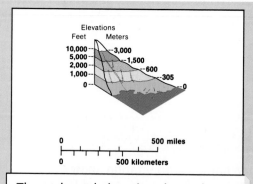

The scale and elevation shown here might appear on a physical map.
▶ Which color is used to show 1000 feet (305 m)?

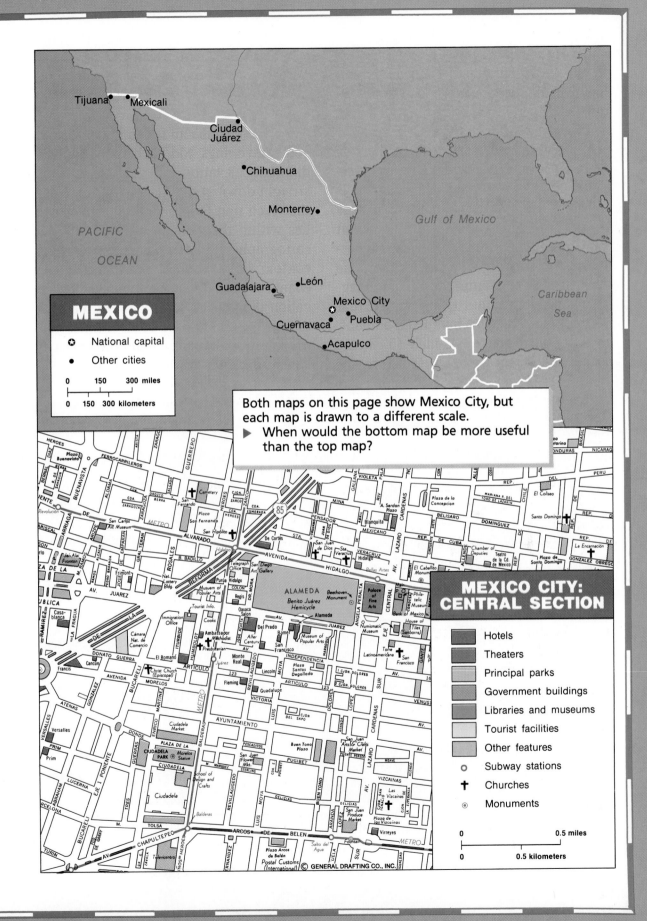

MEXICO

✪ National capital
● Other cities

0   150   300 miles
0   150   300 kilometers

Both maps on this page show Mexico City, but each map is drawn to a different scale.
▶ When would the bottom map be more useful than the top map?

MEXICO CITY: CENTRAL SECTION

Hotels
Theaters
Principal parks
Government buildings
Libraries and museums
Tourist facilities
Other features
○ Subway stations
✝ Churches
◉ Monuments

0   0.5 miles
0   0.5 kilometers

© GENERAL DRAFTING CO., INC.

Showing Elevation Maps are a useful way to show differences in elevation. For this purpose a series of lines, called **contour lines,** is often used. A contour line connects points of the same elevation. If you follow one contour line on a map, every place on that line will have the same elevation.

One can think of a contour line as being a little like a ring that would be left if a glass pitcher of milk was not refrigerated daily. The ring would be at the same level all the way around the pitcher. Imagine a full pitcher and then imagine that the milk was lowered by a fixed amount, say enough to make a 2-inch (5.08-cm) space. If the milk stayed at that level for a while, another ring would form. If this process were to be repeated at 2-inch intervals, a set of "contour lines" would be created.

Now imagine an island in contour. It could have rings, too, each one showing a different elevation. If you could look straight down at the island, you could see that each ring (contour) at a higher level lies within the next lower ring. Often, a cartographer will add colors between the contour lines to show more clearly the changes in elevation. The colors make elevation differences stand out. By learning to read maps that have contour lines, you can learn a great deal about differences in land elevation.

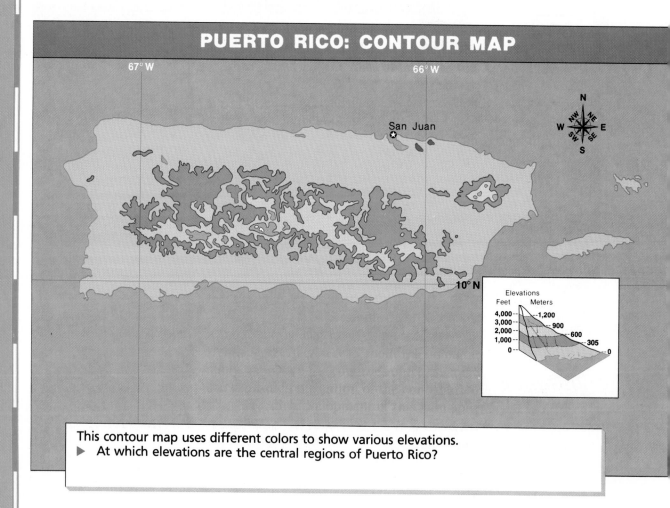

PUERTO RICO: CONTOUR MAP

Elevations	
Feet	Meters
4,000	1,200
3,000	900
2,000	600
1,000	305
0	0

This contour map uses different colors to show various elevations.
► At which elevations are the central regions of Puerto Rico?

UNDERSTANDING CONTOUR LINES

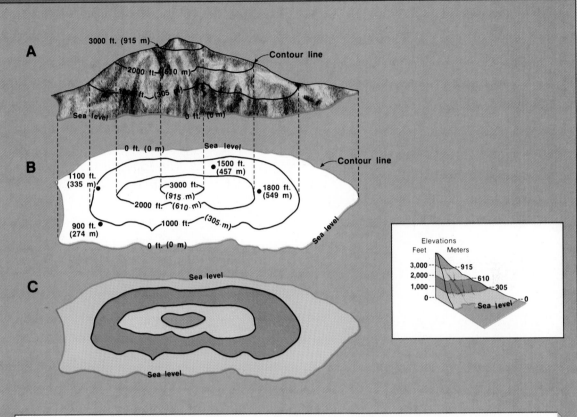

A
3000 ft. (915 m)
Contour line
2000 ft. (610 m)
ft. (305 m)
Sea level
0 ft. (0 m)

B
0 ft. (0 m)
Sea level
Contour line
1100 ft. (335 m)
1500 ft. (457 m)
3000 ft. (915 m)
1800 ft. (549 m)
2000 ft. (610 m)
1000 ft. (305 m)
900 ft. (274 m)
0 ft. (0 m)
Sea level

Elevations
Feet   Meters
3,000 --   915
2,000 --   610
1,000 --   305
0 --   0
Sea level

C
Sea level
Sea level

On drawing A, find the contour line marked 1000 feet (305 m). Then find the same contour line on drawing B.
▶ What color in the key at the right shows elevations that are between 1000 feet and 2000 feet (305 m and 610 m)?

Any point on a contour line is at the same elevation as all other points on that line.
▶ How does the drawing show this?

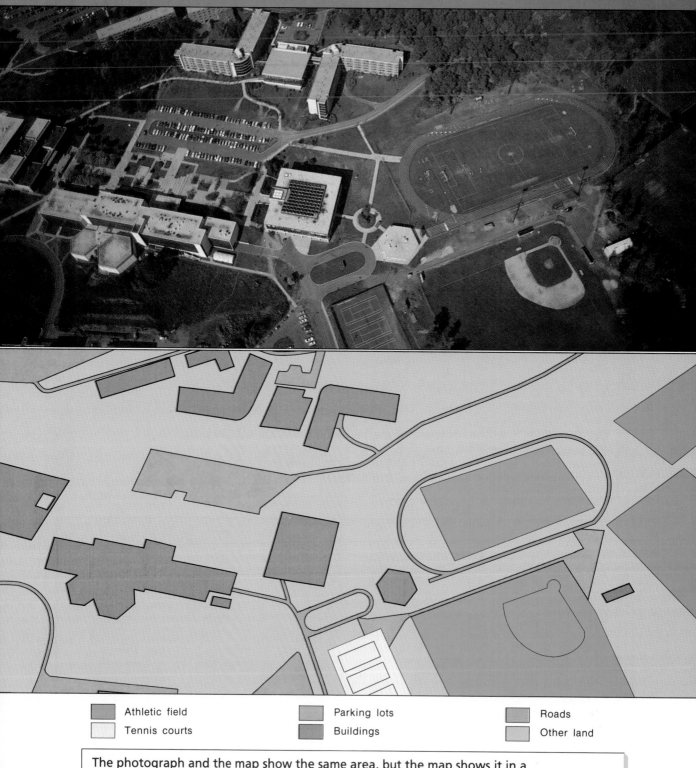

Athletic field

Tennis courts

Parking lots

Buildings

Roads

Other land

The photograph and the map show the same area, but the map shows it in a special way. Symbols on the map represent the most important features in the photograph.

▶ Are any features shown in the photograph not shown on the map?

C. From Photograph to Map

Cartographers, or mapmakers, need accurate information about the earth's surface to make maps. How do they get this information, you might wonder. Vital information comes from photographs taken from airplanes flying high above the surface of the earth. These photographs show where things are, such as roads, buildings, rivers, forests, and farms.

Why don't we just use the photographs instead of maps to locate things? There are important differences between photographs and maps. Photographs show many things about the real world that do not appear on most maps. However, maps include some important information that does not appear on photographs.

For example, the names of countries, cities, rivers, and lakes do not appear on photographs. Those are things that must be added by the cartographer. The cartographer can show boundaries of countries and states and use colors to show differences in elevation. Maps can also show the distribution of crops and natural resources, a comparison of climates in different regions of the earth, and much more.

Look at the map and photograph on the facing page. Both the map and the photograph show the same building complex. What does the photograph show that does not appear on the map?

To make sure that their maps are accurate, cartographers must make careful measurements.
▶ Which tools can you identify?

LESSON **2** *REVIEW*

THINK AND WRITE

A. Why is scale useful on maps?

B. In which ways can elevation be shown on maps?

C. When, do you think, would a photograph be more useful than a map?

SKILLS CHECK

MAP SKILL

Look at the map of Puerto Rico on page 12. Explain the features of this map in your own words.

15

Maps for Many Purposes

THINK ABOUT WHAT YOU KNOW

A student sitting beside you has just challenged you to list as many different types of maps as you can in the next minute. Begin!

STUDY THE VOCABULARY

landforms   **profile**
relief   **vertical exaggeration**
perspective

FOCUS YOUR READING

What types of maps are in common use today?

A. Maps with Boundaries and Cities

Maps can tell you much more than distances and elevation. One commonly used map, a political map, provides a great deal of information. For example, the political boundaries of countries and states are indicated by the use of color.

Political maps usually show the locations of capital cities and other major cities of states or countries. The symbol ⊛ is often used to show any national capital. The symbol ● is often used to show other major cities. Usually, lines of latitude and longitude are shown on political maps as well as a scale of miles as part of the key. Find these features on the map on page 17.

Sometimes a smaller map, called a locator map, will appear along with a larger map. A locator map does just what its name suggests. It helps you locate the subject of the main map within a larger area of the world. Look at the map of Ecuador on this page. You probably knew that Ecuador was a country in South America, but you may not have been sure of exactly where Ecuador is located. Now you know! The locator map shows Ecuador along the western coast of South America.

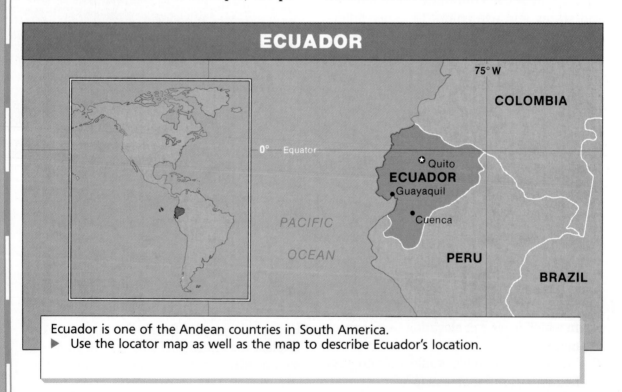

ECUADOR

Ecuador is one of the Andean countries in South America.
► Use the locator map as well as the map to describe Ecuador's location.

Barranquilla
Maracaibo Caracas
10° N
Barquisimeto Valencia
Orinoco River

Medellín
MALPELO I.
(COLOMBIA)
Bogotá
Cali
COLOMBIA

VENEZUELA

Georgetown
GUYANA
Paramaribo
SURINAME
Cayenne
French
Guiana
(FR.)

U.K. —UNITED KINGDOM
FR. —FRANCE

Quito
0°
ECUADOR
Guayaquil

Manaus
Amazon River

Equator

Belém

Fortaleza

B R A Z I L

Recife

PERU

10° S
Callao
Lima

Arequipa
Lake
Titicaca
La Paz
BOLIVIA
Sucre

Brasília
(Federal
District)

Goiânia

Salvador

20° S

PACIFIC
OCEAN

SAN FÉLIX I.
(CHILE)
SAN AMBROSIO I.
(CHILE)

PARAGUAY
Asuncion

Belo
Horizonte

Campinas
São Paulo
Curitiba
Santo
André
Rio de Janeiro

ATLANTIC
OCEAN

Tropic of Capricorn

Paraná River

Pôrto Alegre

San
Justo
Cordoba
CHILE
30° S

JUAN FERNÁNDEZ IS.
(CHILE)

Santiago

Rosario
Buenos Aires
Morón
Lomas
de Zamora

URUGUAY
Montevideo

Rio de la Plata

ARGENTINA

40° S

FALKLAND IS. (U.K.)
(MALVINAS IS.)

Strait of
Magellan

50° S

90° W   80° W   60° W   50° W   40° W   30° W

**SOUTH AMERICA:
POLITICAL**

⊛   National capitals
•   Other cities

0   500 miles
0   500 kilometers

This political map shows the countries of South
America as well as some important cities.
▶ Which national capitals are located on
or near the coastline?   **17**

B. Maps with Physical Features

You know that the earth's surface includes features such as mountains, valleys, and plains. These features of the earth are called **landforms**. Differences in the elevation of landforms on a map are called **relief**. Places that have large differences in elevation, such as mountains and valleys, have what is referred to as high relief. Places that have little difference in elevation, such as plains areas, have low relief.

A map that shows landforms is called a physical map. Look at the map of Canada on page 19. Notice the map title and the key. This particular key shows that different colors stand for different ranges of elevation on the map. Which color is used to show the elevation range of 700 to 1,500 feet (200 to 500 m)?

The way things look from a given point according to their size, shape, distance, and so on is called the **perspective**. Most maps are drawn as if the reader were directly over the area shown on the map.

Sometimes a map is drawn at an angle, as if the viewer were looking at it from the top of a high mountain.

At other times it is useful to show a land surface from the side, as if it has been cut away. A map or diagram drawn from this perspective is called a **profile**, or a cross section. Profiles are useful for showing differences in land elevation and for showing the underground structure of the earth.

While it may not seem true, the actual heights of mountains and depths of the oceans are quite small compared with distances between places on the earth. At a scale of 1 inch (2.5 cm) to 100 miles (161 km), two towns 100 miles (161 km) apart would be 1 inch (2.5 cm) apart on a map. Using this same scale, however, a mile-high mountain would have to be shown as a tiny fraction of an inch (or centimeter) in height. That great a difference presents a problem in drawing a profile.

Cartographers solve the problem by using two scales. The scale for height is

THREE PERSPECTIVES

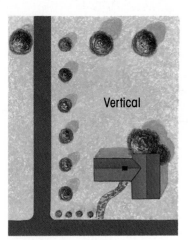
Vertical

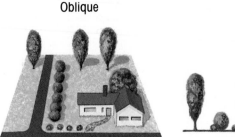
Oblique

Profile

The drawings show the same area, with a home, a roadway, trees, and bushes. Each drawing shows the area from a different perspective.
▶ From which angles are the different perspectives drawn?

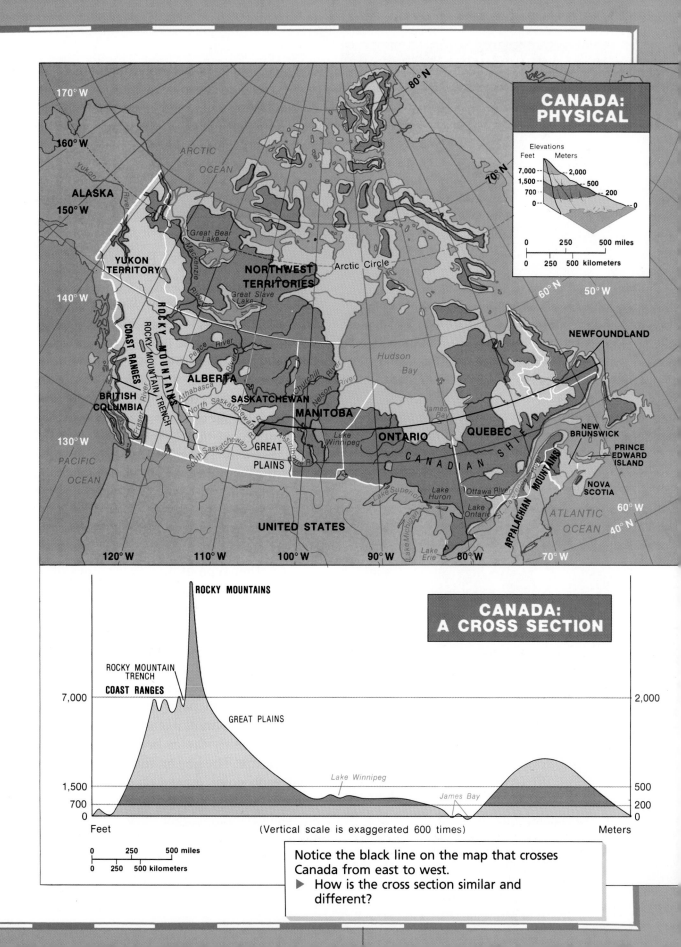

CANADA: PHYSICAL

Elevations
Feet | Meters

7,000 -- -- 2,000
1,500 -- -- 500
700 -- -- 200
0 -- -- 0

0   250   500 miles
0   250   500 kilometers

170° W
160° W
ALASKA
150° W
140° W
130° W

ARCTIC OCEAN

YUKON TERRITORY

NORTHWEST TERRITORIES

Great Bear Lake

Mackenzie River

Great Slave Lake

Arctic Circle

80° N

70° N

60° N

50° W

COAST RANGES

ROCKY MOUNTAINS

ROCKY MOUNTAIN TRENCH

BRITISH COLUMBIA

Fraser River

Peace River

Athabasca River

ALBERTA

North Saskatchewan R.

South Saskatchewan R.

SASKATCHEWAN

MANITOBA

GREAT PLAINS

Assiniboine R.

Lake Winnipeg

Churchill River

Nelson River

Hudson Bay

James Bay

ONTARIO

Lake Superior

Lake Michigan

Lake Huron

Lake Ontario

Lake Erie

QUEBEC

CANADIAN SHIELD

Ottawa River

St. Lawrence River

NEWFOUNDLAND

NEW BRUNSWICK

PRINCE EDWARD ISLAND

NOVA SCOTIA

APPALACHIAN MOUNTAINS

ATLANTIC OCEAN

60° W

40° N

PACIFIC OCEAN

UNITED STATES

120° W   110° W   100° W   90° W   80° W   70° W

CANADA: A CROSS SECTION

ROCKY MOUNTAINS

ROCKY MOUNTAIN TRENCH

COAST RANGES

GREAT PLAINS

Lake Winnipeg

James Bay

7,000

1,500
700
0
Feet

2,000

500
200
0
Meters

(Vertical scale is exaggerated 600 times)

0   250   500 miles
0   250   500 kilometers

Notice the black line on the map that crosses
Canada from east to west.
▶ How is the cross section similar and
different?

THE AMERICAS: COFFEE AND BANANAS

- • Coffee
- • Bananas

THE AMERICAS: WHEAT AND CORN

- • Wheat
- • Corn

Both North and South America produce many agricultural crops.
▶ Which three crops are grown in large quantities along the eastern coast of Brazil?

exaggerated, or much larger, in relation to the scale for distance. This process is called **vertical exaggeration**.

The amount of vertical exaggeration is given on the profile of Canada on page 19. It says, "Vertical scale is exaggerated 600 times." This means that the heights have been drawn to appear 600 times larger than the distances.

C. Maps for Special Purposes

Distribution Maps There are many other types of maps that are in use today. One type you will find throughout this book is called a distribution map. A distribution map shows the distribution of a certain quality — such as climate, crops, or resources — in a country or region.

The maps on this page show the distribution of four crops produced in the Americas. Distribution maps help you understand why some types of agriculture or industries develop in certain parts of the world. For example, in which part of South America is most of the wheat grown?

Another type of map that shows distribution is a *choropleth* (KOR uh pleth) map. A choropleth map uses different colors to show the distribution of something in a region or in the world. The colors also show the quantity, or how much of, that something each region has.

The map on page 9 is a choropleth map of average annual temperature. In this case, the quality that is being compared is temperature. The key on the map explains what each color means on the map. For example, on that map you can see that purple shows regions that have an average annual temperature above 80°F (27°C). Which color is used to signify the lowest range in temperature? You can use the

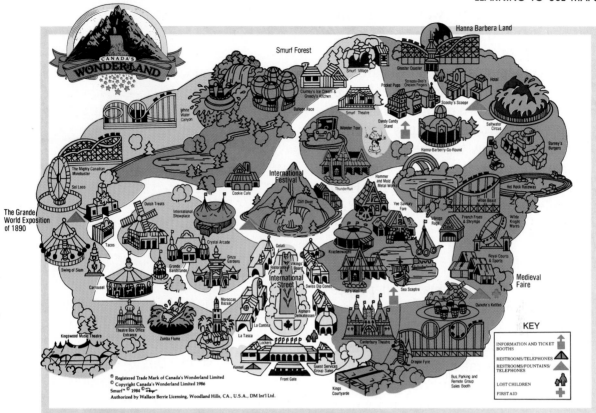

Symbols and drawings are used to represent places and objects on this map of Canada's Wonderland, an amusement park.
▶ Where are the information and ticket booths located?

same choropleth map to find the regions in the world with similar temperatures and with very different temperatures. Other choropleth maps compare such things as how much of a certain crop is produced and how much of a certain natural resource is mined in a certain region or in the world.

Special-Interest Maps Maps are often made for amusement parks, historical sites within a town, or tourist areas. They help orient the visitors so that they can find their way around and take advantage of the facilities available. The key sometimes has symbols for human features rather than natural features. These can easily be

recognized and located on the map. What is the symbol used for first-aid stations on the map entitled "Canada's Wonderland"?

Sometimes a special-interest map will show only certain symbols in the key. Other symbols are drawn on the map on the spot where they are located, and they are labeled. Find the *Ghoster Coaster* on the map. What other attractions on the map do you find interesting?

Historical Maps Another type of special-purpose map is a historical map. Historical maps are often about voyages, discoveries, trade routes, or battles for independence. Look at the historical map on page 22. Read the title. What is the subject of the map? Which areas of the world are shown? Does the map have a grid?

The key, or legend, that accompanies a historical map must be studied carefully for its correct interpretation. For example, on the map key shown on the map entitled *Pizarro's Route*, you need to pay attention to the purple arrow and the direction of that arrow to follow the route of Francisco Pizarro. Now notice the map scale. How many miles are represented by one inch on the map?

D. Other Maps

There are, of course, many other types of maps. You probably listed some of them when you began this lesson. Did you list a map of vegetation regions? Such a map shows where natural features — rain forests, deserts and semideserts, grasslands — are located. A population density map shows where the largest number of people live in the world or in a certain part of the world. Road and city maps guide travelers.

An atlas is a collection of maps used for reference. A Social Studies textbook usually has an atlas near the back of the book. Sometimes an atlas will have a variety of types of maps. The Atlas in this book features physical maps of the continents of the world, several climographs

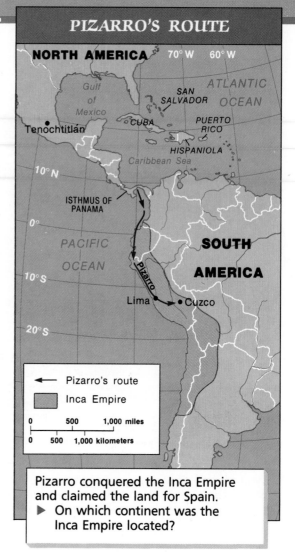

Pizarro conquered the Inca Empire and claimed the land for Spain.
▶ On which continent was the Inca Empire located?

of the world and political maps of the world and of the United States. Turn to pages 592 to 602 to preview these maps before you answer the Think and Write questions below.

LESSON **3** REVIEW

THINK AND WRITE

A. What are three features of a political map?
B. How is color often used on a physical map?
C. When would a special-purpose map be of particular use?
D. When would you use an atlas?

SKILLS CHECK

WRITING SKILL

Imagine that you and your family are planning a three-week vacation trip to Canada. You are in charge of getting together the maps you might need. In an explanatory paragraph or two, tell which maps you will need. Explain why.

Projections

If you ever made meatballs or cookies, you may have at first made them in a ball shape and then flattened them out. What happened when they were flattened out?

spherical   projection
distortion

Why do all flat maps have distortion?

A. Representing the Earth

The Problem of Distortion No map or photograph printed on a flat sheet of paper can show the earth perfectly. This is because the earth is **spherical**, or ball-shaped. The surface is curved. It cannot be flattened without **distortion**.

Distortion means "a changing of the form of" something. If you have ever worked with modeling clay, you know that the models are distorted, or pulled out of shape, when they are stretched or twisted. You can get an idea of the distortion involved in making a map of the earth on a flat sheet of paper if you peel an orange. As you peel, try to keep at least half the skin

FROM GLOBE TO MAP

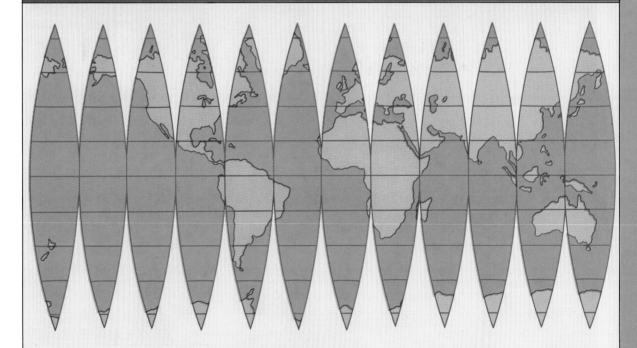

For this map, the "skin" from a globe has been peeled and laid out flat.
▶ Why is it necessary to "split" the continents?

unbroken. Now try to flatten the curved orange skin. You cannot do this without tearing the skin. The cartographer has the same problem when he or she tries to show the earth on a flat page.

The only way to accurately show the earth is to draw it on a globe. But a globe is not a handy form for most maps. It cannot be very large because a very large globe will not fit in a room. A curving surface like that of a part of a globe also must be rigid. It could not be folded, rolled up for storage, or carried around in one's pocket. Imagine taking a globe as your guide on an automobile trip.

What qualities should an accurate map of the earth have? First, such a map should show the true direction between any two points on the map. Second, the map should show the shapes of land-masses and water bodies correctly. Third, it should show all areas in their proper size relationship to each other. Fourth, it should have the same scale throughout.

Only a globe can have all four of these qualities at the same time. A flat map can only show some of these qualities. The choice of which qualities a cartographer will select depends upon the use for which the map is made.

Map Projections Cartogaphers have invented map **projections** to deal with the problem of selecting what map quality to show correctly on any map. A projection is a way to show a drawing of the earth on a flat surface. For example, a map that is to be used for navigation should show directions as straight lines. That way it is easy to plan the course for a ship or an airplane.

A globe cannot be folded, rolled up, or carried around in your pocket, yet a globe has many uses.
▶ How can you use a globe in school?

B. The Mercator Projection

Early Mapmaking The most famous projection for navigation was developed in 1568 by Gerardus Mercator (juh RAHR dus mer KAYT ur). He worked at a time when European navigators were sailing to many parts of the world. There was a great need for accurate maps for navigation. Mercator invented a projection, called the Mercator projection, that showed compass directions as straight lines. This was very useful for sailors because they could see the direction between point A and point B easily. The map below is an example of a Mercator projection. Notice that directions are shown as straight lines.

Mercator drew his projection by stretching the parts of the map close to the poles so that all parallels and meridians crossed at right angles. North and south were always top and bottom. East and west were always right and left. A Mercator projection makes it easy to see that Oslo, Norway, is west of St. Petersburg, in the former Soviet Union. Both are located at about 60°N.

Distortion in Projections Although a Mercator projection is good for finding di-

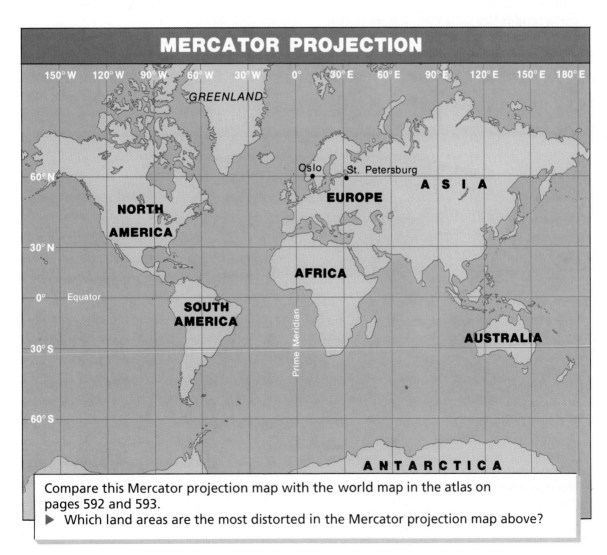

MERCATOR PROJECTION

Compare this Mercator projection map with the world map in the atlas on pages 592 and 593.
▶ Which land areas are the most distorted in the Mercator projection map above?

rections, it is not helpful for comparing the sizes of different landmasses. This is because the sizes of land and sea areas have been changed to keep the directions accurate. Between the 50th parallels and the Equator, the distortion is fairly small. The sizes of the polar areas, however, are greatly exaggerated. That is why Greenland looks as big as South America in a Mercator projection, such as the one on page 25. Greenland is really only about one-sixth the size of South America.

You know that this book is about Canada and Latin America. Canada is close to the North Pole, but most of Latin America is near the Equator. In a Mercator projection of these areas, Canada appears much larger than South America. In reality, the opposite is true. South America is far larger than Canada. You can see this by comparing the size of North America on the Mercator projection with its size on the other map projections shown on this page and page 27.

C. An Improved Projection

A far better kind of projection for comparing countries or continents is one that reduces the distortion of land areas. This type of projection is called an equal-area projection. Compare the sizes of Greenland and South America on the equal-area projections on this page and page 27. On which map does South America appear larger?

The equal-area projection on this page accurately shows land and water sizes but it does not show the shapes cor-

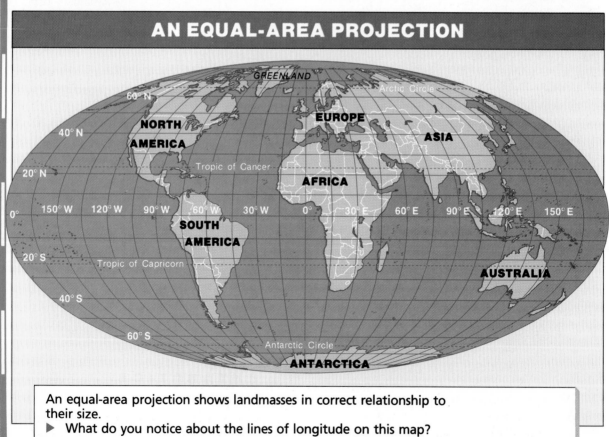

AN EQUAL-AREA PROJECTION

An equal-area projection shows landmasses in correct relationship to their size.
▶ What do you notice about the lines of longitude on this map?

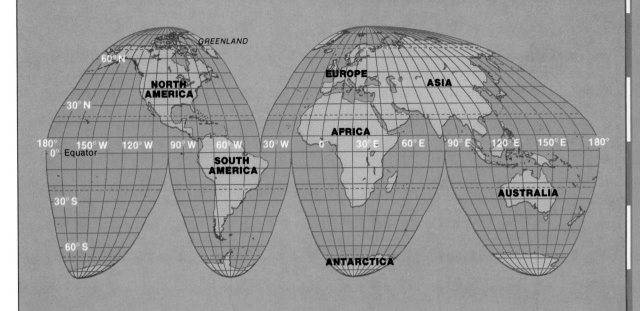

Another type of equal-area projection is an interrupted projection.
▶ How is the distortion over water reduced in an interrupted projection?

rectly. The distortion increases toward the poles. The projection shown on this page has the advantage of reducing the distortion of areas and shapes. It does this by breaking the map up, somewhat as you would do to get an orange peel to lie flat. Such a map is called an interrupted projection. The name comes from the interrupting, or breaking, of the projection. In this type of projection, parts of the water areas are "split" so that the shapes of the large landmasses are shown correctly. The land areas in the outer part of an interrupted projection are not as distorted as they would have been in a Mercator projection. Because they show land sizes the way they really are, interrupted projections are also equal-area projections.

LESSON 4 REVIEW

THINK AND WRITE

A. Why is there distortion when the earth's surface is shown on a flat map?

B. What advantages and disadvantages does Mercator's projection have?

C. How have the equal-area projections improved upon the Mercator projection?

SKILLS CHECK

MAP SKILL

Compare the equal-area interrupted projection map on this page with the Mercator projection on page 25. List as many reasons as you can to prove that the newer map is an improvement over Mercator's map.

Time and Time Lines

THINK ABOUT WHAT YOU KNOW

Think about different clocks and different types of watches you use or have seen. How do they compare with ancient methods of telling time, such as by using a sundial or an hourglass?

STUDY THE VOCABULARY

A.M.
P.M.
standard time zone

International
Date Line
time line

FOCUS YOUR READING

How have methods of telling time changed over the years?

A. Measurement of Time

Hours The idea of having 12 hours in a natural day, or daylight, is very old. Over 5,000 years ago the ancient Egyptians divided the daylight time into 12 parts. But the Egyptian hours were not like the hours we use now. The length of an Egyptian hour changed with the seasons, just as the length of a natural day does. The hours we use, of course, are all of the same length whether it is summer or winter. Can you imagine what problems and confusion there would be if we had short hours in winter and long hours in summer?

A.M. and P.M. The Romans thought noon, the time when the sun is directly overhead in the sky, was an important time

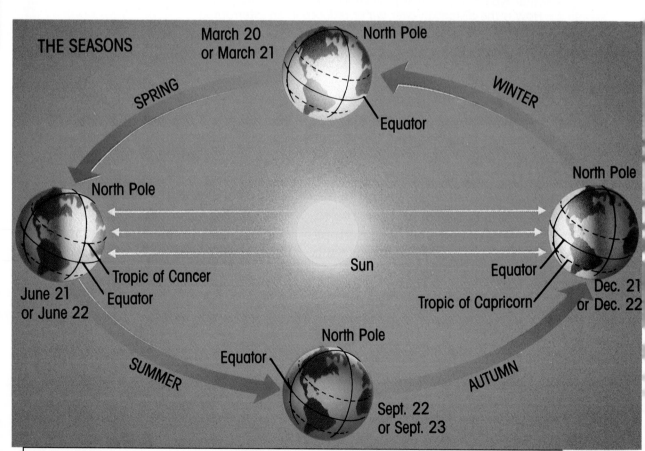

THE SEASONS

March 20 or March 21

North Pole

Equator

SPRING

WINTER

North Pole

North Pole

Sun

Equator

Tropic of Cancer

Equator

June 21 or June 22

Tropic of Capricorn

Dec. 21 or Dec. 22

North Pole

Equator

SUMMER

AUTUMN

Sept. 22 or Sept. 23

The tilt of the earth as it orbits, or travels around, the sun is the cause of our seasons.
► Which dates mark the start of winter in the Northern Hemisphere?

THE EARTH'S ROTATION

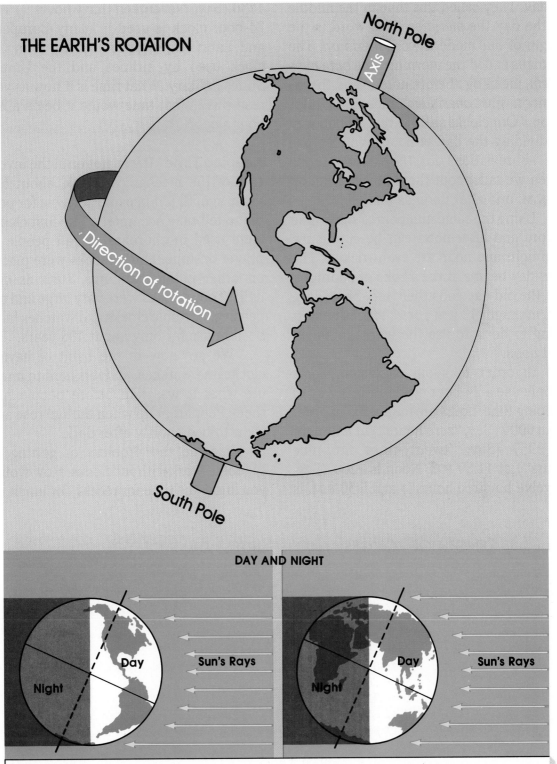

North Pole

Axis

Direction of rotation

South Pole

DAY AND NIGHT

Night | Day | Sun's Rays

Night | Day | Sun's Rays

As the earth rotates, only one half of it can be lighted by the sun. The other half is in darkness.

▶ In what direction does the earth rotate?

of day. They called this time in the middle of the day the *meridies*. This word is the origin of our modern word *meridian*. The Romans called the morning time *ante meridiem*, meaning "before noon," and the afternoon *post meridiem,* meaning "after noon." Our clocks still use this Roman way of dividing the day at noon. We also use the abbreviations for the Roman terms when we talk about the time before noon as **A.M.** and after noon as **P.M.**

Using the same numbers to show time before and after noon can be confusing. Midnight and noon are even trickier. The new day begins at the stroke of midnight, but the old day ends then, too. Should we call midnight 12 A.M., or 12 P.M.? The best thing to do is to use the words *midnight* and *noon.*

In order to avoid confusion, some people use a 24-hour clock. In this way of keeping time, hours are numbered in order from 0000 (Say, "zero hours") at midnight to 2359 (Say, "twenty-three fifty-nine hours") at 11:59 P.M. Noon is 1200 (Say, "twelve hundred hours") and 5:30 P.M. is 1730 (Say, "seventeen thirty hours.") The 24-hour clock is used in many European and Latin American countries. It is the clock used by airlines and the United States military. What time is it now as you read this? What time would it be on a 24-hour clock?

Keeping Time It was not until the invention of the mechanical clock, about 600 years ago, that it became possible for people to tell time accurately. The first clocks were used in churches to call people to prayer on time. Later, clocks were placed on other public buildings, such as city halls. These clocks were very large and expensive. Portable clocks and watches have been in use for only about 400 years.

We are now in the habit of having clocks and watches, and it is hard to imagine what it was like before people had them. People got up when the sun rose and went to bed shortly after dark.

Imagine the problem of getting to school or work without clocks. How would you know the time for recess, for lunch, or

LENGTH OF LONGEST AND SHORTEST DAYS OF THE YEAR

Latitude north or south	Longest day (Hours:Minutes)	Shortest day (Hours:Minutes)	Time difference (Hours:Minutes)
0° (Equator)	12:07	12:07	0:00
10°	12:43	11:33	1:10
20°	13:21	10:55	2:26
30°	14:05	10:12	3:53
40°	15:02	9:19	5:43
45°	15:38	8:46	6:42
50°	16:23	8:04	8:19
60°	18:53	5:52	13:01
66 1/2° (Arctic and Antarctic Circles)	24:00	0:00	24:00

After you find the latitude in your area by looking at the atlas map on page 594, you can use the table.
▶ What is the length of the longest day in your area?

(Left) An early mechanical 12-hour clock and (above) a 24-hour clock are shown.

▶ Why is the 24-hour system used by airline personnel and others?

(Clockwise) Early ways of telling time included a water clock, an hourglass, and a sundial.

▶ Why, do you think, are they not popular today?

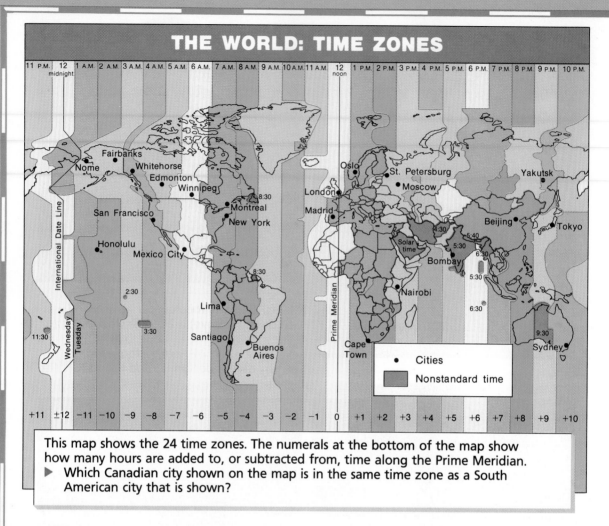

THE WORLD: TIME ZONES

| 11 P.M. | 12 midnight | 1 A.M. | 2 A.M. | 3 A.M. | 4 A.M. | 5 A.M. | 6 A.M. | 7 A.M. | 8 A.M. | 9 A.M. | 10 A.M. | 11 A.M. | 12 noon | 1 P.M. | 2 P.M. | 3 P.M. | 4 P.M. | 5 P.M. | 6 P.M. | 7 P.M. | 8 P.M. | 9 P.M. | 10 P.M. |

| +11 | ±12 | -11 | -10 | -9 | -8 | -7 | -6 | -5 | -4 | -3 | -2 | -1 | 0 | +1 | +2 | +3 | +4 | +5 | +6 | +7 | +8 | +9 | +10 |

Cities •
Nonstandard time

This map shows the 24 time zones. The numerals at the bottom of the map show how many hours are added to, or subtracted from, time along the Prime Meridian.
▶ Which Canadian city shown on the map is in the same time zone as a South American city that is shown?

for going home in the afternoon? How could people know when to leave to catch a bus, a train, or an airplane for a trip? The invention of clocks truly changed the way people live!

B. Time Zones

Have you ever heard a television announcer say that a program will be shown at 8 P.M. Eastern Time and 7 P.M. Central Time? Why should a television program be shown at two different times? The answer is that the world is divided into time zones. These time zones, called **standard time zones**, have been created to make clock time the same for large parts of the earth.

There are 24 standard time zones on the earth, one for each hour of the day. The starting point for the world's time zones is the Prime Meridian, at 0°. Most time zones cover about 15° of longitude in a band going from pole to pole. All places within each zone have the same time, regardless of the exact position of the sun in the sky. Many of the time zone boundaries do not follow the meridians exactly. They have been changed to follow the boundaries of countries or states. That way all parts of a country or large sections of a country can have the same clock time.

Altogether, the United States has eight time zones. The 48 *contiguous* states of the United States have four time zones. *Contiguous* means "touching," or "bordering." The 48 contiguous states are all the states except Alaska and Hawaii. Alaska and Hawaii are apart from the other states and do not touch them.

You have probably heard of these four time zones in the contiguous United States — the Eastern, Central, Mountain, and Pacific zones. The states of the Atlantic coast are in the Eastern Standard Time Zone. Most states in the middle part of the country east of the Rocky Mountains are in the Central Standard Time Zone. The states in the mountainous parts of the West are in the Mountain Standard Time Zone. The states of the Pacific coast are in the Pacific Standard Time Zone.

Study the map of the time zones of the world. Pick out one zone. Notice that in the zone to its east, the time is one hour later, while in the zone to its west, the time is one hour earlier. It is important to remember: Time gets earlier as you move to the west and gets later as you go east. If a television program is shown at the same time in all 50 states, as is sometimes done for live broadcasts of sports events or political speeches, it will be seen at different hours, depending on which time zone people are in. If the President addresses the nation from Washington, D.C., (Eastern Time Zone) at 8 P.M., the broadcast will begin in Chicago

Sports events are often shown "live" on television in all 50 states.
▶ If a sports event, such as the one shown, is on television at 6:00 P.M. Eastern time, what time will people in the Central time zone see it?

(Central Zone) at 7 P.M., in Denver (Mountain Zone) at 6 P.M.; and in Los Angeles (Pacific Zone) at 5 P.M. In Alaska (Alaska Zone), it will be 4 P.M. In Hawaii (Hawaii-Aleutian Zone), the President's speech will be heard live at 3 P.M. The United States stretches across six time zones from Maine to the Aleutian islands of western Alaska. (The westernmost Aleutians are in the same zone as Hawaii.) If you flew from New York to Hawaii, you would set your watch back six hours. The former Union of Soviet Socialist Republics (the Soviet Union) is the only country that has more time zones than the United States. It has eleven time zones.

The International Date Line The explorer Magellan (muh JEL un) sailed on the first recorded voyage around the world in 1519. Magellan's crew carefully recorded each day of the trip in the ship's log. They thought the date when they returned to Spain was Sunday, September 7, 1522.

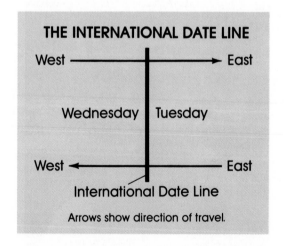

THE INTERNATIONAL DATE LINE

West ————————→ East

Wednesday | Tuesday

West ←———————— East

International Date Line

Arrows show direction of travel.

At the International Date Line, the date changes.
▶ If it is September 30 east of the line, what is the date west of it?

Much to their surprise, they found that the date in port was Monday, September 8, 1522. What had happened to the missing day? Had the ship's crew miscounted?

Magellan's ship went clear around the world, sailing to the west. As the crew sailed, they slowly gained time on the sun. By sailing all the way around the world, they actually took away a full day of earth rotation! So both the crew's record and the date in the Spanish port were correct.

Anyone who travels around the earth will have a similar experience. If you go around the earth from east to west, clock time gets earlier and a day is lost. If you go from west to east, clock time gets later and you gain a day. In order to make up for this gain or loss of time, it is necessary to have a place on the earth where days gained or lost can be adjusted.

The **International Date Line** is an imaginary line that marks the place where each calendar day begins. It roughly follows the meridian of 180°, just about in the middle of the Pacific Ocean. If you are on an airplane that crosses the International Date Line, the date will change. If the plane is traveling west toward Asia, you must skip a day (think of taking a day off the calendar). If you cross the International Date Line on Sunday, it will be Monday on the other side. If the plane is traveling east toward America, a day is repeated (think of putting a day back on the calendar). If you cross the Date Line on Thursday, it will be Wednesday on the other side of the line. International travelers must understand how time changes and day changes work in order to schedule travel times and appointments. The International Date Line is part of the standard time system that is used throughout the world.

Time lines let you see and compare the amount of time between events.
▶ About how much time passed from Cortés's conquest of the Aztecs
to Pizarro's conquest of the Incas?

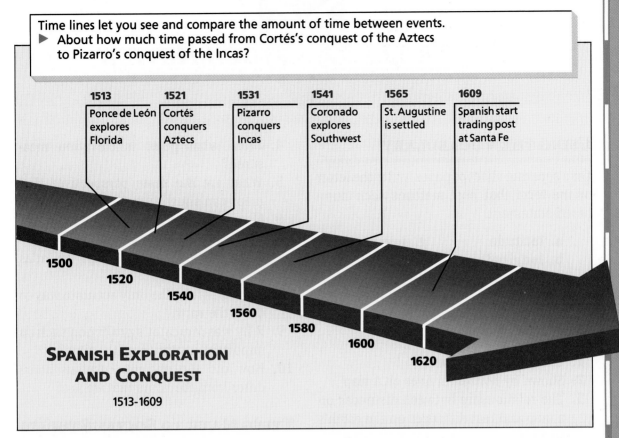

1513	1521	1531	1541	1565	1609
Ponce de León explores Florida	Cortés conquers Aztecs	Pizarro conquers Incas	Coronado explores Southwest	St. Augustine is settled	Spanish start trading post at Santa Fe

1500
1520
1540
1560
1580
1600
1620

SPANISH EXPLORATION
AND CONQUEST

1513-1609

C. Time Lines

Just as a map shows the locations of objects on the earth, a time line shows the locations of events in time. Like a map, a time line has a scale, but the scale represents years rather than distances. Markers are placed equal distances apart on a time line to enclose spaces that stand for a certain amount of time. On the time line shown above, each 11/16-inch space stands for 20 years. On a time line showing many events that occurred over a longer period of time, a different scale would be used. For example, the scale of 1 inch (2.5 cm) to represent 100 years might be used.

Notice that black lines connect the events and the appropriate locations on the time line. This makes it easy to understand developments in the progress of time. Throughout this book, you will find time lines to help you understand *when* things happened, just as you will find maps to show you *where* things are located.

LESSON 5 REVIEW

THINK AND WRITE

A. What do we still use today in measuring time that was used long ago?

B. Summarize what standard time zones are.

C. How do time lines help you to better understand historical events?

SKILLS CHECK

THINKING SKILL

"There is no time like the present." is a famous saying. Think of at least two ways that you can interpret this saying. Share your ideas with some classmates.

MAP SKILLS HANDBOOK REVIEW

USING THE VOCABULARY

On a separate sheet of paper, write the letter of the term that best matches each numbered statement.

a. latitude
b. longitude
c. hemispheres
d. scale
e. elevation
f. cartographer
g. perspective
h. relief
i. projection
j. International Date Line

1. The height of the land
2. Shown by horizontal lines on a map
3. The relationship between distances on a map and real distances on the earth's surface
4. An imaginary line that marks the place where each calendar day begins
5. Differences in the elevation of landforms on a map
6. The way things look from a given point by their size, shape, and distance
7. Equal halves of the earth
8. Shown by vertical lines on a map
9. A way to show a drawing of the earth on a flat surface
10. A person who makes maps

REMEMBERING WHAT YOU READ

On a separate sheet of paper, answer the following questions in complete sentences.

1. From where does the word *orientation* come?
2. For what are geographic coordinates used?
3. Why would it be difficult to use a map without a scale?

4. From what point is elevation measured?
5. What are the three perspectives that maps can show?
6. How is a political map different from a physical map?
7. Name three kinds of maps an atlas might include.
8. Why is a globe the only accurate way to draw the earth?
9. Why was Mercator's projection such an important invention at the time?
10. How did the ancient Egyptian hours differ from the hours that we use?

TYING MATH TO SOCIAL STUDIES

In the metric system, the distance between two places is measured in kilometers. A mile is equal to 1.609 kilometers. If you know the distance between two places in miles, you can figure it out in kilometers. To convert miles to kilometers, multiply the distance in miles by 1.609. Convert the distances between New York and these world cities from miles to kilometers: Cairo — 5,602 miles; Hong Kong — 8,054 miles; Mexico City — 2,094 miles.

THINKING CRITICALLY

On a separate sheet of paper, answer the following questions in complete sentences.

1. Does climate vary according to latitude or longitude?

2. Name five reasons why people use maps.
3. How does the length of longitude lines on a Mercator projection compare with those on an equal-area projection?
4. Explain why you think either the 12-hour clock or the 24-hour clock is better.
5. List three things you might need a map for in the near future.

SUMMARIZING THE CHAPTER

On a separate piece of paper, draw a graphic organizer like the one shown here. Copy the information from this graphic organizer on the one you have drawn. Under the main idea for each lesson, write three words or phrases that support the main idea.

CHAPTER THEME

Maps and globes provide a wealth of information about people and the earth. To interpret maps, it is necessary to understand scale, symbols, latitude, longitude, and projections.

LESSON 1
Map features help us find the locations of things on the earth.

1. Geographic coordinates
2. _____
3. _____

LESSON 2
Maps help us show the relationship between things on the earth.

1. Elevation
2. _____
3. _____

LESSON 3
There are different maps for different uses.

1. Political maps
2. _____
3. _____

LESSON 4
Projections are a way of showing a drawing of the earth on a flat surface.

1. Mercator projection
2. _____
3. _____

LESSON 5
The measurement of time has evolved through the years.

1. Standard time zones
2. _____
3. _____

COUNTRIES OF THE
WESTERN HEMISPHERE

	FLAG	TOTAL AREA	POPULATION AND DENSITY	ECONOMY	MAJOR EXPORT
ANTIGUA AND BARBUDA — St. Johns — N. AMERICA		171 sq mi 443 sq km	78,400 458 per sq mi 177 per sq km		Machinery
ARGENTINA — Buenos Aires — S. AMERICA		1,072,156 sq mi 2,776,884 sq km	31,900,000 30 per sq mi 11 per sq km		Wheat
BAHAMAS — Nassau — N. AMERICA		5,386 sq mi 13,950 sq km	249,000 46 per sq mi 18 per sq km		Petroleum
BARBADOS — Bridgetown — N. AMERICA		166 sq mi 430 sq km	256,000 1,542 per sq mi 595 per sq km		Electrical parts
BELIZE — Belmopan — N. AMERICA		8,867 sq mi 22,966 sq km	179,814 20 per sq mi 8 per sq km		Sugar
BOLIVIA — La Paz — S. AMERICA		424,162 sq mi 1,098,580 sq km	7,193,000 17 per sq mi 6 per sq km		Natural Gas
BRAZIL — Brasília — S. AMERICA		3,284,426 sq mi 8,506,663 sq km	147,400,000 45 per sq mi 17 per sq km		Coffee
CANADA — Ottawa — N. AMERICA		3,851,809 sq mi 9,976,185 sq km	26,300,000 7 per sq mi 3 per sq km		Motor Vehicles
CHILE — Santiago — S. AMERICA		292,257 sq mi 756,946 sq km	13,000,000 44 per sq mi 17 per sq km		Copper
COLOMBIA — Bogotá — S. AMERICA		439,735 sq mi 1,138,914 sq km	32,316,939 73 per sq mi 28 per sq km		Coffee

38

■ Agriculture ☐ Industry ■ Services ☐ Not Available

		FLAG	TOTAL AREA	POPULATION AND DENSITY	ECONOMY	MAJOR EXPORT
COSTA RICA	N. AMERICA San Jose		19,652 sq mi 50,899 sq km	3,000,000 153 per sq mi 59 per sq km		Coffee
CUBA	N. AMERICA Havana		44,218 sq mi 114,525 sq km	10,500,000 237 per sq mi 92 per sq km		Sugar
DOMINICA	N. AMERICA Roseau		289 sq mi 749 sq km	81,200 281 per sq mi 108 per sq km		Bananas
DOMINICAN REPUBLIC	N. AMERICA Santo Domingo		18,657 sq mi 48,322 sq km	7,000,000 375 per sq mi 145 per sq km		Sugar
ECUADOR	S. AMERICA Quito		109,483 sq mi 283,561 sq km	10,500,000 96 per sq mi 37 per sq km		Crude Oil
EL SALVADOR	N. AMERICA San Salvador		8,260 sq mi 21,393 sq km	5,100,000 617 per sq mi 238 per sq km		Coffee
FRENCH GUIANA	S. AMERICA Cayenne		35,135 sq mi 91,000 sq km	114,600 3 per sq mi 2 per sq km		Shellfish
GRENADA	N. AMERICA St. George's		133 sq mi 344 sq km	100,000 752 per sq mi 290 per sq km		Cocoa
GUATEMALA	N. AMERICA Guatemala City		42,042 sq mi 108,889 sq km	9,198,448 219 per sq mi 84 per sq km		Coffee
GUYANA	S. AMERICA Georgetown		83,000 sq mi 214,970 sq km	800,000 10 per sq mi 4 per sq km		Bauxite

■ Agriculture ☐ Industry ■ Services ☐ Not Available

	FLAG	TOTAL AREA	POPULATION AND DENSITY	ECONOMY	MAJOR EXPORT
HAITI N. AMERICA — Port-au-Prince		10,714 sq mi 27,749 sq km	5,609,000 523 per sq mi 202 per sq km		Coffee
HONDURAS N. AMERICA — Tegucigalpa		43,277 sq mi 112,087 sq km	5,000,000 116 per sq mi 45 per sq km		Bananas
JAMAICA N. AMERICA — Kingston		4,471 sq mi 11,580 sq km	2,500,000 559 per sq mi 216 per sq km		Aluminum
MEXICO N. AMERICA — Mexico City		761,600 sq mi 1,972,544 sq km	86,700,000 114 per sq mi 44 per sq km		Crude Oil
NICARAGUA N. AMERICA — Managua		49,579 sq mi 128,410 sq km	3,500,000 71 per sq mi 27 per sq km		Coffee
PANAMA N. AMERICA — Panama City		33,659 sq mi 87,177 sq km	2,400,000 71 per sq mi 28 per sq km		Bananas
PARAGUAY S. AMERICA — Asuncion		157,043 sq mi 406,741 sq km	4,200,000 27 per sq mi 10 per sq km		Cotton
PERU S. AMERICA — Lima		496,222 sq mi 1,285,215 sq km	21,400,000 43 per sq mi 17 per sq km		Copper
PUERTO RICO N. AMERICA — San Juan		3,435 sq mi 8,897 sq km	3,300,000 961 per sq mi 371 per sq km		Chemicals
ST. KITTS-NEVIS N. AMERICA — Basseterre		118 sq mi 306 sq km	45,000 339 per sq mi 131 per sq km		Sugar

	FLAG	TOTAL AREA	POPULATION AND DENSITY	ECONOMY	MAJOR EXPORT
St. Lucia N. AMERICA — Castries		238 sq mi 616 sq km	148,183 623 per sq mi 240 per sq km		Bananas
St. Vincent & the Grenadines N. AMERICA — Kingstown		150 sq mi 389 sq km	100,000 667 per sq mi 257 per sq km		Bananas
Suriname S. AMERICA — Paramaribo		63,251 sq mi 163,820 sq km	400,000 6 per sq mi 2 per sq km		Aluminum
Trinidad and Tobago N. AMERICA — Port of Spain		1,980 sq mi 5,128 sq km	1,200,000 628 per sq mi 606 per sq km		Crude Oil
United States N. AMERICA — Washington, DC		3,615,123 sq mi 9,363,169 sq km	250,885,000 69 per sq mi 27 per sq km		Machinery
Uruguay S. AMERICA — Montevideo		68,536 sq mi 177,508 sq km	3,000,000 44 per sq mi 17 per sq km		Meat
Venezuela S. AMERICA — Caracas		352,143 sq mi 912,050 sq km	19,734,968 56 per sq mi 22 per sq km		Crude Oil

WHY STUDY LATIN AMERICA AND CANADA?

Latin America and Canada share the Western Hemisphere with the United States. The history and development of the Americas reflect the interaction of people, resources, and ideas among nations.

▶ *In winter, the Rideau Canal in Ottawa, Canada, becomes the world's largest skating rink.*

CHAPTER 1
EXPLORING LATIN AMERICA AND CANADA

*T*he Western Hemisphere is divided into regions that have diverse physical features, climates, and cultural heritages.

This New World

THINK ABOUT WHAT YOU KNOW

Imagine that you are a student living in Europe in the year 1400. You are looking at a map of the world. Explain why North and South America are not shown on the map.

STUDY THE VOCABULARY

mainland	strait
territory	cartographer

FOCUS YOUR READING

How did some of the different parts of the Americas get their names?

A. Amerigo Vespucci's Famous Statement

In past days I wrote to you of my return from the new countries; and it is lawful to call it a new world, because none of these countries were known to our ancestors. I have found a new continent in that southern part; more populous and full of animals than our Europe, or Asia, or Africa, and even more temperate and pleasant than any other region known to us.

You have just read the words of Amerigo Vespucci (ah me REE goh ves-POO chee), an Italian explorer who sailed to America in 1499. Notice the similarity between Vespucci's first name, Amerigo, and the name *America*. As you can easily figure out, the Americas were named after Amerigo Vespucci.

How did that happen? Why weren't the Americas named in honor of Christopher Columbus? After all, Columbus had sailed to America seven years before Vespucci!

The answer lies in a decision made by a mapmaker. You will read more about that shortly.

B. Islands or Continents?

At the time Christopher Columbus made his famous voyages, people in Europe believed that all the major land areas in the world had already been discovered. Many people thought that Asia and the surrounding islands were much closer to Europe than they really are. They were unaware that if they sailed west, they would find two huge continents between Europe and Asia. They were also unaware of the existence of the vast Pacific Ocean.

The discoveries of Columbus and other daring explorers surprised Europeans. They thought the new lands could be nothing more than islands near Asia in the Atlantic Ocean. Little by little, as more explorers tried to sail around these supposed islands, the true shape and size of the New World became apparent.

This portrait of Columbus was done by an Italian artist in 1519.
▶ How would you describe Columbus based on this portrait?

45

John Cabot and his son Sebastian are shown on the left. Jacques Cartier, discoverer of the St. Lawrence River, is shown on the right.
▶ What qualities did these explorers probably have in common?

C. Several Names for Canada

John Cabot The mysteries of the great Atlantic Ocean and the promise of riches in a new land lured other adventurers. John Cabot, an Italian sailor, was sponsored by England, and in 1497 he sailed from Bristol, England, in a small ship called the *Matthew*. He took a northern route across the Atlantic and landed on islands off the coast of Canada. His trip took only 35 days, an extremely fast time for those days.

Like Columbus, Cabot thought he had reached Asia. He sailed along looking for ways to reach the **mainland**. The mainland is the main part of a country or continent. Cabot coasted around an area he called "New Found Land." Part of the shore where he sailed still carries that name. As you may have guessed, it is the island of Newfoundland. Because Cabot sailed for England, the English later would call the new land British North America.

Jacques Cartier France challenged England's claim to the **territory**, or area of land. In 1534 the king of France instructed a French sailor named Jacques Cartier (zhahk kahr tee AY) "to discover certain islands and lands where it is said a great quantity of gold and other precious things are to be found." With a crew that included many convicts from the local jail, Cartier sailed from France's western coast. He made a good crossing and explored the western coast of Newfoundland. Then fog set in. Cautiously he made his way to the northern entrance of the St. Lawrence River, passing through the **strait** called the Strait of Belle Isle. A strait is a narrow body of water that connects two larger bodies of water. He crossed the mouth of the St. Lawrence River. Cartier later explored Prince Edward Island. He said he saw "the fairest land that could possibly be seen, and fields of wild corn and peas in bloom." Because Cartier sailed for France, he named this land New France.

What about the name *Canada*? According to one story, Cartier stopped while journeying up the St. Lawrence River to ask some Native Americans where he was.

They answered "Kanata," an Indian word for "village." Cartier thought the word referred to the land and therefore he named the land Canada. So this northern neighbor has had three names: *British North America*, *New France*, and *Canada*.

D. New Maps of the World

The Land Called America Martin Waldseemüller (VAHLT zay myool ur) was a German schoolteacher. However, he was also a **cartographer**, or mapmaker. He read a pamphlet in which Vespucci described his discoveries. Waldseemüller used the pamphlet to make a map of the

Very early maps, such as those made by the Greek scholar Claudius Ptolemy (TAHL uh mee) in the second century, were helpful to early navigators.
▶ Although the map has errors, what do you see that are still on maps?

world in 1507. As the New World had not yet been named, Waldseemüller decided to name it for Amerigo Vespucci. He called the land America, based on the explorer's first name.

Mercator's Distinction What about the terms *North America* and *South America*? They first appeared on a map in 1537. A Flemish cartographer, Gerardus Mercator, knew astronomy and mathematics and had great artistic ability. He tried to make accurate and attractive maps to guide sailors. Waldseemüller's map really had not even included North America. The land he had named America was actually the continent of South America. Mercator, who keenly followed news of voyages and discoveries, had learned more about the Americas. It was clear that there was a northern and a southern part to the Americas. Mercator decided to use the names *North America* and *South America* to distinguish between them.

Some navigators were slow to accept the new Mercator projection map. One navigator made the following statement about 100 years later: "I could wish all seamen would give over the sailing by the

The Netherlands, in Western Europe, became the center for printed map production during Mercator's time.
▶ For what is Mercator famous?

false plain charts, and sail by Mercator's chart, which is according to the truth of navigation. But it is a hard matter to convince any of the old navigators."

LESSON *1* REVIEW

THINK AND WRITE

A. Why did Vespucci think the land that he had explored should be called "a new world"?

B. Why did many people, including Columbus, think the lands in the Americas were nothing more than islands?

C. What do *British North America*, *New France*, and *Canada* have in common?

D. What serious mistake was made by Waldseemüller in his map of the world in 1507?

SKILLS CHECK

MAP SKILL

Use a map to find the Atlantic Ocean and the Pacific Ocean. Between which continents does each ocean lie?

The Americas and the Americans

THINK ABOUT WHAT YOU KNOW

Think about the word *America*. What does the word mean to you?

STUDY THE VOCABULARY

region   Latin America
Anglo-America   peninsula
heritage

FOCUS YOUR READING

In which ways can the lands of the Americas be grouped?

A. Regions in the Western Hemisphere

The Hemispheres The Equator divides the earth into hemispheres, or equal halves as you may recall. The half of the earth north of the Equator is called the Northern Hemisphere. The half south of the Equator is called the Southern Hemisphere. The line formed by the Prime Meridian (0°) and the 180° meridian also divides the earth. The half of the earth lying west of the Prime Meridian is called the Western Hemisphere. The half of the earth east of the Prime Meridian is called the Eastern Hemisphere. When you think of the earth divided at the Equator, you can easily see that the Americas are in both the Northern Hemisphere and the Southern Hemisphere. However, when you think of the earth divided by meridians, you can see that the Americas are totally within the Western Hemisphere.

Different Types of Regions There is another way to consider the earth. The term geographers often use is **region**. A region is an area that shares some common characteristic or feature, such as culture. Maps are used to show different types of regions. Since there are different features emphasized on maps, a country can belong to several regions.

B. Anglo-America

Canada and the United States The Western Hemisphere can be divided into two large cultural regions. One is **Anglo-America**. *Anglo-* is a word root meaning "English" or "England." Canada and the United States make up the region referred to as Anglo-America. Find Canada and the United States on the map on page 50. Then, on the map of the Western Hemi-

Parades are held in Canada and the United States in memory of ties to British beginnings.
▶ What instrument is being played?

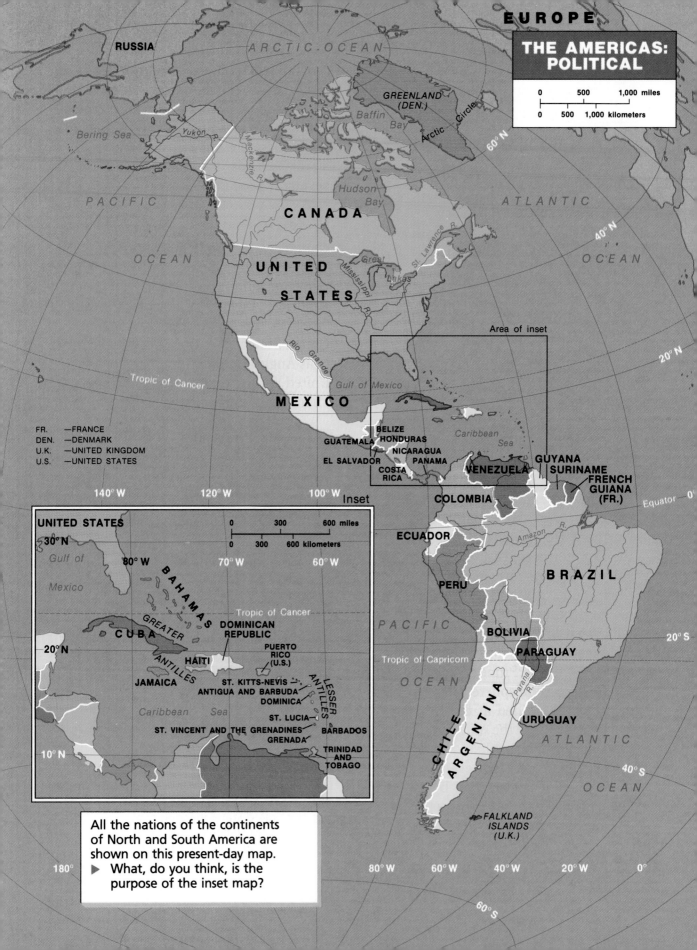

EUROPE

RUSSIA

ARCTIC OCEAN

THE AMERICAS: POLITICAL

| 0 | 500 | 1,000 miles |
| 0 | 500 | 1,000 kilometers |

GREENLAND
(DEN.)

Baffin
Bay

Bering Sea

Yukon

Arctic
Circle

60° N

PACIFIC

Mackenzie R.

CANADA

Hudson
Bay

ATLANTIC

40° N

OCEAN

St. Lawrence R.

Great
Lakes

OCEAN

UNITED

STATES

Mississippi R.

FR. —FRANCE
DEN. —DENMARK
U.K. —UNITED KINGDOM
U.S. —UNITED STATES

Rio Grande

Tropic of Cancer

Gulf of Mexico

20° N

Area of inset

MEXICO

BELIZE
GUATEMALA HONDURAS
NICARAGUA
EL SALVADOR PANAMA
COSTA
RICA

Caribbean
Sea

VENEZUELA

GUYANA
SURINAME
FRENCH
GUIANA
(FR.)

COLOMBIA

Equator 0°

ECUADOR

Amazon R.

BRAZIL

PERU

20° S

BOLIVIA

Tropic of Capricorn

PARAGUAY

PACIFIC

Paraná R.

OCEAN

URUGUAY

ARGENTINA

CHILE

ATLANTIC

40° S

FALKLAND
ISLANDS
(U.K.)

OCEAN

60° S

140° W   120° W   100° W

Inset

Inset

UNITED STATES

30° N

Gulf of
Mexico

80° W

| 0 | 300 | 600 miles |
| 0 | 300 | 600 kilometers |

70° W   60° W

BAHAMAS

Tropic of Cancer

CUBA

GREATER

DOMINICAN
REPUBLIC

20° N

ANTILLES

HAITI

PUERTO
RICO
(U.S.)

JAMAICA

ST. KITTS-NEVIS
ANTIGUA AND BARBUDA
DOMINICA

LESSER
ANTILLES

Caribbean   Sea

ST. LUCIA

ST. VINCENT AND THE GRENADINES
GRENADA

BARBADOS

10° N

TRINIDAD
AND
TOBAGO

180°

All the nations of the continents
of North and South America are
shown on this present-day map.
▶ What, do you think, is the
purpose of the inset map?

80° W   60° W   40° W   20° W   0°

sphere on page 51, locate the two countries again, shown as Anglo-America.

A Common British Heritage Many people in Anglo-America share a common British **heritage** and a common language, English. A heritage is something passed on to people from their great-grandparents and others before them. The British heritage of Anglo-America is made up of all the ideas and customs of the United States and Canada that can be traced to British beginnings. The system of laws, ideas about democracy, and even a sense of kinship or attachment to Britain are all part of the Anglo-American heritage.

When we say that Canada and the United States share a British heritage, however, that does not mean the two countries are exactly alike in their ways of life. For example, Canada's system of government more closely resembles the British system than does the government of the United States.

C. Latin America

The Region of Latin America The Spanish and Portuguese languages come from Latin, the language of the Roman Empire. The Roman Empire once included Spain and Portugal. People from these two countries settled most of the land in the Western Hemisphere that is south of the United States. Because these people spoke Spanish or Portuguese, each a Latin language, the area became known as **Latin America**. Mexico, Central America, the Caribbean islands (West Indies), and South America make up Latin America. Find them on the map on page 50. Find Latin America on the map on this page.

An Iberian Heritage Much of the region of Latin America has an Iberian heritage.

That is, most of the colonists who came to Latin America were from Spain and Portugal, two countries located on the Iberian Peninsula. A **peninsula** is a piece of land that reaches out into the sea from a larger body of land. The languages, ways of life, and economic and political systems in much of Latin America come from the Iberian heritage. You know that Canada and the United States share an Anglo-American heritage but that the two countries are not exactly alike. The same thing is true with regard to Latin America. The countries may share an Iberian heritage,

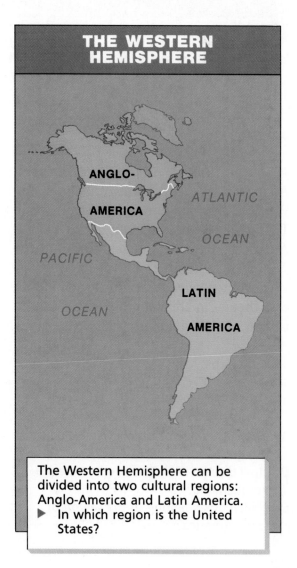

THE WESTERN HEMISPHERE

ANGLO-AMERICA

ATLANTIC OCEAN

PACIFIC OCEAN

LATIN AMERICA

The Western Hemisphere can be divided into two cultural regions: Anglo-America and Latin America.
▶ In which region is the United States?

In Argentina, a dance troupe and musicians in a park provide entertainment.
Like other countries in Latin America, folk dances remain popular.
▶ What dance in Anglo-America somewhat resembles the dance shown here?

but no two countries of Latin America are exactly alike.

A Shared Name   All the people living in Anglo-America and Latin America in the Western Hemisphere are "Americans." That's because both regions are part of the Americas. By what names are all these "Americans" known? The people in Canada call themselves Canadians, and others call them Canadians too. People in the United States generally call themselves Americans. When they travel to other countries, the term *North American* more closely defines their nationality. *United Statians* would sound awkward. Latin Americans generally call themselves by their own nationalities—Peruvian, Colombian, Brazilian, Panamanian, and so on. They often call themselves or are called Latin Americans. In the same manner, Latin Americans often refer to the people who live in the United States as North Americans.

LESSON *2* REVIEW

THINK AND WRITE

A. What are some of the ways we can group the lands in the Americas?
B. How did the region of Anglo-America get its name?
C. Which areas belong to the region of Latin America?

SKILLS CHECK

THINKING SKILL

Sometimes people are known by a name given to them because of the city, state, or special area in which they live. For example, people who live in Ohio are known as Ohioans. With your classmates, think of other names for "Americans."

A View from Above

THINK ABOUT WHAT YOU KNOW

Think of the outstanding physical features of the region in which you live. Which of these features might you expect to find in Canada and in Latin America?

STUDY THE VOCABULARY

tundra   plateau
plain   volcano
prairie   basin

FOCUS YOUR READING

What are the major physical features of Canada and Latin America?

A. Canada's Northern Location

America's Physical Features Imagine that you have been chosen to take a free guided sightseeing trip on a jet plane from northern Canada to South America. Of course, you'll be flying rather high, so you won't be able to see details such as towns and roads. Only the largest physical features will be easily seen. Just the same, you can still learn a great deal about the Americas and their lands. The map shows your flight route.

Canada—A Vast Land You begin your trip far to the north, flying over Canada. Below, an immense land, bordered on the east by the Atlantic Ocean and on the west by the Pacific Ocean, sprawls from the Arctic Circle southward. Canada takes up nearly a quarter of all the land in the Americas. It is the largest country in area in the Americas and the second largest in the entire world. Only Russia covers more area.

Canada also has one of the most northerly locations of any country in the world. It claims territory up to the North Pole, although much of it is under the water and ice of the Arctic Ocean.

The Barren North Flying southward over the barren north, you see below you a great expanse of **tundra**, or treeless ground. The long dry cold of winter makes it impossible for trees to survive.

The Canadian Shield As you continue southward over Canada, you see a most imposing region, the Canadian Shield. It is a great horseshoe-shaped region that stretches from the Arctic Ocean southward. You can see forested hills and mountains as well as flat lands. The guide mentions that the elevations range from

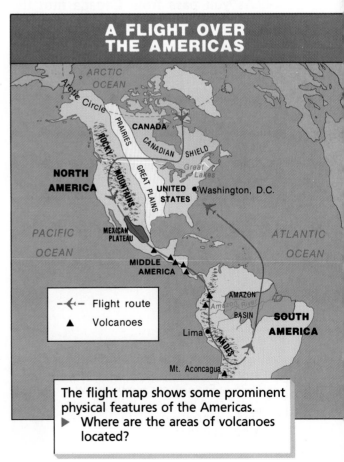

The flight map shows some prominent physical features of the Americas.
▶ Where are the areas of volcanoes located?

600 feet to over 3,500 feet (183 m to over 1,066 m) above sea level and that the shield covers about one half of the total area of Canada. Now you spot a chain of five lakes that you recognize as the Great Lakes. Your guide remarks that the Great Lakes form the world's largest chain of lakes.

The Canadian Prairies Heading westward along the Canadian–United States border, you pass over a long stretch of **plains**, or a flat area. You learn from the guide that the southern part of these plains is called the **prairies**. Soon you are flying over the impressive Rocky Mountains. What a sight!

B. Toward Latin America

As you pass from Canada into the United States, you look for a borderline separating the two great nations of Anglo-America. You cannot find one, since many physical features of Canada are also part of the United States. The long border between Canada and the United States really was fixed by agreement between the two countries.

Now that you're over the western part of the United States, it's time for the pilot to punch navigational coordinates into the plane's computer so that you can head for Latin America. In which direction will the jet fly?

If you look carefully at the map on page 53, you can see that the correct answer is southeast. Most of Latin America is east of Canada and the United States. Lima, Peru, on the west coast of South America, is nearly due south of Washington, D.C., which is on the east coast of North America.

In 1535, a Spanish conqueror drew a city plan for Lima, Peru, with streets around a central area.
▶ What is in this main area?

C. Flying over Latin America

Middle America Rising below you, and throughout most of northern Mexico, is a large **plateau**, called the Mexican Plateau. A plateau stands like a giant table, a level area raised above the surrounding land. Rugged mountains form both the eastern and western sides of the plateau. To the north the plateau extends into the United States. To the south it becomes a chain of large **volcanoes**. Volcanoes are openings in the earth, usually at the top of a cone-shaped hill or a mountain, out of which gases, rock, ashes, and lava may pour. The guide explains that each of the three highest snowcapped volcanoes rises over 17,000 feet (5,181 m). As you are passing over Central America, you see more volcanoes. Central America appears as a long, narrow strip of land between North America and South America. You can see that Mexico, Central America, and the islands of the Caribbean are a fragmented, or broken-up, area. This whole region is sometimes called Middle America. Find Middle America on the map on this page.

South America Look out your window as the plane heads south along the west coast of South America. You can see another rugged chain of mountains that extends along the entire length of the continent of South America. These are the Andes, the longest chain of mountains anywhere in the world. They run unbroken over 4,000 miles (6,436 km), from Venezuela in the north all the way to the southern tip of South America. They are extremely high. Only in Asia can you find mountains higher than the Andes. Aconcagua (ah kawn KAH gwuh), a mountain in western Argentina, is the highest mountain in the Western Hemisphere. It is

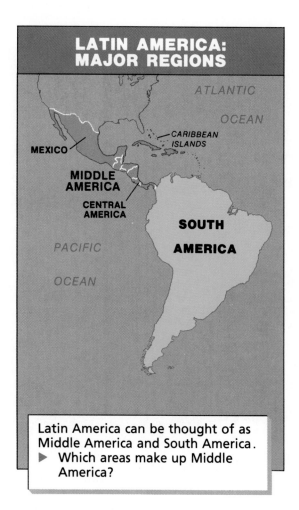

LATIN AMERICA: MAJOR REGIONS

Latin America can be thought of as Middle America and South America.
▶ Which areas make up Middle America?

22,834 feet (6,960 m) high. However, it does not stand alone. As you fly along the western coast, you count at least a dozen more mountains that are almost as high.

You have been flying south, and now the plane turns northward as you near the end of your trip. After flying some distance, the plane is over South America's largest lowland area, the Amazon Basin. A **basin** is a broad, flat valley. A vast *rain forest* covers most of the Amazon Basin. A rain forest is a forest with a thick growth of trees in a place with heavy rainfall. The huge Amazon rain forest covers an area about two-thirds the size of the United States! You also can see the outline of a great river winding its way through the

Look at these photographs in a clockwise direction. There are valleys, volcanoes, mountains, tundra, and plains.
▶ What other physical features do you see?

rain forest toward the Atlantic Ocean. It's the majestic Amazon River. With a length of about 4,000 miles (6,436 km), it's the world's second longest river. Only the Nile River in Africa is longer. Even the Nile, however, does not carry as much fresh water as the Amazon. Twenty percent of all the fresh water that empties into the oceans of the earth comes from the Amazon.

Now you're homeward bound. The view from the air has certainly been enchanting. Which places would you like to visit for a close-up view?

D. Other Physical Features of the Americas

To find out how things would look close up, you'll have to leave the comfort of the pressurized plane and get down on the ground. Before you step outside, here's a little north-to-south preview of some of the places you'll read about in this book. Try to imagine that you are visiting these places right now.

On a crisp, clear March or April night in Canada's far northern arctic region, up in the sky you see a natural electric-light show. The dancing bluish-green colors are the aurora borealis, or northern lights. Early the next day, you trek across the frozen tundra, where summer temperatures do not rise above 50°F (10°C) and winter temperatures can take a nose dive to −50°F (−10°C).

You shed your heavy clothing and put on lightweight clothing. Be sure you wear

Angel Falls. While you're in the area, you take a steamship from the Amazon River's Atlantic mouth and sail 2,300 miles (3,700 km) all the way to Iquitos (ee KEE-tohs), Peru. When you finish your trip along the world's longest naturally navigable river, you decide to head for the fertile flat plains known as the Pampas of Argentina. There you see fields of wheat, herds of cattle, and the famous Argentine cowhand.

Then you might head still farther south to a plateau between the Andes and the Atlantic Ocean at the tip of South America. The Spanish explorers named this area Patagonia (pat uh GOH nee uh), from a word meaning "big feet." They used this name because the Indians who lived there were tall and wore large boots stuffed with grass. Part of Patagonia is desert — a cold, barren region used mainly for ranching and sheep raising.

So from northern lights dancing above the frozen tundra, through mountains and forests, across rivers and plains, you have caught a glimpse of the incredible variety of this hemisphere you call home. Are you ready now for your great American adventure? Not quite. It would be a good idea to learn something more about the weather you're likely to experience in the Americas.

shoes for hiking. In Mexico and Central America, you climb rugged mountains and get a closer view of the mighty volcanoes. In the dense forest of northern South America, you are awed by the breathtaking beauty of the world's highest waterfall,

LESSON **3** REVIEW

THINK AND WRITE

A. What are some of Canada's major physical features?

B. In which directions did the imaginary flight travel from Canada to Latin America?

C. What are some of the outstanding physical features of Middle America and of South America?

D. How would you sum up the physical characteristics of Canada and Latin America in one or two sentences?

SKILLS CHECK

WRITING SKILL

Iquitos and Lima both are cities in Peru. Find each city in the Gazetteer and on a map. Write a short explanation of the location of each city.

Seasons and Climates in the Americas

THINK ABOUT WHAT YOU KNOW

You have learned some things about the regions of the Americas. Imagine that you are planning a vacation trip to several countries in the Americas. What types of clothing might you need for different parts of your trip?

STUDY THE VOCABULARY

weather	tropics
precipitation	temperate zone
temperature	frigid zone
climate	

FOCUS YOUR READING

What affects seasons and climates in the Americas?

A. Different Seasons North and South of the Equator

It's January 1, New Year's Day. A holiday is a time for fun, so how about a nice family picnic in the park? That sounds good to me, but first, why not go to the beach? It surely would be pleasant to lie out in the sun and then go for a swim. That warm ocean water would feel good. Summer is the best season! Summer? How can it be summer on January 1? Isn't that winter?

It may be winter in much of the United States, but it isn't winter everywhere in the Americas. Refer to the diagram on page 28. Notice that the sun's light seems to move across the earth as the year progresses. In summer in the Northern Hemisphere, the direct sun rays strike at or near the Tropic of Cancer. In winter they hit at

or near the Tropic of Capricorn, in the Southern Hemisphere. These two parallels ($23\frac{1}{2}°$N and $23\frac{1}{2}°$S) are important because they are the limits of the direct sun rays. The more directly the rays strike the earth, the more energy reaches the ground to heat it. This is one reason why it is warm or cold in certain seasons.

Direct rays of the sun strike the earth somewhere between the Equator and the Tropic of Cancer from the start of spring (March 20 or 21) in the Northern Hemisphere to the end of summer (September 22 or 23). They strike between the Equator and the Tropic of Capricorn from the start of fall (September 22 or 23) to the end of winter (March 20 or 21). This means that the seasons are reversed in the two hemispheres.

Growing Up on the Yucatán On the morning of March 21, Carla awoke early. She had been anticipating this day for

Both the Yucatán and the Dominican Republic are in the Northern Hemisphere within the tropics.
▶ What is their typical climate?

In addition to the slithering snakelike figure that can be seen twice a year, the pyramid at Chichén Itzá holds other interests. The total number of steps is 365, including the top platform, and there are 52 side panels.
▶ How does this confirm facts found on this page and the next about the Maya?

many weeks. Her family was going to see the massive temple pyramid known as El Castillo (kahs TEEL yoh), "the castle." It was built by the Maya (MAH yuh), American Indians who began a great civilization around the year A.D. 300. El Castillo has a total of 365 steps and 52 carved panels.

Carla lived in the city of Mérida (ME-ree dah) on the Yucatán (yoo kah TAHN) Peninsula, Mexico. About 75 miles (121 km) east are the Maya ruins of Chichén Itzá (chee CHEN eet SAH). From the time she was a little girl, Carla had walked among the many ruins uncovered in the jungle area. She was amazed by stories her parents told of the Maya culture and the Indians' knowledge of astronomy, mathematics, art forms, and building techniques.

Today's visit, however, was special. When Carla and her family arrived at Chichén Itzá, they would join a crowd of 30,000 people, many of whom had traveled from other parts of Mexico and even from other countries just to be there at this particular time of the year.

On or about March 21 and September 21, the sun crosses the plane of the Equator, making night and day of equal length all over the earth.

Because the calendar and seasons fascinated the Maya, they built the castle in an extraordinary way. Something unusual happens twice a year, and Carla was about to witness it.

As the sun set, it sent a shadow along the steps of the pyramid. The remaining area, where there was light, resembled a

The dry land (left) in parts of Mexico is in sharp contrast to the rain forest (right).
► How would you describe their differences?

snake slithering along the steps. It seemed to be heading toward the nearby sacred well of the Maya. Then the sun set, and the snake vanished.

B. Temperatures and Latitude

Weather and Climate What's the **weather**, or present condition of the air, like? To answer that question, you usually refer to **precipitation** or **temperature** or both. Precipitation is moisture that falls from the air as rain, snow, sleet, or hail. Temperature is the amount of heat in something such as air. If you study the weather in the Americas, you see that both precipitation and temperatures vary from place to place. For example, northern Mexico is arid, or dry. Places that get enough rain to grow trees and crops are called humid **climates**. *Climate* means "the normal pattern of weather in an area

over a period of time." Some places, such as northern Canada, are cold most of the year. They have frigid, or cold, climates.

In general, temperatures are warmer near the Equator and colder at the North and South Poles. Sometimes the world is divided into three regions based on temperature differences. Refer to the map shown on page 61 as you read about these climate divisions.

The Tropics The region of warm climates near the Equator is called the **tropics**. Another name for this area is the low latitudes. That's because it is near or at the latitude of 0°, or the Equator. The only place the sun ever will be directly overhead in the sky is in the tropics. It is generally warm to hot here all year. Temperatures change very little from month to month during the year. Most countries of Latin America are in the tropics.

The Temperate Zones Just on either side of the tropics are lands of middle latitudes. Find them on the map. They have a warm summer season but a cool winter season. These areas, one in the Northern Hemisphere and one in the Southern Hemisphere, are called the **temperate zones**. *Temperate* is a word that means "neither very hot nor very cold, but between the two extremes." However, *temperate* does not accurately describe this region. The land may be quite hot in summer and very cold in winter. The weather can change from warm and sunny to cold and stormy in a matter of minutes. On the map below, notice how much of North and South America are in the temperate zones.

The Frigid Zones At the far ends of the earth, around the North and South Poles, are the **frigid zones**. These are cold areas, also called polar regions, located in the high latitudes. The climate in these regions consists of long, cold winters and short, cool summers. Near the North and South Poles, snow and ice never melt in the cool summer season. Parts of Canada and Alaska are in the frigid zone. In which climate zone would you prefer to live?

C. Temperatures and Elevation

Have you ever wondered why some mountains are covered with snow all year round? You know that latitude determines the three zones: tropical, temperate, and

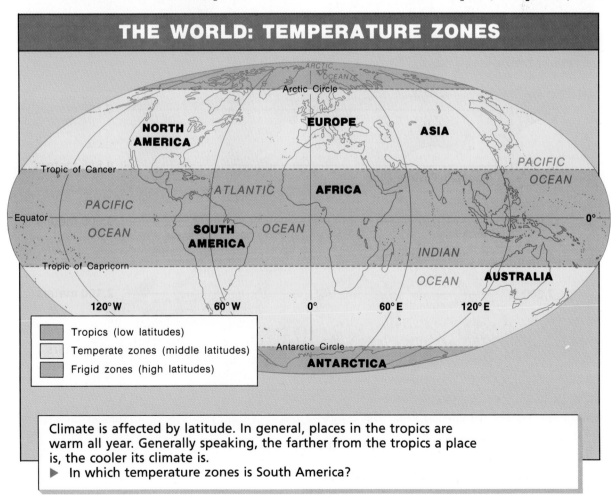

THE WORLD: TEMPERATURE ZONES

Tropics (low latitudes)
Temperate zones (middle latitudes)
Frigid zones (high latitudes)

Climate is affected by latitude. In general, places in the tropics are warm all year. Generally speaking, the farther from the tropics a place is, the cooler its climate is.
▶ In which temperature zones is South America?

frigid. Other things on the earth also affect climate. An increase in elevation causes cooler temperatures. The higher up you go, the cooler it gets. In Ecuador, for example, there are high mountain peaks located very close to the Equator. The best-known are Chimborazo (chihm buh RAH zoh) and Cotopaxi (koh tuh PAK see). Both rise to a height of approximately 20,000 feet (6,096 m) and are snowcapped all year long, even though they are in the tropics. These mountain peaks are cold because of their high elevation.

The people of Latin America call the climates that are found at the different elevations by different names. Low elevations, where temperatures are warm, are called *tierra caliente* (tee ER uh ka lee EN-tee), which is Spanish for "hot lands."

The middle elevations, neither very hot nor very cold, are called *tierra templada* (tem PLAH duh), "temperate lands." Unlike temperatures in the middle-latitude temperate zones, temperatures in the *tierra templada* are always about the same. There is no winter or summer. The middle-latitude temperate zones, of course, do have those seasons.

High elevations are called *tierra fría* (FREE uh), "cold lands." These areas are not so high as to be permanently snowcapped. However, they are cold enough so that people dress warmly, and tropical crops will not grow there.

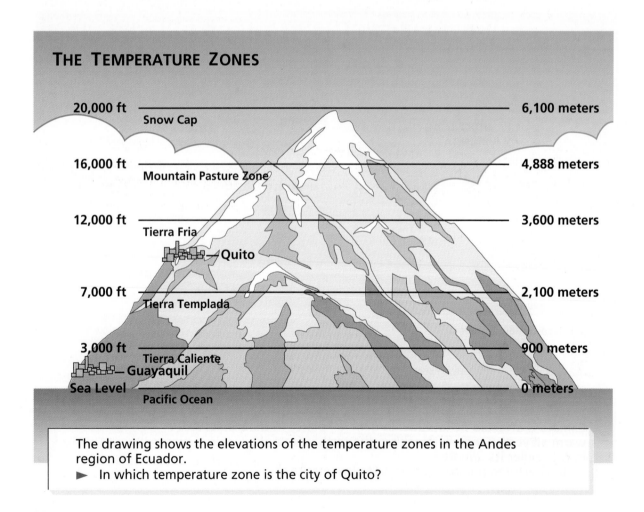

THE TEMPERATURE ZONES

20,000 ft	6,100 meters
Snow Cap	
16,000 ft	4,888 meters
Mountain Pasture Zone	
12,000 ft	3,600 meters
Tierra Fria	
Quito	
7,000 ft	2,100 meters
Tierra Templada	
3,000 ft	900 meters
Tierra Caliente	
Guayaquil	
Sea Level	0 meters
Pacific Ocean	

The drawing shows the elevations of the temperature zones in the Andes region of Ecuador.

► In which temperature zone is the city of Quito?

D. Climates and Seasons

Steady Tropical Climates You know that temperatures do not vary greatly from season to season in the tropics. Close to the Equator the temperatures may change only a few degrees between summer and winter. For example, the city of Manaus (man NOUS), in the Brazilian rain forest, records its highest average temperature in September and its lowest in January. The September temperature is 82.2°F (28°C), and the January figure is 79.2°F (26°C). That's a difference of only 3°F (2°C). That does not mean that there are no real seasons in the tropics. Instead, the seasons are different.

Rainy and Dry Seasons The region of the tropics usually has two seasons. One is the rainy season. The other is the dry season. The exact months for these seasons vary throughout the tropics, depending in part on latitude and in part on elevation. Countries in such climates generally have a dry season of only a few months. Almost all the rainfall happens during the rainy season. It doesn't rain all day long, but often a shower falls every day. The shower

A statue of the rain god is found in Mexico, in Chapultepec, one of the world's largest parks.
▶ What else might be in the park?

may be very brief, and the rest of the day will be bright and sunny. From time to time there are heavy rainstorms. Thunder roars and rain streams down in torrents.

LESSON **4** *REVIEW*

THINK AND WRITE

A. Summarize the way the seasons differ in the Northern Hemisphere and in the Southern Hemisphere.
B. What are three different climate zones set by latitudes?
C. How would you explain the three climate zones set by elevation?
D. What types of seasons are there in the tropical areas?

SKILLS CHECK

MAP SKILL

Look at the map titled THE WORLD: TEMPERATURE ZONES found on page 61. Parts of how many continents lie in the middle latitudes? Which two continents do not have any land in the middle latitudes? Which two continents have land that can be found in three different temperature zones?

PUTTING IT ALL TOGETHER

USING THE VOCABULARY

Anglo-America   temperature
heritage   tropics
Latin America   temperate zone
precipitation   frigid zone

On a separate sheet of paper, write the term from the list above that best completes each sentence.

1. Two names for cultural regions in the Americas are _____ and _____.
2. The two most important features to name when you describe a region's climate are its _____ and its _____.
3. The part of South America that contains the rain forest is in the climate zone called the _____.
4. Cold areas near the North and South Poles are called the _____.
5. The _____ of Latin America is Iberian.

REMEMBERING WHAT YOU READ

On a separate sheet of paper, answer the following questions in complete sentences.

1. Why weren't the Americas named for Christopher Columbus?
2. Who discovered an area and called it "New Found Land"?
3. Which Frenchman named this same land Canada?
4. Which geographic areas belong to the region of Anglo-America?
5. The area in the Western Hemisphere that includes all of the land south of Anglo-America bears what name?

6. What is the northern area of Canada called that is barren and treeless?
7. Which term describes a level area that is raised above the surrounding land?
8. What makes Middle America different from Latin America?
9. What are the three different temperature zones?
10. How does the elevation affect the temperature of a place no matter what its latitude is?

TYING POETRY TO SOCIAL STUDIES

Haiku poems are a tradition in Japan. They consist of three lines with five syllables in the first line, seven syllables in the second line, and five syllables in the third line. These poems most often show a happening in nature. It may be a small detail, as in the poem below, or an impressive event. Here is one example.

The Tundra
A polar bear suns   (5)
on floating ice. Summer heat   (7)
means fifty degrees (F)!   (5)

Read the poem aloud and count the syllables in each line. Your count should match the number in parentheses after each line.

As you were introduced to the Americas in this chapter, you may have imagined being in one of the places described. Create your own haiku poem about one of these places. Look back to the descriptions on pages 53–57 for inspiration.

THINKING CRITICALLY

On a separate sheet of paper, write your answers in complete sentences.

1. Why, do you think, did sailors from Europe not discover the Americas before 1492?
2. What benefits are there from having both a British and an Iberian heritage in the Americas?
3. Your plane can land in three places — one in Canada, one in Middle America, and one in South America. Name the three places you would choose and tell why.
4. Which climate region has been changed the least by people living there? Explain your answer.
5. Describe how your yearly schedule would be different if you lived in a temperate zone in the Southern Hemisphere.

SUMMARIZING THE CHAPTER

On a separate sheet of paper, draw a graphic organizer like the one shown here. Copy the information from this graphic organizer on the one you have drawn. Under each heading, fill in the blanks with facts you learned from that lesson. The first one has been done for you.

CHAPTER THEME
The Western Hemisphere can be thought of in terms of its regions, different heritages, physical features, climates, and even the order of the seasons of the year.

LESSON 1
The Western Hemisphere was mapped by Europeans who named different regions.

1. America named for Amerigo Vespucci
2. North and South America named by Mercator, a mapmaker
3. Canada named by Cartier

LESSON 2
Cultural Regions

1. _____
2. _____

LESSON 3
Physical Features

1. _____
2. _____
3. _____
4. _____
5. _____
6. _____

LESSON 4
Climate Regions

1. _____
2. _____
3. _____

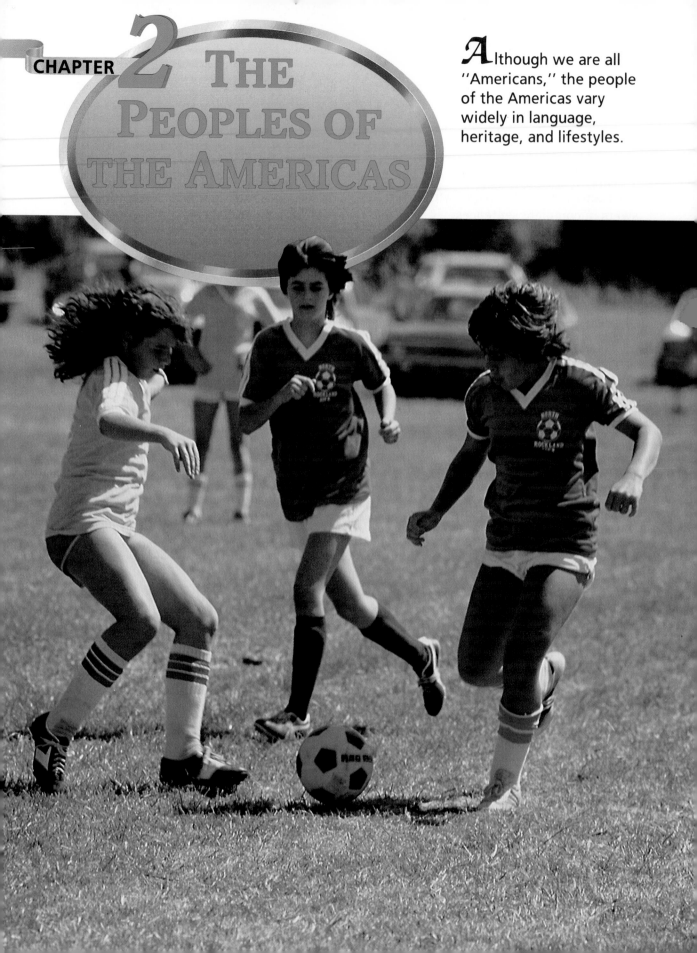

2 THE PEOPLES OF THE AMERICAS

*A*lthough we are all ''Americans,'' the people of the Americas vary widely in language, heritage, and lifestyles.

Foreign Things

THINK ABOUT WHAT YOU KNOW

Make a list of some of the ordinary things you do every day that might seem unusual to visitors from another country.

STUDY THE VOCABULARY

culture   dominion
colony

FOCUS YOUR READING

How do people of the Americas differ from country to country?

A. Being a Foreigner

It was Fernanda's first full day in the United States, and she was feeling a bit confused. Fernanda had come from Buenos Aires, Argentina, as part of a student exchange program. For the next five months, she would be living with the Warners, her host family in the United States. She would be attending the local public school. When Fernanda first heard about the exchange program, the idea of living in the United States sounded great. Now she wasn't so sure. The Warners were nice and friendly, but they certainly had some strange habits. Take their meals, for example. They had their big meal in the evening, and they ate it at 5:30 P.M. Could she ever get used to eating dinner that early? Fernanda wondered. How could she get by with such a tiny lunch? In Argentina, lunch was the biggest meal and dinner came much later at night.

Imagine if the situation were reversed and you were living in Argentina. You probably would feel very much the way Fernanda did. As you learn about the different peoples of Latin America and Canada, try to remember that what seems strange to you makes perfectly good sense to the peoples of other countries. That's because of the difference in **cultures**.

Culture includes the customs, way of life, values, and beliefs of a certain people. The ideas, skills, arts, tools, and even the language of a people are also part of their culture. To know other peoples and countries, try to understand their cultures.

B. Different Languages Spoken

Suppose someone said to you, "Don't put your runners on the chesterfield. If you eat anything, be sure to use a serviette." Would you know what the person meant? A Canadian would. In Canada, runners are tennis shoes or sneakers. A chesterfield is a couch, and a serviette is a napkin. So you see, even when people from different countries speak the same language, the words they use can have different meanings.

Sidewalk cafes in Latin America serve snacks late in the afternoon.
▶ What advantages are there to outdoor cafes?

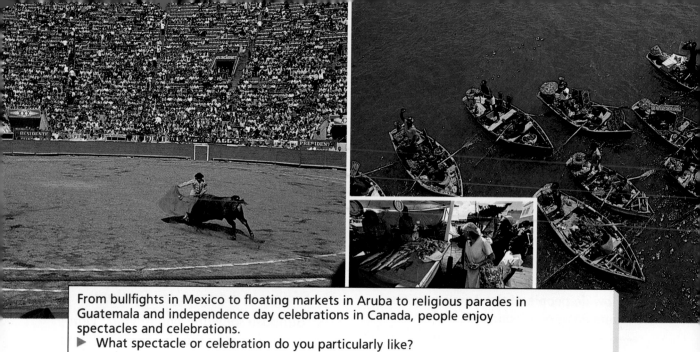

From bullfights in Mexico to floating markets in Aruba to religious parades in Guatemala and independence day celebrations in Canada, people enjoy spectacles and celebrations.
▶ What spectacle or celebration do you particularly like?

There are over 2,000 different languages spoken in the world today. Most people in the United States and Canada, as well as some in the West Indies, speak English. Most of the other nations in the Americas are Spanish-speaking. Brazilians speak Portuguese. Haitians and some other West Indians speak French. French is also a very important language in Canada. In fact, both French and English are official languages in Canada.

There's another kind of language that varies across cultures. It is body language. Body language includes gestures, facial expressions, and even how closely people stand to one another when they are speaking.

C. Different Foods

In the United States, many people usually put ketchup on French fried potatoes. In Belgium, a country in Western Europe where this kind of fried potato was "invented," people enjoy their fries with mayonnaise. Many Canadians prefer vinegar with theirs.

Argentines eat an enormous amount of beef. That's because Argentina is an important cattle-raising country. Many people in the Caribbean area prefer fish and seafood. Can you guess why? Both Argentina and the Caribbean are part of Latin America, but the people in these areas have varying food preferences.

Some people in the United States think that all Latin American food is very spicy. That's because the Latin American food that people in the United States know best comes from Mexico. Each Latin American country has its own special foods and eating habits, and much Latin American food is not at all spicy. If you wanted a taco or tortilla in Brazil, for example, you would have to go to a Mexican restaurant. As you saw with Fernanda, even the size and time of meals may change across cultures.

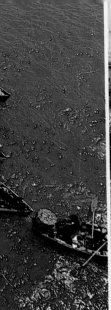

D. Celebrating Holidays

People in the United States celebrate a special holiday called the Fourth of July. It's also known as Independence Day because it honors the date on which the Declaration of Independence was approved in 1776. That document declared that the 13 **colonies**, or settlements, were no longer British possessions. Canadians also have their independence celebration in July. On July 1, they celebrate Canada Day, also called Dominion Day. It is in honor of the British North America Act of 1867, which made Canada a **dominion**. A dominion is a self-governing nation that has close ties with Great Britain. You will learn about Canada's path to independence when you study Chapter 21.

Each of the countries of Latin America has special holidays. Some holidays are in memory of independence or of the deeds of great people. Many others are religious celebrations.

It is important to realize that holidays, like so many other things you have read about in this lesson, vary across cultures. All people celebrate, but they often celebrate different things in different ways. People really are alike and different at the same time!

LESSON 1 REVIEW

THINK AND WRITE

A. Why is it important to learn something about the cultures of other people and countries?

B. What are the main languages that are spoken in the Americas?

C. What are some ways that eating habits differ?

D. What kinds of holidays do people celebrate in the Americas?

SKILLS CHECK

THINKING SKILL

When people move and settle in another country, they bring with them their customs and languages. Think about and then write your comments about some advantages and some disadvantages people have when they cling to their heritage. Have a discussion with your classmates to share your ideas.

Our Interdependent Hemisphere

THINK ABOUT WHAT YOU KNOW

Each day of our lives, we depend on other people to do or make things for us. What are some of the ways we depend on others?

STUDY THE VOCABULARY

interdependent	imports
industry	exports
immigration	landlocked

FOCUS YOUR READING

Why are the nations of the Western Hemisphere important to one another?

A. Belonging to a System

When you were in the jetliner looking down on the Americas, you noticed that the Western Hemisphere has many different parts. You also saw that almost all of those parts were connected to form a massive area of land.

The countries of the Americas are all individual nations. Together they are part of a system. That means that things happening in one country may affect the lives of people living in another country.

When bad weather ruins coffee crops in Colombia, people in the United States may have to pay more money to buy coffee at the grocery store. When Canada and Mexico develop new natural gas fields, it can help lower heating costs in the United States. Thinking about systems can help you see the many ways in which individual countries are connected to a larger world and the many ways in which countries are **interdependent**. *Interdependent* means "relying or depending on one another."

B. Learning From Others

When I, Dr. Gerald Greenfield, was a young boy, I loved to play cowboy. I wore a cowboy hat and whirled a lariat, or lasso, made from clothesline. Like most of my friends, I thought of the cowboy as a true United States hero.

In this painting, a cowhand is shown in action.
► What is this cowhand holding in his hand?

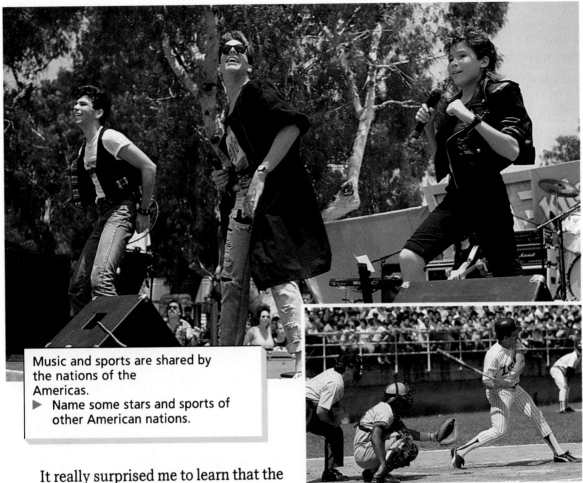

Music and sports are shared by the nations of the Americas.
▶ Name some stars and sports of other American nations.

It really surprised me to learn that the first cowboys came from Mexico! They brought with them the lariat, chaps, and the cowboy hat and boots, along with numerous other things related to the cattle **industry**. An industry is a branch of manufacturing, business, or trade.

Latin American music has been popular in the United States for years. Your grandparents probably heard Argentine tango music on the radio, and your parents may have listened to popular bands playing bossa nova music from Brazil when they were in school. You may have heard reggae, a type of music from Jamaica, or listened to the music of many popular Latin American bands.

The United States has also learned much from Canada. For example, much

has been learned about how to deal with cold winters. Think about Canada's location, and you'll probably guess why.

Snowshoes were used by early Canadian Indians, and the dogsled comes from the Inuit (IHN oo wiht), or Eskimos, of Canada's Far North. Have you ever worn or seen people wearing ski parkas to keep warm? Parkas come from Canada too.

The United States in turn has given much to the other nations of the Americas. Movies, music, and television shows from the United States all enjoy great popularity throughout the Americas. Baseball, a sport developed in the United States, has spread to Canada, Mexico, Central America, and much of the Caribbean.

C. Migration Across Borders

Heritage from Nearby Nations Perhaps the most important contribution of Canada and Latin America to the United States is people. Many people in the United States can trace their heritage to Canadian or Latin American origins.

Immigration Today most of the Latin American population in the United States is the result of **immigration** during this century. *Immigration* means "the act of coming into a new country to live." Cubans have come to the United States, chiefly to the city of Miami in Florida. Mexicans have moved into the United States, especially into California and Texas. Mexican influence in part of the United States, however, is very old. The southwestern United States once belonged to Mexico and came into the United States with a largely Mexican population.

After African Americans, Mexicans are the second largest *minority* in the United States. A minority is a group of people who make up less than half of the total number. Other minorities include Nicaraguans and people from other Latin American countries who live in other large cities of the United States as well as in many small towns. Many Canadians, especially French Canadians, live in the northern parts of New York, Vermont, New Hampshire, and Maine.

A group of people from other nations are sworn in as United States citizens.
▶ Why might a person want to become a citizen?

Travel Within the Americas People also visit other countries in the Americas. Sometimes it's for pleasure. At other times, business takes them abroad. Each year about one third of all foreign visitors to the United States come from Canada and Latin America. In turn, Canada and Latin America are popular destinations for United States travelers.

D. Uniting the Americas Through Trade

Many Imports The last hamburger you ate may have come from a cow raised in Honduras. If you drink orange juice, there's a good chance that it comes from Brazilian oranges. The United States **imports**, or brings in, many other valuable products from Latin America and Canada. For example, the United States imports some of its oil and natural gas from Canada, Mexico, and Venezuela (ven uh-ZWAY luh). Your local grocery store or supermarket probably sells bananas, sugar, coffee, spices, fish, and canned beef that come from Latin America.

Canadian workers build many of the Ford and General Motors cars sold in the United States. In 1988, Volkswagen started selling a car called the Fox. The Fox is made in Brazil. Mexico also manufactures cars. Many of them are sold in the United States.

Exports from the United States Of course, trade is not a one-way street. The United States **exports** many products to the other nations of the Americas. *Export* means "to ship products, usually for sale, to another country." Canada and Latin America are very good customers for United States producers. About one third of all United States exports go to Western

Thousands of on shore and off shore oil wells are in operation in Venezuela.
▶ What type of workers are needed for this industry?

In 1990 Canada produced 969,862 automobiles, of which 819,428 were exported to its best customer, the United States.
► Approximately what percentage of passenger cars made were sold to the United States?

Hemisphere countries. That makes the Western Hemisphere the largest regional market for United States goods. Canada alone accounts for about half of that trade.

E. Disagreement Among Good Neighbors

Just as with individuals, countries that are friends do not always agree. Countries may have different opinions as to what is right, and what is very important to one country may not be as important to another. In part this comes from the cultural differences you learned about earlier. In part it's because the problems that countries face may be very different. For example, people in the United States often worry about eating too much and becoming overweight. In some countries of the Americas, however, not getting enough to eat can be a problem. In addition, countries often see issues in terms of their own interests. They try to do things that are to their advantage. However, what is favorable for one country may be unfavorable for another.

The nations of the Americas differ on many issues. Canada and the United States have argued about the control of pollution that causes acid rain, or rain that is full of pollutants. Bolivia has long tried to get Chile to allow it access to the sea. Bolivia became **landlocked** as a result of a war with Chile in the nineteenth century. *Landlocked* means "being shut in on all sides or nearly all sides by land."

F. Cooperation Among the Americas

The nations of the Americas, try to

avoid war with one another. They have joined together to promote common interests. Almost all nations of the Americas belong to the Organization of American States, generally known in the United States by its initials, OAS. Respect for the independence and equality of all the hemisphere's nations is a basic principle of the OAS. It promotes cooperation among the nations of the Americas and tries to resolve disputes among its member countries.

Countries of the Americas who do not belong to the OAS, can be observer nations and send representatives to the OAS who observe and report back.

Headquartered in Washington, D.C., the OAS sponsors many cultural exchanges among countries, including art shows, musical performances, and theater presentations. It also gives money to students to help them study in other countries of the Americas. Perhaps someday you will receive an OAS scholarship. If so, which country will you pick for your study abroad? This book may help you decide.

Daniel Ortega, once a Nicaraguan leader, spoke before the OAS.
▶ Why might a leader of a country speak to the OAS?

LESSON **2** *REVIEW*

THINK AND WRITE

A. What does it mean to be part of a system?
B. What are some of the things that the nations of the Americas have learned about from one another?
C. Name at least four groups of people who have immigrated to the United States.
D. Why is there trade among the nations of the Americas?
E. What are some of the reasons why the nations of the Americas may disagree with one another?

F. How does the OAS promote cooperation in the Americas?

SKILLS CHECK

WRITING SKILL

Make a list of things you eat, wear, or possess that are imports. Then, as you can, arrange the items in categories, by the countries from which they came. Write a paragraph about some of your observations.

LEARNING TO APPRECIATE ALL AMERICANS

As you are learning in Chapter 2, people in the various countries of North and South America come from different backgrounds. In order for our countries to prosper and provide a good life for everyone, the various groups of people must understand and be able to get along with each other.

In the past, textbooks presented the history of the Americas mainly from the point of view of the white majority, whose roots were in Europe. The contributions and struggles of the Native, African, Hispanic, and Asian Americans were given little space. In some cases, these groups were portrayed according to stereotypes, or false pictures of what all members of the group were like.

For many years, members of minority groups have been calling on American schools to present a more well-rounded, truthful picture of the roles of minorities in American history. Textbooks today are trying to meet this challenge.

For example, social studies textbooks now tell about the European conquest of the Western Hemisphere from the Native American's point of view as well as the European. Students learn about the achievements of the great civilizations of the Maya, the Aztecs, and the Incas, as you will in Chapter 4 of this book.

The bringing of Africans against their will to the Western Hemisphere is a blot on the histories of both North and South America. By learning about the injustices of slavery, you can better appreciate the struggles of African Americans for freedom and equal opportunity. You can also appreciate their achievements in the face of discrimination.

To understand the culture of Americans, it is important to learn about the history of the peoples and nations of the Western Hemisphere. As you read about the immigration of people from many nations to the countries of North and South America, you can grow in appreciation of the contributions of those people to the development of this hemisphere.

Thinking for Yourself

On a separate sheet of paper, answer the following questions in complete sentences.

1. Which groups of Americans feel they have been ignored or misrepresented in books about our history?
2. Have you ever read anything that presented a stereotype of a particular group of people living in the Western Hemisphere? How did it make you feel?
3. Do you think that learning about injustices against one's group will hurt or help a student of your age? Give reasons for your opinion.
4. What do you think are the best ways to learn to appreciate all Americans?

Latin Americans and Canadians

THINK ABOUT WHAT YOU KNOW

Suppose someone asked you to describe a typical student in your school. Why might that be difficult for you to do?

STUDY THE VOCABULARY

ancestor   mestizo
expedition   mulatto

FOCUS YOUR READING

Which different peoples make up the populations of Canada and Latin America?

A. Latin America's Rich Heritage

What does a typical Latin American look like? That question really has no good answer. Depending on which country you consider, the majority of the people may or may not have similar roots. Therefore, some Latin Americans are tall, but others are short. There is a wide variety in skin tones too.

The first people to live in the area we now call Latin America were Native Americans, or American Indians. The **ancestors** of those Indians crossed a land bridge from Asia to America many thousands of years ago. An ancestor is a person on one's family tree, such as a great-grandparent. You will learn more about their journey in Chapter 3. The people that Europeans thought were the original inhabitants of the Americas were descendants of the first immigrants to the region.

Their number had grown to many millions by the time Columbus sailed to America. Native Americans are still a very important part of the population in parts of Latin America, such as Guatemala and the central Andes. American Indian influence is apparent in the culture of many countries, particularly with regard to foods, handicrafts, art, and music.

B. Africans and Asians as Workers

Blacks came to Latin America with early explorers and military **expeditions.** An expedition is a long journey undertaken for a specific purpose, such as to explore or to place military forces in a region. Some of these blacks were free citizens of Spain or Portugal, and others were slaves. Later, Europeans transported blacks from Africa in large numbers across the Atlantic to work as slaves on the farms and in the mines of the colonies.

Many of the nations of Latin America abolished slavery when they achieved independence. Others held onto slavery until almost the end of the nineteenth cen-

Military bands in Jamaica play in parades and for social functions.
▶ Why do most people enjoy music?

Students of Indian heritage take a break during the school day.
▶ What, do you suppose, are the two buildings in the background?

tury. You can see African influence throughout much of Latin America. It is especially strong throughout the West Indies and Brazil.

Some of the remaining European colonies in Latin America still needed workers. England and the Netherlands had other colonies in Asia. The English brought workers from India to European colonies in the Caribbean area. The Dutch brought workers from Indonesia. Many people whose ancestors came from India still live in Trinidad and Guyana, former English colonies, and in Suriname, a former Dutch colony. Suriname also has a large population that is of Indonesian heritage.

For a period in the nineteenth century, Peru actively tried to attract Chinese laborers. Many Chinese moved to Peru to work in the mines. Chinese laborers were also brought into Canada in the 1870s to work on the Canadian Pacific Railway.

C. The Mixing of Different Peoples

Mexicans point with pride to their Native American heritage. In fact, most Mexicans living today have some Indian ancestry. That's because in Mexico the mixing of different peoples has been going on almost from the moment Europeans first conquered the Indian peoples who lived there. The mixing of peoples has occurred throughout most of Latin America, adding to the variety of the population.

The mixing of peoples created two important new groups: **mestizos** (mes-TEE zohz) and **mulattoes** (muh LAHT-ohz). Mestizos of Latin America are people of mixed European and American Indian ancestry. Mulattoes are people of mixed black and white ancestry.

Today, mestizos form the largest part of the population in Mexico, Central America, and the northern Andes. Mulattos make up the largest population group in parts of Brazil and on many of the islands of the West Indies.

D. Canadians from Many Places

You have learned that Canada belongs to Anglo-America, so you know that much of its population is British. However, long before it became a part of Anglo-America, Canada was settled by the French. They came as colonists during the seventeenth and eighteenth centuries. Today, French Canadians make up about one third of Canada's population. Like the rest of the Americas, Canada has received immigrants from many parts of the world. Some of the major groups who have immigrated are the Germans, the Italians, the Dutch, and the Scandinavians.

Canada also has a Native American population. When Europeans first came to Canada, they found a land that was settled, farmed, hunted, and fished by various American Indians. You will learn about some of these peoples in Chapter 3.

Historical Pictures Service - Chicago

This 1844 painting is entitled *Christmas in Canada: Going to Church*.
▶ Why might the Frenchman shown be carrying a rifle?

LESSON *3* REVIEW

THINK AND WRITE

A. Make notes about the first people who lived in Latin America, and then write a summary.
B. How did Latin America's need for laborers affect its population?
C. Why is the mixing of peoples important in Latin America?
D. What different groups of people have settled in Canada?

SKILLS CHECK

MAP SKILL

Find and read the entries in the Gazetteer for the Caribbean islands and the West Indies. Describe how these two areas are related by forming a clear definition of your own.

Where People Live

THINK ABOUT WHAT YOU KNOW

Think about cutting a pizza into slices for yourself and three friends. If you wanted the pieces to be equal in size, what would the pie look like? Suppose you wanted your slice to be twice as large as each friend's slice. Draw two pictures to show the difference.

STUDY THE VOCABULARY

population density   metropolitan area
epidemic   primate city
natural increase   rural area

FOCUS YOUR READING

How does population vary throughout the Americas?

A. Graphing the Americas

Using a Pie Graph Three giant countries take up about two thirds of all the land in the Americas. One good way to present this type of information about places is by using graphs. Graphs are like maps in that they allow the reader to see similarities and differences easily. The different types of graphs that are described and shown in this lesson compare the sizes and populations of some American countries.

A pie graph is good for showing what percentage each part takes up of the whole thing that is being considered. The pie graph on this page shows how much of the total area of North and South America is taken up by each of the five largest countries. It also shows that Canada, the United States, and Brazil are the three countries that take up about two thirds of all the

land. How much land does that leave for the other 32 nations and colonies of the Americas?

B. Wide Variety in Population

Using a Bar Graph Brazil's mammoth Maracaña soccer stadium seats 200,000 people. It is large enough to hold the combined populations of St. Christopher–Nevis and also St. Lucia, two independent island nations in the West Indies. As you might guess, Brazil has a very large population. You can compare the populations of countries by using bar graphs. A bar graph is better than a pie graph for comparing amounts, but it is not as good as a pie graph for showing parts of a whole.

The bar graph on the next page shows the ten countries in the Americas that have

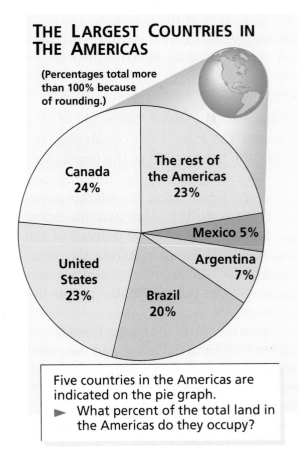

THE LARGEST COUNTRIES IN THE AMERICAS

(Percentages total more than 100% because of rounding.)

Canada 24%
The rest of the Americas 23%
Mexico 5%
Argentina 7%
Brazil 20%
United States 23%

Five countries in the Americas are indicated on the pie graph.
► What percent of the total land in the Americas do they occupy?

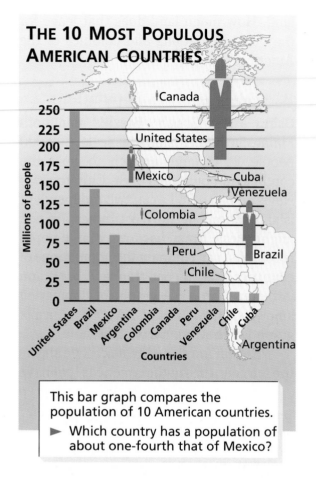

THE 10 MOST POPULOUS AMERICAN COUNTRIES

Millions of people

This bar graph compares the population of 10 American countries.

► Which country has a population of about one-fourth that of Mexico?

land is known as **population density**. Population density is the average number of people in a certain area. Graphs made in the United States show the number of people per square mile to indicate population density. Latin American countries and Canada use the number of people per square kilometer.

Some countries have a high population density. That means they have a great number of people relative to the amount of land. What does it mean to have low population density. Look at the country tables on pages 38–41. Find the columns that give information about population density. Compare that information with that on the bar graphs on this page. Do countries with the largest populations also have the highest population densities?

C. Changes in Population

Using a Line Graph Here's a riddle. Two students were asked how many countries in Latin America had populations of over 100 million. One student replied, "None." The other student said, "One." Both students were right. How can that be?

The answer to this riddle is really very simple. The students were asked the question at different times. The first student was asked the question in 1972, when Brazil had a population of 98 million. The other student was asked the question today.

The best type of graph to use if you want to show how something changes over time is a line graph. The line graph on page 83 shows the population growth in Anglo-America and Latin America from the year 1650. By looking at it you can learn several things about the population of the Americas. For example, you should

the largest populations. The height of a bar indicates the size of the population: the higher the bar, the larger the population. You can easily see that the United States, Brazil, and Mexico have much larger populations than do the other nations. Brazil and Mexico have over 50 percent of the people of Latin America. Adding the population of the United States would account for around two thirds of all the people living in the Americas!

Find the top of the bar for Canada and run your finger to the left to find the population. Doesn't Canada's population seem small in comparison to its size? After all, Canada has more land than any other country in the Americas. The relationship between population and size or extent of be able to tell if population is growing slowly or rapidly. It also lets you compare the growth of population in Anglo-America with that in Latin America.

If you look at the slant of the lines showing population growth, you can make some predictions about the future of the people of the Americas. Predictions, as you know, are educated guesses based on trends and patterns of information. Most predictions about the future involve looking at a change that is taking place and guessing whether or not it will continue in the same way.

Do you think the population in Latin America will continue to grow quickly? As you answer this question, you are making a prediction.

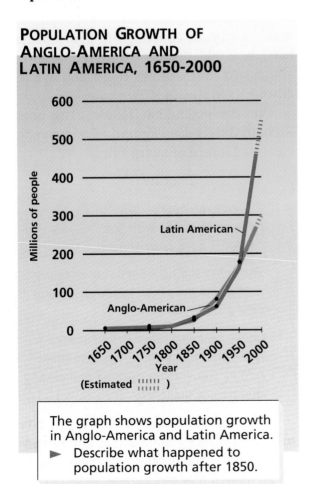

POPULATION GROWTH OF ANGLO-AMERICA AND LATIN AMERICA, 1650-2000

The graph shows population growth in Anglo-America and Latin America.
▶ Describe what happened to population growth after 1850.

D. Health Measures and Population Growth

Many years ago in the United States, children commonly died from diseases like smallpox and diphtheria. Then vaccines against these diseases were invented. Children received the vaccines at a very young age. As a result those diseases disappeared almost entirely. You were probably vaccinated before you were first enrolled in school.

Vaccination is an example of a public health measure. Public health measures also include making sure that water systems provide pure drinking water and that wastes are disposed of properly. Another health measure is the guarding against conditions that can cause an **epidemic**. An epidemic is the rapid spread of disease among a large number of people. Improved public health programs throughout Latin America have made people's lives healthier. They also have contributed to Latin America's high rate of population growth. People live longer, fewer young children die, and mothers have healthier babies.

Now population in Latin America is growing from **natural increase**. *Natural increase* means the change in population that comes from differences in the number of births and deaths. If more people are born in a year than die, the population increases. Migration can also cause changes in population. The combination of natural increase and population gained or lost by migration is called the *rate of population growth*.

In the United States and Canada, health conditions are generally better than in Latin America. Even so, Anglo–America's rate of population growth is not as high as Latin America's. That's because the birth rate in Anglo America is lower.

E. Cities in the Americas

Metropolitan Areas Greater Mexico City has over 20 million people. A city with its immediate surrounding cities and towns is called a **metropolitan area**. The word *greater* before the name of a city indicates a metropolitan area. Mexico City is not only the largest city in the Americas, but it is the largest city in the entire world! The Brazilian city of São Paulo (soun POU loo) is the largest in South America. It has around 18 million people. About 11 million people live in Buenos Aires (BWAY-nus ER eez), the capital of Argentina. Canada's leading metropolitan area is Toronto with around 3 million people. Montreal is a close second. What is the population of the largest city in your area?

It doesn't take a million people to make a city, of course. One figure often used is 2,000 people. By that measure, about two thirds of all Americans live in cities.

In the poem that follows, the poet Richard García used figurative language to create a picture of a large city.

The City Is So Big

The city is so big
Its bridges quake with fear
I know, I have seen at night

The lights sliding from house to house
And trains pass with windows shining
Like a smile full of teeth

I have seen machines eating houses
And stairways walk all by themselves
And elevator doors opening and closing
And people disappear.

Three views of the city of Toronto show development both above and below street level.
▶ Describe what you see.

Throughout Latin America the city with the largest population in each country is usually the capital city. One way to get an idea of the importance of the capital

The primate city of Buenos Aires, shown on the left, looks as though buildings occupy space for many miles. Córdoba, shown on the right, appears much less crowded.
▶ Why, do you think, do many people prefer to live in large cities?

city of a country is to compare its population with that of the second largest city.

Primate Cities A city whose population is over two and one-half times the size of the country's next largest city is called a **primate city**. In Latin America, primate cities have nearly all the important businesses, industries, cultural and educational institutions, and government offices. The finest hospitals, tallest buildings, and greatest job opportunities of the country are found there. Look at the photographs on this page. Which quick observation can you make from the photographs?

Buenos Aires is a good example of a primate city. It is about ten times larger than Argentina's second largest city,

which is Córdoba (KOR duh buh). About one third of all Argentines live in Buenos Aires. If New York City had that portion — one third — of the population of the United States, it would be a city of around 85 million people!

F. Different Population Patterns

Most Canadians live within 100 miles (161 km) of Canada's long border with the United States. As you can see from the map on page 570, most of Canada's important cities, from St. John's in the east to Vancouver in the west, are located between latitudes 40°N and 50°N. Severe cold and difficult land make life in the north very hard, so few people settle there.

In Mexico and Central America, most of the large cities are in the mountains.

In rural areas, it is not uncommon for people and animals to travel along the same unpaved road.
▶ What are the cowhands doing?

There are fewer large population centers near the coasts. You find that same pattern of population development along the west coast of South America and in the country of Venezuela.

Along South America's east coast, you see a different pattern. There, the large cities are near the coast. Many are important ports, such as Buenos Aires, Rio de Janeiro (REE oh day zhuh NER oh), and Recife (ruh SEE fuh).

Throughout Latin America, centers of high population density are isolated, or set apart, from one another. They are not all clustered in one large area as they are in Europe or in the eastern part of Anglo-America.

What about the people in Latin America who do not live in cities? Most of their houses have electricity, but people often get water from wells or streams. Many roads are unpaved. Dust billows up on hot, windy days. When it rains hard, the unpaved roads become thick with mud. There are few schools or medical facilities nearby. People shop at open-air markets or small stores. That's the reality for much of the **rural area**, or the countryside, where most of the farming population lives in Latin America.

LESSON 4 REVIEW

THINK AND WRITE

A. What are the three largest countries of the Americas in area?

B. What did you learn by looking at the bar graph about population?

C. Which has the larger population, Anglo-America or Latin America?

D. What makes population grow?

E. What makes primate cities different from other cities in Latin America?

F. Summarize where most people live in Canada and in Latin America.

SKILLS CHECK

THINKING SKILL

Refer to the pie graph and the bar graph on pages 81 and 82. Imagine that someone tried to put the information from the pie graph on the bar graph and vice versa. What, in your opinion, would be the result?

2 PUTTING IT ALL TOGETHER

USING THE VOCABULARY

culture	mestizos
dominion	population density
interdependent	epidemic
industry	natural increase
immigration	metropolitan area
import	primate city
export	rural area
ancestor	

On a separate sheet of paper, write the number of the definition and the term from the list that matches the definition.

1. leaving one's homeland and moving to another nation to live
2. customs, way of life, values, and beliefs of a certain people
3. average number of people in a certain area
4. person on one's family tree
5. rapid spread of disease among a large number of people
6. self-governing nation that has close ties with England
7. a large city with its immediate surrounding cities and towns
8. relying or depending on one another
9. to ship products, usually for sale, to another country
10. a city whose population is over two and one-half times the size of the country's next largest city
11. branch of manufacture, business, or trade
12. people of mixed European and American Indian ancestry
13. to receive products from another country for sale in your country
14. an excess, or extra number, of births over deaths
15. countryside, where most of the farming population lives

REMEMBERING WHAT YOU READ

On a separate sheet of paper, answer the following questions in complete sentences.

1. What two languages are most commonly spoken in the Americas?
2. What are the official languages in Canada?
3. How are the countries of the Americas interdependent?
4. Name the two largest minority groups in the United States.
5. Which states in the United States have had large numbers of immigrants?
6. From which countries in the Americas does the United States import oil and natural gas?
7. What food items are imported from Latin America?
8. Where do the greatest number of people live in Canada?

TYING LANGUAGE ARTS TO SOCIAL STUDIES

Write an imaginary business letter to the tourist board of a country in the Americas requesting travel information. Be specific about what kinds of transportation you wish to use, places of interest you want to visit, and when you want to make your trip.

THINKING CRITICALLY

On a separate sheet of paper, answer the following questions.

1. Name any group of people who have immigrated to your state. Tell what you know about their language, customs, food, and holidays.
2. Pick one immigrant group and tell some of their achievements and contributions to life in the United States.
3. Discuss a recent news event that shows how two countries in the Western Hemisphere are interdependent. Tell what happened and how the two nations were affected.
4. Describe the metropolitan area nearest you. On a map, show the cities and towns. Tell why they were included.
5. What are the advantages and disadvantages of living in a primate city? Tell why you would prefer one over the other.

SUMMARIZING THE CHAPTER

On a separate sheet of paper, draw a graphic organizer like the one shown here. Copy the information from this graphic organizer to the one you have drawn. Under each heading, fill in the blanks with facts you learned from this chapter.

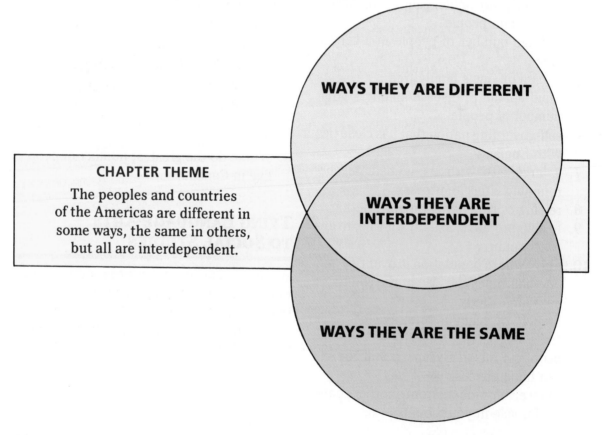

CHAPTER THEME

The peoples and countries of the Americas are different in some ways, the same in others, but all are interdependent.

WAYS THEY ARE DIFFERENT

WAYS THEY ARE INTERDEPENDENT

WAYS THEY ARE THE SAME

REVIEW
COOPERATIVE LEARNING

In this unit you learned that the Western Hemisphere regions of Canada, the United States, and Latin America are interdependent. One important aspect of this interdependence is the cultural exchange among these nations. You have learned that culture is the customs, way of life, values and beliefs of a certain people. What do you think it would be like to visit Canada or Latin America? How much different do you think our culture is from theirs?

PROJECT

Work with a group of classmates to discuss what you already know about the cultures of Canada and Latin America. Even if you have not visited either region, you may have seen programs or read magazines or books about these different cultures.

● Discuss each region. Think of the people, food, languages, sports, clothing, holidays, and anything else that comes to mind. Each person should contribute at least one idea. Record the group members' responses.

● Then imagine that you will be visiting either Canada or Latin America. As a group, vote on one region everyone would most like to visit. Have one member look at a map and choose a city for all of you to visit.

● Write a journal entry about an imaginary visit to that city. Each group member can choose from the following topics:

    PEOPLE THAT I MET
    A SPORTING EVENT I ATTENDED
    A FESTIVAL I ATTENDED
    AN UNUSUAL SITE THAT I SAW
    A PROBLEM I ENCOUNTERED
    VISITING A FAMILY'S HOME

● As you write about your experience, try to include as many details as you can. Imagine yourself in the place before you begin writing. Hear the sounds around you. Is this country very different from our country? Describe what you feel. Are you afraid or do you feel excitement and curiosity? Don't be concerned if you have little information about your imaginary visit. Later in this book you will learn a lot more about both Latin America and Canada.

PRESENTATION AND REVIEW

After each group member has finished his or her journal entry, hold another group meeting. Read your entry to the group. Then discuss how to combine the journal entries into one composition. Decide on the order of events. Choose one or two people to add transitional sentences that will help make the journal entries a whole piece. Have one member read the "travelogue" to the class. How might your group have improved the composition?

REMEMBER TO:
● Give your ideas.
● Listen to others' ideas.
● Plan your work with the group.
● Present your project.
● Discuss how your group worked.

A. WHY DO I NEED THIS SKILL?

Imagine that you are a weather reporter on the five o'clock news. You want to show your viewers the average temperature in March over the last 50 years. Would you show them 50 different numbers, one for each year? Probably not, at least if you want to keep your job. The best approach would be to make a graph. Using a line graph, you could show your viewers 50 years' worth of information in just a few seconds.

A graph is a visual way of organizing and presenting information. Graphs are used to show, clearly and simply, how things are related to one another. For example, our imaginary graph of average March temperatures shows how the temperature changes from year to year. Since the graph uses lines, it is easy to see whether the temperature has gone up or down from one year to the next.

B. LEARNING THE SKILL

There are many different kinds of graphs. The most common graphs are pie graphs, bar graphs, line graphs, and pictographs.

A pie graph shows how a whole is divided into parts, much as a real pie is cut into slices. Pie graphs are useful for showing *percentages*. For example, we could make a pie graph showing what percentage of the world's total land mass each continent occupies. Note that the parts of a pie graph, when added together, must equal 100 percent.

A bar graph can also be used to compare sizes, percentages, and quantities. But the parts of a bar graph do not have to equal 100 percent when added together. The bar graph below illustrates the population of the five largest states in the United States. The vertical line of this graph (called the *vertical axis*) is marked in millions to show the

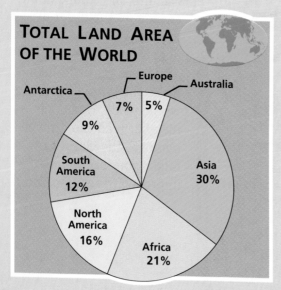

TOTAL LAND AREA OF THE WORLD

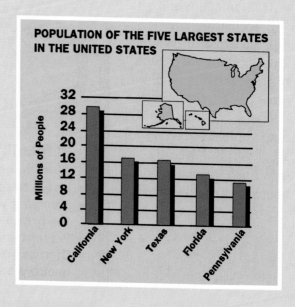

POPULATION OF THE FIVE LARGEST STATES IN THE UNITED STATES

number of people in each state. The horizontal line (called the *horizontal axis*) is marked to indicate each of the five states.

A line graph is usually used to show information that is connected in some way. For example, a line graph could be used to show the population growth in Mexico over the past ten years. This information could be represented as a continuous line, since the population grows from day to day. Turn to page 83 in Chapter 2. The line graph on that page shows the actual growth and the projected growth in population for Anglo-America and Latin America.

A pictograph is a chart that uses picture-symbols. Each picture-symbol stands for a fixed amount. The pictograph below shows the number of people living on each continent. Each human figure in the graph stands for 100 million people.

C. PRACTICING THE SKILL

1. On the pie graph, which continent is the smallest and which is the largest?
2. About how many people live in the state of Florida?
3. What state in the United States has the highest population?
4. About how many people live on the continent of Europe?
5. Which continent has a higher population, Africa or Asia?

D. APPLYING THE SKILL

Find out the high or low temperatures in your hometown for the past five days. Make a line graph showing these temperatures.

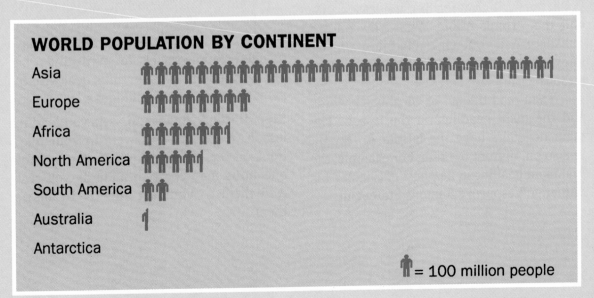

WORLD POPULATION BY CONTINENT

Asia

Europe

Africa

North America

South America

Australia

Antarctica

= 100 million people

A. WHY DO I NEED THIS SKILL?

This social studies book presents information about people, places, and events. Each lesson contains material that you must try to remember and learn. In this Skillbuilder, you will learn to use a strategy, or plan of action, for reading social studies lessons. It is called **SQR**. These letters, SQR, stand for **Survey**, **Question**, and **Read**. You may have used it already to study other subjects. SQR can help you to organize and remember the important information found in this book as well as in other books.

B. LEARNING THE SKILL

There are three steps in the SQR strategy. These steps are described below.

Step 1: Survey the lesson. **Survey**, in this case, means "to look over what you will read so as to get a general idea of the contents." Begin surveying by reading the lesson title and the "Think About What You Know" question. Ask yourself, "What do I already know that I can relate to the topic of the lesson?"

Then read the list of vocabulary words and the main headings in the lesson. The main headings have the letters **A.**, **B.**, **C.**, and so on, in front of them. For example, the first main heading in Lesson 1 of Chapter 1 is "Amerigo Vespucci's Famous Statement."

Look at any pictures, maps, charts, and other illustrations in the lesson. You can get a general idea from them about what you will be studying in the lesson.

At this point, make some guesses or predictions about the lesson, based on what you have observed so far.

Step 2: Ask questions. Think of any questions you may have about the lesson from the survey you just did. Use the words **who**, **what**, **where**, **when**, **why**, and **how** for help in thinking of questions.

Next, read the questions that appear throughout the lesson. For example, the "Focus Your Reading" question at the beginning of the lesson will help you focus on the main idea of the lesson. Also, read the questions that relate to the pictures and other illustrations. Then, read the questions in the "Lesson Review" section at the end of the lesson.

Fold a sheet of paper in half lengthwise. On the left half, jot down the questions you plan to be able to answer when you have finished reading the lesson. Write about five or six questions that you think deal with the most important facts and ideas.

Step 3: Read the lesson. As you read the lesson, write short answers to your questions on the right half of your paper. Other questions may come to mind as you read. Add them to your list and try to answer them.

C. PRACTICING THE SKILL

Practice using SQR for Lesson 2 of Chapter 1, "The Americas and the Americans." Follow the three steps. Refer to the "Using the SQR Strategy Chart" for help in remembering the steps.

USING THE SQR STRATEGY

Step 1: Survey
- Read the lesson title and the "Think About What You Know" question to recall what you already might know about ideas that relate to the topic.
- Read the vocabulary words, headings, and questions. Also look at the visuals in the lesson.
- Use this information to make some guesses or predictions about what will be in the lesson.

Step 2: Question
- Ask yourself some questions, using the words **who**, **what**, **where**, **when**, **why** and **how.**
- Read the questions in the lessons throughout the chapter.
- Jot down the questions you plan to be able to answer when you have finished reading.

Step 3: Read
- Read to answer the questions on your list.
- Write answers to the questions.
- Ask and then answer other questions that come to mind as you read.

D. APPLYING THE SKILL

SQR can help you learn and remember important material in your social studies book. Besides being a good textbook-study help, SQR is a useful method to use when you study for a test. Save your SQR questions and answers and use them to review a chapter before a test.

As you read the next chapter, which is about the first Americans, use the SQR study strategy. It should help you to understand and remember the material.

THE PEOPLES OF
THE WESTERN HEMISPHERE

The Western Hemisphere – that half of the earth that includes North and South America – was home to many groups of peoples before the time of Columbus.

▶ *These ear ornaments of gold, lapis lazuli, and turquoise were made by artisans from the Chimú kingdom of coastal Peru. The jewelry dates from pre- Columbian times.*

CHAPTER 3

THE FIRST AMERICANS

*T*housands of years ago a "bridge" of land connected America and Asia. The earliest Americans traveled across that bridge from Asia, in search of food.

Searching the Distant Past

THINK ABOUT WHAT YOU KNOW

This lesson deals with Native Americans, the first people to live in the Americas. Have a class discussion on all the things you know about early Americans.

STUDY THE VOCABULARY

prehistoric	migration
pre-Columbian	land bridge
archaeologist	nomad
artifact	extinct

FOCUS YOUR READING

Who were the first people to reach the Americas?

A. Clues from the Past

Prehistoric Times   History is the study of the recorded past, but how do historians know what happened long ago? Usually they search written records, such as books, official government papers, and newspapers. What if there are no written records of a time or place and there is no one left to tell what it was like? How can people learn about a **prehistoric** time or place? *Prehistoric* means "the time before history was written." Some writers call the period before Columbus reached America **pre-Columbian** times.

Archaeologists and Artifacts   A scientist who studies the prehistoric past is called an **archaeologist** (ahr kee AHL uh-jihst). Because there are no written records, archaeologists must use other ways of learning about the people who lived in the past.

Archaeologists learn about the past by studying **artifacts**, or things people have made. Artifacts may include the remains of large buildings, such as temples and forts, as well as remains of small objects, especially tools, weapons, and ornaments. They also may be pieces of pottery or household items. All of these artifacts are clues to how people lived in the past.

Sometimes archaeologists discover a human skeleton or even a preserved body. These human remains can give scientists many clues about people who lived long ago. They can indicate how tall the people were, whether they ate well, what they ate, and even what diseases they had. The more artifacts and human remains that archaeologists can study, the greater the amount of information they can learn about people of the past.

Many clues to the past, including ornaments, pottery, and tombs, have been found in Peru.
► What do the clues tell you?

B. Out on a Dig

Archaeologists actually do dig up the past. It takes a lot of planning and a great deal of hard work by many people to uncover artifacts of people who lived long ago.

Before the excavation starts, the director of the excavation decides where and how to dig, organizes the transport of equipment to the site, and generally sees that everything is ready by the time the work force arrives.

The work force includes many people with special talent. For example, some workers must know how to use survey instruments, draw patterns of stones or sections of soil, and measure the position of finds. An important member of the team is the photographer who takes pictures of the site and the artifacts as the work progresses and records each photograph.

Here is part of an archaeologist's description of one excavation, or dig, he worked on.

By 9:15 A.M. everyone is at work. The major activity to be seen is digging. The workers are also finding things, such as bones, pots, stone tools, and charcoal. These are being put into bags or containers marked to indicate precisely where they were found. Every different area of soil, every hole, every wall, every patch of stones has its own number and description. These may run into the hundreds of thousands on the average dig, or excavation.

Teotihuacán, the oldest pre-Columbian city in Middle America, dates back to about 100 B.C. Archeologists continue to search there for clues to the past.
▶ How is the pyramid at Chichén Itzá (on page 59) similar to this earlier one?

C. Across a Land Bridge

North America Tall forests rose up from the land. Fish swam in rivers and lakes. Many different types of animals roamed the plains. Birds soared through the skies, but no people lived there.

Travelers from Asia That land was North America many thousands of years ago. The research of archaeologists shows that the first human beings who arrived in the Americas had traveled from Asia. No one knows exactly when these people first came to the Americas. Archaeologists estimate it was between 15,000 and 50,000 years ago.

These people were the ancestors of the Native Americans that early European explorers, such as Columbus and John Cabot, found living in the Americas. Columbus, as you recall, mistakenly believed he had reached the East Indies, or Asia. Because of that, he called the people he saw *Indians*. In a way, the name *Indian* was appropriate. The ancestors of the people Columbus called Indians really *had* come from Asia.

You may be asking yourself how these people made their way from Asia to North America so many thousands of years ago. How did they cross the water that separates the two continents? The map on this page shows the route those first Americans probably followed in their **migration**, or moving, from Asia to North America.

Use of a Land Bridge The ancestors of the American Indians were able to cross from Asia to North America on a **land bridge**. A land bridge is a piece of dry land that connects larger landmasses, such as islands or even continents. Asia and North America were once connected by a land bridge.

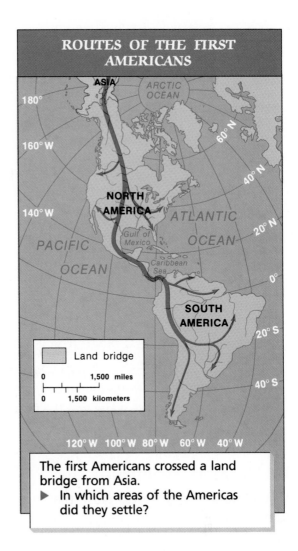

ROUTES OF THE FIRST AMERICANS

The first Americans crossed a land bridge from Asia.
▶ In which areas of the Americas did they settle?

The Bering Strait Today a stretch of sea just 50 miles (80 km) wide separates North America and Asia at the place where the two continents are closest to each other. The Bering Strait is the name of this body of water.

The water of the Bering Strait is only 150 feet (46 m) deep now, but thousands of years ago the oceans were about 300 feet (91 m) lower. The land that now is covered by the water of the Bering Strait was dry. The first people were able to *walk* from Asia to North America without crossing any water at all!

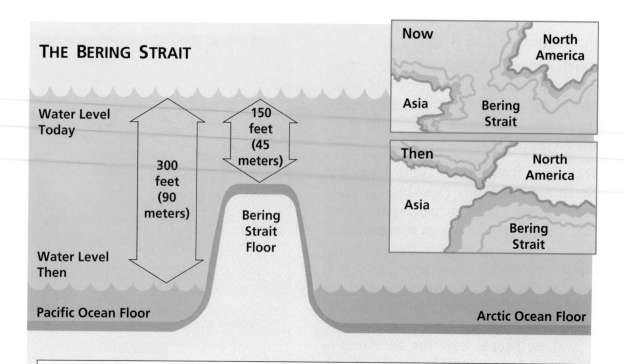

THE BERING STRAIT

Now

North America

Asia

Bering Strait

Then

North America

Asia

Bering Strait

Water Level Today

300 feet (90 meters)

150 feet (45 meters)

Bering Strait Floor

Water Level Then

Pacific Ocean Floor

Arctic Ocean Floor

The diagram shows that the floor of the Bering Strait was above water when the first Americans used it as a land bridge.

► How much above water was the floor of the Bering Strait at that time?

D. The First Migrations

Why People Migrated Now that you know *how* these early people came to North America, you may be wondering *why* they came. These people were hunters who crossed the land bridge while tracking game for food. They were **nomads**. Nomads are people who have no permanent homes and who travel constantly in search of food. The early nomads had only simple tools for hunting. They used clubs, slingshots, and pointed wooden spears to kill their prey. With such simple tools and no permanent settlements, they left little trace of their passage. That's why it is difficult to know exactly when the people came and how many of them there were. Even so, the research of archaeologists and other scientists allows us to make some good guesses.

The bands of hunters would have been small. They were probably made up of 10 to 30 related people — men, women, and children. Most scientists believe the land bridge was open for several thousand years and during at least two different times. Many small groups of hunters could have crossed from Asia to North America during those times. The most recent people to have crossed from Asia are the Inuit, or Eskimos. They came by sea within the past 2,000 years, long after the land bridge at the Bering Strait was flooded.

From Alaska to South America The earliest Americans first set foot on the continent of North America in what is now Alaska. Slowly, over many generations, they made their way south and spread out into the plains, forests, and mountains of North America. Eventually, they found their way to the farthest tip of South America.

It must have taken hundreds and hundreds of years for North and South America to become occupied. This would have happened long after the first people who crossed the land bridge had died. By 1492 — the time of Columbus — all of the Americas, except the highest mountains and the driest deserts, were settled.

E. The Great Extinction

The woolly mammoth looked much like an elephant, but it had a hairy skin. Its tusks grew as long as 16 feet (5 m). The saber-toothed tiger, a fierce beast 6 feet (2 m) long, got its name from the two long teeth that curved down from its upper jaw.

You can't find either of these animals in a zoo or in any place in the entire world today. That's because they no longer exist. They and many other animals became **extinct**, or died out, between 10,000 and 6,000 years ago. The number of animals that died was so great and the time during which they disappeared so short that this 4,000-year period has been given the name "the great extinction."

Scientist know such animals lived in North America because their remains have been found in many places. One of the most famous sites where the remains of these animals have been uncovered is Rancho La Brea (BRAY uh) in California. Although the city of Los Angeles has grown up around Rancho La Brea, the site has been preserved as a park.

La Brea is Spanish for "the tar." Some

American Museum of Natural History

The tusks of the woolly mammoth were 50 percent longer than the tusks of an elephant. The tusks curved back so they were not useful as weapons.
▶ How might the woolly mammoth have put its tusks to use?

Visitors to Hancock Park in Los Angeles, California, can go to a museum and the Rancho La Brea pits to see the replicas of extinct creatures.

▶ What facts did those who built these life-size replicas need to consider?

of the land of Rancho La Brea has places where oil seeped from the ground and hardened into sticky tar. Over a very long period of time, between 15,000 and 40,000 years ago, many animals became trapped in the tar and died. Because the tar preserved the animals' bones, scientists can study the remains and learn about life long ago.

Many animals that are now extinct were trapped in the tar at the La Brea site. Mammoths, camels, horses, bison (buffalo), wolves, and other animals have been found in the tar. Over 2,400 saber-toothed cats alone have been dug from the tar at La Brea!

The animals found in America by the early nomads from Asia were extremely large. In addition to the mammoths, there were beavers as large as modern bears, large wolves called dire wolves, and bison that were much larger than those that live today.

The early hunters certainly didn't have a shortage of game to hunt. Probably they needed to watch out that they did not become the prey of saber-toothed cats or wolves themselves! The oldest artifacts of stone spearpoints can be dated to be about 12,000 years old. Hunters before that time must have used very crude weapons.

What caused the great extinction? Some scientists believe that the hunters who came across the land bridge from Asia caused it. Animals were easy prey for the hunters, who moved across the center of North America and probably killed animals in great numbers for food, bone, and skins as they went.

There is no doubt that Indian hunters

10,000 years ago did kill some of the large animals that became extinct. Preserved skeletons of mammoths and giant bison have been found with stone spearpoints still stuck in the bones. Other remains show signs that the animals were eaten after they were killed.

Could the hunters have killed so many animals so fast they became extinct? There is no sure answer to this question. Someday, new evidence may be uncovered to help scientists find out what really caused the great extinction. For now, we know only that the animals died out at about the same time that skilled hunters seem to have arrived in North America.

LESSON *1* REVIEW

THINK AND WRITE

A. How are historians and archaeologists alike, and how are they different?
B. How do archaeologists learn about the past?
C. Summarize how the first Native Americans got to North America.
D. What are some things that archaeologists know about the first Americans?
E. Where is Rancho La Brea, and what can be seen there?

SKILLS CHECK

MAP SKILL

Find *Bering Strait* in the Gazetteer and on the map on page 100. Which two bodies of water does it connect? Which two continents does it separate? With your classmates, arrive at a definition that includes the exact location of the Bering Strait.

YOU DECIDE: SHOULD SOME ANIMALS BE ALLOWED TO BECOME EXTINCT?

You learned in this chapter that some animals that were once plentiful in the Western Hemisphere have disappeared completely. Among these animals that are now extinct are the woolly mammoth, saber-toothed tiger, and bison. Some of them vanished because they were over-hunted. Others died out for reasons unknown.

Scientists classify animals in different categories called species. There are about a million different species of animals in the world. Some of them live in the wild, while others are under the control of people. Within each species, there are different types of the animal called breeds.

Many species and breeds of animals are disappearing at the present time. Some disappear because of uncontrolled hunting and fishing. Other animals die because the habitat in which they had lived was destroyed. As the human population on earth increases, more and more land is cleared to make room for homes, farms, industries, and transportation. When habitats are gone, animals die out. Pollutions of the water, soil, and air by chemicals are also causes of animal deaths.

No Wild Animals Should Become Extinct

Some scientists feel that all species of animals in the wilds must be saved. They argue that if one animal disappears, it disrupts the balance of nature in that habitat. Animals in one habitat depend on each other as sources of food. When one is gone, all are affected. Scientists also urge that we keep all species alive so we can study them.

All Farm Breeds Should Be Saved

Some scientists say it is dangerous to rely on only the most productive breeds of farm animals. It was reported recently that if a very contagious disease spread through our cattle herds, we would lose a large part of our food supply. If cattle were fed grains contaminated by chemicals from soil or water pollution, the same thing would happen. Other breeds might be needed then to develop new crossbreeds that have more resistance to disease or who have other valuable traits. "Don't throw the genes [traits] away," a conservationist warned. "Your grandchildren might need them."

Some Wild Animals Can Become Extinct

To care properly for the world's growing population, some people argue that we must destroy some animal habitats. People are more important than animals. We should concentrate on improving the standard of living for all people, even if it means losing some animal species.

Raise Only the Most Productive Farm Animals

A controversy is growing among farmers about whether certain breeds of domesticated animals should be saved. During the last century, scientists have tried to breed farm animals to be more productive. We now have cows that produce large quantities of milk. Scientifically bred chickens lay more and larger eggs. Sheep have been bred to produce better wool and much tastier meat. Some hardy breeds though not productive, like the Texas Longhorn cattle, are disappearing. As was reported in *Newsweek* magazine, "Roughly half of our farm animals are in danger of disappearing forever."

Thinking for Yourself

On a separate sheet of paper, write your answers in complete sentences.

1. What reasons are given for saving all wild species from extinction? Do you agree? Explain.
2. According to some scientists, why should we preserve all breeds of farm animals?
3. Do you agree that all farm breeds should be saved? If not, what rules would you make for whether a breed should be saved or not?

Different Ways of Living

Imagine that you are one of the first Americans and you live out in the wilderness. How do you get enough food to eat? What kinds of things do you need in order to survive?

STUDY THE VOCABULARY

subsistence	shifting agriculture
domesticate	civilization
manioc	specialization
irrigation	surplus

FOCUS YOUR READING

What are some ways that early Native American people got food?

A. Getting Food

What do you do when you are hungry? Well, you may take something from the refrigerator. Perhaps you go out to a restaurant. Of course, the early Native Americans couldn't do that. How, then, did they get their food? They had to gain their **subsistence** from the lands on which they lived. *Subsistence* means "a way of keeping alive."

By the time that Europeans first arrived in the Americas at the end of the fifteenth century, Native Americans had developed many different ways of living. Many Indians were still surviving by hunting and by gathering wild food. Others had discovered farming. They were planting such crops as corn, beans, pumpkins and potatoes.

However they managed to get their food, the people then had to prepare it. That wasn't easy. Animals had to be skinned, cut up, and cooked. Grains might need to have certain parts removed and then be ground and baked. All this had to be done by hand and often with only simple tools.

Storing food also was difficult. After all, there were no refrigerators. Meat could be cut into strips and dried in the sun and wind. That was a long process.

The need for food caused some Indian groups to roam from place to place. Others remained settled in one area. Some of them lived in small groups, and others lived in large cities that were the capitals of mighty empires. No matter where the people lived, the obtaining and preparing of food had to be considered.

Even today, some Indians live in homes built on stilts over lakes and rivers.
► What foods might they eat?

Lake dwellers used bows and arrows to hunt aurochs.
▶ Why was this task both difficult and dangerous?

Where fish were plentiful, fishing became very important for the Indians' subsistence. On the northwest coast of North America, fish, game, and other wild food was so plentiful that a very full Indian culture developed.

Most areas of hunting, gathering, and fishing were not rich in food supplies, so only small Indian populations could survive. Hunting, gathering, and fishing were common in the colder and drier parts of North and South America. The Inuit of the Far North were hunters. So were the Indians of the northern forests. Hunters also lived in the plains areas and in the deserts of the present-day western United States and Mexico. In South America, hunters lived mainly in the deserts, plains, and cold areas in the south.

C. More Food Through Agriculture

The Indians were good farmers. They learned how to **domesticate** plants. To domesticate is to cultivate certain plants (or to tame certain animals) to make them more useful for people. All of the agricultural plants we have today are domesticated plants.

American Indians domesticated corn, potatoes, tomatoes, chili peppers, squash, pineapples, many kinds of beans, and **manioc** (MAN ee ahk). Manioc is a tropical plant similar to the potato. Manioc plants have become very important plants in many parts of the world.

Agriculture was practiced by American Indians in most places in which crops could be grown. In North America the Indians of the eastern part of the continent, from what is now southern Canada to Florida, grew crops of corn, squash, beans, and other plants. Crops were also grown in

B. Hunters, Gatherers, and Fishers

Snares and Traps Hunting for food was done in many different ways. Indian hunters made several kinds of snares and traps to catch small game. They also used spears, bows and arrows, slingshots, and bolas (BOH luz). A bola was made by tying two or more rocks to the ends of leather or twine strips, one rock on each strip. The strips, about 2 feet (60 cm) long, were then tied together at the free ends. When thrown at the feet of a running animal, a bola would get tangled in the animal's legs, causing the animal to fall down and be caught.

Picking and Collecting Gathering was another important way Indians got their food. They picked berries, dug up roots, and collected small animals. They even ate insects and grubs when necessary.

Craftspeople in the well planned city of Chan Chan specialized in the mass production of pottery.
▶ What might they have made?

burned in small patches. Burning the forest helps to clear the ground for planting. The ashes of the burned plants add nutrients to the soil for future crops. These areas are then planted with a mixture of crops that grow well in the tropics. The Indians planted in a haphazard manner, not in the neat rows of modern agriculture. Two crops, or perhaps three, are grown before the land is allowed to return to forest. The soils are too poor to support crops for a longer time.

Simple Tools The early American Indians did not have plows. Instead, they used hoes and digging sticks to work the ground. Farming required a lot of hand labor, but it was often very productive.

parts of present-day southwestern United States and northern Mexico. Columbus found Indian farmers living on the islands of the Caribbean when he first came to America. Farming Indians also lived in Central America and in all the tropical parts of South America.

D. Special Tools and Techniques

Making Use of Irrigation Not all land is good for farming. Sometimes special farming methods, or ways, are needed for crops to grow. For example, in areas where there is little rainfall, **irrigation**, or the bringing of water to crops, is necessary. Indian farmers in the dry southwestern United States, northern Mexico, and the central Andes all used irrigation.

In the forest areas of South America **shifting agriculture** was common. In shifting agriculture, also called slash-and-burn agriculture, the forest is cleared and

E. Civilization and Surplus

A Cultural Stage **Civilization** is the stage in a culture marked by a high level of science and government. Civilized societies typically have cities and large-scale trade. They have complex religions and well-developed arts and crafts. Almost every civilization has some written form of language. People in a civilization usually are divided into different social classes. For example, there might be an upper class of nobles who enjoy more power and have a higher standard of living than the rest of the people.

Another feature of civilization is **specialization**. Instead of each person doing much the same thing, people have different roles or functions in specialization. For example, long ago there might have been a warrior group, whose only job was fighting. There might have been merchants to take care of trade. Think of some other specialized roles people might have had long ago.

Although cutting down trees is a way to clear land for farming, many trees are destroyed.
▶ Why do some people continue to do this?

Advantages of Surplus The key to civilization is **surplus**. A surplus is an extra amount, something more than is absolutely necessary. Remember how much work it was for the first Americans to get enough food to survive. That didn't leave them much time for anything else. Also, since those people barely had enough food to ensure their survival, they could not afford to support people who did not get their own food.

With domestication of agriculture and improved farming methods, food was not as scarce. One person could produce enough to feed several people. That made it possible for some people to do things other than grow food. They could specialize in things such as studying the heavens and making pottery. With enough surplus, whole classes of people could be supported through the labor of others. Some surplus could be stored for emergencies.

Another advantage of surplus was that it allowed people to remain in one spot rather than move around in constant search of food. People had time to establish cities with majestic buildings.

The production of a surplus remains important today. Imagine what it would be like if you had to grow and prepare all your own food, make all your clothing and tools, and build your own shelter. You surely would not have much time left in your day for other things.

LESSON **2** *REVIEW*

THINK AND WRITE

A. What problems did the early Americans have because of their need for food?

B. How were hunting and gathering similar?

C. Explain the success that the American Indians had with plants.

D. What were some of the methods used by American Indians to farm the land?

E. What is surplus, and why is it important in order for civilization to take place?

SKILLS CHECK

WRITING SKILL

Jot down your typical daily schedule. Then reread the last paragraph in this lesson. Make a new daily schedule based on that style of life. Compare and discuss your findings with your classmates.

Indian Groups in 1492

THINK ABOUT WHAT YOU KNOW

Think about the house you live in and the foods you eat. In what ways might they be different if you lived in another climate?

STUDY THE VOCABULARY

llama   tributary
thatch   palisade
leaching

FOCUS YOUR READING

What were some of the Indian groups that lived in Latin America both before and at the time of Columbus?

A. Arawaks and Caribs

When Columbus landed on the island of Hispaniola in the Caribbean, he was fascinated by the people he found living there. He described them in his journal.

> *The inhabitants of this island are so liberal with their possessions that no one who has not seen them would believe it. If one asks for anything they have, they never say no. On the contrary, they offer a share to anyone, with demonstrations of heartfelt affection, and they are immediately content with any small thing, valuable or valueless, that is given them.*
>
> *They have no religion, but all believe that power and goodness dwell in the sky, and they are firmly convinced that I have come from the sky with these ships and people. They are men of great intelligence, for they navigate all these seas, and they give a marvelously good account of everything.*

These people whom Columbus so admired were the Arawaks (AH rah wahks). They, along with the Caribs (KAR ihbz), were the main Indian peoples of the Lesser Antilles (an TIHL eez). Locate the Lesser Antilles on the Atlas map of the world on page 592. The Caribs first lived on the mainland of South America around the Guianas. About 100 years before the arrival of Columbus, some Carib groups invaded the Lesser Antilles. The Arawaks fled to islands farther to the north.

Both the Arawaks and the Caribs were part of a larger cultural group called the Circum-Caribbeans. The word *circum-Caribbean* refers to the geographic location. All the peoples of this group lived

around the Caribbean Sea. In Latin, the word *circum* means "about" or "around." The Circum-Caribbean Indians belonged to the same cultural group, which means that their cultures shared some important common features.

Most of what we know about these Indian peoples comes from accounts written by Spanish explorers. From those reports, it seems that these peoples organized themselves into *chiefdoms*. A chiefdom is a small group of people ruled by a person called a chief. Usually, several small chiefdoms joined together to create larger, more powerful groupings.

The Circum-Caribbean Indians generally lived in villages and farmed the land. Since they lived near the sea, fishing also provided food. Depending on the group and where it lived, however, methods of farming varied. Some groups used shifting agriculture, the slash-and-burn method. Others used irrigation to water their crops. They grew many different vegetables, including manioc. Indians who lived in lowland areas had all sorts of tropical fruits.

B. The Chibchas

The Biggest Chiefdom In the highlands of what is today Colombia, the Chibchas organized a very large chiefdom. In fact, it was bigger than that of any other Circum-Caribbean Indian group. Around 300,000 Chibchas lived in five different political groupings. Each one was ruled by a powerful chief.

Each chief received very special treatment. When he went out, he was carried on a litter, or platform, that was covered in gold. As the chief's procession moved along, attendants threw flowers in front of his litter. People bowed and looked away when they approached the chief. This showed their respect.

The Importance of Religion Religion was of great importance to the Chibchas. Each of the chiefdoms had temples and priests. The elaborate religious ceremonies usually involved some sort of sacrifice. Sometimes the sacrifice was a human being. At other times the Chibchas offered their gods beautiful textiles or objects of gold.

Chibcha Crafts The Chibchas had great skill in arts and crafts. They fashioned gold into all sorts of objects to decorate their temples and to wear for jewelry. Chiefs might wear elaborate chest plates, necklaces, and crowns. Precious stones, espe-

Columbus found the Arawaks to be gentle people, as you learned when you read his journal entry.
▶ How is their gentleness shown in this piece of art?

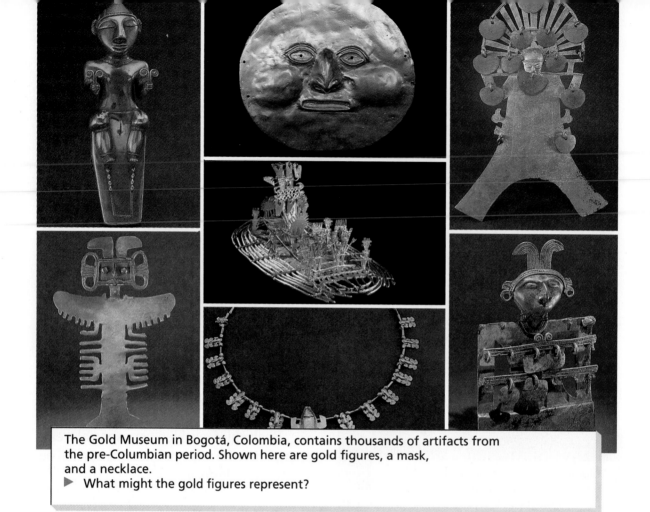

The Gold Museum in Bogotá, Colombia, contains thousands of artifacts from the pre-Columbian period. Shown here are gold figures, a mask, and a necklace.

▶ What might the gold figures represent?

cially emeralds, were used as jewelry. The Chibchas would make a small cut in a person's skin and insert a stone directly into it. They also made jewelry and other decorative objects from copper, shell, and bone. Many of these beautiful objects can be seen today in the famous Museo de Oro ("Gold Museum") in Bogotá, the capital of Colombia.

C. The Onas in the Southern Plains

Patterns of Nomad Travel You have learned that nomads move from place to place in search of food. However, the nomads of neither the past nor the present should be thought of as simply wandering about. Usually their travels show patterns that reflect the seasonal movement of the animals they hunt plus the growing seasons of the plants they gather.

Nomadic Ways of Living If you moved around often, would you want to carry a great many things with you? Would you put much effort into building a house? Probably not. Nomadic people usually have relatively few possessions. They do not erect large public structures, such as temples or palaces for their rulers. Because food generally is hard to find, such groups usually are small. Also, there is not much surplus to support a ruling class.

Throughout the nations that are known today as Argentina, Chile, Uruguay, and Paraguay, there lived many different groups of hunters and gatherers. One such group was the Onas of Argentina.

Because horses were not brought to the Americas until the Spanish arrived, the Onas originally hunted on foot. There was no big game around. The Onas stalked the guanaco, a hoofed mammal related to the camel. Guanacos have a height at the shoulder of around $3\frac{1}{2}$ feet (1 m) and a length of around $5\frac{1}{2}$ feet (2 m). The **llama** and the alpaca, both common in South America, probably are domesticated versions of the guanaco. They are used as pack animals and as sources of wool.

Small Bands of Onas The Onas grouped together in bands made up of several families. Usually between 50 and 100 were in each band. That's certainly a far cry from the chiefdoms of the Chibchas! Leadership of a band was given to the oldest male. There were no other leaders — no nobles, no full-time priests, no craftspeople. Each Ona band hunted a particular area. It probably did not exceed 20 square miles (52 sq km). Hunting in another band's territory could lead to war.

Uses for Guanaco Skins The clothing and shelters of the Onas were simple. From the skins of the guanaco, the Onas made loose sleeveless coats, or mantles. Guanaco skins stretched on poles served as shelters, which were nothing more than windbreaks. Since winter often is cold on the plains of Argentina, the Onas must have been a very hardy people.

D. Araucanians in Chile

A Large Araucanian Population Also in the same area, but in fertile lands in central Chile, lived the Araucanians (ar aw KAY-

Llamas are valued as pack animals since each can carry loads of as much as 130 pounds (59 kg).
▶ Describe the scene pictured.

nee unz). Estimates of the total Araucanian population around the time the Spaniards arrived run from 500,000 to 1,500,000. There were three Araucanian groups, each occupying a particular region: the Picunches in the north, the Mapuches in central Chile, and the Huilliches in the south.

Mighty Araucanian Warriors The Huilliches were famous for their skill as warriors. They quickly took to the horse and successfully fought the Spanish. After independence, they fought the Chileans. Toward the end of the nineteenth century, after more than 300 years of struggle, they suffered their final defeat and were forced onto reservations. Alonso de Ercilla y Zúñiga, a Spanish soldier who had fought against them, wrote a great poem called "La Araucana" ("The Araucanian"), in which he acknowledged their bravery. A portion of his poem is on page 114.

Beardless men, robust of gesture
Theirs are full-grown, shapely bodies
Lofty chests and massive shoulders
Stalwart limbs and steely sinews.

They are confident, emboldened,
Dauntless, gallant, and audacious,
Firm inured to toil and suffering,
Mortal cold and heat and hunger.

This poem may be a bit difficult to understand, but a second look may help you see how the courage and strength of the Araucanians impressed Ercilla y Zúñiga. In the last two lines, he remarks how they bear up to all hardships, including hard work, bad weather, and lack of food.

Both the Huilliches and Mapuches used shifting agriculture. The potato was one of their most important crops. Those living in coastal areas fished and trapped. They also kept large herds of llamas.

Araucanians used poles and **thatch** to make houses. Thatch is grass that is matted together to make a roof or walls. They also made baskets, nets, and rope. They knew how to work wood and stone, and they also made pottery. Weaving was another Araucanian skill, which resulted in fine, colorful blankets.

E. People in Tropical Forests

The region of the great Amazon rain forest and the vast basin drained by the mighty Amazon River was home to many different Indian groups. They were farmers and fishers. Most of them lived in small villages. Farming in the forest was not easy. There was not that much good land to farm. Also, once land was cleared, it soon lost fertility because of **leaching**. Leaching is the carrying off by rainwater of much of the soil's minerals, which crops need for growth. This problem still occurs today in Latin America when farmers clear the rain forests.

When the land could no longer support them, the forest Indians moved on to new locations. They lived in pole-and-thatch houses that were easy to build. They slept in hammocks. The rain forest dwellers often traveled by water, using dugout canoes. Many **tributaries** of the Amazon River flow throughout that region. A tributary is a stream or river that flows into a larger stream or river.

Villages usually were small. Sometimes a single large building housed the entire community. Such a house, shaped something like a large loaf of bread, might be as much as 200 feet (61 m) long. Even

Forest Indians are shown, as well as a palisade village in Venezuela.
▶ Why do some Indian groups still prefer to live a traditional life?

behind it. This fence or wall was needed for defense. A line of stakes set up like this is called a **palisade**, so this type of settlement is called a palisade village. The palisade had importance because many of the Indian groups fought with one another.

Among important forest Indians were the Tupinambas, who had moved south from the Amazon along the coast of Brazil. The Tupinambas were one of the many groups that spoke the language called Tupi. Tupi speakers believed in a hero figure known as "the Grandfather." According to legend, somewhere there was a "land of the grandfathers" where they would lead happy lives. Many Tupi-speaking Indians moved out of the Amazon region in search of this promised land.

The Tupinambas lived in very large settlements behind a double row of palisades. They fished and grew crops. They behaved very courteously to one another. However, they also were very fierce people and warred on their neighbors. When they made war, they usually would eat many of the people they captured.

As mentioned earlier, some Native Americans lived in very large cities. In fact, three groups of Native Americans established very advanced civilizations. You will learn about these remarkable peoples in the next chapter.

those large houses were made with poles and thatch. The forest Indians arranged their villages in a special way. They stuck big pieces of wood in the ground, forming a kind of fence, and then placed their houses

LESSON 3 REVIEW

THINK AND WRITE

A. How were the cultures of the Circum-Caribbean Indians alike?
B. What were some important features of the Chibchas' culture?
C. Why do nomads live very simply?
D. What have you learned about the Araucanians?
E. Of what use were palisades?

SKILLS CHECK

THINKING SKILL

Imagine that you have taken a trip in a time machine. It has placed you as a member of a Latin American Indian group in the 1400s. Who are you? Where are you? What are you doing?

USING THE VOCABULARY

> prehistoric
> nomads
> extinct
> domesticate
> irrigation
> shifting agriculture
> specialization
> surplus
> leaching
> tributary

On a separate sheet of paper, write the words that fit with the following definitions.

1. Term used for animals or plants that completely die out
2. Another name for slash-and-burn farming
3. Tribes or other groups of people who move from place to place
4. Having an extra amount
5. A stream or river that flows into a larger one
6. Before events were written down
7. To raise animals or plants for people's use
8. System whereby people have special jobs, such as warriors, merchants, or priests
9. Bringing water into an area for crops
10. The carrying off by rainwater of the soil's minerals

REMEMBERING WHAT YOU READ

On a separate sheet of paper, answer the following questions in complete sentences.

1. What type of artifacts are sometimes found at an archaeologist's excavation?
2. What is meant by a dig?
3. How did the earliest people come to settle in the Americas?
4. What discovery did scientists make at Rancho La Brea?
5. Describe the kinds of weapons the early Native Americans used for hunting.
6. How did domesticating plants and animals help the early Indians?
7. How do surpluses of food help people develop a civilization?
8. Describe the civilization of the Chibcha Indians.
9. What was the life of nomadic tribes like?
10. What happened to the rain forest land of the Amazon a few years after it was cleared for farming?

TYING SCIENCE TO SOCIAL STUDIES

Animals that are in danger of becoming extinct are put on the endangered list. Find out about an endangered animal species in the Western Hemisphere. Do some research in the library to find out what is being done to save that animal. A good place to find this information is in a current science, nature, or news magazine. Use the *Readers' Guide to Periodical Literature* to locate the issue you want or ask a librarian to help you. Write a one page summary of what you have learned and share it with your classmates.

THINKING CRITICALLY

On a separate sheet of paper, write your answers in complete sentences.

1. Pretend you are an archaeologist in a future time. On a dig in the United States, you find a refrigerator from 1990. What does this refrigerator tell you about the ways of people living in the 1990s?
2. Name some plants and animals that people have domesticated in the current time.

What uses, other than food, do these plants and animals have?

3. What are some specialized jobs that members of your community do?
4. Would you rather have lived in a hunting and fishing tribe or a tribe that farmed and raised livestock? Tell why.
5. Why did the tribes who lived near the Caribbean develop a similar way of life?

SUMMARIZING THE CHAPTER

On a separate piece of paper, draw a graphic organizer like the one shown here. Copy the information from this graphic organizer on the one you have drawn. On each blank line, write some fact about the subject mentioned that you learned from the chapter.

CHAPTER THEME
The first Americans were from different Indian groups with distinct ways of living.

HOW DO WE KNOW ABOUT THE FIRST AMERICANS?
1. artifacts
2.

DIFFERENT WAYS OF LIVING
1.
2.
3.
4.

INDIAN GROUPS IN 1492
1. Arawaks and Caribs
2. Chibchas
3.
4.
5.

CHAPTER 4

THE GREAT INDIAN CIVILIZATIONS

Long before Europeans landed in America, the Maya, Aztecs, and Incas had established mighty empires in Central and South America.

The Rise of Empires

THINK ABOUT WHAT YOU KNOW
Look through the illustrations in this chapter for clues to the cultures of the Aztecs, Incas, and Maya. How, do you think, do these people compare with the Indian peoples you read about in Chapter 3?

STUDY THE VOCABULARY
nuclear America
empire

FOCUS YOUR READING
How did great civilizations develop in Latin America?

A. Great Civilizations in the Americas

Major Indian Civilizations Perhaps you think of atomic bombs or power plants when you see the word *nuclear*. The word *nuclear* relates to "central" or "in the middle of." Some archaeologists and anthropologists use the term **nuclear America**. What they mean is the ancient cultural centers of America. The term *nuclear America* refers to the areas of the three great Indian civilizations—the Maya, the Aztec, and the Inca.

Nuclear America included two areas. One area was in the part of Middle America that today makes up the southern half of Mexico and northern Central America. The other area covered most of the Andes Mountains on the west coast of South America. Find the two areas on the map.

The Maya The Maya once ruled the lands in Middle America that now make up the Yucatán Peninsula, Guatemala, Belize, and the western parts of Honduras and El Salvador. The earliest traces of a Maya village have been dated at 2500 B.C. By around A.D. 250, the Maya had created a civilization with cities and temples as well as active trade and productive farms in the rain forests of the tropical lowlands.

The Aztecs The Aztecs first settled in the area of Middle America that is now Mexico City about A.D. 1200, a little over 300 years

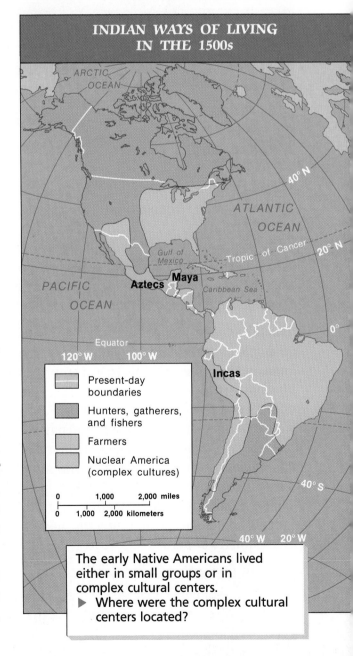

INDIAN WAYS OF LIVING IN THE 1500s

Present-day boundaries

Hunters, gatherers, and fishers

Farmers

Nuclear America (complex cultures)

0   1,000   2,000 miles
0   1,000   2,000 kilometers

The early Native Americans lived either in small groups or in complex cultural centers.
▶ Where were the complex cultural centers located?

Paintings can help you learn about historical events, such as Aztec life. Stonework, such as this Inca fortress, tell about the past, too.
▶ What did you learn from these visuals?

before the Spanish conquest. They built a great city called Tenochtitlán (tay nawch-tee TLAHN) and carried on active trade with the Maya and other Indian groups. Aztec agriculture supported a very large population. The Aztecs had huge armies that conducted wars of conquest.

The Incas The largest and richest **empire** in nuclear America was created by the Incas in the fifteenth century. An empire is all the territories and people under the control of a powerful nation. The Inca Empire extended from the southern part of the present South American country of Colombia to northern Chile and Argentina, a distance of over 3,000 miles (4,827 km). That empire included the entire central part of the Andes region and the nearby coastal parts of Peru.

B. The Growth of Civilization

Archaeologists have discovered a history of civilization in nuclear America that dates back thousands of years. The accomplishments from those early times paved the way for two later periods. The *Classic Period* ran from around A.D. 1 to A.D. 1000. The *Postclassic Period* followed, and it ended with the arrival of the Spaniards.

During the Classic Period, magnificent pyramids were erected. The Indian civilizations in central Mexico left us other signs of their wealth and power at that time. Advances in pottery and weaving continued. The study of time and the heavens also received much attention. Then, for reasons that remain puzzling and unclear, the Classic Period came to a sudden end. Archaeologists have uncovered many Classic settlements that had either been destroyed or abandoned. The end seems to have come to all those settlements at about the same time.

Maybe these centers fell to invaders. Some archaeologists suggest that this "Classic collapse" was a longer process

Tikal, a Maya city in the jungles of Petén in western Guatemala, was abandoned around 700 years before the Spanish conquest.
▶ How large a population do you think it had?

that saw food production unable to keep up with population growth.

C. New Empires

The Postclassic Period was the time when the great empires of the Aztecs and Incas rose to power. Like other empires before them, they grew through conquering other peoples or states.

As you might imagine, the conquered peoples disliked losing their independence. Revolts were common as the conquered peoples tried to regain their freedom. Also, as conquering empires grew wealthier, groups within the ruling class struggled with one another.

By the time of the Spanish conquest in the sixteenth century, the Maya civilization already had collapsed. War gripped the Inca Empire as two Inca nobles each claimed to be the rightful king. The Aztec Empire, however, seemed at the height of its power.

LESSON **1** *REVIEW*

THINK AND WRITE

A. What are the names of the three great Indian civilizations of nuclear America?
B. What achievements were made during the Classic Period?
C. What important events happened during the Postclassic Period?

SKILLS CHECK

WRITING SKILL

Refer to the map of Tenochtitlán on page 122. Pick one item, such as towers, from the key. Use the symbol or the color to find your selected item wherever it appears on the map. Then write a detailed description of this item, including its location and its importance to the city.

The Aztec Empire

THINK ABOUT WHAT YOU KNOW

The Aztecs, as you know, had one of the great civilizations in the Americas. Think of some of the things you have learned about civilization. What things would you expect to find in the Aztec civilization?

STUDY THE VOCABULARY

causeway   **pochteca**
chinampa

FOCUS YOUR READING

What was Aztec society like?

A. The Aztecs' Arrival in the Central Valley of Mexico

Mexicas, the Early Aztecs The Aztecs, known around A.D. 1200 as the Mexicas (ME hee kahs), began a long, wandering journey from northern Mexico toward the central valley. They carried with them their tribal god, whose name meant "Humming Bird of the South." He was god of war and the sun. They believed that this god would lead them to a special place.

An Aztec Legend According to Aztec legend, the god told them to make their home on the spot where they saw an eagle perched on a cactus with a serpent in its mouth. Again according to legend, the Aztecs saw the eagle on an island in Lake Texcoco in Mexico's central valley. There they stopped and made their home, building the city of Tenochtitlán. Today the eagle and serpent are shown on the flag of Mexico.

B. A Rise to Power

Tenochtitlán, the Central City At its height, the Aztec Empire included millions of people. Even though no one knows exactly how many people there were, it seems clear that the Aztec Empire had a population equal to the large European countries at the time! Tenochtitlán alone, which may have had as many as 300,000 people, was larger than any European city. Along the shores of Lake Texcoco were other cities. These cities were connected to Tenochtitlán by a system of **causeways**,

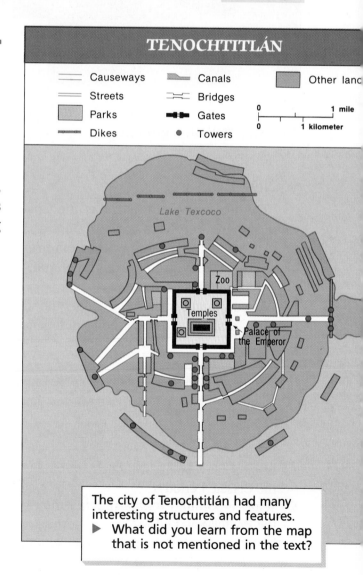

TENOCHTITLÁN

Legend:
— Causeways   ▨ Canals   ▨ Other land
═ Streets   ⇌ Bridges
▭ Parks   ▪■▪ Gates
┈ Dikes   ● Towers

0 ———— 1 mile
0 ———— 1 kilometer

Lake Texcoco
Zoo
Temples
Palace of the Emperor

The city of Tenochtitlán had many interesting structures and features.
► What did you learn from the map that is not mentioned in the text?

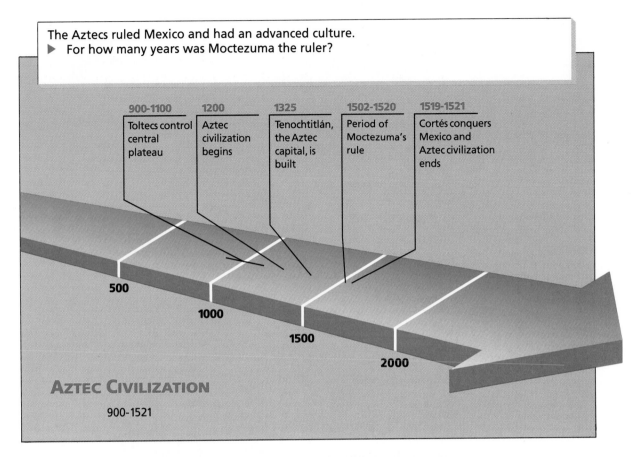

The Aztecs ruled Mexico and had an advanced culture.
▶ For how many years was Moctezuma the ruler?

900-1100 Toltecs control central plateau

1200 Aztec civilization begins

1325 Tenochtitlán, the Aztec capital, is built

1502-1520 Period of Moctezuma's rule

1519-1521 Cortés conquers Mexico and Aztec civilization ends

500
1000
1500
2000

AZTEC CIVILIZATION
900-1521

or raised earthen roads, built across the lake. Bridges on the causeways allowed canoes to go from one part of the lake to another.

Island Gardens, or Chinampas A productive agriculture helped support the large population of Tenochtitlán. The Aztecs planted corn and other crops in irrigated fields around Lake Texcoco. They built more islands from layers of reeds, other plants, and mud in the shallow water of the lake. The islands covered most of the southern part of the lake and were planted with crops that produced large amounts of food. These island gardens were called **chinampas** (chih NAHM pahs). One Aztec crop was tomatoes. The English word *tomato* comes from the Aztec word *tomatl*, meaning "the swelling fruit."

C. Aztec Warfare

The Aztec Conquerors The Aztecs carried on constant wars with neighboring peoples. They fought with wooden swords that had sharp stone blades. They also used bows and arrows as well as spears. Their armor was padded cotton made into suits fitted to the body. This armor worked well against the weapons of other Indians. However, it was little protection against the steel swords, arrows, muskets, and cannons of the Spaniards.

The main purpose of the Aztec wars was to capture enemy soldiers so that thousands could be sacrificed, or offered, to the gods. Captives were brought to Tenochtitlán. There they were led up the steps of a great pyramid on the top of which stood a temple. In front of the temple stood the sacrificial altar. While drums boomed,

This is an example of the work of Diego Rivera (1886–1957), a famous Mexican painter.
▶ What can you tell about Aztec life from this painting?

each unlucky captive was held down on the altar. The sharp knife of an Aztec priest flashed in the sun, and in an instant the victim's chest was opened. The priest then reached in, grabbed the heart, and held it aloft for all to see. In this manner, the Aztecs sacrificed thousands of people each year.

D. Cycles of Creation and Destruction

Religious Beliefs What was the reason for all these sacrifices? The answer lies in the Aztec religion. That religion had a number of important beliefs. In common with other groups in Middle America, the Aztecs believed that the world had been created and destroyed several times. Ultimately, they believed their world would again end in disaster. The Aztecs thought

that their special purpose in life was to delay that destruction. They sacrificed to the god of war and the sun to keep the sun in the sky and avoid destruction for as long as possible.

Priestly Powers Many other Aztec gods controlled natural forces. For example, there was a god of rain and a god of wind. These gods also required attention, although they might not have demanded human sacrifice. Life was very insecure, since the gods could cause all sorts of problems if they became unhappy. It was important, therefore, to know what the gods wanted. The priests supposedly had the ability to interpret signs of the gods' pleasure or unhappiness. Priests had enormous power in the Aztec society.

USING SOURCE MATERIAL

THE GREAT CITY OF TENOCHTITLÁN

Tenochtitlán, the Aztec capital, fell to the Spanish conqueror Hernándo Cortés. You will read about the conquest in Chapter 5. When Cortés first saw Tenochtitlán and walked about the city, he was very impressed. In a letter written to the king of Spain on October 30, 1520, Cortés described some of what he had seen. In part of that letter, Cortés tells about the city's markets.

> *The city has many open squares in which markets are continuously held. One square in particular is twice as big as that of Salamanca [a city in Spain] and completely surrounded by an arcade where there are more than sixty thousand folk buying and selling daily. Every kind of merchandise is for sale there, whether of food, or ornaments of gold and silver, or precious stones, snails, and feathers.*

> *There is a street of game where they sell all manner of birds that are to be found in their country, including hens, pigeons, parrots, owls, eagles, and sparrow hawks. They also sell rabbits, hares, deer, and small dogs which they breed especially for eating.*

> *All kinds of vegetables may be found there. There are many different sorts of fruits including cherries and plums very similar to those found in Spain. They sell honey obtained from bees.*

> *They have colors for painting of as good quality as any in Spain, and of as pure shades as may be found anywhere. A great deal of chinaware is sold of very good quality and including earthen jars of all sizes for holding liquids, pitchers, pots, tiles, and an infinite variety of earthenware all made of a very special clay and all decorated and painted in some way.*

Understanding Source Material

1. How can you tell that Tenochtitlán was a large city?
2. What are some of the things that impressed Cortés?
3. What does this letter tell us about Aztec crafts?

The Sun Stone, also called the Aztec Calendar, dates back to the fifteenth century.
▶ What might be represented on the stone?

The priests also understood the great ceremonial calendar. It told of holy days that called for happy celebrations with song and dance. It also told of other days that were solemn and required fasting. The Aztecs believed that the calendar, if properly understood, could foretell the future.

E. Nobles and Commoners

You may recall that civilization and the importance of specialization were mentioned earlier. Aztec priests are an example of specialization. The priests were supported by the efforts of other people.

They did not grow their own food or make their own clothes. Priests enjoyed power and privilege. The priests formed part of the upper class.

Aztec society, like all complex societies, had different social classes. People at the top—nobles, high priests, and people important in the military and government—had lives of luxury, with fine houses, clothing, and jewelry. The largest class was made up of commoners, such as farmers, servants, and craftspeople. In Aztec society, commoners were organized into *clans*, or groups, made up of many different families. Each clan joined people together throughout their lives. Members of a clan all lived in the same district. Merchants formed yet another class in Aztec society, separate from the commoners.

The Aztecs carried on a great deal of trade with other Indian nations. Traders, or **pochtecas** (pohch TAY kahs), also acted as spies when they went to other Indian cities. They brought back not only goods but also valuable information, such as any signs of unrest in the Empire or possible danger to the Aztec traders. Like the commoners, traders lived in their own district. However, traders were prosperous.

LESSON **2** REVIEW

THINK AND WRITE

A. Why did the Aztecs decide to settle near Lake Texcoco?

B. How did the Aztecs grow food around Lake Texcoco for their large population?

C. Why did the Aztecs make war on their neighbors?

D. What were the religious beliefs of the Aztecs?

E. What were some of the different classes in Aztec society?

SKILLS CHECK

WRITING SKILL

Today, Lake Texcoco is dry. The city of Tenochtitlán no longer exists. Write a free-verse description of the lake or the city that begins with these words: If (Lake Texcoco or Tenochtitlán) existed today, what a wondrous sight it would be.

The Maya of Central America

THINK ABOUT WHAT YOU KNOW

This lesson deals with the Maya who, among other things, were successful astronomers. What are some things you know about the solar system that the Maya may have learned also?

STUDY THE VOCABULARY

observatory

glyphs

FOCUS YOUR READING

Why can we say that the Maya had a great civilization?

A. Lowland Maya

A Large Maya Area The Maya were at the height of their power from approximately A.D. 600 to A.D. 900. They expanded throughout a large area that included almost all of present-day Guatemala and Belize, substantial portions of Honduras and El Salvador, and the Yucatán section of southeastern Mexico. That area includes both highlands and lowlands. It was in the lowlands, however, that the Maya made some of their outstanding advances.

Maya Achievements The fame of the Maya does not rest on conquest. Instead, the Maya are remembered for their achievements in astronomy, mathematics, and the arts. The remains of their graceful pyramids and temples still excite wonder and command respect today. Imagine how grand they must have been at the height of their glory so many years ago!

Many Important Cities Unlike the Aztecs, whose power centered in the single city of Tenochtitlán, the Maya had many important centers. Their largest city was Tikal (tih KAHL), in the far north of modern-day Guatemala. The city covered only around 6 square miles (16 sq km), but it may have had a population of around 10,000 people. It served as the center for a larger area with a total population that may have reached 45,000.

B. Temples and Pyramids as Places of Power

The Fame of Tikal Every year, tourists flock to Tikal. There, rising high out of the tropical growth, they see five magnificent pyramids. Two stand at either end of the

One of the nearly 3,000 structures in Tikal is shown here. Tikal was important as a ceremonial center.
▶ Why, do you think, did the Maya build temples atop pyramids?

127

Great Square, or public plaza. Perched at the very tops of these stone structures are temples. These were used only by priests or rulers. The tallest of Tikal's pyramid-temple structures towers some 212 feet (65 m) above the ground. Cylinder-shaped stones, many of them with elaborately carved bases, are found throughout the city.

Restored Ruins in Chichén Itzá In the Yucatán, the city of Chichén Itzá, which was mentioned in Chapter 1, was a particularly sacred place. Among the restored ruins of this ancient city are one enormous ball court and eight smaller ones. Courts of this type appear throughout the Aztec and Maya areas. Exactly what type of game was played on such courts remains unclear. Archaeologists believe that the game had religious importance.

At Chichén Itzá also is a round building called El Caracol. In Spanish, *caracol* means "snail." Inside is a spiral stairway which curves like a snail's shell. The shape of this building is very unusual for a Maya temple. Archaeologists believe it was an **observatory**. An observatory is a place for studying the sky.

Ceremonial Centers It appears that Maya cities were ceremonial centers. Not many people actually lived in them. People went to these cities only for religious celebrations and to trade goods. Priests and their assistants were the main full-time residents.

Archaeologists digging at a site in northern Yucatán, however, believe that they have found at least one Maya city that actually had a large number of permanent residents. They have uncovered ruins of what look like dwellings for ordinary people. It seems that this city may have had as

After the Toltecs conquered the Maya at Chichén Itzá, they changed the appearance of El Caracol.
▶ How does this fact help you understand the text material?

many as 50,000 different structures and a population even larger than that of the Aztec city of Tenochtitlán!

C. The Importance of Priests

Why would the Maya build so many centers just for priests? Imagine all the work it must have taken just to carve out the stone blocks used for the pyramids and temples. Think of the time and effort it took to actually build those giant structures, especially at a time when such work was done without powerful machines.

Like the Aztecs, the Maya believed in many different gods, and for each god there were special ceremonies. Life's most important moments, from birth to death, all required certain rituals by priests. Also like the Aztecs, the Maya believed that there had been other creations and destructions of the world. Good and evil battled in the present. If the powers of good held the upper hand, then the rains fell and harvests were good. Evil powers might bring drought and hurricanes. Once again, it was the priests who understood these things.

D. The Solar Year

Study of the Heavens In their efforts to understand the gods and the nature of the universe, the Maya priests studied the heavens. They believed, as did civilized peoples in other parts of the world at that time, that the positions of the sun, moon, and stars influenced events on earth. They believed that the heavens also held clues to the future of the world.

Keeping Records As they watched the heavens, the Maya priests kept a written record of what they saw. They used a writing system of **glyphs** (glihfs). A glyph is a combination of picture writing and of symbols standing for words, sounds, and ideas. Royal scribes used glyphs to write many books. Glyphs were also carved into tall stone columns in and around the city temples. These glyphs, some of which still remain, tell the history of the Maya rulers. Specialists have deciphered some of the Maya glyphs. Many, however, remain a puzzle.

The careful observations of the sky, combined with the use of glyphs to keep records, taught the Maya many things. They could predict when eclipses of the moon and sun would occur. They also charted the course of the planet Venus and understood the solar year.

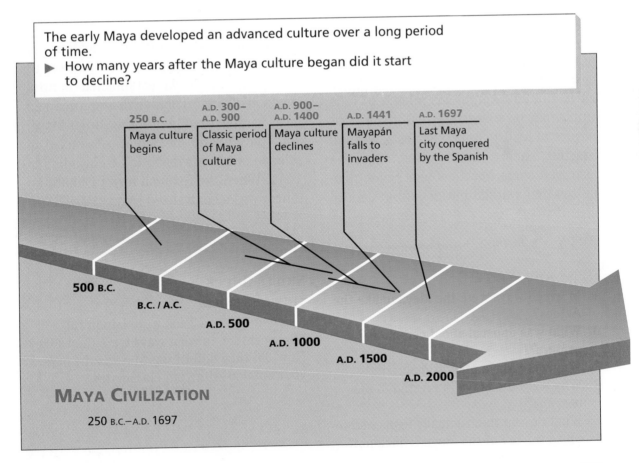

The early Maya developed an advanced culture over a long period of time.
▶ How many years after the Maya culture began did it start to decline?

250 B.C. Maya culture begins

A.D. 300–A.D. 900 Classic period of Maya culture

A.D. 900–A.D. 1400 Maya culture declines

A.D. 1441 Mayapán falls to invaders

A.D. 1697 Last Maya city conquered by the Spanish

500 B.C.

B.C. / A.C.

A.D. 500

A.D. 1000

A.D. 1500

A.D. 2000

MAYA CIVILIZATION
250 B.C.–A.D. 1697

An accurate estimate Another impressive invention of the Maya was their calendar. It divided the year into 365 days. The Maya also worked out a correction between that calendar and what they figured to be the real length of the solar year: 365.2420 days. Our present astronomy sets the solar year's real length at 365.2422 days. So the ancient Maya, without any telescopes, came remarkably close to our best calculation.

E. Collapse of the Classic Maya

After about 1,000 years the Maya civilization collapsed. Though not every Maya ceremonial center fell at once, by around A.D. 900, all those places of power had been abandoned. The rain forest soon crept forward and covered the pyramids and temples.

What happened to the Maya? Why did they abandon their cities? Many answers have been suggested. As you learned earlier in this unit, problems related to food supply may have been the reason. Perhaps plagues of locusts ruined harvests. Natural disasters, such as earthquakes, may have destroyed some Maya centers. Some people say that warlike invaders from central

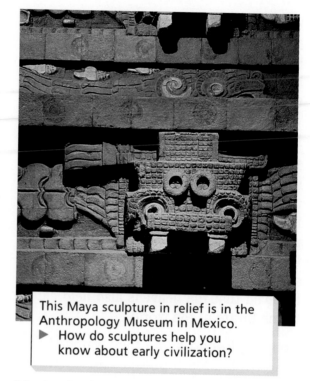

This Maya sculpture in relief is in the Anthropology Museum in Mexico.
▶ How do sculptures help you know about early civilization?

Mexico broke the Maya civilization. All of these are possibilities.

In the area of northern Yucatán, the Maya remained. From a city known as Mayapán, the Maya established control over a wide area. Their civilization seemed more warlike than that of the earlier Maya, and they made no great advances in science or art. Mayapán fell to invaders in 1441. When the Spanish arrived, there no longer was a centralized Maya state.

LESSON **3** REVIEW

THINK AND WRITE

A. In which ways were the Maya unlike the Aztecs?
B. What was unusual about ceremonial centers?
C. Why were Maya priests important?
D. Why were the Maya interested in the heavens?
E. What do you think actually happened to cause the fall of the Maya civilization?

SKILLS CHECK

THINKING SKILLS

Chichén Itzá and Tikal were important Maya centers. In what ways were they alike? How did they differ from Mayapán? Share your opinion with your classmates.

The Inca Empire

A. A Mighty Empire

The Largest Indian Empire In the mountainous land of Peru, an Indian people who spoke a language called Quechua (KECH wah) built a mighty empire. These Indians, later known as the Incas, ruled the largest American Indian empire. It stretched from modern-day Ecuador all the way along the west coast of South America to Chile's present capital, the city of Santiago. That's a distance of about 3,000 miles (4,827 km). Locate the Inca Empire on the map on page 134.

The Inca capital was Cuzco (KOOS-koh), a city high in the Andes. Cuzco may have had a population of 100,000. It must have rivaled Tenochtitlán in splendor.

Inca Roads and Walls Unlike the Maya and the Aztecs, the Incas had no written language. They were not inventors or scientists. Rather, they built an amazing number of fine roads and bridges. Inca masons cut stones so exactly that they were able to build walls without using any

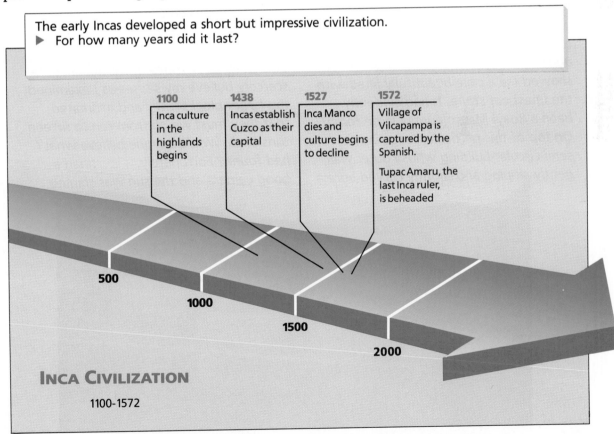

The early Incas developed a short but impressive civilization.
▶ For how many years did it last?

1100 — Inca culture in the highlands begins

1438 — Incas establish Cuzco as their capital

1527 — Inca Manco dies and culture begins to decline

1572 — Village of Vilcapampa is captured by the Spanish.

Tupac Amaru, the last Inca ruler, is beheaded

500 1000 1500 2000

INCA CIVILIZATION
1100–1572

FROM: # Lost City of the Incas

By: Hiram Bingham
Setting: Machu Picchu, Peru

Hiram Bingham, an archeologist from the United States, "discovered" Machu Picchu in 1911. Actually, Indians who lived in that region were aware of the ruins but had no appreciation of their great importance. In this part of the story, Bingham, his interpreter who spoke Quechua, and a small boy assigned to be the guide have just left the farmers' hut in search of some ruins.

*W*e scrambled along through the dense undergrowth, climbing over terrace walls and in bamboo thickets where our guide found it easier going than I did. Suddenly without any warning, under a huge overhanging ledge the boy showed me a cave beautifully lined with the finest cut stone. It had evidently been a Roayl Mausoleum [a large tomb]. On top of this particular ledge was a semi-circular building whose outer wall, gently sloping and slightly curved bore a striking resemblance to the famous Temple of the Sun in Cuzco. This might also be a Temple of the Sun. It followed the natural curvature of the rock and was keyed to it by one of the finest examples of masonry I had ever seen. Furthermore, it was tied into another beautiful wall, made of very carefully matched ashlars [square-cut building stone] of pure white granite, especially selected for its fine grain. Clearly, it was the work of a master artist. . . . Owing to the absence of mortar, there were no ugly spaces between the rocks. They might have grown together.

. . . It fairly took my breath away. What could this place be? Why had no one given us any idea of it? . . . I could scarcely believe my senses as I examined the larger blocks . . . and estimated that they must weigh from ten to fifteen tons each. Would anyone believe what I had found? Fortunately, . . . I had a good camera and the sun was shining.

This photograph reveals an overall view of "The Lost City of the Incas." The city is on a mountain called Machu Picchu, high in the Andes.

▶ Why, do you think, did the Incas choose such a place for their fortress city?

mortar, a cement mixture to hold the stones together.

Even today, despite the passage of time and the terrible earthquakes that have rocked Ecuador and Peru, many old Inca walls still stand, and old Inca roads are still used. The Incas terraced the sides of mountains for farming and built elaborate irrigation systems.

An Inca Legend Where did the Incas come from? Archeologists may some day uncover artifacts from excavations that will provide information. Inca legend tells the following story:

The Sun created a son and a daughter, set them upon an island in Lake Titicaca (tee tee KAH kah), gave them a staff of gold, and bade [instructed] them settle where the staff disappeared into the ground. The brother and sister—the future king Manco Capac and the future queen Mama Ocllo—traveled north to the valley of Cuzco, where the golden staff disappeared into the ground. Here they stayed and founded the city of Cuzco about A.D. 1200.

Whether this Manco Capac of the legend ever lived is not clear. Once again, however, the patient work of archaeologists has revealed pre-Inca communities. Like the Aztecs, the Incas benefited from cultures that came before them.

B. Inca Expansion

Most of the Inca Empire was gained between 1438 and 1493 under the reign, or rule, of a king, called an Inca. The empire was built through conquest. The peoples and the land the Incas conquered became part of the empire. Local chiefs often kept their power if they cooperated. However, they had to take orders from the Incas.

The Inca Empire required much from the conquered people. Some of those peoples' lands were taken from them. The people still worked the land, but the harvest belonged to the Inca state. The Incas also imposed the **mita,** a system of forced labor. Under this system, people owed a certain amount of work to the Inca state. The roads and fortresses of the Inca Empire were built with this mita labor.

Sometimes people in a newly conquered area did not accept Inca rule. If they rose up in revolt, Inca armies would move quickly to squash outbursts. Then people from that rebellious area, sometimes entire villages, would be forced to leave. The Incas resettled them in an older, more secure part of the empire. Their place was taken by loyal Inca subjects.

C. Holding an Empire Together

The power of the Inca rule certainly helped the Incas keep order. In addition, the Incas demanded that people learn their Quechua language, the language of Cuzco. That, too, helped create unity.

Such a large empire also needed a good communication system. You have learned that the Incas were builders of roads. They built them to connect the parts of their empire. One system of roads ran through the Andes all the way from what is now Colombia to Argentina. The other followed the coast from northern Peru to northern Chile. The Inca road system was about 9,500 miles (15,285 km) long!

The Incas did not have wheeled carts or wagons, and they did not have animals,

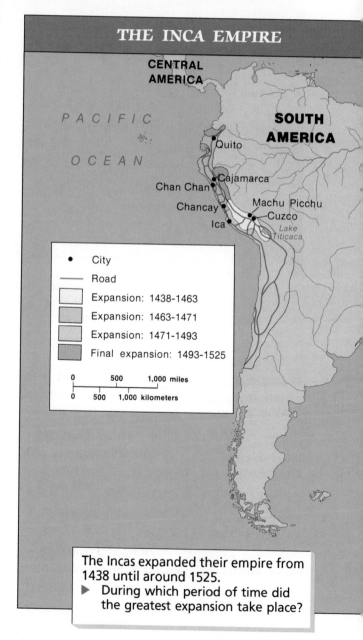

THE INCA EMPIRE

The Incas expanded their empire from 1438 until around 1525.
▶ During which period of time did the greatest expansion take place?

such as horses, for riding. They used llamas as pack animals. Because the roads were intended for people on foot, large bridges were not needed. Deep canyons were crossed by rope bridges. Some of these spanned distances of 400 to 500 feet (122 to 152 m). Steep slopes had steps cut into them for people on the mountain trails.

If a message had to be delivered quickly, runners carried the message between stations on the road. The stations were set at 8-mile to 15-mile (13-km to 24-km) intervals. At each station, the arriving runner would pass his message on to a rested man, who would run to the next station. In that way, messages were delivered with surprising speed.

As you have learned, the Incas did not know writing. What happened if messages contained information about quantities that would be difficult to memorize? The **quipu** (KEE poo) was one thing that helped. The quipu was made up of a series of strings. Each of the strings was knotted at particular places to indicate a particular quantity. It is clear that the Incas understood the mathematical idea of place value. The quipu was similar to the Chinese abacus. In fact, it appears that the Incas used some type of abacus for making calculations.

D. Skilled at Crafts

Gold and Silver Metalwork Gold was a metal sacred to the Incas, who believed it was the sweat of the gods. Thousands of gold ornaments decorated their temples. Silver was nearly as important, and the Incas had much of that metal too. They were fine metalworkers and produced gold and silver ornaments and utensils of great beauty. Unfortunately, most of the Inca

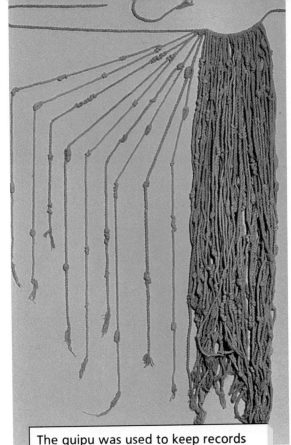

The Granger Collection

The quipu was used to keep records of quantities.
► How might a farmer have used a quipu?

metalwork was lost when the Spaniards took over the Inca Empire. They melted the gold and silver into bars to ship to Spain. However, some has been saved and can be seen in museums in Colombia, Ecuador, and Peru.

Builders of Temples Like the Aztecs and the Maya, the Incas built huge stone temples. Many of these were high up in the mountains, so the Incas built stone stairways leading to them. Usually, they dedicated the largest temple to the sun. In their religion, the sun held great importance. Remember the legend about the first Inca king and queen, Manco Capac and Mama Ocllo, being created by the sun. In fact, the Incas are sometimes known as "the people of the sun."

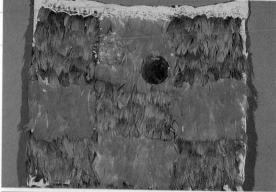

Artifacts of the Incas include articles that are woven and a feathered tapestry.
► What details do you notice?

E. An Argument About Inca Rule

Throughout the great Inca Empire, farmlands were divided into three parts. One part was given to farming communities for the use of the people. Another part of the land belonged to the Incas' gods. Most of the crops from this land were put into storage, to be used if crops failed or if there was an earthquake or other natural disaster. The third part of the land belonged to the government. That land was used to support the Inca and the government officials.

The Inca state gave out food in times of need and helped care for the sick. Because of this, some people say that it was kind and caring. According to one of the early Spaniards who wrote about the Incas, "The Incas always did good work for their subjects, never permitting them to be burdened with excessive tribute or outraged in any way." Other writers have pointed out that it was the ordinary people who did all the work. That's why the Inca state wanted to keep the people healthy. You may wish to read more about the Incas and then decide for yourself what kind of rulers they were.

LESSON **4** REVIEW

THINK AND WRITE

A. What were the strengths of the Inca civilization?

B. How did the Inca state grow so large and still keep order?

C. How did the Inca rulers keep track of what was going on in their empire?

D. At what kinds of work were the Inca skilled?

E. How would you describe Inca rule?

SKILLS CHECK

MAP SKILL

Use the Gazetteer to find what Cuzco and Lake Titicaca have in common. Then find each place on the map on page 134.

USING THE VOCABULARY

nuclear America   mita
observatories   complex cultures
empire   chinamapas
glyphs   quipu
causeway   pochtecas

On a separate sheet of paper, write the term that would best complete the sentence.

1. The Maya studied the stars from buildings called _____.
2. Another name for a raised road above a body of water is a _____.
3. An _____ consists of all the territories and people under the control of one powerful nation.
4. The Incas knew about place value. This is shown by their use of the _____.
5. When anthropologists speak of _____ _____, they mean the great ancient Indian cultural centers.
6. The Aztecs grew crops in island gardens named _____.
7. The Incas demanded _____, or forced labor, from conquered peoples.
8. Aztec traders known as _____ were also often government spies.
9. The Maya system of writing used symbols called _____.
10. The areas of America where civilizations developed are called _____ _____.

REMEMBERING WHAT YOU READ

On a separate sheet of paper, answer the following questions in complete sentences.

1. Nuclear America included which civilizations and areas?
2. How were the Aztecs able to grow enough food to feed their very large population?
3. Why were the Aztecs a warlike nation?
4. In Aztec society, what privileges did the priests enjoy?
5. What were the greatest achievements of the Maya?
6. What was unusual about Maya cities?
7. What might have destroyed the Maya Empire?
8. What did the Incas demand of conquered peoples that helped create unity in their empire?
9. How did the Incas communicate with other parts of their empire?
10. What are the two arguments about the Incas' way of ruling their people?

TYING MATH TO SOCIAL STUDIES

The Maya calculated that each solar year —one complete orbit of the earth around the sun—took 365.2420 days. Modern astronomers, with their high-powered telescopes and computers, have found the solar year to be 365.2422 days. An extra day is added to the calendar in special years called leap years. Which month is that day added to? What is the date?

A leap year is added to every year that can be divided evenly by four. Which of these years are leap years: 1940, 1928, 1963, 1990? The years that mark hundreds such as 1300 and 1900 are not leap years. Only those in which the century number can be divided by four, such as 1600 or 2000, are leap years. Name any four leap years that have passed and any four that are to come.

On a separate sheet of paper, answer the following questions in complete sentences.

1. What events can lead to the collapse of great empires that have conquered other peoples?

2. Why were so few Spanish soldiers able to defeat the mighty Aztec warriors?

3. How do you think archaeologists figured out what the Maya used their cities for?

4. What is the benefit to a civilization of having a system of writing?

5. What are some features that the Aztec, Maya, and Inca civilizations had in common?

SUMMARIZING THE CHAPTER

On a separate sheet of paper, draw a graphic organizer like the one shown here. Copy the information from this graphic organizer to the one you have drawn. On each blank line, write some facts about the subject mentioned that you learned from the chapter.

CHAPTER THEME

The great Indian civilizations — the Maya, Aztec, and Inca — were advanced in many ways and left behind a valuable heritage.

	MAYA	AZTECS	INCAS
TIME PERIOD			
CITIES			
RELIGION			
ACHIEVEMENTS			
SOCIAL CLASSES			
RECORD-KEEPING SYSTEMS			

COOPERATIVE LEARNING

As you learned in Unit 2, the Americas were inhabited by advanced civilizations long before the arrival of Europeans. Imagine the Spaniards' surprise at finding the great pyramids of the Aztecs and the Maya, the roads and temples of the Incas, and the great cities.

One way to imagine these things is to put yourself in the place of one of the adventurers who has been sent by Spain in search of gold and riches. Your first duty, however, is to prepare a description of the new land and its peoples for the king of Spain.

PROJECT

With a group, choose one of the Native American civilizations to describe. Each member of your group should assume the role of a specialist. You will be expected to add information by using your special skill. Depending on size, your group might consist of some of the following specialists:

- a cartographer, who will draw a map of the city or village

- a translator, who will interview the chief or king

- an engineer, who will observe the architectural features of the city or surrounding territory

- a military specialist, who plans to meet the Native Americans and describe the people

- an artist, who will provide a drawing of the people in traditional dress and show them working crops, attending ceremonies, and so on

- a religious specialist, who will observe and describe the religious beliefs and rituals

Use Chapters 3 and 4 to gather information for your task. Use your school library or an encyclopedia if you need additional information. Try to stay as close to the facts as possible. You can use your imagination to add details, however.

Each member of the group should work on an assigned task. Then the group should meet to decide the order in which these individual parts will be put together in a single presentation to the king. The presentation should be oral. Even the illustrated maps and drawings should be described orally.

PRESENTATION AND REVIEW

The members of the group should speak before the class as if they were making a presentation to the king of Spain. Classmates should act as the king's advisors. Afterward the class can ask questions about the new country and how Spain could benefit from it.

Meet with your group to discuss your presentation. What facts could you have included to make your description more complete? In what other ways could your description have been improved?

REMEMBER TO:
- Give your ideas.
- Listen to others' ideas.
- Plan your work with the group.
- Present your project.
- Discuss how your group worked.

A. Why Do I Need This Skill?

Imagine that you have gone to France for the summer to visit a distant relative. While there, you hear some amazing news: your town has declared its independence from the United States. You read everything you can find about this incident in the French newspapers. Then a friend of yours sends you a firsthand account of the event. Your friend's report is very different from what you've been reading in the papers in France.

Assuming that your friend is trustworthy, which account of the story would you believe? Most likely you would believe your friend, since your friend has experienced the event directly. In the study of history, firsthand accounts of events are called **primary sources**. Primary sources are almost always the best sources of historical information, since they are the closest you can get to actually "being there."

A **secondary source** is any information that is based on other people's accounts of an event. When primary sources are hard to find, historians often rely on secondary sources. This textbook is a secondary source. This textbook also contains many examples of primary sources.

B. Learning the Skill

Below are two accounts of the first moon landing, on July 20, 1969. The first account is a transcription of the actual words of astronauts Neil Armstrong, Edwin "Buzz" Aldrin, and Michael Collins as they spoke to each other and to Mission Control in Houston. Following that is an account of the same event from a secondary source.

Primary Source

Armstrong: Houston, Tranquility Base here. The Eagle has landed.

Mission Control: Tranquility, we copy you on the ground. You got a bunch of guys about to turn blue. We're breathing again. Thanks a lot.

Collins: Fantastic!

Armstrong: Houston, that may have seemed like a very long final phase.

Mission Control: Roger, we copy. It was beautiful from here, Tranquility. Over.

Aldrin: We'll get to the details of what's around here, but it looks like a collection of just about every variety of shape. . . . It looks as though some of the rocks and boulders are going to have some interesting colors to them. Over.

Mission Control: Rog, Tranquility. Be advised there are lots of smiling faces in this room and all over the world. Over.

Secondary Source
"Tranquility Base here. The Eagle has landed." The words of Commander Neil A. Armstrong crackled across 240,000 miles (384,000 km) of space to planet Earth. The date was July 20, 1969, the time 4:17 P.M., Eastern Daylight Time. Some 6 1/2 hours later, Armstrong stepped out of the landing craft Eagle and onto the surface of the moon.

Back on Earth a billion people watched the scene on television.

C. PRACTICING THE SKILL

On a separate sheet of paper, write *primary* next to each primary source of information and *secondary* next to each secondary source.

1. Letters describing the Amazon basin, from a boat captain traveling along the Amazon River
2. The diary of a Spanish explorer to America
3. A photo of Mexico City taken from an airplane
4. A biography of Christopher Columbus
5. A magazine article on how the Incas built their roads

D. APPLYING THE SKILL

Suppose you are going to Mexico City for a vacation with your parents. Your class has read about Mexico City in its textbook and asks that you bring back as much information as possible about life in Mexico City. Make a list of the primary and secondary sources you could bring back to your class.

A. WHY DO I NEED THIS SKILL

In this social studies textbook, the authors present many facts about the history of various cultures in the Western Hemisphere. Facts are events that have really happened or things that can be proved to be true.

Additionally, there are authors who base their writings on historical events. You have probably read stories, myths, poems, and plays that tell something about history. These writings are considered literature, and their main purpose is to entertain or inspire readers. The authors use the historical events as backgrounds for their stories. By reading literature that deals with historical events, you can gain insight into the feelings, attitudes, and day-to-day lives of people who lived at different times in history.

There are several types of literature that deal with history. The next column lists some of the more common types of literature.

TYPES OF LITERATURE

Historical fiction is literature based on historical events. Some facts are used, but much information is made up by the writers.

Poetry is rhythmic verse that helps you imagine various feelings and events. It may or may not be written in rhyme.

Dramas, or plays, are stories that are intended to be performed by actors.

Myths, legends, and tales are stories that are often based on historical events. However, they also include exaggeration or made-up information.

Autobiographies, **diaries**, **journals**, **letters**, **and biographies** are about true happenings. They are often written by the people who have experienced what is described. Examples of this type of literature include diaries, journals, letters, and autobiographies. A story of a person's life written by someone else is a biography.

B. LEARNING THE SKILL

When you read literature, it's a good idea to actualize. You know that the word *actual* means "not just possible, but *real*." When you actualize, you make something realistic. As an example, in Chapter 4 you read an excerpt from a letter Cortés wrote to the king of Spain, telling about the Aztec capital, Tenochtitlán. This letter presents a first-person account of what Cortés saw and experienced in the open markets of this great Aztec city.

To help yourself understand and enjoy the pieces of literature in this social studies book, try one of the following strategies as you read.

STRATEGIES TO HELP YOURSELF ACTUALIZE

Pretend that you are a character taking part in the events that are described. Try to feel the excitement or fear that the character must have felt. For example, how would you feel if you were Cortés walking through the market square among 60,000 Aztec citizens buying and selling goods?

Imagine that you are an observer watching what is going on. For example, what is it like to be a shopper browsing through the Tenochtitlán markets?

Visualize the event. Think of the colors, the smells, and the sounds that you are experiencing. For example, what might you see, smell, or hear as a merchant selling live game, such as wild ducks and deer, in the market?

C. PRACTICING THE SKILL

Select one of the strategies for reading literature and use it as you reread the excerpt from the letter that Cortés wrote to the king of Spain. See if the events Cortés describes on page 125 "come alive" for you.

Then use the pretend, imagine, and visualize strategy as you reread the excerpt in Chapter 4 from Hiram Bingham's autobiography *The Lost City of the Incas,* in which he describes his exploration of the Inca civilization in South America. In this excerpt, he describes his discovery of Machu Picchu, an ancient Inca city on a mountaintop. As you read this piece, try to "step into history" and actually feel the excitement Bingham must have felt as he discovered this wondrous Inca city.

D. APPLYING THE SKILL

Use the pretend, imagine, and visualize strategy as you read other literature excerpts in this textbook. Here's a warning: You may feel so much a part of the situation described that you will want to read the entire piece of literature! Reading literature about social studies can be interesting, informative—and fun!

Res fuerat quondam prestans, & Gloria summa
Orbis subiectus Cefaris Imperio,
Hic longe prestat, cuius nunc Orbis Eous,
Et Nouus, atq̃ alter panditur Aufpitijs.

EUROPEANS ARRIVE
IN LATIN AMERICA

Spain and Portugal sent explorers and
conquerors to Latin America and then
established colonies there. After several centuries, the
people in the colonies waged fierce struggles to win independence.

▶ *This hand-colored woodcut map showing Tenochtitlán and the Gulf of Mexico was
included in a book on the conquest of Mexico published in 1524.*

cim cū dimidia, ita q̃ duo magni puncti continent
viginti quinq̃ leucas. Cōtinet autē leuca quatuor

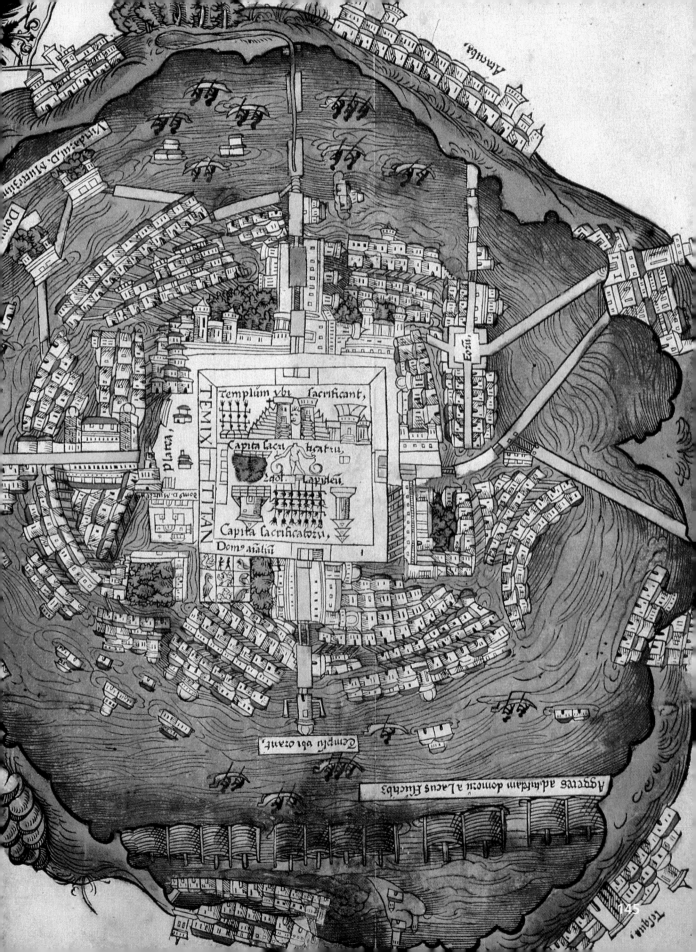

145

CHAPTER 5

THE CONQUEST OF LATIN AMERICA

*A*fter discovering that Latin America offered wealth, many explorers from Spain and Portugal set out on great expeditions. In their quest, the Europeans conquered the mighty Indian civilizations.

The Granger Collec

An Age of Discovery

THINK ABOUT WHAT YOU KNOW

Think about a time when you "discovered" how something worked. How did your success make you feel?

STUDY THE VOCABULARY

maritime	monarchy
capital	nationalism

FOCUS YOUR READING

Why did Europeans set sail on voyages of discovery?

A. The Meaning of Discovery

At one time in your life, you probably felt that you had discovered static electricity. Did you truly *discover* it? After all, static electricity existed long before you were even born.

When we talk about the discovery of America we face a similar problem. Did Columbus truly discover the New World? Wasn't it there all along? Sometimes, in fact, Native Americans point out that their ancestors discovered America thousands of years before the voyage of Columbus. And they add, "Columbus didn't discover us. We knew who we were all along!"

Since it is true that Columbus was not the first person to come to America, why do we remember and celebrate his accomplishment? The reason is that in the centuries before Columbus, people in Europe did not know of America's existence. As you recall from Chapter 1, Europeans were surprised at the discoveries of Columbus and other early explorers. Because of Columbus's voyages, Europeans began to realize that their views of how the world looked were wrong. So in this sense, Columbus deserves credit as a pioneer in Europe's discovery of the New World.

B. Europe on the Move

The Europe that Columbus sailed away from late in the fifteenth century had changed a great deal in the previous few centuries. It would continue to change in the coming centuries. Large cities in Europe had become prosperous. Their wealth came mostly from trade. As that trade grew, it created still more opportunity for riches. Cities also became important financial centers. They had merchant and banking houses.

The commercial activity in such Italian cities as Genoa, Florence, Venice, and Milan explains why so many of the early explorers were Italian. Merchant houses in

On his first voyage, Columbus landed on three Caribbean islands.
▶ What might Columbus have said on these occasions?

The riches of Italy are suggested by this painting of Venice in 1496.
► What structure do you see in the background?

cities had been sponsoring **maritime** expeditions throughout the Mediterranean Sea. *Maritime* means "having to do with shipping or sailing."

New business and financial organizations also developed. The first public bank was created early in the fifteenth century. All of this made more **capital**, or money, available to support high-risk undertakings, such as voyages of discovery and the establishing of colonies.

C. Nation-states and New Rivalries

New Political Units The political map of Europe changed as well in the 1400s and 1500s. Individual kings became stronger and took power away from other nobles. After a time, some of these rulers established **monarchies**. A monarchy is a country ruled by a king or queen. The special thing about these new political units, called nation-states, was that they had definite boundaries. They united people who had the same backgrounds and religious beliefs. This sameness was very important, and people who were seen as different had a very difficult time.

For example, in the 1490s, just around the time that Columbus sailed, Queen Isabella of Spain gave people of the Islamic and Jewish faiths a choice: Either convert to Catholicism or leave the country. In other countries, people who were not members of the official national religion could remain, but they did not have any political rights.

Reasons for Rivalry Religion was a reason why these new nations fought with one another. For example, Protestant England often was an enemy of Catholic France and Spain. However, a much more important cause of rivalry was a spirit of **nationalism**. Nationalism is a devotion to one's country. It often includes a belief that the nation to which one belongs is better than other nations. Nationalism led many nations to compete with one another for power and wealth.

D. The Orient Trade as the Key to Power

Do you have a pepper shaker at home? Grains of pepper similar to those in your container were once so valuable that nations spent fantastic sums of money for them. In fact, pepper and other of today's common spices were among the main attractions for European traders doing business with the Orient.

As you may recall from the earlier discussion about ways that Native Americans got food, keeping food from spoiling was very difficult. Europeans used spices to preserve foods. Spices also covered up the foul taste of slightly rotted meats and gave exotic flavor to the foods eaten by the upper classes. Such spices did not grow anywhere in Europe. Since they were rare, useful, and much in demand, spices became very valuable.

The Orient, then sometimes called the Indies, had other costly luxury goods, such as the silks and perfumes that Europe's nobles desired. Fine dishes of porcelain were also made in the Orient.

The profitable trade goods from the Orient were moved over land through the Middle East and across the Mediterranean

The Granger Collection

This box was made in the Orient in the 1400s.
▶ Why did Europeans want such works of art?

Sea. After other overland journeys, they reached the countries of western Europe. At every step in this trade process, the merchants involved profited by raising prices. By the time these trade goods finally reached Europe, their prices had risen enormously. So gold and silver from western Europe, always in short supply, flowed into the hands of these merchants.

The riches of the Orient, therefore, held great promise for many of the new nation-states. If a nation could trade directly with the Indies, it could buy luxury goods at lower prices and then profit by selling them at higher prices to other European nations.

LESSON **1** *REVIEW*

THINK AND WRITE

A. In what sense is it correct to say that Columbus discovered America?

B. What changes took place in Europe that helped bring on an age of discovery?

C. Why did nation-states compete with one another?

D. Why did western European nations want to have direct trade with the Indies?

SKILLS CHECK

THINKING SKILL

You read in this lesson that the Europeans of the 15th century valued what we would consider to be common spices today. Make a list of some items that we consider to be very valuable today that you feel will be very common and easily available 500 years in the future.

Early Exploration

THINK ABOUT WHAT YOU KNOW

Imagine that you are about to take a trip to a place that neither you nor anyone you know has ever visited. What will you do to prepare for your trip?

STUDY THE VOCABULARY

circumnavigate
landmass

FOCUS YOUR READING

Who were the important explorers of Latin America?

A. Christopher Columbus's Western Route to the Indies

When I was in elementary school, we always learned about Christopher Columbus. Every year. After a while it got pretty boring. Oh, it was a good enough story, I guess.

There was poor Columbus, convinced that the world was round when everyone else thought it was flat. Finally, after being laughed out of all the royal courts of Europe, he got some help in Spain. Off he sailed, across the Atlantic, with three small, leaky ships. He discovered the New World, but it was named after someone else. Columbus died a poor man.

Well, I'm certainly not going to tell you that story. It still bores me. More important, *it's wrong*!

As you probably know, most educated people of Columbus's day believed the world was round. Columbus had trouble getting support for two reasons. First of all, he asked for a great deal. Sure, he would take the personal risk of sailing, but he wanted someone else to put up all the money. What's more, he demanded special honors and a good percentage of all the profits. As he himself reminded Queen Isabella of Spain, he was to be "Admiral-in-Chief of the Ocean Sea and Viceroy and Perpetual Governor of all the islands and mainlands" that he discovered.

The second reason he had trouble getting support was scientific. Most of the learned specialists at the royal courts thought Columbus had figured things incorrectly. They were right. Columbus had underestimated the amount of water separating Europe from China. That's why, when he reached the New World, he thought he had sailed far enough to be off the coast of China.

Columbus's three ships—the *Niña*, the *Pinta*, and the *Santa María*—were fairly small, but they were fit for travel on the sea and manned by experienced sailors. Spain not only supported his first

Columbus's ship can be compared in this art to the U.S.S. New Jersey.
► How would you say they compare?

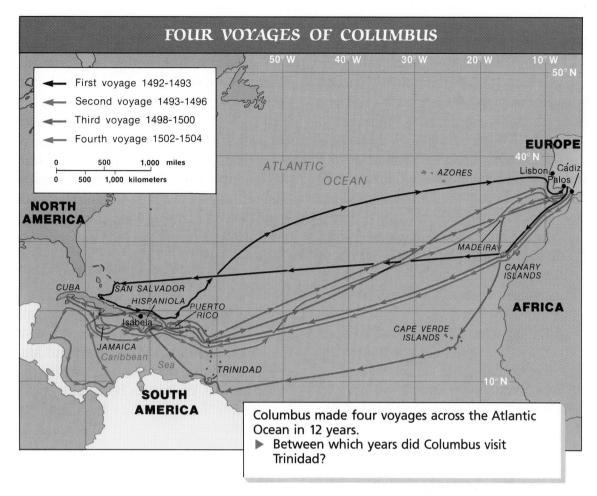

FOUR VOYAGES OF COLUMBUS

First voyage 1492-1493
Second voyage 1493-1496
Third voyage 1498-1500
Fourth voyage 1502-1504

Columbus made four voyages across the Atlantic Ocean in 12 years.
▶ Between which years did Columbus visit Trinidad?

voyage but sent him back three more times, even though he never returned with a really valuable cargo. Portugal probably profited far more from one voyage made by Vasco da Gama than Spain did from the four voyages of Columbus. Of course, Da Gama really had reached the Indies, but Columbus had not. While Columbus died a bitter man because he had lost his personal claim to the new lands, he certainly was not poor.

Should we forget about Columbus? Absolutely not. First of all, he was a fantastic sailor. Unlike so many of the Portuguese, whose expeditions kept within sight of a coastline, Columbus sailed completely away from land. Although he had some instruments that helped him navigate, he did most of his steering by the stars. Imagine sailing for over eight weeks across unknown waters without any map or chart to guide you!

A man of great skill and courage, Columbus had a bold idea. He tried to prove it. Now that, all by itself, makes a very good story.

B. Cabral's Discovery of Brazil

Portugal's claim to territory in the New World came from a bold sailor also. But though Columbus actually *intended* to sail west, not east, the discoverer of Brazil *set out* to sail *east*!

Vasco da Gama had just returned to Portugal with a cargo of spices. Portugal naturally wanted to send another expedition as quickly as possible. So on March 8, 1500, an expedition of 13 ships, led by

151

Pedro Álvares Cabral (AHL vuh rihsh kuh BRAHL) sailed from Portugal on a voyage around the southern tip of Africa to India. About six weeks later, at 17 degrees south latitude, something unexpected happened. The expedition sighted land!

Cabral went ashore and claimed the land in the name of the king of Portugal. He called his discovery the *Ilha de Vera Cruz*. That means "Island of the True Cross." You can see from that name that Cabral had no idea he had reached the mainland of a new continent. Cabral sent a ship back to Portugal with news of his discovery and then went on to India.

The discovery of Brazil was an accident. Or was it? How could an experienced sailor like Cabral get so far off course?

One reason for suspicion is that, in 1494, Portugal and Spain had signed the *Treaty of Tordesillas*. The treaty drew a north-to-south line across the Atlantic Ocean to divide the areas of Spanish and Portuguese exploration. Everything to the west of that line would belong to Spain; everything to the east would be Portugal's.

The line passed through the eastern portion of Brazil. Did Portugal already know about Brazil when it negotiated with Spain? We may never learn the answer to that question.

C. Magellan's Voyage Around the World

Imagine taking a sea voyage that lasts almost three full years! That's how long it took an expedition led by Ferdinand Magellan (muh JEL un) to **circumnavigate**, or sail around, the world. Born in Portugal, Magellan wound up sailing for Spain.

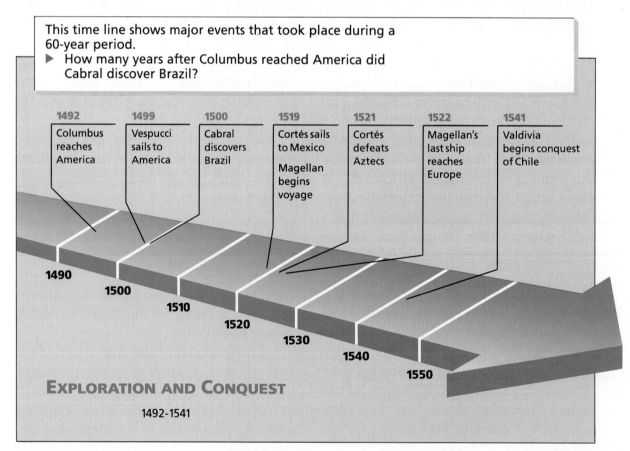

This time line shows major events that took place during a 60-year period.
▶ How many years after Columbus reached America did Cabral discover Brazil?

1492	1499	1500	1519	1521	1522	1541
Columbus reaches America	Vespucci sails to America	Cabral discovers Brazil	Cortés sails to Mexico / Magellan begins voyage	Cortés defeats Aztecs	Magellan's last ship reaches Europe	Valdivia begins conquest of Chile

1490   1500   1510   1520   1530   1540   1550

EXPLORATION AND CONQUEST

1492-1541

Pedro Álvares Cabral is shown taking possession of Brazil.
▶ Guess what he thought he had discovered.

In September of 1519, at the age of 39, Magellan set sail across the Atlantic on a voyage that truly proved the world was round. His goal was to find a water passage through the New World that would lead to the Indies. Like Columbus, Magellan hoped to reach the Indies by sailing west.

By that time, of course, various expeditions to the New World had shown that the Americas formed a great continent.

Magellan thought there was a way through that great **landmass**. A landmass is a very large area of land, such as a continent. He thought he would find it to the south, near present-day Argentina. When Magellan reached the Río de la Plata, he found only fresh water. If the river really went through to another ocean, it would have had some salt water in it. So Magellan continued sailing south. By March, bitter winter began to set in. Magellan made camp on the cold and barren coast, far to the south on the continent.

With the arrival of better weather in August, he again set sail searching for a passage. After a two-month journey, the expedition found an opening. On the ships sailed, and kept on for over five weeks, until finally they were through to another ocean. That passage is known as the Strait of Magellan. By comparison with the treacherous waters of the strait, the ocean seemed very calm. So Magellan called it the Pacific. (In Spanish, *pacífico* means "calm" or "peaceful.")

Magellan had accomplished much. However, it took the one remaining ship in the expedition until 1522 to reach home, and when it did, Magellan was not aboard. He was killed in the Philippine Islands as he helped one local ruler fight another.

LESSON *2* REVIEW

THINK AND WRITE

A. Why should Columbus be remembered?
B. How did Cabral discover Brazil?
C. What did Magellan's expedition accomplish?

SKILLS CHECK

THINKING SKILL

Imagine that you are about to interview one of these famous explorers — Columbus, Cabral, or Magellan. You want to give the explorer a chance to set the record straight. What is the one question you will ask to have answered?

The Conquest of Mexico

THINK ABOUT WHAT YOU KNOW

Think about what you have learned about the Aztecs. Imagine that you are a Spanish spy who has been gathering information for the king of Spain. What strengths and weaknesses of the Aztecs will you report?

STUDY THE VOCABULARY

Royal Fifth
ally

FOCUS YOUR READING

How did the Spanish conquer the mighty Aztecs?

A. Hernando Cortés

By 1515, Spain's colonies included Hispaniola, Cuba, and other lands around the Caribbean Sea. None of these lands had yielded the great riches that Spain hoped for. Still the Spanish colonists dreamed of great wealth to be discovered in America. Their dreams were fed by rumors of rich Indian civilizations on the mainland of the unexplored lands.

Hernando Cortés was one such colonist. Born in Spain in 1485, Cortés went to Hispaniola in 1504. Soon he moved to Cuba, where he became a successful landowner. He was not satisfied. He wanted the wealth and fame that would come to the discoverer of new lands. Cortés also wanted to convert the Indians to Christianity.

His chance came when Diego Velázquez (dee AY goh vuh LAS kes), the governor of Cuba, ordered a fleet to sail to the shores of Mexico. Cortés was made commander of the fleet. One fifth of any wealth that was found had to be set aside for the Spanish crown. That was known as the **Royal Fifth**. The remainder of the wealth, as well as the governorship of the conquered lands, would belong to Velázquez.

Cortés left Cuba in 1518 with 11 ships, about 550 soldiers, 100 sailors, 14 cannons, and 16 horses. This small army conquered one of the greatest kingdoms in the world at that time.

B. Cortés Lands in Mexico

Doña Marina As Cortés's expedition made its way from Cuba to the Yucatán and then west along the coast of Mexico, it gained an important addition—an Aztec princess whom the Spaniards called Doña Marina (DOH nyah muh REE nuh). Among the Indians she was known as *La Malinche*.

The Granger Collection

This Aztec drawing shows both Aztecs and Spaniards.
▶ From the viewpoint of the Aztec, what is happening?

As a young girl, Doña Marina had been sold as a slave and taken to the coast. Doña Marina knew Nahuatl (NAH waht-ul), the language of the Aztecs, as well as Maya, a language understood by one of the members of the expedition. When Cortés's words were translated from Spanish into Maya and then into Nahuatl, Cortés could talk with the Aztecs. Doña Marina told Cortés about the Aztec ruler Moctezuma (mohk tay SOO mah) and his empire. That information later helped Cortés defeat the Aztecs.

The Spaniards landed near the present-day city of Veracruz, on the east coast of Mexico. Cortés did not know it at the time, but the date of his landing in 1519 was very important. It was to influence the whole course of the conquest.

C. The Legend of Quetzalcóatl

Amazing Coincidences An Aztec god-man was Quetzalcóatl, who was also the feathered serpent god. According to Aztec belief, another god many years before had forced Quetzalcóatl to leave Mexico. He fled to the sea and sailed away on a magic raft, promising to return someday to destroy his enemy.

The year on the Aztec calendar in which Quetzalcóatl was supposed to return was 1519 on the European calendar, the very year that Cortés landed in Mexico. In another amazing coincidence, the day Cortés landed, April 22, happened to be Quetzalcóatl's special day on the Aztec calendar. Quetzalcóatl was thought to be tall and fair-skinned with a full beard. Cortés was tall, fair-skinned, red-haired, and wore a full beard. Is it any wonder that Moctezuma thought Cortés was the god Quetzalcóatl?

Doña Marina was of great help to Cortés in conquering the Aztecs.
▶ In which two ways was she an aid to Cortés?

Moctezuma's Decision Because Moctezuma believed that Cortés was Quetzalcóatl, he did not attack. Instead, he sent messengers with gifts, trying to persuade Cortés to leave. According to one Aztec account, "While the messengers were away, Moctezuma could neither sleep nor eat, and no one could speak with him. He was lost in despair, in the deepest gloom and sorrow."

When those messengers returned, their descriptions of the Spaniards made things worse. They spoke of the cannon. "It comes shooting sparks and raining fire. If the cannon is aimed against a mountain, the mountain splits and cracks open. If it is aimed against a tree, it shatters the

155

This museum display shows two views of Tenochtitlán—a wall mural, in the background, and a scale model—for visitors to observe.
► How are the two views different?

tree into splinters." This report terrified Moctezuma.

D. The March to Tenochtitlán

Cortés spent nearly four months at Veracruz, training his soldiers and learning what he could about Moctezuma and the Aztecs. Finally, he was prepared to march to Tenochtitlán.

As you know, Tenochtitlán lay on Lake Texcoco in the central valley of Mexico on a high plateau. Cortés and his army had to climb over a 10,000-foot (3,048-m) mountain pass to get to the plateau. They had to go through other cities on the plateau before reaching the valley of Mexico. One of these was Tlaxcala (tlahs KAH-lah), the capital of an independent state that had not been conquered by the Aztecs. The Tlaxcalans sent an army to attack Cortés.

The Indians were no match for the Spaniards. The well-disciplined Spanish troops with their muskets and cannons killed many warriors. The Spaniards' horses terrified the Tlaxcalans, who believed the horses were gods that could not be killed. After the Spaniards defeated the Tlaxcalans, Cortés treated them so well that they became his **allies,** or supporters, against the Aztecs.

E. The Sad Night

A Warm Welcome Cortés and his army reached the Aztec capital in early November. Moctezuma welcomed them and treated them like visiting royalty. He gave them the use of a palace and plenty of food to eat. Moctezuma still believed Cortés was a god.

Cortés realized that he would have to gain control of Moctezuma to rule in Mexico. He talked the king into moving to the palace with the Spaniards. Cortés pretended that Moctezuma was his guest. In reality, he had made the great ruler his prisoner. Moctezuma's people grew unhappy with his friendship toward the Spaniards. However, they didn't want to attack the Spaniards while they held Moctezuma captive.

Serious Fighting During a time when Cortés was temporarily out of Tenochtitlán, his men killed a group of Aztecs who were celebrating an important religious occasion. The Aztecs demanded that the Spaniards who were responsible for the deaths be killed. When Cortés came back in June of 1520, he told Moctezuma to calm the Aztecs. By this time, however, other Aztec leaders no longer believed in Moctezuma, and they began to fight the Spaniards. Moctezuma died at that time. According to the Spaniards, he was stoned to death by the Aztecs when he asked them to stop fighting.

With Moctezuma gone, there was no one to protect the Spaniards, so Cortés ordered a retreat from Tenochtitlán. He set the night of June 30, 1520, as the time to leave. Loaded down with around a million dollars in gold they had looted from Moctezuma's treasure house, the Spaniards retreated across the long causeway that connected the city with the lake shore. The Aztecs attacked from all sides. Many of the Spaniards drowned in the lake, pulled under by the weight of the gold they carried. Cortés lost over half his army in the battle, but he and most of his officers escaped. They called the night of the battle *La Noche Triste*, which is Spanish for "the sad night."

F. The Fall of the City

Cortés made his way back to Tlaxcala, where he and his army rested and recovered from their wounds. With the help of the Tlaxcalan army, Cortés built ships so that he could attack Tenochtitlán from the lake. By April of 1521, Cortés was ready. Meanwhile, smallpox was raging throughout Tenochtitlán, killing hundreds of Indians and weakening the Aztec forces.

La Noche Triste, or "the sad night," is shown in this painting.
▶ Explain what happened as Cortés and his army made their retreat.

Cortés and his army are shown in battle with the Aztecs.
▶ Why were the Aztecs at a disadvantage in the attack?

The Granger Collection

The Spaniards attacked from the lake and along the causeways. The Aztecs put up a fierce battle, killing many Spaniards and their Tlaxcalan allies. Cortés decided that the only way to defeat the Aztecs was to destroy their city. He surrounded the city, closing it completely to all trade with the outside. After a while, food and water gave out. Although weak from thirst, hunger, and disease, the Aztecs still held out. A new Aztec emperor, Cuauhtémoc, led a courageous resistance.

Cortés finally attacked the city directly. Battering rams knocked down the barricaded causeways. The Spanish troops stormed in. Bit by bit the city was destroyed. By August of 1521, the Aztecs were defeated.

In his book *Cortés and the Downfall of the Aztec Empire*, Jon Manchip White ponders the victory of Cortés and the end of the world of the Aztecs.

Cortés had set out with a score of ships and a handful of men towards an unknown shore. His intention had been to establish a modest colony and amass a modest fortune. Even in his broadest imaginings, he had not pictured the discovery of a vast kingdom, its monuments certainly as grand as those of Europe, ruled by an emperor more wealthy, more powerful, and more feared than his own.

If Cortés had failed to reach his goal, our world would have been different. But reach it he did. On that night of agony, death, and rain, the world of Spain was superimposed on the world of Mexico. The far-ranging community of Spanish-America was born.

LESSON 3 REVIEW

THINK AND WRITE

A. Why did the Spaniards go from the Caribbean islands to the mainland?

B. How did Doña Marina help Cortés?

C. Why did Moctezuma think Cortés was Quetzalcóatl?

D. What made the Tlaxcalans decide to become allies of Cortés?

E. Summarize why the Spaniards decided to leave Tenochtitlán?

F. How did the Spaniards finally defeat the Aztecs?

SKILLS CHECK

WRITING SKILL

Use the actualizing strategy to imagine that you are "observing" Cortés. Choose any episode that you read about in the life of Cortés. Try to imagine what is happening. Then write a paragraph or two about what you have observed.

The Conquest of the Incas

THINK ABOUT WHAT YOU KNOW

You now know how Cortés conquered the Aztecs. What advice do you think he would have given to someone who wanted to conquer the Inca Empire?

STUDY THE VOCABULARY

conquistador   civil war
isthmus   treason

FOCUS YOUR READING

In what ways were the conquests of the Incas and Aztecs similar?

A. Francisco Pizarro's Expedition

First Spanish Settlement In the same way that the islands of Hispaniola and Cuba served as bases for exploring the mainland around the Caribbean, Panama became a jumping-off place for voyages to the South American mainland. Panama had been founded by the famous Spanish explorer and **conquistador** (kahn KWIHS-tuh dor), or conqueror, Vasco Núñez de Balboa (bal BOH uh). He founded a colony at Darién, on the Isthmus of Panama, that was to be the first lasting Spanish settlement on the mainland of America. An **isthmus** is a narrow strip of land with water on either side. It connects two larger bodies of land. In 1513, Balboa crossed the isthmus and became the first European to see the ocean that Magellan a few years later would call the Pacific.

Stories of a rich land to the south floated around Panama. Everyone there already knew about the great wealth of the Aztec Empire. They also knew that

Cortés's conquest had made him a very wealthy man.

The Dream of Wealth It was not until 1524 that a plan for an expedition was launched. Its two leaders were Francisco Pizarro (pih ZAHR oh) and Diego de Almagro (ahl MAH groh). Neither man could read or write. Both were soldiers who had come to the New World to get rich, yet neither man had made his fortune. The dream of wealth remained, even though both Pizarro and Almagro already were over 50 years old.

The two decided to work together to search for and conquer the rich kingdom said to be in South America. They didn't have much money, so they took on a wealthy third partner, a priest named Fernando de Luque (LOO kay). In addition to

After the Spanish settled in Darién, Panama, they used it as a base for explorations to other lands in the Americas.
▶ Why was Darién a good base?

159

Pizarro is shown on the outskirts of the city of Cajamarca, ready for a major attack against Atahualpa and his army.
▶ What weapons do Pizarro and his army have that may have been unknown to the Inca people?

money, de Luque brought another advantage. He was a close friend of the governor of Panama. The governor gave the partners permission to organize the expedition, but he demanded a share of the profits. So Fernando de Luque raised the money and remained in Panama. Almagro got the ships, supplies, and crew together. Pizarro led the expeditions.

The Rich Inca Empire After several attempts ended in failure, Pizarro sailed down the coast from Ecuador and reached Tumbes (TOOM bays), an Inca town in northern Peru. There he went ashore and saw with his own eyes substantial buildings and much gold and silver. Now he knew for sure that the stories of a wealthy empire were true!

Approval from Spain Pizarro sailed back to Panama to get support for a new expedition, but the governor was not impressed. Pizarro then sailed all the way back to Spain to speak to the king. Since Cortés was there at that very time, it is possible that Pizarro spoke with Cortés. Perhaps because of Cortés's success, the king approved Pizarro's plan.

Preparation for the Battle In 1531, Pizarro, now officially a governor and captain-general of Peru, once more set out for Peru from Panama. With him went 180 men and 27 horses. By 1532, Pizarro had conquered Túmbes. Then with some additional soldiers from Panama, he made ready to invade the Inca stronghold high in the Andes.

B. Pizarro and Emperor Atahualpa

A Ruthless Emperor Pizarro was lucky because he faced a weakened kingdom. The previous Inca had died in 1527. In his will he had divided the kingdom between his two sons. After a while, the brothers fought over the kingdom in a **civil war**. A civil war is a war between parts of the same country. One brother, Atahualpa (ah tah WAHL pah), was cruel. He took his brother captive and put him in prison just before Pizarro and his men climbed the Andes to meet the Incas. He also had many members of the imperial family executed so that they could not challenge his right to rule.

In November of 1532, Atahualpa was camped with his army of about 30,000 warriors, near the city of Cajamarca (kah-huh MAHR kuh). Pizarro had with him 106 foot soldiers and 62 horsemen. After sending word for Atahualpa to meet him in Cajamarca, Pizarro laid a trap for the Inca.

Secure in his power, and as a man of daring, the Inca ruler entered the city being carried on a golden litter. A group of Indians went before him, sweeping the dust from the roadway.

From their hiding places, Pizarro's men attacked. Pizarro himself leaped up and grabbed Atahualpa. Many Indians were killed. The Spaniards did not lose a single soldier.

As the daring Inca ruler, Atahualpa was often carried through the streets on a throne placed on a litter.
▶ What happened to him because of his daring?

Gold and Silver Treasures Atahualpa tried to buy his freedom. He promised to give the Spaniards enough gold to fill a whole room and enough silver to fill a second room. Pizarro agreed.

It took two months for the Indians to deliver enough gold and silver to ransom Atahualpa. The Spaniards melted down all the golden objects—fine plates, goblets, and ceremonial pieces—into bars to more easily divide the treasure.

During that time, Atahualpa sent word to have his brother killed. That way, he believed, the Spaniards would have no choice but to accept him as Inca. Pizarro decided that freeing Atahualpa was too great a risk. He therefore had the Inca tried for **treason**, or the betrayal of his country, and put to death.

C. The March on Cuzco

With Atahualpa dead, Pizarro left Cajamarca and marched to Cuzco, the Inca capital. The Spaniards captured the city in November of 1533 with the aid of Inca nobles still loyal to Atahualpa's brother. With resistance in Cuzco crushed, the Spaniards grabbed everything of value they could find. Pizarro's fortune had by then risen to nearly $17 million in estimated value.

When the Incas ruled, the main square of Cuzco was an open area. Later it became the Plaza de Armas.
► Who might have wanted to make some changes in the central city?

Meanwhile, Diego de Almagro came from Panama to join the conquest. He and Pizarro quarreled over dividing the country. They became enemies. In 1538, after Almagro seized Cuzco, a civil war followed as Spaniards fought Spaniards. Almagro was executed by Pizarro's brother, Hernando. Pizarro was murdered later by a group of men led by Almagro's son. Then the Spanish king sent a representative to bring peace to the land.

LESSON **4** REVIEW

THINK AND WRITE

A. What was Panama's connection with the conquest of the Incas?
B. Summarize the life of Atahualpa.
C. What happened to Pizarro after the conquest?

SKILLS CHECK

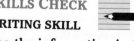

WRITING SKILL

Use the information in this lesson to write two cause-and-effect sentences. Write one about Pizarro. Write the other one about Atahualpa. Begin each sentence with the word *because*.

Spanish Exploration Continues

THINK ABOUT WHAT YOU KNOW

Think of some cities in the United States that have Spanish names. Use the Atlas if you need help. Why, do you think, do they have Spanish rather than English names?

STUDY THE VOCABULARY

settlement
colonization

FOCUS YOUR READING

What other parts of the Americas did the Spanish explore?

A. The Search for El Dorado

According to legend, El Dorado was a golden kingdom. Fabulous wealth awaited the person of vision and daring who could find and conquer it. Anything seemed possible in this strange new land. After all, the Spaniards already had seen people, plants, and animals never before known to them. Small numbers of Spaniards had even triumphed over mighty empires. Thus, Spanish explorers set out to find new wonders and search for more treasure.

B. Cabeza de Vaca's Journey

To the north and east of Panama, a group of around 300 men led by Pánfilo de Narváez (nahr VAH es) landed in Florida in 1528. Narváez explored along the Gulf Coast of Florida. Attacked by Indians and beset by disease and starvation, Narváez's men decided to try to reach another Spanish **settlement**, or colony, in northeastern Mexico. They built five barges, and sailed off along the Gulf shoreline.

Two of the barges made it to Galveston Island in present-day Texas. There, a cold winter and inadequate supplies took a heavy toll. By spring, most of the Spaniards had died. Just about all of the survivors left. Alvar Nuñez Cabeza de Vaca was sick, so he stayed behind. Cabeza de Vaca spent several years in eastern Texas, living among the Indians and trading with them.

Then, in 1533, he met up with three members from Narváez's original party. They told Cabeza de Vaca that they alone had survived. The four agreed to try again to get to Mexico City, the new capital city the Spaniards had built on the ruins of Tenochtitlán.

They began that journey the following year. For two more years they traveled on, helped by Indian guides. The four Spaniards finally reached Mexico City in 1536. So from the time he began sailing west-

In legend, the ruler of El Dorado covered his body with gold dust each day and washed it off each night in a lake.
► How might the term *El Dorado* be used today?

163

ward in the Gulf of Mexico, Cabeza de Vaca had spent over eight years wandering through what would become the Southwest of the United States!

C. The Growth of Spain's New World Empire

Sebastián de Benalcázar, one of Pizarro's men, went north from Peru and conquered Quito (KEE toh), in today's Ecuador, in 1534. From there he went on to Colombia, where he founded the cities of Cali (KAH lee) in 1536 and Popayán (paw pah YAHN) in 1537.

In 1541, Pedro de Valdivia marched south from Peru to conquer Chile by authority of Pizarro. The Araucanian Indians of Chile fought bravely, and Valdivia and his band of conquerors were nearly all killed. Valdivia lived long enough to found Santiago, now the capital of Chile.

One person who greatly helped Valdivia was a Spanish woman named Inés de Suárez (SWAHR ez). Not only did she fight along with the men but she also tended the men's wounds and encouraged them when they began to give up hope of surviving.

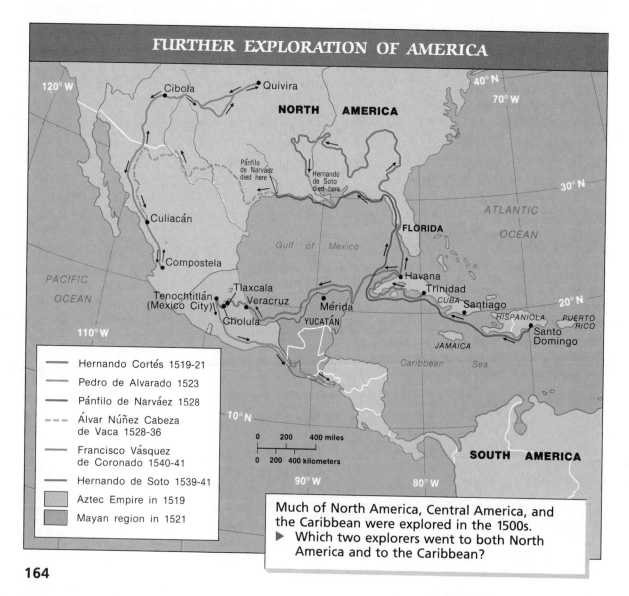

FURTHER EXPLORATION OF AMERICA

Hernando Cortés 1519-21
Pedro de Alvarado 1523
Pánfilo de Narváez 1528
Álvar Núñez Cabeza de Vaca 1528-36
Francisco Vásquez de Coronado 1540-41
Hernando de Soto 1539-41
Aztec Empire in 1519
Mayan region in 1521

Much of North America, Central America, and the Caribbean were explored in the 1500s.
► Which two explorers went to both North America and to the Caribbean?

A Spaniard named Pedro de Mendoza founded Buenos Aires in 1536 and built a fort there. After the little fort was destroyed by Indians the next year, the Spaniards moved up the Paraná and Paraguay rivers to found Asunción, the present capital of Paraguay. Asunción became the center of Spanish **colonization** in the southeastern part of South America. A colonization can mean a settlement in one land ruled by the government of another country.

In 1541, Francisco de Orellana and other explorers went into the Amazon rain forest and became lost. They found a tributary of the Amazon River. After making crude boats, they floated 2,000 miles (3,218 km) to the Atlantic Ocean. Orellana and his group were the first Europeans to sail the Amazon.

People from Peru settled western Argentina in the 1550s and 1560s. For many years this area was part of Peru. Buenos Aires was resettled in 1580, which completed the Spanish conquest in South America. In less than a century after Columbus's first voyage, Spain had established the largest empire in America. The map on pages 164–165 shows you the pattern of the Spanish conquests.

CONQUESTS IN SOUTH AMERICA

Francisco Pizarro 1531–1534

Pedro de Mendoza 1536

Pedro de Valdivia 1540–1541

Francisco de Orellana, 1541–1542

Inca empire

0   500 miles
0   500 kilometers

The routes of four Spanish explorers are shown on the map.
▶ Which explorer journeyed the farthest in the shortest amount of time?

LESSON **5** REVIEW

THINK AND WRITE

A. How did the story of El Dorado affect the Spaniards?
B. What area did Cabeza de Vaca explore?
C. What other places were explored by the Spaniards?

SKILLS CHECK

MAP SKILL

Look at the map on this page to locate the following cities founded by the Spaniards: Quito, Buenos Aires, Asunción, and Cuzco. Use the Gazetteer to find out which of these cities is not a national capital today.

USING THE VOCABULARY

maritime	conquistador
capital	civil war
nationalism	isthmus
circumnavigate	treason
La Noche Triste	colonization

On a separate sheet of paper, write the number of the definition and the term from the list that matches the definition.

1. Fighting between parts of the same country
2. Money that can be invested
3. Betrayal of one's country
4. Love of one's country
5. Settlement in one land ruled by the government of another
6. To travel around the world by ship
7. Spanish word for *conqueror*
8. A battle in which the Aztecs killed many of Cortés's soldiers
9. A narrow strip of land with water on either side which connects two larger pieces of land.
10. Shipping and sailing in general

REMEMBERING WHAT YOU READ

On a separate sheet of paper, answer the following questions in complete sentences.

1. What do people mean when they say that Christopher Columbus "discovered" the New World?

2. How did nationalism and the desire for trade lead to the exploration of the New World?
3. Why was it important for European nations to have a more direct trade route to the Indies?
4. Why was Cabral's discovery of Brazil important?
5. Who was the first navigator to sail around the world?
6. Why did Moctezuma believe that Cortés was the god Quetzalcóatl?
7. How did Moctezuma help Cortés conquer the Aztecs?
8. How did Pizarro conquer the Incas?
9. Who was the first European to travel through what is now the American southwest?
10. By then, which country had established the largest empire in the Americas?

TYING LANGUAGE ARTS TO SOCIAL STUDIES

Pretend to be one of the explorers discussed in this chapter and write one journal entry of your adventures in the New World. Write about the sights, sounds, events, and feelings you experienced on that day or series of days. You may prefer to write about your adventures in a letter to a good friend back home. Have your letter tell about a series of events and your reactions to them. Your observations of the new lands and peoples would also be of interest to your friend.

THINKING CRITICALLY

On a separate sheet of paper, answer the following questions in complete sentences.

1. Nationalism is still important today. Describe a recent news event that shows that nationalism is still strong.
2. In Chapter 4, you learned that superior weapons helped the Spanish conquer the Aztecs. How did coincidence, fear, and disease also help the Spaniards win?
3. How did both Cortés and Pizarro use the idea of "divide and conquer" to defeat the Indians?
4. How did greed lead to disaster for *both* Pizarro and Atahualpa?
5. How do parts of the Americas still show the influence of Spanish culture today?

SUMMARIZING THE CHAPTER

On a separate sheet of paper, draw a graphic organizer like the one shown here. Copy the information from this graphic organizer to the one you have drawn. Under each heading, fill in the blanks with facts you learned from that lesson.

CHAPTER THEME
The Spanish and the Portuguese conquered Latin America.

LESSON 1
An Age of Discovery
1. _____
2. _____

LESSON 2
Early Discoveries
1. _____
2. _____

LESSON 3
Conquest of Mexico
1. _____
2. _____
3. _____

LESSON 4
Conquest of the Incas
1. _____
2. _____
3. _____

LESSON 5
Further Exploration
1. _____
2. _____
3. _____

CHAPTER 6

COLONIZING LATIN AMERICA

*W*ith each passing century, the frontier outposts established by Spain and Portugal became settled communities. They had their own special characteristics and ways of life.

The Granger Collection

Governing the Colonies

THINK ABOUT WHAT YOU KNOW

Think about how the Incas ruled their large empire. Decide whether or not you think Spain faced some of the same problems in trying to rule its colonies.

STUDY THE VOCABULARY

viceroy   encomienda
viceroyalty   encomendero
labor

FOCUS YOUR READING

How did Spain govern its colonies?

A. A Long Colonial Period

Sometimes people become impatient when studying things that happened a long time ago, especially when those things are not very exciting. Maybe you feel that way, but look at it this way. If you want to be able to understand today's Latin America, it is important that you know something about the years when all of Latin America was made up of colonies.

Spain established its first New World colony on Hispaniola at the time of Columbus's second voyage, in 1494. Most of Spain's colonies didn't gain independence until about 1824. So as you can see, the colonial period in Spanish America lasted well over 300 years. Portugal's rule lasted just about that long in Brazil. In fact, Latin America has a much longer history as an area of colonies than as a region of independent countries.

In this lesson you'll take a look at some of the important institutions and events in the colonial history of Spanish America. As you study this lesson, think back on what you learned about the conquest of Latin America. How will that information help you to better understand the colonization of Latin America?

B. Spain's Viceroyalties

New Spain and Peru The conquistadors governed in Spain's colonies for the first few years after the Spaniards conquered Latin America. Spain feared that the conquistadors might grow too powerful and independent. Cortés, for example, had Spanish soldiers and Indian rulers who were more loyal to him than to Spain. The crown moved quickly to take away power from the conquistadors in an effort to solve this problem.

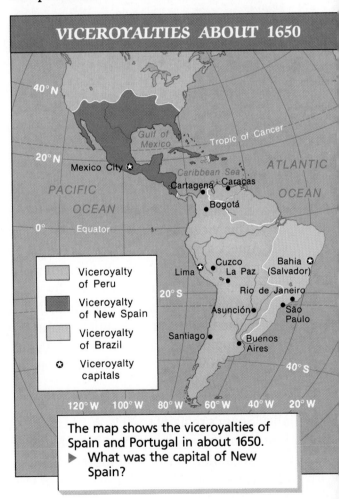

The map shows the viceroyalties of Spain and Portugal in about 1650.
▶ What was the capital of New Spain?

Churches and stores within an arched walkway around the plaza in Cuzco, Peru, were built in Spanish style.
▶ What else was in the plazas?

Spain appointed **viceroys**, or rulers who represented the crown in the colonies and replaced the conquistadors. Each viceroy ruled an area called a **viceroyalty**. At first there were two viceroyalties in Spanish America—New Spain and Peru.

The capital of New Spain was Mexico City. This viceroyalty covered all of Spanish America north of Panama as well as most of the islands of the West Indies. It stretched far into territory that is now part of the United States. At one time, New Spain also included the Spanish colony in the Philippine Islands, more than 10,000 miles (16,090 km) across the Pacific Ocean from Mexico.

The viceroyalty of Peru consisted of all of Spain's remaining New World claims. Lima, known as the "City of the Kings," was its capital. Peru's vast mineral wealth of silver and gold made it the richer of the two viceroyalties.

New Granada and La Plata Later on, as part of an administrative reform, the Spanish government created two new viceroyalties—New Granada in 1717 and La Plata in 1776. As you can see from the map on page 169, both were carved out of the viceroyalty of Peru. Bogotá became the capital of New Granada. Buenos Aires was La Plata's capital.

C. A Powerful Church

A plaza, or square, stood at the center of every colonial town or city. Two buildings dominated each plaza. One of these buildings always was for the government. In a small city it was a town hall. In a capital, such as Mexico City or Lima, it was the palace of the viceroy.

The other important structure on the plaza was a church. Churches ranged in size from humble wooden buildings in the smaller towns to stone cathedrals with gold finishes in the more important cities. The church and the government building symbolized the two great powers in colonial Spanish America.

Priests took part in most of the early voyages of discovery. They accompanied the great conquerors, and after the physical conquest, priests continued to work for the spiritual conquest of the New World. They spread their religion among the Indians. Often they learned Indian languages and in some cases translated the Bible into those languages. They also established schools. Sometimes, unfortunately, they destroyed many of the Indians' religious objects, such as idols of their gods. The priests thought that destroying such objects would show the Indians that the Christian God was more powerful than the Indians' gods.

Over the years, the church gained great wealth. People left money to the church and asked that prayers be said for them after their death. Well-to-do people sometimes willed the church enormous amounts of money to show their faith. After a while, the church became the largest owner of land in the colonies. It also held great amounts of silver and gold. Then, too, the church had great power because the people felt church activities were important to them.

D. Control of Indian Labor

Neither mines nor land can produce anything without **labor**, or work. The Native Americans, therefore, were seen as a valuable resource. As with the other New World resources, the Spanish crown wanted to make the rules for how the Indians could be used. Although the rulers expected the Indians to do most of the hard work, they did not want the colonists to continue treating the Indians badly. They also wanted the Indians to learn to speak Spanish and to become Christians.

To carry out their plans for the Native Americans, the Spanish rulers created **encomiendas** (en koh mee EN duz). An encomienda was a group of Indians that was placed in the care of a Spanish colonist called an **encomendero**. The encomendero was also to be responsible for the religious training. In return, the Indians had to work the encomendero's land for a certain number of days each month. They also had to pay a tax in the form of goods they produced from their own land. The Indians were not slaves, but their lives were tightly controlled.

Usually an encomienda consisted of an Indian village or part of a village, but some of the encomiendas were even larger.

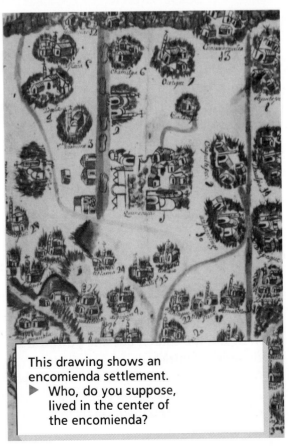

This drawing shows an encomienda settlement.
▶ Who, do you suppose, lived in the center of the encomienda?

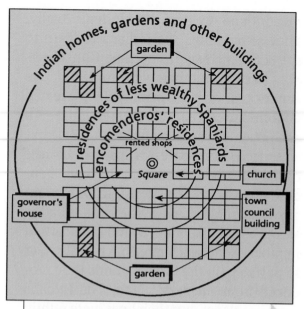

Indian homes, gardens and other buildings

residences of less wealthy Spaniards

encomenderos' residences

garden

rented shops

Square

church

governor's house

town council building

garden

The encomenderos owned the best houses in the center of the encomienda.
▶ Why, do you suppose, did they rent out some space facing the square?

One of the largest encomiendas in Spanish America was owned by Cortés. It had 22 villages and nearly 100,000 Indians who lived in a territory of 25,000 square miles (64,750 sq km). This encomienda was in the valley of Oaxaca (wah HAH kah), in the southern part of Mexico.

E. Spain's Problems in Enforcing Its Laws

Writing laws is one thing, but making them work is quite another matter. In fact, one of the things that made a viceroy successful was knowing when it was best to ignore the laws that came from Spain. The viceroys knew local conditions far better than did the officials in Spain. A law could make good sense to those officials but no sense at all to the viceroy.

The distance between Spain and the colonies also created problems. Remember, this all took place long before the age of steamships or airplanes. There was no telegraph, telephone, or radio for sending messages. Think about a viceroy who was living far north of Mexico City. Imagine the time and difficulty involved in sending a message to the king in Spain and then getting an answer back. A messenger would have had to travel by land to the nearest port and wait for a ship to arrive. The ship would not have sailed until its cargo was loaded. Then the journey to Spain would have taken many weeks. How long do you think the complete trip would have taken?

LESSON **1** *REVIEW*

THINK AND WRITE

A. Why is it important to learn about Latin America's colonial period?
B. Why did Spain and its viceroys organize viceroyalties?
C. Why did the church become powerful in Spain's colonies?
D. What purpose did the encomienda have?
E. What reasons are given for Spain's problems in enforcing its laws in the colonies?

SKILLS CHECK

MAP SKILL

Use the Atlas map on pages 592–593 as well as the inset map of Europe to locate Spain. Then try to answer the question at the end of this lesson. Write a paragraph or two to support your answer. Base your answer on what you found out by studying the Atlas map and the inset map.

The Colonial Trade

A. Spain's Control of Commerce

You may recall that a desire for the spices and silks of the Orient caused European nations to undertake voyages of exploration. Spain's colonies in the Americas did not have the luxury goods of the Orient, but they did have gold, silver, and important agricultural products. Spain wanted to keep other nations out of its colonies. Spain wanted a **monopoly**, or complete control, over the trade its colonies had with other countries. To gain control over **commerce**, Spain limited the ports through which goods could be shipped into and out of the distant colonies. Commerce is the buying and selling of goods and services.

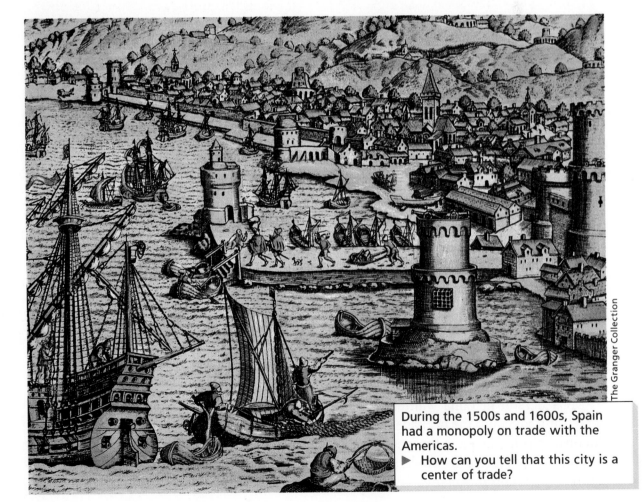

The Granger Collection

During the 1500s and 1600s, Spain had a monopoly on trade with the Americas.
► How can you tell that this city is a center of trade?

173

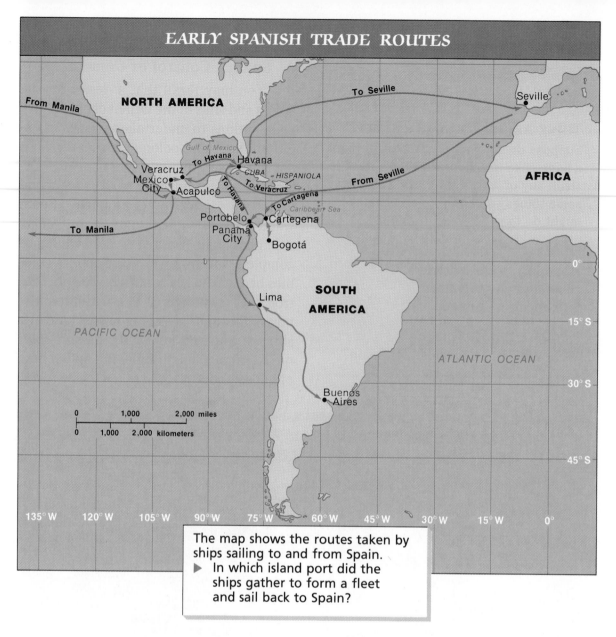

EARLY SPANISH TRADE ROUTES

The map shows the routes taken by ships sailing to and from Spain.
▶ In which island port did the ships gather to form a fleet and sail back to Spain?

At first, all goods shipped to the Americas had to pass through Seville in Spain. Later, the city of Cádiz received permission to ship goods to the colonies. In America the ports that received goods from Spain were Veracruz in Mexico and the ports of Portobelo in Panama and Cartagena in Colombia.

If a person in Lima wanted to send something to Spain, the package would be put on a ship and taken to the west coast of Panama. From there it would cross the Isthmus in Central America by mule to Portobelo on the Caribbean coast. At Portobelo it would be put on the next ship for Spain.

Havana, on the island of Cuba, was an important port too. Its fine harbor guarded the passage between Cuba and Florida. That was the main route for ships leaving the Caribbean on the way to Spain.

B. Fleets for Protection and Control

Dangers to Ships Ships left Veracruz, Portobelo, and Cartagena in small fleets, or groups of ships. At Havana they would gather in one great fleet to sail for Spain. It was dangerous for a single ship or even a small fleet to leave Havana alone. There were **buccaneers**, or pirates, near Cuba and Florida ready to attack. A large fleet was harder to attack, and it could be protected by warships. Some Spanish fleets had as many as 90 ships!

Some ships were sunk in **hurricanes**, the powerful tropical storms that sweep through the Caribbean region. Now, over 400 years later, treasure hunters and archaeologists search for the remains of sunken Spanish ships to recover the treasures they carried.

Other Problems The long trade routes between Spain and its American colonies caused other problems too. The colonists sometimes ran out of things they needed. It usually took months, and often years, for goods to travel from Spain to the colonies. Even messages from the king or queen to colonial officials took a long time to arrive.

Worse still, the cost of shipping added to the price of goods that were exported to the colonies from Spain. Each time a ship was loaded or unloaded, the cost of its contents rose. A bale of cotton carried from Peru to Spain might have increased 200 times in cost by the time it was made into cloth and sent back to Lima. The wealthy people were the only ones who could afford to buy imported goods.

Pirate ships raided Spanish ships, but today, divers sometimes search for the treasures within sunken ships.
► What found treasures are shown?

FROM:

A Voyage to South America

By: Jorge Juan and Antonio de Ulloa
Setting: Portobelo Fair in Panama

Jorge Juan and António de Ulloa (oo YOH ah), two Spanish scientists, wrote a historical account of a voyage that they made to South America. One of their stops was in Portobelo. They knew that only one fleet a year called at Spain's Caribbean ports. When the fleet arrived, there was a great fair that lasted 40 days. Merchants came from all over the colonies. In this literature selection, the two men relate their impressions of the Portobelo fair.

The ships are no sooner moored in the harbor than the first work is to erect a tent made of the ship's sails in the square. The proprietors of the goods are present in order to find their bales by the marks which distinguish them. These bales are drawn on sledges, to their respective places by the crew of every ship, and the money given them [for their labor] is proportionally divided.

Whilst the seamen and European traders are thus employed, the land is covered with droves of mules from Panama, each drove consisting of about 100, loaded with chests of gold and silver, on account of the merchants of Peru. Some unload them at the ex-change, others in the middle of the square. Yet, amidst the hurry and confusion of such crowds, no theft, loss, or disturbance, is ever known.

The ships being unloaded, and the merchants of Peru, together with the president of Panama, arrive, and the fair begins. After prices are settled, contracts are signed and made public. Thus no fraud can take place. The purchases and sales, the exchanges of money are transacted by representatives from Spain and Peru. After this, everyone begins to dispose of goods — the Spanish representatives loading their chests of money and those of Peru sending away the goods they have purchased. And thus, in forty or less days, the fair of Portobelo ends.

C. Pirates and Privateers

Challenges to Spain "I would like to see," said Francis I, king of France, "the will of our common ancestor Adam, which left all the riches of the New World to Spain and Portugal."

Francis I wanted France to share in the wealth of America. Other nations felt that way too. England and the Netherlands, both important commercial nations, also wanted "a piece of the action."

"Legal" Pirates The rulers of England, France, and the Netherlands could not attack Spanish ships directly without starting a war. However, they could not be blamed, the rulers reasoned, if pirates attacked the Spanish treasure ships. So their ship captains were given permission to attack Spanish ships. Such "legal" pirates were called **privateers**. Pirates, legal or illegal, were not always punished for their deeds. Often they were treated like heroes in their countries.

Privateers and buccaneers caused many problems for Spain. They sank or captured Spanish ships and took Spanish treasure. They even raided ports in Spain and the colonies.

Sir Francis Drake The most famous privateer was an Englishman named Sir Francis Drake. For nearly 25 years he terrorized Spain and its colonies. In 1572, Drake sailed from England to Panama, where he raided the port and captured mule trains carrying 30 tons (27 t) of Peruvian silver. He received a hero's greeting in England when he returned.

In 1577, Drake set out again, sailing through the Strait of Magellan to the Pacific Ocean. He traveled up the western coast of the Americas as far as the present state of Washington, claiming land in North America for England. He returned home as the first English sailor to go around the world. Queen Elizabeth I made Drake a knight in 1581.

Spain's Losses Additional raids on Spanish ships and Spanish ports weakened Spain. In 1588, the English navy defeated the Spanish **armada**, or fleet of armed ships, that was sailing to invade Britain. The loss was so great to Spain that it was never able to recover.

With the weakened navy, Spain could not easily defend its colonies in the Caribbean. It had never colonized the small islands in the Lesser Antilles because they seemed to have little value. Now these islands were easy prey for Spain's enemies. Between 1623 and 1650, the English, French, and Dutch colonized most of the islands in the Lesser Antilles.

Queen Elizabeth is shown making Francis Drake a knight.
► Describe the ceremony from clues in the illustration.

A coastline view of Port-au-Prince, Haiti, is shown. *Haiti* is a word that means "mountain country."
▶ Does the name seem to apply?

Spain's colonies in the Greater Antilles were also attacked. England took Jamaica in 1655. Though Spain held the eastern part of Hispaniola, French buccaneers and colonists settled the western part of Hispaniola at the beginning of the seventeenth century. The French colony was called St. Domingue (san duh-MANG). Today it is the country of Haiti.

D. Bourbon Reforms

Beginning in 1700, Spain's rulers came from the Bourbons, a great European royal family. They changed colonial policy to make things work more efficiently. Ships, as long as they had licenses from the crown, could sail to the New World whenever they wanted. When they arrived, they could trade directly with several different ports. So colonial merchants no longer had to take their goods on long land journeys to fairs at the few ports. Also, more Spanish cities were allowed to trade directly with the colonies. Little by little, more of a free trading system developed.

Spain's commerce with its colonies began to rise. Economic activity in the colonies also increased. The Bourbon changes had some good effects.

LESSON **2** REVIEW ─────────────

THINK AND WRITE
A. How did Spain try to control trade with its colonies?
B. Why did Spain establish a fleet system?
C. In your own words, explain the meaning of the remark that Francis I made.
D. What did the Bourbons do to revive trade?

SKILLS CHECK
THINKING SKILL

Sir Francis Drake was a famous privateer. He became an English hero after he terrorized Spain and its colonies for many years. Try to form some judgments about Drake. It may help you to start your thinking in this way: "On the one hand, ____." Then switch to the opposite view: "On the other hand, ____ ." Share your ideas with some classmates.

Living in Colonial Latin America

THINK ABOUT WHAT YOU KNOW

In this lesson, you'll read that a place called a hacienda (hah see EN duh) was its own little world in some ways. Name some things you would expect to find in a place that was "its own little world."

STUDY THE VOCABULARY

land grant	peninsular
hacienda	Creole
debt peonage	social class

FOCUS YOUR READING

What was life like in colonial Latin America?

A. The Development of Great Estates

Land Ownership You already know that Latin America is a very large region. Much of it has mountains and rain forests. There also is desert. That limits the amount of good land that is available for farming and ranching. Even so, considering the small number of colonists and the large amount of territory, you might think that almost everyone in colonial Latin America had a piece of good land.

That is not what happened. Instead, a small number of people gained control over almost all of the good land. This pattern of land ownership exists throughout much of Latin America even today. It is important to see how it got started.

One way of dividing the land among the colonists was by **land grants**. A land grant was land given, or granted, to a colonist by the king. Many encomenderos, such as Cortés, received land grants as rewards for their service to Spain.

Indian Losses Another way for Spanish colonists to get land was to claim unused land. Sometimes colonists would falsely say that Indian land was not being used so that they could claim it. Although the Indians had farmed the land for many years, they did not have deeds, or official papers proving ownership. If they went to court to try to protect their rights, Spanish judges would not usually give them a fair hearing. Many Indian villagers lost their land.

When the encomienda system was ended in the eighteenth century, most of the good land in the Spanish colonies was held in estates called **haciendas**. The haciendas were owned by Spaniards or colonists and worked by Indians. The Indians got the poorest land.

Chocó Indians living in parts of Panama and Colombia today often have poor land.
▶ How are the people shown using this land?

The hacienda in some ways was its own little world. One portion of the land was used for grazing sheep or cattle. Another was used for farming. Some forest land was kept to provide wood.

The hacienda sometimes had its own church and a priest who lived on the estate. Workers who wanted to buy things would get them at the hacienda store. They could buy on credit, since the hacienda owner could deduct the amount from their wages. Owners also charged interest for purchases made on credit. Over a time, many workers became so deeply in debt that they never could hope to pay off what they owed. That kept them tied to the land. This system of using debt to control workers is called **debt peonage**.

B. Sugar, Plantations, and Slaves

Another type of estate found in the Americas was the *plantation*, or great farm. The British, French, and Dutch discovered that the islands of the Caribbean were ideal places for growing sugarcane. Because there was a large European market for sugar, the British, French, and Dutch started plantations on the Caribbean islands. The plantations needed many workers to plant and harvest the sugarcane and to refine it into sugar. Since there were not enough people on the islands to supply the needed labor, workers had to be found. The source of labor was the continent of Africa.

African slaves had been brought to the Americas from the beginning of the

A TYPICAL HACIENDA IN COLONIAL LATIN AMERICA

Fields
Fields
Church
Owner's Home
Workshop
Stables
Plaza
Skilled Worker's Home
Store
Skilled Worker's Home
Overseer's Home
Gardens
Gardens

A hacienda was a private estate with high walls. The walls were there to protect the hacienda from bandits.
► Compare the hacienda-owner's home, the overseer's home, and a skilled worker's home. In which ways do they differ?

Cuba is one country in the world whose major wealth depends on sugar.
▶ Why is sugarcane cut by hand, do you suppose?

C. The Importance of Social Class

People who came to the colonies from Spain were known as **peninsulars** (puh-NIHN suh lurz). The word *peninsular* means "from the peninsula." Spain is on the Iberian Peninsula.

Colonists who were born in the Americas were called **Creoles** (KREE ohlz). Both peninsulars and Creoles owned large farms, had slaves or servants, and held good jobs. All the important offices in the government and the church were held by the peninsulars. They had a higher place in colonial society than the Creoles.

You learned in Chapter 2 that racial mixing produced two new groups of people — mestizos and mulattoes. They often worked as artisans, or craftspeople. They also worked as laborers, household servants, and farmhands. As the Indian population dwindled, mestizos made up most of the haciendas' work force.

The mestizos and mulattoes did not belong to the same **social class** as the peninsulars. Social class is a person's place in society, based on birth, wealth, or the kind of work one does. A person's social class is still very important in most of Latin America. Often a person's chance for success in life depends on the social class to which that person belongs.

D. Cities as Centers for Activities

Spain's colonies were not just places of great landed estates. They also had fine cities. Spain founded the cities as centers for administering its colonies and for defense against its European enemies. Coastal cities with fortress walls and cannons pointed outward toward the oceans helped guard against privateers. Some cities were very important for commerce.

colonization period, but the number of African slaves in Spain's colonies was small. With the coming of sugar plantations, slavery grew as never before. Thousands of African slaves were brought to the islands of the Caribbean. They provided the labor to run the plantations. One Spanish colony that had an extremely large number of slaves was Cuba. Cuba became an important center for sugar. Today more than half of the people in the West Indies are descendants of Africans who were brought to the West Indies as slaves.

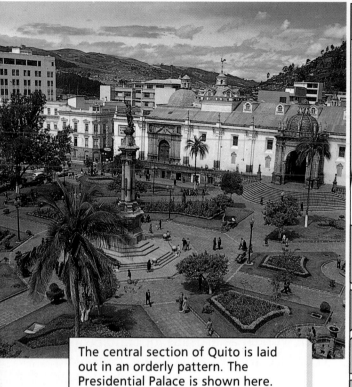

The central section of Quito is laid out in an orderly pattern. The Presidential Palace is shown here.
▶ Find it on the map at the right.

QUITO, ECUADOR

City block

Plaza, park

① Indian Market
② National Museum
③ La Compania Church
④ Presidential Palace
⑤ Cathedral
⑥ Plaza Independencia
⑦ Archbishop's Palace
⑧ Municipal Palace
⑨ Bolívar Theater
⑩ Sports Stadium

The map shows part of the Quito area that has been declared a national monument.
▶ Which buildings are around the plaza?

Others served as centers for mining regions. The greatest cities of the empire were Mexico City and Lima. Smaller cities and towns throughout Spain's colonies also had importance in their local areas.

Remember that each Spanish city had a central plaza, or square, and the most important public building as well as the church always fronted directly on the plaza. Going out from the plaza, the streets were neatly arranged to create a series of rectangles. Though today many people prefer to live in the suburbs, at that time the wealthiest people lived in the central part of cities. In fact, the closer they lived to the plaza, the richer they were!

LESSON 3 REVIEW

THINK AND WRITE

A. Explain how land was divided up and used in colonial Latin America.
B. Why did plantations develop?
C. What factors determined social classes in colonial Spanish America?
D. How, would you say, were small cities and large cities similar as centers for activities?

SKILLS CHECK

WRITING SKILL

Imagine that you are a peninsular or a Creole. Where do you live? What kind of work do you do? Do you have slaves or servants? Give yourself a name and write a short story to tell about your life.

182

Brazil: A Portuguese Colony

THINK ABOUT WHAT YOU KNOW

Suppose you collect stamps, especially ones with pictures of famous people. If someone offered to sell you a stamp collection that had few "people" stamps, how eager would you be to purchase it? Explain why you might change your mind if you knew that a rival collector was interested in purchasing those stamps.

STUDY THE VOCABULARY

captaincy   bandeirante
economy   fazenda

FOCUS YOUR READING

How did Portugal's colony of Brazil compare with Spain's colonies?

A. Slow to Colonize

When Christopher Columbus returned to Spain after his first voyage, he received a hero's welcome. Almost immediately, Spain established a colony on Hispaniola. However, when Cabral sent Portugal notice of his discovery of Brazil, it produced very little excitement. After all, with the voyage of Vasco da Gama, Portugal had already found a route to the Indies. What riches did Brazil hold? Just a dyewood known as *pau brasil*, or brazilwood. (This is the origin of the name *Brazil*.)

So Portugal made no swift move to establish its power in the New World. It took Portugal about 30 years before it even established a city in Brazil! It founded São Vincente (soun vee SAYN tuh) in 1532 mainly to defend its colony against the Spaniards, French, and Dutch who wanted to colonize the area.

B. The Captaincy System

Large Land Grants That same fear that other nations might try to take Brazil also sparked the first Portuguese attempt to establish more settlements in Brazil. However, with all of Portugal's activities in Asia and Africa, the Portuguese king, John III, had little money to spend on Brazil.

In 1533, King John decided to divide the colony into several large grants of land called **captaincies**. He gave them to people in Portugal who agreed to send settlers and to develop farming and trade in their

LATIN AMERICA ABOUT 1700

Legend:
- Spanish colonies
- Portuguese colonies
- French colonies
- English colonies
- Dutch colonies

0   1,000 miles
0   1,000 kilometers

Spanish, Portuguese, French, English, and Dutch colonies had been established in the Americas by 1700.
▶ Where were the Spanish colonies?

Bahia, now known as Salvador, was the capital of Brazil for two centuries. It was during this time that John III began a new policy to insure the successful settlement of Brazil.
▶ Why was Bahia probably chosen as the center of activity?

land grants. The settlers were to protect their areas from invaders. They were also to encourage the people they found living there to become Christians. Since the person who received a land grant was to pay for everything, the settling of Brazil would not cost Portugal any money at all!

John III carved all the immense territory of Brazil into only 15 captaincies. These grants of land were enormous. Each was as large as a small country. The Portuguese crown provided little overall control, and each captaincy functioned almost as a separate country.

Only two captaincies had success — Pernambuco (pur num BYOO koh) in the northeast and São Vicente to the south, near the present-day city of Santos. In both cases, trade in brazilwood and the development of a sugar industry made them profitable.

A New Policy The obvious failure of the captaincies led to a new policy. John III appointed a governor-general who was to oversee all the individual territories. This man, Tomé de Sousa (toh MAY day SOO-suh), had served as a soldier in both India and Africa. In 1549, with a fleet of six ships carrying around 1,000 people, he arrived in Bahia (buh HEE uh), today called Salvador. Bahia, with its fine harbor, became Brazil's first capital. Tomé de Sousa enjoyed great success. At last Brazil would have effective settlement.

C. A Challenge from the Dutch

In 1580 the countries of Spain and Portugal were joined under the rule of Philip II of Spain. For the Brazilians, that meant trouble. They had to stop trading with the Dutch, an enemy of Spain. Dutch ships had carried most of Brazil's sugar to the European markets.

The Dutch tried to get back into the sugar trade by attacking Brazil. It took them many years. Finally, in 1630, they captured important sugar-producing areas near the city of Recife, on the northeastern coast of Brazil.

While the Dutch were in Brazil, they improved the way in which sugarcane was grown. Production and profits increased. Recife became a prosperous commercial center. The Portuguese colonists, however, did not benefit much. The Dutch sent the profits they made back to the Netherlands. Furthermore, they caused the Portuguese colonists added worry by trying to introduce Protestant Christianity in Brazil. The Portuguese colonists feared that it would replace their Catholic religion.

In 1641 the Portuguese colonists rebelled. By 1654 they had reclaimed all of Brazil for Portugal. The Dutch left for the West Indies, taking with them their knowledge of the sugarcane business.

D. Strength of the Economy

You remember that at first Brazil seemed to offer little of value except for the dyewood. Sugar changed the **economy**. The economy is the production and management of resources.

The Portuguese had brought sugarcane to Brazil. It grew well in the coastal lands. As in the Caribbean islands, there were few Indians to help harvest and mill the cane. Because of that, blacks were brought from Africa to help develop the sugarcane business in Brazil.

At first, only a few thousand colonists and African slaves lived in Brazil. By the end of the eighteenth century, there were hundreds of thousands of colonists and slaves in the Portuguese colony.

At the entrance to the huge Ibirapuera Park in São Paulo, there is a monument in tribute to the pioneers who settled Brazil. It is 165 feet (50 m) long. Known as the Pioneer's Monument, it is sometimes called "Don't Push."
▶ Why would people use a nickname for a serious piece of sculpture?

From 1550 to 1650, Brazil provided almost all of the sugar Europe needed. Later, the Dutch changed that when they began growing sugar in the Caribbean after being driven from Brazil. Portugal received more profit from sugar than from all of its Asian and Indian trade. Brazil also had other riches. Tobacco and cotton grew well there, and good grazing lands supported a growing cattle industry. Most of these activities, especially the rich sugar industry, took place in northeastern Brazil.

E. Brazil's Golden Century

The colonists in the southern part of Brazil were poor. They were too far from markets to grow sugarcane for profit, and they had found no other way to get rich. Many of them continued the search for wealth by exploring the interior of the continent. The people who went on these expeditions were called **bandeirantes** (bahn day ee RAHN tes). Most of them came from São Paulo, then a small village but now Brazil's largest city in population.

At first the bandeirantes raided missions where Indians had been taken to live and work. They captured the defenseless Indians and sold them as slaves. As they went farther into the center of Brazil, the bandeirantes pushed the edges of the Portuguese colony into Spanish America.

The bandeirantes had their greatest success in 1698, when they discovered gold in a province that was later named Minas Gerais (MEE nus zhuh RYS). *Minas Gerais* is Portuguese for "general mines." This discovery set off a gold rush that led to the settlement of central Brazil. The gold boom lasted for nearly 100 years. It was because of the gold rush that Rio de Janeiro, the port nearest to the goldfields, became the new capital of Brazil in 1763.

Both fazenda owners and wealthy Brazilian individuals owned slaves.
▶ Compare the number of slaves shown in these two paintings.

F. Large Estates and Slavery

Like the Spanish colonies, Brazil also had great estates. There they were called **fazendas** (fuh ZEN duz). The estate owner was called a *fazendeiro*. The richest fazendeiros enjoyed enormous power. They lived in fine houses and controlled the lives of many relatives and workers. A fazendeiro's influence reached beyond his estate to nearby villages and towns. Local government officials could not go against the fazendeiro's wishes. They depended on his good will. Besides, the royal officials were far away, but the fazendeiro lived close by. Many loyal followers would obey his orders rather than the law.

Unlike most of the Spanish colonies, Brazil had a very large number of slaves. Over 2 million Africans entered Brazil as slaves during the colonial period. Africans

The Granger Collection

influenced Brazilian culture in many areas, including food, religion, and folklore. They labored not only on the fazendas but also in mines and cattle ranches. They provided much of Brazil's labor.

One Portuguese priest of the seventeenth-century, Father António Vieira (an-TOH nee oh vee AY ee ruh), criticized slavery with these words in one of his sermons.

> *Few masters, many slaves. Masters richly dressed, slaves despised and naked. Masters banqueting, slaves dying of hunger. Masters swimming in gold and silver, slaves loaded down with irons.*

Slavery in Brazil continued throughout the colonial period. In fact, slavery lasted until almost the end of the nineteenth century.

LESSON 4 REVIEW

THINK AND WRITE

A. Why did Portugal think Brazil was unimportant?

B. How did John III try to colonize Brazil?

C. Why were the Dutch interested in Brazil?

D. Name five industries that were important to Brazil's economy in colonial times.

E. How did the discovery of gold affect Brazil?

F. Summarize what the fazendas were like.

SKILLS CHECK

WRITING SKILL

Use the Gazetteer to find one important way in which São Vicente, Rio de Janeiro, and Salvador are alike. Also find one important fact that mentions dates. Then write an explanatory paragraph that begins by telling how the three cities are alike. Continue your paragraph by telling how each one is unique.

6 PUTTING IT ALL TOGETHER

USING THE VOCABULARY

encomienda	peninsular
monopoly	Creole
privateers	captaincy
hacienda	economy
debt peonage	bandeirantes

On a separate sheet of paper, write the word or words from above that best complete the sentences.

1. A group of Indians entrusted to Spaniards for their protection was called an _____.
2. When a country keeps complete control over the trade of one of its colonies, it has a _____.
3. "Legal" pirates who attacked Spanish trading ships were known as _____.
4. A _____ was a large estate in the Spanish colonies of America.
5. The production and management of a country's resources is called its _____.
6. A _____ was a person of Spanish descent who was born in one of the colonies.
7. _____ is a system that results when laborers owe money to their employers.
8. The colonists who explored the interior of Brazil were called _____.
9. A colonist who had been born in Spain was called a _____.
10. A _____ was a large grant of land in Brazil given by the king of Portugal to a colonist who promised to send more settlers there.

REMEMBERING WHAT YOU READ

On a separate sheet of paper, answer the following questions in complete sentences.

1. Whom did Spain appoint to take away power from the conquistadors in the New World?
2. What two buildings were always found in the town plazas of Latin America?
3. How did Spain control the trade of its colonies?
4. Why was it dangerous for single trading ships or even small groups to sail for Spain?
5. Why did the Portobelo fair last so long?
6. Why couldn't Spain defend its colonies in the Caribbean?
7. Why were African slaves imported to the Americas?
8. Which class of people held the most power in colonial Spanish America?
9. What crop raised Brazil's economy?
10. How did the discovery of gold change Brazil?

TYING ART TO SOCIAL STUDIES

Work with a group of classmates to create a mural showing life on a hacienda or a fazenda. Review the chapter and its illustrations for details about the different groups of people, the buildings, and the activities on these estates. You may also need to do some research on this topic. List your ideas for the mural and develop a plan with your group. Then sketch the mural in pencil on a large sheet of white paper. Finally, paint or color the mural and present it to your class.

THINKING CRITICALLY

On a separate sheet of paper, answer the following questions in complete sentences.

1. In your opinion, were the Indians better off than slaves under the encomienda system?
2. What were the results of the rivalry that England and Spain had over the wealth of the colonies?
3. How might have the governments of Spain and Portugal assigned land ownership in Latin America fairly?
4. How did the sugar plantations change life in the Spanish and Portuguese colonies?
5. Why did Brazil develop more slowly than the Spanish colonies?

SUMMARIZING THE CHAPTER

On a separate sheet of paper, draw a graphic organizer like the one shown here. Copy the information from this graphic organizer to the one you have drawn. On each blank line, write some facts about the subject mentioned that you learned from the chapter.

CHAPTER THEME	The colonization of Latin America created a whole new social order and way of life.
LESSON 1 **The viceroys take over the governing of the colonies.**	1. _____ 2. _____ 3. _____
LESSON 2 **Spain tries to control trade with the colonies but has problems.**	1. _____ 2. _____ 3. _____
LESSON 3 **Life in colonial Latin America becomes different for each social class.**	1. _____ 2. _____ 3. _____ 4. _____
LESSON 4 **Brazil develops more slowly than the colonies of Spain**	1. _____ 2. _____ 3. _____ 4. _____

CHAPTER 7

INDEPENDENCE COMES TO LATIN AMERICA

Latin America gained its independence as a result of several separate movements which differed from one another in important ways. A number of bold leaders and their followers contributed to these heroic efforts.

The Latin American Struggle

THINK ABOUT WHAT YOU KNOW

At some time you may have thought about being grown up and living on your own instead of being dependent on your parents. List some of the advantages and disadvantages of being independent.

STUDY THE VOCABULARY

revolt   opposition
revolution   revolutionist
depose

FOCUS YOUR READING

What triggered the Latin American movement for independence?

A. Napoleon's Invasion of Spain

For 300 years, Spain and Portugal held their colonies in the Americas. As the nineteenth century began, those colonies were enjoying considerable success. Even so, during the first two or three decades of the century, **revolts** broke out throughout Latin America. A revolt is an act of rising up, or rebelling, against the government. A **revolution** is a complete change or the overthrow of a government. By 1825, Spain had lost all its American possessions except Cuba and Puerto Rico. Brazil had written its first constitution.

What accounts for that change? One way of finding an answer is to look for a spark—that is, some special event that really stirred things up. For Latin America, that spark was Napoleon's invasion of the Iberian Peninsula.

Napoleon Bonaparte (BOH nuh-pahrt) came to power in France in 1801. In 1808, the French army occupied Madrid,

the capital of Spain, and took control of the Spanish government. Napoleon **deposed**, or removed, the Spanish king and made his own brother Joseph the new ruler. Were the colonists in Latin America willing to obey that foreign king?

The Spanish colonists' answer was a resounding "No!" They declared their loyalty to Ferdinand VII, the deposed monarch, and they revolted against Joseph. That meant that for the first time in three centuries, they had to take complete charge of their own affairs. By the time the rightful monarch was back on the throne, many colonists had experienced independence. They wanted to keep their independence, so they continued in revolt. This time, it was against the Spanish king.

Spanish colonists in Latin America protest the removal of the king from the throne of Spain.
▶ Explain the words on the sign.

B. Factors Leading to Independence

Resentment developed in the colonies. The Creoles, the American-born Spanish colonists, were the **opposition** to Joseph Bonaparte, the king of Spain. The opposition is the group of people who disagree with the group in power. The Spanish-born peninsulars still had the best jobs and the highest places in society. They remained loyal to the new king because their favored positions in society now depended on him.

The Creoles felt they deserved what the peninsulars had. They saw an opportunity to get back at the peninsulars. The split between Creoles and peninsulars was not something new. The break had developed over a long period of time. There were other such causes in Latin America.

People in the colonies were unhappy because Spain was profiting from their resources. The colonists themselves wanted the money from their mines and farms. Why should the resources of the Americas go to Spain when the colonists could use them?

Other Revolutions After Britain's North American colonies rebelled in 1775, some people in Spain's colonies heard about it and met with Thomas Jefferson, Benjamin Franklin, and other United States **revolutionists**. A revolutionist is someone who is in favor of, and even takes part in, a revolt.

Some years later, France had a revolt. Its slogan was Liberty, Equality, Fraternity. Revolutionary France issued its Declaration of the Rights of Man and of the Citizen. When Napoleon took power in 1799 in France, the French Revolution ended, but

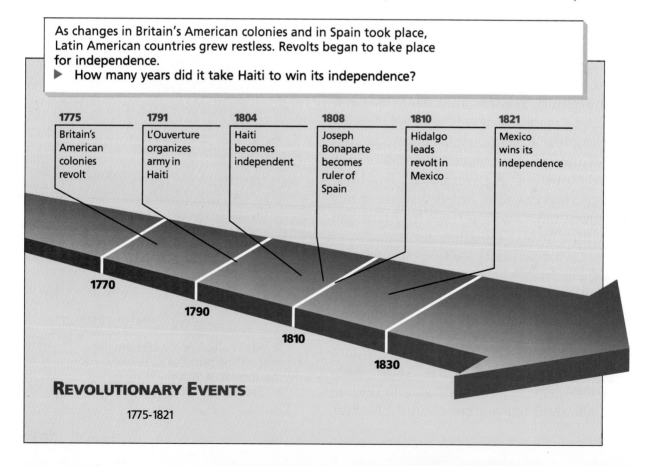

As changes in Britain's American colonies and in Spain took place, Latin American countries grew restless. Revolts began to take place for independence.
▶ How many years did it take Haiti to win its independence?

1775 Britain's American colonies revolt

1791 L'Ouverture organizes army in Haiti

1804 Haiti becomes independent

1808 Joseph Bonaparte becomes ruler of Spain

1810 Hidalgo leads revolt in Mexico

1821 Mexico wins its independence

1770

1790

1810

1830

REVOLUTIONARY EVENTS
1775–1821

its ideas did not. In fact, one Creole in Latin America translated the French Declaration into Spanish. For that, the Spaniards put him in prison.

C. Revolt in Haiti

An Independent Colony After the French Revolution, one of the first things the new French government did was to outlaw slavery in all French colonies. In St. Domingue, now Haiti, the black slaves outnumbered the planters by about 20 to 1. The slaves began to leave the plantations. Some formed outlaw bands that raided and burned towns and farms.

In 1791, Toussaint L'Ouverture (tou-SAN loo ver TOOR) organized outlaw bands into a revolutionary army. A former slave and the grandson of an African king, Toussaint was a natural leader and military commander. The rebellion went on for

In 1791, slaves in St. Domingue revolt against their French rulers. Toussaint L'Ouverture (bottom), led the successful revolution.
▶ Describe the battle scene.

ten years. In 1801, the revolutionary army controlled the entire island of Hispaniola.

Napoleon sent a large army to put down the rebellion. The fighting was fierce, but gradually the French controlled the island. Toussaint was tricked into surrendering. He was put in a French prison, where he died in 1803. The rebels kept on fighting. At the same time, yellow fever killed over 50,000 in the French army. The rebels were victorious. In 1804 the former colony, under its new name, Haiti, became the first independent nation in Latin America.

D. Several Separate Wars

When other Latin Americans rose in revolt, they did not create just one revolt. Instead, three separate wars occurred. You will read about them in the next lessons.

One such war took place in Mexico, one in northern South America, and one in the southern part of South America. Latin America as a whole did not have one general who played the role George Washington played in the United States. It did not have one authority directing the wars.

Each of the three areas had a different experience. In some places, independence came relatively easy. In others, it involved long and bloody struggles.

La Citadelle Laferriere, a mountaintop fort, was built by Haiti's King Henri Christophe.
▶ How might a fort be used?

In some cases, these wars were also struggles over who should rule once independence was achieved. So wars for independence also became civil wars.

LESSON *1* REVIEW

THINK AND WRITE

A. How did Napoleon's invasion of Spain affect the colonies?
B. What were some of the factors that led to independence in Latin America?
C. How did Haiti achieve independence?
D. What other independence movements were there in Latin America?

SKILLS CHECK

WRITING SKILL

There is a proverb that says, "The wish is father to the thought." Use this proverb as the title for a paragraph. In your paragraph tell how this proverb applies to an event or a revolt described in this lesson.

Independence for Mexico

THINK ABOUT WHAT YOU KNOW
Think about religious leaders you know or have heard about. What reasons might cause such leaders to be spokespersons for independence?

STUDY THE VOCABULARY
guerrilla

FOCUS YOUR READING
Who were the leaders of Mexico's independence movement?

A. The Grito de Dolores

A Leader for Independence "Down with bad government. Death to the Spaniards!" Known as the Grito de Dolores (GREE toh day doh LOH rays), which means the "Cry of Dolores," these words became the battle cry of the Mexican independence movement. The words were spoken by Father Miguel Hidalgo (mee-GEL hih DAL goh), the priest of the small village of Dolores. The date was September 16, 1810. Each year on September 16, the people throughout Mexico celebrate Independence Day.

Born in 1753 in Mexico to a middle-class Creole family, young Miguel grew up on a hacienda where his father was the resident manager. At the age of 24, he received his degree from the University of Mexico and four years later was ordained as a priest.

In 1803, Father Hidalgo went to Dolores. There, he tried to improve the lives of the poor mestizos and Indians of the village. There, too, he met a man who invited him to join a book club. This club did not discuss literature. It plotted revolution.

School children look at Diego Rivera's mural of Father Hidalgo rallying his followers in Dolores.
► What is Hidalgo holding?

The government learned of the plan. It moved quickly to arrest the club members. Hidalgo and other leaders received word that the government had searched the house of one of the group's members and found guns and ammunition. Was everything lost? Should they run away? Instead of fleeing, they began a revolt.

Hidalgo called the people of Dolores together at the church. The assembled group of Indians and mestizos listened as their priest asked, "Will you free yourselves? Will you recover the lands stolen 300 years ago from your forefathers by the hated Spaniards?" Then they cheered loudly as he concluded the meeting with the thrilling words of the Grito de Dolores.

B. The End of Hidalgo's Revolt

Father Hidalgo's cry set off a great response among the poor people. Soon he had a large army, perhaps as many as 50,000 people. The army was made up not of trained soldiers but of men, women, and even children. Most were Indians and mestizos. Many had no weapons except their farm tools and their great anger. They were willing to fight.

At first they were able to defeat the weak Spanish army. They killed any Spaniard they found. They robbed farms and towns. Hidalgo could not stop them. All he could do was keep his forces in motion as news of the rebellion spread throughout Mexico.

Father Miguel Hidalgo (left) led the first revolt against the Spanish in Mexico. José María Morelos continued the fight.
▶ Who were Father Hidalgo's followers?

This 1834 painting shows Father Hidalgo (left) crowning Mexico and breaking the chains binding Mexico to Spain.
▶ What symbol does the artist use for Mexico?

The Creoles might have joined in the rebellion, but they were too frightened to do so. After all, Hidalgo's followers had reason to dislike them as well. The Creoles didn't want the lower class to gain control, so they supported the Spanish army.

As the Spaniards began to gain strength, many people simply left Hidalgo's army and went back home to their farms. Remember, they were poor people, and if they did not tend to their crops, they might have nothing to eat during the coming year. So Hidalgo's army grew smaller and weaker.

In 1811, Hidalgo was captured, convicted of treason, and executed by a firing squad. Although Hidalgo had failed to free Mexico, the country honors the courageous priest as its first revolutionary hero.

C. José María Morelos

The fight that was begun by Hidalgo continued. Another priest, José María Morelos (moh RAY lohs), came to lead the rebellion. Father Morelos, a mestizo, organized and trained an army. By 1813, he controlled most of southern Mexico.

Morelos called a congress to meet in November of that year. Morelos spoke of the Aztecs and of Cuauhtémoc's valiant defense of Tenochtitlán.

The group declared Mexico independent and wrote a constitution for the new country, but the Spanish army kept on fighting. By 1815 it had defeated the rebel army and captured Morelos. Like Hidalgo before him, he was convicted of treason and executed by the Spaniards.

With those first leaders dead, the

These soldiers are marching in an Independence Day parade being celebrated in Mexico City.
▶ On what day is it celebrated?

struggle for independence was carried on by small bands of **guerrillas** (guh RIHL-uz). Guerrillas are groups of fighters who are not usually part of a regular army. They fight on their own. Five years after the death of Morelos, only two guerrilla bands remained to oppose the Spaniards, and together they had only 3,000 men.

D. Iturbide Changes Sides

In 1821, Agustín de Iturbide (ah goos-TEEN day ee toor BEE day), a colonel who commanded the Spanish army in southern Mexico, decided to join the rebels. Iturbide then drew up a plan for Mexican independence. It was called the Plan de Iguala (ih GWAHL uh), after the town where it was proclaimed. In the plan,

the rebels promised to support the Roman Catholic Church. They also promised to fight for equal rights for all citizens, whether they were born in Mexico or in Spain.

Instead of criticizing Spain, Iturbide praised that country for all it had given Mexico. So, unlike the revolts of Hidalgo and Morelos, Iturbide's movement did not frighten the Creoles and the Spaniards. In fact, many Spanish and Creole officers joined Iturbide in the fight for Mexico's independence.

The rebels defeated the remaining Spanish troops within a year. Iturbide's victorious army entered Mexico City. After 11 years of fighting, Mexico had become an independent nation.

LESSON *2* REVIEW

THINK AND WRITE

A. Why do Mexicans celebrate September 16 as their Independence Day?
B. Why did Hidalgo's revolt fail?
C. How were the revolts of Morelos and Hidalgo similar?
D. Why did many Creoles and Spaniards support Iturbide?

SKILLS CHECK

THINKING SKILL

As you have read, Father Hidalgo is honored as one of Mexico's first revolutionary heroes. Compare and contrast Hidalgo to George Washington, one of America's first revolutionary heroes.

Independence for South America

THINK ABOUT WHAT YOU KNOW

Look at a relief map of South America. What physical features might have made it difficult for an army to march from one part of the continent to another part to help in the fight for independence?

STUDY THE VOCABULARY

liberate   Llanos
llanero   diplomat

FOCUS YOUR READING

Why is Simón Bolívar known as the great Liberator?

A. Francisco de Miranda

Just about the same time that Hidalgo's revolt ended in Mexico, the fight for Venezuela's independence began. Its leader, Francisco de Miranda (mee RAHN-dah) had already led an interesting and unusual life. Born in 1750 of Spanish parents in Caracas, Venezuela, Miranda became an officer in the Spanish army. Later he held the rank of general in the army of France. During a long stay in London, Miranda plotted revolution in Latin America and spoke about putting an Inca noble at the head of a great nation in South America. He also visited the United States, where he met many of that country's revolutionary leaders.

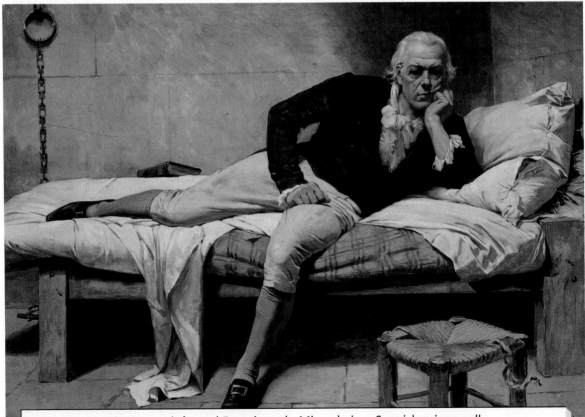

This painting depicts a defeated Francisco de Miranda in a Spanish prison cell, shortly before his death in 1816.
▶ What do you think is on Miranda's mind?

Arturo Michelena, *Miranda En La Carraca,* 1986, Galeria de Arte Nacional, Caracas. Photo: Petre Maxim.

Simón Bolívar points the way for his soldiers over the rugged snow-capped Andes Mountains.
▶ What country is named for Bolívar?

B. Bolívar, the Great Liberator

After Miranda's capture, Simón Bolívar (see MAWN boh LEE vahr) took command of the struggle. Bolívar became the most famous and successful leader of all in the fight for independence throughout Latin America.

Bolívar was born into a rich Venezuelan Creole family in 1783. His parents died when he was very young, and Bolívar was cared for by his mother's family. Because Bolívar was not doing well with his studies, he was placed in the care of a servant who became his greatest teacher as well as a "big brother." At the age of 16, he went to Spain, where he lived for three years. At the age of 19, he married the daughter of a Spanish nobleman and took his new wife back to Venezuela. Bolívar's wife died less than a year after they were married.

When his wife died, Bolívar tried to forget his sorrow by returning to Europe. He visited France, where he saw the results of the French Revolution. Bolívar vowed to liberate his country.

He returned to Venezuela and was one of the people who asked Francisco Miranda to lead the fight for independence. After Miranda's capture, Bolívar fled to Colombia, which was then a part of the viceroyalty of New Granada. He returned to Venezuela in 1813 at the head of an army and took Caracas, the capital, from the Spaniards.

The next year, a newly strengthened Spanish army forced Bolívar to flee once more. He tried, without success, to invade Venezuela again in 1816.

In 1817, Bolívar gained the support of an important man, José Antonio Páez (PAH ays). He was a **llanero** (lyah NAYroh), or cowhand, from the **Llanos**, or plains, of Venezuela. With the help of Páez

In 1806, Miranda sailed from the United States in a small ship with a little army and attempted to **liberate**, or free, Venezuela. Finding little support from the people, he fled to England.

Two years later, after Napoleon had deposed the Spanish king, the Venezuelans were more willing to think about rebelling against Spain. In 1810, at the age of 60, Miranda was called back to lead the revolutionary army. Miranda and his followers began the fight for Venezuela's independence from Spain the following year.

Unfortunately, Miranda was not a strong military leader. The Spanish army fought so hard that Miranda feared a major defeat. He surrendered his army in 1812 and tried to escape but was captured. He died in a Spanish prison in 1816.

and the llaneros, Bolívar at last began a successful war for independence. By 1819 the rebels had defeated the main Spanish force in Venezuela.

C. Triumphant Rebels

The Battle of Boyacá Bogotá was the capital of the viceroyalty of New Granada. Bolívar's army met the Spaniards at a place called Boyacá (boi yuh KAH), about 60 miles (97 km) north of Bogotá. To get there, Bolívar and his army of 3,000 men had to pass through an extremely cold wilderness, climb high into the Andes, and cross icy mountain passes 2 miles (3 km) above sea level.

Most of the army's horses died on that march, and many of Bolívar's men became ill. Even so, after some days of rest, they defeated the Spanish army at the battle of Boyacá in August of 1819. It was the most important battle in the struggle for independence in northern South America. It liberated most of New Granada, in the area that is now Colombia.

The Battle of Carabobo The victorious Bolívar, officially proclaimed as the Liberator of New Granada, returned to Venezuela in 1820. There, he organized three divisions with a total of 6,500 foot soldiers and cavalries in preparation for another attack around the town of Carabobo. Bolívar had successfully won a battle there some years earlier, and he knew the area well. On June 24, 1821, Bolívar's army defeated the last sizable Spanish army in Venezuela. This battle assured the independence of Venezuela.

With both Colombia and Venezuela secured, Bolívar turned his attention to Ecuador, which was also part of New Granada. It was freed with little fighting in 1822. Now all of northern South America had gained independence from Spain!

The battle at Carabobo was a great victory for Simón Bolívar. It marked the end of Spanish rule in Venezuela.
▶ What weapons are being used?

WHAT MAKES A PERSON GREAT?

Some people call a person great because he or she changed the world — by making a discovery that benefited humankind or by leading people through a crisis such as war, revolution, or disaster. Others call people great whose art, music, literature, or teachings inspire us and ignite our imaginations.

Simón Bolívar, the Liberator of South America, has been called great by many historians. All the persons described in the following paragraphs have been called great by some people. Which of their achievements add up to greatness? Read about each of them and decide for yourself.

Zora Neale Hurston

She was a writer in the 1920s and 1930s whose work has become popular today. In addition to writing her own stories and novels, she was an anthropologist (a scientist who studies human cultures) who collected folk tales from the American South and from Jamaica and Haiti. Hurston also studied and wrote about the Maya cultures of Middle America.

José Batlle y Ordóñez

Batlle was the president of Uruguay from 1903 to 1907 and 1911 to 1915. He was hailed as a great leader and a man of vision who made Uruguay into a peaceful and prosperous model democracy. Batlle sponsored many laws that helped his people — laws such as old-age, workers' pension, and minimum wage laws and laws to improve public health and education services.

Gabriela Mistral

Gabriela Mistral is the pen name of a Chilean poet who won the Nobel Prize for literature in 1945. She was the first Latin American to receive this honor. Once a rural school teacher, she came to have great influence over the whole educational system of Chile. In her later years, she was a diplomat for her country.

Gabriela Mistral

Langston Hughes

An American poet, short story writer, and playwright, Langston Hughes translated Gabriela Mistral's poems into English. Hughes also translated the works of Mexican, Cuban, and Haitian authors for American readers. One of America's best-known writers, Hughes won the Spingarn Medal given by the NAACP in 1960 for his contribution to African American culture.

Carlos Juan Finlay

This Cuban doctor at the turn of the century saw yellow fever weaken and kill thousands of people living in the tropics. He was the first to pinpoint the cause of this feared disease: a virus transmitted by a certain kind of mosquito. Yellow fever had previously halted work on the Panama Canal. After widespread destruction of the mosquitoes, workers were able to complete the project.

Thinking for Yourself

On a separate sheet of paper, answer the following questions in complete sentences.

1. Which of these people would you consider the greatest? Explain why you think so.
2. Which person or persons would you like to know more about? Give some reasons for your interest.
3. Name a person living today whom you would include in a list of great people. Why do you consider that person to be great?

Carlos Juan Finlay

The Granger Collection

Langston Hughes

D. Revolt in Argentina

On May 25, 1810, the people of Buenos Aires rebelled against Napoleon's rule in Spain. They declared their loyalty to Ferdinand VII, the deposed king of Spain. The city did not really become independent on that day. Yet even now, May 25 is celebrated as Argentina's Independence Day.

Buenos Aires was the capital of the viceroyalty of La Plata. That viceroyalty had many provinces. They included areas that later became parts of Argentina, Bolivia, Paraguay, and Uruguay.

The main influence for the rebellion came from Mariano Moreno. He had much in common with Benjamin Franklin of the United States. Like Franklin, Moreno had a newspaper in which he promoted his ideas. He started a national library and organized a census bureau. He argued for ideas that Franklin would have liked, such as personal freedom, a free press, and national independence.

Despite his good works, Moreno had many enemies. They forced him to resign from the ruling council of Buenos Aires. Even so, his enemies named him to Great Britain as a **diplomat**. A diplomat is someone who represents the government in important dealings with other nations. Moreno died at sea in 1811, before reaching Britain.

The people of the city of Buenos Aires tried to unite the provinces of La Plata under their control. In 1813 they gave those lands the name *United Provinces of La Plata*. In 1816 the United Provinces of La Plata declared independence from Spain, but the Argentine army still had to defeat the Spanish army. That was done under the leadership of José de San Martín (sahn mahr TEEN).

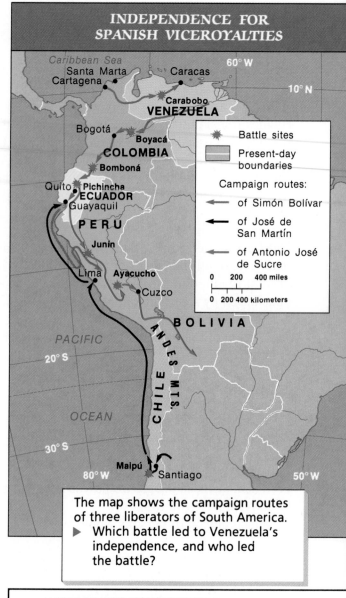

INDEPENDENCE FOR SPANISH VICEROYALTIES

Battle sites
Present-day boundaries
Campaign routes:
of Simón Bolívar
of José de San Martín
of Antonio José de Sucre

0 200 400 miles
0 200 400 kilometers

The map shows the campaign routes of three liberators of South America.
▶ Which battle led to Venezuela's independence, and who led the battle?

BATTLES FOR INDEPENDENCE

Battle of Maipú
San Martín liberates Chile, 1818.

Battle of Boyacá, 1819
Bolívar liberates Colombia.

Battle of Carabobo, 1821
Bolívar liberates Venezuela.

San Martín captures Lima, Peru, 1821.

Battle of Pichincha, 1822
Sucre and Bolívar liberate Ecuador.

Battle of Ayacucho, 1824
Bolívar and Sucre liberate Peru.

José de San Martín (left) leads his army through the Andes Mountains to fight the Spanish in Chile.
► What made this a hard trip?

E. San Martín, Liberator of the South

The Daring Andes Crossing José de San Martín was born in Argentina in 1778. He went to Spain as a child. He became a soldier and earned a high rank in the Spanish army. In 1812 he went to Buenos Aires, where he offered to help fight for independence in South America.

In 1814, San Martín was appointed head of the rebel army. He later resigned and was made governor of Cuyo (KOO-yoh), a province near the Uspallata Pass, the main pass over the Andes.

Actually, San Martín had a plan to defeat the Spaniards. The plan was to cross the Andes by way of the Uspallata Pass and help the Chileans become free. The Chileans then would help him drive the Spanish forces from Peru. This was a daring plan. The trail over the Andes was steep and rugged. At high elevations it is cold and windy, and there is little oxygen in the air.

By early 1817, San Martín had trained an army and was ready to march with 10,600 mules, 1,600 horses, and 700 head of cattle. Bernardo O'Higgins, a Chilean revolutionary leader, and his troops joined San Martín's army. The crossing of the high, rugged Andes was one of the most difficult feats in military history.

Using block and tackle, the army hoisted cannons up the steep slopes. Many soldiers suffered from a sickness caused by the lack of oxygen. This is commonly called altitude sickness. Fortunately, few soldiers died, but the animals fared very poorly. By the time the expedition reached Chile, over half the mules and around two thirds of the horses had died. Those that survived were near death.

San Martín's bold move across the Andes allowed him to surprise the Spanish army in Chile. He defeated the Spaniards and took Santiago, the capital of Chile. When the remaining Spanish troops were defeated, Chile became independent.

The Battle of Ayacucho, led by Sucre, freed Peru from Spain.
▶ What problems did soldiers fighting in the mountains face?

San Martín spent most of the next two years bringing together enough ships to move his army to Lima. He reached Lima, Peru, in 1821. The people of the city decided in favor of independence from Spain. They welcomed the rebel army. San Martín controlled Lima, but the Spanish forces still ruled the rest of the country.

F. The End of Spanish Power

Bolívar and San Martín, the two great generals of independence, met in Guayaquil, in present-day Ecuador, on July 26 and 27, 1822. The details of that meeting are not clear, but San Martín soon withdrew from Peru and later went to Europe. Bolívar remained to complete the liberation of South America.

Bolívar's army went to Peru in 1823. By that time his revolutionaries had become experienced soldiers. The Spanish forces were no match for Bolívar. The first victory was fought with only lances and sabers by Bolívar's cavalry against a large Spanish cavalry. Several months later, Bolívar turned command of the army over to a trusted lieutenant, a Venezuelan named Antonio José de Sucre (SOO kray). Bolívar also continued in the fight along with an army of Colombians and Venezuelans.

Sucre led the rebels in the battle of Ayacucho (ah yah KOO choh). It was the final battle to free Peru. Sucre's rebels attacked and defeated a much larger force of Spaniards and loyal Creoles in a violent battle in December of 1824. Bolívar and his forces received much praise.

By the beginning of 1825, only one part of South America was still under Spanish control. That was the area called Alto Peru. Soon Sucre's troops defeated the last Spaniards there, and the independence of South America was complete.

A MESSAGE FROM BOLÍVAR

The great Liberator did not have a happy end. Although South America became independent, Bolívar's dream of a great unified nation failed. In September of 1830, Gran Colombia broke up into the nations of Ecuador, Colombia, and Venezuela. By that time, Bolívar, disillusioned with political struggles, had decided to leave Colombia. He planned to sail to Europe. But he did not live long enough to make that trip. Sick from a disease of the lungs called tuberculosis, he died on December 17, 1830. That very month, knowing he was near death, he gave a final message to the people of Colombia.

> You have witnessed my efforts to establish liberty where tyranny once reigned. I have labored unselfishly, sacrificing my fortune and my peace of mind. My enemies have played upon your credulity [readiness to believe, even without proof] and destroyed what I hold most sacred — my reputation and my love of liberty.

> As I depart from your midst, my love [for you] tells me that I should make known my last wishes. You must all work for the supreme good of a united nation: the people, by obeying the present government in order to rid themselves of anarchy; the ministers, from their sanctuary, by addressing their supplications to Heaven; and the military, by unsheathing the sword to defend the guarantees of organized government.

> Colombians! My last wishes are for the happiness of our native land. If my death will help to end party strife and to promote national unity, I shall go to my grave in peace.

Understanding Source Material

1. Why was Bolívar unhappy?
2. What did he say he tried to accomplish?
3. What did he think was needed for Colombia to be successful?

Dom Pedro I, the son of King John of Portugal, ruled Brazil from 1821 to 1831.

▶ How did the artist show that Pedro was an emperor?

G. Brazil's Different Road

Napoleon Bonaparte, who had provided the spark for independence in Spain's colonies, was even more directly responsible for the independence of Portugal's colony of Brazil. Napoleon's army invaded Portugal in 1807. As the French army neared the capital city of Lisbon, the Portuguese royal family fled to Brazil. They took with them the entire royal court —some 1,000 people—and the gold and jewels of the royal treasury. Nearly 50 ships were needed to carry all the people and their belongings!

The court went to Rio de Janeiro, Brazil, and Rio became the capital of the Portuguese empire. Brazil itself officially received the rank of kingdom. That meant it was equal to Portugal. Rio de Janeiro remained the capital for 14 years.

When the threat from Napoleon ended, the Portuguese king and his court moved back to Portugal. That was in 1821. His son Pedro stayed behind to govern the colony. Many Brazilians did not want to return to being merely a colony. Besides, Brazil was so big, and Portugal was just a tiny country. As one Brazilian leader remarked, Portugal seemed to treat Brazil "as if we were a handful of miserable slaves," even though Brazil "was more powerful with more resources than Portugal."

Then, in 1822, the Portuguese government demanded that Pedro return to Portugal. He refused. When the Portuguese troops in Rio de Janeiro prepared to force Pedro to leave, they found no support among the Brazilian people and militia of the city. Instead, the troops were forced to leave! Brazil then became independent, with Pedro as its emperor.

LESSON **3** REVIEW

THINK AND WRITE

A. How did the first attempt to gain independence in South America turn out?

B. How would you describe Bolívar, the revolutionary leader?

C. Why do we remember the battle of Carabobo?

D. How did independence begin in Argentina?

E. Why did San Martín want to liberate Chile?

F. Whose army fought the final battle for independence in South America?

G. How did Napoleon Bonaparte influence Brazilian independence?

SKILLS CHECK

In this lesson, you read about some South American leaders for independence. What adjectives would you select to describe each leader?

USING THE VOCABULARY

revolts	diplomat
opposition	Llanos
guerillas	depose
revolutionist	llanero
revolution	liberated

On a separate sheet of paper, write the word from the list above that best completes the sentence.

1. Toussaint L'Ouverture was a _____ who helped make Haiti an independent nation.
2. _____ are soldiers who are not members of a regular army.
3. New Granada was _____, or freed, from Spain in 1819.
4. Napoleon Bonaparte decided to _____, or get rid of, the Spanish king in 1808 and make his brother ruler.
5. Latin America's history is filled with many _____ against the government.
6. "Cry of Dolores" was the battle cry of the peasants during the Mexican _____.
7. A _____ does the same job in Venezuela as the cowboy does in the United States.
8. The _____ are the plains of Venezuela where cattle graze.
9. The rebels faced _____ from those citizens loyal to the present government.
10. A _____ represents his or her country to the government of another nation.

REMEMBERING WHAT YOU READ

On a separate sheet of paper, answer the following questions in complete sentences.

1. Who was Napoleon Bonaparte?
2. By what year were most Latin American countries independent?
3. Name the chief way independence was achieved in Latin America.
4. Who helped Toussaint L'Ouverture win independence for Haiti?
5. What was Father Hidalgo's role in the fight for Mexican independence?
6. Which of the colonies were liberated by Simón Bolívar?
7. How was Mariano Moreno of Argentina much like Benjamin Franklin?
8. Who was the liberator of the southern part of South America?
9. In what year did Brazil finally become independent?
10. Why did the Brazilians want to be free of Portugal?

TYING LANGUAGE ARTS TO SOCIAL STUDIES

Imagine that you are the editor of an American newspaper in the early 1800s. Form your opinion of one of the struggles for independence described in this chapter. Write your opinion in an editorial.

Thinking Critically

On a separate sheet of paper, answer the following questions in complete sentences.

1. How might Toussaint L'Ouverture, the revolutionary leader in Haiti, have been influenced by the American Revolution?
2. Why did Iturbide's revolt succeed in gaining independence for Mexico when other revolts, such as those of Hidalgo and Morelos, failed?
3. What conditions lead people to revolt against their government?
4. Why do native soldiers have an advantage when they fight a foreign army in their native land rather than in the foreigner's land?
5. Tell why you admire one of the leaders described in this chapter.

Summarizing The Chapter

On a separate sheet of paper, draw a graphic organizer like the one shown here. Copy the information from this graphic organizer on the one you have drawn. Under the main idea for each lesson, write facts that support that main idea.

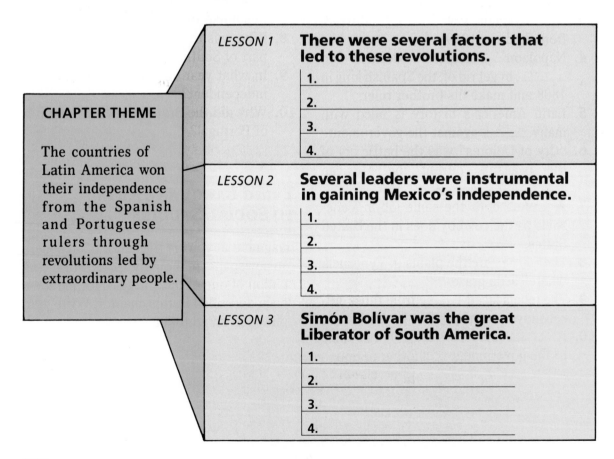

CHAPTER THEME

The countries of Latin America won their independence from the Spanish and Portuguese rulers through revolutions led by extraordinary people.

LESSON 1 **There were several factors that led to these revolutions.**
1.
2.
3.
4.

LESSON 2 **Several leaders were instrumental in gaining Mexico's independence.**
1.
2.
3.
4.

LESSON 3 **Simón Bolívar was the great Liberator of South America.**
1.
2.
3.
4.

COOPERATIVE LEARNING

In this unit you read about events that occurred during an important period in Latin America's history. This period, from the early 1500s to the early 1800s, saw tremendous growth and change. Many brave men and women contributed to the expansion and freedom of Latin America during this time.

PROJECT

In Chapter 5, you learned about the discovery of the Americas by European explorers. In Chapter 7, you learned how the Latin American people fought for their freedom from European dominance. Imagine that you could conduct television interviews with a few of the adventurous European explorers, such as Ferdinand Magellan, or some of the freedom fighters who helped to liberate Latin America, such as Símon Bolívar.

● To conduct your interviews, use a talk show format, involving each member of the group. In your group, decide whom you would like to interview from the following list: Ferdinand Magellan, Doña Marina, Hernándo Cortés, Moctezuma, Francisco Pizarro, Father Miguel Hidalgo,

Francisco de Miranda, Símon Bolívar, José de San Martín. One member should be the host of the show, however.

● Before you begin, help each other in developing a list of questions and answers for the interviews. You can use your textbook for factual information about the person, but try to also be imaginative with your questions and answers. Try to write at least four questions and answers for each person being interviewed.

● After you have finished your questions and answers, practice the interviews. If you are taking the part of one of the famous people, you may wish to write some notes on index cards in order to remember your answers. If you are the host, you may want to plan the order in which you will ask questions.

PRESENTATION AND REVIEW

When you have finished practicing the interviews, present your talk show to the class. Afterwards, meet in a group again to discuss the outcome of your show. Were you able to keep the attention of the class? If not, why? How could you have improved your talk show?

REMEMBER TO:
- Give your ideas.
- Listen to others' ideas.
- Plan your work with the group.
- Present your project.
- Discuss how your group worked.

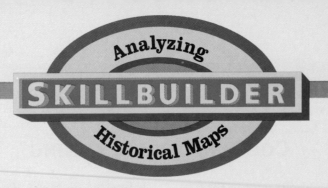

A. WHY DO I NEED THIS SKILL?

There are a variety of maps that you can refer to if you need information. Some maps, such as political or distribution maps, show very specific information. Another specific type of map is a historical map. Historical maps help you understand things as they were, or as they happened, in the past.

B. LEARNING THE SKILL

One type of historical map shows something that happened a long time ago. The map on the next page shows the voyages of some early explorers, including Italian-born Amerigo Vespucci. Vespucci wrote letters about his voyages. One of his letters came into the hands of a German mapmaker. As a result, the Americas were named after Amerigo Vespucci.

As the map shows, Vespucci took part in two well-documented voyages. Each voyage is marked on the map with a different colored line. The years in which the voyages took place are listed in the map key. The first voyage started in Spain in 1499, reached the northern coast of modern Brazil, and kept on traveling northwest along the coast. As soon as the ship reached the most northern part of South America, it turned straight north, passing between Cuba and Haiti.

Vespucci's second voyage started in Portugal in 1501, and as soon as he reached the most eastern part of Brazil, he went south along the coast. Before turning back, Vespucci went beyond the point where the city of Buenos Aires is today.

C. PRACTICING THE SKILL

Refer to the map showing the voyages of early explorers and answer these questions.
1. Did Vespucci ever reach the North American continent?
2. In which direction did Vespucci's ship turn as soon as it reached South America during his 1501–1502 voyage?
3. Use the scale on the map to estimate the distances sailed in each of Vespucci's voyages. Which voyage was longer?
4. Which other two explorers are shown on this map?
5. Which explorer sailed along the coast of Florida?

6. Which explorer sailed south from the island of Hispaniola?

7. Which two explorations took place during the same year?

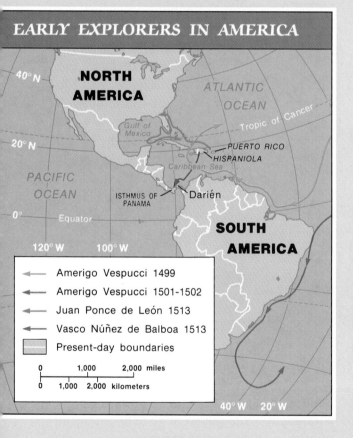

EARLY EXPLORERS IN AMERICA

NORTH AMERICA

ATLANTIC OCEAN

40°N

Tropic of Cancer

Gulf of Mexico

20°N

PUERTO RICO

HISPANIOLA

Caribbean Sea

PACIFIC OCEAN

ISTHMUS OF PANAMA

Darién

0° Equator

SOUTH AMERICA

120°W   100°W

← Amerigo Vespucci 1499
← Amerigo Vespucci 1501-1502
← Juan Ponce de León 1513
← Vasco Núñez de Balboa 1513
▭ Present-day boundaries

0   1,000   2,000 miles
0 1,000 2,000 kilometers

40°W   20°W

D. APPLYING THE SKILL

You learned in Chapter 5 that Pedro Álvares Cabral led an expedition in 1500. The goal of the expedition was to reach India. The ships sailed from Portugal toward the southern tip of Africa. About six weeks into the voyage, at about 17° south latitude, something unexpected happened. They sighted land. Cabral went ashore and claimed the land in the name of the king of Portugal. Cabral had reached modern Brazil. He sent a ship back to Portugal with news of his discovery. The expedition then continued to India.

Based on the information in the preceding paragraph, make your own historical map. Outline the entire voyage of Pedro Álvares Cabral. Refer to the world map in the Atlas, on pages 592 and 593, in order to correctly outline the geographical areas noted in the above paragraph. Your map does not have to be detailed, but try to be as accurate as possible. Also, locate the 17 degree south latitude line and mark it on your map. When you are finished drawing the route of the Cabral expedition on your map, compare your map with a classmate's to see if you both outlined the same route.

Understanding SKILLBUILDER Author's Viewpoint

A. WHY DO I NEED THIS SKILL?

Authors and other writers sometimes express their beliefs and attitudes when they write. This is called an author's *viewpoint*. You, as a reader, should be aware of any writer's viewpoint so you can decide if you agree or disagree with it.

B. LEARNING THE SKILL

Writers show or express their viewpoints when they write to *persuade* an audience. In this type of writing, a writer wants the reader to feel a certain way, to believe in something, or to buy something. A letter to an editor or an advertisement are examples of persuasive writing.

Writers may also express viewpoints when they write to *inform*. Your social studies textbook is an example of something written to inform. However, writers generally try to present facts, not their viewpoints, when they write to inform.

Viewpoints can be either valid or biased. *Valid viewpoints* are ones that are based on facts and reasons. *Biased viewpoints* are based on emotion. They may be based on faulty arguments.

The table on the next page describes four steps to follow to recognize an author's viewpoint. Apply the steps to the paragraph on page 151 that begin with these words: Should we forget about Columbus?

The author seems to have a viewpoint —he thinks that it is important that people remember Columbus. How does he indicate this? He makes the statement, "He was a fantastic sailor." The author is expressing his feelings about Columbus. Is the author's viewpoint valid or biased? You can tell that it is valid because the author supports his statement about Columbus with facts and reasons. Do you agree or disagree with the author's viewpoint regarding Columbus?

How can you tell if an author's viewpoint is biased? If the author of the above paragraph had simply said that Columbus was a fantastic sailor and did not go on to support this statement, the author's viewpoint would be considered biased.

C. PRACTICING THE SKILL

Try to determine if there is a viewpoint expressed in each of the following paragraphs, which have been purposely changed from the original paragraph on page 158 of this textbook. Use the steps in the table to look for valid and biased viewpoints. For each paragraph, write answers to the following questions on a sheet of paper.

A. Does the writer express a viewpoint? If yes, what is the viewpoint?
B. What words or phrases are clues that the writer has a viewpoint?

C. Is the viewpoint valid or biased? Explain your answer.

Paragraph 1
Cortés and his brave soldiers decided that the only way to defeat the uncivilized Aztecs was to destroy their city. The clever Cortés surrounded the savages' city, closing it completely to all trade with the outside. After a while, food and water gave out. Although weak from thirst, hunger, and disease, the foolish Aztecs still held out.

Paragraph 2
The barbaric Cortés decided that the only way to defeat the defenseless Aztecs was to destroy their city. He surrounded the city, closing it completely to all trade with the outside. Because of this cruel act, the Aztecs' food and water gave out. Although weak from thirst, hunger, and disease, the noble Aztecs still held out.

After you have finished, read the first paragraph on page 158. Decide whether or not the author expressed a viewpoint.

Steps to Understanding an Author's Viewpoint
1. As you read, look for descriptive words or phrases that may express a particular attitude or feeling.
2. Think about how those words and phrases tell what the author's feeling or attitude is toward a person, event, or topic.
3. Decide if the author's viewpoint is valid or biased. Look for facts that support what the author says.
4. Decide if you agree or disagree with an author's valid viewpoint.

D. APPLYING THE SKILL

Read letters to the editor on the editorial page in your local newspaper. Try to figure out the writers' viewpoints and decide if they are valid or biased. Then decide if you agree or disagree with the valid viewpoints.

Remember, it is all right for a writer to express a viewpoint. Just be certain that you, as a reader, recognize expressed viewpoints and that you know the difference between valid and biased viewpoints.

Unit 4

MIDDLE AMERICA FROM INDEPENDENCE TO TODAY

Middle America includes Mexico, Central America, and the countries of the Caribbean. The many nations of the region vary in their histories and in their development.

▶ *Famous Mexican artist Diego Rivera (1886-1957) painted this mural depicting Tenochtitlán. The mural hangs in the National Palace in Mexico City.*

217

CHAPTER 8

MEXICO

Mexico's varied landscape includes mountain ranges, coastal lowlands, a vast plateau, and a range of volcanoes. Its history is varied as well, from early Spanish rule to the present-day republic.

Mexico's Land and Climate

THINK ABOUT WHAT YOU KNOW
What comes to mind when you think about Mexico? Make a list of some of those things, such as what the land and climate are like.

STUDY THE VOCABULARY
summit   **semiarid**
lava

FOCUS YOUR READING
What are Mexico's main physical features?

A. Mexico's Location

Mexico's Neighbors Mexico is roughly triangular in shape and lies in the southern part of North America. The United States is Mexico's neighbor to the north. The two countries share a border that is about 2,000 miles (3,218 km) long. For more than half this distance, the border follows a river, the Rio Grande. Every year many people cross the border between Mexico and the United States. Some people travel to shop or to enjoy a vacation. Others look for jobs or for a place to retire.

Guatemala and Belize, two of the smaller countries of Central America, share Mexico's southern border. You will read about the countries of Central America in Chapters 10 and 11.

Coastal Regions Mexico's east coast borders the Gulf of Mexico and the Caribbean Sea. By looking at the map on page 220, you can see that the Gulf of Mexico and the Caribbean Sea are separated by the Yucatán Peninsula and Cuba.

The Gulf coastal plain and the Yucatán Peninsula form a major coastal region. Most of the area is low and flat. It is suitable for tropical farming. Veracruz, where Cortés began his expedition, is on this coastal plain.

The west coast of Mexico touches the Pacific Ocean and the Gulf of California. In Mexico, the Gulf of California is called the Sea of Cortés. The peninsula that is called Baja (BAH hah) California, or Lower California, separates the Sea of Cortés from the Pacific Ocean.

In southern Mexico, between rugged mountains and the Pacific Ocean, there is another coastal region. There, near the Isthmus of Tehuantepec (tuh WAHNT uh-pek), a long and narrow coastal plain begins. It stretches across the border into Guatemala. The Isthmus of Tehuantepec is the narrowest part of Mexico.

B. Rugged Mountains and a High Plateau

A Country of High Altitudes More than half of Mexico is more than 3,000 feet

Tall mountains loom over Puerto Vallarta, a coastal town along the Pacific Ocean.
▶ What kind of trees grow here?

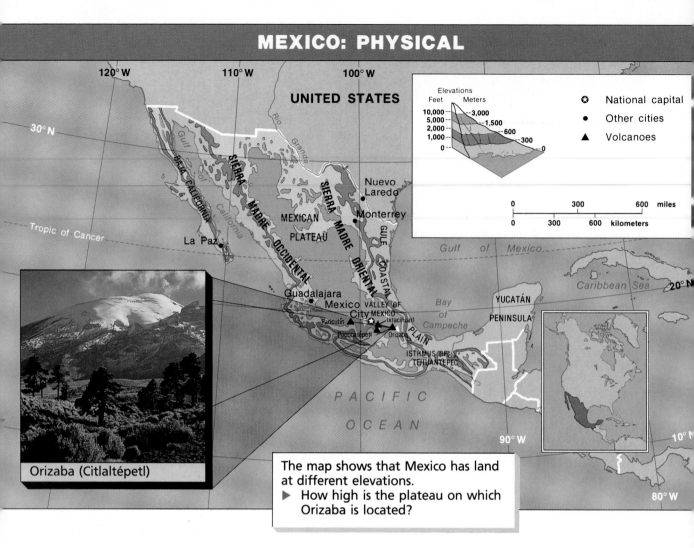

Orizaba (Citlaltépetl)

The map shows that Mexico has land at different elevations.
▶ How high is the plateau on which Orizaba is located?

(914 m) above sea level. The Mexican plateau is about 3,500 feet (1,067 m) high at Ciudad Juárez, a city on the border with the United States. It slowly rises toward the south, reaching a height of about 8,000 feet (2,438 m) near Mexico City. Much of the plateau is desert.

Mountain Ranges The Mexican plateau has a mountainous surface. Its northern section has long, narrow mountain ranges separated by broad, flat basins. Steep and rugged mountains border the plateau on its east and west sides. The western range is called Sierra Madre Occidental (MAH-dray ahk suh DENT ul), or Western Sierra Madre. The eastern range is called Sierra Madre Oriental (or ee ENT ul), or Eastern Sierra Madre.

The western mountains are not only steep and rugged but also very high. There are only a few ways of crossing these high mountains. The city of Guadalajara (gwah-dul uh HAHR uh) is 800 miles (1,287 km) south of the United States border. In all that distance, only two routes make an east-west crossing of the mountains. One route is a highway and the other, a railroad. The railroad goes through a very deep canyon called Copper Canyon. People travel from all around the world to ride the train through Copper Canyon.

The Sierra Madre Occidental range stretches to the Sea of Cortés. A number of

rivers that are used for irrigation flow out of the mountains to the sea. The valleys along the rivers form one of Mexico's most important agricultural areas.

The Sierra Madre Oriental range is nearly as steep and rugged as the Sierra Madre Occidental, but it is not as high. Many more roads and railroads cross the Sierra Madre Oriental. They connect the coastal plain along the Gulf of Mexico with the cities of the Mexican plateau.

C. Mexico's Volcanoes

Famous Volcanoes The southern part of the Mexican plateau ends in a range of volcanoes. Most of Mexico's volcanoes are small, but some are large and well-known. Two such volcanoes are Popocatépetl and Ixtacihuatl (ess tah SEE waht ul). These famous landmarks can be seen on a clear day from Mexico City, some 40 miles (64 km) away.

Although both volcanoes are over 17,000 feet (5,182 m) high, they are not the highest volcanoes in Mexico. That honor goes to Orizaba (aw ree SAH bah), also called Citlaltépetl (see tlah TAY pet-ul). Look at the photo on page 220. Citlal-tépetl rises 18,700 feet (5,700 m) above sea level. Because these three volcanoes are so high, the snow never melts from their **summits**, or peaks.

Most of Mexico's people live in the basins in the general area of the high volcanoes. One of these basins, the Valley of Mexico, was the home of the Aztec Empire. Today, Mexico City, the city with the largest population in the Americas, is located there.

A Young Volcano New volcanoes still develop in Mexico. One of the most famous of this century is Paricutín (pah-ree koo TEEN), in the central part of the

These pictures show four different regions of the Mexican plateau.
▶ Why might Mexico be called a country of contrasts?

Popocatépetl and Orizaba (top and middle) are snow-capped year round.
▶ What might the climate be like in Baja California (bottom)?

country. On February 20, 1943, the ground suddenly began to shake, and a crack opened up in the earth, much to the dismay of a terrified farmer who was planting his cornfield nearby. When smoke began to rise from the crack, the villagers of San Juan Parangaricutiro (pah rahn gah ree-koo TEE roh) realized that a volcano was growing in the cornfield. The **lava**, or melted rock, eventually covered the whole village. The elevation of this volcanic mountain, called Paricutín, is now 9,213 feet (2,808 m) above sea level.

D. A Variety of Climates

Is Mexico a tropical land? Look at the map on page 220, and you'll see that about two thirds of its landmass lies north of the Tropic of Cancer. This area has a temperate climate because of its latitude. Also, since much of Mexico has a high elevation, even some parts that lie in the tropics have a temperate climate. Look back to the diagram on page 62. There you see the temperature zones and how temperature is affected by elevation. The high elevations of tropical Mexico are in the tierra fría — the cold zone. Other areas, such as the Gulf coastal plain, are in the tierra caliente — the hot zone.

Mexico is one of the driest countries in Latin America. Over half the country has either a desert climate or a **semiarid** climate. A semiarid climate is dry, but not as dry as a desert. The driest parts of Mexico are Baja California and along the northern Pacific coast. Look at the climograph for La Paz on the next page. It shows the climate of Baja California. A climograph shows both temperatures and precipitation. Notice that the numbers on the left show temperatures — both in Fahrenheit and in Celsius. The numbers on the right

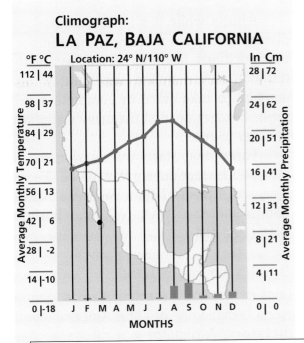

Climograph:
LA PAZ, BAJA CALIFORNIA
Location: 24° N/110° W

°F °C

112 | 44
98 | 37
84 | 29
70 | 21
56 | 13
42 | 6
28 | -2
14 | -10
0 | -18

In Cm

28 | 72
24 | 62
20 | 51
16 | 41
12 | 31
8 | 21
4 | 11
0 | 0

Average Monthly Temperature

Average Monthly Precipitation

J F M A M J J A S O N D

MONTHS

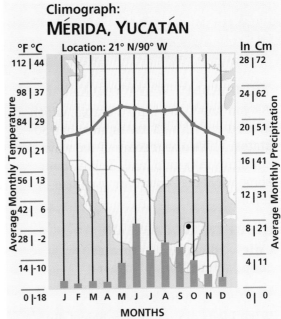

Climograph:
MÉRIDA, YUCATÁN
Location: 21° N/90° W

°F °C

112 | 44
98 | 37
84 | 29
70 | 21
56 | 13
42 | 6
28 | -2
14 | -10
0 | -18

In Cm

28 | 72
24 | 62
20 | 51
16 | 41
12 | 31
8 | 21
4 | 11
0 | 0

Average Monthly Temperature

Average Monthly Precipitation

J F M A M J J A S O N D

MONTHS

Compare the climates of La Paz and Mérida.

► Which of the two Mexican cities has the drier climate?

show precipitation—in centimeters and in inches. Climographs are useful for comparing different kinds of climate.

Compare the climograph for La Paz with the one for Mérida. Mérida is on the northern end of the Yucatán Peninsula.

Notice that Mérida has more precipitation, in general, than La Paz.

The most humid parts of Mexico are at the southern end of the Yucatán Peninsula and along the Gulf coastal plain. There are heavy thundershowers in those places nearly every day.

LESSON 1 REVIEW

THINK AND WRITE

A. For what reasons do people cross the border between Mexico and the United States?

B. In a sentence or two, describe Mexico's location by noting its southern, eastern, and western borders.

C. Why are several volcanoes in Mexico well-known?

D. Compare the climate of Mexico with the climate of your state. What are the similarities and the differences?

SKILLS CHECK

MAP SKILL

Look at maps in the Atlas, especially the map of the world on pages 592–593, to find out which Latin American lands border the Gulf of Mexico and the Caribbean Sea. List those Latin American lands by countries and by islands.

Mexico in the Nineteenth Century

THINK ABOUT WHAT YOU KNOW

As you know, the United States, which started out with 13 states, now has 50 states. Think about some of the ways that countries may gain land. Think about some ways that countries may lose territory.

STUDY THE VOCABULARY

exile	dictator	rurales
coup	rebellion	invest

FOCUS YOUR READING

What kinds of political problems did Mexico have in the nineteenth century?

A. A Time of Unrest

In Chapter 7 you learned that Augustín de Iturbide led Mexico to its independence from Spain in 1821. He used his position to have himself declared emperor of Mexico, but he really had little support in the new country. Early in 1823, one of his own commanders led a revolt that forced Iturbide into **exile** in Europe and ended the empire of Mexico. Exile is the removal by force from one's homeland. During the next 50 years, Mexico had many setbacks. It lost around half of its land to the United States. It was attacked by France and occupied by the French army. Mexico also had several civil wars.

You can see that the new nation went through a very difficult period. Often, the defeated side in an election would accuse the other side of dishonesty and act to overthrow the new government. The sudden overthrow of a government by force is called a **coup** (koo).

After a while this kind of turmoil, or disturbance, gave military leaders important positions. Winning an election really did not assure that a candidate would manage to take office or complete a full term. Leaders needed the army's support in order to rule.

Three men stand out as shapers of Mexico's history during this period. These men are Antonio López de Santa Anna, Benito Juárez (HWAH res), and Porfirio Díaz (DEE ahs).

B. Mexico Loses Land

Loss of Central American Lands Santa Anna became one of Latin America's first **dictators**. A dictator is a ruler who has complete authority and power over a country. Santa Anna had led the revolt against Iturbide. As president of Mexico, Santa Anna often ignored the law and the rights of the people.

Antonio López de Santa Anna, a dictator, was Mexico's president 11 times between 1833 and 1855.
▶ Describe Santa Anna's clothing.

The Granger Collection

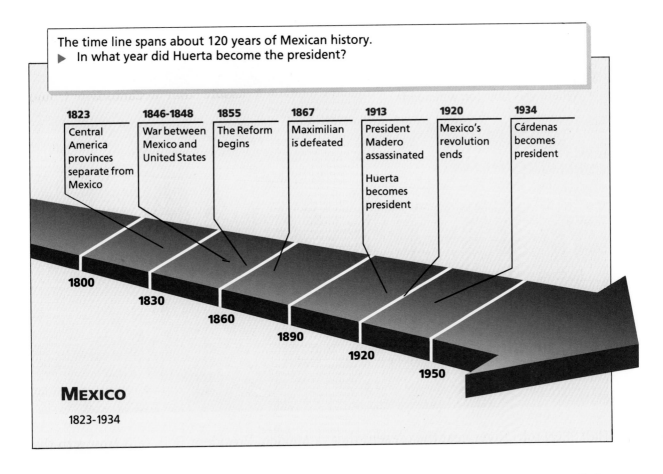

The time line spans about 120 years of Mexican history.
▶ In what year did Huerta become the president?

1823
Central America provinces separate from Mexico

1846-1848
War between Mexico and United States

1855
The Reform begins

1867
Maximilian is defeated

1913
President Madero assassinated

Huerta becomes president

1920
Mexico's revolution ends

1934
Cárdenas becomes president

1800
1830
1860
1890
1920
1950

MEXICO

1823-1934

In 1821, when Mexico won its freedom from Spain, it had more than twice as much land as it now has. The present Central American lands of Guatemala, Honduras, Nicaragua, and Costa Rica were part of Mexico. Two years later they broke away.

All or part of what are now the states of Arizona, California, Colorado, Kansas, Nevada, New Mexico, Oklahoma, Texas, Utah, and Wyoming also belonged to the newly independent Mexico. Soon those lands were lost as well.

Loss of Texas and Other Land People from the United States began to settle in the area of present-day Texas about the time that Mexico became independent. By 1830 there were over 20,000 United States citizens settled in Texas and only a few thousand Mexican citizens. Many of the people living in Texas at that time became unhappy with Mexican rule.

In 1836 the people in Texas rebelled against Mexico and declared Texas an independent country. A United States settler, David Burnett, was named president of the new country.

The Alamo Santa Anna, determined to squash the Texas revolt, organized an army of 6,000 and marched north from Mexico City. In February of 1836, his army attacked a band of about 180 Texans at the Alamo, a mission outside the town of San Antonio. Everyone at the Alamo was killed. "Remember the Alamo!" became the battle cry of Texans.

After his victory at the Alamo, Santa Anna moved his army to the San Jacinto

225

Here Mexican general Santa Anna surrenders to a wounded Sam Houston after the battle at San Jacinto.
► Where was Houston wounded?

(juh SEEN toh) River near the present-day city of Houston, Texas. There, in April 1836, Texans led by Sam Houston surprised Santa Anna. Only two Texans died, but over 600 Mexican soldiers were killed, and Santa Anna was captured.

Sam Houston made a bargain with Santa Anna. The defeated general agreed to recognize the independence of Texas. In return, Santa Anna would be set free. Santa Anna did not make good on his pledge. In fact, he did not have the power to do so. However, even though Mexico did not acknowledge the loss of Texas, it made no further move to attack. In 1845, Texas became the twenty-eighth state in the United States.

C. More Lost Land

War with the United States The United States and Mexico clashed over where to mark the borderline between Texas and Mexico. President Polk sent troops to the disputed territory. Then Mexican troops attacked one of the smaller troops and killed several soldiers. Polk used this incident as an excuse to declare war on Mexico in 1846. Many Americans, including Congressman Abraham Lincoln, opposed the war. At that time, the issue of slavery was becoming very important in the United States.

Some people believed the war was just a plot by slaveholders to add more slave states to the United States. Others, however, had sympathy for the desire of Texans to become part of the United States. They agreed with President Polk's description of the border clash with Mexico as an act of war: "American troops have been fired upon on American soil."

Again Santa Anna led the Mexican army. He could not stop the advancing troops of the United States. They reached

Mexico City in September of 1847. Teenage boys from the Mexican military school died trying to defend their capital in the last battle.

Treaty of Guadalupe   Peace came in 1848 with the signing of the Treaty of Guadalupe Hidalgo (gwahd ul OOP hih DAHL-goh). It was at this time that Mexico lost nearly half of its territory, including California, to the United States under the terms of the treaty. The terms also included payment of $15 million to Mexico.

In 1853, Santa Anna sold more land to the United States. That land, now the southern parts of Arizona and New Mexico, is known as the Gadsden Purchase. It is named after James Gadsden, the man who arranged the sale for $10 million.

Many people in both countries felt the United States had taken advantage of Mexico almost from the time the first settlers arrived in Texas. Those feelings affected relations between Mexico and the United States for many years.

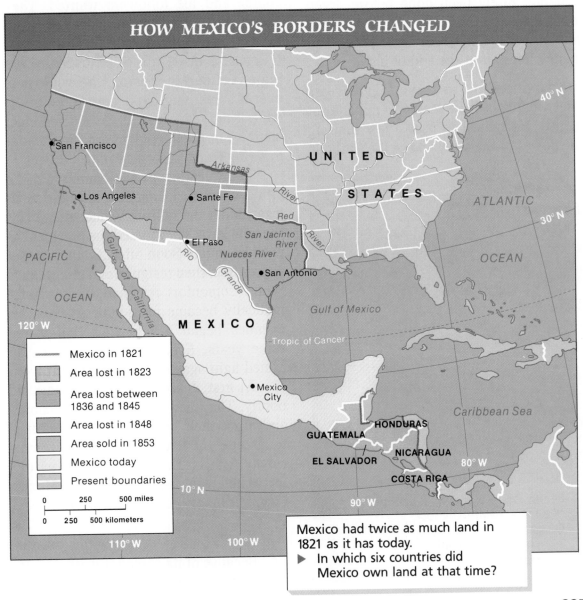

HOW MEXICO'S BORDERS CHANGED

San Francisco

Los Angeles

UNITED

Arkansas

Sante Fe

STATES

ATLANTIC

Red

San Jacinto River

El Paso

Nueces River

PACIFIC

OCEAN

Rio Grande

San Antonio

OCEAN

Gulf of Mexico

Gulf of California

MEXICO

Tropic of Cancer

Caribbean Sea

Mexico City

HONDURAS

GUATEMALA

NICARAGUA

EL SALVADOR

COSTA RICA

40° N

30° N

120° W

10° N

80° W

90° W

100° W

110° W

Mexico in 1821
Area lost in 1823
Area lost between 1836 and 1845
Area lost in 1848
Area sold in 1853
Mexico today
Present boundaries

0   250   500 miles
0   250   500 kilometers

Mexico had twice as much land in 1821 as it has today.
▶ In which six countries did Mexico own land at that time?

D. Benito Juárez as a Leader

A Native American President Benito Juárez was a Zapotec (ZAP uh tek) Indian from the state of Oaxaca in southeast Mexico. His mother and father died when he was very young. As a youth, he worked as a servant. Juárez later became a lawyer and entered politics. In 1847 he became governor of Oaxaca. Benito Juárez was considered to be an honest governor. He worked to improve education. He opened his office to Indians, something that had rarely been done before. Even more unusual, the state treasury, which was empty when Juárez took office, had money left in it at the end of his term.

Juárez and Reform Laws Eight years later, Juárez became Mexico's minister of justice. He helped to pass a law limiting the power of the army and of the Catholic Church in Mexico. The law took from soldiers and priests many of the privileges they enjoyed. Another law forced the Catholic Church to give up most of its land. Until that time, the Catholic Church had owned about half the farmland in Mexico.

These laws were the first of a number of laws meant to give freedom and a better life to more people in Mexico. The laws were called La Reforma, "The Reform."

In 1857 a new constitution was made law. It included many of the reforms that Juárez and his followers wanted. They hoped that these reforms would keep Mexico free of dictators. The new constitution also made the chief justice of the Supreme Court the person who would take over if something happened to the president. That year, Juárez was elected chief justice. The president was Ignacio Comonfort (ihg NAHS yoh   koh mawn FORT).

Many leaders of the church and the army, who were losing their land and privileges under the reform, blamed Juárez for the new laws. They forced the president to put him in jail. Soon after, Comonfort set Juárez free, then resigned and left Mexico. When Comonfort resigned, Juárez automatically became president. At that, his enemies began a **rebellion** that lasted three years. *Rebellion* often means "an armed fight against the government."

At first, Juárez and his followers did poorly. They had to flee from the capital and move their headquarters three times to escape the enemy. Things improved slowly, and by the end of 1860, Juárez's forces had won. Juárez returned to Mexico City, but his troubles were not over.

E. The French Occupation

Because of its constant wars, Mexico owed many debts to other countries. The

Benito Juárez is shown in a section of a mural painted by José Orozco.
▶ Why did the wealthy object to his reforms?

Maximilian is shown as he surrenders on May 15, 1867.
► Why was Maximilian not accepted by the Mexicans?

French decided to get their money back by force. In 1862 a French army landed at Veracruz and began the attack on Mexico. The Mexicans fought hard to defend their country, but the French army was stronger. The French took Mexico City and named Maximilian, who was a young Austrian prince, as the emperor. Juárez and his government fled to the north.

Maximilian tried to be a good ruler. However, most of the Mexican people would not accept a ruler who was forced on them by another country. The French army kept Maximilian in power. In 1865, France removed its army from Mexico to deal with problems at home. Maximilian was left with a small, poorly equipped force. It was no match for the army of Juárez, which returned from the north and captured Maximilian. He was tried and shot the next month.

The Return of Juárez Juárez returned to Mexico City and won reelection as president in October. He worked hard to bring peace to Mexico and to continue the work of reform. He died in office in 1872. Mexicans remember Juárez not only as a great patriot who fought Maximilian but also as a person who tried to make things better for the Mexican people. Many of the changes he fought for were also issues later on, during the time of the Mexican Revolution.

F. Porfirio Díaz, President to Dictator

Juárez had fought hard for his country, but he was not able to solve Mexico's many problems. The nearly 50 years of unrest, from 1823 to 1872, had done a great deal of damage. Bandits roamed the countryside. Even city streets were not entirely safe. Farmland lay unused, and mines were idle. The unpaved dirt roads were impassable most of the time. There were only about 400 miles (644 km) of railroads in the whole country. Mexico was in deep trouble.

Porfirio Díaz became president in 1876. His campaign slogan was "Effective

It was the job of the rurales to make the country safe and to keep law and order in rural Mexico.
▶ Why were the rurales feared?

When Díaz took office, he moved quickly to establish his own authority. To make the country safe from bandits, Díaz formed a rural police force, the **rurales** (roo RAH lays). Some say Díaz got the worst bandits in the country to join the police force by paying them more than they could earn by robbing. The poor of Mexico lived in fear of the rurales.

To end the political problems that were tearing the country apart, Díaz used what became known as "bread or the club." That is, he granted favors to people who helped him. People who opposed him were put into prison or even put to death.

To help the economy, Díaz invited foreign countries to **invest** in Mexico. To invest is to use money to build businesses or factories or to develop resources in order to earn more money. The money that was invested in Mexico was used to build factories, to search for oil, and to put mines back into production. Thousands of miles of railroads were built. On the surface, Mexico seemed to become rich. Most of the money, however, went to a few powerful families and to the foreign investors. No money went to the landless poor.

suffrage [right to vote], no reelection." Actually, he ruled as a dictator for 35 years! During that time, he did bring order to Mexico, and the country enjoyed some good economic success. However, as you will see, Díaz's policies also caused a lot of harm.

Born in 1830 to a poor family, Díaz was a mestizo. He rose to power through the army and was a general under Juárez. Díaz later led a revolt against him in 1871.

LESSON 2 REVIEW

THINK AND WRITE

A. In what ways did Mexico experience unrest during its early years of independence?

B. How did Texas become an independent nation?

C. In your judgment, what were the main reasons why Mexico lost so much land to the United States?

D. How did Benito Juárez try to change Mexico?

E. What was the cause of Maximilian's loss of power?

F. How did Porfirio Díaz control Mexico?

SKILLS CHECK

THINKING SKILL

Choose one of the Mexican leaders mentioned in this lesson. In your mind, prepare yourself to report on that person's success or failure as a leader. Then meet with some classmates and share your reports.

230

Mexico in the Twentieth Century

THINK ABOUT WHAT YOU KNOW

This lesson deals with a Mexican revolution. Think about why people revolt. Make a list of some possible reasons.

STUDY THE VOCABULARY

democracy   ejido
peon   expropriate

FOCUS YOUR READING

Why is the Mexican Revolution important?

A. Díaz's Policies

In 1910, at the age of 80, Díaz began his eighth term as president. Rather than unrest, there was law and order in Mexico. Foreign capital, especially from the United States, was pouring in. The budget was balanced and modernization was taking place.

Despite these achievements, Díaz's years as head of the Mexican nation had brought many problems. The rich had grown richer, and the poor had become poorer. A few families had built large haciendas — some of more than a million acres (405,000 ha) — from land taken from Indians or from poor mestizos. During the rule of Díaz, Indian villages lost land that they had held for centuries.

In the countryside, poor Indians and mestizos could not make enough money to feed and house themselves decently. In urban Mexico, too, poor people lived difficult lives. The absence of political freedoms created anger in most Mexicans.

In 1908, Francisco Madero had written a book calling for more **democracy** in Mexico. Democracy is government of, for, and by the people. Two years later, using Díaz's old slogan "Effective suffrage, no reelection," Madero ran for the presidency. Díaz jailed Madero but then released him after the election.

That was a big mistake. Madero fled to Texas. Safe from the dictator's reach, he encouraged armed uprisings to remove Díaz from office. His plan was put into effect in November of 1910. Díaz resigned, and Madero was elected president.

While Mexico's president, Díaz established a strong military dictatorship.
▶ What groups did Díaz favor?

231

Villa (in presidential chair), with Zapata (holding large hat), and María Gutiérrez (inset), briefly occupy Mexico City in 1914.
▶ For whom did they want to make life better?

B. The Long Revolution

Zapata and Other Leaders Within a year, a full-scale revolution had begun. It lasted until 1920. It was fought chiefly by rebel armies in the countryside and claimed 1 million lives. The best-known rebel leaders were Emiliano Zapata (sah-PAH tah) and Pancho Villa (VEE yah).

Like Father Hidalgo during the struggle for independence, and like Juárez during La Reforma, Zapata and Villa wanted to make life better for Mexico's poor. Zapata and Villa joined the revolution. Both men attracted many followers—Indians, hungry peasants, ranch workers, and greedy outlaws—who clashed with federal troops and plantation owners.

Zapata led the band of poor people, mostly Indians, who wanted to have land. Villa was an outlaw who believed in taking from the rich and sharing with the poor. He and his followers raided haciendas whenever they could. They were more interested in getting some of Mexico's wealth than they were in having land to farm.

Madero, along with Zapata and Villa, was not against helping the poor, but he thought political changes would come first. He wanted to have free elections and a constitutional government. When Madero did not listen to the demands of Zapata and Villa right away, the poor people stopped supporting him. Madero began to lose power quickly.

Huerta's Term as President A general of the army, Victoriano Huerta (WAIR-tah), caused Madero's final downfall. In February of 1913, Huerta's soldiers arrested Madero and other members of his government. Madero was forced to resign. Four days later, Huerta's men murdered Madero and his vice president as they were being taken from the national palace to prison.

Huerta himself was overthrown in 1914 by the combined forces of four revolutionists: Zapata, Villa, Venustiano Carranza (kah RAHN sah), and Álvaro Obregón (oh bray GOHN). After Huerta's downfall, the four fought among themselves for control of the country. By 1916, Carranza controlled most of the country of Mexico.

C. A New Constitution

Carranza called together a group of citizens to write a new constitution for Mexico. The new constitution, which became effective in 1917, made many changes in the government of Mexico.

The most important part of the new constitution stated that, for the good of the people, the government could take private property away from its owners. Using that law, the government was later able to take land from the hacienda owners and give it to people who had no land.

The new constitution said that Mexico's mineral and oil wealth belonged to the Mexican people. It also recognized labor unions and established an eight-hour work day. That was well before the United States had similar laws.

The Granger Collection

Rebel leader Pancho Villa, shown here riding with his supporters, was one of many who fought for power in Mexico. He believed in taking from the rich and giving to the poor.
► Who were the other well-known rebel leaders?

D. Many Changes

Small Percent of Landowners Before the revolution, most of Mexico's farmland was in huge haciendas owned by the wealthy. The people who lived and worked on the haciendas were called **peons** (PEE unz). Over 95 percent of the people of Mexico had no land of their own. Most people wanted to be free of the haciendas and to own their own farms. Many of those people joined the revolution.

New Form of Ownership After 1920, the government broke up haciendas to give land to the peons. The government feared that, as in the past, the peons might have the land taken from them. To protect them, it set up a new kind of property, the **ejido** (ay HEE doh). An ejido was land given to a whole village rather than to one family. The land was owned by all the people who worked it. Since the land could not be sold or rented, the peons were protected from losing it.

Pride in Mexican History The revolution also helped create a new sense of Mexican history. The accomplishments of the Aztecs and other Indian peoples became a source of pride. The unfair treatment of the Mexican people by past rulers also was acknowledged.

For example, on several public buildings in Mexico City, the government had artists paint murals. These murals were about the Aztec religion, historical events, and scenes of the Spanish conquest. Other murals showed how hacienda owners and government officials became rich by taking advantage of Mexico's poor people. The artists showed why the revolution had been fought. The artists used both European and American Indian painting techniques to create the murals.

This section of a mural painted by David Siqueiros depicts the Mexican Hat dance, Mexico's national dance.
▶ Why might it be called a hat dance?

Three great artists—José Clemente Orozco (oh ROHS koh), Diego Rivera (ree-VAY rah), and David Alfaro Siqueiros (see-KAY rohs)—painted these murals. Orozco and Siqueiros had fought in the revolutionary army. All three artists became famous in Mexico and also all over the world.

E. Land Reform Under Cárdenas

The president of Mexico who most completely followed the ideals of the revolution was Lázaro Cárdenas (KAHR day-nahs). He was president from 1934 to 1940. Cárdenas turned more hacienda land into ejidos than any other president, giving farms to millions of poor peons.

Cárdenas also **expropriated**, or took over, the oil fields in Mexico that were owned by foreign companies. He placed the oil industry under government ownership. Cárdenas made this move because of a dispute with the oil companies over pay for their workers. The Mexican courts had ordered a large pay raise for the striking workers, but the oil companies refused to pay it.

Expropriating the oil industry was daring because the companies were owned by people in the United States and other countries. That did not happen. Eventually, the companies were paid a small part of their claims for their property. Cárdenas retired from office as one of Mexico's most respected presidents.

Cárdenas takes the oath of office to become Mexico's 19th president.
► Why was he one of Mexico's most respected presidents?

LESSON *3* REVIEW

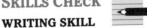

THINK AND WRITE

A. Why were poor people unhappy with Porfirio Díaz?

B. How did the Mexican revolution begin?

C. What are some of the important features of Mexico's 1917 constitution?

D. How did the revolution change Mexico?

E. Why is Lázaro Cárdenas remembered?

SKILLS CHECK

WRITING SKILL

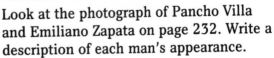

Look at the photograph of Pancho Villa and Emiliano Zapata on page 232. Write a description of each man's appearance.

USING THE VOCABULARY

expropriate
rebellion
dictator
peon
semiarid
exile
summit
ejido
lava

The following statements are false. On a separate sheet of paper, rewrite each statement replacing the underlined word with a term above to make it a true statement.

1. The top of a mountain is its <u>cliff</u>.
2. A place that has a bit more rainfall than a desert is <u>tropical</u>.
3. A <u>president</u> has complete control over which laws will be made in his country.
4. A political <u>immigration</u> took place when the government was overthrown.
5. That <u>hacienda</u> was owned by all of the members of the community.

REMEMBERING WHAT YOU READ

On a separate sheet of paper, answer the following questions in complete sentences.

1. What river flows along the United States and Mexican border?
2. What type of physical feature covers more than half of the area of Mexico?
3. Can Mexico be considered a tropical country? Explain.
4. Under what terms did Mexico lose nearly half its territory to the United States?
5. Which man was considered to be the first leader to give more freedom and a better life to the majority of people in Mexico?
6. How did the Austrian Maximilian come to rule Mexico?
7. What, do you think, does the term *Porfirian Peace* refer to?
8. Which man was able to rally enough support to be elected president and force Díaz to resign?
9. What changes came to Mexico as a result of the revolution?
10. What was Lazaro Cardenas's daring move as president?

TYING MUSIC TO SOCIAL STUDIES

In Mexico, as in many countries, music is an important part of the culture. There are many popular songs in our own country that have a Mexican flavor. Many Mexican folk songs tell about the struggles of the people. Perhaps you can write your own folk song by using a recording of instrumental Mexican music and adding your own words to tell a story about some of Mexico's history.

THINKING CRITICALLY

On a separate sheet of paper, answer the following questions in complete sentences.

1. If you had been a Mexican in the years 1830 to 1848, what might you have resented about the United States?
2. How did La Reforma affect each of the following groups: the army, the Catholic Church, the Indians and poor people?
3. Compare Pancho Villa with Robin Hood. Tell why you do or don't think that Villa was right in taking from the rich to give to the poor.
4. Try to imagine life on an ejido in Mexico. What would some of its advantages be for a farming family?
5. Why, probably, did the Mexicans change unfair conditions through revolution rather than by more peaceful means?

SUMMARIZING THE CHAPTER

On a separate sheet of paper, draw a graphic organizer like the one shown here. Copy the information from this graphic organizer to the one you have drawn. Under each heading, fill in the blanks with facts you learned from that lesson.

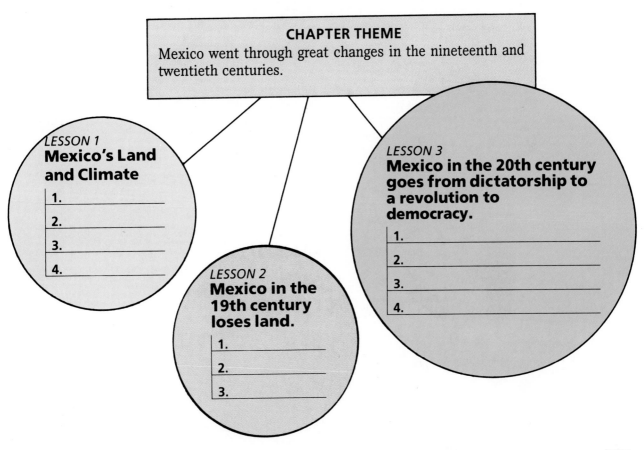

CHAPTER THEME
Mexico went through great changes in the nineteenth and twentieth centuries.

LESSON 1
Mexico's Land and Climate
1. _____
2. _____
3. _____
4. _____

LESSON 2
Mexico in the 19th century loses land.
1. _____
2. _____
3. _____

LESSON 3
Mexico in the 20th century goes from dictatorship to a revolution to democracy.
1. _____
2. _____
3. _____
4. _____

MEXICO TODAY

odern-day Mexico is a land of contrasts. Some farmers still cultivate plots just large enough to feed their families, while Mexico City has the largest population of any city in the Americas.

Making a Living in Mexico

THINK ABOUT WHAT YOU KNOW

List some jobs you might like to have when you grow up. Which of these jobs do you think would be most in demand in Mexico?

STUDY THE VOCABULARY

manufacturing
gross national
  product
reserves
subsistence farm
erosion
commercial farm

FOCUS YOUR READING

How do Mexicans earn a living?

A. The Importance of Industry

Hecho en Mexico means "Made in Mexico." If you looked through a Mexican department store, you'd find those words stamped on almost every item.

Mexico is one of the most industrialized countries of Latin America. From its factories come iron and steel, glass, chemicals, paper, cement, textiles, electrical equipment, and many other things. The **manufacturing** of automobiles is a major industry in Mexico. Manufacturing is the making of goods, especially by machinery on a large scale. In 1991, manufacturing accounted for about 30 percent of the value of Mexico's domestic economy.

Mexico's main manufacturing area stretches from Veracruz on the east coast to Guadalajara, near the western side of the Mexican plateau. Mexico City and the cities of Puebla, Cuernavaca (kwer nuh-VAH kuh), Toluca, Querétaro (ke RE tah-roh), and León (lay OHN) are part of this area.

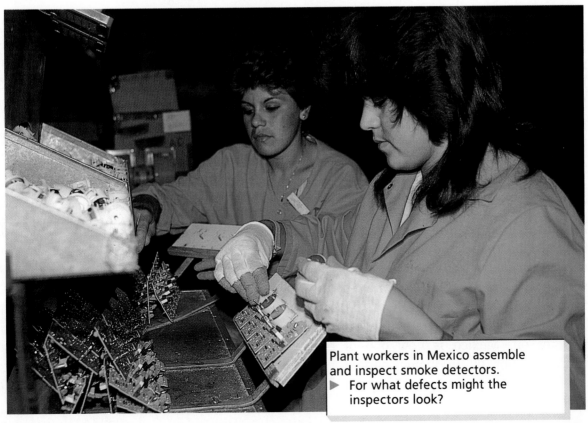

Plant workers in Mexico assemble and inspect smoke detectors.
▶ For what defects might the inspectors look?

Tourism is also big business in Mexico. In 1985, over 10 percent of Mexico's **gross national product** came from tourism. Gross national product, often just called GNP, is the total value of a nation's goods and services produced and sold in a single year. It takes more than nice weather and scenery to attract tourists. It requires good advertisements, hotels, restaurants, and tourist agencies along with efficient transportation systems. You probably can figure out why the tourist industry provides many employment opportunities for Mexicans.

B. Natural Resources

Mineral Wealth Since the time of the Aztecs, the mines of Mexico have produced vast quantities of precious metals. Mexico still is one of the world's leading producers of silver.

Copper, iron, lead, zinc, gold, mercury, and other metals also are taken from Mexico's mines. At one time most of the metals were exported to other countries to be made into manufactured goods. Now Mexico uses more of its minerals to make products both to sell in Mexico and to export to countries around the world.

The Importance of Oil Mexico's most important mineral resource today is oil. You learned that after the revolution, Mexico expropriated the oil holdings of foreign countries. In the 1970s, the price of oil rose quickly. Mexico drilled new oil wells in the southeastern part of the country and offshore in the Gulf of Mexico. These new wells tapped into an enormous pool of oil. Mexico is now one of the world's major oil-producing nations. In 1990 Mexico's wells pumped about 2.7 million barrels of oil a day.

These men work with a rig, or equipment for drilling oil.
▶ What characteristics might a good oil driller possess?

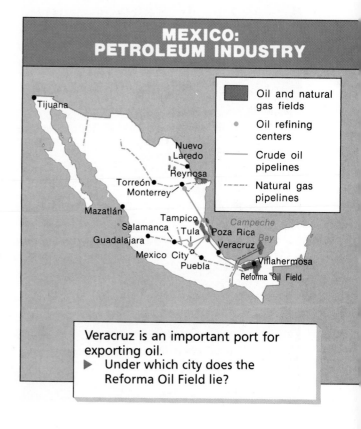

Veracruz is an important port for exporting oil.
▶ Under which city does the Reforma Oil Field lie?

240

In 1991 Mexico's crude oil **reserves** totaled 56.4 billion barrels, good for seventh place among the world's nations. Reserves are the supplies, such as oil, that are still available in the ground.

The United States imports more petroleum from Mexico than from any other country. In 1973, Mexico sent only about 16,000 barrels of oil to the United States each day. By the early 1990s, Mexico had become the second largest supplier of oil to the United States.

Natural Gas Mexico also has plentiful supplies of natural gas, which is usually found with petroleum. In 1980 Mexico began to export natural gas to the United States. Today Mexico is among the world's leading producers of natural gas liquids.

C. Agriculture in Mexico

Small Plots of Land About 41 percent of Mexico's labor force works in agriculture. You may remember that after the revolution, President Cárdenas broke up many large estates so that he could distribute land to the peons. However, presidents after Cárdenas did not give this policy so much attention.

Today, land in Mexico is still divided in a very unequal fashion. About one half of the farmers work with simple tools on small plots of land called **subsistence farms**. A subsistence farm is one on which members of a family grow food chiefly for themselves. Only a small amount of the crop is sold.

About half of Mexico's farmland is planted with *maize*, or corn. It was Mexico's most important crop in Aztec times, and it still is. Maize is the main crop on subsistence farms.

Because subsistence farmers are

In Chiapas, Mexico, this farmer uses a simple method of plowing.
► Why is an ox a useful beast?

poor, they cannot buy expensive farm equipment. Instead, most of them use a wooden plow pulled by an ox. Often the land they plow is hilly. On such land, plowing should follow the contours of the land. That is, it should go around the hillside, not up and down the hill. Contour plowing helps to stop **erosion**, or the wearing away of the soil. Many subsistence farms have land that has been damaged by erosion because the farmers did not use contour plowing. Finding ways to improve the lives of the subsistence farmers is a major problem for the government.

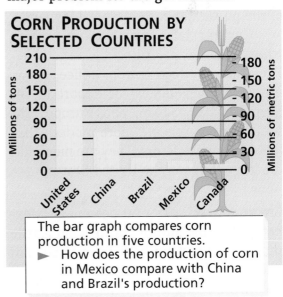

CORN PRODUCTION BY SELECTED COUNTRIES

The bar graph compares corn production in five countries.
► How does the production of corn in Mexico compare with China and Brazil's production?

241

Both in the states of Chihuahua (left) and Sinaloa (right), land is used for cultivating crops and for cattle ranching.
▶ How would you describe the land shown?

Large Farms Mexico's large commercial farms produce many crops. Commercial farms are farms that raise crops for sale rather than for home use. Most of Mexico's commercial farms are in the irrigated oases of the north and in the tropical lowlands.

Commercial farms grow maize, wheat, rice, beans, fruits, and vegetables. They also produce cotton, coffee, sugar, fruits, and vegetables for export to the United States, Japan, and Europe. The commercial farms are more modern than the subsistence farms. They are much like the large farms in the United States.

Grazing Land Over 30 percent of Mexico's land is pasture, or grazing land. Cattle and sheep ranching have been important since the 1500s, when the first farm animals were brought in by the Spaniards.

Ranching is most important in the northern part of the Mexican plateau. This area is too dry for farming. There are still some large haciendas there. On these haciendas there is enough land to graze herds of cattle and sheep. Some of the haciendas have deep wells to provide water for the livestock.

D. Finding Jobs

There are not enough jobs in Mexico for all the people who want to work. Even for people who have jobs, wages are low compared with what workers earn in Anglo-America. As Mexico's population grows, the lack of jobs is likely to grow worse.

Low wages and difficulty in finding work have caused many people to leave Mexico. Usually they come to the United

242

States. In 1942, the United States was involved in World War II. With so many of its citizens in the armed forces, the United States needed agricultural workers. The presidents of the two countries signed an agreement that allowed Mexicans to work on farms in the southwestern United States. These Mexicans were called *braceros* (bruh SAIR ohz), or day laborers.

In 1964 the bracero agreement between the United States and Mexico ended. Yet the same needs have continued. The Mexicans need work and the United States needs inexpensive labor.

The United States has immigration laws that regulate who can come to this country to live and work. These laws include quotas that set exactly how many people may come to the United States from another country. The laws also make immigrants meet other requirements.

Because of the quotas and other requirements, many Mexicans cannot enter the United States legally. Some try to enter illegally. These illegal immigrants are often called *undocumented workers* because they enter without the required immigration documents.

The governments of the United States and Mexico are trying to solve the problem

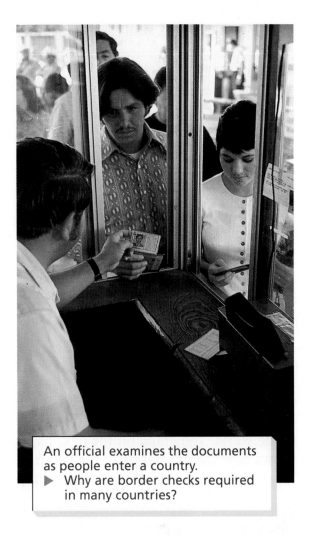

An official examines the documents as people enter a country.
▶ Why are border checks required in many countries?

of undocumented workers. It is hard to find an answer that will help the people of both countries.

LESSON **1** *REVIEW*

THINK AND WRITE

A. What are two of the major forms of employment in Mexico?

B. Why are oil, natural gas, and metals important to Mexico's economy?

C. Compare and contrast a subsistence farm with a commercial farm.

D. Why are some Mexican laborers having a hard time getting jobs?

SKILLS CHECK

WRITING SKILL

Imagine that you are applying for a job in Mexico that relates to tourism. Write a few paragraphs. Begin by stating the job you would like to have. Then tell what you plan to do in that job to attract tourists to Mexico.

LESSON 2

The People of Mexico

THINK ABOUT WHAT YOU KNOW

Recall what you learned about Mexico's geography in Chapter 8. In which part of the country do you think most Mexicans live?

STUDY THE VOCABULARY

urban   squatter settlement
migrant

FOCUS YOUR READING

Why is population growth a problem in Mexico?

A. Rapid Population Growth

Mexico has more people than any other Spanish-speaking country. It is also one of the most rapidly growing countries in the world. The graph on the next page shows how the population of the country has grown since 1940. You can see that

Mexico's population has more than quadrupled in 50 years. Some population experts predict that by the year 2100, Mexico will have around 200 million inhabitants.

Rapid population growth causes many problems. All of a country's services have to grow just to keep up with population. So from health care to garbage disposal, public services feel the strain of Mexico's growing population.

Education is another area affected. Imagine how many new schools Mexico must build to educate its young people. After all, over half of all the Mexicans are under the age of 20! What other services need to grow to keep up with the increase in the population?

B. Population Patterns

Over half of Mexico's people live in a wide area across the middle of the country, between the Gulf of Mexico and the Pacific Ocean. Locate this area on the map on page 246. Mexico City is in this wide area.

A classroom scene in Mexico City is shown here.
▶ What similarities are there to a classroom in the United States?

POPULATION GROWTH IN MEXICO

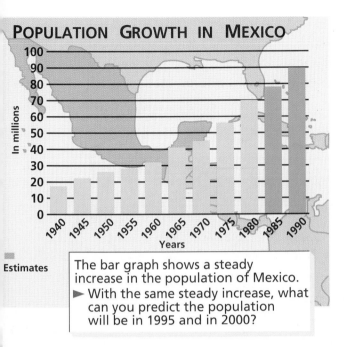

In millions

100
90
80
70
60
50
40
30
20
10
0

Years
1940 1945 1950 1955 1960 1965 1970 1975 1980 1985 1990

Estimates

The bar graph shows a steady increase in the population of Mexico.
► With the same steady increase, what can you predict the population will be in 1995 and in 2000?

Throughout this broad region are many little valleys and villages. Each valley looks different from the others, and each has its own way of life. In Indian areas, even the language changes from valley to valley. People call these valleys *patrias chicas* (PAH tree ahs CHEE kahs), which is Spanish for "little countries." Many Mexicans, especially Indians, are more attached to their patrias chicas than they are to the country of Mexico.

The northern part of Mexico is one of the least populated parts of the country because it is so dry. Most of the people who do live in this area live in oases, where water can be found.

Another part of Mexico that has few people is the Yucatán Peninsula. The most populated part of the Yucatán Peninsula is the northern one third. It has been the home of the Maya and their descendants for thousands of years.

C. From Countryside to City

In 1910, four out of five Mexicans lived on farms or in small villages. Today, over half the people of Mexico live in **urban** areas. *Urban* means "having to do with the city rather than the countryside." Each year more and more people in rural areas leave their homes and move to cities. Study the pie graphs on this page. Notice the rise in urban population.

People who leave one place to live in another place within their country are called **migrants**. Why do they change locations? There are many reasons. Remember that primate cities usually have most of a country's industries and modern services. That certainly is true in Mexico. You also know that it is not possible to make a good living by farming a tiny plot of land, so some people move to the cities to find work. Others want to go to school, or they think that the cities offer them the opportunity for a better life. Mexican cities cannot easily house all migrants. Many of the migrants are poor. Many cannot afford to buy even the simplest houses.

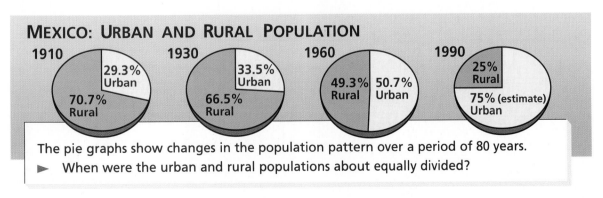

MEXICO: URBAN AND RURAL POPULATION

1910
29.3% Urban
70.7% Rural

1930
33.5% Urban
66.5% Rural

1960
49.3% Rural
50.7% Urban

1990
25% Rural
75% (estimate) Urban

The pie graphs show changes in the population pattern over a period of 80 years.
► When were the urban and rural populations about equally divided?

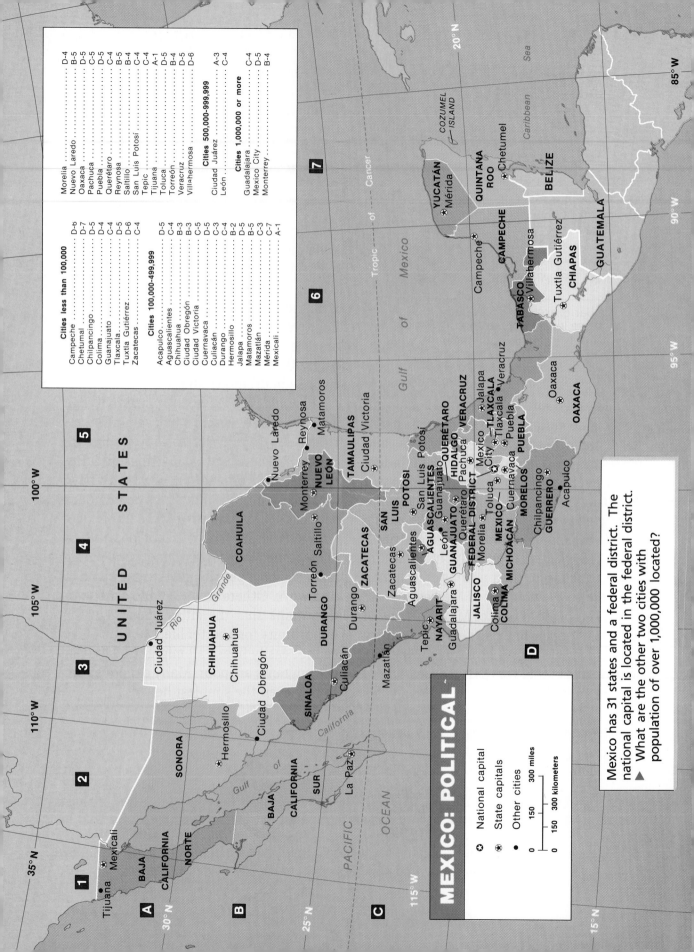

MEXICO: POLITICAL

Cities less than 100,000

Campeche	D-6
Chetumal	D-7
Chilpancingo	D-5
Colima	D-4
Guanajuato	C-4
Tlaxcala	D-5
Tuxtla Gutiérrez	D-6
Zacatecas	C-4

Cities 100,000-499,999

Acapulco	D-5
Aguascalientes	C-4
Chihuahua	B-3
Ciudad Obregón	B-3
Ciudad Victoria	C-5
Cuernavaca	C-3
Culiacán	C-3
Durango	C-4
Hermosillo	B-2
Jalapa	D-5
Matamoros	B-5
Mazatlán	C-3
Mérida	C-7
Mexicali	A-1

Cities 500,000-999,999

Morelia	D-4
Nuevo Laredo	B-5
Oaxaca	C-5
Pachuca	D-5
Puebla	C-4
Querétaro	C-4
Reynosa	B-5
Saltillo	B-4
San Luis Potosí	C-4
Tepic	C-4
Tijuana	A-1
Toluca	D-5
Torreón	B-4
Veracruz	D-5
Villahermosa	D-6

Cities 500,000-999,999

Ciudad Juárez	A-3
León	C-4

Cities 1,000,000 or more

Guadalajara	C-4
Mexico City	D-5
Monterrey	B-4

Mexico has 31 states and a federal district. The
national capital is located in the federal district.
▲ What are the other two cities with
population of over 1,000,000 located?

Scale:
0   150   300 miles
0   150   300 kilometers

Legend:
✪ National capital
✪ State capitals
● Other cities

Poor migrants are forced to live on unused land at the edge of a city. There they build houses from scraps of lumber, tin, and even cardboard. Such areas are called **squatter settlements**. They are found around rapidly growing cities everywhere in Latin America. Ciudad Netzahualcóyotl (syoo DAHD net sah wahl-KOH yoht ul), called Ciudad Netza, is a squatter settlement near Mexico City. Over a million people live there.

People often think that squatter settlements are giant slums filled with crime. This is not correct. Squatter settlements usually are stable neighborhoods — that is, neighborhoods in which people live for years. Neighbors know one another, and children play in the streets and vacant lots.

Residents try to improve their houses by adding better materials in place of the scraps with which their houses were first made. They may add rooms for their children. Squatter settlements give new migrants who have little or no money a chance to get started in the cities.

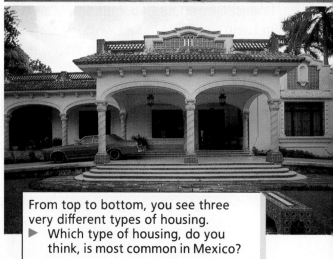

Of course, Mexican cities also have neighborhoods for the middle classes and the rich. In the past, most wealthy people liked to live near the central plazas of the downtown areas. Today, the wealthy neighborhoods of Mexican cities are in the suburbs, at the edges of the towns, and away from the older sections.

From top to bottom, you see three very different types of housing.
▶ Which type of housing, do you think, is most common in Mexico?

LESSON **2** REVIEW

THINK AND WRITE

A. What problems are caused by rapid population growth in Mexico?
B. Why do most of the people in Mexico live in the middle areas of the country?
C. For what reasons do people move from the countryside to the city?

SKILLS CHECK

THINKING SKILL

Think about the opportunities for Mexicans of school age who live in squatter settlements of cities. What are some inexpensive ways that they can enjoy and improve their lives? Consider recreation, education, and culture.

A Visit to Mexico City

THINK ABOUT LIFE IN MEXICO

Do you live in a large city? If not, have you ever visited or seen pictures of a really large city? List some of the ways in which large cities differ from small towns.

STUDY THE VOCABULARY

artisan

FOCUS YOUR READING

What features make some of Mexico's cities important?

A. Visiting Mexico City

Are you ready for a trip to Mexico City? This great national capital has the largest metropolitan population of any city in Latin America. In fact, with over 20 million people, its metropolitan area has the largest population of any urban area in the Americas.

Mexico City is the business center of the country. It has the most jobs, the best schools, the finest shops, and the best entertainment. Visitors to Mexico City find plenty to see and do there. Remember, Mexico City has a very long history. You can visit Aztec ruins, take a walking tour of colonial buildings, and visit modern museums and amusement parks.

A good starting point is the Zócalo, the great plaza right at the heart of Mexico City. Around the Zócalo you see the city's most important buildings. On one side is the largest and oldest cathedral in Latin America. On another side is the National Palace, a government building that is the office of Mexico's president. Shops fill the street across from the National Palace. There are also Aztec ruins, some of which were not found before the 1970s.

The Cathedral in Mexico City, with twin towers, is a majestic structure.
► What other buildings for worship, would you expect, are in the city?

From the Zócalo you can walk down Avenida Juárez. The Palace of Fine Arts is located on this avenue. During six months of the year, the National Opera company gives performances. Concerts are also given in the palace by the National Symphony Orchestra.

Another popular attraction in the cultural center is the Ballet Folklórico de México. This dance troupe is internationally famous. It tours the world from time to time to present its spectacular program of Mexican folkdances. Avenida Juárez leads to Paseo de la Reforma. The names of these streets commemorate Benito Juárez and the reform movement he led in the nineteenth century. Paseo de la Reforma is Mexico City's most important street. Along Reforma are seven traffic circles. Each traffic circle has a monument in the center. One of the most famous monuments honors the independence of Mexico. It is named El Angel, or "The Angel."

Tall buildings line both the Avenida Juárez and Paseo de la Reforma. These buildings house the businesses, banks, shops, and government offices in which many of the people of the city work. At the end of Paseo de la Reforma is Chapultepec (chuh POOL tuh pek) Park, one of the most famous city parks in the world. It seems as

The Ballet Folklórico often appears outside Mexico as well as in Mexico.
▶ What would you expect to see at one of the performances?

if every family in Mexico City is at the park on Sundays—visiting the zoo with its world-famous pandas, enjoying the amusement park rides, or watching the entertainers perform under the trees. Chapultepec Castle, where Mexico's rulers once lived, sits high up on one of the hills in the park. It is now Mexico's National Museum of History.

B. Two Other Mexican Cities

Guadalajara Mexico's second largest city, Guadalajara, has 3 million people, only about one-sixth the population of Mexico City. Located northwest of Mexico City, Guadalajara became a rich commercial center during the 300 years of Spanish rule in Mexico. Much of the wealth was spent on elaborate buildings, wide avenues, and beautiful landscaping. In Guadalajara you can still see many Spanish colonial buildings and churches that were built hundreds of years ago.

If you were to go to Guadalajara, you would probably want to visit Mercado Libertad, or Liberty Market in English. There you could buy many different kinds of food and souvenirs. The busiest market day is Friday, when merchants bring their handicrafts and freshest produce to sell. Many people travel a long way to sell their goods at this popular marketplace.

Guadalajara is a center for glassmaking and pottery making. You can visit factories to watch **artisans**, or craftspeople, at work making glass and pottery. Guadalajara is also a growing city known for its musical entertainment. It is the home of the famous *mariachis* (mar ee AH cheez), the strolling musicians of Mexico. Each October the people of Guadalajara enjoy a holiday called the Autumn Festival. The

Today, Chapultepec Castle, shown here, is a museum.
▶ What might be shown in the museum?

Mariachi bands play both classical and traditional music.
▶ Where might people see and hear these musicians?

city has open-air concerts and bullfights and other sports events. There are also exhibits of many different kinds of handmade goods.

Monterrey Mexico's third largest city is Monterrey (mahn tuh RAY). Founded in 1596, Monterrey is about 300 miles (483 km) south of San Antonio, Texas. This city of about 3 million people is the most important manufacturing center in Mexico after Mexico City. Over 75 percent of Mexico's iron and steel comes from Monterrey. It is also an important center for making glass, cement, chemicals, and beverages. Monterrey has a well-known technical institute that trains scientists, engineers, and managers for Mexico's businesses and factories.

Under an urban renewal project, Monterrey has taken on the appearance of a modern city. A 100-acre (41-ha) plaza with the State House, City Hall, and other buildings, extends for a number of blocks. Named the Grand Plaza, it was dedicated in 1985.

C. Indian Culture in Oaxaca

Oaxaca, in southern Mexico, is a city known as a center of Indian culture. Benito Juárez, whom you read about in the last chapter, worked and went to school in Oaxaca. In his day, the city had only a few thousand people. Today, it has a population of about 200,000.

Oaxaca is in a large valley surrounded by the Sierra Madre. Most of the people who live in the valley earn their living by working their small farms and by making cloth and pottery to sell in the markets. The city is a center of trade for most of southern Mexico.

Like most visitors to Oaxaca, you might be interested in seeing the Indian markets, which are a short ride from the

People in Oaxaca enjoy a relaxing afternoon in the zócalo.
▶ What activities do you see taking place?

city. There you can buy Indian handicrafts, such as woolen shawls called *serapes* (suh RAH peez), embroidered clothing, pottery, and leather goods.

Oaxaca has several colonial churches. One is the church of Santo Domingo, a few blocks from the center of the city. Part of the church is now a museum. Near Oaxaca are the important Indian ruins of Monte Alban and Mitla. They are two of the most important archaeological sites in southern Mexico. Some of the sites there date back to the seventh century B.C.

LESSON **3** *REVIEW*

THINK AND WRITE

A. What are some ways in which Mexico City is important to Mexico?
B. How does Guadalajara compare with Mexico City?
C. Which would you prefer to visit — Oaxaca or one of the other Mexican cities mentioned in this chapter? Give at least two reasons for your answer.

SKILLS CHECK

MAP SKILL

Look in the Gazetteer for *Mexico City*, *Guadalajara*, *Monterrey*, and *Oaxaca* to find out which city has the most northern location and which has the most southern location. Then use the information to find each city on the map of Mexico on page 246.

Government and Politics

THINK ABOUT WHAT YOU KNOW

Think about the United States political system. With your classmates, discuss how people are elected to public office.

STUDY THE VOCABULARY

republic   interest

deputy

FOCUS YOUR READING

What economic as well as political challenges does Mexico face?

A. The Republic of Mexico

Mexico began as an empire and then, as you have learned, experienced civil war and dictatorship. Today, Mexico is a **republic**—that is, it has an elected leader, a president, rather than a king or queen. The official name of the country is los Estados Unidos Mexicanos, or the United Mexican States.

Mexico has 31 states and a federal district for its national capital, Mexico City. Each state elects two senators, as do the states in the United States. Each state also elects **deputies**, or representatives. The number of deputies from each state depends on the population of the State. Deputies are like members of the House of Representatives in the government of the United States.

B. The PRI and Politics

How long can a revolution last? The effects or influence of a great revolution can be felt for hundreds of years. However, the revolution itself must give way to a more orderly situation.

Since the Revolution of 1910, Mexico really has had only one major political party. This new political party came to power in Mexico in 1929. The Institutional Revolutionary Party, or the PRI as it became known in Mexico, has continued to control the country almost unchallenged. There are other political parties in Mexico. Some of these parties' candidates have won elections to city governments and even to Mexico's congress. But only the PRI candidates have won the presidential elections in Mexico. Because they have so much power, the PRI elected officials can decide how the Mexican government will act.

The powerful position of the PRI helped to bring peace and order to Mexico. Land reform was often mentioned, but very little redistribution of land occurred. Under the PRI, Mexico has concentrated on industrialization and economic growth.

As you learned, Mexico achieved considerable success with its development plans. However, problems of inequality and poverty did not disappear.

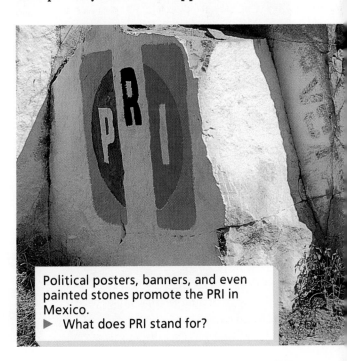

Political posters, banners, and even painted stones promote the PRI in Mexico.
▶ What does PRI stand for?

Can a country have a democracy with only one real political party? The United States has two major political parties. Candidates from these two political parties run for office and are elected by the American people. This election process is not the same in Mexico. For many years in Mexico the PRI was the only political party. A party as large as the PRI had to represent the interests of many different groups. For example, organized labor groups belonged to the PRI and so did peasant groups. Since representatives of many different groups all tried to influence policy, there was a democracy of a sort inside the PRI.

C. A Troubled Economy

Although Mexico is a country with valuable resources, productive commercial farms, and many industries, it is also a country with very big debts. When Mexico discovered its large oil reserves, the government began many costly projects. It borrowed billions of dollars from banks in foreign countries to build new office buildings, factories, refineries, hotels, dams, and many other things. Those projects were all intended to make jobs for Mexico's people and to improve the economy. The loans were to be repaid from the oil Mexico would sell.

Large office buildings (left) and housing projects (right) were built in Mexico during the oil boom.
► Why were they built then?

Oil refineries, such as this one in Mexico, employ many different workers in their plant.
► What jobs might people have?

FOREIGN DEBT OF SELECTED NATIONS

Debt in millions of dollars			Debt as % of GNP	
	1970	1986	1970	1986
Mexico	5,966	91,062	17%	76%
Argentina	5,171	43,012	23%	52%
Brazil	5,128	97,162	12%	38%

The chart shows three nations whose debts and percentage of debts to GNP were similar in 1970.
► How did these patterns change in 1986?

When banks lend money, they charge **interest**. The interest is usually a percentage of the amount borrowed and is charged by the lender. So to pay a debt, the borrower must pay back the original amount borrowed plus the interest.

In 1981 the price of oil began to fall worldwide. It continued to fall throughout the 1980s. So Mexico could not earn enough to pay its debts. Just paying the interest on its loans was very difficult.

This caused the value of Mexico's money to go down and the cost of food and goods to go up. When added to the population growth, Mexico's economic problems became even more serious.

D. New Opposition

As Mexico struggled with its economic problems, criticism of the PRI grew. People said that the government had mismanaged the oil industry and the economy. The PRI, it was said, had lost touch with the people. It no longer worked for the ideals of the revolution.

In 1988 it was time to elect a new president. PRI leaders chose Carlos Salinas de Gortari as their party's candidate. A former minister of planning, he was 40 years old, and had graduate degrees in economics and government from Harvard University in the United States. Would the PRI candidate win easily?

FROM:

My Heart Lies South

By: Elizabeth Borton de Treviño
Setting: Monterrey, Mexico

When Elizabeth Borton, a native of California, married Luís Treviño, a native of Monterrey, Mexico, she learned to accept and appreciate a number of new customs.

In this selection, she tells about one of the customs that is observed in Latin America.

. . . Monterrey held pitfalls in a part of the language I never dreamed of. These were the names.

My husband's father's name was Porfirio Treviño Arreola. . . . My husband's name is Luís Treviño Gómez, for his mother's name as a girl had been Adelita Gómez Sánchez. On her marriage she became Adelita Gómez de Treviño. It will be seen that children use the father's name first and the mother's name last. Women keep their maiden name intact, merely adding "de" (belonging to) and the husband's name. Thus I became Elizabeth Borton de Treviño. Properly written in the old Spanish style, my name would have carried both my husband's father's and mother's names, thus: Elizabeth Borton de Treviño Gómez. Sounds complicated, but it has its virtues. . . .

For example, let us suppose two young things are rattling on about Pepe [nickname for José] Morones. Their mother, to get it straight, stops them and says, "Whom do you mean?" The reply is his full name. "José Morones Maldonado." "Ah," thinks Mamacita [affectionately, little mother]. "They mean the son of Adalberto Morones Calderon, who married Concha Maldonado Becerra." Everything is cleared up. . . . My kind sister-in-law Adela arranged a dancing party in our honor to introduce me to her friends. About 50 couples had been invited. My head began to swim after the third introduction and by the end of the evening I was lost. I had met Sr. [abbreviation for Señor] de la Garza y Garza, Sr. Garza Gonzalez, Sr. Gonzalez Garza, Sra. [abbreviation for Señora] Gonzalez de Garza y Garza, Nena Garza de Gonzalez, Sr. Treviño Garza, Sr. Treviño Gonzalez-Garza, Nena Garza de Treviño, Sra. Treviño de Treviño, and so on and so on, mostly Garza Gonzalez and Treviño in endless combinations. These happen to be the most common family names in Monterrey. . . .

This time something unexpected happened. Another strong political party established itself. In the past, only the National Action Party, known as the PAN, had challenged the PRI. Now the opposition also included the National Democratic Front, a party led by Cuauhtémoc Cárdenas, son of the extremely popular past president Lázaro Cárdenas. You may recall that Cuauhtémoc was the name of the last Aztec emperor who defended Tenochtitlán against the Spaniards. By his name alone, then, Cárdenas seemed to represent something special, the Aztec past and the ideals of the great revolution.

Salinas de Gortari won, but the official vote count gave him only slightly over half the vote, the smallest winning percentage ever. Cárdenas received 31 percent and the PAN candidate, 17 percent. The opposition parties won four Senate seats and had great support in Mexico City.

In the early 1990s it seemed that the PRI's stranglehold on national politics might be coming to an end. That wasn't the only change. President Salinas encouraged economic reforms to strengthen the private sector and reduce the number of government-owned corp-

Mexican President Carlos Salinas meets with President Bill Clinton.
▶ What subjects might these two leaders discuss?

orations. These reforms helped the country's economy to grow, and they created more jobs for the Mexican people. President Salinas also supported developing a North American Trade Zone, a free trade area to include Mexico, Canada, and the United States. You can read more about this proposal for the North American Free Trade Agreement (NAFTA) on page 584.

LESSON *4* REVIEW

THINK AND WRITE

A. In what ways is the government of Mexico similar to that of the United States?
B. How can the PRI be considered democratic?
C. What problems does Mexico face in the present?
D. Why was the 1988 presidential campaign and election important?

SKILLS CHECK

WRITING SKILL

"Live and learn" is a famous saying. It means that each person—and even each country—should learn from the past in order to build a better future. In a paragraph or two, explain how this saying can be applied to something you read about in this chapter.

CHAPTER 9 — PUTTING IT ALL TOGETHER

USING THE VOCABULARY

gross national product (GNP)	squatter settlement
manufacturing	urban
commercial farm	interest
subsistence farm	deputy
erosion	reserves
republic	migrants
	artisans

On a separate sheet of paper, write the number of the definition and the term from the list that matches the definition.

1. making of goods
2. neighborhood of the poor
3. having to do with the city
4. percentage charged on an amount borrowed
5. farms that raise crops for sale
6. people leaving one place to live in another part of their country
7. craftspeople
8. country with an elected leader rather than a king or queen
9. value of a nation's goods and services for one year
10. extra supplies to be used later

REMEMBERING WHAT YOU READ

On a separate sheet of paper, answer the following questions in complete sentences.

1. What are some of Mexico's important natural resources?
2. Who are braceros?
3. What are some problems that are caused by Mexico's rapid growth in population?
4. What is Ciudad Netza?
5. What interesting sights can you see in Guadalajara?
6. Which city is a center of Indian culture?
7. What form of government does Mexico have?
8. How many states does Mexico have?
9. Name the two major political parties in Mexico.
10. Describe the current president of Mexico.

TYING MATH TO SOCIAL STUDIES

Call or visit three banks in your town or city. Ask these questions at each bank.

1. How much interest does each pay on a savings account?
2. How much interest does it charge on a personal loan?
3. If you borrowed $3,000 for two years, what would your total payments to the bank add up to?

Based on the information you get, answer these questions on a separate paper.

1. Where would you prefer to open a savings account?
2. Where would you take out a loan?
3. How much money would you pay in interest on the loan of $3,000 in two years to the bank of your choice?

THINKING CRITICALLY

On a separate sheet of paper, answer the following questions in complete sentences.

1. If you grew up as the child of a poor laborer, how might you make a change and become a well-paid professional in Mexico?
2. How might subsistence farmers in Mexico improve their lives?
3. What makes Mexico an interesting place to visit?
4. Why is it better to have several political parties in a country instead of just one?
5. Mexico's economy is in trouble because of debts to foreign banks. The government cannot pay back the debts because the price of oil has gone down. In which ways might the government solve this problem?

SUMMARIZING THE CHAPTER

On a separate sheet of paper, draw a graphic organizer like the one shown here. Copy the information from this graphic organizer to the one you have drawn. Under each heading, fill in the blanks with facts you learned from that lesson.

CHAPTER THEME
Mexico is highly industrialized and has many natural resources, but it also has many economic problems.

LESSON 1
Mexicans face a job shortage and low pay in spite of economic growth.

1. _____
2. _____
3. _____

LESSON 3
Mexico's cities have much to offer natives and tourists.

1. _____
2. _____
3. _____

LESSON 2
Mexican population has increased rapidly causing many problems.

1. _____
2. _____
3. _____

LESSON 4
Politics in Mexico have slowly emerged into a form of multi-party democracy.

1. _____
2. _____
3. _____

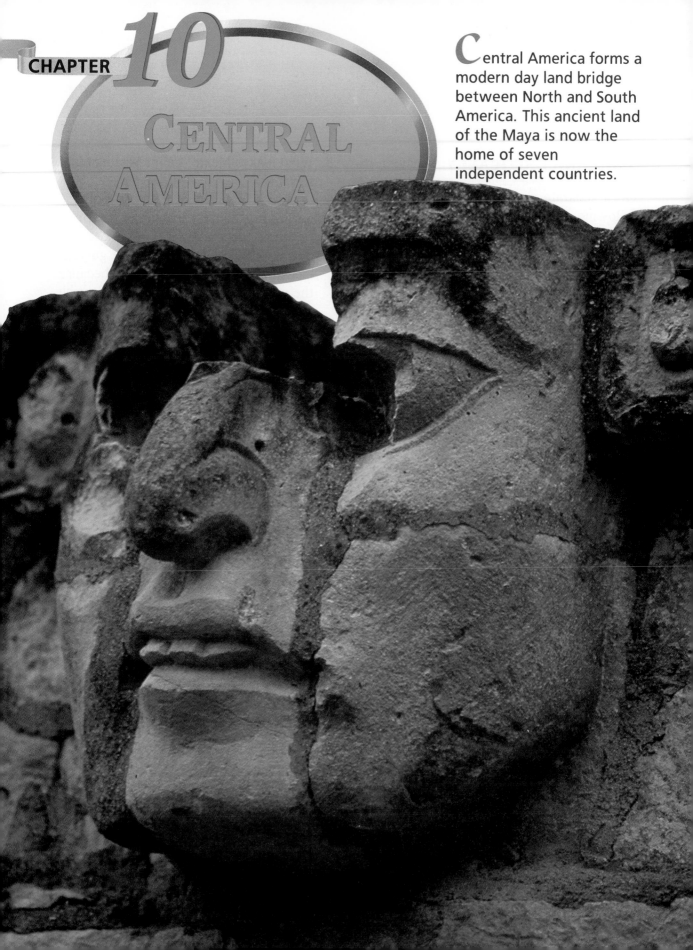

CHAPTER

10

CENTRAL AMERICA

Central America forms a modern day land bridge between North and South America. This ancient land of the Maya is now the home of seven independent countries.

Land Between the Seas

THINK ABOUT WHAT YOU KNOW

Discuss with your classmates some of the things you know about volcanoes. What happens when a volcano erupts?

STUDY THE VOCABULARY

fault

FOCUS YOUR READING

What are some of the important features of the land and climate in Central America?

A. Mountains and Lowlands

Unlike the land bridge that connected Asia and North America and disappeared thousands of years ago, there is another land bridge that still exists. It is Central America. Once a group of volcanic islands that rose from the sea, the region is today a narrow strip of land that connects North America with South America. Central America is made up of seven countries — Guatemala, Belize, El Salvador, Honduras, Nicaragua, Costa Rica, and Panama. Find each country on the map on the next page.

There are several highland areas with mountains and volcanoes in Central America. One mountain chain not far from the Pacific coast stretches some 1,200 miles (1,931 km), from southern Mexico all the way to Panama. Other long, narrow mountain ranges rise in Guatemala, Honduras, and Nicaragua. These mountains stretch like ribs from the interior to the Caribbean coast. Between the mountains are low valleys.

Lowlands run along both sides of Central America's mountainous spine. A coastal lowland stretches along the Pacific coast of Central America from Guatemala to Panama. It is one of Central America's

Countries of Central America are linked by the Pan American Highway.
▶ What natural features are in this part of El Salvador?

90° W

MEXICO

TURNEFFE IS.

EL PETEN ✪ Belmopan

BELIZE

Gulf of Honduras

BAY IS.

San Pedro Sula

Tajumulco
13,845 ft ▲ GUATEMALA
(4,220 m) ▲ ●Quezaltenango
Santa María
12,375 ft   ✪ Guatemala City
(3,772 m) ▲ Fuego
Lake Atitlán 12,346 ft.
         (3,763 m)

HONDURAS

Lake Izabal

Coco River

Lempa River

Izalco ✪ San
7,749 ft. Salvador
(2,362 m)

☆ Tegucigalpa

MISKITOS IS.

EL SALVADOR

NICARAGUA

León ●

Lake Managua

Managua ✪

Bluefields ●

● CORN IS.

Lake Nicaragua

15° N

10° N

Irazú
11,260 ft.
(3,432 m) ▲

COSTA RICA

San José ☆ ▲ ● Limón

Mt. Chirripó ▲
12,530 ft
(3,819 m)

ISTHMUS OF PANAMA

PANAMA ✪ ● Panama City

Gulf
of
Panama

REY I.

COIBA I.

COLOMBIA

85° W

80° W

75° W

Lake Nicaragua

○ National capitals
● Other cities
▲ Volcanoes

Elevations
Feet   Meters
12,000 --   -- 3,658
9,000 --   -- 2,743
5,000 --   -- 1,524
2,000 --   -- 610
1,000 --   -- 305
500 --   -- 152
0 --   -- 0

0   100   200 miles

0   100   200 kilometers

The physical map shows that Central America has extremes in its elevation.

▶ In which Central American country is the highest volcanic peak located?

most important commercial farming areas. The lowlands on the Caribbean side of Central America are larger. However, the soil there is poorer for farming than it is on the Pacific coast.

B. Volcanoes and Lakes

Many of Central America's mountains are volcanic. Although Volcán Tajumulco at 13,845 feet (4,220 m) and Atitlán at 11,633 feet (3,546 m) in Guatemala are not as high as Orizaba in Mexico, these volcanoes are still impressive. The active volcanoes in Central America frequently erupt, hurling out hot gases and lava.

Volcanoes may not seem pleasant to

you, but they certainly provide fertile soil for farming. They also provide beautiful scenery. Imagine sailing on a lake surrounded by the towering heights of majestic volcanoes. That's what you would see from a boat on Guatemala's Lake Atitlán (ah tee TLAHN), considered by some people to be one of the world's most beautiful lakes. You'd enjoy a similarly spectacular view from Lake Nicaragua, the largest lake in Central America.

It might surprise you to learn that neither of these lakes would exist if it weren't for volcanoes. That's because the lakes were formed as a result of volcanic activity and **faults**. A fault is a break in the earth's solid rock layer. Faults form when pressure inside the earth causes the rock to break and move. Scientists think that Lake Nicaragua was part of a bay in the ocean at one time. Volcanic activity filled in a low area in the bay and separated the water from the ocean, creating a lake. Lake Atitlán was created when large volcanoes made a huge dam that blocked streams flowing from nearby mountains.

Besides being the largest lake in Central America, Lake Nicaragua is the largest lake between the Great Lakes and Lake Titicaca in Peru. It is also among the 25 largest lakes in the world with an area of 3,100 square miles (8,029 sq km). About 20 young volcanic cones, many active, extend along the margins of both Lake Nicaragua and Lake Managua.

Long before the Panama Canal was built, several countries considered building a canal from the Caribbean to Lake Nicaragua, then across Lake Nicaragua with a cut through to reach the Pacific Ocean. Spain even surveyed the area for a route as early as the eighteenth century. The United States and Great Britain formed a treaty for a joint project in 1850. Treaties in 1901 and 1914 gave the United States sole right to build a canal. Even after the Panama Canal was opened, the United States had an interest in a canal through Nicaragua. Finally, in 1971, the option to build a canal there was cancelled.

(Left) Volcanoes stand guard over Guatemala's Lake Atitlán.
(Right) This is a bird's-eye view inside of Irazú, a volcano in Costa Rica.
▶ Find Irazú on the map on page 262. How high is the volcano?

C. Tropical Regions in the Petén

The Petén is an area that covers the northern third of Guatemala and lies in the southern part of the Yucatán Peninsula. The Petén is a low limestone plateau. Much of the tropical forests and jungles that cover the Petén have not been cleared since the days of the Maya. Tall trees keep sunlight from reaching the ground, and there is very little undergrowth.

In recent years, however, Guatemala has built roads into the Petén so that forests can be cleared and farms started. Guatemalans from other areas have eagerly moved there to take advantage of the opportunity. Other people concerned with the environment worry about these kinds of projects. That's because although tropical rain forests cover only 16 percent of the earth's surface, they house about 50 percent of the earth's animals. The tropical forests are home to many different kinds of animals, such as monkeys, parrots, deer, ocelots, jaguars, and peccaries. Peccaries look like small pigs. The forests also help to recycle carbon dioxide and oxygen into the air.

Tikal, a famous Maya city, is located in the Petén. It was a significant center of Maya culture. Many ancient ruins have been found in Tikal. Because this area has been declared a national park, the wildlife there remains undisturbed.

D. Climate Varies

The Dry Lowlands Can you imagine a place where there's no rain at all for half of the year? That's what it's like in the Pacific coast lowlands of Central America. The region has a tropical climate with a long dry season. The dry season usually lasts for about six months. The other six months of the year are rainy, with short, but often heavy, showers nearly every day. Overall, precipitation averages less than 100 inches (254 cm) per year.

Plants and animals such as these are native to Central America's tropical forests.
▶ What, do you think, might happen to some plants and animals as forests are cleared?

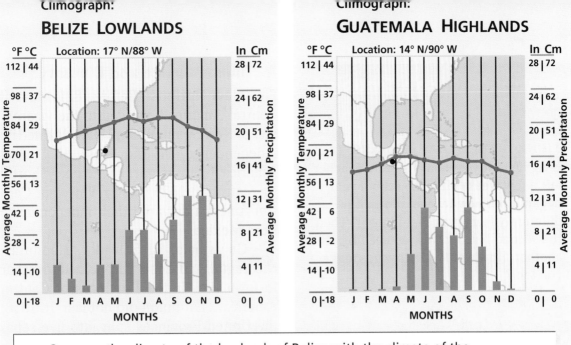

Climograph:

BELIZE LOWLANDS

°F °C   Location: 17° N/88° W   In Cm

Climograph:

GUATEMALA HIGHLANDS

°F °C   Location: 14° N/90° W   In Cm

Compare the climate of the lowlands of Belize with the climate of the Guatemalan highlands.
► Which region is cooler and drier?

The Rainy Lowlands In contrast, the lowlands on the Caribbean coast have a rainy tropical climate year round. Precipitation is usually over 100 inches per year. If a dry season occurs, it is very brief.

The Effects of Elevation Though all of Central America lies in the tropics, various elevations create the temperature zones learned about in Chapter 1. The lowland,

the tierra caliente, has a warm climate. At the middle land, the tierra templada, the climate becomes temperate. In the higher land, the tierra fría, it is cool.

The capitals of Guatemala, Honduras, and Costa Rica are in the tierra templada. The capitals of El Salvador, Nicaragua, Belize, and Panama are in the tierra caliente. Find the names of these capital cities on the map of Central America on page 262.

LESSON **1** *REVIEW*

THINK AND WRITE

A. Describe the land of Central America.
B. What is the connection between volcanoes and two of the major lakes in Central America?
C. Why is Guatemala trying to clear the tropical forest covering the Petén?
D. For each different climate zone in Central America, give one reason why people would or would not want to live in that climate.

SKILLS CHECK

MAP SKILL

Look up *Lake Nicaragua* in the Gazetteer and find something about it that is very unusual. Then locate Lake Nicaragua on the map on page 262. How do the map and information you read about in this section help you understand the Gazetteer entry?

Central America's Troubled History

THINK ABOUT WHAT YOU KNOW

Imagine that your social studies teacher left a few weeks after the school year began. Your new teacher did things differently from your first teacher. Then the second teacher was replaced by still another. How would the changes make you feel?

STUDY THE VOCABULARY

civil rights   **literacy rate**
terrorist

FOCUS YOUR READING

What problems have the countries of Central America faced since gaining independence?

A. Independence and Disunity

Five New Nations Before 1821, most of Central America belonged to the viceroyalty of New Spain. When Mexico gained its independence, so did most of Central America—but as part of Mexico. Shortly thereafter, in 1823, the provinces of Central America declared their independence from Mexico.

Guatemala, El Salvador, Honduras, Nicaragua, and Costa Rica joined together to form the United Provinces of Central America. That union did not last. In 1838, the United Provinces split into five separate republics.

These new nations continued to have difficulties. Rule by dictators, the occurrence of frequent coups and civil wars, and *intervention* by other nations caused slow economic growth. Intervention can mean the act of one country going to another

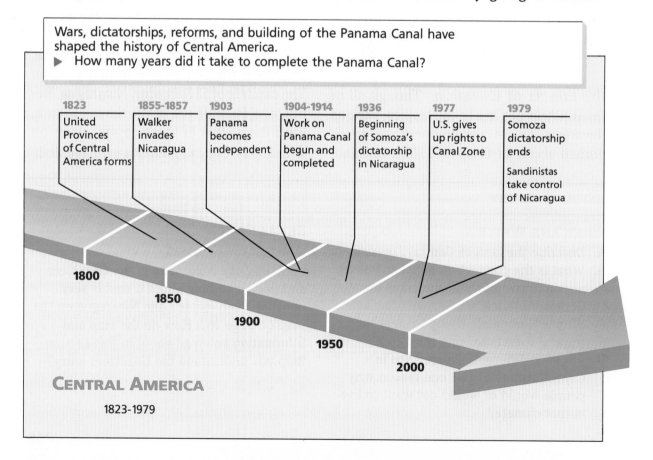

Wars, dictatorships, reforms, and building of the Panama Canal have shaped the history of Central America.

▶ How many years did it take to complete the Panama Canal?

1823	1855-1857	1903	1904-1914	1936	1977	1979
United Provinces of Central America forms	Walker invades Nicaragua	Panama becomes independent	Work on Panama Canal begun and completed	Beginning of Somoza's dictatorship in Nicaragua	U.S. gives up rights to Canal Zone	Somoza dictatorship ends Sandinistas take control of Nicaragua

1800
1850
1900
1950
2000

CENTRAL AMERICA
1823-1979

Banners wave in Belize City when Belize became independent in 1981.
▶ What, do you think, do the words on the front banner mean?

country to stop some action or help settle a dispute that is taking place there. Throughout, the Indian and peasant peoples of these countries suffered greatly.

Two More Nations The other two Central American nations became independent under very different circumstances. Panama, which was in the viceroyalty of New Granada, gained independence as a part of Colombia after Simón Bolívar defeated the Spaniards. It became a separate republic in 1903. Belize began as a British colony. For many years it was called British Honduras. Belize became independent in 1981.

B. Problems in Honduras

During its 160 years as an independent country, Honduras has had 126 changes in government as well as 16 constitutions! Such frequent changes, of course, have made it difficult for Honduras to progress.

Foreign companies, such as the United Fruit Company and the Standard Fruit Company, developed large plantations in Honduras, where they grew bananas. These companies often played a role in Honduran politics. Because the economy of Honduras depended on this one crop, many foreigners called Honduras a *banana republic*.

In 1957, Hondurans finally enjoyed free, honest elections. However, six years later, the military deposed the president and took over the government. *Depose*, you will remember, means "to remove from office or from a position of authority."

In 1969, Honduras went to war with El Salvador. This war was fought because for many years people from El Salvador

Honduras is a major banana-exporting country.
▶ In which temperature zone is Honduras located? Refer to the map on page 61.

went to Honduras looking for work or for farmland. The Hondurans wanted the jobs and land that migrants from El Salvador took, so they tried to send the Salvadorans home.

In the 1980s, a war in neighboring Nicaragua caused new problems for Honduras. Nicaraguans who were opposed to the Nicaraguan government established military bases in Honduras. The Nicaraguan army attacked those bases. The United States, which also opposed the government of Nicaragua, sent troops, on training missions, and supplies to Honduras.

Some Hondurans became very disturbed with this situation. They did not want Nicaragua invading their country, but they also resented the ever-growing United States presence in their country. They feared that neither side really cared about the interests of Honduras.

C. Reform in Guatemala

Election of a President Like Honduras, Guatemala went through many years of dictatorship. In 1944, a revolution resulted in the overthrow of the last dictator. The government that came to power wanted to improve the lives of the Guatemalans. The first president of Guatemala, Juan José Arévalo (ah RAY vah loh), was elected in 1945. When his term ended in 1950, the first election in many years was held. The winner was Jacobo Arbenz Guzmán, who had served as minister of defense.

The governments of Arévalo and Arbenz tried to give Guatemalans political freedom and other **civil rights**. Civil rights are the rights of citizens to such things as life, ownership of property, and equal treatment under the law. Other reforms attempted to improve education and better the standard of living of the Indians.

Military Control In 1954 a military coup ended the Arbenz government. The United States helped the coup. It said that enemies of the United States really controlled the Arbenz government. Also, some people in the United States government were upset because the Guatemalans had expropriated the land of American companies in Guatemala. Among those companies was the United Fruit Company, which owned vast plantations in Guatemala. For about the next 30 years, the military controlled Guatemala's government.

Many Guatemalans who opposed the military turned to violence. Guatemala suffered frequent warfare between the guerrillas and the government. **Terrorists**, both on the side of the guerrillas and the government, kidnapped or murdered hundreds of people. Terrorists are people who use fear or violence to force others to do what they want them to do.

In the late 1970s, the guerrillas moved into the western part of the country, where most of the Indians live. The army fought back fiercely. Thousands of Indians were killed or driven from their homes by both the guerrillas and the army. The Indians suffered in a war they did not begin and in which many of them did not take sides.

D. A Different Pattern in Costa Rica

There's something about Costa Rica that makes it very unusual, not just in Central America but in the entire world. It has no army! Here's how that happened.

In 1948, Costa Rica had a revolution. The army sided with the government that was overthrown. After the revolution, the new government decided that the country did not need an army. The police could keep order inside Costa Rica. The neighboring countries, Nicaragua and Panama, seemed to pose no threat, and the money it

This coffee plantation near the city of Antigua, Guatemala, is almost completely surrounded by forests.
▶ What do you see in the background?

cost to keep an army could be used for education and public health. Therefore, the army was disbanded.

Other things also set Costa Rica apart from its neighbors. It has a long history of democratic and stable government. It also has excellent schools, and about 90 percent of the people can read and write. This **literacy rate** ranks among the highest in the world. Literacy rate is the percentage of people in an area who can read and write. Few of Costa Rica's people are extremely poor or extremely rich. Most of the land is held in small farms rather than in large haciendas or plantations.

What accounts for Costa Rica's different development? That question has several answers. First of all, farmers, not conquistadors, settled Costa Rica. Land and resources were owned by more than a few families. As a result, there are no large underprivileged groups, such as the Indians of Guatemala. Many of Costa Rica's people own their land and grow coffee or other commercial crops. So poverty is not as big a problem in Costa Rica as it is in other Latin American countries.

Two high school students stop to talk beside a fruit stand in the capital city of San José.
▶ In what language is the sign above the fruit stand?

For those reasons, the great differences between rich and poor that are found in most of Latin America did not develop in Costa Rica. Social class differences have less importance in Costa Rica than elsewhere in Latin America. Most people are in the middle class.

LESSON 2 REVIEW

THINK AND WRITE

A. What happened to the region of Central America after it gained independence from Spain?

B. In a few sentences, summarize the problems that Honduras has had with its neighboring countries.

C. Contrast the period of reform with the troubled times in Guatemala.

D. In what ways does Costa Rica differ from the other republics of Central America?

SKILLS CHECK

THINKING SKILL

You have probably heard about and seen pictures on television showing violent outbreaks in some Central American countries. Think about Costa Rica—a country without an army. With your classmates, discuss whether or not you think Costa Rica should have an army.

Nicaragua

THINK ABOUT WHAT YOU KNOW

Part of this lesson tells about civil war in Nicaragua. Why would people who live in the same country fight a war with one another? Make a list of some possible reasons.

STUDY THE VOCABULARY

socialism

FOCUS YOUR READING

What kinds of governments has the country of Nicaragua had?

A. Nicaragua and the United States

In 1855, a United States citizen named William Walker invaded Nicaragua as a liberator to spread democracy, ran for the presidency, and won easily! Five years later he was captured by the British and handed over to a Honduran firing squad. During the early period of its independence, Nicaragua, like the other republics in Central America, faced dictators, coups, and foreign interference throughout the nineteenth century.

In this century, Nicaragua's problems have continued. In 1912, United States Marines landed in Nicaragua to prevent a civil war and to protect United States interests in the area. The Marines stayed in Nicaragua from 1912 to 1925 and again from 1927 to 1933.

Many Nicaraguans did not like having American Marines in their country. One such person was Augusto César Sandino. Between 1927 and 1934 he fought a guerrilla war against both the United States Marines and the Nicaraguan army, called the National Guard. Sandino was killed in 1934 by members of the National Guard.

In 1936, Anastasio Somoza began one of the longest continuous dictatorships in Latin American history. Until 1979, he, one of his sons, or a Somoza–chosen candidate was president of Nicaragua. Over those years, the National Guard remained loyal to the Somoza leadership. The Somoza family piled up enormous personal wealth that was invested in land and businesses.

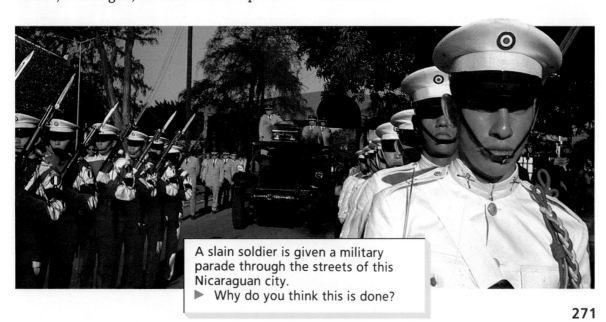

A slain soldier is given a military parade through the streets of this Nicaraguan city.
▶ Why do you think this is done?

B. The End of the Somoza Leadership

In 1972 a terrible earthquake caused major damage to the city of Managua — Nicaragua's capital. Some 10,000 Nicaraguans died. Relief poured in from many countries and international agencies. Then some disturbing news began to come out of Nicaragua. President Anastasio Somoza, Jr., and his allies had taken much of the relief money to use as their own.

Even before the earthquake, many people in Nicaragua had grown weary of Somoza's long dictatorship. A guerrilla army that called itself the Sandinista Liberation Front, after the rebel leader Augusto Sandino, had been organized back in 1961. Many of its members, who became known as Sandinistas, were peasants who did not have land to farm. Somoza's misuse of the relief money helped spark a wider opposition and brought new supporters to the rebel army. Women led some of the fighting units.

In 1979, the Sandinistas launched an attack. The Nicaraguan president, Luis Somoza, went into exile in Florida. A new government was set up along the lines of **socialism**. Socialism is a system of government in which land and industries are controlled by the government rather than by individuals or private companies.

C. Sandinistas and Contras

Some of the people who had been in Somoza's National Guard escaped across the border into neighboring Honduras. There they began planning to overthrow the Sandinistas. Since they were against the revolution, they were called contras, or counterrevolutionaries. In Spanish the word for "counter" is *contra*.

A man surveys the damage to Managua after the earthquake of 1972.
▶ Why, do you think, are his nose and mouth covered?

FROM:

Selected Poems of Rubén Darío
Translated by: Lysander Kemp

Rubén Darío was born in Nicaragua on January 18, 1867. From the age of 14, he used the pen name Rubén Darío whenever he signed his poems and stories. His actual name was Félix Rubén García.

At the age of 19, he began a lifetime of travel throughout South America, Europe, and the United States, with periodic visits to his homeland. He died in Nicaragua in 1916.

Darío was a leader in the literature movement known as Modernism. He gained fame and respect throughout the world and was called "the prince of Spanish-American Literature."

The poetry of Rubén Darío has been translated from Spanish into English and into other languages. One of the translations appears below. In "Evening," his love of nature is evident.

Evening

The siesta hour has passed,
the sunset hour is nearing,
and there is a touch of coolness now
on this sun-stricken tropic coast.
There is a breath of ocean air
and the west pretends to be a forest
lit with a purple flame.

The crabs are marking the sand
with the illegible scrawl of their claws
and sea shells, color of roses, of gold
reflections, and little snails, and bits
of starfish, are a singing carpet
when you walk these harmonious shores.
And when Venus shines,
imperial love of the godlike evening,
you can hear in the waves the sound
of a lyre or the song of a siren.
And a star like that of Venus glows in my soul.

Contras, in the fight against the Sandinistas, stand at attention awaiting inspection.
► Why, do you think, is the camp in the forest?

Some of the men and women who had fought with the Sandinistas also became unhappy with Nicaragua's new rulers. They thought the Sandinistas themselves were becoming dictators and that Cuba and the Soviet Union had too much influence in the government. Many of these people went to Costa Rica, where some formed another group of Contras. With the Nicaraguan economy only one third of what it was in 1979, and workers' wages down considerably in the last 10 years, the Sandinista government faced difficult times.

LESSON 3 REVIEW

THINK AND WRITE

A. Briefly describe the political situation in Nicaragua from 1855 until 1979.
B. What were two of the causes that resulted in the downfall of the Somoza rule?
C. Why did some Nicaraguans oppose the Sandinistas?

SKILLS CHECK

THINKING SKILL

Imagine that you are living in Nicaragua at the time of one of the rulers mentioned in this lesson. You don't approve of the government, but you love your country. What will you do? Discuss your feelings and ideas with some classmates.

Panama and the Canal

THINK ABOUT WHAT YOU KNOW

You learned in an earlier chapter that Magellan found a water passage around South America. Suppose the United States wanted to send goods from its East Coast to its West Coast by ship. Why wouldn't using the Strait of Magellan be a good way to ship those goods?

STUDY THE VOCABULARY

ratify
lock

FOCUS YOUR READING

What events led to the building of the Panama Canal?

A. A Route Between the Atlantic and the Pacific

The Need for a Canal The battleship *Oregon* steamed out of San Francisco. The year was 1898, and the United States and Spain were at war. The United States needed the *Oregon*'s firepower in the Caribbean Sea. The mighty ship began its long journey along the western coast of the United States and around South America. The trip took 67 days. By the time the *Oregon* actually reached the Caribbean the war was nearly over! The United States Congress decided that a shorter route from the Pacific to the Atlantic Ocean was needed. A canal had to be built across the country of Panama.

Earlier Efforts Others had tried before. In fact, almost from the moment Balboa first saw the Pacific Ocean, Europeans hoped to find an easy route between the Atlantic and Pacific oceans. The first route was a rough mule trail built by the Spaniards to carry goods across Central America. It took days to travel the 40-mile (64-km) trail between Portobelo and Panama City. Today, preserved in a Panamanian national park, you can see parts of this centuries-old trail.

A railroad, built across Panama in 1855, cut travel time from days to hours. Still the problem of moving ships from one ocean to the other remained.

In 1881, a French company started to build a canal across Panama. After nine years the company had spent all of its money, but it had built only a few miles of canal. Thousands of workers had died from tropical diseases, chiefly yellow fever and malaria.

Working Toward a Treaty Although the French company had failed, the United

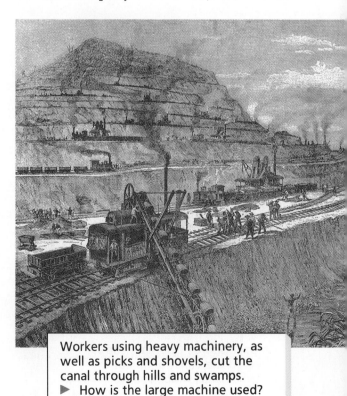

Workers using heavy machinery, as well as picks and shovels, cut the canal through hills and swamps.
▶ How is the large machine used?

275

States still believed that a canal could be built across Panama. However, since Panama was at that time part of the country of Colombia, the United States first had to negotiate a treaty with Colombia. The Colombians wanted more money for the canal rights than the United States was willing to pay. The Colombian legislature refused to **ratify**, or approve, the treaty. Without Colombian approval there would be no canal in Panama.

Then in 1903, a revolt against Colombia broke out in Panama. The Colombian navy set out to stop the revolution, but the fleet was blocked by United States ships sent to aid Panama. Panama became an independent nation. Less than two weeks later, the United States and Panama signed a canal treaty.

Colonel George Goethals (top), directed the construction of the Panama Canal, which opened in 1914.
▶ How did the canal change travel?

B. George Goethals

The United States began work on the Panama Canal early in 1904. The person who is best known for the building of the Panama Canal is George Washington Goethals, then a colonel in the United States Army Corps of Engineers. Of Dutch ancestry and hailing from Brooklyn, New York, the colonel served as chief engineer on the Panama Canal from 1907 until its completion in 1914.

At the height of the excavations, some 60 steam shovels operated throughout the day. Every day, about 500 trainloads of dirt were hauled away. More than 45,000 laborers worked under Goethals. Most of them were English-speaking West Indian blacks. Many of the West Indians stayed on in Panama after the canal was built. Today, there are many English-speaking blacks who live in Panama.

On August 15, 1914, the Panama Canal was officially opened. Since then, thousands of ships carrying billions of tons of cargo have used the Canal. Today, it takes an average of 15 to 17 hours for a ship to pass through the Canal, a distance of 50.7 miles (81.6 km). You may wonder why it takes that many hours.

The Canal has several different elevations in its length, so **locks** allow ships to go through. A lock is an enclosed part of a canal with a gate at each end so that the water level and ships can be raised or lowered. Ships move from one elevation to another. This procedure takes time, but when ships reach either end of the Canal, they are at the proper water level to sail away.

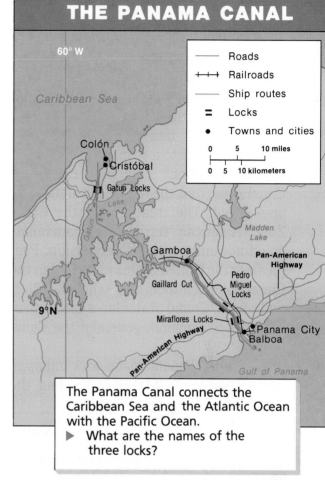

THE PANAMA CANAL

The Panama Canal connects the Caribbean Sea and the Atlantic Ocean with the Pacific Ocean.
▶ What are the names of the three locks?

Two oceangoing ships pass through the Miraflores Locks.
▶ What is the land like in this part of Panama?

277

C. Panama Canal Treaties

Can you imagine living in a country where a strip of land owned by foreigners cuts your country in half? For many years, that was the situation in Panama. The 1903 Panama Canal treaty gave the United States the rights to a strip of land on either side of the Canal. This land, called the Canal Zone, runs the full length of the Panama Canal. The treaty made the Canal Zone American territory. Panamanians could not enter without permission. People from the United States who lived in the Canal Zone had their own schools, police, and courts. United States laws, rather than the laws of Panama, governed the Canal Zone.

Even so, Panamanians grew unhappy about the United States controlling the Panama Canal and the Canal Zone. Riots broke out in 1964. The United States and Panama began talks about a new treaty. In 1975, Brigadier General Omar Torrijos, then the leader of Panama, spoke eloquently to the United Nations Security Council: "When your ships sail through the Canal, those ships are sailing through 50 miles of our not-so-peaceful history."

Panamanians have not always felt well treated by the United States. As you learned, many Panamanians resented United States control of the Canal Zone. They also disliked the fact that United States citizens working in the Canal Zone received higher wages than Panamanians who worked there.

Debate in the United States over

When the Panama Canal was built, its locks were big enough for any ship afloat. In the years following, much larger ships have been built. Now there are hundreds of ships that are too large to pass through the Panama Canal.
▶ What do you predict may happen to the canal in the future?

In 1977, United States President Jimmy Carter (seated left) and Panamanian General Torrijos signed a new treaty giving most of the control of the canal and Canal Zone to Panama.
▶ Why might Panama want to take control?

whether to "give the Canal back" to Panama also added to bad feelings. Many important people in the United States said Panama was not capable of properly operating the Canal. Panamanians thought such remarks were insults to their nation. Because of this past history, Panama has been very sensitive about its interactions with the United States.

Finally, in 1977, United States President Jimmy Carter and General Torrijos signed two new treaties. Panama now controls most of the Canal Zone. The United States controls the Canal itself and has military bases there. It also has the right to defend the Canal against any attack. Panama gains complete control of the Canal and the Canal Zone on December 31, 1999.

LESSON *4* REVIEW

THINK AND WRITE

A. For what reasons did people in Europe and the United States believe that a canal was needed?

B. Summarize the planning and building of the Panama Canal.

C. Explain two differences of opinion that the United States has had with Panama.

SKILLS CHECK

WRITING SKILL

Imagine that the year is 1975. You are a Panamanian who is unhappy about the control that the United States has over the Canal. Write a persuasive paragraph in which you give reasons against that control.

10 PUTTING IT ALL TOGETHER

USING THE VOCABULARY

civil rights
literacy rate
socialism
ratify
locks

On a separate sheet of paper, write the word or words from above that best complete the sentence.

1. The legislature would not _____, or approve the treaty.
2. A political system in which land and industry is controlled by the government is called _____.
3. To pass through the Panama Canal, a ship has to pass through several _____ that move it higher or lower.
4. The _____ of a citizen in the United States include life, liberty, ownership of property, and equal treatment under the law.
5. Because about 90 percent of its people can read and write, Costa Rica's _____ ranks among the highest in the world.

REMEMBERING WHAT YOU READ

On a separate sheet of paper, answer the following questions in complete sentences.

1. Central America is made up of which seven countries?
2. What difficulties have most of the countries of Central America had since they gained their independence?
3. Why has it been difficult for Honduras to progress?

4. What important reason did the United States have for helping the military coup in Guatemala?
5. How is Costa Rica different from its neighbors?
6. What are the reasons for this difference in Costa Rica?
7. Why did the Sandinistas overthrow the Somoza government?
8. What reasons did the Contras have for opposing the Sandinistas?
9. What did the 1903 Panama Canal treaty do for the United States?
10. In 1977, what was agreed to by the two new treaties between the United States and Panama?

TYING SCIENCE TO SOCIAL STUDIES

Central America has many volcanoes, some of which erupt frequently. Find out more about how volcanoes form or what happens when they erupt. Present your information in a simple diagram. Add labels, as necessary, and add a few important facts.

THINKING CRITICALLY

On a separate sheet of paper, answer the following questions in complete sentences.

1. How do land and climate affect where population centers will develop?
2. Why has there been such a troubled history for many of the republics of Central America?
3. Describe the present government of Nicaragua. Is it, in your opinion, a fair government helpful to all the people?
4. Do you think the United States is right in its plans to give the Panama Canal to Panama? Explain your answer.
5. Do you think the United States would be wise to be without an army? Explain your answer.

SUMMARIZING THE CHAPTER

On a separate sheet of paper, draw a graphic organizer like the one shown here. Copy the information from this graphic organizer on the one you have drawn. Beside each lesson heading, fill in the blanks with facts you learned from that lesson.

CHAPTER THEME

Most of the nations of Central America have a history of instability.

LESSON 1
Central America has various physical characteristics.

1. _____
2. _____
3. _____

LESSON 2
The countries of Central America have had to solve many problems since gaining independence.

1. _____
2. _____
3. _____

LESSON 3
Nicaragua has had several different kinds of government.

1. _____
2. _____
3. _____

LESSON 4
The Panama Canal is important to U.S. and world trade.

1. _____
2. _____
3. _____

CHAPTER

11

CENTRAL AMERICA TODAY

Central America is home to over 25 million people of a wide variety of ethnic origins. Agriculture — especially bananas, cotton, and coffee — is the mainstay of the Central American economy.

A Diverse Population

THINK ABOUT WHAT YOU KNOW

What different types of people make up the population of the United States? For what reasons might you expect to find these same types of people in Central America?

STUDY THE VOCABULARY

profit

FOCUS YOUR READING

What different peoples make up the population of Central America?

A. Differences in Population

Population, Current and Future Over 25 million people live in Central America, mostly on the Pacific side of the isthmus, a narrow strip of land that has water on each side and that joins two larger bodies of land. The population is growing rapidly. By the year 2000 there will be more than 40 million Central Americans if the present growth rate continues.

The population of Central America includes most of the major ethnic groups found throughout Latin America. There are several different Indian peoples and mestizos as well as descendants of Africans and Europeans.

Population Patterns If you look at individual countries, rather than at the whole region, you see a lot of variation in population patterns. For example, with around nine million people, Guatemala, which is about the size of Ohio, has the largest population of any Central American country. Belize, the smallest country in population, has about 180,000 people.

El Salvador, which is about the size of Massachusetts, has the region's highest population density—about 632 people per square mile (244 people per sq km). Nicaragua, by contrast, has about 73 people per square mile (28 people per sq km). Over half of the Nicaraguans live in cities, but only 30 percent of Hondurans live in cities.

B. The Descendants of the Maya

Working Independently Great Maya ancestors once ruled the land, but today the descendants of the ancient highland Maya live difficult lives. The Maya make up over half the population of Guatemala, some 4.6 million people, clustering chiefly in the western highlands. Over 23 different Indian languages are spoken today in Guatemala.

CENTRAL AMERICA: AREA AND POPULATION

Country	Area	Population (1990 Estimate)
Nicaragua	49,579 sq mi (128,410 sq km)	3,606,000
Honduras	43,277 sq mi (112,087 sq km)	5,261,000
Guatemala	42,042 sq mi (108,889 sq km)	9,340,000
Panama	33,659 sq mi (87,177 sq km)	2,423,000
Costa Rica	19,652 sq mi (50,899 sq km)	3,032,000
Belize	8,867 sq mi (22,966 sq km)	180,400
El Salvador	8,260 sq mi (21,393 sq km)	5,221,000

The countries of Central America vary in size and in population.

► Find the two countries that have around the same population. How do they compare in size?

Most of Guatemala's Indians are subsistence farmers who grow and make nearly everything they need. They farm tiny plots of land where they grow maize, beans, squash, and other vegetables. Some Maya grow wheat and vegetables to sell at the markets. They also make things, such as furniture, woolen blankets, textiles, and pottery to sell at the markets. The **profit,** or gain made by selling goods, is very small. That is because the handcrafted articles require a long time to make. In addition, the articles are mainly purchased by other Indians, who bargain and buy at the lowest prices that they can. Often people travel hundreds of miles with over 100 pounds (45 kg) on their backs.

The Indian markets of Guatemala are important to the Guatemalan Indians' way of life. The markets take place in the plazas on two or three days of the week. Since many of the Indians have traveled long distances, they bring social and political news to pass on to others. The market is also a place to meet new people and to discuss problems and share ideas.

Working for Others Because they cannot survive on the small profits they make, many Indians leave their homes and farms for part of the year to work on plantations. In the past, they had to do this even if they did not want to. The Indians had to work a certain number of days each year for the government or for plantation owners. The government required them to carry identification cards that showed whether they had done so. That practice ended around 45 years ago, but many Indians still must work for low wages on plantations or coffee farms for their subsistence.

You read about the patrias chicas in Mexico in Chapter 9. They are like little

Indian markets, like this one in Chichicastenango, are an important part of Indian life.
▶ Name some products for sale.

In 1992, Rigoberta Menchu was awarded the Nobel Peace Prize in recognition of her efforts to help the Indian peoples of Guatemala.
▶ What in the photograph tells you that Rigoberta Menchu is proud of her heritage?

countries within the larger country itself. The Indians of Guatemala also think of themselves more as part of their *patrias chicas* than as part of their country. Within their *patrias chicas*, the Indians of Guatemala have achieved success as farmers, craftspeople, and traders. Outside their communities, however, they often are not as successful at finding jobs.

Growing Up in Guatemala In this excerpt, Rigoberta Menchu, an Indian woman from the Quiche (kee CHAY) region of Guatemala, tells about her childhood. She grew up speaking an Indian language, but she also learned Spanish when she was ten years old.

In Guatemala we Indians have no childhood. I started working for a living when I was eight years old on the plantations of the large landowners on the South Coast. My mother was always exhausted, picking coffee or cotton while carrying her newborn baby on her back, and [there were] my other five brothers and sisters around her, hungry. Since the children who don't work are not fed by the owners, she never earned enough. We migrated from the highlands to work on the plantations because my father had only a small piece of land that didn't produce much, only a small amount of corn and beans that lasted for four or five months. The rest of the year we were forced to go to the plantations. That was what our lives were like, and that's why I say I never had a childhood.

C. Miskito and Cuna Indians

In Honduras and Nicaragua, the Miskito (muh SKEE toh) live along the coast of the Caribbean Sea and along rivers flowing to the coast. Many Miskito have intermarried with blacks. Cuna Indians live on islands off the Caribbean coast of Panama and along the coast itself.

The Miskito and the Cuna Indians live by fishing and by growing crops in small plots. For additional income, the Miskito hunt and sell large sea turtles; the Cuna grow coconuts and bananas for sale.

The Cuna Indians live in special areas called *comarcas*. They have their own government in the comarcas, and they can make their own laws.

The Miskito have had problems because of the unrest in Nicaragua and Honduras, and they have rebelled. The Miskito do not think of themselves as belonging to either country. They want their independent rights respected.

Some Miskito have taken refuge in other neighboring countries of Central America. Others have continued to fight to protect their rights. In 1982, over 10,000 Miskito in Nicaragua were forced to relocate, or move to another location.

D. Other Peoples

Mestizos live in most of the highlands and Pacific coastal lands. They make up about 90 percent of the populations of Honduras and El Salvador. They are also a chief part of the populations of Nicaragua, western Panama, and eastern Guatemala.

(Top) On an island off Panama's coast a Cuna woman does a kind of needlework. Boys in a Miskito village in Nicaragua play basketball.
▶ What skills are needed for each activity?

Throughout most of Middle America, the distinction between mestizo and Indian depends on culture. Mestizos, in contrast to Indians, are people who speak Spanish and whose customs and way of dress are European or Western.

In Costa Rica, there have not been large populations of Indians since the Spanish conquest. Most of the Indians who did live there died of European diseases shortly after the Spaniards came. The settlers married other settlers, so the Costa Rican population is largely people of European descent. Costa Rica also has received substantial foreign immigration, especially from Germany. Also, many United States citizens have retired in Costa Rica. In fact, United States citizens make up the largest block of non-Hispanic foreigners living in Costa Rica.

Blacks make up about 2 percent of Costa Rica's population. Most of them live on the Caribbean coast. In the 1600s and 1700s, the English brought blacks from their colonies in the West Indies to Belize to help cut lumber. Other blacks escaped from slavery and found their way to other parts of the coast of Central America. Sometimes the blacks mixed with Indians, such as the Miskito, creating Afro-Indian populations.

About half of the population of Belize has African ancestry.
▶ Using the chart on page 38, about how many people is this?

In Costa Rica and Panama, most of the black population came during the late 1800s and early 1900s. Blacks were brought from the West Indies to work on banana plantations, to build railroads, and to work on the Panama Canal. Since many of them were brought from Jamaica and Barbados, where most of the people speak English, their descendants today also speak English. Panama City and Colón, both in Panama, have significant numbers of English-speaking blacks. Blacks also are a significant group in Nicaragua, comprising about 9 percent of the population. They, too, speak English.

LESSON 1 REVIEW

THINK AND WRITE

A. How would you describe the population of Central America?
B. What are living conditions like for the Indians of Guatemala?
C. Who are the Miskito?
D. What other peoples live in Central America?

SKILLS CHECK

THINKING SKILL

Use the population table on page 283 to make a bar graph that shows a comparison of populations of all the Central American countries.

LESSON 2

Central American Economy

THINK ABOUT WHAT YOU KNOW

You have already learned something about the land and climate of Central America. Do conditions seem favorable for agriculture? Give your reasons.

STUDY THE VOCABULARY

common market
tariffs

FOCUS YOUR READING

What kinds of activities help the economy in Central America?

GUATEMALA AND EL SALVADOR: SELECTED EXPORTS

(value in millions of dollars)

Exports	Guatemala	El Salvador
Coffee	452	543
Cotton	74	38
Bananas	71	0
Cardamon	61	0
Sugar	47	35

The chart shows the earnings from five products.
► About how many times greater was the value of coffee than sugar in each country?

A. Tropical Products

Bananas and cotton grow on large plantations in the tropical lowlands. Coffee bushes dot the mountain slopes in the tierra templada. Together, bananas, cotton, and coffee account for more than 50 percent of the value of Central America's exports.

Coffee production began in the highlands of Costa Rica in the middle of the 1800s. From there, coffee production spread to El Salvador, Guatemala, and Nicaragua. El Salvador, which has no banana crop, relies on its coffee exports. Guatemala and Costa Rica are also major exporters of coffee. Central American coffee, which is of very high quality, is sold chiefly to buyers in Germany and the United States.

Most cotton is grown on the Pacific coastal lowlands of Nicaragua, El Salvador, and Guatemala. In Guatemala and El Salvador, cotton is second to coffee in value. Study the table on this page. What are the other chief products that El Salvador and Guatemala export?

During the past 20 years or so, cattle have become an important export product. Central America ships large amounts of beef to the United States. Most of that beef goes to large restaurant chains or food companies where it is made into hamburger, lunch meat, and other products.

B. A Big Business from Bananas

The United Fruit Company Every morning throughout the United States, people slice bananas over their cereal. This nutritious and inexpensive tropical fruit is a major export of Central America.

For nearly 70 years, United States companies controlled the banana business in Central America. The largest company was the United Fruit Company, established in 1899. It owned ports and thousands of acres of land. It also owned the longest railroad in Central America. The company even had some power over the governments of Central American countries.

In the 1950s and 1960s, some people in Central America grew unhappy with

288

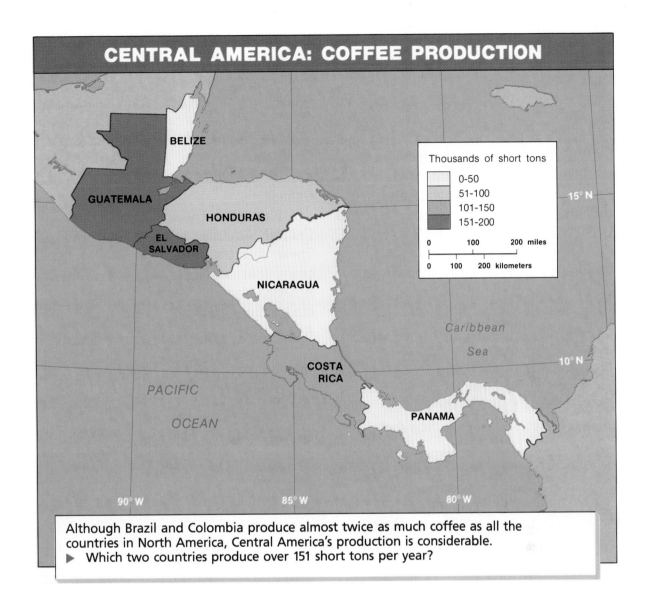

CENTRAL AMERICA: COFFEE PRODUCTION

Thousands of short tons

- 0-50
- 51-100
- 101-150
- 151-200

BELIZE

GUATEMALA

HONDURAS

EL SALVADOR

NICARAGUA

COSTA RICA

PANAMA

PACIFIC OCEAN

Caribbean Sea

15° N

10° N

90° W   85° W   80° W

0   100   200 miles
0   100   200 kilometers

Although Brazil and Colombia produce almost twice as much coffee as all the countries in North America, Central America's production is considerable.
▶ Which two countries produce over 151 short tons per year?

how much power the United Fruit Company had. Central American plantations brought foreign investors great profits, people reasoned, but the nations of Central America received very little in return.

People urged United Fruit to share ownership of some plantations with the governments or citizens of the countries in which they were located. That way, more of the profits from the plantations would remain in the Central American countries. United Fruit did sell its railroads and ports in some countries.

Other Banana Growers In part because of those changes, smaller growers were able to get into the banana business. Today, even though the large plantations still produce much of the banana crop, smaller growers and cooperative farms have grown in importance. However, the produce of these smaller holdings is bought by the large corporations, which then ship it abroad. Bananas and other export crops bring money into Central America, creating wealth for plantation owners and money to run the government.

C. Subsistence Farming

The large farms, ranches, or plantations that grow export crops have most of the good land. In Guatemala, for example, around 2.5 percent of the people own around 65 percent of the land.

Little good land exists to begin with, so there is not enough land to grow food for the people. In fact, Central America has to import basic grains, such as wheat and rice. Poor people cannot find land to farm, and they cannot afford the costly foods. The most important crops that are grown on subsistence farms in Guatemala, El Salvador, and Honduras are the same as those grown in Mexico. Maize, squash, beans, and peppers are the foods that were also favorites of the Maya and Aztecs. Many people today still eat beans and rice or tortillas, and these foods provide them with complete proteins in their diets.

The cool highlands, where many of Guatemala's Indians live, have a good climate and fertile soil. Cabbage, broccoli, brussels sprouts, and cauliflower grow well there. The vegetables are sold in markets in Guatemala and other Central American countries. An increasing share goes to markets in the United States and Canada.

Farmers in the southern countries of Central America grow different crops. These farmers raise manioc and other crops that originally came from South America and the Caribbean. This is because the Indians of southern Central America were related to the Indians of South America and the Caribbean. They shared the same likes and dislikes in food. Rice is also an important food of southern Central America. It grows in the rainy lowland areas of these lands.

(Left) Guatemalan Indians make tortillas the same way their ancestors did. (Right) Crops grown on subsistence farms are sold in markets.
▶ What vegetable grain is used in tortillas?

D. A Common Market

It does no good to produce things if you cannot sell them. That's where the idea of a **common market** comes in. In a common market, each member country agrees to lower **tariffs,** or taxes, on products from the other member countries. When a government places high taxes on goods coming in from another country, those goods become more expensive. Why does a country do that? Well, it knows that if foreign goods are expensive, the people will have to buy the goods produced in their own country. That may sound like a good idea, but it can cause problems. For one thing, people in such a country are paying more than they would have to if goods traded freely.

In 1960, the nations of Central America decided to eliminate tariff barriers between their countries. That made prices lower. It also combined the consumer markets of the individual countries to make one large market.

The Central American Common Market (CACM) began operating in 1962. It has brought many new industries to Central America. Most of the industries are in Guatemala and El Salvador. These countries have better transportation, more

Attending a 1986 meeting to discuss trade agreements are the leaders of five Central American countries.
▶ Why are these meetings needed?

electricity, and more skilled workers in industries than the other Central American countries have.

It should not surprise you to learn that Costa Rica, Honduras, and Nicaragua felt the agreement helped Guatemala and El Salvador more than it helped them. Other disputes among the nations of the region have hurt the CACM, but it has not died completely. In 1986, Central American leaders met in Guatemala to discuss ways to make the common market more effective. Those efforts continue today. Even so, Central American nations trade far more with the United States than they do with one another.

LESSON 2 REVIEW

THINK AND WRITE

A. What tropical products grow in Central America?

B. Why are bananas important for the economy of Central America?

C. Why is it difficult for poor people to get land to farm?

D. In a few sentences, summarize what a common market is.

SKILLS CHECK

WRITING SKILL

Imagine that you are living in Central America in the 1960s. Write a persuasive letter to the United Fruit Company. Give reasons why you think the company should share ownership of the banana business with you and other citizens of the country.

Living in Central America

THINK ABOUT WHAT YOU KNOW

In what ways are the lives of people in cities in the United States different from the lives of people in the countryside, and in what ways are they similar?

STUDY THE VOCABULARY

sorghum
tradition

FOCUS YOUR READING

How can some of the larger cities in Central America be described?

A. A Trip to the Highlands

For a closer look at how people live in Guatemala, why not take a coast-to-highland journey. You'll begin in the port of Champerico, which is at about sea level along the Pacific coast. You'll travel all the way to the mountain city of Quezaltenango (ke sahl te NAHNG goh), nearly 8,000 feet (2,438 m) above sea level.

The sand on the Pacific coast beaches of Guatemala is dark gray in color and very coarse because it comes from volcanic ash. The sand gets very hot because of its dark color. So don't try walking barefoot on the beach! You'll need to have your feet in good condition for the trip.

Leaving Champerico, you travel north toward the mountains. It's a clear day, so you can see the mountains rising in the distance. The high volcanoes are easy to pick out. Your trip will take you along the side of Santa María, the nearest of the volcanoes.

On the highway to Retalhuleu (ret uh-loo LE oo), a large town and an important farming center, you pass large farms where you see cotton, corn, and **sorghum** growing. Sorghum is a grain that can be used to feed cattle and other livestock. It is used on the cattle ranches here.

Just before reaching Retalhuleu, you see a large, low building. It's the local market. People sell almost every kind of food imaginable. Stalls are stacked with bananas, tomatoes, onions, pineapples, and many other vegetables and fruits that really look appealing. There's also clothing for sale and pots and pans too. No wonder so many people come here to buy things.

It's difficult to leave the market, but there's so much to see. Retalhuleu is one of the most beautiful cities in Guatemala, so you had better continue.

There's a plaza and a beautiful old church right in the center of the city. Across from the church are government

When walking in this quiet area, one cannot help but notice the volcano.
► What else do you notice about this area?

buildings and the city hall. Stores, restaurants, and a movie theater line the other two sides of the plaza.

In the center of the plaza is a bandstand. The city band gives free concerts there each Sunday and Thursday evening. The public concert is an old Latin American **tradition** that is still followed in some places. A tradition is something that people have done for years and years. Think how pleasant it must be to sit on a bench in the plaza on a warm tropical evening, listening to the band and watching the people stroll by.

B. Plantations and Indian Villages

Unfortunately, you just don't have time to stay. In fact, it's time to leave Retalhuleu and follow the road as it climbs into the mountains. The plantations now begin to change. Instead of cotton, sugarcane grows in the fields beside the road.

The road continues to rise. Look for some tall trees that have small bushes with shiny dark-green leaves growing under them. Those bushes are coffee plants, which grow best in the shade. It's just about harvest time, so you can see the bright-red berries that contain the beans from which coffee is made.

Up ahead, steam rises from the small, bare cone of a volcano. The cone is a part of the volcano Santa María. In 1902 this volcano erupted, causing great damage to crops and villages. Remember that volcanic eruptions also have their benefits since they enrich the soil for crops.

As you journey up the road, now passing through the the temperature zone called the tierra templada, you see many Indian villages. By the time you reach Quezaltenango, in the tierra fría, you will be seeing the small fields of the Indian

An Indian couple leave their village and head for the market to trade and sell their wares.
▶ What might be in the basket?

farmers that dot the hillsides. The main crop is corn, but you can see fields planted in onions, cabbages, carrots, and other vegetables. The Indian villages near Quezaltenango have many vegetable farms.

Indians walk along the road. The women are dressed colorfully. Each village has its own colors and designs for clothing. People who know the colors and designs can easily tell the village in which a person lives. It may surprise you to learn that the tradition of wearing the same style of clothing within a given area has been observed for centuries.

In just another few miles, you will reach Quezaltenango. Quezaltenango looks very much like a colonial Latin American city. Rows of white-painted houses with tile roofs line its narrow stone-paved streets. The weather in Quezaltenango is cool. You had better put on a sweater or jacket.

293

Guatemala City, the largest city in Central America, is surrounded by volcanoes.
► How would you describe the city?

Well, that's the end of your journey. You've traveled only about 70 miles (113 km), but you have climbed nearly 8,000 feet (2,438 m) and passed through several climate zones.

C. Capital Cities

Guatemala City Compared with a giant such as Mexico City, Central America's capital cities do not seem very large. The largest of them, Guatemala City, the capital of Guatemala, has slightly under 2 million people. Since it is by far the largest city in Guatemala, it is a primate city.

Guatemala City rests on a plateau some 5,000 feet (1,524 m) above sea level, surrounded by towering volcanoes. This elevation gives the city a lovely temperate climate. You cannot find many old buildings in Guatemala City, since much of the

city was rebuilt after a series of earthquakes in 1917 and 1918 almost completely destroyed the capital. A 1976 earthquake also caused considerable damage. However, the newer buildings in the central section of the city received little damage.

Walk along tree-lined La Reforma avenue and you can see tall buildings and statues of famous Guatemalans. Many of the city's tallest buildings, including hotels and apartment buildings, are on this avenue.

San Salvador The capital of El Salvador is in a high valley at an elevation of 2,000 feet (610 m). Like Guatemala City, San Salvador is ringed by mountains. Again as in Guatemala City, you won't find any old colonial buildings. In 1854, the original city of San Salvador was devastated by a great earthquake. The city then was rebuilt in a safer location. Tremors, such as one in 1986, frequently shake San Salvador. Even though many of the newer buildings have been specially designed to withstand earthquakes, there are times when a great deal of damage results. Poor people's homes, which are not well built, are often destroyed.

Tegucigalpa A city where you can see many fine old colonial buildings is Tegucigalpa (tuh goo suh GAL puh), the capital of Honduras. It lies off the region's main earthquake fault line. Tegucigalpa is in the mountains, at an altitude of 3,000 feet (914 m), and much of the city is hilly. Adding to the natural beauty of the setting are many old streets that have a series of steps leading to the next level.

Managua Nicaragua's capital has a picturesque location on the southern shore of Lake Managua, about 24 miles (39 km) from the Pacific Ocean. Along the lake is a boardwalk where people in Managua promenade, or take leisurely walks, especially on weekends and holidays. Nearby, buildings once stood around the central plaza of the city. In 1972 an earthquake destroyed nearly all of the buildings. The government at that time decided not to rebuild the city's center, so now other buildings form a big ring, like a giant doughnut, around the empty heart of the city.

San José Costa Rica's capital lies in a broad, fertile valley, the center of an important agricultural area. San José has a metropolitan population of about 1 million, and it is Costa Rica's industrial

Tegucigalpa (top) and San José (bottom) are smaller than most Latin American capitals.
▶ What do capital cities have in common?

center. About two thirds of the nation's industrial production takes place in San José. The city is impressive, with an interesting blend of old and new buildings. You can walk down wide avenues lined with tall buildings or poke your way along narrow streets with small wooden houses.

Panama City   After the famous buccaneer Henry Morgan sacked the old city of Panama in 1671, Spain built a new, heavily fortified city nearby. Today it is called Panama City. It is Panama's capital as well as its largest city. It's also a major manufacturing center. On a stroll through Panama City, visitors enjoy the mixture of old and modern architecture.

Old Panama, nearby, has been restored. In the Plaza de Francia are monuments to members of the old French canal company as well as to Carlos Finlay, the Cuban physician who discovered the cause of yellow fever. You read about him on page 203. Yellow fever, you may recall, killed many of the people who worked for the French canal company. Near the plaza is the old sea wall built by the Spanish to protect the city from pirates.

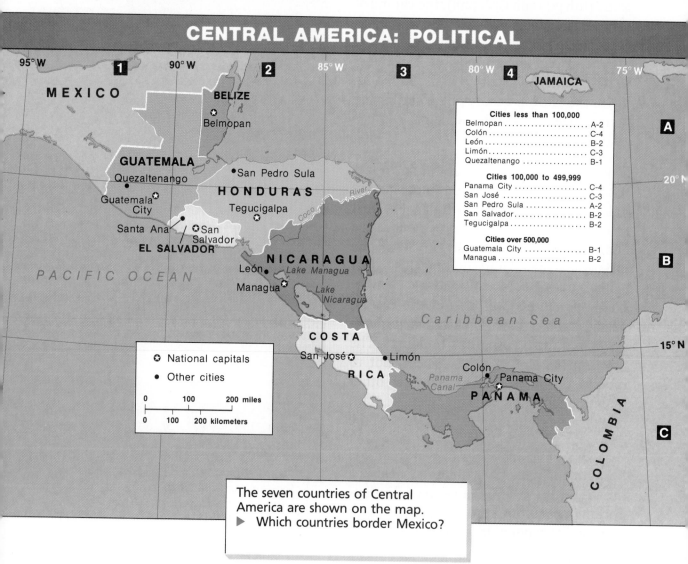

CENTRAL AMERICA: POLITICAL

Cities less than 100,000
Belmopan A-2
Colón C-4
León B-2
Limón C-3
Quezaltenango B-1

Cities 100,000 to 499,999
Panama City C-4
San José C-3
San Pedro Sula A-2
San Salvador B-2
Tegucigalpa B-2

Cities over 500,000
Guatemala City B-1
Managua B-2

☉ National capitals

• Other cities

0   100   200 miles

0   100   200 kilometers

The seven countries of Central America are shown on the map.
▶ Which countries border Mexico?

Panama City (top), on the Pacific, is a modern industrial city. Belize City (left), once the capital of Belize, has been replaced by Belmopan.
▶ Why might the little bridges be needed?

Belmopan In 1970, Belmopan became Belize's capital. It is a very small city with only a few thousand inhabitants. The former capital, Belize City, is really Belize's most important urban center. Much of the land nearby is swampy and subject to flooding, so most of the houses are built on piles to raise them above the ground. Because of this swampy condition, the capital was moved to Belmopan.

LESSON **3** *REVIEW*

THINK AND WRITE

A. How would you describe and summarize the city of Retalhuleu?

B. What important crop grows in the tierra fría highlands of Guatemala?

C. Compare the appearances today of the central sections of the cities of Guatemala City, Tegucigalpa, and Managua.

SKILLS CHECK

MAP SKILL

Find the entries for Panama City, Belmopan, San Salvador, and San José in the Gazetteer. Locate each city on the map on page 296. Then write a short explanation of where each city is located.

A Search for Lasting Peace

THINK ABOUT WHAT YOU KNOW

You have already learned something about the war in Nicaragua. Look at the map of Central America on page 296. Which countries do you think would have the most concern about that conflict and why?

STUDY THE VOCABULARY

ration
human rights

FOCUS YOUR READING

Why has it been difficult to achieve lasting peace in Central America?

A. Civil War in El Salvador

Civil war broke out in El Salvador in 1979 and continued through 1991. A guerrilla group called the Farabundo Martí National Liberation Front opposed the United States-backed government. Agustín Farabundo Martí had been a labor leader in El Salvador in the 1920s, and he was thought of as a hero by the members of the guerrilla group.

Many people in El Salvador who opposed the government disappeared off the streets and were never heard from again. The United States did not want to support a government that allowed the disappearance and probable killing of its own people. On the other hand, the United States feared that the rebels had Communist ties with the countries of Nicaragua, Cuba, and the former Soviet Union.

The United States-supervised election of 1984 brought José Napoleón Duarte (DWAHR te) to the presidency. He himself had once been tortured by the military government. He declared his willingness to speak with the rebel groups. However, Duarte suffered from ill health in 1988 and his control of the government weakened. In 1989, Alfredo Cristiani was elected President, and the raging war continued.

Finally, in January 1992 the government of El Salvador and its guerrilla foes signed a peace treaty. In return for the promise of the guerrillas to lay down their arms, the government of El Salvador agreed to make some political and economic changes.

B. Developments in Nicaragua

The situation in Nicaragua remained tense also. Nicaragua's economy slumped 50 percent during Sandinista rule. The country became the poorest nation in the Western Hemisphere. Per capita income was under $300. The war with the contras cost about $12 billion. When consumer goods became scarce, supplies were **rationed.** To ration is to limit the amount of scarce items, such as meat or gasoline, that

In 1992 the people of El Salvador celebrate the signing of a peace treaty, ending the long civil war.
▶ What is a civil war?

goods became scarce, supplies were **rationed**. To ration is to limit the amount of scarce items, such as meat or gasoline, that each person can buy. Opponents, or people who disagreed with the government, blamed the failing economy on the Sandinistas' socialist policies. The Sandinistas said that the war with the Contras was the cause of Nicaragua's economic difficulties. Violations against **human rights** became regular occurrences in Nicaragua. *Human rights* refers to freedom of speech, religion, and the press without government censorship. It often suggests rights of the people that have not yet been recognized. In some, cases the Sandinistas were responsible. In others, the Contras were to blame.

A presidential election was held in Nicaragua in February of 1990. The voter turnout was heavy, and the election was monitored by many international observers.

In a stunning victory, Violeta Barrios de Chamorro defeated Daniel Ortega, the leftist president. Chamorro was the candidate of the party called UNO (United National Opposition). The party was formed from 14 groups united mainly because of their dislike for Ortega's leadership. This meant that the new president was faced with a difficult task to insure the support of 13 groups. In addition, Sandinistas held control of the Legislature. President George Bush, commenting on the election result said, "It moves us one step closer to the day when every nation in this hemisphere is a democracy."

C. War in Panama

In May of 1989, after presidential elections were held, General Manuel Antonio Noriega accused the United States of interference and cancelled the election

Guillermo Endara views Panama City from a rooftop, after becoming the President of Panama in 1989.
► What problems does he face?

results. Many Latin American leaders denounced the voiding of the election. International election observers, including former President Jimmy Carter, said that Guillermo Endara had beaten Noriega's candidate, a man named Carlos Duque, by a landslide.

A Panamanian attempt to oust Noriega in October 1989 failed. The following December, United States troops invaded Panama. Tanks and rocket-firing helicopters destroyed the headquarters of the Panamanian Defense Forces. Within minutes, President Guillermo Endara took power. Noriega sought political asylum in the Vatican Embassy in Panama City.

After days of bombings and sniper fire, much of the capital was in ruins. Over 20,000 people were homeless. As the days of fighting continued, most of Noriega's forces surrendered.

Noriega spent ten days inside the embassy before surrendering to the United States authorities. He was accused of illegal drug trafficking and was brought to Florida for trial.

299

D. International Perspectives

The conflict in Nicaragua, like the conflict in El Salvador, caused problems for neighboring countries. For example, refugees as well as rebel groups moved back and forth throughout the region. As the conflict grew, it threatened all the other Central American republics. It had become a regional issue.

The situation in Central America had still wider international importance. The United States stood on one side of the conflict, and the Soviet Union stood on the other. Latin Americans worried that their own interests would be lost in a clash between the two superpowers.

Latin Americans tried to take matters into their own hands. In 1983, representatives from Colombia, Mexico, Venezuela —the Latin American nations closest to the Central American republics—and Panama assembled to find a way to bring peace to the region. They met on the Panamanian island of Contadora, so they came to be known as the Contadora Group. They called for a cease-fire and for negotiations to end the fighting.

Their proposal received the official support of the Organization of American States (OAS). Four nations—Brazil, Argentina, Uruguay, and Peru—gave special help as a "Contadora Support Group."

E. The Árias Peace Plan

While the Contadora Group continued searching for a way to achieve peace, the fighting in Central America continued. The next year, 1984, bold action was taken

The Contadora Group, made up of leaders from countries in Central and South America, meet to discuss political issues and to find a way to end the fighting.
► Why, do you think, do these leaders want to end the war?

(Left) Children eagerly reach out to shake the hands of Costa Rica's President Oscar Árias. (Right) Árias accepts the Nobel Peace Prize in 1987 for his peace plan for Central America.

▶ Why, do you think, might Árias be a good role model?

by the nations that were most directly affected. These were the republics of Costa Rica, Guatemala, Honduras, Nicaragua, and El Salvador. The president of Costa Rica, Oscar Árias Sánchez, worked out a peace plan that was agreed to by the heads of the other four republics. For this, he received the 1987 Nobel Peace Prize. Árias accepted the award in the name of his country by saying, "It has been given to a magnificent country and to the values we share: freedom, peace, and democracy."

The Contadora Group and the OAS both backed the Árias Peace Plan. They said it represented the best hope for peace in Central America. Signing a peace plan is one thing. Making it work is quite another. Developments in Nicaragua and El Salvador are signs of progress. The increasingly active role of the Organization of American States and the United Nations also improved the chances for peace. Still, as one U.N. official put it, "With peace negotiations, the rule is that nothing is agreed until everything is agreed."

LESSON 4 REVIEW

THINK AND WRITE

A. Why, do you suppose, did the United States supervise Duarte's election?

B. What happened in Nicaragua as the war continued?

C. Summarize the war in Panama.

D. What is the Contadora Group?

E. Why did Oscar Árias Sánchez win the Nobel Peace Prize?

SKILLS CHECK

WRITING SKILL

Imagine that you have been awarded the Nobel Peace Prize. What did you do to receive such an honor? Will you share this honor with another—as President Árias did in his acceptance speech? Write the acceptance speech that you will give.

CITIZENSHIP AND AMERICAN VALUES

YOU DECIDE: DOES A COUNTRY NEED AN ARMY?

Throughout history, various countries have been at war. Some nations have attacked others to gain more land. Others have gone to war to seize resources that would make them rich. Still others have waged war to gain power.

Maintaining armed forces is quite expensive. The total number of men and women in uniform in the United States is well over two million. Can you imagine what it takes to clothe and feed that many people? It takes billions of dollars. On top of that, money is needed to pay salaries and provide needed equipment. Some of the airplanes used by the armed forces cost hundreds of millions of dollars.

Because of the threat of war, some countries spend much money for the military and neglect the needs of their people. There are many people in the United States who feel that not enough money is spent for education, housing, health, and human needs. They believe that too great a percentage of the national budget goes for defense. The Soviet Union has had this problem for many years. It is only recently that they have decided to cut military spending and concentrate on supplying their people with consumer goods.

The Central American nations have been in turmoil for decades. The cost in human suffering has been enormous. But, as a tourist slogan goes, "Costa Rica is different." What makes Costa Rica different is that it does not have an army. Since the army was abolished in 1948, this small country has lived in peace, prosperity, and democracy.

All Countries Need Armies

Even if there were world peace, nations would still need armies to protect themselves against invasion from other nations that have kept their armies. Peace treaties are always being broken. There will always be greedy and selfish people who will come to power and try to use war to gain more territory, resources, and power.

A national army can prevent civil war by defending the government against attack from those who wish to seize power. Without an army to defend it, a democratic government might not be able to remain in power. Potential dictators could easily arm their followers and take over.

Some, Perhaps All, Countries Can Survive Without Armies

If all countries agreed to live in peace, no nation would need an army. If peace were guaranteed by a treaty, all nations could disarm and spend their "peace dividend" on better living conditions for all their citizens.

If basic needs were met, people would have no reason to rebel against the government. They would also have no need to attack other countries.

A police force would be enough to protect law-abiding citizens in a democratic country. An army would not be necessary.

Thinking for Yourself

On a separate sheet of paper, write your answers in complete sentences.

1. Pick one opinion under either heading and tell why you agree or disagree with it.
2. What could be done so that all the countries of the world could be safe without armies? Make a list of your ideas, including even those that would be very hard to put into practice.
3. Pick one idea from your list that you think has a chance of making the world more peaceful. Tell how you would put your plan into effect and what results you hope for.

11 PUTTING IT ALL TOGETHER

USING THE VOCABULARY

> **tradition**
> **tariffs**
> **common market**
> **sorghum**
> **ration**
> **profit**

On a separate sheet of paper, write the numbers 1 through 5. Then write the words from the list that would correctly complete the sentences in the paragraphs below.

Farming is the chief economic activity in Central America. Farmers used to grow crops only to feed themselves and their families. These subsistence farmers were forced to _____ food if they could not grow enough. Many farmers worked on large plantations that grow food to sell for _____. One of the crops still grown is _____, a grain. Several of the Central American countries have formed a _____ in which _____ are lowered to make trade among countries easier.

REMEMBERING WHAT YOU READ

On a separate sheet of paper, answer the following questions in complete sentences.

1. What are the two main ethnic groups found in Central America?
2. Which Central American country has the largest population?
3. Which crops account for over 50 percent of the value of Central American exports?
4. Where is most of the good farmland found in this region?
5. What kinds of crops do the subsistence farmers grow?
6. Which different climate zones would you travel through on a coast to highland tour in Guatemala?
7. What natural disaster has caused destruction in many Central American cities?
8. Which major cities are important manufacturing centers?
9. Which countries have had continuing outbreaks of civil war?
10. Who received the Nobel Prize for working out a peace plan that was agreed to by the heads of the Central American republics?

TYING MATH TO SOCIAL STUDIES

Some population figures have been stated in this chapter. Use these and a copy of an almanac to get the most recent population figures for the seven countries of Central America. Create a bar graph showing these population findings. Use a calculator to find the total population in Central America. It would also be interesting to look up population density figures for these nations and compare them on another bar graph.

THINKING CRITICALLY

On a separate sheet of paper, answer the following questions in complete sentences.

1. How would you explain the different ways of life of the Indians and the mestizos in Central America?
2. Do you think the CAMC (Central American Common Market) is a good idea? Explain your answer.
3. Compare the life of a subsistence farmer with that of a plantation owner. First, tell how they are different. Next, mention any similarities in their lives.
4. Why are local marketplaces still so popular in Central American towns and cities?
5. Why do civil wars continue to break out in some Central American nations?

SUMMARIZING THE CHAPTER

On a separate sheet of paper, draw a graphic organizer like the one shown here. Copy the information from this graphic organizer on the one you have drawn. Under the main idea for each lesson, write the facts that support the main idea.

CHAPTER THEME
Central America today is trying to unite economically in a common market and to secure peace and democracy within its countries.

LESSON 1
Central Americans are of different races.

1.
2.
3.
4.

LESSON 3
The capital cities are small compared with Mexico City.

1.
2.
3.
4.
5.

LESSON 2
Agriculture dominates the Central American economy.

1.
2.
3.
4.

LESSON 4
Central America has been a war zone in recent years.

1.
2.
3.
4.

CHAPTER **12**

THE CARIBBEAN

The Caribbean Sea is separated from the Atlantic Ocean by a long string of islands, which stretch from near the tip of Florida to the northern coast of Venezuela.

An Area of Differences

THINK ABOUT WHAT YOU KNOW
This chapter is about the Caribbean islands, sometimes called the West Indies. They include Cuba, Jamaica, and the Bahamas. When you think about these islands, what images come to your mind? Make a semantic map, using the names of the islands and some words to describe them.

STUDY THE VOCABULARY

continental island	**trade winds**
volcanic island	**windward**
limestone island	**leeward**

FOCUS YOUR READING

What are some of the differences among the Caribbean islands?

A. Important Passageways

The Caribbean islands, or West Indies, are like a fence. The fence's "gates" are the passageways, or openings, through which ships can move into and out of the Caribbean Sea. These give the West Indies a strategic location, since the Caribbean Sea covers more than 1 million square miles (2,590,000 sq km).

Look at the map on page 308. There you'll see the three groups of islands that make up the West Indies: the Bahamas, the Greater Antilles, and the Lesser Antilles. On the map they seem to form a long curved line between Florida and Venezuela. To the east of the line of islands is the Atlantic Ocean. To the west are the Caribbean Sea and the Gulf of Mexico. No ship can enter or leave the Caribbean Sea without passing close to one of the Caribbean islands.

The most important "gates" lie in or near the Greater Antilles. Find them on the map on page 308. Most ships must use these passages to get to the Panama Canal and to ports of the Caribbean and the Gulf of Mexico.

B. Continental Islands of the West Indies

Some islands are part of the same kinds of rock formations that make up the mainlands of continents. That's why we call them **continental islands**. The Greater Antilles and Trinidad are continental islands.

Cuba, the largest island of the West Indies, is also a continental island. With an area of 44,218 square miles (114,525 sq km), it is about the size of the country of Honduras or the state of Pennsylvania. Compared with the other continental islands of the West Indies, Cuba has more flat land and fewer mountains. It also has more and better farmland.

Sugarcane is Cuba's main crop, but fruits and vegetables are also grown.
▶ How is this scene similar to farm scenes in Central America?

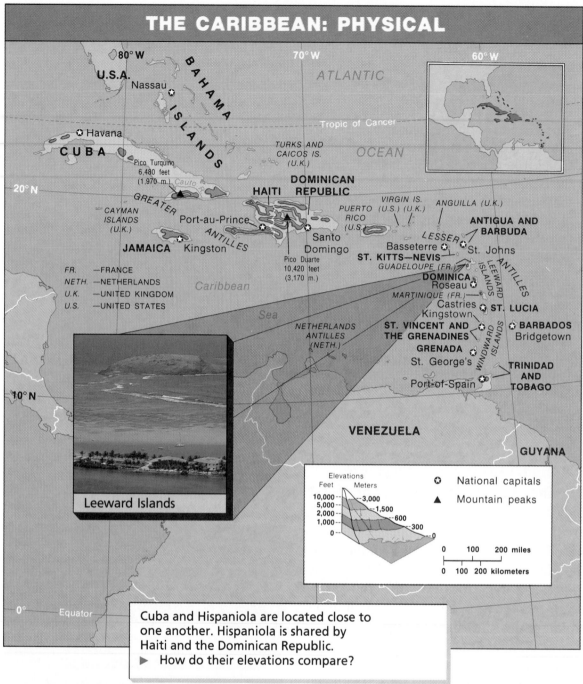

Leeward Islands

Elevations		
Feet	Meters	
10,000	3,000	
5,000	1,500	
2,000	600	
1,000	300	
0	0	

⊛ National capitals

▲ Mountain peaks

0   100   200 miles

0 100 200 kilometers

Cuba and Hispaniola are located close to
one another. Hispaniola is shared by
Haiti and the Dominican Republic.
► How do their elevations compare?

Hispaniola, another continental island, is the second largest island and has the highest mountains of the Caribbean area. Pico Duarte (pee koh DWAHRT ee), in the central part of the island, rises over 10,000 feet (3,048 m) above sea level. The eastern end of Hispaniola has broad, flat valleys between mountain ranges. The Dominican Republic and Haiti share the island, two thirds and one third respectively. Most of the people of the Dominican Republic live in the fertile valleys. Haiti, which is on the western end of Hispaniola, is rugged and mountainous.

Narrow plains circle near the coasts of two other continental islands — Jamaica and Puerto Rico. The plains rise to mountainous spines in the center of the islands. Trinidad is the smallest of the continental islands. It is slightly smaller than the state of Delaware. The low mountain range in northern Trinidad is a continuation of the South American Andes. Hills and plains make up the rest of Trinidad.

C. Volcanic Islands and Limestone Islands

Some islands are **volcanic islands**. Think about the word *volcanic*, and you'll probably figure out why some islands are called volcanic islands. These islands are the tops of volcanoes that extend above the surface of the sea. They are cone-shaped and may reach elevations of 5,000 to 6,000 feet (1,524 to 1,829 m). Because of that, volcanic islands sometimes are called high islands.

If you could dive deep into the waters of the Caribbean Sea and the Gulf of Mexico, you would find a large platform made of rock called limestone. That type of rock often forms at the bottom of oceans and seas. The Bahamas are **limestone islands**. The peninsulas of Yucatán and Florida are also made of limestone.

The limestone reaches the surface of the sea in many other places as well, making small, low islands. The limestone islands do not reach elevations over 1,500 feet (450 m), so they sometimes are called low limestone islands.

The high islands receive more rainfall than the low islands. They have more streams, better soils, and can grow a wider range of crops than the low islands.

In the Lesser Antilles there are two rows of islands. The islands in the eastern, or outer, row are limestone. The others are volcanic. The Virgin Islands of the United States are volcanic islands. All the islands in the Bahamas are low limestone islands.

St. Lucia (top) is a volcanic island. The Bahamas (bottom) have low elevations, few above 200 feet (61 m).
▶ What type are the Bahama Islands?

D. Where Trade Winds Blow

In the seventeenth and eighteenth centuries, captains and sailors aboard tall ships traded tales about winds and currents. Fair winds meant the journey would be a success. Foul winds meant failure.

Merchant ships heading from Europe to the West Indies were aided by steady winds blowing almost constantly in one direction. These winds sped the ships westward to the islands. Since their ships were loaded with goods to be traded, the sailors called these helpful winds **trade winds**. We call them that today too. The trade winds that blow in the West Indies come from the northeast, so they are called the northeast trade winds.

The northern and eastern coasts of the Caribbean islands face the trade winds. Those are the **windward** coasts. The word

The Dominican Republic has constant trade winds and even some hurricanes.
► What difficulties result when hurricanes wash out roads?

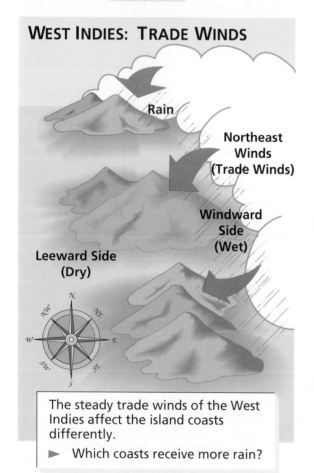

WEST INDIES: TRADE WINDS

Rain

Northeast Winds (Trade Winds)

Windward Side (Wet)

Leeward Side (Dry)

The steady trade winds of the West Indies affect the island coasts differently.
► Which coasts receive more rain?

windward means "facing the wind." The windward coasts receive warm, moist air from the sea all year. Rain falls as the warm, moist air rises over the islands.

The southern and western coasts of the islands of the West Indies are sheltered from the trade winds. The coast of an island that faces away from the wind is the **leeward** coast. As you have probably guessed, the word *leeward* is the antonym of *windward*. It means "facing away from the wind." The leeward side of an island is much drier than the windward side.

The city of San Juan is on the northern, or windward, coast of Puerto Rico. Ponce, another city, is on the southern, or leeward, coast of Puerto Rico. San Juan receives nearly 61 inches (155 cm) of rain each year, but Ponce, on the leeward coast, gets an average of only 36 inches (91 cm).

E. A Tropical Rain Forest

The United States National Forest System has only one tropical rain forest. Where could it be? Here's a hint. The forest's official name is the Caribbean National Forest, but people know it as El Yunque (YOONG kay). Need more help? The forest covers 28,000 acres (11,340 ha) in the Luquillo (loo KEE oh) Mountains, and it receives over 100 billion gallons (379 billion L) of rainfall annually! This is due in part to its windward location. If you guessed that the rain forest is in Puerto Rico, you're exactly right.

El Yunque is Puerto Rico's largest forest. The peaks of the mountains in which the forest is located are drenched by rain, winds, and fog. People say that some moisture falls for part of each minute of each day in the rain forest. That makes a perfect environment for the more than 240 kinds of trees that grow in El Yunque. Mosses, ferns, vines, and all kinds of beautiful flowers also grow wild in the forest.

El Yunque is a refuge for wild birds, including such endangered species as the Puerto Rican parrot and the peregrine falcon. The coquí (koh KEE), a tiny tree frog, seems to "sing" its own name. This tree frog numbers in the millions.

The coqui (insert) is a small tree frog found in El Yunque rain forest.
▶ What other creatures might be found there?

For visitors, El Yunque provides a scenic road on which they can drive through much of the rain forest. There is also a visitors' information center, an observation tower, and miles of rugged trails for people who enjoy hiking.

LESSON **1** *REVIEW*

THINK AND WRITE

A. How would you describe the location of the Caribbean islands?

B. Compare two of the continental islands.

C. How are volcanic islands different from limestone islands?

D. How did the trade winds get their name?

E. What makes El Yunque special for the United States?

SKILLS CHECK

MAP SKILL

Use the map on page 308 to locate continental, volcanic, and limestone islands. Then list the names of several of the islands. Add some other information about each of the islands that you have listed.

Island Nations and Colonies

THINK ABOUT WHAT YOU KNOW
Many of the Caribbean islands are very small. List two or three problems that small islands might experience in trying to exist as independent nations. Think of ways they might solve these problems.

STUDY THE VOCABULARY
department
federation

FOCUS YOUR READING
What different kinds of governments are there in the Caribbean islands?

A. European Colonies

During the seventeenth century, several European nations established colonies on the Caribbean islands. One of the main reasons for this activity was sugar. Sugarcane not only grew well in the West Indies but also brought fortunes as a product for trade. You will learn about the sugar industry in the next chapter.

In some cases, the colonies became independent nations. In other cases, they remained linked to the European countries. For example, Martinique chose to be an overseas **department** of France. A department is one of the parts of France, somewhat like a state. The island of Guadeloupe became a French department in

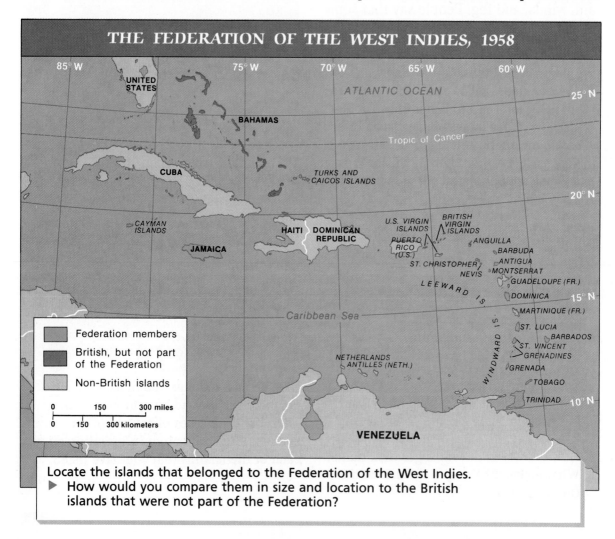

THE FEDERATION OF THE WEST INDIES, 1958

Federation members

British, but not part of the Federation

Non-British islands

0   150   300 miles
0   150   300 kilometers

Locate the islands that belonged to the Federation of the West Indies.
▶ How would you compare them in size and location to the British islands that were not part of the Federation?

1946. Read the table on this page. It lists a number of Caribbean islands and island groups and gives their political statuses and relationships with larger nations.

B. The British West Indies

Moves Toward Independence For many years the British controlled a number of Caribbean islands. Jamaica, the Bahamas, the Leeward Islands, the Windward Islands, Barbados, Trinidad, Tobago, and some of the Virgin Islands belonged to the British Empire. About the middle of the twentieth century, people in the British West Indies began to push for independence.

A Union of Colonies Most of the islands in the British West Indies are small and have only a few resources. The British government feared that such small areas would not survive alone. The British decided to unite their West Indies colonies under one government before granting them independence. This **federation**, or union, of British colonies was called the Federation of the West Indies. Formed in 1958, it included all the islands in the British West Indies except the British Virgin Islands and the Bahamas.

The Federation of the West Indies had troubles from the start. Jamaica and Trinidad, the largest islands, were fairly prosperous, but many of the small islands were very poor. People in Jamaica and Trinidad worried that their resources would be used to support the poorer islands. The distances separating the island nations also interfered with unity. Jamaica, for example, was 1,000 miles (1,609 km) from the nearest member of the federation.

The End of the Federation As you might expect, the Federation of the West

INDEPENDENCE IN THE CARIBBEAN

Nation	Date
* Antigua and Barbuda	1981
* Bahamas	1973
* Barbados	1966
Cuba	1898
* Dominica	1978
Dominican Republic	1844
Grenada	1974
Haiti	1804
Jamaica	1962
* St. Kitts-Nevis	1983
* St. Lucia	1979
* St. Vincent and the Grenadines	1979
Trinidad and Tobago	1962

* Starred nations are former West Indies Associated States.

Study the chart showing island nations.
► How many years elapsed between the time the first and the last island was free?

After 165 years of colonial rule, the British flag is lowered for the last time in Port of Spain, Trinidad.
► How must the people have felt?

313

CONTROLLING POWERS IN THE CARRIBEAN

Nation	Island(s)	Status	Nation	Island(s)	Status
France	Guadeloupe	Overseas department	Netherlands	Netherlands Antilles	Part of the Kingdom of the Netherlands
	Martinique	Overseas department			
Great Britain	Anguilla	Dependency	United States	Puerto Rico	Associated Commonwealth Territory
	British Virgin Islands	Dependency		U.S. Virgin Islands	
	Cayman Islands	Dependency			
	Montserrat	Dependency			
	Turks and Caicos Islands	Dependency			
	Bermuda	Self-governing dependency			

The table lists islands that are not completely independent. They are controlled by other nations.
► Which islands are not controlled by European nations?

Indies did not last long. In 1962, Jamaica and Trinidad became independent. The small island of Tobago (toh BAY goh) joined with Trinidad to make the two-island country of Trinidad and Tobago. Barbados gained independence in 1966.

That left only the very small and very poor islands. Some of them once again became colonies, later called dependencies, after the Federation of the West Indies failed. Other islands have since become fully independent.

C. The United States Virgin Islands

Rhode Island, the smallest state in the United States, is nine times larger than the three islands that make up the United States Virgin Islands—St. Thomas, St. John, and St. Croix. In 1917, the United States purchased St. Thomas, St. John, and St. Croix from Denmark for $25 million. The islands are located in the Lesser Antilles, about 40 miles (64 km) east of Puerto Rico, another United States possession.

In 1927, Congress passed a law granting United States citizenship to the people of the Virgin Islands. All resident citizens who are 18 or older can vote in local elections. However, these citizens of the Virgin Islands cannot vote in any United States national elections, such as presidential elections.

A governor, who is elected for a four-year term, runs the islands. The capital of the Virgin Islands is Charlotte Amalie (uh-MAHL yuh), on St. Thomas.

LESSON *2* REVIEW

THINK AND WRITE

A. What islands have connections with France?

B. What are two reasons why the Federation of the West Indies wasn't successful?

C. Summarize the political powers granted to the United States Virgin Islands.

SKILLS CHECK

THINKING SKILL

What types of help might the dependent islands have requested over the years from the countries that controlled them? Share your ideas with a small group of your classmates.

LESSON 3

Cuba: Delayed Independence

THINK ABOUT WHAT YOU KNOW

Look at the map of the West Indies on page 308. Think about why the United States might consider Cuba to be a particularly important island.

STUDY THE VOCABULARY

policy   personalismo
communist   literacy

FOCUS YOUR READING

In what ways does Cuba differ from the rest of Latin America?

A. Cuba's Struggle for Independence

Cuba's Great National Hero Back in the 1820s, when the wars for independence in the Americas ended, Spain still held two Caribbean colonies: Cuba and Puerto Rico. In 1895, Cuba began a war for its independence, after several earlier attempts to gain freedom had failed. José Martí, who would go down in history as Cuba's greatest national hero, led that struggle.

Spain had expelled Martí from Cuba many times because of his revolutionary ideas. For nearly fifteen years, from 1881 to 1895, he lived in the United States. In Tampa, Florida, Martí made a famous speech calling for an independent Cuba as a land of freedom. He urged, "Let us place around the star of our new flag this formula of love triumphant: 'With all, and for the good of all.'" Martí returned to Cuba in 1895. He died in one of the first revolts against Spanish rule.

The Start of a War As fighting continued, the many United States citizens living in Cuba felt threatened. The United States companies that had invested in Cuban sugar plantations also felt uneasy. The United States sent the battleship *Maine* to

The Granger Collection

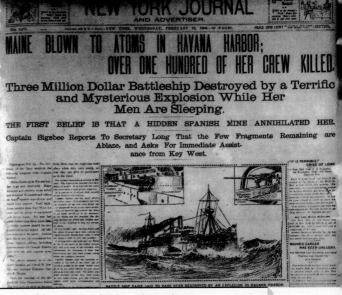

The destruction of the battleship *Maine* was started by an explosion that also caused the ship's ammunition to go up in flames.
► According to the newspaper shown, what did the early reports say?

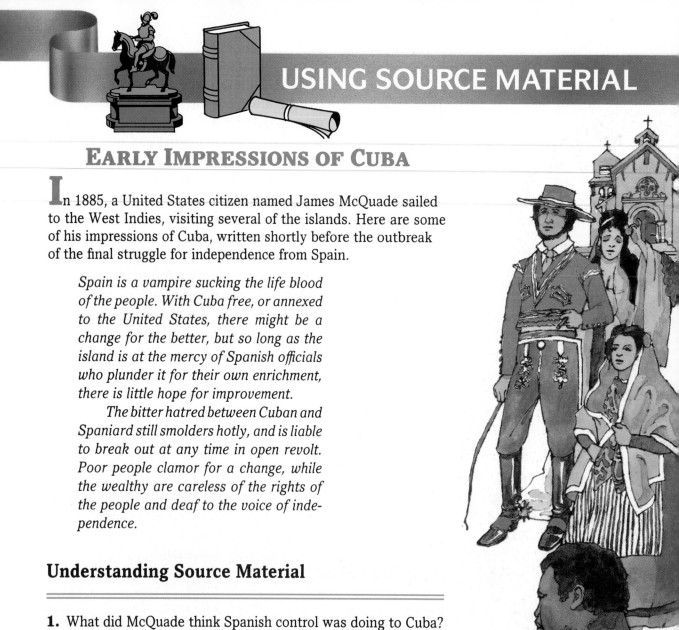

USING SOURCE MATERIAL

EARLY IMPRESSIONS OF CUBA

In 1885, a United States citizen named James McQuade sailed to the West Indies, visiting several of the islands. Here are some of his impressions of Cuba, written shortly before the outbreak of the final struggle for independence from Spain.

> *Spain is a vampire sucking the life blood of the people. With Cuba free, or annexed to the United States, there might be a change for the better, but so long as the island is at the mercy of Spanish officials who plunder it for their own enrichment, there is little hope for improvement.*
>
> *The bitter hatred between Cuban and Spaniard still smolders hotly, and is liable to break out at any time in open revolt. Poor people clamor for a change, while the wealthy are careless of the rights of the people and deaf to the voice of independence.*

Understanding Source Material

1. What did McQuade think Spanish control was doing to Cuba?
2. What things made it seem likely that a revolt would break out in Cuba?

Havana to protect United States citizens and their investments. Then, without warning, on February 15, 1898, a great explosion ripped through the *Maine*, killing many of the sailors.

No one knows to this day exactly why the *Maine* exploded. At the time, United States newspapers fixed the blame on Spain. They ran pictures showing the great battleship sinking amidst smoke and flames. With the slogan "Remember the Maine!" as a battle cry, the United States backed Cuba and declared war on Spain. The Spanish-American War had begun.

B. United States Control

The United States forces quickly defeated the weak Spanish forces. As a result of its victory, the United States gained title to Spain's colonies of Puerto Rico and the Philippines. United States troops occupied Cuba for four years. The Cubans still wanted to be independent, but the United States government believed they could not govern themselves. Finally, in 1901, an agreement was made to free Cuba, but the United States kept the right to send troops to Cuba whenever there were problems. The agreement was known as the Platt Amendment.

The Platt Amendment kept Cuba from having complete independence. The United States held power over the Cuban government. Several times during the years from 1901 to 1934, United States troops went to the island to maintain order and to protect United States citizens.

In 1934, the Platt Amendment was ended by another agreement between the United States and Cuba. Under the new agreement, Cuba became completely independent. This agreement, known as the

In the 1940s, President Roosevelt (second from left), greeted President Batista of Cuba (fourth from left) as he arrived in the United States for a goodwill visit.
▶ Why, do you suppose, did Batista make this visit?

Good Neighbor Policy, was part of a new Latin American **policy** begun by President Franklin Delano Roosevelt. A policy is a plan of action. Under the Good Neighbor Policy, the United States agreed to stay out of the affairs of Latin American countries.

C. Fidel Castro's Revolution

Independence did not bring political freedom to Cuba. By 1933, Fulgencio Batista had gained power, and he controlled Cuba's government off and on for 25 years. Then, in 1959, Fidel Castro forced Batista out. The Cuban revolution had begun. After he took office, Castro spoke about the poor conditions in Cuba. He said, "What did the Revolution find when it came to power? Three million people [Cuba's total population was around 6 million then] did not enjoy the advantages and comforts of electricity. Three and a half million lived in huts, shacks, and slums, without the slightest sanitary facilities."

At first, Castro enjoyed popularity in the United States as well as in Cuba. Soon, however, some people in the United States began to suspect that one dictator had replaced another. United States companies that had holdings in Cuba worried about their future.

They had reason to worry. Castro expropriated the property of businesses in Cuba owned by United States citizens. The United States then stopped buying sugar from Cuba. Cuba's economy was badly hurt because most of Cuba's income came from sugar exports to the United States. Castro turned to the Soviet Union for help. In 1960, Cuba and the Soviet Union signed a trade agreement, and soon Cuba became an ally of the Soviet Union. An ally is a country or person united with another country or person for a special purpose.

During a Cuban conference in 1989, President Gorbachev of the Soviet Union stands to the left of Fidel Castro.
▶ What might Gorbachev do there?

D. The Flight of Many Cubans

Castro had many of the people who opposed him put to death or sent to prison. He placed all the large farms under government control. He also took over many private businesses, such as industries and banks. Cuba was becoming a **communist** country. In a communist country, all property is owned by the community although the government controls all property and industry. The government of such a country is controlled by one party, the Communist party.

Over 700,000 Cubans who were unhappy with Castro's policies poured out of Cuba to the United States and to other Latin American countries. Cuba lost most of its physicians, lawyers, engineers, and other professional people. Many of those people now live in southern Florida, the part of the United States nearest Cuba.

Many Cubans have fled Cuba to escape Communist rule and arrived in the United States.
▶ Describe the scene shown.

E. Cuba Today

Fidel Castro, a very forceful man, rules on the strength of his own personality rather than with the support of a strong political party. The Spanish name for that kind of leadership is **personalismo.** It means "leadership by personality." Most Cubans who have stayed in their country after the revolution believe that Castro is a good leader for Cuba. Few of them are true believers in communism.

Castro's government began programs to increase **literacy.** *Literacy* means "the ability to read and write." The countryside has received a great deal of attention, particularly to foster better health and sanitation. The government also fought against racism in Cuba and has tried to give more equal treatment to women. The slums that so commonly ring the cities of Latin America scarcely exist in Cuba.

However, people in Cuba do not enjoy full freedom of speech or of the press. They cannot really vote Castro out of power. In this regard, Castro is like a dictator. The end of the Cold War, the collapse of communism, and changes in the Soviet Union meant the end of Soviet financial support for Cuba. These events also hurt Cuba's trade. In the early 1990s, as Castro hung onto power, the economic woes of Cuba grew.

LESSON 3 REVIEW

THINK AND WRITE

A. Summarize how Cuba was aided by the United States in 1898 in its fight for independence.

B. Summarize the Platt Amendment.

C. How did Cuba become an ally of the Soviet Union?

D. Why did many Cubans flee to other countries?

E. Make a checklist to show what Cuba has gained and what it has lost since Castro became its leader.

SKILLS CHECK

WRITING SKILL

Select one event you read about in this lesson as the topic for a short report. Add several details from the text to support your topic.

Puerto Rico: A Blend of Cultures

THINK ABOUT WHAT YOU KNOW

Puerto Rico was colonized by Spain, but for nearly 100 years it has been part of the United States. Discuss with your classmates how the cultures of both Spain and the United States may have affected Puerto Rico.

STUDY THE VOCABULARY

commonwealth

FOCUS YOUR READING

What political changes took place in Puerto Rico after the Spanish-American War?

A. Puerto Rico After Spain

After the Spanish-American War, many United States citizens wondered what to do with Puerto Rico. The initial answer came in 1900, when the Foraker Act officially made Puerto Rico a United States possession. The President of the United States appointed the island's governor, cabinet, and part of the legislature. That left the House of Deputies as the only elected branch of government.

The Jones Act of 1917 gave United States citizenship to all Puerto Ricans unless they specifically refused it. That meant all rights guaranteed by the Constitution of the United States applied to inhabitants of Puerto Rico.It was an additional 31 years before Puerto Ricans enjoyed the right to elect their own governor.

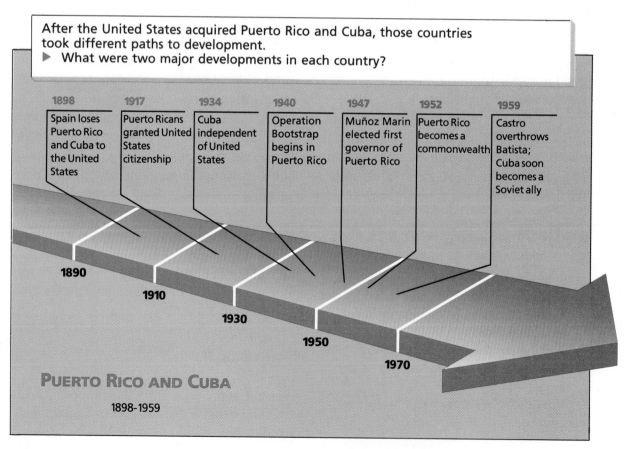

After the United States acquired Puerto Rico and Cuba, those countries took different paths to development.
▶ What were two major developments in each country?

1898	1917	1934	1940	1947	1952	1959
Spain loses Puerto Rico and Cuba to the United States	Puerto Ricans granted United States citizenship	Cuba independent of United States	Operation Bootstrap begins in Puerto Rico	Muñoz Marin elected first governor of Puerto Rico	Puerto Rico becomes a commonwealth	Castro overthrows Batista; Cuba soon becomes a Soviet ally

1890   1910   1930   1950   1970

PUERTO RICO AND CUBA

1898-1959

Both Pablo Casals (seated), a famous Spanish cellist, and Governor Muñoz Marín (standing, left), sign autographs for admirers.
► Why do people want autographs?

B. Luis Muñoz Marín

In 1948, for the first time, Puerto Rico's residents went to the polls to choose their own chief executive. They elected Luis Muñoz Marín (moo NYAWS mah REEN). He had been elected president of the Puerto Rican Senate in 1940 with the platform of the Popular Democratic party.

Muñoz Marín worked very hard to improve the island's economy. Even before he became governor, he had helped work out a plan, called *Operation Bootstrap*, to develop Puerto Rico. You will learn more about this successful plan in the next chapter.

Luis Muñoz Marín served four terms, from 1950 until 1965. During his first years in office, another important change in Puerto Rico's relationship with the United States took place. In 1950, the United States Congress authorized Puerto Rico to write a new constitution that would give the island's people more control over their own affairs. Two years later, the new constitution received approval. Muñoz Marín once had said, "What counts is what a country *wants* to be. If a country wishes to be a democracy, it should be treated like one." It seemed the United States had heard his words.

C. Puerto Rico as a Commonwealth

The new Puerto Rican constitution established the free associated state. This name indicates that Puerto Rico's freedom is bound by its association, or relationship, with the United States. That kind of arrangement is called a **commonwealth**. The word *commonwealth*, when used without an initial capital letter, means a

As a self-governing commonwealth, the nation of Puerto Rico has a governor and a legislative assembly elected by the citizens for four-year terms.
▶ What issues might be discussed at an assembly?

political unit that is somewhat like a state, in which the people hold the ruling power. Puerto Ricans were granted the power to make their own local laws and elect their own officials. Since they are United States citizens, Puerto Ricans can travel freely in the United States and live on the mainland if they wish. They do not need passports to enter the United States mainland, as people from many Latin American nations do. Immigration quotas for the rest of Latin America do not apply to Puerto Rico.

However, Puerto Rico's representative to the United States Congress has no vote. Puerto Ricans cannot vote in the elections for the United States President. Also, they do not pay federal income tax.

Because of Puerto Rico's association with the United States, it seems very much like the United States in some ways. In other ways, however, there is also a strong Spanish influence.

LESSON 4 REVIEW

THINK AND WRITE

A. How did Puerto Rico become a United States possession?

B. What did Luis Muñoz Marín do for Puerto Rico?

C. From what two United States responsibilities are the people of Puerto Rico excused?

SKILLS CHECK

THINKING SKILL

From what you have read so far, compare Puerto Rico with one other Caribbean island. Share your ideas with a classmate.

Haiti and the Dominican Republic

THINK ABOUT WHAT YOU KNOW

In the sense that they share the same island, Haiti and the Dominican Republic are close neighbors in general. Think about neighbors. Do they always get along? Are they usually pretty much alike in the way they think and act? Discuss some of your ideas about neighbors with your classmates.

STUDY THE VOCABULARY

dialect
junta

FOCUS YOUR READING

How do the experiences of Haiti compare with the experiences of the Dominican Republic?

A. An Island Divided

A Two-Nation Island They share the same island of Hispaniola, but Haiti on the west and the Dominican Republic on the east have very different cultures. The whole island belonged to Spain at first, but France took over the western part in 1697. The western part was known then as St. Domingue. The eastern part, known then as Santo Domingo, remained Spanish. The western part was renamed Haiti in 1804 when it became independent. In 1844, the eastern part became known as the Dominican Republic.

In the seventeenth and eighteenth centuries, thousands of Africans were brought to St. Domingue to work as slaves on the sugar plantations. Few Africans were brought to Santo Domingo to work on the cattle ranches. So many Africans came to St. Domingue as slaves that today

The history of Hispaniola has often been marked by unrest and dictatorships.
► Who held control for the longer period—Trujillo in the Dominican Republic or the Duvaliers in Haiti?

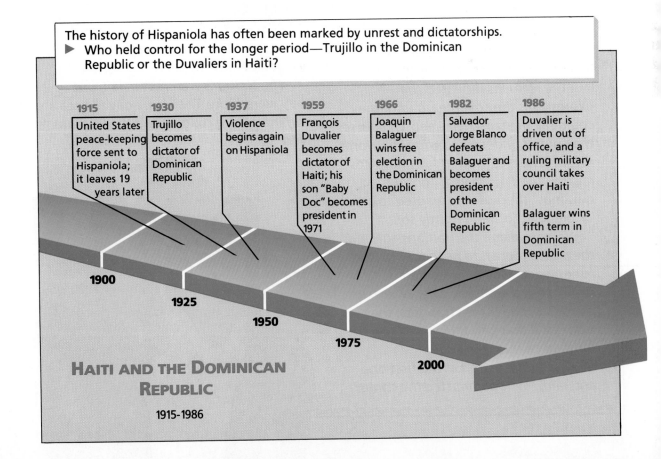

1915 United States peace-keeping force sent to Hispaniola; it leaves 19 years later

1930 Trujillo becomes dictator of Dominican Republic

1937 Violence begins again on Hispaniola

1959 François Duvalier becomes dictator of Haiti; his son "Baby Doc" becomes president in 1971

1966 Joaquin Balaguer wins free election in the Dominican Republic

1982 Salvador Jorge Blanco defeats Balaguer and becomes president of the Dominican Republic

1986 Duvalier is driven out of office, and a ruling military council takes over Haiti

Balaguer wins fifth term in Dominican Republic

1900   1925   1950   1975   2000

HAITI AND THE DOMINICAN REPUBLIC
1915-1986

FROM:

The Haitians in the Dominican Republic

Setting: The Dominican Republic
Time: About 1930

This adapted folktale from the Dominican Republic is one of many stories that appear in the book *The King of the Mountains: A Treasury of Latin American Folk Stories.*

One day three Haitians went over the mountains into the green land of the Dominicans to look for work. The Haitians spoke only French.

"We have a serious problem," said one.

"We must learn the language of this country if we want good jobs," said the second.

"Let's listen to people talk. Then we'll repeat what they say, and we'll learn Spanish," said the third.

The Haitians repeated the expressions they overheard until they could say them in their sleep. Of course, they didn't understand what the words meant. They learned to say, "nosotros mismos" *(we ourselves),* "porque quisimos" *(because we wanted to),* and "Y bien hecho" *(and rightly so)....*

In one village the Haitians entered, the police there had been told to look for escaped convicts who had committed a terrible crime. When the police saw the three strangers, they suspected them, so the police took the Haitians before the judge.

The judge glared at the first one and said, "Who committed the crime? If you know who it was, tell us who did it."

"Nosotros mismos," answered the first Haitian.

"Ah! So you confess to the crime! Why did you do it?"

"Porque quisimos," answered the second.

"You will all be properly punished for your crime. You'll be hanged for it. We will make an example of you," shouted the judge.

"Y bien hecho," said the third Haitian, proudly showing that he, too, could speak Spanish.

"I'm glad you realize that," cried the judge. "Take them away to be hanged at dawn."

The Haitians were put in jail, but they were lucky. That same day the real criminals were caught, and the Haitians were set free.

most of the people of Haiti are black. The mulatto population is small. In Santo Domingo, the African and European populations were more evenly balanced. As a result, today mulattoes are the largest population group in the Dominican Republic.

French Haitians have kept a large part of their African heritage, but French influence is also present. For example, the Roman Catholic religion is practiced by many people. The official language of Haiti is French. However, most of the people speak a **dialect** called Creole. A dialect is a form of a language that is used in a certain area or by a certain people. The Haitian dialect combines French, Spanish, African, and English words. In that way it's similar to the Cajun dialect spoken by some people in the United States city of New Orleans.

Spanish Influence The culture of the Dominican Republic is chiefly Spanish. The nation clearly belongs to Spanish Latin America. Because of its ties with Spain on and off over the years, Dominicans feel more of a relationship to Puerto Ricans and Cubans than to Haitians.

B. Trouble on the Island

United States Marines landed on Hispaniola in 1915 and occupied both Haiti and the Domincan Republic until 1934. Because of the continuing unrest on the island, the United States sent the Marines to protect United States investments and to guard against anything that might interfere with ships using the recently completed Panama Canal. While in Haiti, the Marines also helped build roads, schools, and sanitary facilities.

A classroom in a small school in Haiti is shown here.
▶ How might a classroom in a large city in Haiti be different?

After the Marines left, Haiti suffered seemingly endless military coups and dictatorships. In 1959, François Duvalier (frahn SWAH doo VAL yay) became president. Five years later, he had himself made president for life! When François Duvalier died in 1971, his 19-year old son, Jean-Claude, became president for life. Opposition to the long Duvalier family dictatorship grew stronger. In 1986, Jean-Claude Duvalier resigned as president and left Haiti. A military **junta** (HOON tuh) took over. A junta is a group of people who rule as a committee. Such a group usually uses force to gain control of a country.

Haitians rejoiced at the prospect of freedom. Instead, they found only more terror. General Prosper Avril led a military junta that ruled for 18 months. Following a week of violence and political turmoil, Avril submitted his resignation in March of 1990 and fled into exile.

A provisional president was quickly named. She was the Supreme Court Justice. Ertha Pascal-Trouillot (troo YOH) became the first woman president in Haiti's history. When a reformist priest, Jean-Bertrand

In March 1993, Jean-Bertrand Aristide, exiled president of Haiti, met with President Clinton at the White House.
▶ What might be the purpose of this meeting?

Aristide, won the presidency in a free election, it seemed as if Haiti might finally enjoy peace. Then in September 1991, the military unseated him. The OAS, the UN, and the United States have since been working very hard to help Aristide regain his presidency. With this help, the Haitian people may finally see their dreams for peace and happiness come true.

C. Democracy in the Dominican Republic

The Trujillo Rule The Dominican Republic also suffered a harsh dictatorship. Rafael Trujillo (rah fah EL troo HEE yoh) either headed or controlled the Dominican Republic between 1930 and 1961. Trujillo was a caudillo, or military dictator, much like Díaz had been in Mexico and the Somozas in Nicaragua. He ruled with an iron hand and brought peace to the country. Roads and ports were built, and sugar production was improved. However, he and his family came to control much of the country's land and businesses. Unless they belonged to the upper class, Dominicans had little personal freedom and many lived in poverty.

In 1961, another election took place. Trujillo announced that he had been elected for a second term. During the same year he was assassinated.

Other Leaders Joaquín Balaguer (hwah-KEEN bah lah GER) became president and tried to bring democracy to the Dominican Republic. He resigned under pressure in 1962. In a democratic election, Juan Bosch became the first freely-elected leader of the country in 38 years. Of the 1.6 million eligible voters, 1.1 million had cast their votes. The country adopted a new constitution. Peace did not last long. The army revolted later that same year.

President Balaguer won a fifth term as head of the Dominican Republic.
▶ What qualities must he have to win the vote so often?

In 1965 another revolution began, and fighting broke out in the streets of Santo Domingo, the capital. The United States sent Marines to help United States citizens leave the city safely and to prevent an anti-United States government from taking over. Later, a peace-keeping force made up of soldiers from countries belonging to the Organization of American States (OAS) was sent to the Dominican Republic. The peace force remained until 1966. Later that year, Balaguer returned to power. He was reelected for two more terms. However, the falling prices of sugar and rising oil cost slowed down economic growth. In 1978 Balaguer was defeated by Antonio Guzmán.

In 1982, something remarkable happened. When his term of office ended, President Antonio Guzmán stepped down voluntarily. He was the first president in the country's history to do that. Salvador Jorge Blanco was elected president. In 1986, at the age of 76, Joaquín Balaguer again became president of the Dominican Republic. It was the fifth time he had held that position. His election helped continue the country's move toward a more open and democratic political system.

LESSON 5 REVIEW

THINK AND WRITE

A. List some of the major differences between Haiti and the Dominican Republic.
B. Why did the United States Marines occupy Haiti and the Dominican Republic?
C. In a few sentences, describe the five leaders mentioned who ruled the Dominican Republic.

SKILLS CHECK

WRITING SKILL

You learned about Rafael Trujillo, a harsh dictator. You read that there was little personal freedom under his rule, and many people lived in poverty. You also read that he brought peace to the Dominican Republic. How was this possible? In a paragraph or two, write your thoughts in answer to the question.

CHAPTER 12 PUTTING IT ALL TOGETHER

USING THE VOCABULARY

trade winds	windward coast
federation	policy
ally	literacy
communist	commonwealth
dialect	junta

On a separate sheet of paper, write the word or words from the list that best complete the sentence.

1. All countries want to achieve a 100 percent rate of _____, so that all their citizens can read and write.
2. People in Haiti speak a _____ of French that includes some African and some Spanish words.
3. The _____ of the West Indies was a union of the governments of many islands.
4. In a _____ country, all business as well as industry is controlled by the government.
5. A military council that rules a country is known as a _____.
6. The _____ are steady winds that blow westward toward the Caribbean Sea.
7. A government's foreign_____ is its plan of how to act toward other nations.
8. Jamaica and Canada are part of the Brit-
9. The _____ gets more rain than the leeward coast.
10. An _____ of the United States is Great Britain.

REMEMBERING WHAT YOU READ

On a separate sheet of paper, answer the following questions in complete sentences.

1. What are the three types of islands in the Caribbean Sea?
2. Where is El Yunque, the tropical rain forest?
3. Which islands in the West Indies are part of the United States?
4. Why did the United States help Cuba become an independent nation?
5. What did the United States gain as a result of the Spanish-American war?
6. What was President Roosevelt's "Good Neighbor Policy"?
7. Why did many Cubans leave after Castro took power?
8. How did Cuba become an ally of the Soviet Union?
9. In what ways is Puerto Rico like a state in the United States?
10. In a few sentences, tell how Haiti and the Dominican Republic suffered under dictatorships.

TYING MUSIC TO SOCIAL STUDIES

Join with some classmates in a group to study the music of one of these Caribbean countries: Puerto Rico, Jamaica, Trinidad, Haiti, or Cuba. Look for tapes or records of the music. Perhaps you can borrow some from your school or public library. Present one record or tape to the class and tell something about the music and its performers. The class might make a tape of their favorite "Caribbean Rhythms."

THINKING CRITICALLY

On a separate sheet of paper, answer the following questions in complete sentences.

1. Why were the islands of the Caribbean valuable to their European rulers?
2. Why is it important that the rain forest of El Yunque be protected?
3. Why, do you think, do even small nations want to be independent?
4. What advantages do small nations receive from being part of a federation or a commonwealth?
5. What are the advantages and disadvantages of living under communist rule in present-day Cuba?

SUMMARIZING THE CHAPTER

On a separate sheet of paper, draw a graphic organizer like the one shown here. Copy the information from this graphic organizer on the one you have drawn. Under each lesson heading, fill in the blanks with facts you learned from that lesson.

CHAPTER THEME
The lands, cultures, and histories of the Caribbean nations are quite varied.

LESSON 1
An Area of Differences

1. Three kinds of islands
_____
_____
_____

2. Three kinds of wind
_____
_____
_____

LESSON 2
Types of government

1. _____
2. _____
3. _____

LESSON 3
Cuba: A Long Struggle for Independence

1. _____
2. _____

LESSON 4
Puerto Rico becomes a U.S. possession and improves its economy.

1. _____
2. _____

LESSON 5
Haiti and the Dominican Republic — Contrasts

1. _____
2. _____

13

THE CARIBBEAN TODAY

*S*ince the time of the British Empire, many of the Caribbean islands have produced wealth through the cultivation of sugar. Not all of these islands, however, enjoy a high standard of living.

Many Different Islands and Peoples

THINK ABOUT WHAT YOU KNOW

Think about the 50 states in the United States. Compare any two of them by size and population.

STUDY THE VOCABULARY

tone language
patois

FOCUS YOUR READING

How do the islands of the Caribbean differ from one another?

A. Variety in Languages

Buenos dias! Bon jour! Goede dag! Good day! In Spanish, French, Dutch, and English, pleasant greetings are exchanged between people in the Caribbean. These languages reflect the different European nations that colonized the islands.

Throughout the British West Indies, on islands such as Jamaica, Barbados, and Dominica, people speak English.

The Netherlands Antilles includes two groups of islands. Curacao and Bonaire are just north of Venezuela. Another island, Aruba, became a self-governing member of the Netherlands in 1986. The other group, which is made up of three islands, is located between the Virgin Islands and St. Kitts. Dutch is the official language in these islands.

As you may recall, most of the islands of the West Indies have populations of African descent. Many African languages are **tone languages**. In a tone language, a word's meaning changes according to how the word is sounded. A word sounded with a high note has a different meaning from that same word sounded with a low note. This tone characteristic gives the spoken languages of the West Indies a musical quality. On many Caribbean islands, whatever the official language, there is also a local dialect, or **patois** (PA twah), that mixes African and European words.

B. Variety in Population and Size

Only 45,000 people live on the islands of St. Kitts and Nevis. Together the two

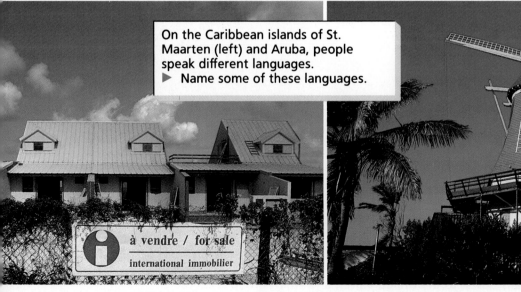

On the Caribbean islands of St. Maarten (left) and Aruba, people speak different languages.
▶ Name some of these languages.

à vendre / for sale
international immobilier

islands have a land area of only 118 square miles (306 sq km). At the other extreme, Cuba has 44,218 square miles (114,525 sq km). Over 10 million people live on Cuba. The Bahama Islands, lying southeast of Florida, number about 700. Those 700 islands total 5,386 sq mi (13,950 sq km). Only around 20 of the 700 islands have people living on them. The population of the Bahamas totals about 250,000. As you can see, the islands of the Caribbean vary enormously in size and population.

Dominica, originally owned by the French but taken over by England, has an area about a quarter of the size of the state of Rhode Island. Around 81,000 people live on Dominica. The small islands of Antigua and Barbuda, which gained their independence from Great Britain in 1981, form a very small nation. The entire population is under 100,000. St. Johns, the capital of Antigua and Barbuda, has only 27,000 people. Antigua and Barbuda are at the southern end of the Leeward Islands.

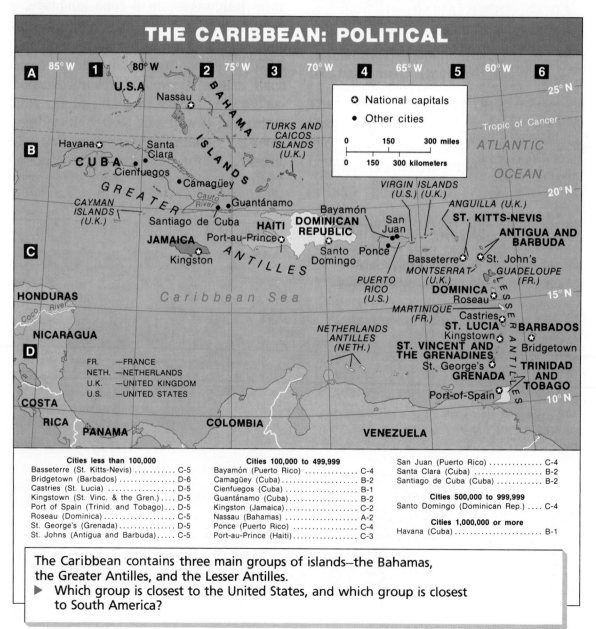

THE CARIBBEAN: POLITICAL

Cities less than 100,000	Cities 100,000 to 499,999	
Basseterre (St. Kitts-Nevis) C-5	Bayamón (Puerto Rico) C-4	San Juan (Puerto Rico) C-4
Bridgetown (Barbados) D-6	Camagüey (Cuba) B-2	Santa Clara (Cuba) B-2
Castries (St. Lucia) D-5	Cienfuegos (Cuba) B-1	Santiago de Cuba (Cuba) B-2
Kingstown (St. Vinc. & the Gren.).... D-5	Guantánamo (Cuba) B-2	
Port of Spain (Trinid. and Tobago)... D-5	Kingston (Jamaica)................... C-2	**Cities 500,000 to 999,999**
Roseau (Dominica) C-5	Nassau (Bahamas) A-2	Santo Domingo (Dominican Rep.) C-4
St. George's (Grenada) D-5	Ponce (Puerto Rico) C-4	**Cities 1,000,000 or more**
St. Johns (Antigua and Barbuda)..... C-5	Port-au-Prince (Haiti)................ C-3	Havana (Cuba) B-1

The Caribbean contains three main groups of islands—the Bahamas, the Greater Antilles, and the Lesser Antilles.
▶ Which group is closest to the United States, and which group is closest to South America?

By contrast, over 7 million people live in the Dominican Republic, which is about the size of New Hampshire and Vermont combined. Jamaica, the third largest Caribbean island, has a population of 2.5 million. Most people live in the metropolitan area of the capital city, Kingston.

C. Large Cities on the Islands

Santo Domingo Christopher Columbus had a brother named Bartholomew. In 1496, Bartholomew founded the city of Santo Domingo. Today this city of 1 million people is the capital of the Dominican Republic. Much of the city was rebuilt after a hurricane nearly destroyed it in 1930. Fortunately, the hurricane did not destroy all of the city's fine old colonial buildings. In Santo Domingo you can see the Cathedral of Santa María. Diego Columbus, a son of Christopher Columbus, laid the first stone for the church in 1514. The body of Christopher Columbus rests in a tomb in the church. His body was shipped to the island as he had requested.

Among Santo Domingo's main industries are the processing of sugar, tourism, and shipping. A main tourist attraction is La Atarazana, a group of buildings dating from 1507. Built as warehouses to store trade goods awaiting shipment abroad,

Diego Columbus lived in the Alcazar de Colón, a mansion and fortress.
▶ How might it be used today?

these now-restored buildings house interesting shops and restaurants.

Havana There are two other large cities in the Caribbean Islands: Havana, Cuba's capital, and San Juan, the capital of Puerto Rico. You will learn about San Juan later in this chapter. Havana, with a population of over 2 million, is Cuba's business and industrial center. The city's factories turn out a variety of products, from sugar and cigars to shoes. Many of the nation's imports and exports pass through Havana's port.

LESSON **1** *REVIEW*

THINK AND WRITE

A. Why are so many different languages spoken in the Caribbean islands?
B. Compare the population and land area of Cuba with those of Antigua and Barbuda.
C. What are the three largest cities in the West Indies?

SKILLS CHECK

MAP SKILL

Locate *Santo Domingo* and *Havana* in the Gazetteer and on the map on page 332. Find two ways in which they are alike and two ways in which they are different. Write your answers in two complete sentences.

Growing Sugar: Then and Now

THINK ABOUT WHAT YOU KNOW

Make a list of some of the foods people eat that contain sugar. Make another list of foods to which some people add sugar.

STUDY THE VOCABULARY

byproduct **provision grounds**
overseer **refinery**

FOCUS YOUR READING

How has the growing of sugarcane been particularly important to the larger islands of the West Indies?

A. Europe's Sweet Tooth

Some people bake with it. Other people worry that they eat too much of it. The "it" is sugar, and almost everyone in the United States consumes some every day.

Sugarcane, from which most sugar comes, grows well in tropical and semitropical climates. The cultivation of sugarcane probably began around 8,000 years ago. Exactly where it first started remains unknown. The most likely locations are the islands of the South Pacific and the northeastern part of India.

During the seventh century A.D., much of Christian Europe fought wars against the Muslims in an area known today as the Middle East. Around the year 636, some people returning to Europe from the wars carried cane sugar back with them. The sugar was unusual. Before then, the only available sweeteners were fruit crystals and honey. However, sugar, like pepper, was rare and cost a great deal of money. It was so expensive that even extremely wealthy people could not afford it.

As trade grew over the next few centuries, beverages such as tea and coffee also gained popularity in Europe. That made sugar even more desirable as a sweetener. Then the Europeans, beginning their explorations on the Atlantic and around Africa, tried to plant sugarcane. The Portuguese, for example, planted sugarcane along the coast of West Africa.

The New World, however, provided the best conditions for growing this important plant. Columbus carried sugarcane to Hispaniola on his second voyage. By the early 1500s, the first sugar mill had been built. Cortés helped develop sugar in Mexico. The Portuguese planted it in northeastern Brazil. The sugar boom was on!

B. Sugar from Cane

The stalks of sugarcane grow from 7 to 15 feet high (2 to 5 m) and have a diameter of around 2 inches (5 cm). Inside those stalks is a sugary juice. Getting that juice out of the cane and making it into sugar takes a lot of work.

To begin with, the cane must be cut down. Harvesting the cane takes both good timing and speed. The cane must be cut quickly when it is ready. If too much time goes by, the sugar content is lost.

Back in the 1600s and 1700s, workers cut down the cane by hand, using long knives. This hot and difficult job required the labor of a great many people. After the cane stalks were cut, they were washed, shredded, and then crushed in a machine. The crushing of the cane took place in a mill. Water or animal power was used to move the millstone.

By crushing the cane, the liquid called cane juice is extracted, or pressed out. That juice needs to be heated and passed through filters to purify it. Back in the

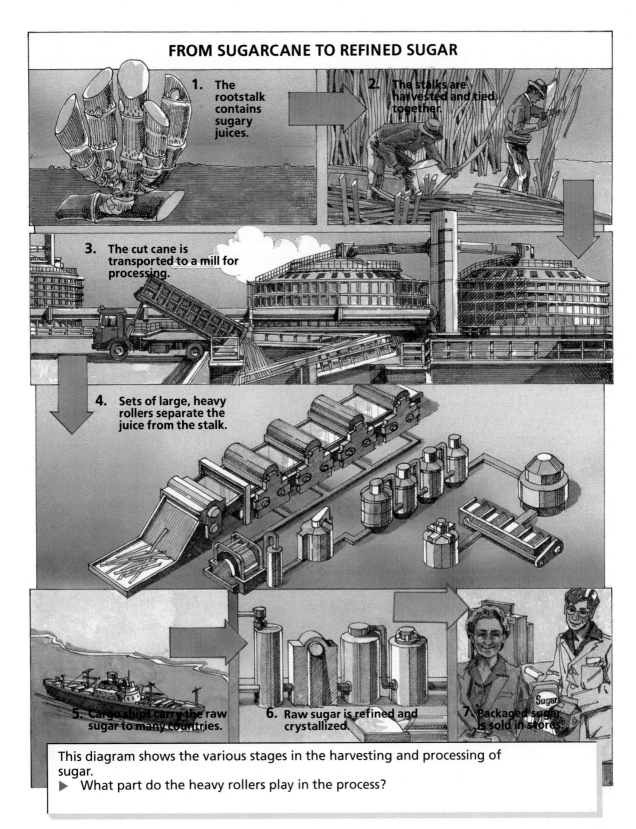

FROM SUGARCANE TO REFINED SUGAR

1. The rootstalk contains sugary juices.

2. The stalks are harvested and tied together.

3. The cut cane is transported to a mill for processing.

4. Sets of large, heavy rollers separate the juice from the stalk.

5. Cargo ships carry the raw sugar to many countries.

6. Raw sugar is refined and crystallized.

7. Packaged sugar is sold in stores.

Sugar

This diagram shows the various stages in the harvesting and processing of sugar.

▶ What part do the heavy rollers play in the process?

1600s, people heated the juice in cauldrons, or large metal pots, over open wood fires. The wood came from the forests. In time, the constant cutting destroyed the forests. The planters then began to burn the fiber from the cane stalks.

New World sugar mills produced a relatively low grade of sugar, often known as "raw" sugar. It was called raw because it was not pure enough. Because the colonial mills used inefficient procedures, they often got more molasses than sugar. Molasses is a **byproduct** of sugar refining. A byproduct is something produced in the course of processing a desired product. You may recall another byproduct mentioned in the discussion of the oil industry. Petrochemicals are produced in the processing of petroleum.

At first, molasses seemed to have no value, so planters just threw it away. Later, people used it to make an alcoholic drink called rum. In the 1600s and 1700s, merchants in colonial New England traded with the West Indies for molasses. In fact, trade between the British colonies in North America and the sugar-growing islands of the West Indies became very important. Prior to the start of the American Revolution, Massachusetts and other colonies traded food, lumber, and other goods with the British West Indies as well as with the French sugar-producing islands.

This trade was vital to the West Indies. On the smaller islands, so much land was needed to grow sugarcane that little was set aside to grow food. Food could be imported more cheaply than it could be grown.

C. Workers and Sugarcane

Sugarcane Plantations During the 1700s, sugar production reached its peak in Haiti, Jamaica, and many islands of the Lesser Antilles. Sugarcane was grown on large plantations owned by European families. A plantation had one purpose: to grow sugarcane at a profit. **Overseers**, or hired supervisors, often managed the plantations.

Slave Laborers A large labor force was needed to do the work. The sugar planters were responsible for bringing over most of the Africans for slaves throughout the West Indies. They also brought most of the Asian workers to Trinidad.

Plantation owners did not pay the slaves. The plantations in Haiti and Jamaica usually had **provision grounds** for

This drawing shows the slave laborers at work in the sugarcane fields.
▶ What are the overseers doing?

Today, people in the islands still enjoy a variety of produce grown in fertile land. Some visit an outdoor market in St. George's, Grenada.
▶ Why do people buy rather than grow produce?

the slaves. Provision grounds were areas where slaves could grow food for themselves. In these provision grounds, slaves grew a mix of plants, originally from Asia and Africa, such as okra, yams, and plantains. Other plants included corn, squash, manioc, and papaya. Okra is a green vegetable. Yams are like sweet potatoes. Plantains are a fruit similar to bananas, but they must be cooked before they are eaten. Papayas are a delicious tropical fruit that comes in different sizes. Many grocery stores and fruit markets in the United States today sell these fruits and vegetables. Which ones have you seen or eaten?

D. Plantations Decline

In the 1800s the plantations began to have problems. In Haiti the long war for independence had destroyed the large plantations. They were never rebuilt, although some Haitian rulers of the early 1800s tried to rebuild them. The plantation owners had all fled, and the former slaves did not want to go back to work on the plantations. Haiti, once the richest colony in the West Indies, became the poorest country of the Americas!

Other islands in the West Indies also saw production decline. Not long after Haiti gained independence, France declared that slavery was illegal. Other European nations followed France's lead. That made workers harder to find, and the workers now had to be paid. In many places the soil had become worn out after more than 100 years of overuse, so crops didn't grow as well.

Competition from other producers also hurt the islands. Sugar beets were being used to make sugar in Europe. Then in the early 1900s, sugar from Asia broke the West Indies' monopoly on the production of cane sugar.

Pictured is a large refinery in the Dominican Republic. Raw sugar is washed, purified, and filtered.
▶ What are some uses of sugar?

E. The Sugar Industry Today

Workers in most countries still cut cane by hand. They use steel cane cutters. The blades of these large knives are about 18 inches (46 cm) long and 5 inches (13 cm) wide. The cane cutter has a hook on the back. Workers use the hook to strip the leaves from the stalks.

The big difference today is in the processing. The sugar is processed in large **refineries**. A refinery is a place where a raw material, such as sugar, is purified.

Modern sugar refineries use machines, operated by electricity, to squeeze out the cane juice, to evaporate some of the juice, and to separate liquid from syrup. The refining process also uses special filters and chemical processes.

The number of countries growing sugarcane and refining sugar has grown. Even countries with temperate climates grow and process beets for sugar. Nevertheless, the world trade in sugar remains very high. Much of the world still has a sweet tooth!

LESSON *2* REVIEW

THINK AND WRITE

A. How did sugarcane come to be grown in the Americas?

B. Summarize the process used long ago to produce sugar.

C. What is the connection between slavery and sugar?

D. What were two of the causes of the decline in sugar production in the 1800s?

E. What are some important ways in which the sugar industry has improved over the years?

SKILLS CHECK

WRITING SKILL

Choose a point of view. Will you be *for* the continued production and use of sugar, or will you be *against* the production and use of sugar? State your point of view in writing. Then give several strong reasons to support the stand you took.

LESSON 3

Making a Living in the West Indies

THINK ABOUT WHAT YOU KNOW

Suppose you were a grown-up and needed a job, but you lived in a place where jobs were scarce. Think of some things you could do to find work.

STUDY THE VOCABULARY

emigrate
resort

FOCUS YOUR READING

How do the economies of the islands in the West Indies differ?

A. A Weak Economy in Some Islands

"I have to be going now. There's no work for me here." With these words, Andrew kissed his wife and children and set off on the road that led to the coast. When he reached the coast, he found hundreds of other men like himself waiting there patiently. They, too, had families to support but could find no work.

"Who's hiring today?" Andrew asked one of the men.

"There's a big plantation on Trinidad that needs hands for the harvest," the man replied. Andrew thought about his life. Living on a small island of the British West Indies certainly had its drawbacks. The island had few resources and few jobs. So he, like most of the men, had to leave the island to find work.

For the past three years, Andrew had gone to the larger islands to work on big commercial plantations. He didn't like leaving his wife behind, but she had to stay home to do the farming and gardening and run the household while he was away. Andrew didn't like being away from his children either. Would there ever be a time, he wondered, when the family could always be together? Maybe they could **emigrate** to England. To emigrate is to leave one country to settle in another. Andrew's two brothers had emigrated to England a few years ago.

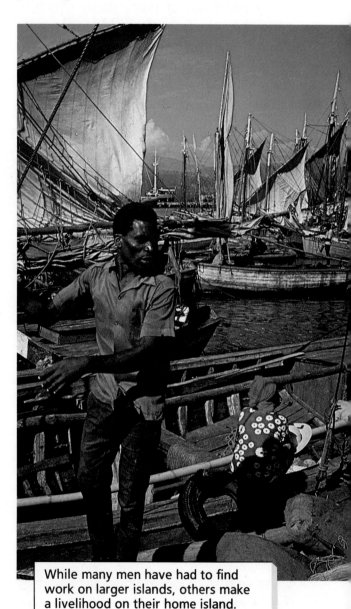

While many men have had to find work on larger islands, others make a livelihood on their home island.
▶ How might this Jamaican make a living?

339

B. Agricultural Products and Mineral Wealth

Commercial Sugar Farms Not all West Indian workers face the same problems as Andrew's. Some of the islands have large commercial farms. A single commercial sugar farm today may cover hundreds of acres. Such a farm has its own modern refinery and roads or railroads by which to carry the cane from the fields to the mill. From there, the sugar is taken to modern ports and shipped to other countries. In Cuba, the making of sugar is still the most important economic activity. The govern-ment sets a goal for the size of the harvest. If Cuban workers meet or exceed that target, it's cause for celebration.

Other Sources of Income Today, most Caribbean countries have other sources of income as well. For example, Cuba also exports tobacco and food products. Jamaica has rich bauxite deposits. Trinidad has oil and natural gas resources that contribute to its economy. Even tiny Grenada has a specialty. It produces 60 percent of the world's supply of nutmeg.

Recently, some industries have come to the Dominican Republic and Haiti as

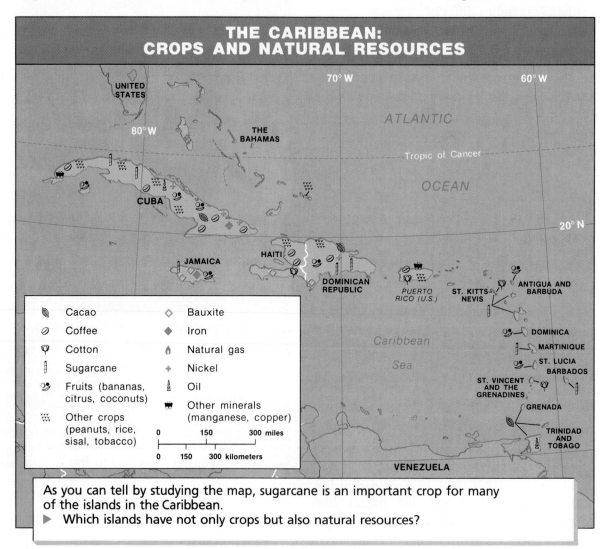

THE CARIBBEAN: CROPS AND NATURAL RESOURCES

Legend:
- Cacao
- Coffee
- Cotton
- Sugarcane
- Fruits (bananas, citrus, coconuts)
- Other crops (peanuts, rice, sisal, tobacco)
- Bauxite
- Iron
- Natural gas
- Nickel
- Oil
- Other minerals (manganese, copper)

0   150   300 miles
0   150   300 kilometers

As you can tell by studying the map, sugarcane is an important crop for many of the islands in the Caribbean.
▶ Which islands have not only crops but also natural resources?

On Bonaire (top) and Barbados (bottom), industries employ skilled workers.
▶ What are these workers doing?

well as to other islands. Some companies in the United States and Europe have moved parts of their businesses to the Caribbean to take advantage of the low wage rates for workers. In some cases, workers in small plants assemble parts that have been manufactured elsewhere to make the finished products. *Assemble* means to put together. Clothing is an example of a product that is often assembled in the West Indies.

C. Tourism in the Caribbean

"And here we are among the rich, green, wild beauty of these Caribbean islands." A British traveler to the West Indies wrote those words around 130 years ago. They could have been written today. The beauty of the islands continues to draw tourists from all over the world. Especially when it is cold in their home countries, people flock to the beautiful beaches and warm weather of such places as Jamaica, Martinique, Curaçao, and the Virgin Islands.

Most of the tourists are North Americans and Europeans since it is easy to get to the Caribbean islands from mainland North America and from Europe. The islands offer a great variety of cultures. Nearly any tourist would feel at home on some island of the Caribbean.

341

(Left) Vacationers in Antigua enjoy the pool and the sea. (Right) Young people in Aruba entertain visitors with steelband music.

▶ Why do resorts appeal to vacationers?

Many large **resorts** have been built to attract tourists. A resort is a place that appeals to people for a vacation. Puerto Plata, in the Dominican Republic, has built a new international airport to speed tourists to its resorts. San Juan, the historic capital of Puerto Rico, has quaint old areas as well as modern resorts for tourists. Both Montego Bay and Ocho Rios in Jamaica have many resort hotels. Montego Bay has its own airport. Nearly every island in the Lesser Antilles has resorts. Some are small and simple. Others are large, luxurious, and expensive. So the islands provide the tourists with pleasant vacations and, at the same time, provide many jobs for thousands of people who live on the Caribbean islands.

LESSON 3 REVIEW

THINK AND WRITE

A. Why do some men find it necessary to leave their homes in the British West Indies, at least for a time?

B. What are some of the important economic activities in the West Indies?

C. What attractions draw tourists to the islands in the Caribbean?

SKILLS CHECK

THINKING SKILL

In this lesson, you read about someone who had to leave his island home to find work on a larger island. The smaller island had few resources and few jobs. What hope do you see for people in similar situations? What creative solutions can you think of to solve their problems? Discuss your ideas with some classmates.

A Closer Look at Puerto Rico

THINK ABOUT WHAT YOU KNOW

You know that Puerto Rico has been a possession of the United States for almost 100 years. In what ways would you expect Puerto Rico to be similar to the United States? In what ways would you expect it to be more like other West Indian islands?

STUDY THE VOCABULARY

light industry   plebiscite
per capita
    income

FOCUS YOUR READING

Why has Puerto Rico prospered more than most islands in the Caribbean?

A. One City, Several Cities

It is a historic old city, founded in 1521, yet it is a modern, bustling capital. It is a center for business, government, and industry. It also is a beautiful tropical resort, lined with beaches and studded with palm trees. San Juan, Puerto Rico's capital, is all this and more.

The Spanish explorer Juan Ponce de León, who roamed Florida searching for the fountain of youth, was the founder of San Juan and served as Puerto Rico's first governor. Today, with a population of about 437,000 and a metropolitan population twice that number, San Juan is Puerto Rico's leading city. Its fine harbor, on the northeast coast, also makes it the island's chief port. Why not take a quick tour of the city.

In 1955 the Institute of Puerto Rican Culture was set up to encourage the arts. Shown here is the school of art and music in Old San Juan.
▶ What courses might be taught at this school?

B. Sights of Old San Juan

You're on your way to Old San Juan. To find it, you'll have to walk down to the harbor. As you look out into the harbor, you will see a peninsula. Three old Spanish forts — El Morro, San Cristóbal, and San Gerónimo — still stand on that peninsula. Remember, Spain had many enemies, especially in the Caribbean. It built the forts to help protect Puerto Rico from raids by the English and French.

Old San Juan is not very large — only an area of seven square blocks. Many of the buildings have been restored to their original colonial style. It still doesn't look exactly as it did in the old days, but Old San Juan has a special charm. Some of the streets are still paved with small grey-blue blocks that came from iron furnaces in Spain. Sailing ships carried these blocks as ballast on their voyages over to the New World. Ballast is weight added to ships. Old sailing ships that were built to carry cargo had to add ballast for stability when they sailed with empty cargo holds.

While you're enjoying today's Old San Juan, close your eyes and imagine that you're in the sixteenth century. High on the fortress, cannons face out toward the sea. The city itself seems safe, completely encircled by a tall wall, over 40 feet (12 m) high. Day and night, guards patrol the area and look beyond the wall to scan the horizon for enemy ships. Other patrols are alert, ready to fight off any enemy attack. Now, at sunset, hinges squeak as soldiers push against the six wooden doors that allow access to the city. Slowly the great doors swing shut. With the guards wide awake, the city within prepares to sleep.

A rampart, or embankment (insert), surrounds El Morro fort and castle.
▶ Why was the rampart necessary for such a large fort?

The Le Lo Lai festival features performers of colorful folk dances. The dances depict episodes from historical and culture events in Puerto Rico.
▶ How, do you suppose, did folk dances originate?

C. Other Attractions in San Juan

It's time to move on to the Condado and Isla Verde sections of San Juan. There people enjoy the sun, water, and cool breezes of the trade winds during the day. In the evenings they can eat in fine restaurants. Le Lo Lai (lay loh LYE) dance performances are given nightly to introduce visitors to Puerto Rico's colorful heritage.

If you prefer, you can head for Río Piedras, the business heart of the city, with tall office buildings and large shopping centers. The Plaza Las Américas — the largest shopping mall in the Caribbean — and the Hiram Bithorn Baseball Stadium are located there. The large stadium is usually filled with enthusiastic fans who really enjoy baseball.

D. Other Cities in Puerto Rico

"It's so sunny here that even the cows wear sunglasses." That's something that a cabdriver in Ponce, Puerto Rico's second

The busy Río Piedras section has many tall buildings, including the Roosevelt Tower.
▶ Why do cities have tall buildings?

345

Puerto Ricans and tourists alike visit the cathedral (top) and the building called the Old Firehouse.
▶ Compare these two old buildings.

largest city, might tell visitors. Located on the south side of the island, Ponce has the hottest climate in Puerto Rico.

La Perla Theatre and the magnificent Ponce Museum of Art are popular places for everyone to visit. The Tibes (TEE bays) Indian Ceremonial Center, the oldest cemetery uncovered in the Antilles, is nearby.

A statue of Christopher Columbus stands in the plaza of the western port city of Mayagüez (mah yah GWES). Mayagüez, Puerto Rico's third largest city, is quieter than either San Juan or Ponce, and it has fewer tourists. The city, almost completely destroyed by an earthquake in 1918, has been rebuilt. Today it is home to the Mayagüez Zoo, known for its Bengal tigers and its bird and reptile collections. The Tropical Agricultural Research Station of the United States Department of Agriculture conducts tours to show the exotic plants, trees, and flowers that grow all over the island.

In the Plaza Colón in Mayagüez, there is a monument with a statue.
▶ To whom, would you guess, is the statue dedicated?

A technician and production line workers (insert) are in a Puerto Rican pharmaceutical factory.
▶ What precaution are they taking?

E. Manufacturing in Puerto Rico

You may recall that Luis Muñoz Marín served several terms as governor of Puerto Rico. Why did the people keep voting him back into office? Part of his popularity came from his economic policy. At the time when the United States still appointed Puerto Rico's governor and Muñoz Marín was in the Puerto Rican Senate, he helped to develop a plan called Operation Bootstrap.

Operation Bootstrap called for many changes to promote the island's social and economic development. As governor, Muñoz Marín worked hard to put the plan into effect. Land reform broke up large farms, and the land was given to farm workers. As a result of improved education, more people learned to read and write. In the cities, dwellings that were sturdier and cleaner replaced many squatters' settlements.

Part of Operation Bootstrap encouraged industrial development. Mainland companies began many **light industries** on the island. Light industries are industries that use small machines and few raw materials to produce goods. From the new factories came electronic equipment, appliances, textiles, and clothing. Businesspeople have also invested in industry. Over 1,600 manufacturing plants have been created since Operation Bootstrap first began. As a result, the island is fast becoming a major producer and exporter of electronic products, chemicals, and clothing.

Puerto Rico was once a poor country. Today it has a **per capita income** that is among the highest in all of Latin America. Per capita income is the total amount of money that a nation's people earn in a year divided by the total population. Puerto Rico's per capita income rose from $125 a year in the early 1940s to over $5,600 a year in 1989. However, unemployment is still a problem. In the early 1990s the official unemployment rate stood at about 17 percent.

Demonstrators, in a political march, carry flags and banners.
▶ Why might they be doing this?

F. The Fifty-first State?

"We affirm the right of Puerto Rico to assert its own personality, either through statehood or independence." Those words were written around 50 years ago by Luis Muñoz Rivera, the father of Muñoz Marín. He was a newspaper editor and politician who spent much of his life trying to get the United States to allow more independence for Puerto Rico. Today, the question of Puerto Rico's political status remains an important issue.

Some people think Puerto Rico should be an independent country. Others want Puerto Rico to become the fifty-first state in the United States. A **plebiscite** was held in Puerto Rico in 1957. A plebiscite is a vote to see how people feel about a question or problem. It is like an opinion poll. Over 60 percent of those who voted wanted Puerto Rico to remain a commonwealth.

The debate over statehood for Puerto Rico continues today. However, one thing is clear. Few Puerto Ricans want the island to be independent. They believe that Puerto Rico's association with the United States brings them many advantages.

LESSON **4** REVIEW

THINK AND WRITE

A. What are the three major areas of San Juan?

B. What did Old San Juan look like in colonial times?

C. Why do people go to Condado and Isla Verde?

D. What are the names and locations of two other cities in Puerto Rico?

E. How did Operation Bootstrap change Puerto Rico?

F. What major issue divides Puerto Rico today?

SKILLS CHECK

MAP SKILL

Look up *San Juan* and *Ponce* in the Gazetteer and also find them on the map on page 332. What feature of location do these cities have in common?

USING THE VOCABULARY

light industries
refinery
tone language
emigrate
per capita income

patois
plebiscite
overseers
provision grounds
byproducts

On a separate sheet of paper, write the correct definition — **a** or **b** — and the term it defines.

1. **a.** industries that use small machines
   b. industries that make lightweight products
2. **a.** a place where sugar cane is grown
   b. a place where sugar is processed
3. **a.** a language that is spoken loudly
   b. a language in which a high or low tone changes a word's meaning
4. **a.** to leave one region to live in another
   b. to travel for pleasure by ship
5. **a.** average earnings of the leaders
   b. average earnings per person in a country
6. **a.** a local dialect of a language
   b. a dance step
7. **a.** a mineral
   b. a vote to show how people feel about an issue
8. **a.** supervisors of slaves
   b. owners of slaves
9. **a.** ability to earn a living
   b. land for slaves to grow their own crops for food
10. **a.** products used in pet foods
    b. products that result from processing another product

REMEMBERING WHAT YOU READ

On a separate sheet of paper, write your answers in complete sentences.

1. Why might you say that the Caribbean islands have variety?
2. When was sugar first imported to Europe?
3. Describe briefly the trade that linked sugar and molasses to slavery of the Africans.
4. When did slavery become illegal in the West Indies?
5. Name three sources of income, besides sugar, that the Caribbean nations have.
6. Which three cities in the Caribbean are the largest and most important?
7. Why is Ponce de León important in the history of Puerto Rico?
8. Why did sixteenth-century San Juan need forts, high walls, and soldiers to guard it?
9. How did Governor Muñoz Marín's economic policy "Operation Bootstrap" help Puerto Rico?
10. Which form of government, would you say, do most Puerto Ricans favor?

TYING LANGUAGE ARTS TO SOCIAL STUDIES

Read a current magazine article about the Caribbean. Write a one-page summary and illustrate it with a picture (or a copy of one) from the magazine.

THINKING CRITICALLY

On a separate sheet of paper, write your answers in complete sentences.

1. Which island in the Caribbean would you most like to visit? Explain why.
2. Some United States light industries have moved to the Caribbean because wages for workers are lower there. What problems does this cause for some factory workers living in the United States?
3. Why should people preserve and restore old buildings that are historical? Explain their value or importance.
4. What are some of the medical problems a person might have as a result of eating too much sugar?
5. Describe one or more of the local industries of the city, town, or rural area in which you live.

SUMMARIZING THE CHAPTER

On a separate sheet of paper, draw a graphic organizer like the one shown here. Copy the information from this graphic organizer to the one you have drawn. Under each heading, fill in the blanks with facts you learned from that lesson.

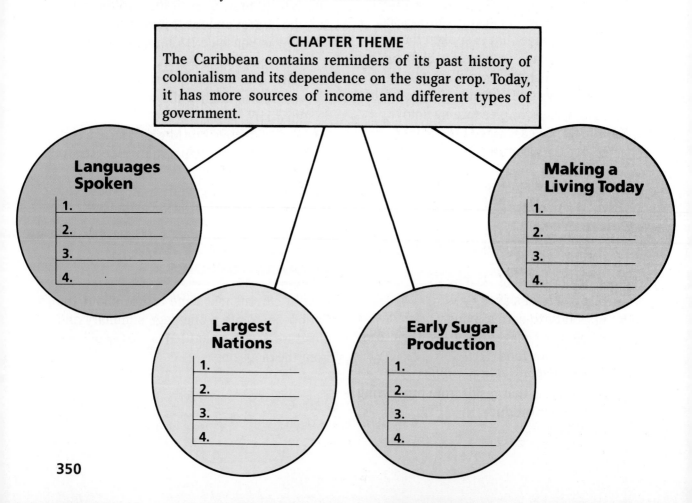

CHAPTER THEME
The Caribbean contains reminders of its past history of colonialism and its dependence on the sugar crop. Today, it has more sources of income and different types of government.

Languages Spoken
1. _____
2. _____
3. _____
4. _____

Making a Living Today
1. _____
2. _____
3. _____
4. _____

Largest Nations
1. _____
2. _____
3. _____
4. _____

Early Sugar Production
1. _____
2. _____
3. _____
4. _____

COOPERATIVE LEARNING

When travelers prepare for a visit to a foreign country, they may read guidebooks. A guidebook is an information book for a traveler. It gives directions to points of interest. It also gives information about the climate, physical features, and the culture. Some guidebooks also provide historical information. How would you go about writing a guidebook?

PROJECT

In Unit 4, you read about Middle America. With a group of classmates, compose a guidebook for one or more of the countries of Middle America. Your guidebook will be used by a group of students that is going on a tour of Middle America.

● In your guidebook you will want to include at least the following information:

1. What are the points of interest, both natural and man-made? Include such attractions as important cities, ancient ruins, scenic lakes, volcanoes, and so on.

2. What is daily life like there for city dwellers? For country dwellers? Where do most of the people live?

3. On what is the economy of the country based? For example, what are the main industries or crops?

● To decide what will be in your guidebook, hold a meeting. Then divide tasks among group members.

Depending on the number of students in the group and the information your guidebook will include, your group might divide the tasks as follows:

● One group member could write about visiting important historical sites such as temples, monuments, and buildings.

● Another group member could write about religious practices.

● A third group member could draw pictures to illustrate what has been written for the guidebook.

● One group member could draw a map of the region and label where the important places to visit are located.

● Another group member could prepare the cover, title page, and table of contents for the guidebook.

PRESENTATION AND REVIEW

When your guidebook is complete, present it to the rest of your class. As a group, try to answer any questions the class may have about the country or countries described. Ask the class what additional information could be included in your guidebook.

After your presentation, meet as a group to decide whether or not your guidebook is effective. Could tourists use it to learn important information about the places described? What things could you do to improve it?

REMEMBER TO:
● Give your ideas.
● Listen to others' ideas.
● Plan your work with the group.
● Present your project.
● Discuss how your group worked.

A. WHY DO I NEED THIS SKILL?

Have you and your family ever planned a long trip by car? If you are going to several places that are long distances apart, you will want to know how long it will take to get from place to place. To find out the distances between places, you can use a mileage chart. A mileage chart tells you approximately how many miles it is from one city to another.

B. LEARNING THE SKILL

Imagine that you are planning a trip through Mexico. You will be visiting several of these cities: Ciudad Juárez, Mazatlán, Mérida, Mexico City, Tijuana, Tuxtla Gutiérrez, and Veracruz. Try to locate these cities on the map of Mexico on page 246. You can find the approximate distances between cities on the map by using the scale of miles. But if you want to know more exact *highway* distances, consult a mileage chart.

The mileage chart on the opposite page shows the distances between the cities listed above. Note that the same cities are listed alphabetically across the top and down the left-hand side of the chart.

To find the distance between two cities, locate one city on the left-hand side of the chart. Then move your finger across the row of numbers to the right of that city until you find the number in that row below the other city. This number is the mileage between the two cities.

For example, suppose you are in Mexico City and you want to know how far you will have to travel to get to Tijuana. Find Mexico City in the left-hand column. Then move your finger across the row of numbers to the right of Mexico City until you find the number in that row that falls directly below Tijuana. The mileage chart should tell you that it is 1,834 miles from Mexico City to Tijuana.

C. PRACTICING THE SKILL

Using the mileage chart, answer the following questions.

1. What is the distance from Veracruz to Tijuana?

2. What is the distance from Mérida to Veracruz?
3. How far is it from Tuxtla Gutiérrez to Ciudad Juarez?
4. What is the total distance you would have to travel if you drove from Mérida to Tuxtla Gutiérrez to Veracruz?
5. Which is the greater distance to travel — from Mexico City to Veracruz or from Tijuana to Mérida?

D. APPLYING THE SKILL

Make a mileage chart containing the following information about four cities in the United States.

New York City to Boston: 215 miles
New York City to Chicago: 790 miles
New York City to Los Angeles: 2,875 miles
Boston to Chicago: 965 miles
Boston to Los Angeles: 2,985 miles
Chicago to Los Angeles: 2,050 miles

HIGHWAY MILEAGE CHART	Ciudad Juárez	Mazatlán	Mérida	Mexico City	Tijuana	Tuxtla Gutiérrez	Veracruz
Ciudad Juárez		877	2,522	1,247	899	1,932	1,507
Mazatlán	877		2,015	705	1,129	1,392	975
Mérida	2,522	2,015		974	2,808	818	695
Mexico City	1,247	705	974		1,834	687	265
Tijuana	899	1,129	2,808	1,834		2,521	2,099
Tuxtla Gutiérrez	1,932	1,392	818	687	2,521		429
Veracruz	1,507	975	695	265	2,099	429	

A. WHY DO I NEED THIS SKILL?

If you read that Brazil has 147 million people, you would have some idea of how big Brazil is in terms of population. If you were told that Brazil has almost two-thirds the population of the United States, you would have an even better idea.

Authors often organize ideas by making comparisons. Comparisons tell how persons, places, ideas, or events are alike and different. If you are able to recognize and make comparisons, it will be easier for you to understand and remember what you read.

B. LEARNING THE SKILL

Writers of social studies books use comparisons to make ideas clearer. For example, on pages 332–333 of Chapter 13, the text reads as shown below.

> "Dominica, originally owned by the French but taken over by England, has an area about a quarter of the size of the state of Rhode Island. Around 312,000 people live on Dominica. . . . By contrast, over 7 million people live in the Dominican Republic, which is about the size of New Hampshire and Vermont combined."

Here the size of Dominica is compared with the size of Rhode Island, and the population of Dominica with the population of the Dominican Republic. The words *by contrast* signal that a comparison of the populations shows how they are different.

On occasion, a text question will ask the reader to compare ideas. For example, the "Focus Your Reading" question for Lesson 1 in Chapter 13 asks how the Caribbean Islands differ from one another. Paying attention to questions like this will help you to better understand how the things you read "fit together."

C. PRACTICING THE SKILL

In Chapter 11 you read about Central America today. On pages 294–297, there are descriptions of the capital cities of several Central American countries. These countries have many similarities and differences. They can be compared and contrasted in many ways.

One way to organize comparisons is to make a **comparison chart** like the one shown. Write the people, places, or things to be compared in the left-hand column. Then write characteristics that they may share in a row across the top. Then fill in the empty boxes with plus or minus signs to show which of the things being compared have each characteristic (+) and which do not (−). Compare one row with the next to find out how the things being compared are alike and different.

Copy the comparison chart on a sheet of paper and complete it. The capital cities of

PLACES TO COMPARE		CHARACTERISTICS				
Capital City	Country	struck by earthquakes	rebuilt after earthquakes	has old colonial buildings	has mountains	is on a lake or ocean
Guatemala City	Guatemala	+	+	−	+	−
San Salvador	El Salvador					
Managua						
San José						
Panama City						

five Central American countries are listed in the first column. The second column gives the country in which each city is located. You'll need to complete this column.

Fill in each row of empty boxes with plus and minus signs (the first row is done for you). For example, in Chapter 11 you learned that Guatemala City has been struck by earthquakes (a plus), was rebuilt after the earthquakes (a plus), does not have any old colonial buildings (a minus), is ringed by mountains (a plus), and is not located on any body of water (a minus).

Use the information in the chapter to fill in the boxes for the other cities. Then go back to the lesson and find more characteristics that some of these capital cities share.

Add these new characteristics to your chart and complete the expanded chart.

Finally, review the chart by noting how these cities are alike and how they are different.

D. APPLYING THE SKILL

In Chapter 14 you will learn about the Northern and Andean countries of South America. Look for and make comparisons as you read about these countries. Some comparisons will be made directly in the text. Others, you'll have to make yourself. Construct a comparison chart to show how these countries are alike and different in their lands, climates, and peoples.

Unit 5

SOUTH AMERICA FROM INDEPENDENCE TO TODAY

The vast continent of South America includes 13 nations. Although similar in some ways, the nations are very different in other ways.

▶ *The Andean highlands of Peru are made up of towering, snowcapped mountains and broad valleys and plateaus.*

356

The different physical features of the northern and Andean countries of South America range from the high, rugged chains of the Andes Mountains to tropical forests, lowlands, and coastal plains.

Land and Climate: Colombia, Venezuela, and the Guianas

THINK ABOUT WHAT YOU KNOW

Think about places you know of that have many high mountains. What other physical features would you expect such places to have?

STUDY THE VOCABULARY

selva	savanna
cordillera	mesa

FOCUS YOUR READING

What are the major regions of the northern countries of South America?

A small village in Colombia nestles in the Andean foothills.
▶ Would you like to live there?

A. Northern South America

If you sailed east from Panama along the northern coast of South America, you'd pass five nations — Colombia, Venezuela, Guyana, Suriname, and French Guiana. Find each nation on the map on page 360. Colombia is the only country in South America to border both the Pacific Ocean and the Caribbean Sea. From the standpoint of their location, Venezuela and Colombia, and the Guianas — Guyana, Suriname, and French Guiana — are in northern South America.

Venezuela and Colombia are sometimes counted among the Andean nations, with Ecuador, Peru, and Bolivia, because the Andes Mountains run through all five countries. Even though the Guianas are also in northern South America, they have little in common with the other countries of that region. Instead, the Guianas share a close cultural heritage with the islands of the West Indies.

NORTHERN AND ANDEAN COUNTRIES: PHYSICAL

Caribbean Sea

Cristóbal Colón
19,020 ft.
(5,797 m)

Caracas La Guaira

TRINIDAD
AND
TOBAGO

ATLANTIC

OCEAN

10° N

PANAMA

Lake
Maracaibo

SIERRA NEVADA
DE MÉRIDA

VENEZUELA

Orinoco River

LLANOS OF THE ORINOCO

Georgetown

Paramaribo

GUYANA

Cayenne

SURINAME

FRENCH
GUIANA

Nevado del Ruíz
17,716 ft. (5,400 m)

WESTERN CORDILLERA

CENTRAL CORDILLERA

EASTERN CORDILLERA

Meta

Bogotá

CHOCO

COLOMBIA

Tolima
18,425 ft.
(5,616 m)

GUIANA HIGHLANDS

Pasto

Quito

Cotopaxi
19,347 ft.
(5,897 m)

Huila
18,865 ft.
(5,750 m)

Amazon

River

ECUADOR

Chimborazo
20,561 ft.
(6,267 m)

Marañón

Equator

0°

A N D E S

PERU

BRAZIL

River

Huascarán
22,205 ft.
(6,768 m)

Yungay

10° S

PACIFIC

Lima

Machu
Picchu

Cuzco

OCEAN

Lake
Titicaca

La Paz

BOLIVIA

ALTIPLANO

Lake
Poopó

Sucre

GRAN CHACO

Sajama
21,391 ft.
(6,520 m)

Tropic of Capricorn

PARAGUAY

CHILE

ARGENTINA

URUGUAY

Legend

✪	National capitals
•	Other cities
▲	Mountain peaks

Elevations

Feet	Meters
10,000	3,000
5,000	1,500
2,000	600
1,000	300
0	0

0   200   400 miles

0   200   400 kilometers

Lake Titicaca

The highest navigable lake in the world is Lake Titicaca. It is
130 miles (209 km) long and it is situated 12,506 feet (3,812 m)
above sea level.
▶ Between which two countries does it form part of the boundary?

360

The Andes form the most important physical feature of South America. In fact, these high mountains extend all the way south, through Chile. In northern South America, however, the mountains are only one part of the story. Along with highland areas, you'll also find lowlands, coastal plains, tropical forests, and volcanoes in the countries of Colombia, Venezuela, Guyana, Suriname, and French Guiana.

Most of the people of Colombia live in and around the large cities in the highlands of the Andes. In contrast, most of the people living in the countries of Guyana, Suriname, and French Guiana live in the coastal areas.

B. Regions in Colombia

Lowland Region With more than 440,000 square miles (1,140,000 sq km) of land, Colombia is the fourth largest country in South America. It is larger than the states of California and Texas combined. About 60 percent of Colombia's land is a vast lowland that lies to the east of the Andes. The northern section of this lowland forms part of the Llanos (LAH-noz), or plains, of the Orinoco. The southern section is **selva**, or tropical forest. The Colombian selva forms part of the great tropical forest of the Amazon Basin that covers nearly all of the middle of South America. Very few people live in Colombia's southern section.

Mountain Ranges In southern Colombia, the Andes divide into three large, high mountain ranges that cover 30 percent of Colombia's land. The three mountain ranges, or **cordilleras** (kor dihl YER uz), are called the Western Cordillera, the Central Cordillera, and the Eastern Cordillera.

The valleys of two large rivers, the Cauca and the Magdalena, separate the three cordilleras. Find the three ranges on the physical map on page 360.

Active Volcanoes Some of the peaks of the Andes are active volcanoes. An active volcano is one that is erupting, has erupted in the recent past, or shows signs of erupting in the future. In 1985, Nevado del Ruiz, one of the active volcanoes in the Colombian Andes, erupted. The eruption itself was not very great, but heat from the volcano melted the snow on its peak. The melting snow caused great mud slides that killed over 20,000 people. The mud slides also completely destroyed the city of Armero. In March of 1988, Colombians experienced some anxious moments when Nevado del Ruiz again began to rumble. Fortunately, this time the volcano simply belched some smoke and then returned to rest. Like earthquakes, volcanic eruptions are a serious natural hazard in many parts of Latin America.

Some people who lived nearby were affected by the threatened eruption of Nevado del Ruiz in 1988.
▶ What are the people doing?

C. Venezuela and the Guianas

Venezuela is smaller than Colombia, with just over 350,000 square miles (906,500 sq km), but it is far from being a tiny country. It is over twice the size of California. The Eastern Cordillera of Colombia splits into two ranges as it enters Venezuela. One range, the Sierra de Perijá (pay ree HAH), continues northward, forming part of the border between Venezuela and Colombia. The other range, the Sierra Nevada de Mérida (ME ree dah), extends northeast. The Sierra Nevada de Mérida, together with the highlands that continue along part of Venezuela's coast, are called the Andes highlands.

Maracaibo Lowland Between the two great sierras, there is a large, V-shaped lowland called the Maracaibo lowland. Lake Maracaibo, the largest lake in South America, fills part of this lowland. The Maracaibo lowland has the second greatest number of people in Venezuela. The Maracaibo lowland area is Venezuela's most important oil producing region.

Venezuela's Llanos The Llanos cover an area some 600 miles (965 km) long from the Orinoco River basin westward into Colombia. Find the Llanos on the physical map on page 360. In the past, the Llanos area was a land of giant cattle ranches. There were very few towns or small farms. Even today, only 9 percent of Venezuela's population lives there. The Venezuelan government has tried to bring farming and industry to parts of the area. Although the discovery of oil has brought more people to the area, the population remains small.

Guiana Highlands Beyond the Orinoco River are the Guiana Highlands. They extend south and east in Venezuela to the border between Brazil and the Guianas.

Lake Maracaibo is among the world's largest producers of oil.
▶ What other activities might this large lake provide?

The upper Orinoco River, in Venezuela, has 436 tributaries. It is one of the three main rivers in South America. The Caroní is one of the tributaries.

▶ Into what body of water does the Orinoco River flow? (See map on page 360.)

This large area includes forests, rivers, and **savannas**, which are tropical grasslands. Giant **mesas**, or flat-topped mountains, rise above the forests. Some of these mesas are so large they have rivers flowing across them. When the rivers flow over the sides of the mesas, they form large waterfalls. Angel Falls, the world's highest waterfall, drops 3,212 feet (979 m) from the top of a mesa in the Guiana Highlands.

Lowlands in the Guianas Lowlands make up much of the Guianas. The coast is low and swampy. Nearly all the people, towns, roads, and farms are located in a narrow strip along the coast. There the swamps have been drained, canals have been dug, and pumps have been brought in so that the land will not be flooded by the sea or by the many rivers that flow to the coast.

Inland from the narrow strip of settled land, dense tropical forests (selvas) can be found. Some of them have hardly been explored. The forests have valuable wood that as yet has not been cut for lumber.

D. Climate in the Northern Countries

You would never need a winter coat in the north-coast lowlands of South America. The north coast lies in the tropics, so it's warm there the year round. Since the temperature does not change much through the year, the seasons are defined by the amount of precipitation. There is a dry season and a rainy season.

In the rainy season, the highlands usually receive enough rainfall for farming. However, a part of the Andes highlands of Venezuela stays very dry. There the government has built irrigation projects so that more crops can be grown. Even with irrigation, only a little farming can be done during the dry season in this area.

FROM:

Angels Four

By: David Nott
Setting: Guiana Highlands of Venezuela

In January of 1971, four men climbed the face of Angel Falls. That is, they climbed Auyán-Tepuí, or Devil Mountain, a 250-square-mile (648-sq-mi) plateau in the Guiana jungle of southeastern Venezuela. After ten days and nine nights, they completed their ascent.

In the selection below, David Nott, one of the climbers, describes his feelings as he views Auyán-Tepuí for the first time.

. . . *We came to a level stretch, rounded a bend, and there before us was the Auyán-Tepuí, stretching for miles on either side, soaring 3,000 feet up from the jungle.*

The mind slips gears trying to take in a colossus like this, especially when you encounter it unexpectedly. I recalled docking a ketch in a busy port months before and sleeping on board. In the morning there was a great freighter alongside. It had berthed in the night and now, at dawn, suddenly loomed immense above me. But compared with this wall ahead, the freighter seemed a toy. The Auyán-Tepuí was like a separate planet rearing over the rim of the world!

We began tracing routes up it, as climbers will. It was difficult to grasp the scale. I peered at a fissure in the face — a thin dark scar running up a third of its height — and realized with a jolt that you could tuck a hundred-story skyscraper into it.

A smooth slab of rock above the fissure was as large as six football fields laid end to end in pairs, 900 feet high, 300 wide. If we climbed that far, we would still be a thousand feet from the top. . . .

The falls and our point of attack were still miles to the south. But it was the same wall.

"So, we're going to be four days and nights on that, John? said Straub.

"I hope it's only four," said Timo.

It was going to be ten.

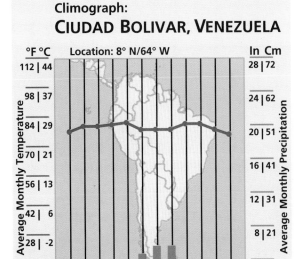

Climograph:
CIUDAD BOLIVAR, VENEZUELA

Location: 8° N/64° W

Average Monthly Temperature (°F | °C): 112 | 44, 98 | 37, 84 | 29, 70 | 21, 56 | 13, 42 | 6, 28 | -2, 14 | -10, 0 | -18

Average Monthly Precipitation (In | Cm): 28 | 72, 24 | 62, 20 | 51, 16 | 41, 12 | 31, 8 | 21, 4 | 11, 0 | 0

MONTHS: J F M A M J J A S O N D

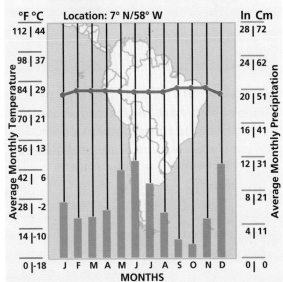

Climograph:
GEORGETOWN, GUYANA

Location: 7° N/58° W

Average Monthly Temperature (°F | °C): 112 | 44, 98 | 37, 84 | 29, 70 | 21, 56 | 13, 42 | 6, 28 | -2, 14 | -10, 0 | -18

Average Monthly Precipitation (In | Cm): 28 | 72, 24 | 62, 20 | 51, 16 | 41, 12 | 31, 8 | 21, 4 | 11, 0 | 0

MONTHS: J F M A M J J A S O N D

Ciudad Bolivar, Venezuela, and Georgetown, Guyana, have almost the same temperature.
► Which city has a wetter climate?

If you want to go to one of the rainiest places in the entire world, head for the Chocó (choh KOH). This area of the northwest coast of Colombia, near Panama, receives 350 inches (889 cm) of rain per year. The difficulty of building a road through the swamps of this area is one reason the Pan-American Highway has never been completed between Panama and Colombia.

In the Llanos, the grass dies and small streams may dry up during the long dry season. Then in the rainy season, heavy rainfalls often flood low areas. The long dry season and the lowland flooding in the rainy season make farming difficult in the Llanos. They also limit the growth of trees, accounting for the grassy plant growth.

Moving south toward the Amazon Basin, the dry seasons become shorter. Forest begins to replace the grass of the Llanos, and soon you are in dense selvas. The selvas are broken by grassy savannas. There, the soils are poor or often flooded.

LESSON 1 REVIEW

THINK AND WRITE

A. Briefly describe the locations of the countries of northern South America.

B. What are some major regions of Colombia?

C. What happens to the Andes when they enter Venezuela?

D. How does climate vary along South America's Caribbean coast?

SKILLS CHECK

MAP SKILL

Locate *Orinoco River* in the Gazetteer. What are the names of two of its tributaries? Find them on the physical map on page 360.

Land and Climate: Ecuador, Peru, and Bolivia

THINK ABOUT WHAT YOU KNOW
Think about what you learned about the countries of northern South America. What similar physical features would you expect to find in the three Andean countries nearby?

STUDY THE VOCABULARY
ocean current   alpaca
Altiplano

FOCUS YOUR READING
Why is elevation an important factor in Ecuador, Peru, and Bolivia?

A. Coast, Mountains, and Forest

The countries of Ecuador, Peru, and Bolivia are in the central part of the Andes. They stretch from the Pacific coast, across the Andes, and into the lowlands of the Amazon Basin. The lands of Ecuador and Peru can be divided into three regions: the coast, the mountains, and the forest. Bolivia has two of these regions: the mountains and the forest. Bolivia also has large areas of savanna and brushy land.

Why isn't there a coastal region in Bolivia? Look at the map on page 360. Bolivia is one of two landlocked countries in South America. A landlocked country is one that has no seacoast. All goods shipped into and out of Bolivia must cross a neighboring country. Look again at the map of South America. Locate the other landlocked country.

These scenes in Bolivia show its different physical features, such as a river valley (top) and Lake Titicaca (bottom).
▶ Compare the middle scene with the others.

B. Coastal Areas of Peru and Ecuador

The Peruvian Desert Can you imagine a place where it rains only once in ten years? That's what it is like in some parts of Peru's coastal desert, the narrow belt of land between the Andes and the sea. Since it is dry, the Peruvian desert has little or no natural vegetation.

It seems strange that a place so dry should often be covered with fog, but that is the case. What causes this fog? The answer lies in an **ocean current**, called the Peru Current. An ocean current is a regular movement of the surface water caused mostly by winds and differences in water temperature. A stream of very cold water flows from south to north, offshore from about the middle of Chile all the way to Ecuador. The cooling of the moist ocean air as it crosses the Peru Current causes fog. Instead of falling as rain, the moisture forms a low cloud of fog. The Andes trap the cloud near the coast, so fog covers the area like a giant blanket.

Coastal River Valleys Over 40 rivers flow to the sea from the Peruvian Andes. For centuries before the coming of the Spaniards, Indian farmers used water from these rivers to irrigate land for crops. Today the coastal river valleys are among Peru's most important farming areas. Lima, Peru's capital, is in the valley of the Rímac (REE mahk) River, one of these coastal rivers.

Ecuador's Coast The Peru Current ends near Ecuador. Here the coast is hot and wet. For many years people were afraid to live on the coast of Ecuador because of the danger of diseases such as malaria and yellow fever. Today, most of the tropical dis-

The photographs above show how land is used in different parts of Peru.
▶ Which of the photographs also shows a volcano?

eases have been controlled. Now the coast is one of the most rapidly growing parts of Ecuador.

C. Avenue of the Volcanoes

Over 30 great volcanoes loom above the series of high mountain basins in Ecuador. That's why the area is often called the Avenue of the Volcanoes. One of these, as you may recall, is Cotopaxi. It is the world's highest active volcano, towering to 19,347 feet (5,897 m).

The mountain basins, separated one from another by still higher areas, have been the centers for highland settlements since long before the Spaniards arrived. Near Peru the basins give way to long, narrow mountain ranges that run the length of Peru. Here you see some of the most beautiful mountains and valleys in all of Latin America. However, this area is a dangerous place in which to live. In 1970, for example, a landslide caused by an earthquake completely buried the city of Yungay, killing 20,000 people. Several other towns in the same valley were also badly damaged. In all, over 50,000 people were killed in a matter of minutes.

In southern Peru, the Andes widen to form still more basins. Higher and larger than those of Ecuador, the basins continue all the way through Bolivia. Cuzco, the ancient Inca capital, is in a basin 11,500 feet (3,505 m) above sea level in the Andes of Peru.

D. The Altiplano

Would you like to ride in a boat on the highest navigable lake in the world? Then head for Lake Titicaca (tiht ih KAH kuh). It is situated on the Altiplano, the high plateau near the border between Peru and Bolivia. The Altiplano is over 500 miles (805 km) long and averages about 85 miles (137 km) in width. It truly is high,

Mardi Gras parades and dances about Inca warfare take place in Bolivia.
▶ Why are such activities important?

Bolivian farmers cultivate crops in a riverbed during the dry season.
▶ What words would you use to describe the Altiplano?

ranging from about 12,500 feet (3,810 m) to over 15,000 feet (4,572 m).

The border between Peru and Bolivia crosses Lake Titicaca, dividing the lake between the two countries. The Peruvian railroad ends on the northern shore of the lake, and the Bolivian railroad ends on the southern shore. A large boat carries freight and passengers across the lake.

The Altiplano is mostly a bleak, barren place, too high for trees to grow and without enough rain to keep grass green. Nonetheless, about 70 percent of Bolivia's people live in or around the Altiplano. The elevation of the land near Lake Titicaca is a bit lower than most of the rest of the Altiplano, and the lake water keeps temperatures a little warmer. Therefore, many small farms dot the land near the lake. Herds of sheep, llamas, and **alpacas** graze on the sparse grass of the higher Altiplano. Like the llama, the alpaca is a small member of the camel family. Llamas and alpacas are raised for wool, although the wool of the alpacas is finer. The llamas are also used to carry loads.

E. The Forest Region

A rugged land of steep slopes, deep canyons, and rushing rivers — that's the forest region on the eastern slopes of the Andes, between the elevations of 10,000 and 2,000 feet (3,048 and 610 m). The forest region has another part that's made up of the lower slopes of the eastern Andes and of the Amazon lowlands to the east. Forest covers very large areas of the land in Ecuador as well as in Peru. Bolivia is another country that has some large areas of forest.

It would be hard to find a greater contrast than that between the bare, cold Altiplano and the warm, green forested lowlands. The difference between the two often seems even greater because in many places just a short distance separates the high plateaus and basins from the beginnings of the warm, humid forests.

The tranquil beauty of this lowland forest is uninterrupted by human life.

▶ Why is this region not as developed as the Altiplano?

Because of its more pleasant climate, you might expect the lowland forest region to be a popular place to live. Surprisingly, the rugged slopes and canyons of the highland forests have been developed more. That's because they are close to the communities of the highlands and because they have better farming conditions than the lower areas.

F. Bolivia's Lowlands

Bolivia doesn't have a seacoast, but it does have lowlands. The lowlands are to the east of the Andes. The northern half of these lowlands is in the Amazon Basin. Only part of this northern area is forested. The rest is poorly drained, and floods occur during the rainy season. Like the Llanos of the Orinoco, this part of the Amazon Basin is a grassland. It is used mainly for cattle grazing.

Grass, brush, and low forest cover the southern half of Bolivia's lowlands. This area forms part of the Gran Chaco, a dry region that also covers about half of Paraguay and much of northern Argentina.

LESSON **2** *REVIEW*

THINK AND WRITE

A. What are the three regions of Ecuador and Peru?

B. Why does fog often cover Peru's coastal desert?

C. Why are the high mountain basins important?

D. What is the Altiplano?

E. What two parts make up the forest region of the Andes?

F. What are the Bolivian lowlands mainly used for?

SKILLS CHECK

THINKING SKILL

You read that the bare, cold Altiplano is more developed than the warm, green lowland forest region with its pleasant climate. Much of the land in Ecuador, Peru, and Bolivia is in the forest region. Do you think that this region will be developed in the future? Share your ideas with some classmates.

Since Bolívar

THINK ABOUT WHAT YOU KNOW

Suppose you and another person both wanted to be class president, and each of you had the support of some important people in the class. Even if you lost, how would you try to get everyone to work together after the election was over?

STUDY THE VOCABULARY

redistribution

FOCUS YOUR READING

What type of political rule did Venezuela and Colombia experience after they achieved independence?

A. Disunity and Disorder

The United States of South America —what a large and mighty nation that would have been! As you have learned, however, even the great Liberator, Simón Bolívar, could not keep Gran Colombia, first formed in 1820, from breaking up into separate nations. Venezuela and Ecuador withdrew from Gran Colombia in 1830, about two months before Bolívar died. The remaining portion became the nation of Colombia.

Each of the new nations went through difficult times. Venezuela and Colombia became lands of violence, ruled by caudillos and dictators. Revolts and unrest made democratic politics impossible. Happily, however, both countries finally achieved considerable progress. You will read about both Venezuela and Colombia, the two countries north of Ecuador, Peru, and Bolivia in this lesson. In the next lesson, you will read about what happened to Ecuador.

B. Dictators Rule

A hero of independence became Venezuela's first caudillo. José Antonio Páez had helped Simón Bolívar defeat the Spanish army in Venezuela. Páez ruled Venezuela from 1830 to 1846 and from 1861 to 1863.

Shortly after Páez, another caudillo, Antonio Guzmán Blanco, came to power. He dominated the country from 1870 to 1889, although he was not in office for the whole period. Guzmán Blanco, much like Porfirio Díaz in Mexico, was a dictator who brought peace to a country troubled by civil wars and bandits. He ordered the building of roads and telegraph lines to connect the parts of the country. Foreign companies first began to invest in Venezuela during the time that Guzmán Blanco was in office.

In 1908, a third dictator, Juan Vicente Gómez, came into office and controlled the

Vice-president Gómez seized control while the president of Venezuela was away for medical treatment.
► Describe Gómez as a ruler.

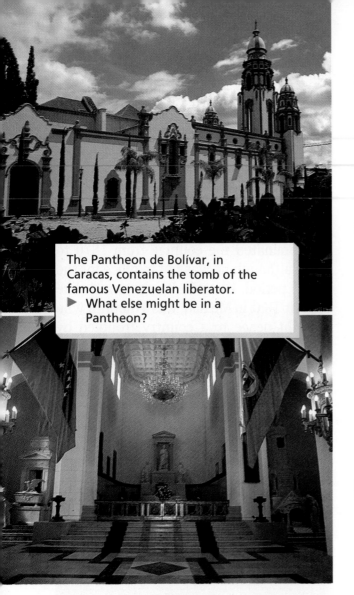

The Pantheon de Bolívar, in Caracas, contains the tomb of the famous Venezuelan liberator.
▶ What else might be in a Pantheon?

C. Rómulo Betancourt and Democracy

The Last Dictator Venezuelan military planes dropped bombs on Caracas. Rioting broke out, and then a general strike took place. Finally, the latest in a long line of dictators, Marcos Pérez Jiménez, fled the country. It was 1958, and Venezuela had had its fill of dictators. An honest, peaceful election brought Rómulo Betancourt to the presidency and brought democracy to Venezuela.

Land Reform Betancourt, who came from a lower-middle-class family, started an important program of land reform. His government established the National Agrarian Institute to break up the large estates and distribute their holdings to landless farmers. The dividing of large land holdings into smaller parcels so that more people can own land is called **redistribution**. Betancourt finished out his full five-year term and then turned the government over to his freely elected successor. Venezuela has had a democratic government ever since.

D. Liberals and Conservatives in Colombia

Civil War The War of the Thousand Days raged in Colombia from 1899 to 1902. Over 100,000 people died. Did some foreign enemy cause this tragedy? The answer is no. The War of the Thousand Days was a civil war, one of the numerous conflicts between Colombia's Liberal and Conservative parties.

Political Disagreements The two parties disagreed about the kind of government that Colombia should have. Conservatives wanted the nation's president to have most of the power. They also

country until 1935. It was during the Gómez rule that Venezuela's valuable oil reserves began to be tapped. Gómez encouraged foreign companies to develop the oil fields, and then he used the oil profits to build a strong army. He also took some of the oil profits for his own use. In fact, Gómez took a percentage of almost all government operations and used it to make himself one of the richest men in all of South America. On one of his many large properties, he built a palace that was over 1,000 feet (305 m) long and that had more than 100 rooms!

wanted the Roman Catholic Church to play a very strong role in national affairs. Liberals thought the elected representatives in the legislature should have as important a voice in government as that of the president. They also believed in separating the church from the government. However, the Conservatives held power until 1930.

Period of Violence Colombia's political problems grew even worse in 1948. The assassination of a popular newspaper publisher set off riots in the capital. Those riots began ten years of undeclared war between the two parties. As many as 200,000 people died. The period became known as *La Violencia,* which is Spanish for "the violence."

In 1957, the two political parties agreed to quit fighting and to work together. They agreed to take turns with the presidency, alternating from one party to the other each term for four terms, or 16 years. They also agreed to share the important government jobs.

The first president elected under the agreement was a Liberal. After his term ended, a Conservative president was elected. Before the end of the fourth term, the two parties decided to keep the agreement for one more term, until 1978.

E. Guerillas And Drugs

Colombia solved one type of violence, but others remained. Over the past 20 years, several different guerrilla groups have fought against the government. The guerillas are not strong enough to take over the country, but they are strong enough to cause a great deal of damage.

They also call attention to their opposition to the government. For example, in

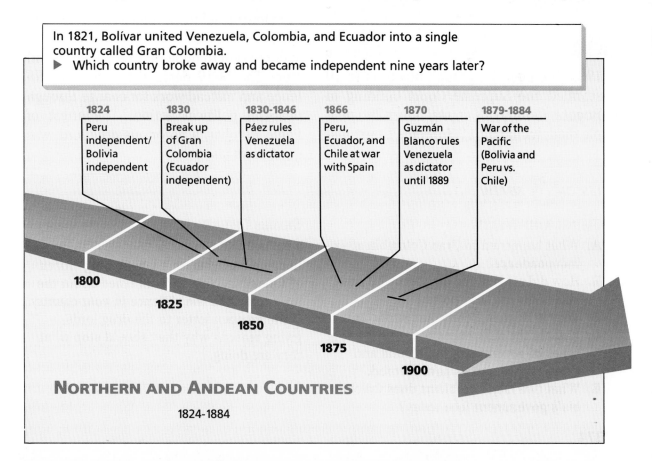

In 1821, Bolívar united Venezuela, Colombia, and Ecuador into a single country called Gran Colombia.
▶ Which country broke away and became independent nine years later?

1824	1830	1830-1846	1866	1870	1879-1884
Peru independent/ Bolivia independent	Break up of Gran Colombia (Ecuador independent)	Páez rules Venezuela as dictator	Peru, Ecuador, and Chile at war with Spain	Guzmán Blanco rules Venezuela as dictator until 1889	War of the Pacific (Bolivia and Peru vs. Chile)

1800
1825
1850
1875
1900

NORTHERN AND ANDEAN COUNTRIES

1824-1884

In Colombia, soldiers are shown burning drugs (top). Gálan (bottom) hoped to put an end to drug traffic.
▶ How did the drug lords spread terror in Colombia?

1985, the guerrilla group known as M-19 stormed the Supreme Court building in Bogotá, Colombia's capital. Over 200 people died, including 11 Supreme Court justices. Three years later, M-19 kidnapped Álvaro Gómez, a former presidential candidate of the Conservative Party, and held him for eight weeks.

Violence also results because Colombia has the world's largest drug rings. They make enormous profits from growing, processing, and selling illegal substances, such as cocaine and marijuana. Some experts think that the drug traffic brings in more money than any of Colombia's legal exports.

The leaders of the drug trade, called drug lords, have private armies that are as well equipped as the government's own troops. The drug lords have waged a campaign of terror against the government, murdering dozens of judges and other public officials. In 1989 Senator Luis Carlos Galán, the presidential candidate of the Liberal party, was assassinated. Two other presidential candidates were slain as the drug lords tried to stop the election. In the early 1990s, however, Colombians have some reason to hope that La Violencia will stop. The M-19 decided to abandon violence and instead work for change through peaceful political action. The arrest of Pablo Escobar, a notorious drug lord, was good news also.

LESSON 3 REVIEW

THINK AND WRITE

A. What happened to Gran Colombia after independence?
B. How did some of the dictators who ruled Venezuela use their power?
C. Why is Rómulo Betancourt important?
D. Explain the differences between the types of government the Liberal and Conservative parties have favored.
E. What two major problems does Colombia's government face today?

SKILLS CHECK

WRITING SKILL

Imagine that you are a law-abiding citizen of Colombia. You are concerned about the drug trade and the violence in your country. Write an open letter to the drug lords, giving reasons why they should stop what they are doing.

LESSON 4

Three Indian Lands

THINK ABOUT WHAT YOU KNOW
Suppose everyone in your class worked on a special project, but only a few of your classmates received credit for it. How would that make you feel?

STUDY THE VOCABULARY
regionalism
inflation

FOCUS YOUR READING
In what ways are the histories of Ecuador, Peru, and Bolivia similar?

A. A Troubled Heritage

Treatment of Indians Independence brought no benefits to most of the people who lived in the central Andes. The Indians, who formed the majority of the population in Ecuador, Peru, and Bolivia, lived on haciendas in the highlands. Landowners treated the Indians almost like slaves, making them live and work under very harsh conditions. Only a few Indians spoke Spanish. They were not allowed to vote or to have other rights of citizenship. Serious differences grew among the ruling groups over the ways the Indians were treated. The differences have become greater over the years and are still the cause of many political battles.

Regional Loyalties In some lessons, you have read about different types of regions. The differences have contributed toward a strong sense of **regionalism** among the people of the central Andes. *Regionalism*, in this case, means "the devotion to one's own particular region rather than to the nation as a whole." It may remind you of the patrias chicas, which you read about earlier.

Regional loyalties caused problems for many of the newly independent nations of the Americas. In Ecuador, Peru, and Bolivia, however, the isolation of mountain settlements and the great differences between the highlands and the lowlands made regionalism even stronger. Partly because of this regionalism, each of the nations of the central Andes has found it difficult to achieve political unity.

B. Landlocked Bolivia

Loss of Land Newly independent in 1825, Bolivia claimed around 850,000 square miles (2,202,000 sq km) of land, including a seacoast and large parts of the Amazon Basin and the Gran Chaco. Today, Bolivia has only about half that land area

In Bolivia, regionalism is strong in the Inca settlements.
▶ In your own words, what is regionalism?

—424,162 square miles (1,098,580 sq km)—and no access to the sea. Bolivia lost much of its land as a result of wars with its neighbors.

War of the Pacific In 1879, Bolivia and Peru began a war with Chile, called the War of the Pacific. The war, which ended in 1884, was fought for control of valuable deposits of nitrates, minerals found in large quantities in the desert along the coast. Nitrates are used to make fertilizers and explosives. Chile won the War of the Pacific, taking Bolivia's coastlands and part of Peru's southern coast. Ever since, Bolivian diplomats have urged their neighboring nations to allow them some access to the sea. Recently, Peru allowed Bolivia access to the Pacific Ocean.

In 1932, Bolivia and Paraguay fought over land in the Gran Chaco. The Chaco War lasted until 1935. Bolivia lost nearly 100,000 square miles (259,000 sq km) of land to Paraguay.

C. Víctor Paz Estenssoro in Bolivia

The average time in office for a Bolivian president used to be less than one year. That wasn't the officially established term of office. It was the result of Bolivia's record as Latin America's most unstable nation.

Until the 1950s, hacienda owners and the military controlled Bolivia. The economy stayed largely in the hands of a few wealthy families. Only three families owned all of Bolivia's tin mines. Tin was, and still is, Bolivia's leading export. Haciendas and mines depended on the labor of Indians, who worked under terrible conditions for low wages.

In 1952, a revolution changed Bolivia. Víctor Paz Estenssoro, a middle-class Bolivian, led this revolution. He had the backing of the mine workers and of people who owned small farms. When the revolution began, the Indians rose up. Without help from the leaders of the revolution, they took over many of the haciendas.

Later, the government nationalized the tin mines and allowed the workers to

President Paz Estenssoro (center) is shown as he once again was voted leader in Bolivia.
▶ What, would you guess, did he probably promise the voters?

help manage them. New election laws gave Indians the right to vote, and education was improved. Paz Estenssoro was president of Bolivia until 1956. He was a strong and able leader.

The revolutionary government stayed in power until 1964. Then the military overthrew the government. That brought Bolivia back to where it had been before Paz Estenssoro. Again, its governments rose and fell, and the economy grew weaker. Just as in Colombia, drug rings became a serious problem.

Inflation was running as high as 15,000 per cent in 1985. *Inflation* means "an economic condition in which the value of money goes down and prices go up." Paz Estenssoro became president once again. He tried to halt Bolivia's slide into debt and drugs by putting into effect economic reforms. The inflation rate was lowered to about 276 per cent. A new president, Jaime Paz Zamora, was elected in 1989. Inflation went down and the political situation appeared stable.

D. A Struggle for Change in Peru

A New Political Party In the 1920s a young Peruvian, Víctor Raúl Haya de la Torre, began a new political party called APRA. The letters stand for the Spanish name of the party, which in English is American Popular Revolutionary Alliance. APRA wanted great changes in Peru. Foreign companies owned much of Peru's natural resources. APRA wanted to nationalize the foreign-owned mining and agricultural companies. The party also wanted equal rights for all citizens of Peru, including Indians.

Haya de la Torre ran for president in 1931, but he lost. APRA, claiming that the vote was not counted honestly, began a

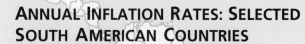

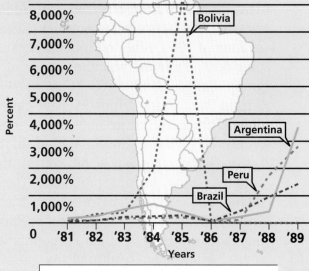

ANNUAL INFLATION RATES: SELECTED SOUTH AMERICAN COUNTRIES

The graph shows the percent of inflation over a nine-year period.
► Between which years did inflation rise in Bolivia?

revolt in the city of Trujillo (troo HEE-yoh). The army struck back, and many supporters of APRA were killed or put in prison. APRA was declared illegal. Even so, Haya de la Torre became very popular, and the party gained support through the 1930s and in the early 1940s. In the late 1940s, APRA was allowed to take part openly in national politics.

An Effort at Reforms In 1968, a group of military officers overthrew the elected president, Fernando Belaúnde Terry, and took control of the government. Unlike most Latin American military governments, this one wanted reforms. The new leaders nationalized foreign-owned farms and mines, began to break up the haciendas in the highlands, and tried to improve the economy. They faced many economic problems and lost popularity, despite their reforms. In 1980, they returned the government to the hands of civilians.

In 1985, Alán García became president. Finally, after 50 years, an APRA member had been elected president. Then in June of 1990, Alberto Fujimori became president. Fujimori was the leader of a group called Cambio 90 (Change 90). Within two years, Fujimori had closed down Peru's legislature and had become almost a dictator. But he promised to restore democracy once he solved the country's most serious problems. These included a violent guerrilla movement known as the Sendero Luminoso, or Shining Path. In 1993, Fujimori's popularity soared when police captured the guerrillas' leader, Amibael Guzman Reynoso.

E. Ecuador's Stormy History

Coastal and Highland Rivalry Ecuador can almost match Bolivia when it comes to a shaky political background. Between 1925 and 1948, for example, Ecuador had 22 different leaders, none of whom finished a full term in office. Conflict between people who live along the coast and people who live in the mountain region is one cause of Ecuador's problems. In colonial times, about 80 percent of Ecuador's people lived in the highlands. The leaders of Ecuador were mainly hacienda owners and other people of Spanish background. Quito was the main city in the country.

At that time, the coast had large cattle ranches and plantations of cacao and sugarcane, but it had few people. African slaves were brought in to work on the plantations.

The Growth of Guayaquil Beginning in the late 1800's, the coast began to grow rapidly, and it became Ecuador's most important agricultural region. By 1972, over 50 percent of the country's people lived there. Guayaquil, located on the coast, had become a larger and more important city than Quito. Quito, however, still held most of the political power.

Alberto Fujimori (right) was elected president of Peru in 1990. He won by a wide margin. This photograph, taken one year later on Independence Day, shows President Fujimori as he prepares to address the nation.
▶ What details in the photograph tell you that Independence Day is an important occasion in Peru?

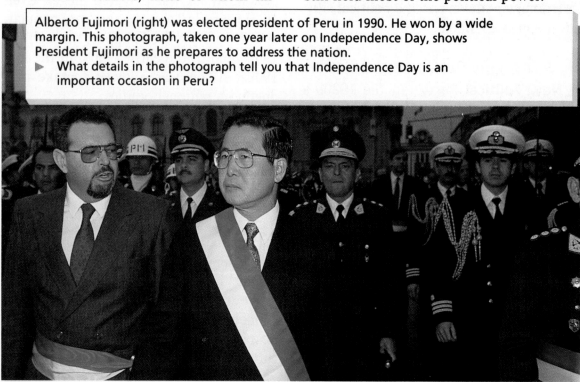

The city of Guayaquil is on the banks of the Guayas River close to the Gulf of Guayaquil.

 Why is this a good port location?

The competition between the two regions—coast and mountains—and the two cities—Guayaquil and Quito—has been very important. The people of the highlands want to keep wealth and power in the hands of the hacienda owners and other rich people. The people of the coast are more interested in the growth of industry and agriculture. They favor reforms to help the farmers and workers.

The Democatric Left Party In 1988, Rodrigo Borja Cevallos became president of Ecuador. Born into a middle-class family in Quito, he had studied to be a lawyer. At the age of 27, Borja Cevallos became a congressman. With some other younger politicians, he organized a new political party in 1970 called the Democratic Left party. This party promised reforms in Ecuador, using democratic means.

In 1992 a peaceful election brought a new president to power—Sixto Durán Bellén. President Durán had been born in Boston, Massachusetts, and had attended college at Columbia University in New York City. A former mayor of Quito, he pledged to carry out free-market reforms.

LESSON 4 REVIEW

THINK AND WRITE

A. What problems have the three central Andean countries had to deal with?
B. How did Bolivia lose much of its land?
C. Who was Víctor Paz Estenssoro?
D. What is APRA?
E. How has competition between coast and mountain people affected Ecuador?

SKILLS CHECK

THINKING SKILL

Think about the competition between the cities of Guayaquil and Quito and the two regions in which they are located. Do you agree more with the ideas of the people of the coast or with the people of the highlands? Perhaps you can appreciate both viewpoints. Get together with some classmates and share your ideas.

USING THE VOCABULARY

mesas	redistributed
savannas	landlocked
ocean current	regionalism
selva	alpaca
inflation	cordilleras

On a separate sheet of paper, number 1 to 10. Write the words from the list that correctly complete the sentences below.

The Andes mountains run through the northern countries on the Pacific coast of South America. The mountain ranges and (1)_____ are very high and cover much land. Between the Andes and the sea, the Peruvian Desert is often covered with fog. This is due to the cooling of moist air by an (2) _____. In the Andes there is a large, very high basin called the Altiplano. In the nearby mountains people herd a camel-like animal called the (3) _____, whose fine wool is made into clothing. East of the Andes in South America is the Amazon Basin. Much of this land is tropical forest or (4) _____. In northern South America are highlands with forests and rivers, as well as (5) _____, or tropical grasslands. There are also flat-topped mountains called (6) _____. All the northern and Andean nations have coastlines, except Bolivia which is (7) _____.

These northern countries have had very unstable governments. In some, (8) _____, or competition between regions, has led to war. There is also much poverty. Some governments have (9) _____ land to poor farmers, but others have opposed this policy. One of the worst problems is high (10) _____, or the rise in prices.

REMEMBERING WHAT YOU READ

On a separate sheet of paper, answer the questions below in complete sentences.

1. Which nations are on the northern coast of South America?
2. In which nations are the Andes mountains found?
3. Which countries make up the Guianas and have a West Indian culture?
4. What happened when a volcano erupted in Colombia in 1985?
5. Describe briefly the Altiplano.
6. What positive things did the dictators of Venezuela—Guzmán Blanco and Gómez—do for their country?
7. How did land reform work under President Betancourt of Venezuela?
8. Why did Indians, mine workers, and farmers of Bolivia revolt in 1952?
9. What problems face Peru today?
10. What do the people of the highlands and the coast of Ecuador disagree about?

TYING MATH TO SOCIAL STUDIES

In Bolivia in 1985, inflation rose to 15,000 per cent. The rate eventually was lowered to 276 per cent. To understand this, let's see what it would cost to buy some foods at these inflation rates. Make a chart on a separate piece of paper. On the left, write *bread $.79 (1 lb.), milk $1.15 (half-gallon), hamburger $2.49 (1 lb.).* Across the top, write *100%, 275%, 1,000%,* and *15,000%.* Use a calculator to find out the new price for each item at each rate of inflation. Fill the chart in with your answers. Discuss with your classmates the effects of such prices on a household budget.

THINKING CRITICALLY

On a separate sheet of paper, answer the following questions.

1. Dictatorships can bring peace and progress but also a lack of freedom. Would you agree to this condition to end a time of hardship? Explain.
2. In Colombia, Liberals and Conservatives took turns running the country every four years for about twenty years. What problems could this cause?
3. Why do drug rings get powerful in some South American countries, such as Bolivia and Colombia, and not in others?
4. Do you think a national government has the right to seize property that belongs to foreign owners and investors? Explain.
5. How can a small group of people control millions of people in a country? Explain.

SUMMARIZING THE CHAPTER

On a separate sheet of paper, draw a graphic organizer like the one shown here. Copy the information from this graphic organizer on the one you have drawn. Under each lesson heading, write four facts about similarities shared by the nations named.

CHAPTER THEME
The northern countries of South America form two groups according to land forms and climate. They share similar histories and other likenesses.

LAND AND CLIMATE

LESSON 1
Colombia, Venezuela, and the Guianas

1. _____
2. _____
3. _____
4 _____

LESSON 2
Ecuador, Peru, and Bolivia

1. _____
2. _____
3. _____
4. _____

GOVERNMENT

LESSON 3
Venezuela and Colombia

1. _____
2. _____
3. _____
4. _____

LESSON 4
Ecuador, Peru, and Bolivia

1. _____
2. _____
3. _____
4. _____

Rich resources from land and sea help shape the economies of the northern and Andean countries. Fish, minerals, coffee, and bananas are examples of the bountiful resources found in this region.

Wealth from Agriculture

THINK ABOUT WHAT YOU KNOW

You have probably heard Colombia mentioned in commercials and seen Colombian products in advertisements. Can you name at least one important Colombian export that is sold in grocery stores in the United States?

STUDY THE VOCABULARY

mechanize	**chuño**
cacao	**cooperative**
foot plow	

FOCUS YOUR READING

What is life like for farmers in the northern and Andean countries of South America?

A. World-Famous Coffee

On the slopes of the Andes in Colombia at the elevation of the tierra templada, the days are warm and the nights are cool. That's a nearly perfect climate for growing coffee trees. Colombian coffee enjoys a worldwide reputation for quality. Coffee accounts for about 60 percent of the value of Colombia's exports.

Colombians grow coffee mainly on small farms. Most are less than 25 acres (10 ha) in size. A very few are larger than 125 acres (51 ha). Single families own or work most of these coffee farms. Everyone in a family helps with the picking when the fruit that holds the coffee beans is ripe. The coffee trees, which are grown in shade to keep them from getting too warm, must be tended carefully.

Coffee beans really are the seeds of a small red fruit that grows in clusters on the coffee trees. The coffee fruit does not ripen all at the same time. To harvest the fruit at its best, workers must visit each of hundreds of trees every few days over several weeks. This work must be done by hand, and it takes a lot of work and time.

Since the coffee is grown in mountainous areas where roads are hard to build, much of the crop even now goes to market on the backs of mules. It would be very difficult to **mechanize** a coffee crop. *Mechanize* means "to replace human and animal workers with machines."

Coffee prices can vary a great deal. If the coffee crops in the main producing countries are large, there may be more coffee offered for sale than buyers want. If that happens, the sellers of coffee have to lower their prices to attract buyers. The price can go so low that farm families can scarcely support themselves. On the other hand, bad weather, such as frosts, may damage crops. If supplies of coffee are low, coffee prices rise. The changes in coffee prices can make planning very difficult.

On a mountaintop farm, workers tie sacks of freshly picked coffee beans.
▶ How will the farmers get the coffee beans to market?

Coffee: From Farm to Factory

1. Young coffee trees growing on a hillside.

3. Frequent raking allows the berries to dry evenly.

2. Picking the berries.

4. Removing coffee beans from the berries.

5. Ground beans being roasted in a processing plant in the United States.

6. Tasting the different batches and blends.

7. Filling the coffee cans.

The photographs and captions tell the general story of coffee from the farm to the factory.
▶ Why are tasters needed?

B. Commercial Agriculture

Mountain Regions In Peru, Ecuador, and Bolivia, farms at the middle elevations of the mountain region produce coffee, bananas, oranges and other citrus fruits, and vegetables. Most of these products are carried into the highlands and to coastal cities for sale.

Valleys and Coastal Areas In Bolivia, two large valleys—Cochabamba (koh chuh BAHM buh) and Tarija (tah REE hah)—are also important farming areas. Located between 6,560 feet and 9,840 feet (2,000 and 3,000 m) above sea level, these valleys are near the mountain region but farther south, where they receive less rain than the mountain region. Their farms produce grains, such as corn, fruits, and vegetables.

The river valleys of Peru's coast have large, irrigated commercial plantations. Much of the processing of sugarcane and other crops takes place right on the plantations. The plantations depend on the Indians, who come from the highlands to work at planting and harvesting times.

Try to guess which country is the largest banana exporter in Latin America. You may be surprised to learn that it's Ecuador! Along Ecuador's coast, bananas are grown on medium-sized farms of about 125 acres (51 ha) instead of on large plantations as in Central America. Packing plants prepare the bananas for shipment overseas. Surplus bananas are used as cattle feed.

In addition to bananas, Ecuador's coastal lands produce sugar, coffee, cooking oil from African oil palms, and **cacao**. Cacao is the seed from which chocolate is made. Ecuador has become one of the world's major cacao producers.

C. Difficult Times for Subsistence Farmers

Leathery-skinned farmers plow their land. A **foot plow** is used by each farmer. The foot plow is made of a stick with a curved end that serves as a handle. A stone or a metal blade is attached to the straight end of the stick. The plow also has a small footrest. The farmer stamps on the footrest, driving the blade into the ground. Then the farmer pulls the curved handle downward, turning the soil over with the blade.

The Incas also used this tool. The foot plow is still the main farming tool for many Bolivian Indians. Using this and other techniques that have been handed down over the centuries, the Indians have gained a modest living from a difficult land. Over

Following the traditional method of their ancestors, Bolivian Indians use foot plows to turn over the land for planting.
▶ Why are no tractors used?

70 percent of Bolivia's people live in the countryside and in small towns and villages. In Ecuador, 64 percent live in rural areas, and in Peru, 57 percent live in rural areas. Most people who live in these regions are highland Indians, and they make a living by farming.

Some Indians who live in villages own the land together and farm it together, much as they did in Inca times. Other village Indians own their own small plots of land, which they farm as families. Village Indians may be very poor, but at least they do own their own land. Many other Indians live on haciendas, where they work for the landowners.

Some of the main crops in the altiplano, or high plateau, are grains such as barley, wheat, and oats, which will grow in cold climates. Quinoa (kih NOH uh), a grain native to the Andes, is an important subsistence crop. Potatoes, which are used to

High in the Andes, a family works hard to terrace the land on their small subsistence farm.
▶ Why, do you think, might it be necessary to terrace the land?

make a food called **chuño** (CHOO nyoh), are also grown. Chuño is made by allowing potatoes to freeze in the cold night air and then setting them out to dry in the sun for several days. Chuño keeps for a long time, and this food can be cooked in stews and porridges.

In Venezuela, too, most farmers live on small subsistence farms. These farms are called *conucos* (koh NOO kohz). In the days when there were few farmers, it was possible to leave land unused for many years between plantings. The forest would grow back, protecting and renewing the soil. Now there are so many farmers and so little land that it is no longer possible to let the forest grow back. The soil has no time to become fertile again, so crops are poor.

Growing Up in the Bolivian Highlands

Along the shore of Lake Titicaca, around 124 miles (200 km) from the Bolivian capital of La Paz, lies the Aymará Indian village of Compí. Located in a valley, Compí has a population of around 1,250. The people earn their livelihood by herding and farming. Often they leave the village to work for wages on neighboring estates. This story

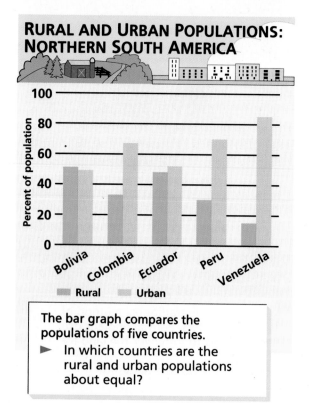

RURAL AND URBAN POPULATIONS: NORTHERN SOUTH AMERICA

Percent of population

Bolivia Colombia Ecuador Peru Venezuela

▬ Rural   ▬ Urban

The bar graph compares the populations of five countries.
▶ In which countries are the rural and urban populations about equal?

will tell you something about the life of Joaquín, a boy of 11.

The sun lit the early morning sky as Joaquín began his journey away from the village and up into the hills. As always in the highlands, the morning was cool and crisp. Joaquín's six-year-old brother, Manuel, walked beside him. They would spend the day herding donkeys and cows. Joaquín would do most of the real work. He knew what to do. After all, he had been herding animals from the time he was four years old.

Now it was his turn to teach this skill to Manuel, just as his older brother and uncle had taught him. Joaquín smiled as he recalled his first herding experience. Like the other children, he began working with the pigs. A few years later, he was trusted to watch the sheep. How proud he had been to herd the larger animals.

He had learned a lot from the older men in his family. In addition to the herding, his father had taught him how to sew hand and with the machine. He also learned how to knit. Girls didn't do sewing. They did weaving and spinning. They also learned how to sell things at the market. Around 3 miles (5 km) away is the town of Jank'o Amaya. The big market attracted people from all over. The women sold handicrafts and food there.

Like most of the boys in Compí, Joaquín liked to fish and swim. Usually he fished off the shore of the lake, using a net. Making nets was something else he had learned to do. Sometimes, though, he got to go out on the big lake with his father and uncles. That really was exciting!

Still, Joaquín liked herding the most. It gave him a chance to think. This year he would be finishing grammar school. His father had never gone to school. That was

Indians travel on Lake Titicaca in boats made of reeds. Their homes are on floating islands on the lake.
▶ Why might reeds be used?

because Compí didn't have a public school when his father was a boy. Joaquín liked studying arithmetic and civics. A lot of his friends didn't attend school regularly because they were needed at home to work.

D. Land Reform

Redistribution Farmers cannot farm without land, but throughout much of Latin America, the wealthy own most of the good land. People who want to help poor farmers have better lives argue for land reform. Land reform changes the pattern of landownership. As you learned in the previous chapter, one way of bringing about land reform is redistribution. This method of land reform was used in Mexico and also in Bolivia after the revolution of 1952.

In Bolivia, land reform led to some small but important changes in farming. Many more Indians in Bolivia now grow crops for market, and they are somewhat wealthier than Indians were before the revolution. Indians now take part in local government in some towns, and they are taking a more active interest in education and farm improvement.

All the villagers work together on this cooperative farm in Peru.
► Why, do you think, might this be better than subsistence farming?

Sharing of Profits Peru provides a different example of redistribution. In 1969, the Peruvian government expropriated the coastal plantations. Instead of dividing land among the farmers, the government created **cooperatives**. A cooperative is a plantation or other business that is owned by its workers. On cooperatives, large commercial crops can still be grown, but the workers share the profits. The workers choose the people who act as leaders.

Forming New Colonies Another type of land reform is sometimes called colonization. You remember that colonization means settlement—often by people from one country in another land. Colonization can also mean giving farmers land that as yet does not have settlements of people. The farmers, or colonists, must clear the land and build farms. In Venezuela, the government has created such new farming areas and started irrigation projects.

Whatever the method of land reform, the purpose is almost always the same. Reformers hope that, as conditions improve, the masses of people will have a better life and the nation will become more stable and democratic.

LESSON *1* REVIEW

THINK AND WRITE

A. Why does it require a lot of work to grow coffee?

B. What are some of the commercial crops that are grown on commercial farms in the Andean countries?

C. What farming technique do many subsistence farmers use?

D. What is the purpose of land reform?

SKILLS CHECK

WRITING SKILL

Use the text material and other information you can find to write an explanatory paragraph about the steps taken in processing coffee beans into coffee.

Earning a Living from Land and Sea

THINK ABOUT WHAT YOU KNOW

If it were possible for you to design a model country, what natural resources would you want that country to have?

STUDY THE VOCABULARY

bauxite
industrial
  complex

guano
petrochemical

FOCUS YOUR READING

What are the major natural resources of the Andean countries?

A. Plentiful Minerals

Colombia produces 90 percent of the world's emeralds. Have you ever seen a genuine emerald? Emeralds come from mines on the slopes of the Eastern Cordillera. Workers mine the emeralds with picks and shovels, in much the same way that Indians mined the gems centuries ago. Colombia's soil also yields precious metals, such as gold, silver, and platinum.

Many minerals that are used by industries are found in Colombia. Colombia is one of the few Latin American countries with large deposits of high-quality coal. Much of that coal is in the mountains, and that makes it hard to ship the coal out. For many years, Colombia exported oil. Now, because industries have grown up in its own country, Colombia uses nearly all of its oil at home. In addition to coal and oil, Colombia has iron and nickel.

Imagine a mountain of silver. That's pretty much what the early Spaniards found high in the Andes of Bolivia. Called the Cerro Rico ("rich hill"), this mountain near Potosí produced about $3 billion worth of silver for Spain after the conquerors discovered the mountain. Potosí, over 13,350 feet (4,069 m) high in the Andes, was the largest city in the Americas for part of the 1600s. Over 156,000 people lived there. Even today, Potosí's population is about 125,000, making it the largest city of its elevation in the world.

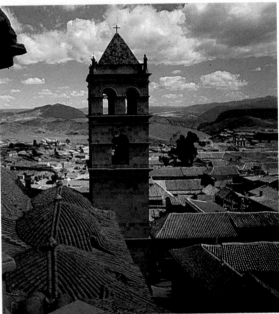

A church tower stands out in this roof top view of Potosí (top). Inside is the Casa Real de la Moneda museum.
► How would you describe Potosí?

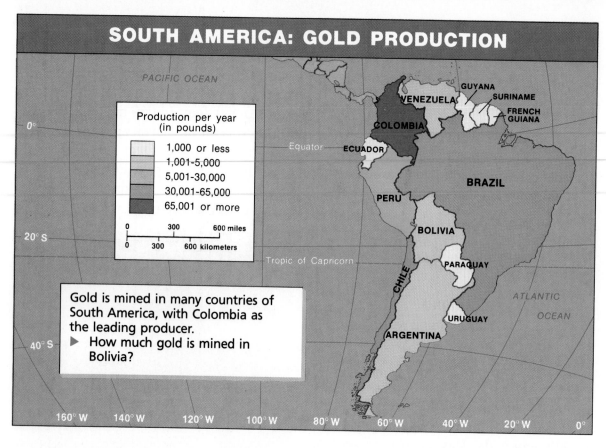

SOUTH AMERICA: GOLD PRODUCTION

Production per year
(in pounds)

1,000 or less
1,001-5,000
5,001-30,000
30,001-65,000
65,001 or more

0   300   600 miles
0   300   600 kilometers

Gold is mined in many countries of South America, with Colombia as the leading producer.
▶ How much gold is mined in Bolivia?

Modern Potosí's wealth comes from tin. Bolivia produces about 13 percent of the world's tin. As you read earlier, tin is a major export of Bolivia. The tin mines are in the eastern highlands. The main mining centers are near the cities of Potosí, Oruro (aw ROOR oh), and Sucre (SOO kray). Small amounts of silver, copper, and zinc still come from Bolivia's mines. The ores of tin and these other metals are found together and can be mined together.

Mining is a difficult and often dangerous job. The workers who have mined Bolivia's tin have not had easy lives. The 1952 revolution brought improved working conditions. In recent years, however, the miners again have suffered from low wages and a lack of job security. You may recall that when Paz Estenssoro again became Bolivia's president in 1985, he tried to stop inflation. One of the things he did was to eliminate state control of mining.

Tin mining was not adding to the economy. As a result of this policy, around 20,000 miners lost their jobs.

By 1986, the cost of tin production in Bolivia had risen to the equivalent of $12 a pound, but its worth was only $2 on the world market. The next year, many miners and their wives started a hunger strike to protest the Bolivian government's policy. One woman, Marina Luna, a mother of four children, expressed the anger and frustration of the miners with these words: "We would rather die of hunger here in this protest than of hunger in our houses. We can't make ends meet. Our children are undernourished because we can't feed them."

In June 1993, Gonzalo Sánchez de Lozado was elected president. Although tin remains expensive to produce, it is still Bolivia's leading export. The problems of tin production and the unemployment of miners continues. The new government will have to find new sources of income to improve the economy.

Peru's mines produce many important minerals, including copper, lead, silver, mercury, iron, and zinc. Most of the important mines are in the highlands. Many mines are underground and go deep into mountains. Foreign companies owned Peru's mines until the revolution of 1968. Now the mines are run by corporations owned by the Peruvian government. Peru's coast has one of the world's largest deposits of phosphates. Phosphates are used for fertilizer.

Both British Guiana and Suriname have huge deposits of **bauxite**. Bauxite is the raw material from which aluminum is obtained. Venezuela's Guiana Highlands also have large reserves of iron ore and bauxite. Small amounts of gold and diamonds are also taken from the Guiana Highlands.

B. Oil-Producing Countries

The name *Venezuela* makes many people think of oil. Until 1981, when Mexico took over the lead, Venezuela was the largest oil producer in Latin America. Venezuela is still the leading producer of oil in South America. It exports most of its oil to the United States.

Venezuela has three areas that produce oil. The oldest and most important oil deposits are near Lake Maracaibo. Many wells have been drilled in this shallow lake. The other oil fields are in the delta of the Orinoco River and in the Llanos north and west of Ciudad Guayana, today Venezuela's fifth largest city.

Oil has brought many changes to Venezuela over the years. At first, the oil wealth went to only a few people — the dictators and their friends. After the overthrow of the dictator Marcos Pérez Jiménez in 1958, the government began to use oil money for programs to help a larger

Smoke pours from the smokestacks of a bauxite factory in Suriname (left). The world's largest iron ore open pit mine is in Venezuela (right).
▶ How is air affected by the smoke?

Venezuela uses some profits made from oil to build cultural centers, such as this one in Caracas.
▶ What kind of entertainment might one see here?

part of the population. Houses, schools, and hospitals were built to help poor people. Oil profits were also used to build large **industrial complexes**. An industrial complex is a group of factories, refineries, or other plants.

Oil fields have also brought wealth to other Andean nations. Bolivia's second most important mineral resource is oil. The oil fields are in the eastern lowlands, south of the city of Santa Cruz. Bolivia refines oil, keeping some for itself and exporting the rest, along with natural gas, to nearby Argentina.

South America's oldest oil fields are on Peru's Pacific coast, near Ecuador. Now the center of Peru's oil industry has moved to the forests of the Amazon Basin. No one knows the size of the selva's oil reserves because much of the area is unexplored. Nevertheless, Peruvians have built a large

pipeline across the Andes to carry oil from the selva to the refineries and ports on the coast.

Oil is Ecuador's only important mineral resource. The first oil fields there were on the Pacific coast, southwest of Guayaquil (gwye ah KEEL). Those oil fields produced enough oil for part of Ecuador's needs, but there was no extra oil for export. In 1969, oil was discovered in the Oriente, the rain forest east of the Andes.

Today, Ecuador is second to Venezuela in the export of oil from South America. In 1987, Ecuador's oil industry suffered a blow when two earthquakes rocked the northeastern part of the nation, causing mudslides and flooding. In addition to leaving thousands of people homeless, these great natural disasters damaged Ecuador's main oil pipeline. This pipeline carried oil from the fields to the refineries at the port of Esmeraldas on the Pacific coast. The pipeline was repaired, and oil remains the leading mineral export.

C. Resources from the Sea

Even before the first rays of the morning sun begin to lighten the sky along the Pacific coast, thousands of fishing boats set out to sea. The Peru Current, flowing in the Pacific, is rich both in oxygen, which fish need to breathe, and in the small sea plants and animals that fish eat. Therefore, many fish are found in the Peru Current. In turn, millions of birds feed on the fish. This food chain — from small sea plants and animals to fish to birds — is valuable to the country of Peru in many ways.

Beginning in the 1950s, Peru began to develop a fishing industry. The main fish caught off Peru is the *anchoveta*, a small, sardinelike fish. The anchoveta is not used directly as food. Instead, this fish is dried and made into fish meal, which is exported for use as fertilizer or cattle feed. Fish meal is Peru's leading industry today. Larger fish, such as tuna, are used for food, but they are less valuable.

Ecuador also gains important revenue from fishing. Much of the fish is processed into canned fish to be sold in grocery stores in other Latin American countries and in the United States.

Another important resource comes from land that is in the sea. Islands off Peru's coast have been nesting areas for birds for thousands of years. Over the years the bird droppings, called **guano**, have built up in large amounts. The guano is as deep as 150 feet (46 m) in places!

The waters off Ecuador are important fishing areas. Here workers unload sardines from a fishing boat.
▶ Why are birds flying overhead?

This person's job was created by Venezuela's huge petrochemical industry.
▶ What might her profession be?

Guano is a very good fertilizer, and Peru's deposits have been mined since before the Spaniards arrived. After the fall of the Incas, few people were interested in guano. In the 1840s, its value was rediscovered. Peruvian guano provided fertilizer for England and other European countries. Guano stayed a major Peruvian export until the 1870s. Then nitrates from southern Peru and Chile began to take its place. Guano is still an important fertilizer used in Peru.

D. Industrial Development

How do industries get started in countries that mainly produce natural resources? By looking at some examples of industry in the Andean countries, perhaps you will see a pattern.

Venezuela, for example, has a sophisticated **petrochemical** industry. A petrochemical is any product manufactured from petroleum. Gasoline, for example, is a petrochemical. Venezuela refines oil and uses oil as well as its petrochemical byproducts to manufacture other things. Much Venezuelan oil is also refined on the nearby Netherlands Antilles island of Aruba. Venezuela also has developed large canning industries. Fruits and vegetables raised in the agricultural areas are processed into juices and other canned foods.

Colombia's main product, coffee, has sparked some additional industries. Coffee beans need to be roasted and packaged. Some of the beans are ground and transformed into instant coffee.

You know that in Peru and Ecuador fishing is big business. When you think about how commercial fishing works, you realize that the building of ships and the making of nets might also be big business. Also, as you have learned, some of the catch gets processed and canned.

What pattern is there in all these industrial activities? Natural resources serve as a base for developing industries. That creates more jobs for more people.

LESSON 2 *REVIEW*

THINK AND WRITE

A. What are some important minerals found in the Andean countries?

B. How has oil been important to some of the South American countries?

C. How are resources from the sea along the Pacific coast used?

D. Choose one natural resource mentioned. How is it used to develop industries?

SKILLS CHECK

THINKING SKILL

In this lesson, you read about industries that were developed because of the natural resources available. Select one natural resource mentioned. Think about industries and jobs that relate to that resource. Discuss your observations with some classmates.

Peoples and Cities of the Andes

THINK ABOUT WHAT YOU KNOW

THINK ABOUT WHAT YOU KNOW

Part of this lesson tells about cities. Think about whether you would prefer to live in a city in a highland region or in a city in a lowland region. List some reasons.

STUDY THE VOCABULARY

bilingual   public housing
barrio

FOCUS YOUR READING

What are the major population groups and cities of the northern and Andean nations of South America?

A. Varied Cultures

Suppose you were traveling through the northern and Andean countries, trying to take pictures of all the different groups of people living there. You'd use quite a lot of film because these countries are home to many different groups of people. For example, in the populations of both Colombia and Venezuela you can see mestizos, whites, blacks, Europeans, Asians, East Indians, and Indians.

Mestizos make up about 68 percent of Colombia's population and about 67 percent of Venezuela's population. By contrast, Indians make up only about 7 percent of Colombia's population and 2 percent of Venezuela's. Most of the Indians live in the lowlands — in the tropical forests and savannas. Only in the southern highlands of Colombia, near the border with Ecuador, are there fairly large communities of highland Indians.

People of African descent — about 10 percent of the population — outnumber Indians in Venezuela. About 5 percent of Colombia's population is black. Blacks came to the coastal areas of both countries during colonial times. Some were escaped slaves from the Caribbean, but most were brought to South America as slaves.

Most of the people of African ancestry still live along the Caribbean coast, but some are on the Pacific coast of Colombia.

ALTITUDES OF SELECTED CITIES: NORTH AND SOUTH AMERICA

12,000 feet	La Paz	3,600 meters
10,000 feet	Quito / Bogotá	3,000 meters
8,000 feet	Mexico City / Santa Fe, New Mexico	2,400 meters
6,000 feet	Denver, Colorado	1,800 meters
4,000 feet	Boise, Idaho	1,200 meters
2,000 feet		600 meters
	Rio de Janeiro	
0 feet		0 meters

The cities of the Andes are the highest in the Western Hemisphere and among the highest in the world.
► How does the altitude of La Paz compare with that of Denver?

Blacks were brought to that area to work as slaves in gold mines. When slavery ended, they became farmers.

Whites, many of them Europeans, make up around 20 percent of the population in both Venezuela and Colombia. Most of them live in highland cities such as Bogotá and Caracas. Many are immigrants who have come to Latin America in the past 40 or 50 years.

B. Highland Indians

More Indians live in the central Andes countries of Peru, Ecuador, and Bolivia than in any other part of South America. Nearly half the population of the three countries, or about 15 million people, is Indian.

As you may recall, the heart of the Inca civilization was high in the Andes. Most of the Indian peoples of Peru, Ecuador, and Bolivia still live in the highlands. They have adapted to the cool climate and thin air of the high altitudes. The capitals of Ecuador and Bolivia are still located high in the Andes.

Quechua, the language that was spread throughout the Andes by the Incas, is the language of the Indians of highland Ecuador, most of Peru, and a large part of Bolivia. In fact, Peru is a **bilingual** nation. It has two official languages. They are Spanish and Quechua. There are around 9.5 million Indians in Peru, accounting for 46 percent of the nation's population. As many as 2 million people in Peru speak only Quechua. The remainder of Peru's population includes mestizos, whites, blacks, Japanese, and Chinese.

Nearly half of Bolivia's highland Indians speak a different Indian language: Aymará (eye muh RAH). Perhaps 10 percent of Peru's Indians, mainly in the southern highlands near the Bolivian border, also speak Aymará. Together, the two Indian groups make up 53 percent of Bolivia's population. The rest of the population is mostly made up of mestizos and whites.

Ecuador shows a different population mix. It has the lowest percentage of Indians of the three central Andean nations —about 25 percent. Mestizos are the largest group—55 percent of the population. Blacks and whites, just about equally divided in number, make up the rest of Ecuador's population.

C. Patterns of Urbanization

Over three quarters of Venezuela's people live in cities and towns. The metropolitan area of Caracas, Venezuela's capital and largest city, has a population of over 3 million. About one out of every eight Venezuelans lives in Caracas. Caracas itself has over 1 million inhabitants and so does Maracaibo, the second largest city in Venezuela.

In this rural village in the Andes highlands, llamas are the main livestock animals.
▶ How are llamas used?

Cities less than 100,000

Bayovar (Peru)	C-1
Cayenne (French Guiana)	B-4
Cuzco (Peru)	D-2
Potosí (Bolivia)	D-3
Sucre (Bolivia)	D-3

Cities 100,000 to 499,999

Arequipa (Peru)	D-2
Armenia (Colombia)	B-2
Barquisimeto (Venezuela)	A-3
Barrancabermeja (Colombia)	B-2
Bello (Colombia)	B-2

Bucaramanga (Colombia)	B-2
Buenaventura (Colombia)	B-2
Buga (Colombia)	B-2
Cabimas (Venezuela)	A-2
Callao (Peru)	D-2
Cartagena (Colombia)	A-2
Chiclayo (Peru)	C-2
Chimbote (Peru)	C-2
Ciénaga (Colombia)	A-2
Ciudad Bolívar (Venezuela)	B-3
Ciudad Guayana (Venezuela)	B-3
Cochabamba (Bolivia)	D-3
Cúcuta (Colombia)	B-2
Cuenca (Ecuador)	C-2
Cumaná (Venezuela)	A-3
Georgetown (Guyana)	B-4
Huancayo (Peru)	D-2
Ibagué (Colombia)	B-2
Ica (Peru)	D-2
Iquitos (Peru)	C-2
Maiquetía (Venezuela)	A-3
Manizales (Colombia)	B-2
Maracay (Venezuela)	A-3
Maturín (Venezuela)	B-3

Neiva (Colombia)	B-2
Oruro (Bolivia)	D-3
Palmira (Colombia)	B-2
Paramaribo (Suriname)	B-4
Pasto (Colombia)	B-2
Pereira (Colombia)	B-2
Piura (Peru)	C-1
San Cristobal (Venezuela)	B-2
Santa Cruz (Bolivia)	D-3
Santa Marta (Colombia)	A-2
Sullana (Peru)	C-1
Trujillo (Peru)	C-2
Tuluá (Colombia)	B-2
Valencia (Venezuela)	A-3
Valledupar (Colombia)	A-2

Cities 500,000 to 999,999

Barranquilla (Colombia)	A-2
Cali (Colombia)	B-2
Guayaquil (Ecuador)	C-2
La Paz (Bolivia)	D-3
Quito (Ecuador)	C-2

Cities over 1,000,000

Bogotá (Colombia)	B-2
Caracas (Venezuela)	A-3
Lima (Peru)	D-2
Maracaibo (Venezuela)	A-2
Medellín (Colombia)	B-2

Most cities in the northern and Andean countries have less than 500,000 people.
▶ Which countries have cities with a population over one million?

Colombia's population is less urban than that of Venezuela. Still, around 65 percent of Colombians live in cities. Isolated regions, such as mountain basins, valleys, and plateaus, have become centers of population in Colombia. The capital, Bogotá, has over 4 million people. Other important cities include Cali and Medellín (may day YEEN). These cities are manufacturing, transportation, and business centers for the surrounding areas.

Of the three nations of the central Andes, Peru is the most urban. About 65 percent of Peruvians live in cities. Lima, the capital, has a metropolitan population of over 5 million. Lima has a number of suburbs that add to the metropolitan population. Bolivia and Ecuador are the least urban of the Andean nations, with around half of their people living in cities. In the remainder of this lesson, you'll learn about the capital cities and some of the other important urban centers.

D. Important Cities

Colombian Cities Bogotá sits on the edge of a large plateau, high in the Andes, at an elevation of 8,070 feet (2,460 m). Bogotá is the regional center for the Eastern Cordillera. That area is the most densely populated part of Colombia.

Bogotá is a city of contrasts. Modern skyscrapers tower over old colonial buildings made of white-painted adobe with red tile roofs. Fashionable shops sell the latest styles in clothing from Europe and United States, and store windows display sophisticated audio and video equipment. The government, however, maintains special artisan centers offering regional handicrafts for sale.

The city of Barranquilla (bah rahn-KEE yah) is at the mouth of the Magdalena River. The Magdalena River is navigable for over 600 miles (965 km) from its mouth. Until a railroad was built in the 1950s, most of the goods that went to Bogotá were shipped from Barranquilla, up the Magdalena to the first rapids, and then carried overland into the mountains to Bogotá. The Magdalena is still an important transportation route, and Barranquilla, with almost 1 million people, is Colombia's most important port.

Venezuelan Cities Caracas, in Venezuela, is the capital, largest city, and economic center of the country. It is sometimes compared to Los Angeles because it has many tall office and apartment buildings, freeways, and shopping centers. Caracas has the appearance of a wealthy, modern city. An impressive sight in Caracas is the magnificent area named Parque Central, with its two 56-story skyscrapers. This city-within-a-city has not only condominiums but shops, offices, supermarkets, a convention center, a museum, and even schools.

As you might expect, there are many statues of Simón Bolívar throughout the city of Caracas. His place of birth and also a summer home in which he lived with his

family are now open to visitors. The tomb of Bolívar is in a national building dedicated to the great Liberator.

Many Venezuelans are well-off, but Caracas has many poor people too. As in most Latin American cities, poor people from the country go to the city looking for better jobs and better lives. Those people live in large squatter settlements scattered around the edges of the city. Such settlements are called **barrios** (BAHR ee ohz). About 35 percent of the population of Caracas lives in barrios.

One thing that everyone in Caracas shares is a pleasant climate. The average temperature is 75° Fahrenheit (24°C), due in part to the elevation of 3,000 feet (914 m). Caracas is often called "The land of eternal spring."

Late at night, Lake Maracaibo looks almost as if prehistoric monsters are rising from its waters. They're really oil *derricks*. A derrick is a tall structure that supports drilling machinery, often over an oil well.

Maracaibo, the second largest city in Venezuela, is in the hot lowlands, on the western shores of the lake. The city has become important because of the large oil fields nearby. Maracaibo has a population of over 1 million.

Peruvian Cities The city of Cuzco, the old Inca capital, held little appeal for the Spaniards because it was high up in the mountains. It was too cold and too far away from the ocean. In 1535, Francisco Pizarro founded a new city in the lowlands about 10 miles (16 km) from the Pacific Ocean. Today that city, called Lima, is Peru's capital and largest city as well as its main center of business and industry.

Lima still has many buildings that date from the days when Peru was a Spanish colony. Some are found on the Plaza de Armas, the old center of Lima. The business district is found near the Plaza San Martín, now the center of the city. In this area are the tall buildings that are found in most modern cities today.

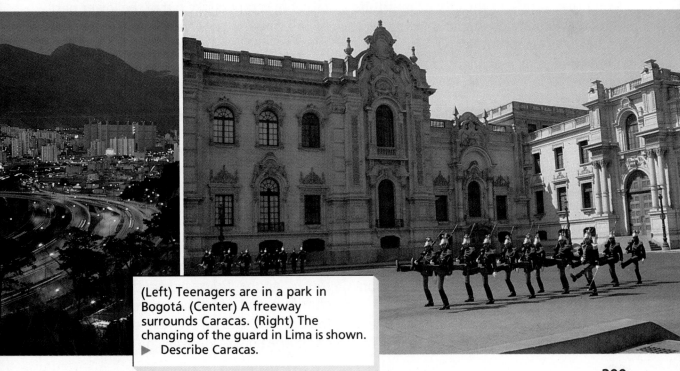

(Left) Teenagers are in a park in Bogotá. (Center) A freeway surrounds Caracas. (Right) The changing of the guard in Lima is shown.
▶ Describe Caracas.

399

La Paz (left) and Quito (center) are both highland cities. (Right) This photo shows a city street in Guayaquil.
▶ What is La Paz surrounded by?

A few of Lima's residents live in some of the old Spanish mansions that remain in the city. There are many apartment buildings and homes in the suburbs for the people of the large middle class. However, many people live in the squatter settlements that surround the city or in **public housing**. Public housing is housing built by the government for people who cannot afford to own or rent their own homes or apartments.

Cities What is the capital of Bolivia? That's a trick question, because Bolivia really has two capitals — La Paz and Sucre! La Paz is the more important of the two. It's the highest capital city in the world, with an elevation of 12,000 feet (3,658 m). Bolivia's official capital is Sucre, which is high in the Andes. Few government offices are in Sucre. Nearly all are in La Paz. The population of La Paz is around 1 million. Sucre's population is over 80,000.

La Paz is in a canyon 1,100 feet (335 m) below the Altiplano. It lies between two cordilleras. These parallel mountain ranges have the three highest mountain peaks in South America. The Spaniards chose that site because it is a little warmer than the Altiplano. However, such a narrow canyon is a poor place for a city. Skyscrapers rise out of the lower part of the canyon, now the city's commercial center. The houses of the poor cling to the canyon's steep sides, looking as if they might slide down at any time.

Ecuadorian Cities Quito, the capital of Ecuador, is another highland city. Even though this city of more than 1 million people is on the Equator, its elevation of 9,446 feet (2,879 m) gives it a cool climate. A modern city with broad avenues, beautiful parks, and luxurious homes in the new suburbs, Quito is best known for its old section, which has narrow streets, tile-roofed adobe houses, beautiful colonial churches, and an Indian marketplace. Find the city of Quito on the map of the Northern and Andean countries on page 397.

Indians have lived in Quito since before the time of the Incas. The Spanish enlarged the city, planned the streets, and built the beautiful churches and houses. The government of Ecuador passed a law that declared the colonial section to be a national monument. No colonial buildings can be destroyed, and no new buildings can be built. As you can imagine, Quito is one of the the best-preserved colonial cities in South America.

In many ways Guayaquil, not Quito, is Ecuador's most important city. Through the port of Guayaquil, on the Guayas River, pass 90 percent of Ecuador's imports and 50 percent of its exports. The city is also Ecuador's chief business and industrial center. At the waterfront there is a statue that portrays the famous meeting between Simón Bolívar and José de San Martín, which took place in Guayaquil in 1822. What changes, do you think, would surprise the two great liberators most if they could visit this region today?

LESSON **3** *REVIEW*

THINK AND WRITE

A. What different peoples make up the populations of Colombia and Venezuela?

B. Where do most of the Indian peoples of the Andean countries live?

C. How is Venezuela's urban pattern different from that of Colombia?

D. Describe two important cities in each country mentioned in this lesson.

SKILLS CHECK

MAP SKILL

Look up *La Paz* and *Sucre* in the Gazetteer. Then locate each city on the map on page 397. Use the information from the text material, the Gazetteer, and the map to write a comparison between the two cities.

USING THE VOCABULARY

bilingual
guano
petrochemical
cooperative
bauxite
cacao
barrio
chuño

On a separate sheet of paper, write the vocabulary word that correctly completes the sentence.

1. Donna speaks English and Italian.
   She's _____.
2. This seed is used to make chocolate.
   It's _____.
3. This raw material is made into aluminum.
   It's _____.
4. These dried potatoes taste delicious in a stew.
   They're _____.
5. Gasoline is one example.
   It's a _____.

REMEMBERING WHAT YOU READ

On a separate sheet of paper, write your answers in complete sentences.

1. What is the ideal climate for growing coffee?
2. Which country is the biggest exporter of bananas and cacao in South America?
3. Why do farms of Indians in many cases yield only enough produce for the family's needs?
4. What are the three methods of land reform used in northern and Andean countries?
5. What are the most important minerals found in these countries?
6. What benefits has oil production brought to Venezuela's people?
7. Which three countries in South America have the largest numbers of Indians?
8. Name two countries in which the majority of people are mestizos.
9. Why is Caracas, Venezuela, compared to Los Angeles?
10. What part of Quito, Ecuador, is the government trying to preserve?

TYING ART TO SOCIAL STUDIES

Make a map of one of the countries discussed in this chapter. Draw an outline map of the country. Make up symbols for important things, such as products, and use them in the map key along with their names. For example, you might symbolize the coffee crop by a coffee bean or by a brown cloth sack that says *Coffee* or *Café*. Then place the symbols on the map in the appropriate areas. Add a title to your map.

THINKING CRITICALLY

On a separate sheet of paper, write your answers in complete sentences.

1. What benefits do people who work in co-operatives enjoy?
2. Many people in this area make only a poor living on their small farms. What could be done to make these farms grow enough to sell and make a profit?
3. Many miners in Bolivia lost their jobs due to the fact that the tin mines were not profitable. What could the government do to find employment for them?
4. Peru has two official languages—Spanish and Quechua. What, do you think, might be the results when a country has two official languages?
5. Write a brief letter to a friend telling about one of the cities described in the chapter and why you would like to visit it.

SUMMARIZING THE CHAPTER

On a separate sheet of paper, draw a graphic organizer like the one shown here. Copy the information from this graphic organizer on the one you have drawn. Under each lesson heading, write four facts that you learned from the chapter about the subject mentioned.

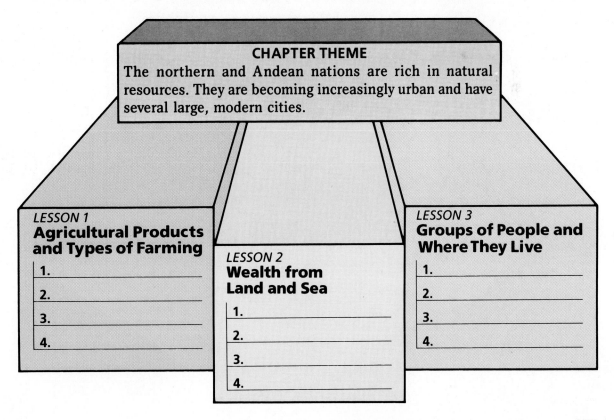

CHAPTER THEME
The northern and Andean nations are rich in natural resources. They are becoming increasingly urban and have several large, modern cities.

LESSON 1
Agricultural Products and Types of Farming
1. _____
2. _____
3. _____
4. _____

LESSON 2
Wealth from Land and Sea
1. _____
2. _____
3. _____
4. _____

LESSON 3
Groups of People and Where They Live
1. _____
2. _____
3. _____
4. _____

16

THE SOUTHERN CONE

*T*he countries in the southern cone of South America include Chile, Paraguay, Uruguay, and Argentina. In varying degrees, all four countries have experienced times of political stability and times of political upheaval.

Land and Climate

THINK ABOUT WHAT YOU KNOW

Use your knowledge gained by studying different types of maps. What predictions can you make about the regions and the climate at this time of year in Chile, Argentina, Paraguay, and Chile?

STUDY THE VOCABULARY

subtropical   **pampero**
quebracho   **rain shadow**

FOCUS YOUR READING

What physical features and types of climate are found in the countries of the southern cone?

A. Four Countries

Southern South America is called the southern cone because, in a way, it is like an ice-cream cone. It bulges out in the north, and then narrows toward the south. Study the map on the next page. You will understand why the comparison is appropriate. Look at the map closely. Antofagasta in Chile and Santos in Brazil are both shown near the Tropic of Capricorn, but on opposite coasts. The distance between the two cities is just over 1,500 miles (2,413 km). Now find the line for 50°S latitude, near the southern tip of South America. There, a distance of only about 275 miles (442 km) separates the coasts of the Atlantic and the Pacific oceans.

Chile, Argentina, Paraguay, and Uruguay are the countries of the southern cone. Chile extends along the Pacific coast like a long, narrow ribbon. Its north-to-south distance runs 2,650 miles (4,264 km), but even at its widest part, Chile is only 221 miles (356 km) from west to east.

That's less than one-tenth its length. Because of Chile's unusual shape, it's hard to judge how large it is, but it is about the size of Texas. Argentina, Chile's neighbor to the east, is the second largest country in South America. It is four times the size of Texas, and it is the eighth largest country in the entire world.

Paraguay and Uruguay are smaller countries. Paraguay is about the same size as the state of California. Like Bolivia, it is a landlocked country. Uruguay, the second smallest independent country in South America, is slightly smaller than the state of Washington.

Most of the land of the southern-cone countries lies south of the Tropic of Capricorn, in the Southern Hemisphere's temperate zone. Only a small part of northern

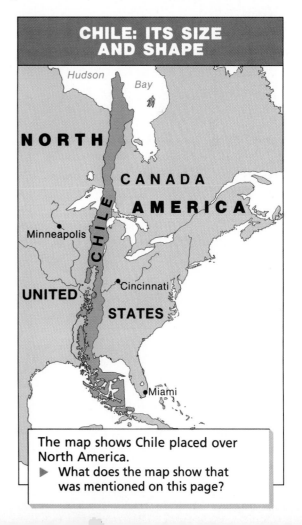

CHILE: ITS SIZE AND SHAPE

The map shows Chile placed over North America.
▶ What does the map show that was mentioned on this page?

THE SOUTHERN CONE: PHYSICAL

BOLIVIA

20° S

PACIFIC OCEAN

ATACAMA DESERT

PARAGUAY

Antofagasta

Tropic of Capricorn

Asunción

Santos

GRAN CHACO

ANDES

CHILE

BRAZIL

30° S

ARGENTINA

Aconcagua
22,834 ft
(6,960 m)

Santiago

URUGUAY

Montevideo

Buenos
Aires

PAMPAS

Gulf of San Matías

40° S

ATLANTIC

PATAGONIA

FALKLAND IS.
(U.K.)

OCEAN

50° S

Strait of
Magellan

TIERRA DEL FUEGO

Cape Horn
Drake Passage

70° W   60° W

○ National capitals

▲ Mountain peaks

Elevations
Feet   Meters
10,000 -- --3,000
5,000 --
2,000 --   --1,500
1,000 --   --600
    0 --   --300
             --0

Land below sea level

0   250   500 miles

0   250   500 kilometers

Mount Aconcagua

The Andes continue into the southern cone.
▶ Where is Aconcagua, the highest peak in the Western Hemisphere, located?

Argentina and the northern half of Paraguay are in the tropics.

Some of the climates of the southern-cone countries are like those of North America, although, as you may recall, the seasons are reversed because the countries are in the Southern Hemisphere.

B. Chile's Three Regions

Even though Chile is on the mainland of South America, Chileans often refer to their country as an island. That's because physical features isolate Chile from its neighbors. The Pacific Ocean lies to the west and south, and a coastal mountain range runs along much of its length. To the east, the Andes form a great barrier between Chile and its neighbor, Argentina.

A Barren Desert On the north, a barren desert, the Atacama, separates Chile from the central Andean countries. Some parts

(Clockwise) In Chile, girls walk in the Atacama Desert, workers harvest grapes, and skiers enjoy the Andes.
▶ Describe each region pictured.

of the Atacama receive scarcely any rain. In fact, there are parts of this desert that never receive rainfall. The Atacama is one of the world's driest regions. This desert portion of Chile is part of a larger stretch of desert that runs along the Pacific coast of South America from Peru through the northern third of Chile.

A Valley Region Central Chile, which really is a valley, is where about 90 percent of the people live. Its climate is like that of California, with hot and very dry summers and mild, humid winters. Since the region is not far from the tropics, this type of climate is sometimes called **subtropical**. A climate like that of central Chile is also called a *Mediterranean climate* because it is like that of the countries around the Mediterranean Sea in Europe. Argentina's Mount Aconcagua rises to the east of Santiago. Its melting snows provide water to irrigate crops during the dry summers.

Mountainous Land The southern third of Chile, on the other hand, has a cool, damp climate. The Andes provide some of the most beautiful scenery in the south. Vacationers from many countries enjoy skiing in the southern Andes of Chile. At higher elevations, a blanket of snow covers the mountains, giving way to forests on the lower slopes. The mountain snows are a major source of water for the farms of Chile and western Argentina. Rivers flow down the mountains and into the Pacific through gaps cut by the glaciers.

C. Paraguay's River

The Paraguay River divides Paraguay into two nearly equal parts. Almost all of

407

Paraguay's people live in the hilly, forested land east of the river. The lower, flat portion of this land becomes flooded yearly. That makes this flood plain a fertile area. The climate in this eastern portion of Paraguay is warm and humid, much like that in the southeastern United States. Across the river to the west lies the Paraguayan part of the region called the Gran Chaco. The climate in the Chaco is much hotter and even more humid than the climate in eastern Paraguay.

Most of the Chaco is a flat land covered with thorn trees, brush, and cactuses. Near the Paraguay River are forests of **quebracho** (kay BRAH choh) trees. *Quebracho* is an Indian word meaning "ax breaker." The quebracho has a very hard wood that has many uses. The tree also yields tannin. Tannin is a chemical that is used to make animal hides into leather.

D. Lands of the Pampas

The Pampas, or fertile plains, lie on both sides of the Río de la Plata and are shared by Argentina and Uruguay. The eastern part of the Pampas is humid. It receives about 20 to 35 inches (51 to 89 cm) of precipitation each year. That is enough to grow wheat, which is the main crop of the area, and many other crops.

Temperatures in the Pampas are mild, although cold winds called **pamperos** blow from the west or southwest in wintertime, bringing freezing temperatures and sometimes even snow. In the western Pampas, the land is dry. Farming without irrigation is very difficult, so the land is used mainly for grazing. North toward the Gran Chaco, cactuses and small trees indicate that the Pampas gradually have become even drier.

In the far west and northwest, along

Livestock in the southern-cone Pampas find feed, but the cattle in the Chaco region are unlucky.
▶ What problems do droughts create?

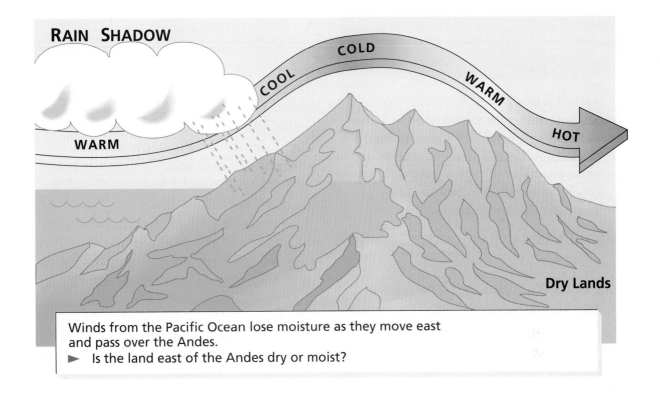

RAIN SHADOW

COOL
COLD
WARM
HOT

WARM

Dry Lands

Winds from the Pacific Ocean lose moisture as they move east and pass over the Andes.
► Is the land east of the Andes dry or moist?

the base of the Andes, are Argentina's oldest cities and agricultural areas. They were settled in the 1500s by people from Peru and Chile. This area supplied mules for the mines of Potosí and other highland mining centers. Streams flowing from the snow-capped Andes bring water to this area.

Patagonia, the southern part of Argentina, is a cool, dry land of grass-covered plateaus and hills. Patagonia is dry because the Andes keep moist air from

reaching the area. Moist air from the Pacific Ocean is forced to rise over the Andes. As it rises, it is cooled. Cooler air cannot hold as much moisture as warm air can, so when the air cools, it loses its moisture as rain or snow. By the time the air reaches Patagonia, on the eastern side of the Andes, it has lost most of its moisture. For that reason, Patagonia is said to be in the **rain shadow** of the Andes. Study the diagram above of the rain shadow.

LESSON *1* REVIEW

THINK AND WRITE

A. What similes can you write to describe the southern cone?
B. What are Chile's three main regions and their climates?
C. How would you describe the Gran Chaco?
D. Compare the eastern and western parts of the Pampas.

SKILLS CHECK

MAP SKILL

Locate *Asunción* and *Montevideo* in the Gazetteer and find two ways in which they are alike. Then locate each city on the map on page 406.

Argentina: In Search of Unity

THINK ABOUT WHAT YOU KNOW

Suppose that your school has five clubs, each led by a president. One day the school's principal decides that all these clubs should work together as part of a single organization. What problems do you think this might produce?

STUDY THE VOCABULARY

gaucho

FOCUS YOUR READING

What kinds of difficulties has Argentina experienced in trying to build a united nation?

A. Beginnings of Unity

When struggles for independence broke Spain's power in southern South America in the early 1800s, most of the former viceroyalty of La Plata formed the United Provinces of La Plata. Despite that name, the United Provinces showed very little unity. It took many years and several wars for the United Provinces to become the country of Argentina.

Caudillos, military dictators, led all of the provinces at first. Then the caudillos fought among themselves, each trying to gain control over the others' provinces. They used **gauchos**, Argentine cowhands, to make up their private armies. The gauchos, you see, were also very skilled fighters. You will learn more about the gauchos in the next chapter.

Juan Perón served a number of terms as president of Argentina. After his death Isabel Perón became president.
▶ How many years was Isabel Perón in office?

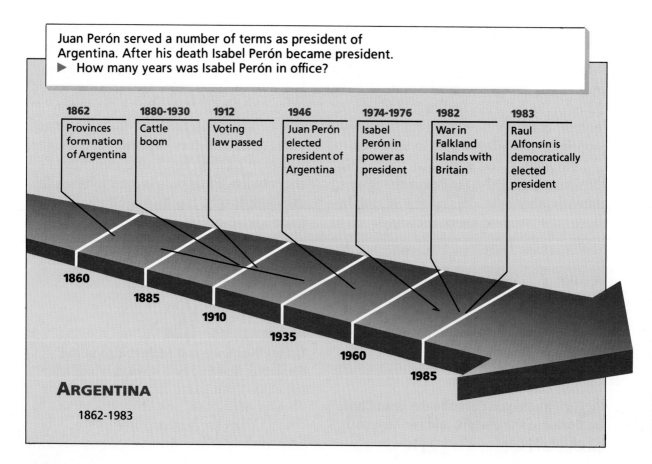

1862	1880-1930	1912	1946	1974-1976	1982	1983
Provinces form nation of Argentina	Cattle boom	Voting law passed	Juan Perón elected president of Argentina	Isabel Perón in power as president	War in Falkland Islands with Britain	Raul Alfonsín is democratically elected president

1860   1885   1910   1935   1960   1985

ARGENTINA

1862-1983

Rosas had a council to inform and advise him.
▶ What, do you think, might Rosas have requested of them?

Some of the provincial caudillos wanted to form a stronger, more centralized union. They took the name *unitarios*, a Spanish word that means "people who favor unity." Other caudillos, however, feared that a strong central government would destroy their power.

B. The Age of Rosas

"Death to the savage, filthy unitarios." That was a slogan encouraged by Juan Manuel de Rosas, who in 1829 became governor of the province of Buenos Aires. Buenos Aires was the richest province, mostly because of the city of Buenos Aires, which was the United Provinces' major port.

Rosas ruled as a dictator. He used a private police force to terrorize his opponents. Those who stood against him received beatings at the hands of Rosas's thugs. Although provincial caudillos stayed in power, Rosas became the supreme caudillo, dominating the other provinces. That was the beginning of a united Argentina.

C. A New Nation

As you might expect, some of the provincial caudillos grew very disturbed with Rosas. They did not want their provinces' interests taking second place to the needs of Buenos Aires. Justo José de Urquiza, a provincial caudillo and longtime Rosas supporter, rose up against the dictator. He led an army of 25,000 men that also included troops from some of the other provinces. The neighboring nations of Brazil, Paraguay, and Uruguay feared Rosas's power in the region, so they also sent reinforcements to aid Urquiza. At the battle of Monte Caseros, in 1852, Rosas suffered defeat. He lived out the rest of his life in exile in England.

Juan Perón and his wife, Eva, ride victoriously along Avenida de Mayo one month before her death.
▶ Why are victory parades held?

After Rosas was overthrown, representatives from all the provinces except Buenos Aires met to decide on a form of government for the union. They wrote a constitution that called for a Congress led by a strong president. By 1862, Buenos Aires had been forced into the union, and the name *Argentina* had been chosen.

For the rest of the century, wealthy ranchers and businesspeople controlled Argentina. They made sure that the person who was elected president would protect their interests. However, in 1889, workers and people from the middle class began to demand free and honest elections. In 1912, a new law made voting secret. It also required all men over 18 years old to vote. Women were not allowed to vote. Free elections took place for a while. In 1930, during a time of economic distress, the army took over the government, ending the short period of democracy.

D. The Peróns

In 1943 a new military junta took over Argentina's government. It included a man named Juan Domingo Perón. Over the next 30 years, he would play a major part in Argentina's politics. Perón became head of the Ministry of Labor. He used that office to gain favor with Argentina's many workers. In 1946, Perón left the army and ran for president. He won the election and then began a program of reform. His government took over foreign-owned businesses and started many programs to help workers.

Perón's second wife, Eva, or Evita, as she was called, played a very important part in the government. She took charge of relations between the government and its major supporters, the workers. Eventually, she also controlled the Ministry of Public Health. Evita ordered Argentina's first successful fight against tuberculosis and malaria. She also had many hospitals and clinics built. In 1947, Argentine women gained the right to vote, largely because of Evita's efforts.

By 1952, Evita was more popular than her husband. The workers knew Evita came from a background like theirs, and they believed she would fight to better their lives. Then, at the height of her power and popularity, Evita Perón became ill and died.

Juan Perón had won a second term as president in 1951, just before Evita died. Her death weakened Perón's popularity, especially among the workers. Then the Argentine economy experienced bad times. The country could not afford the many benefits the Peróns had given to workers. In 1955 the army took over and Perón fled into exile. He first went to Paraguay. Later, he settled in Spain.

E. The Return of Perón

Although Perón was out of Argentina, his memory and influence remained. As the next 25 years brought no solution to the political and economic problems of the troubled country, Perón's popularity grew. In 1973, following several years of increasing unrest and economic distress, the military government decided to allow free elections for a civilian government. One of Juan Perón's followers became president. He allowed Perón, then 77 years old and in poor health, to return to Argentina.

Shortly after Perón returned to Argentina, the president resigned, and new elections were held. Perón ran for president with his third wife, Isabel, as the candidate for vice president. They won by a landslide. Juan Perón died the following year, 1974, and Isabel became president. She was the first woman to serve as president of an American country, but her time in office was brief.

In 1976 the military arrested Isabel Perón and took over the country. That began a truly sad period in Argentine history, during which the military government waged war against its own people. You will learn more about this "dirty war" in the next chapter.

Isabel Perón served for only two years as chief of state.
► Describe the setting in which she is shown here.

LESSON 2 REVIEW

THINK AND WRITE

A. Why didn't the United Provinces of La Plata succeed?

B. How did Rosas begin the process of uniting Argentina?

C. What happened to the United Provinces after the defeat of Rosas?

D. For what reasons was Evita Perón popular in Argentina?

E. How did the military rule Argentina after the Peróns?

SKILLS CHECK

WRITING SKILL

You read that Isabel Perón was the first woman to serve as president of an American country. Write a personal diary entry as Isabel might have written it just before she took office.

Chile: Government for the Upper Class

THINK ABOUT WHAT YOU KNOW

Suppose you were in a class in which the same few students always seemed to get their own way. How would that make you feel?

STUDY THE VOCABULARY

reform	Marxist
agrarian reform	police state

FOCUS YOUR READING

What were the major eras in Chile's political development, and what leaders are associated with them?

A. The Age Of Diego Portales

He never ruled as president, but he held the real power in Chile for seven very important years. His name was Diego Portales. By the age of 23, Portales, who had been born into a wealthy family, had built a prosperous business as a merchant in the city of Valparaíso. There he also started a newspaper. By 1830, at the age of 37, Portales had great influence in Chile.

Portales believed that Chile needed public order and national unity. He distrusted the common people and encouraged the development of commerce and a centralized government.

With its powerful national government, Chile enjoyed stability and economic progress. However, the price the majority of the Chilean people paid for this orderly growth was very high. Since Portales favored the interests of the wealthy few, the upper class received the most benefits. Most Chileans saw very little real improvement in their lives. Equally as bad, they had almost no say in government.

This palace of the president was built in 1805 in Santiago, Chile.
▶ What guard ceremony is shown?

President Alessandri (third from left) is shown with admirals from the United States and Chile.
► Why might a meeting involve naval officers from two countries?

B. Reform in the Twentieth Century

Orderly government and the policies that encouraged business and commerce continued in Chile throughout the nineteenth century. Chile seemed a model of stability. Beneath the surface, however, Chile was a divided land. A small number of upper-class families controlled the land, businesses, and industries of the country. The majority of the population, including members of the working and middle classes, remained relatively poor. Not surprisingly, those who did not share fully in Chile's wealth began to call for **reform**. Reform is a change that stops something that is wrong or unfair, as in government.

In 1920, a man named Arturo Alessandri ran for president. He promised to bring about better living conditions to poor Chileans. For the first time in Chilean history, members of the working and middle classes began to take an active part in politics. Their support helped Alessandri win the presidency.

Alessandri did not have an easy time. In 1924, his enemies sent him into exile, and a military government took over. Alessandri was invited back in 1925, but he was forced out of office again the same year. In 1932, Alessandri again became the president, serving until 1938.

For the next 40 years, Chile elected its leaders democratically. Even so, the Chilean people remained divided. There were still large numbers of poor people and only a few who were well-off.

C. Reforms by Eduardo Frei

Between 1930 and 1970, many Chilean governments tried to transfer land to people who would make it more produc-

415

tive. One of the most important of these attempts at land reform came during the presidency of Eduardo Frei. Between 1964 and 1970, Frei tried to carry out his campaign slogan, "Revolution in Freedom." As head of the Christian Democrats, a liberal political party, Frei called for changes in the tax laws and for **agrarian reform**. *Agrarian reform* is another term for "land and farming improvements." The Frei government tried to promote agricultural labor unions and to increase wages of farm workers.

Frei also called for the "Chileanization" of the copper industry. Foreign companies, mostly from the United States, controlled the mining of copper, Chile's most important industry. Under Frei's new policy, the Chilean government bought 51 percent of the shares of the foreign compa-

nies. Reforms proceeded slowly to avoid creating disorder and alarming the wealthy. Even a modest program of land reform, however, angered Chile's land-owning elite.

D. A Marxist President

A Change in Leadership By 1970, middle-class and working-class Chileans had lost patience. They had expected more from Frei's "Revolution in Freedom." Many of them joined a group that backed Salvador Allende (ah YAYN day) for the presidency. In that election, three main candidates ran for the presidency. Allende won 36 percent of the vote, just enough to become president.

Allende was a **Marxist**. A Marxist is someone who follows the ideas of Karl Marx, a German thinker who lived in the

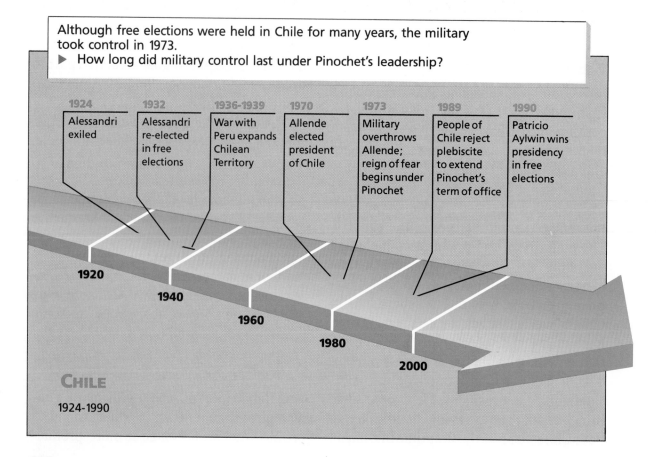

Although free elections were held in Chile for many years, the military took control in 1973.
▶ How long did military control last under Pinochet's leadership?

1924	1932	1936-1939	1970	1973	1989	1990
Alessandri exiled	Alessandri re-elected in free elections	War with Peru expands Chilean Territory	Allende elected president of Chile	Military overthrows Allende; reign of fear begins under Pinochet	People of Chile reject plebiscite to extend Pinochet's term of office	Patricio Aylwin wins presidency in free elections

1920 1940 1960 1980 2000

CHILE
1924-1990

A large billboard in front of a slum area for copper workers proclaims, "We defend copper—We defend Chile."
► Why is copper so important to Chile?

1800s. Marx believed in socialism, which you read about in Chapter 10. You may recall that socialism is a system of government in which land and industries are controlled by the government. Salvador Allende was the first Marxist to become president of a country in the Western Hemisphere in a free election.

After Allende took office in 1970, he greatly increased the number of takeovers of large farms and foreign-owned companies by the Chilean government. He also began programs to raise workers' wages and to give jobs to more people. During Allende's first year in office, workers earned an average of 50 percent more than they had the year before.

Problems for Allende Still, there were many problems. Allende didn't have the backing of the majority of the people. Re-

member, he had received only about a third of the vote. Several parties had joined the group to support Allende when he ran for office. If he didn't please the members of all the different parties, he could not get the Congress to pass the laws he wanted.

Allende also had many enemies. The upper classes and the military did not like his socialist programs. Neither did some middle-class Chileans. In addition, the United States was worried about having a socialist government in South America. For that reason, the United States stopped sending money to Chile and tried to keep other countries from helping Chile.

By 1973, the Chilean economy was in serious trouble. High inflation was causing the workers to lose most of the gains they had made when Allende first came to power. Poor harvests in 1972 and 1973 made matters worse.

Marxist leader Allende is shown making a speech. The sign lists what his platform is for *(para, por)* and against *(contra)*.
▶ What do you think the sign says?

E. A Military Takeover

In September of 1973, the military took over the government. Allende was killed, and Chileans were subjected to the greatest loss of civil rights in Latin American history. A military junta, headed by General Augusto Pinochet (pee naw-CHET), declared that it would "regenerate" Chilean society — that is, change Chilean life for the better.

The new Chile produced by this regeneration was not a pleasant place. The junta did not simply end the reforms begun by Eduardo Frei. It turned democratic Chile into a **police state**, a type of government that uses police, especially secret national police, to keep political opposition down. The new government jailed thousands of Chileans. Many of those jailed were tortured. During its first two years in power, the government killed between 18,000 and 30,000 citizens. The junta banned most labor union activities and outlawed all strikes. It also said that the national Congress would no longer meet. Democratic socialism in Chile had ended.

LESSON **3** *REVIEW*

THINK AND WRITE

A. What were the main beliefs of Diego Portales?

B. Why was the 1920 election of Alessandri important?

C. How did Eduardo Frei try to help the middle-class and working-class people of Chile?

D. Why did Allende's government fall?

E. What happened in Chile when the military took over?

SKILLS CHECK

THINKING SKILL

Select one of the five powerful people discussed in this lesson. Make some notes about the successes and/or failures of that person as an influence on Chile. Share your observations with some classmates.

Paraguay and Uruguay

What would you do if you had two neighbors, both stronger than you, and each one of them wanted you to do only things they thought would help them?

strike

What overall patterns can you see in the histories of Paraguay and Uruguay?

A. A Hopeful Beginning in Paraguay

Two Strong Dictators Known at first as "Supreme One" and later as "Perpetual Dictator," José de Francia took power in Paraguay in 1811 and held it until his death in 1840. Like many Latin American dictators, Francia dealt harshly with those who opposed him. Unlike many dictators, however, he was an honest man, devoted to building a strong nation. Francia began by isolating his small country from its neighbors. No one was allowed to leave or enter the country. He then encouraged new methods in agriculture and stock raising and urged all Paraguayans to work hard for the good of the nation. Francia also established Paraguay's public school system and the nation's first public library.

Carlos Antonio López, described as "vain, fat and incredibly ugly," took over shortly after Francia died, and he ruled Paraguay until 1862. A rancher, who was both less cruel and less personally honest than the previous dictator, Carlos Antonio

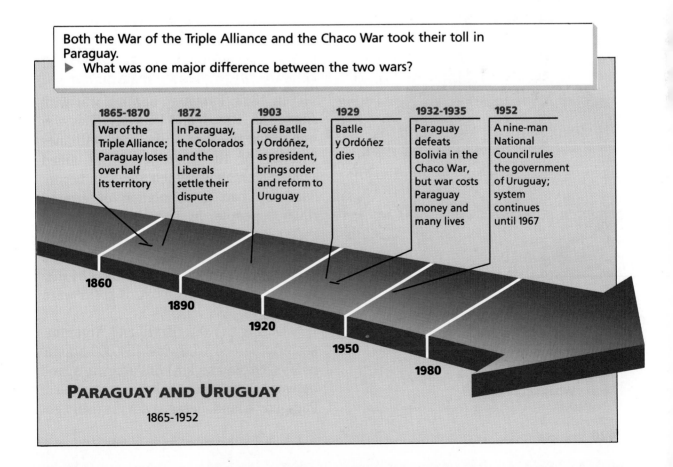

Both the War of the Triple Alliance and the Chaco War took their toll in Paraguay.
▶ What was one major difference between the two wars?

1865-1870	1872	1903	1929	1932-1935	1952
War of the Triple Alliance; Paraguay loses over half its territory	In Paraguay, the Colorados and the Liberals settle their dispute	José Batlle y Ordóñez, as president, brings order and reform to Uruguay	Batlle y Ordóñez dies	Paraguay defeats Bolivia in the Chaco War, but war costs Paraguay money and many lives	A nine-man National Council rules the government of Uruguay; system continues until 1967

1860

1890

1920

1950

1980

PARAGUAY AND URUGUAY

1865-1952

López promoted foreign trade and encouraged the building of roads and railroads. The strong rule of the two dictators, Francia and López, helped make Paraguay one of the wealthiest and most modern countries in Latin America.

By 1862, when Francisco Solano López, Carlos Antonio's son, came to power, the country had enjoyed nearly 50 years of peace. Industry had been developed. Paraguay had a literacy rate that was the highest in Latin America. *Literacy* means "the ability to read and write." There were few large land holdings and few poor peons. The nation also had a large and well-trained army. With 70,000 soldiers, its army was larger than the armies of Argentina, Brazil, and Uruguay combined!

LITERACY TODAY: South America

Argentina	94%	Guyana	86%
Bolivia	63%	Paraguay	84%
Brazil	74%	Peru	80%
Chile	96%	Suriname	65%
Colombia	88%	Uruguay	96%
Ecuador	85%	Venezuela	88%
French Guiana	82%		

The table shows the literacy rates of the 13 South American nations.
▶ Which two South American nations have the highest literacy rate?

Carlos Antonio López was one of two rulers who is honored because he improved the country of Paraguay.
▶ What did López do?

B. Two Major Wars in Paraguay

In 1865, Paraguay began a war with Argentina, Brazil, and Uruguay. This war was called the War of the Triple Alliance because of the three countries allied against Paraguay. When the war began, Paraguay had a population of around 700,000 people. In 1870, when the war ended, Paraguay's population had fallen to only 175,000 people. Most of the nation's men had died during the war. Only 14,000 males remained, and most of them were young boys.

During the war, Brazil and Argentina secretly agreed to divide 154,000 square miles (398,860 sq km) of Paraguay's land between them. They took more than half of Paraguay's land. Paraguay never really got

Drawings in a 1868 magazine show battle scenes between Brazil and Paraguay, and a chaplain encouraging the Paraguayans to surrender.
▶ Why weren't photographs used, do you think?

over the War of the Triple Alliance. To make matters worse, Paraguay fought Bolivia in the Chaco War from 1932 to 1935, again losing many soldiers, and a great deal of money. Paraguay gained only a small area in the northern Chaco. Then, in the next 19 years, Paraguay had 10 different leaders.

A 1954 military coup brought General Alfredo Stroessner (STRES nur) to the presidency in Paraguay. He remained in power for the next 35 years. His secret police force — and his willingness to jail, torture, and kill opponents — kept most people in line. Stroessner was ousted in 1989 by a military coup led by Andres Rodríguez, who was then elected president.

C. Years of Disorder in Uruguay

During the 75 years after becoming an independent nation in 1828, Uruguay experienced some 50 revolutions and coups. Much of the blame for this turmoil rests with Uruguay's two powerful neighbors, Argentina and Brazil.

Back in 1820, both Argentina and Brazil had claimed the land that today is occupied by Uruguay. Brazil refused to accept Argentina's claim. Argentina would not accept Brazil's. When a war between Argentina and Brazil still did not settle the issue, the two nations agreed to recognize the disputed territory in 1828 as the independent nation of Uruguay. Argentina and

Brazil, however, often interfered in the new nation's politics. Argentina wanted a government in Uruguay that would oppose close relations with Brazil. As you might suspect, Brazil supported Uruguayans who opposed Argentina. As a result, disputes between Uruguay's two political parties often wound up involving Uruguay's two large neighbors.

D. José Batlle y Ordóñez

Peace and Reforms Order came to Uruguay only in 1903 with the election of a new president, José Batlle y Ordóñez. He began a far-reaching program of reform. Uruguayans today still refer to *Batllismo*, or the system of social changes promoted by the president. Batlle, whose father had been president of Uruguay from 1868 to 1872, was a large, gruff man who had a

This portrait, and others like it, of President Batlle y Ordóñez hung in many offices and homes.
▶ Why is this probably a real fact?

reputation for physical courage, intelligence, and honesty. A leader of the Colorado party, he served as president from 1903 until 1907 and again from 1911 to 1915.

Batlle brought peace and progress to Uruguay. He pushed for freedom of speech and of the press and for free elections. He also supported the establishing of free public education, including both primary and secondary schools. As well, Batlle gave women the right to vote. Batlle also believed that women should be allowed to attend college. Today, these may not seem like reforms to you, but at the time, they put Uruguay ahead of the United States and the European countries in women's rights.

Batlle's program of reforms also included new rights for working people — the right of workers to organize labor unions and to go on **strike**. A strike is the refusal of workers to go to work. Strikers want to make their employer give them better pay or working conditions. As with his stand on women's voting and education, Batlle's support for labor was advanced for the time. Workers in the United States, for example, did not as yet have the rights granted to Uruguayan workers.

Uruguay's economic development also received Batlle's attention. He promoted an active role for the government in the economy. This included having government establish and fund its own companies when private companies did not seem able to do a good job. Batlle did not accomplish all his goals while in office. However, even after he completed his second term in office, he continued to be an important political figure in Uruguay. He wrote columns in his newspaper, *El Día*, supporting continued reform.

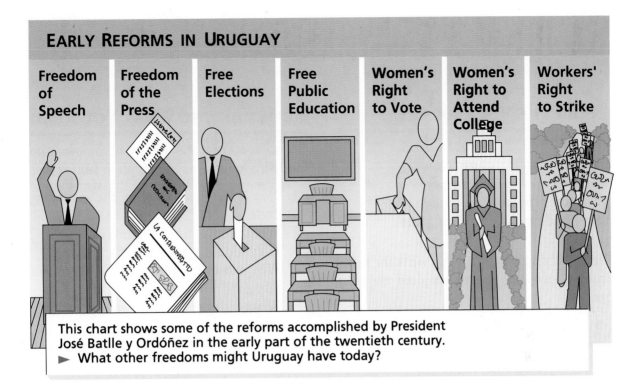

EARLY REFORMS IN URUGUAY

| Freedom of Speech | Freedom of the Press | Free Elections | Free Public Education | Women's Right to Vote | Women's Right to Attend College | Workers' Right to Strike |

This chart shows some of the reforms accomplished by President José Batlle y Ordóñez in the early part of the twentieth century.
► What other freedoms might Uruguay have today?

E. Democracy Ends

No coups. No revolutions. No civil wars. Throughout most of the twentieth century, Uruguay was a model democracy. Ballots, not bullets counted in Uruguay. The country also enjoyed considerable prosperity. Uruguayans lived well. They enjoyed good schools and high rates of literacy. Then, in the 1960s, a failing economy revealed some basic problems in Uruguay. Disorder, banished since the early days of Batlle, returned.

Guerrilla movements grew up in both the countryside and the capital, Montevideo. The sudden explosion of bombs became a common sound in Montevideo. In 1973, the military stepped in, closed the national Congress, and began another period of dictatorial rule until 1985. At that time, Julio Maria Sanguinetti, a civilian, was elected president.

LESSON 4 REVIEW

THINK AND WRITE

A. How did the rule of Paraguay's first two rulers help the country?

B. How was Paraguay changed by the War of the Triple Alliance?

C. Why was Uruguay so unstable during its first 75 years of independence?

D. What do Uruguayans mean when they refer to *Batllismo*?

E. What happened to Uruguay in the 1970s?

SKILLS CHECK

MAP SKILL

Locate *Gran Chaco* in the Gazetteer. What three countries own portions of that region today? Find each country on the map on page 406.

423

USING THE VOCABULARY

reform	subtropical
Marxist	gauchos
strike	pamperos
agrarian reform	quebracho
rain shadow	police state

On a separate sheet of paper, write the terms from above that best complete the sentences.

1. California and central Chile have similar _____ climates.
2. The Argentine cowhands, or _____, were very skilled fighters.
3. The history of Latin America is full of attempts to _____, or change wrong or unfair practices, as in the government.
4. Organized labor unions give people the right to go on _____ to get better pay or working conditions.
5. The _____ tree furnishes tannin, which is used to make animal hides into leather.
6. Cold winds called _____ bring freezing temperatures and even snow to the Pampas.
7. Chile became a _____ in 1973, making life very hard for the people.
8. By _____, Frei promoted agricultural labor unions and tried to increase the wages of farm workers.
9. The _____ occurs when mountains block moisture-bearing winds.
10. Salvador Allende was a _____ who believed in socialism for Chile.

REMEMBERING WHAT YOU READ

On a separate sheet of paper, answer the following questions in complete sentences.

1. Name the countries in the southern cone.
2. What are the three regions of Chile?
3. How did a united Argentina begin?
4. Why was the Argentine leader Perón so popular?
5. What brought about the reform of Chile in the twentieth century?
6. What happened to Chile's government in 1973?
7. In what ways did Paraguay progress between 1811 and 1862, its fifty years of peace?
8. What kind of government did Paraguay have from 1954 until 1989?
9. Which leader set up a far-reaching program of reforms for Uruguay?
10. Why did Uruguay stop being a "model democracy" in 1973?

TYING SCIENCE TO SOCIAL STUDIES

Draw your own diagram to illustrate where a rain shadow occurs. Review page 409 for details. In a short paragraph under your diagram, describe in your own words how the moist air becomes dry.

THINKING CRITICALLY

On a separate sheet of paper, answer the following questions in complete sentences.

1. Write about the similarities and differences of places in the southern cone that compare with areas in the United States.
2. Why, do you think, has it been hard for democracy to succeed in such countries as Argentina and Chile?
3. How could it be said that Chile's history follows the saying that "the rich get richer while the poor get poorer?"
4. Why did Paraguay lose so many soldiers and much land between 1865 and 1870 in the War of the Triple Alliance?
5. Describe what you think it would be like to live in a country under military rule.

SUMMARIZING THE CHAPTER

On a separate piece of paper, draw a graphic organizer like the one shown here. Copy the information from this graphic organizer to the one you have drawn. Under the main idea for each lesson, write facts that support the main idea.

CHAPTER THEME

The countries in South America that make up the southern cone have had many changes of government and very little democracy. Some leaders have brought needed reforms.

LESSON 1
The climates in the southern cone resemble those in the United States.

1. _____ 3. _____
2. _____ 4. _____

LESSON 3
Chile's era of democracy turned to socialism, then to military rule.

1. _____ 3. _____
2. _____ 4. _____

LESSON 2
Argentina's difficulties were many as the country underwent reforms and unified.

1. _____
2. _____
3. _____
4. _____

LESSON 4
Paraguay and Uruguay experienced revolutions and coups. Uruguay was more democratic, but both have had recent periods of military rule.

Paraguay /**Uruguay**

1. _____ 1. _____
2. _____ 2. _____
3. _____ 3. _____

17
THE SOUTHERN CONE TODAY

*I*n the southern-cone countries today, democracy is the rule rather than the exception. The bustling cities of this region show a strong economy and a new hope for the future.

The Economy of the Southern Cone

THINK ABOUT WHAT YOU KNOW

A part of this lesson tells about the growth of the cattle industry in Argentina. Think about the early cattle industry in the "wild west" of the United States. What images come to mind?

STUDY THE VOCABULARY

hydroelectric

FOCUS YOUR READING

What are the major economic resources of the southern-cone countries?

A. A Wealthy Land

Argentina has world importance as a producer of food. The Pampas have a lot to do with that. The flat, treeless plains of the Pampas have rich, deep soils that are especially suited for wheat. Wheat production began on the eastern Pampas, and by the 1880s, it had become an important crop.

The leaves of yerba maté plants produce a tea that is the national drink of three countries.
▶ Which countries might that be?

THE SOUTHERN CONE: CROPS AND NATURAL RESOURCES

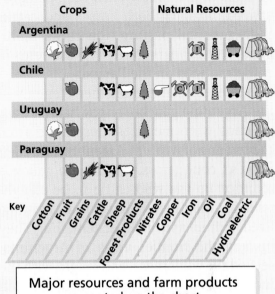

Major resources and farm products are represented on the chart.
▶ Which country produces the greatest variety of crops?

Today, Argentina is one of five great wheat-trading countries in the world. Two of the other countries are Canada and the United States, so you can see that the lands of the Western Hemisphere provide food for people in many other countries. Argentina also stands among the world leaders in exports of rice and corn.

Grapes for wine are grown on the irrigated farms of Mendoza. Argentina produces fine wines, many of which are sold in other Latin American countries, Europe, and the United States. The forests of the Gran Chaco produce quebracho and a plant called yerba maté (YER buh MAH-tay). The leaves of the yerba maté are used to make a tealike drink called maté, which is very popular in the southern cone.

427

B. Cattle and Beef in Argentina

Tall, coarse grasses covered the Pampas in the 1500s. Then the Spaniards arrived, bringing both horses and cattle. With plentiful pasture, the cattle multiplied. As the years rolled by, vast herds of cattle ran wild on the Pampas.

These cattle had one fierce enemy — the Argentine gaucho, or cowhand. These gauchos were mestizos, descended from the Indians of western Argentina and their Spanish conquerors. At first the gauchos rounded up the wild cattle to be slaughtered for their hides. Gauchos at that time lived a free and independent life. They roamed the frontier areas of Argentina, settled the wilderness, and fought with the Indians. They used knives with 14-inch blades (36-cm), for fighting and to cut hides. They also shaved their beards with those same knives.

Beginning in the mid-1800s, the cattle industry began to change. Markets for beef opened up in Great Britain. Argentine ranchers imported improved breeds of cattle to replace the tough Spanish cattle. Gradually the open range disappeared. It was fenced with barbed wire and planted in pasture for the new cattle. Railroads carried cattle and other products from the Pampas to the Argentine ports.

When the age of the open range ended, so did the free life of the gaucho. The gauchos worked as cowhands on ranches. Today in Argentina the gaucho lives on as an interesting figure — a hero of legend, story, and song. A famous poem about gauchos was written by an Argentine named José Hernandez. His poem ran several hundred pages in length! It is called "The Gaucho Martín Fierro." Here are a few stanzas for you to read. Perhaps someday you will read the entire poem.

As soon as the dawn
started to turn red
and the birds to sing
and the hens came down off their perch
it was time to get going
each man to his work

The one whose job was horse-breaking
headed for the corral
where the beast was waiting
snorting fit to burst —
wild and wicked as they come
and tearing itself to bits

Ah, those times! . . . you felt proud
to see how a man could ride
When a gaucho really knew his job,
even if the colt went over backwards
not one of them wouldn't land on his feet
with the halter-rein in his hand.

As you have read, in the early days of the gauchos, the value of cattle came mostly from the hides. The meat had little economic value because it could not be shipped very far without spoiling. So, for much of the nineteenth century, Argentines used two methods to preserve beef, drying and salting.

If your idea of an appetizing piece of beef is a hamburger or a steak, you'll understand why salted or dried beef did not appeal to many people. The hard strips of beef provided nutrition but no taste or flavor. Late in the nineteenth century, the canning industry began. Beef could be processed and canned by using a vacuum process to remove all the air from the container. Without any air in the can, the meat would not spoil. Beef still is canned today. In fact, if you look on your grocer's shelves for cans of corned beef, chances are you'll find that some of it comes from Argentina.

THE SOUTHERN CONE: CATTLE AND SHEEP

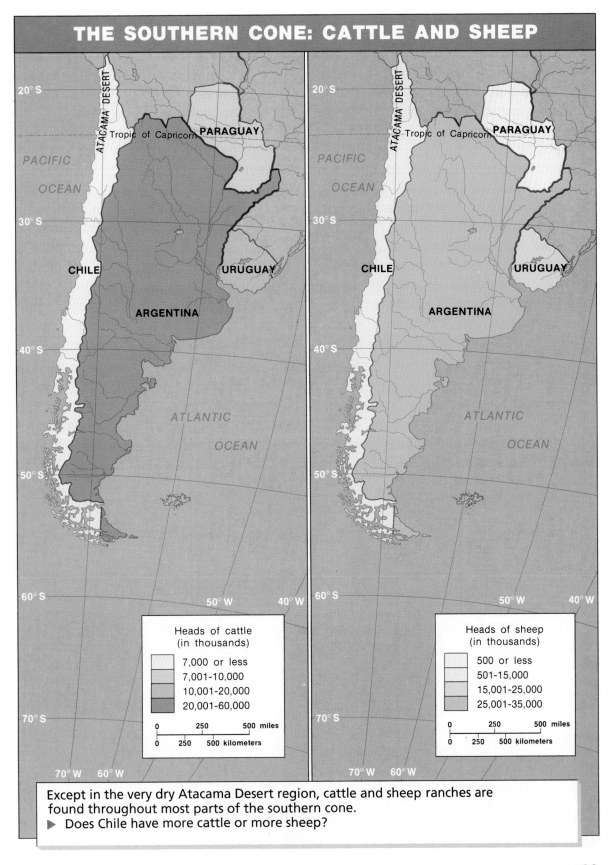

Heads of cattle (in thousands)

- 7,000 or less
- 7,001-10,000
- 10,001-20,000
- 20,001-60,000

0   250   500 miles
0   250   500 kilometers

Heads of sheep (in thousands)

- 500 or less
- 501-15,000
- 15,001-25,000
- 25,001-35,000

0   250   500 miles
0   250   500 kilometers

Except in the very dry Atacama Desert region, cattle and sheep ranches are found throughout most parts of the southern cone.

▶ Does Chile have more cattle or more sheep?

Canned meat was a big improvement over salted or dried meat, but it still did not solve the problem of how to place a tender, juicy Argentine steak on the plate of some consumer in a distant country. Refrigeration and the development of the steamship changed all that. Soon Argentine beef became common in the restaurants and homes of Europe. England, which had very close relations with Argentina at that time, bought an enormous amount of Argentine beef. The cattle industry boomed.

While cattle ranches were taking over the western Pampas, sheep raising was becoming big business in southern Argentina. Wool from the sheep has become another important Argentine product.

C. Stock Raising and Agriculture

Uruguay and Paraguay are grazing countries. Uruguay exports beef, hides, and wool. Paraguay produces cattle, hides, cotton, and tobacco on its farms and wood and tannin from its forests. As you may recall, tannin is used in tanning leather. Most of Paraguay's farms are small. They mainly produce subsistence crops.

Uruguay and Paraguay each produce enough food for their own people. Chile, however, imports more agricultural products than it exports. Central Chile could produce large amounts of grain, fruits, vegetables, and other food crops. However, the land is not well used, and production is small. Wheat and cattle make up about a third of Chile's farm production. Chile's orchards produce apples, grapes, and pears. Fruit and fruit products are Chile's only important agricultural exports.

D. Minerals in Chile

Nearly 2 miles (3 km) long and 980 feet (299 m) deep, Chuquicamata (choo-kee kuh MAHT uh) is the world's largest

Small farms, such as this one in Uruguay, produce only enough for subsistence.
► What is subsistence farming?

(Left) An open-pit mine near Arica, Chile, is shown in operation. (Right) At the Chuquicamata mine, copper has been refined and loaded for transport.
▶ What industries use large amounts of copper?

open-pit copper mine. More copper comes from Chuquicamata than from any other copper mine in the world. El Teniente (ten ee ENT ee) is the largest underground copper mine in the world. Both these mines are in Chile. About 10 percent of the world's copper comes from Chile. El Teniente is in central Chile, only about 95 miles (153 km) from Santiago. Chuquicamata and El Salvador, another important copper mine, are in the Atacama Desert region. Together, the three mines, called the Gran Minería (grahn mee nay REE-ah), account for just about all of Chile's copper. The copper mines were all owned by companies from the United States until 1967, when Chile bought a part interest in them. In 1971 the government expropriated the mines.

Copper makes up 60 to 70 percent of the value of Chile's exports. When the price of copper is high, the Chilean economy is good. When the price of copper is low, there is little money to spare. Chile is like other countries that depend upon a single product to export. The country's

economy goes back and forth from good times to bad, depending on the world price of its special export product.

Iron is the second most important mineral in Chile. The largest iron mines are near La Serena, a city at the southern edge of the desert. Most of the iron is shipped to plants near Concepción, a manufacturing city in central Chile, to be made into steel.

Back in the nineteenth century, nitrates were an important mineral resource in Chile. As you may recall from Chapter 14, nitrates are used as fertilizers. Between 1860 and 1920, nitrates from the Atacama Desert found a good market in Europe. Chile came to control the whole nitrate supply after the War of the Pacific, and nitrates brought in most of the country's export income.

By 1920, manufactured nitrate fertilizers had began to take the place of the natural nitrates of Chile. Today, the mines produce nitrates mainly for use in Chile. Fortunately for Chile, just when nitrates became less important, copper rose in importance.

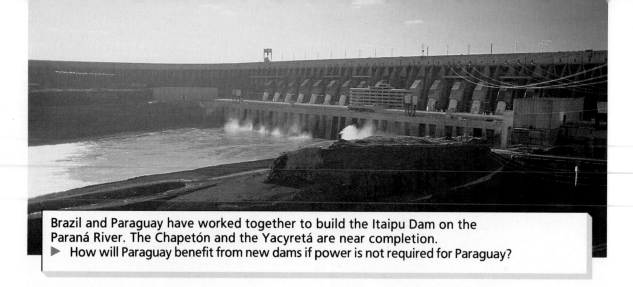

Brazil and Paraguay have worked together to build the Itaipu Dam on the Paraná River. The Chapetón and the Yacyretá are near completion.
▶ How will Paraguay benefit from new dams if power is not required for Paraguay?

E. Power Sources: Present and Future

When it is completed, Chapeton will be the world's largest dam in volume of water. Chapeton is one of several major **hydroelectric** projects in Argentina. The word *hydroelectric* means "electricity produced by water power." Corpus Posadas, one of two joint projects between Argentina and Paraguay, is the sixth largest hydroelectric generator in the world. Paraguay also cooperates with Brazil. In fact, those two countries are presently completing a dam on the Paraná River that will have the world's largest hydroelectric generator. At present, Paraguay has too little industry to use the electricity the new dams will produce. Most of the power will be sold to Brazil and Argentina.

In addition to hydroelectric energy, Argentina also is rich in oil. In fact, it is the third largest producer of oil in Latin America. Most of the oil is found in Patagonia. Smaller oil fields have recently been developed in the far west, along the base of the Andes. Argentina produces enough oil for its own needs but not enough to export.

Chile produces small amounts of oil. Its oil fields are in the far south, near Tierra del Fuego. Chile has important deposits of coal. It is one of the few Latin American countries to have good coal mines.

LESSON **1** *REVIEW*

THINK AND WRITE

A. What are some of Argentina's major agricultural products?
B. How did changes in the cattle industry affect Argentina?
C. How does Chile's agriculture differ from that of Uruguay and Paraguay?
D. What are Chile's most important mineral resources?
E. Why is the Paraná River important to Paraguay, Argentina, and Brazil?

SKILLS CHECK

WRITING SKILL

You read about a number of agricultural industries and natural resources within the southern-cone countries. Select one industry or resource and write a few facts for a poster or advertisement for one of the mentioned countries. Add art, a photograph, or a graph if you wish.

LESSON 2

Peoples of the Southern Cone

THINK ABOUT WHAT YOU KNOW

Perhaps you or someone you know has moved from one city, or even one country, to another. What reasons do people have for moving from one place to another?

STUDY THE VOCABULARY

tenant
estancia

FOCUS YOUR READING

What peoples make up the population of the southern cone?

General Roca's forces fought the Araucanians. The text says that "the Indians were removed from the land."
▶ What do you think that means?

A. War with Indians

"For the Argentine Republic," said General Julio Roca, Argentina's minister of war in the late nineteenth century, "there is no other frontier in the West and the South than the peaks of the Andes and the Ocean."

The Indians of the Pampas thought otherwise. They had lived on the land in the south well before there was an Argentine republic. These Pampean Indians had stood against the invading Spanish. They continued to remain on land that others in Argentina wanted.

In the 1870s and 1880s, change had come to the southern reaches of the Pampas. Booming businesses because of cattle and wheat made the land more valuable. A restless Argentine nation brimmed with energy and enthusiasm. Signs of progress and civilization were everywhere. The Araucanians, however, stood in the way. One group, in particular, the Mapuche, fought to keep Araucanian land.

With a force of 8,000 men, General Roca marched south from Buenos Aires to confront about 2,000 Araucanians, most of them unarmed. A swift victory removed the Indians from the land, opening the way for more settlers. Argentina applauded General Roca. He became a national hero, "the Conqueror of the Desert," and later president of the nation.

B. Emigration from Europe

With its remaining Indian peoples mostly living on reservations, Argentina, unlike some of the other nations of Latin America, never had much of an Indian heritage. It became a land of European immigrants. Remember that immigrants are people who *come into* a country to make it their new home.

433

La Boca is an old neighborhood in Buenos Aires where many descendants of Italian immigrants live.
▶ How would you describe the homes?

A nineteenth-century Argentine political thinker named Juan Alberdi said, "To govern is to populate." Alberdi wanted Europeans to come to Argentina, settle on the land, and help the nation grow. He also believed in building railroads as a way of both improving commerce and helping to build national unity.

Beginning around the 1880s, many Italians decided to emigrate to the Americas. *Emigrate* means "to *leave* one country to settle in another." At that time, Italy was suffering from political distress and poor economic conditions, so emigration seemed like a good move to many people.

Some of these immigrants began small farms on the Pampas, but many more went to **estancias**, or large ranches, to be **tenants**. A tenant is a person who rents land or housing. Each tenant family rented a piece of land in the Pampas. The family had to build a house and plow the land for crops. The land was very hard to plow because it had never been plowed before. At the end of four years, the tenant family had to plant the land in alfalfa for cattle feed and turn it back to the owner. The tenant family then had to move on to another farm or into the city to find work. By 1914, immigrants living in Buenos Aires outnumbered by three to one the people who had been born in Argentina.

C. A European Heritage

The economic opportunity that attracted people to Argentina also brought immigrants to other nations of the Western Hemisphere. Some people went to Canada and the United States. Others headed to Uruguay, Chile, and Brazil. Many Italian-American families in the United States today have relatives living in these other countries of the Western Hemisphere.

These girls in Buenos Aires may have had European ancestors.
▶ From which countries might the ancestors have been?

Since about the middle of the nineteenth century, Spaniards and Germans also were arriving in large numbers in the southern cone region. As a result of this great movement of people across the Atlantic, Argentina, Chile, and Uruguay have a very strong European heritage.

About 97 percent of Argentina's population is of European heritage. In Chile, nearly two thirds of the population has a European background, and about one third is mestizo. In Uruguay, 88 percent of the population is of European ancestry. Only 8 percent are mestizo, and 4 percent are black.

D. Paraguay's Indian Heritage

Paraguay's heritage pattern is different. About 95 percent of all Paraguayans are mestizo. They trace their ancestry to the Guaraní (gwah rah NEE) Indians, who lived in Paraguay long before it was colonized by Spain. In the 1600s, Jesuit Catholic missionaries went to Paraguay to convert the Indians to Christianity. They taught the Indians how to farm, and they built a number of mission settlements. In 1767, Spain decided to expel the Jesuits from all of its colonies. Spain feared the Jesuits were not really loyal to Spain. After that, many Indians and Spaniards married. The result is a large mestizo population.

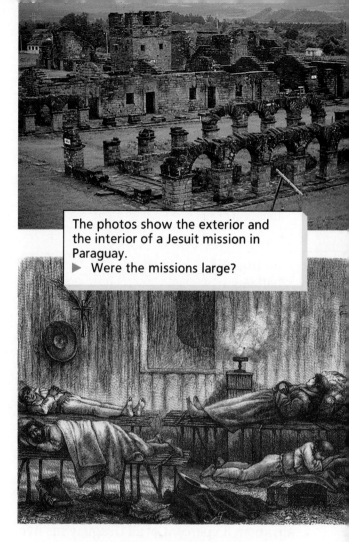

The photos show the exterior and the interior of a Jesuit mission in Paraguay.
▶ Were the missions large?

Paraguayans have kept much of their Indian heritage. Guaraní, the Indian language, is spoken by 90 percent of the people. It is almost an official language. Government documents and publications, as well as newspapers and books, are printed in both Spanish and Guaraní.

LESSON 2 REVIEW

THINK AND WRITE

A. Why did Argentina make war against the Araucanians?

B. What happened to the early Italian immigrants in Argentina?

C. In what way do Argentina, Chile, and Uruguay have similar heritages?

D. Why are the Guaraní important to Paraguay?

SKILLS CHECK

THINKING SKILL

Reread the two sections about heritage in this lesson. Think about how you could make a chart or some graphs based on the information given. With some classmates, discuss different possibilities. Then work out a plan and produce a chart or some graphs.

Cities of the Southern Cone

THINK ABOUT WHAT YOU KNOW

Imagine that you are enrolled in a large school. Half the students in the school all elect to be in one particular classroom. Why might all of them choose that one location?

STUDY THE VOCABULARY

metropolis   estuary
callampa

FOCUS YOUR READING

What are some important features of the major cities in the southern cone.

A. Giant Cities

If you were to guess that any one person from Uruguay lives in the city of Montevideo, there's a 50-percent chance you'd be right. Just about half of Uruguay's 3 million people call Montevideo home. Overall, about 83 percent of all Uruguayans live in cities. That's pretty much the case in Argentina and Chile too. Among the southern-cone countries, only Paraguay is more rural than urban, with only 43 percent of its people living in cities. Asunción, Paraguay's national capital, has only 550,000 people, but that still makes it the largest city in the nation.

In each of the southern-cone countries, the capital is a primate city. You have learned that many of the nations of Latin America have primate cities. However, the primate cities that are also capitals in the southern cone are unusual. There, an extremely large number of people within each nation live in the primate city. For example, about 33 percent of Chileans live in the city of Santiago. About the same percentage of all Argentines live in Buenos Aires. As for Asunción, it is home to 20 percent of Paraguay's population.

B. Buenos Aires: Capital of Argentina

With its broad boulevards, beautiful parks, rows of small eating places along tree-lined streets, fashionable shops, and fine restaurants, Buenos Aires often is called the Paris of South America. Archibald MacLeish, a famous United States author, visited Buenos Aires and came away very impressed. "Buenos Aires," he wrote, "is a great city in the sense in which Paris and London are great cities. It is a twentieth-century **metropolis** [main city] with all the fixings — crowds, avenues, parks, subways, confusion of tongues, screaming of brakes, and shining of movie theaters."

Its population of over 11 million people ranks Buenos Aires among the ten largest metropolitan areas in the entire world! It has the second largest metropolitan population in the Southern Hemisphere, after São Paulo, Brazil.

The economy of the city is based mainly on business, banking, and government. Most companies that do business in Argentina have their main offices in Buenos Aires. All the main government offices are there too. About three quarters of Argentina's manufacturing takes place in Buenos Aires. Meat packing, food processing, and the manufacture of many kinds of goods, such as clothing, furniture, and appliances, are important to the city's economy. Buenos Aires also serves as the nation's chief port.

Almost all of Buenos Aires's old buildings have been torn down to make way for modern office buildings. However, walk to the city's center, the Plaza de

THE SOUTHERN CONE: POLITICAL

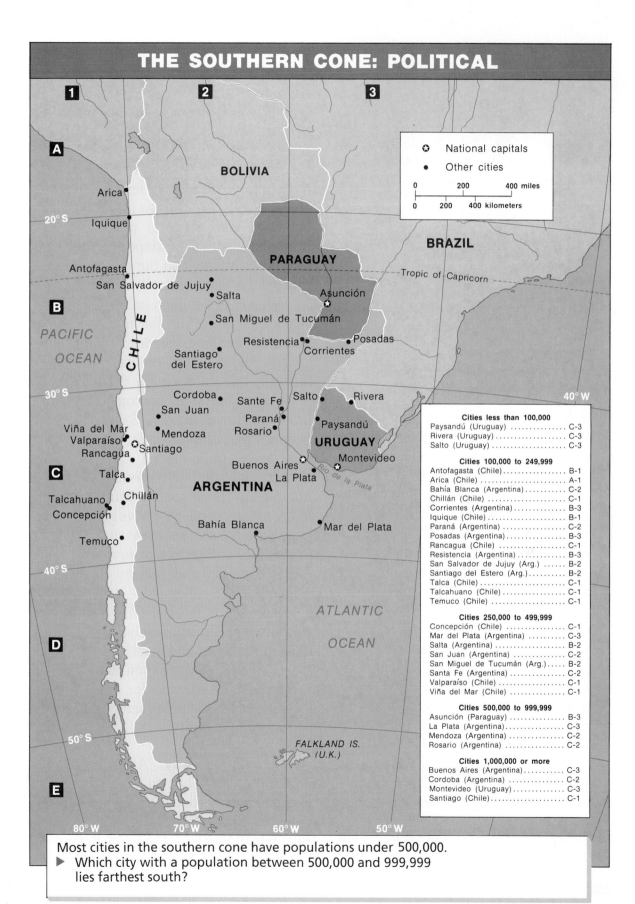

Legend

⊛ National capitals
● Other cities

0 — 200 — 400 miles
0 — 200 — 400 kilometers

BOLIVIA

BRAZIL

PARAGUAY

Asunción

Tropic of Capricorn

PACIFIC OCEAN

CHILE

Arica
Iquique
Antofagasta
San Salvador de Jujuy
Salta
San Miguel de Tucumán
Resistencia
Corrientes
Posadas
Santiago del Estero
Cordoba
San Juan
Sante Fe
Paraná
Rosario
Salto
Rivera
Paysandú
Viña del Mar
Valparaíso
Rancagua
Mendoza
Santiago
Buenos Aires
La Plata
Montevideo
Talca
Chillán
Talcahuano
Concepción
ARGENTINA
URUGUAY
Río de la Plata
Temuco
Bahía Blanca
Mar del Plata

ATLANTIC OCEAN

FALKLAND IS. (U.K.)

40° W

Cities less than 100,000
Paysandú (Uruguay) C-3
Rivera (Uruguay) C-3
Salto (Uruguay) C-3

Cities 100,000 to 249,999
Antofagasta (Chile) B-1
Arica (Chile) A-1
Bahía Blanca (Argentina) C-2
Chillán (Chile) C-1
Corrientes (Argentina) B-3
Iquique (Chile) B-1
Paraná (Argentina) C-2
Posadas (Argentina) B-3
Rancagua (Chile) C-1
Resistencia (Argentina) B-3
San Salvador de Jujuy (Arg.) B-2
Santiago del Estero (Arg.) B-2
Talca (Chile) C-1
Talcahuano (Chile) C-1
Temuco (Chile) C-1

Cities 250,000 to 499,999
Concepción (Chile) C-1
Mar del Plata (Argentina) C-3
Salta (Argentina) B-2
San Juan (Argentina) C-2
San Miguel de Tucumán (Arg.) B-2
Santa Fe (Argentina) C-2
Valparaíso (Chile) C-1
Viña del Mar (Chile) C-1

Cities 500,000 to 999,999
Asunción (Paraguay) B-3
La Plata (Argentina) C-3
Mendoza (Argentina) C-2
Rosario (Argentina) C-2

Cities 1,000,000 or more
Buenos Aires (Argentina) C-3
Cordoba (Argentina) C-3
Montevideo (Uruguay) C-3
Santiago (Chile) C-1

80° W   70° W   60° W   50° W

Most cities in the southern cone have populations under 500,000.
▶ Which city with a population between 500,000 and 999,999 lies farthest south?

The text tells you that the Presidential Palace is pink on the exterior.
▶ What does the photograph tell you about the interior?

Mayo, and you still can catch some flavor of days gone by. There, for example, you'll see the town hall where, in 1810, Mariano Moreno and his fellow citizens declared Buenos Aires independent. You should also pause for a moment at the cathedral, where José de San Martín, a hero of southern South America's independence struggle, is buried. The presidential palace, called the Casa Rosada ("Pink House") because of its color, stands at the far end of the plaza.

Walk west a few blocks to see the national Congress building, where the legislature meets. Then continue along for a bit to Ninth of July Avenue, one of the widest streets in the world. Another street, Florida, is for pedestrians only. No cars are allowed. The street of Florida is a favorite meeting place for the porteños (por TAYN-yohs), or port dwellers, the nickname given to people who live in Buenos Aires.

Porteños love to eat, especially beef, and they love to talk, especially about politics. Late into the night, you'll find them engaging in these favored pastimes in the many fine restaurants, cafeterias, and snack shops on, or near Florida Street.

C. Other Southern-Cone Capitals

Santiago, Chile On a clear day in Santiago, Chile, the snowcapped Andes can be seen in the distance, about 60 miles (97 km) away. Santiago is about 700 miles (1,126 km) to the west of Buenos Aires. The city has been destroyed several times by earthquakes, so only a few old buildings are left. Today's Santiago is a city of new buildings and beautiful parks. Flowing from east to west, the Mapocho River cuts through Santiago, and the several bridges that span it add to the city's charm.

With over 4 million people, the city is also a bustling center for much of Chile's business, banking, government, and industry. About half of the nation's manufacturing takes place in the Santiago area. Although Chile's population as a whole has not grown rapidly, Santiago's has. People from all over Chile, especially its rural areas, have moved to Santiago in search of jobs and better lives. A city cannot quickly create good housing and jobs. Many of the people who have gone to Santiago have not enjoyed great success. They live in huge **callampas**, or squatter settlements. Disease and hunger are all too common in the callampas.

Santiago is not the only city to face this problem. Unfortunately, squatter settlements exist around most of the region's great cities. However, as you learned when you read about Mexico, for many people the squatter settlements can be a starting place for opportunity.

Asunción, Paraguay Asunción stands on the shores of a bay on the eastern bank of the Paraguay River. It's a pleasant city, with tree-lined streets and several parks and public squares. Asunción is far less wealthy than Buenos Aires or Santiago. It

FROM:

Selected Poems of

Gabriela Mistral

Translated by: Langston Hughes

In 1945, the Chilean poet Gabriela Mistral, 1889–1957, became the first Latin American writer to receive a Nobel Prize in literature. Even as a young schoolteacher, she won awards for her poetry. Her subjects are often mothers and children and the love between them. Later in her life, Mistral represented her country at the League of Nations and the United Nations.

Langston Hughes, 1902–1967, a famous American poet and writer, lived most of his life in Harlem in New York. However, he lived in Mexico City, Mexico, as a child. He also spent time in Cuba and in Spain in his adult years. Mistral was a literary friend of Langston Hughes, and he translated many of her poems into English and published them. One of the poems appears below.

Fear

I do not want them to turn
my child into a swallow;
she might fly away into the sky
and never come down again to my
doormat;
or nest in the eaves where my hands
could not comb her hair.
I do not want them to turn
my child into a swallow.

I do not want them to make
my child into a princess.
In tiny golden slippers how could
she play in the field?
And when night came, no longer
would she lie by my side.
I do not want them to make
my child into a princess.

And I would like even less
that one day they crown her queen.
They would raise her to a throne
where my feet could not climb.
I could not rock her to sleep
when nighttime came.
I do not want them to make
my child into a queen.

Avenida 18 de Julio in downtown Montevideo is shown here.
▶ What might the name of the avenue commemorate?

number of interesting sights, including a beautiful theater and the Museum of Natural History. Walk west from Independence Square and in just a little while you'll see Plaza Constitución, or Constitution Square, the oldest plaza in the city. There you can visit the town hall, first built in 1804, where the Uruguayan patriots declared independence from Spain. Before leaving Montevideo, you might as well join many Uruguayans and foreigners and enjoy one of the many beautiful beaches that extend along the waterfront. If you'd rather try a resort, you won't have far to go. It's just a few minutes ride from Montevideo to Punta del Este. This lovely resort has been a meeting place for presidents, foreign ministers, and officials of the Organization of American States.

doesn't have a subway system, and many of its streets lack storm sewers. When the rains fall heavily, the streets flood. Asunción has a colorful botanical garden that includes plants and a museum with Indian and historical exhibitions. The large open markets sell fresh foods, leather goods, pottery, and handicrafts.

Montevideo, Uruguay Founded in 1726, Montevideo also enjoys a scenic location, on the **estuary** of the Río de la Plata, east of Buenos Aires. An estuary is the wide mouth of a river into which the tide flows. With this excellent location, Montevideo serves as Uruguay's main port. Around 90 percent of all the nation's imports and exports pass through Montevideo.

If you want to get the feel of this metropolis, head down to the Plaza Independencia. You'll know it by the statue of José Artigas, the hero of Uruguayan independence. From the square you're close to a

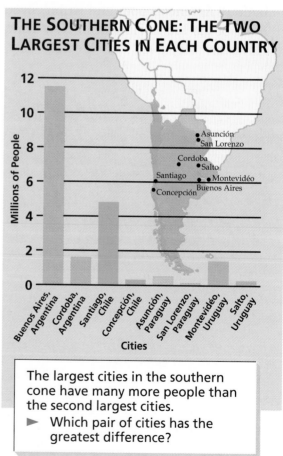

THE SOUTHERN CONE: THE TWO LARGEST CITIES IN EACH COUNTRY

The largest cities in the southern cone have many more people than the second largest cities.
▶ Which pair of cities has the greatest difference?

In this harbor view of Valparaíso, only small vessels are near land.
▶ What types of ships might be anchored farther out to sea?

D. Regional Centers in Argentina

Although Buenos Aires dominates the nation, Argentina also has several smaller cities that are important regional centers. La Plata, the capital of Buenos Aires province, stands at one end of a manufacturing zone that extends to Rosario, some 200 miles (322 km) from Buenos Aires. Córdoba is an important center for the making of transportation equipment.

Tucumán and Mendoza are the major cities of Argentina's west. Both are important agricultural centers. Tucumán is in a sugar-growing area. Mendoza is in Argentina's main wine-producing center. The area's warm, dry summers are ideal for grape growing.

E. Two Chilean Cities

On the Pacific coast, about 75 miles (121 km) west of Santiago, you find Chile's main port and third largest city, Valparaíso (val puh RAH zoh). Goods shipped by sea to and from Santiago go through the port at Valparaíso. As you may recall, the city of Concepción is in an important manufacturing region. Steel is made there, because coal and iron ore are both available. Coal is mined nearby, and iron ore can be shipped cheaply by sea from the mining areas north of Valparaíso. The Concepción area also has textile, paper, glass, and cement industries. Concepción, Chile's second largest city, is near the oil-producing areas in Tierra del Fuego, so it is also an oil-refining and chemical center.

LESSON *3* REVIEW

THINK AND WRITE

A. What is unusual about the population in the southern-cone capital cities?

B. Why do some people say that Buenos Aires is one of the world's great cities?

C. How would you describe Santiago, Asunción, and Montevideo?

D. What are some of Argentina's important regional centers?

E. Why are Valparaíso and Concepción important to Chile?

SKILLS CHECK

MAP SKILL

Use the Gazetteer and the map on page 437 to locate as many cities as you can that are mentioned in this lesson. Then write a short description comparing or contrasting two of the cities.

The Return of Democracy

Think about the leadership of a country being taken over by another country, group, or person. What options do the people have if they do not agree with the takeover?

amnesty

What major political change occurred in the southern cone in the 1980s?

Some Argentine soldiers wait for orders; others inspect damage to buildings in a town.
▶ With whom did Argentina fight?

A. The Dirty War

When the military in Argentina arrested Isabel Perón in 1976 and took over the government, it promised to restore order. To do so, it moved against the various guerrilla groups that had become increasingly bold during the early 1970s. The army and police arrested anyone even suspected of being a guerrilla or of helping the guerrillas. Soon, however, it seemed clear that the generals thought that anyone who criticized the government was on the side of the guerrillas. More and more people were arrested. Often they were tortured or killed. As many as 15,000 people may have been killed by the military and police between 1976 and 1981.

Argentina's economy did well for a while, but things became just as bad as they had been before the military took over. Then, in 1982, Argentina had a brief war with Great Britain. It was fought over some islands in the South Atlantic off the coast of Argentina. Argentina calls the islands Malvinas (mal VEE nus) and claims that they are Argentine territory. Great Britain refers to them as the Falkland Islands and has administered them as British territory since 1833.

Argentina lost the war, and that marked the end for the military government. People began to make fun of the military. The military, they said, wanted to run the country, but it couldn't even run a war properly. A democratically elected president, Raúl Alfonsín, took over in 1983. Argentine citizens rejoiced, but they also wanted justice. The military had waged a "dirty war" against its own citizens, said the people. Should it not stand trial for its crimes? Alfonsín's government courageously put senior officers on trial. This outraged the military and led to several military revolts. Alfonsín's government held on until 1989. When citizens took to the streets to protest high unemployment and the inflation of food prices, Alfonsín left office six months early. The new president, Carlos Saúl Menem, moved quickly to deal with Argentina's economic problems. He also welcomed foreign investment. "We Peronists," said Menem, "cannot continue thinking in 1991 as we did in 1945."

B. The Military in Uruguay

In 1973, tanks rumbled along the streets of Montevideo. The Uruguayan military had taken over the government. Twelve years of repression followed. In Uruguay—as in Argentina, Chile, and Paraguay—opponents of the government "disappeared." They were snatched off the streets or taken from their homes. Some were jailed. Others were killed. Military rule took away all the people's democratic freedoms. Eventually, more and more Uruguayans pushed for a return to democracy.

In 1985, the generals who were ruling Uruguay stepped down. Before they gave up control, however, the generals de-

The soon-to-be president, Julio María Sanguinetti, casts his ballot in the presidential election.
▶ For whom do presidential candidates probably vote?

manded **amnesty**, or freedom from prosecution. They did not want to stand trial for crimes against the Uruguayan people. The new civilian president, Julio María Sanguinetti, helped to pass an amnesty law. He said that amnesty was "an acceptable cost" for political peace, but other Uruguayans disagreed.

C. Hope in Chile

The military had held power in Chile since 1973. Nonetheless, by the end of the 1980s, Chileans had high hopes that their country soon would follow the example of Argentina and Uruguay. General Augusto Pinochet, the president of the Military Junta, had tried to extend his rule by offering a plebiscite on the presidency. A plebiscite is a vote that shows how people feel about a question or a problem. This gave the people of Chile a choice. A "Yes" vote would extend Pinochet's term. A "No" vote would mean that the general would leave office in 1990 so that elections for a new president could be held. The results of the plebiscite made one thing very clear. The people of Chile overwhelmingly said "No" to Pinochet and "Yes" to democracy. Soon Chile inaugurated a new, democratically elected president, Patricio Aylwin.

D. The Dictator of Paraguay

As the elections of 1988 approached in Paraguay, everyone knew who was going to win. General Alfredo Stroessner, the son of a German immigrant, had taken power in 1954. Thirty-four years later he was the world's second longest ruling dictator. The election went as expected, although the opposition parties declared that the results were incorrectly reported. Stroessner won an eighth term, capturing 90 percent of the vote. Then something unexpected occurred. A quick but bloody military coup drove Stroessner from office. A general named Andres Rodríguez led the coup and took over as temporary president. He promised to hold free elections and bring democracy to Paraguay.

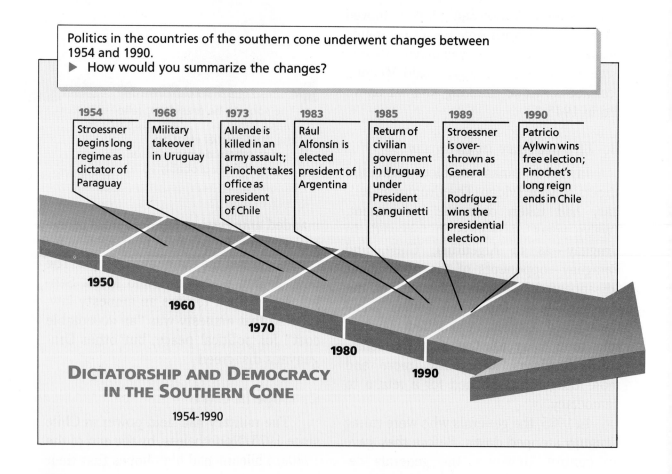

Politics in the countries of the southern cone underwent changes between 1954 and 1990.
▶ How would you summarize the changes?

1954	1968	1973	1983	1985	1989	1990
Stroessner begins long regime as dictator of Paraguay	Military takeover in Uruguay	Allende is killed in an army assault; Pinochet takes office as president of Chile	Rául Alfonsín is elected president of Argentina	Return of civilian government in Uruguay under President Sanguinetti	Stroessner is overthrown as General Rodríguez wins the presidential election	Patricio Aylwin wins free election; Pinochet's long reign ends in Chile

1950 1960 1970 1980 1990

DICTATORSHIP AND DEMOCRACY IN THE SOUTHERN CONE

1954-1990

(Top) President Stroessner walks alongside Pope John Paul II, who is on a visit to Paraguay. (Bottom) In May 1993 Juan Carlos Wasmosy becomes the first freely elected president in Paraguay's 182 years of independence.
▶ Why are Wasmosy's supporters carrying red flags?

Many Paraguayans rejoiced. However, General Rodríguez himself always had supported Stroessner. Opponents said that Rodríguez would simply take the old Stroessner system and dress it in more modern clothes. Rodríguez surprised these critics by allowing more freedom of the press and promoting human rights. He also promised to hand power over to an elected successor in 1993. Rodríguez kept that promise, and for the first time in its history, Paraguay had a democratically elected president, Juan Carlos Wasmosy.

LESSON **4** *REVIEW*

THINK AND WRITE

A. Summarize the events that led to the military's loss of power in Argentina.
B. Tell why you agree or don't agree with the Argentine citizens' demands that the military leaders be put on trial.
C. What were the results of the plebiscite on the presidency in Chile?
D. What predictions would you make about Paraguay's future after Wasmosy's election?

SKILLS CHECK

WRITING SKILL

The Falkland Islands consist of two main islands near Argentina. There are only about 1,800 inhabitants. The islands are more than 8,000 miles from Great Britain but less than 300 miles from Argentina. Take the side of either Great Britain or Argentina. Write a paragraph that tells why you think "your" country should be the sole owner.

445

USING THE VOCABULARY

estuary
callampa
amnesty
estancia
hydroelectric
metropolis

On a separate sheet of paper, write the number of the definition and the word from the list that matches the definition.

1. squatter settlement
2. having to do with electricity produced by water power
3. freedom from prosecution
4. large ranch
5. wide mouth of a river into which the tide flows

REMEMBERING WHAT YOU READ

1. What natural resource has contributed to the importance of Argentina as a world producer of food?
2. Briefly describe the life of an Argentine gaucho in the 1500s.
3. On which mineral does Chile's economy depend?
4. From what countries did people emigrate to settle in the southern cone?
5. Which country, however, has a population that is mostly of mestizo heritage?
6. Does the largest majority of the people of the southern cone live in urban or in rural areas?
7. For what are some of the regional centers of Argentina known?
8. Which two cities are important to Chile? Tell why.
9. What event marked the end of the military government in Argentina in 1982?
10. Did the people of Chile vote "Yes" or "No" on the plebiscite to end the military rule of Pinochet?

TYING POETRY AND ART TO SOCIAL STUDIES

Use the excerpt from the poem "Martin Fierro" by José Hernandez on page 428 about the life of the gaucho. Copy a part of the poem that you like and illustrate it to show details about the life of this legendary hero. If your prefer, look instead for a book about South America that contains information on gauchos and write a short illustrated report.

THINKING CRITICALLY

On a separate sheet of paper, answer the following questions in complete sentences.

1. How could Chile change its economy by making better use of its land?
2. How might the southern cone's power sources make it an important region in the Western Hemisphere?
3. Why, do you think, does the culture of Paraguayans differ from that of the other countries of the southern cone?
4. What is notable about the capital cities of the southern cone?
5. Do you think the countries of the southern cone are progressing toward more democratic governments?

SUMMARIZING THE CHAPTER

On a separate sheet of paper, draw a graphic organizer like the one shown here. Copy the information from this graphic organizer on the one you have drawn. Under each lesson heading, fill in the blanks with facts you learned from that lesson.

CHAPTER THEME

The southern cone today has the possibility of economic well-being and democracy.

LESSON 1
The Economy

1. Argentina –
2. Uruguay –
3. Paraguay –
4. Chile –

LESSON 2
The Different Peoples

1.
2.
3.

LESSON 3
Facts About Important Cities

1. Buenos Aires –
2. Santiago –
3. Asunción –
4. Montevideo –

LESSON 4
Dictatorship and Democracy

1. Argentina –
2. Uruguay –
3. Chile –
4. Paraguay –

18

BRAZIL

*L*atin America's largest country, Brazil, is actually larger than the mainland United States. This vast, populated land has a variety of people, climate, and resources. Its leaders struggle with a huge and complex economy.

Land and Climate

A. A Big Country

Glance at the map shown on this page and you can see why people usually refer to Brazil as "the giant of South America." Brazil occupies about half of all the land in South America. As the fifth largest country in area in the world, Brazil is larger than the 48 states on the mainland of the United States. Because of its great size and location, Brazil shares borders with all but two of the other countries in South America. Locate those two countries on the map of South America, page 17.

North to south, Brazil sprawls 2,670 miles (4,296 km), just about the same as its east-west distance. As you might expect, its land and climate show plenty of variety.

B. Highland Areas

If you don't like high places, Brazil might be just the place for you to visit some day. Less than 1 percent of Brazil's land area has elevations higher than 3,900 feet (1,188 m). Brazil's highest mountain, Pico da Neblina (neb LEE nuh) rises slightly over 9,888 feet (3,014 m). Compare that with the towering height of Cotopaxi in Ecuador.

Brazil's highlands may not be very high, but they make up almost half of the country's territory. The largest of these, the Brazilian Highlands, account for most of the country's highland area. The Brazilian Highlands are really a large plateau in the central and eastern areas of the country. There are two smaller highland areas. Far to the north, Brazil shares part of the Guiana Highlands with Venezuela and the Guianas. A smaller area of highlands, the Paraná Plateau, lies to the south, along the Paraguayan and Argentine borders.

C. Lowlands and Rivers

Narrow Coastal Plains Narrow coastal plains run along the entire length of Brazil's Atlantic coast, a distance of more than 4,658 miles (7,500 km). Most of the plains are in a tropical area. On the coastal plains of northeastern Brazil, the first great sugar plantations were developed.

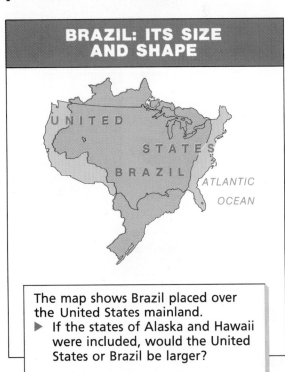

BRAZIL: ITS SIZE AND SHAPE

The map shows Brazil placed over the United States mainland.
► If the states of Alaska and Hawaii were included, would the United States or Brazil be larger?

BRAZIL: PHYSICAL

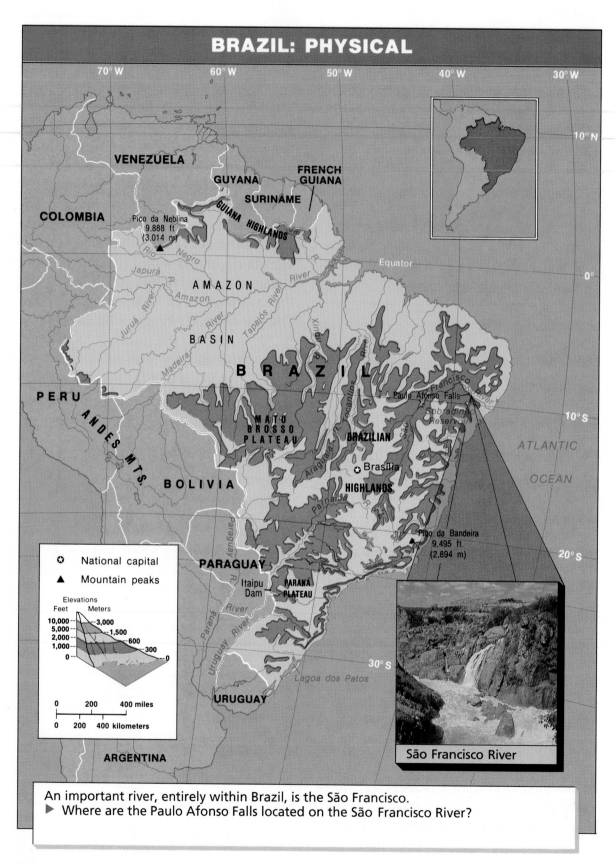

70° W **60° W** **50° W** **40° W** **30° W**

10° N

VENEZUELA

GUYANA

FRENCH GUIANA

SURINAME

COLOMBIA

Pico da Neblina
9,888 ft
(3.014 m)

GUIANA HIGHLANDS

Rio Negro

Japurá

AMAZON

Amazon

Equator

0°

Juruá River

Madeira River

Tapajós River

BASIN

Xingu River

B R A Z I L

PERU

ANDES MTS.

MATO GROSSO PLATEAU

Araguaia R.

Tocantins R.

BRAZILIAN

Francisco River

Paulo Afonso Falls

Sobradinho Reservoir

10° S

ATLANTIC

OCEAN

BOLIVIA

Brasília

HIGHLANDS

Parnaíba R.

Paraguay R.

Pico da Bandeira
9,495 ft.
(2,894 m)

20° S

National capital

Mountain peaks

Elevations
Feet   Meters
10,000 — 3,000
5,000 — 1,500
2,000 — 600
1,000 — 300
0 — 0

PARAGUAY

Itaipu Dam

PARANÁ PLATEAU

Paraná R.

Uruguay River

Lagoa dos Patos

30° S

0   200   400 miles

0   200   400 kilometers

URUGUAY

ARGENTINA

São Francisco River

An important river, entirely within Brazil, is the São Francisco.
▶ Where are the Paulo Afonso Falls located on the São Francisco River?

The Amazon Basin You've already read about another of Brazil's lowland areas, the Amazon Basin. The Amazon Basin occupies about 46 percent of Brazil's area, and it has the world's largest area of dense tropical forest. Most of the Amazon Basin has a low elevation. The lowlands of the Amazon Basin account for about 30 percent of Brazilian territory. They offer many resources, including important commercial woods, such as mahogany and rosewood. This vast lowland area, larger than most of the other nations of Latin America, still has not been fully explored.

Important Rivers Of course, if you think about the Amazon Basin, the Amazon River comes to mind. As you may recall from Chapter 1, the Amazon is the second longest river in the world. Because of the Amazon River's size and extent, it naturally attracts a great deal of attention. However, Brazil does have other important rivers. The São Francisco River, in the eastern section of the Brazilian Highlands, is another important river. From its source in the highlands, it runs some 1,800 miles (2,896 km) north. There, the beautiful Paulo Afonso Falls are found. Below the falls, the São Francisco flows on for another 188 miles (302 km). It empties into the Atlantic Ocean between the northeastern cities of Recife (ruh SEE fuh) and Salvador. Along the middle part of its length, the São Francisco is navigable for about 1,000 miles (1,600 km). This river has considerable commercial importance.

Farther south are two rivers you've already read about—the Paraná and the Paraguay. The Paraná flows south from the Brazilian Highlands. The Paraguay River, a tributary of the Paraná, is nearly as long as the Paraná. The Paraguay River also flows from the Brazilian Highlands. As you learned in Chapter 17, the Paraguay River is the site of important hydroelectric projects. Together the three rivers drain southern Brazil as well as portions of Argentina, Paraguay, and Uruguay.

D. Tropical Brazil

Mainly a Tropical Climate "I live in a tropical country, blessed by the sun."

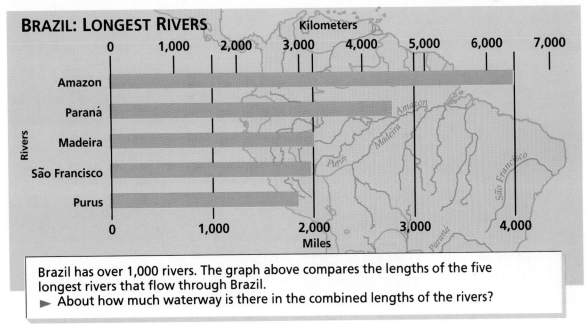

Brazil has over 1,000 rivers. The graph above compares the lengths of the five longest rivers that flow through Brazil.
► About how much waterway is there in the combined lengths of the rivers?

That's the first line of a popular Brazilian song. Most of Brazil lies within the tropics and has a tropical climate. The largest area of rainy tropical climate is in the Amazon Basin. Temperatures there are warm.

Most of the Brazilian coast south of the city of Fortaleza (fawr tuh LAY zuh) also has a rainy tropical climate. A forest like the Amazon selva once covered the coast, but most of it was cleared for lumber or for farmland many years ago.

Savanna Areas The southern part of the Amazon Basin and most of the Brazilian Highlands have a tropical climate that is dry for part of the year. The dry season usually lasts for three to five months. Dry weather and poor soils prevent most trees from growing. The main vegetation of these areas is savanna, with scattered thickets of **scrub**—short, stubby trees. The trees do not grow very high because of the conditions of the land. The Brazilians call these areas *campos cerrados* (KAHM pus suh RAH doh), or "closed fields." They are important cattle-grazing areas.

The northeastern part of Brazil is in an area of high temperatures but little rainfall. In most of northeastern Brazil, there is usually enough rain for cattle ranching, but there are many places where farming is not possible without irrigation.

A Drought Area The length of the dry season of the northeast varies. Sometimes it lasts for only four or five months. At other times the dry season lasts all year. When the dry season is very long, there is **drought**, a long period of dry weather with little or no precipitation. Cattle starve to death or die of thirst, and people move to wetter parts of Brazil to find a way to live. The drought area is called the **sertão** (ser-TOUN). The vegetation of the sertão is a

Cattle graze on pasture land that has been cleared from the forest.
▶ Do you think that the trees are an effective fence to keep the cattle in?

452

(Left) Loggers saw Paraná pines to prepare logs to be shipped.
(Right) A timber raft is tugged along the Rio Negro, a tributary of the Amazon River.
▶ What will happen to the logs next?

forest of cactus, thorn bushes, and certain trees and plants that can survive for months with little or no water.

E. Temperate Brazil

Snow comes every winter to parts of Brazil's southern highlands. Most of Brazil south of the state of São Paulo has a temperate climate. Summers are long and warm, and winters are mild. However, winter cold spells bring freezing temperatures and sometimes snow.

Forests of **araucaria** (ar aw KER-ee uh) trees once covered part of temperate Brazil. These trees are sometimes called Paraná pines. They have soft wood that is useful for lumber. Because of this, the araucaria forests are being cleared rapidly. Some scientists believe that all the araucaria forests will be gone by the year 2000. South of the forests, a part of the Pampas extends north into Brazil. As in Argentina and Uruguay, the Pampas of Brazil are important for cattleraising.

LESSON **1** *REVIEW*

THINK AND WRITE

A. What are some important facts about Brazil's size and location?
B. How would you describe Brazil's largest highland area?
C. Describe the two important lowland areas in Brazil.
D. Summarize the areas of tropical Brazil by their climates.

E. Where is temperate Brazil located?

SKILLS CHECK

THINKING SKILLS

Think about a dry area and an area that has drought. What are some results of the climate in each type of area?

453

YOU DECIDE: SHOULD THE AMAZON RAIN FOREST BE SAVED?

You have already learned that the Amazon rain forest is the world's largest tropical forest. Much of it lies in Brazil, but it also stretches into Venezuela, Colombia, Bolivia, and Peru. The Amazon River, swelled by its more than 1,000 tributaries, flows through the rain forest.

This forest is one of the largest storehouses of natural resources on earth. Over half of the world's plant and animal species are found there. It is also a source of food and other products, such as chemicals used to make different medicines. The rain forest is important because its moist air creates many clouds. These clouds play a crucial role in how heat from the sun is distributed around the globe.

The Amazon rain forest is in grave danger. Large areas are being cleared of trees every day to make room for farms. The forest has become a frontier for Brazilians looking for a better way of life. Loggers constantly level trees to produce lumber to sell. Dams flood vast areas of land, and gold miners pollute and poison the rivers with mercury and other impurities. The Brazilian government refuses to stop the exploitation of the forest. It even encourages it.

This Land Is Needed for Settlers

Brazil has always wanted to settle the Amazon to secure its borders. Since 1970, more than 3 million people have gone north, to the rain forest region, to improve their lives. The government promised, and had provided them with, some schools, hospitals, and other public services, as well as help in developing their farms. However, debt to foreign creditors has kept the government from fulfilling all its promises. The settlers, who now have no resources except their plots of land, are holding on to them. As the cleared land loses its nutrients and becomes useless, more trees are cut down for farmland.

Many other people, such as loggers and gold miners, also make their living by clearing the forest. The Brazilian government argues that it will need help in developing other parts of its economy if the rain forest is not cleared and development of thriving communities does not occur. Most Brazilians who left other parts of Brazil to move to the region still hold on to their dream that life will improve for them.

We Must Save the Rain Forest!

The Amazon rain forest produces clouds of wet air that keep the entire world from overheating. If the rain forest disappears, the atmosphere will get warmer. Scientists warn that if the average temperature of the air rises, even by one degree, it might cause the ice caps at the North and South poles to begin melting. This could cause flooding, especially along coastlines in many parts of the world. Environmentalists also fear that large amounts of carbon dioxide released by burning the trees could poison the atmosphere and create problems worldwide.

The rain forest is home to 200,000 Indians. The destruction of the forest would mean the loss of their habitat. Eighty Indian cultures have already become extinct. The animals of the tropical forest would also lose their habitat and many might become extinct.

The United States and many other countries are trying to convince Brazil to stop the destruction of the rain forest. Scientists, especially environmentalists, are leading the crusade to save the rain forest.

Thinking for Yourself

On a separate sheet of paper, write your answers in complete sentences.

1. Tell which point of view you agree with and why.
2. What are some ways you might convince the Brazilian government to save the rain forest?
3. Over 100 years ago, Americans cleared huge areas of forest to create farms. Did that cause any harm?

Imperial Brazil

THINK ABOUT WHAT YOU KNOW
Imagine that you moved to a new place and formed a big club. Then you move back to where you lived before, but it's far away from the club. What could you do to make sure the club held together?

STUDY THE VOCABULARY
abdicate
regent

FOCUS YOUR READING
What important things happened in Brazil during the time it was a monarchy?

A. Independence or Death

Pedro I Astride his horse by the Ipiranga River, and with his sword raised high, young Prince Pedro issued a defiant grito, or cry: "Independence or Death." The year was 1822. The event signaled the beginning of independence for Brazil.

Pedro, as you learned in Chapter 7, was the son of the Portuguese king, John VI. In 1807, John, his family, and the royal court of about 15,000 people had gone to Brazil to escape the armies of Napoleon. When the threat to Portugal ended in 1821, John returned to his native land. Who, then, would rule Brazil?

That question had great importance because at that very time, as you may recall, much of Latin America had declared its independence. According to one story, John told his son, "Pedro, I fear Brazil might separate itself from Portugal. If so, place the crown on your own head, rather than allow it to fall into the hands of an adventurer."

Independence Day The new Portuguese legislature tried to turn back the clock and make Brazil just a simple colony. That angered many Brazilians. After all, John VI had raised Brazil to the status of a kingdom, and during John's years in Rio de Janeiro, Brazil really had been the center of the worldwide Portuguese empire. Return to colonial status after that? Never! The desire for independence grew quickly. Pedro, then 24 years old, made his cry at Ipiranga on September 7, 1822 — the date that Brazilians celebrate as their independence day.

B. Pedro II

A Child Emperor Pedro I did not have a happy reign. Although Brazilians enjoyed their independence and were proud to have a monarch, they did not quite trust their new ruler. All his advisors were from Portugal, and he seemed more concerned with events in that country than with helping Brazil to prosper. After ten years,

Because Pedro II liked the fresh mountain air north of Rio, he had his summer home built there — and built a city, Petropolis, around it.
► What might the mansion be today?

After a long trip through the United States, Emperor Pedro II sails from New York harbor in 1876.
▶ What is he doing with his hat?

Pedro **abdicated** the throne, and went back to Portugal. To abdicate is to give up a position of power, such as a kingship. However, Pedro passed the crown of Brazil on to his son, who also was named Pedro. At that time, the eldest son of a king usually inherited the throne, so Pedro I's action was not that unusual — except for one thing. His son was only five years old! Certainly the new king was bound to have trouble wearing his father's crown.

Rule by Regents For some time, of course, this very young emperor, officially Pedro II, did not really rule. Instead, advisors acted for him as his **regents**. A regent is someone who rules in place of a king for a time when the king is unable to govern or is away. Such a period, therefore, is known as a regency. In Brazil, it lasted until 1840.

For much of that time, Brazil experienced the same type of turmoil you have read about in the early histories of many other of the new nations of Latin America. Major revolts occurred throughout Brazil's vast territory, and people feared the nation might break up into several smaller countries. In 1844, when Pedro finally reached the age of 18 and was supposed to take the throne, would there even be a Brazilian nation? Pedro didn't wait to find out. Five months short of his fifteenth birthday, he agreed to take on this great responsibility.

C. A Long Reign

Brazil's Gains He began as Brazil's boy emperor. When he left office in 1889, he was a man nearing the end of his life. The changes in Brazil were just as dramatic.

457

Because of Pedro's strong rule, Brazil actually grew in size. It gained some territory through skill in dealing with other nations, and it gained other land through war. Brazil also began to produce an important new product, coffee. Coffee became very popular, especially in the latter part of the nineteenth century. It became Brazil's chief export crop. Today, Brazil is still the world's largest producer of coffee.

The Southeast Prospers Coffee was grown in the Southeast, and as the century wore on, that region grew richer. Beginning in the 1880s, the region attracted many immigrants, especially Italians, to work on the coffee plantations. At that same time, the city of São Paulo experienced growth. It became the collection center for coffee grown throughout the region. From São Paulo, a new railroad, built by British engineers, crossed the steep slope between the highland and the port city of Santos. The growing importance of coffee took place at a time when prices for Brazilian sugar began to go down. The Northeast grew poorer while the Southeast grew richer. Some people said that the Northeast had depended too much on sugar and slavery.

D. Slavery in Brazil

As you may recall, slavery began in Brazil during the colonial era. Slavery continued in Brazil longer than in any other South American country. Brazil participated in the trade of slaves from Africa until 1850. That was long after the other independent countries of Latin America had abolished slavery. Slavery had also ended years before in the West Indian colonies of the British, French, and Dutch. Even after ending its slave trade, Brazil allowed slavery to continue until 1888.

Earlier you learned that producing sugar takes a great amount of labor. For much of the nineteenth century, the large sugar plantations of northeastern Brazil relied almost entirely on slave labor. Because of the end of the slave trade, the price for slaves rose. At the same time, the drop in sugar prices resulted in less money for the northeastern planters. Some planters, therefore, sold their slaves and moved to the Southeast. Then the coffee planters turned around and encouraged more immigration and began using new immigrants as laborers.

The economic base that supported slavery grew weaker, but pressure to end

IMMIGRATION TO BRAZIL: 1884-1913

Countries (of greatest immigration)	1884-1893	1894-1903	1904-1913
Germany	23,000	7,000	34,000
Italy	511,000	538,000	197,000
Japan	-	-	12,000
Portugal	171,000	158,000	385,000
Russia	41,000	3,000	48,000
Spain	103,000	102,000	225,000

BRAZIL

People from many countries immigrated to Brazil. The table shows six countries from which the greatest number of immigrants came.

► From which country did Brazil receive the greatest number of immigrants between 1884 and 1913?

A slave trader is shown trying to sell a man as a slave.
▶ What might this trader have said to convince the buyer?

slavery grew stronger. Joaquim Nabuco, a lawyer and politician from northeastern Brazil, was one of the Brazilians who spoke out forcefully against slavery. He warned, "Slavery is an institution which destroys and degrades everything." Moving slowly but surely, Brazil began to end slavery. In 1871, a law declared children of slaves to be free when they reached the age of 18. This became known as the Law of Free Birth. Then in 1885, another law freed all slaves over the age of 60. One more step remained. Three years later, in 1888, the "Golden Law" put an end to Brazilian slavery. As you will read in the next lesson, it also helped to end the Brazilian empire.

LESSON 2 REVIEW

THINK AND WRITE

A. What made Pedro I decide to declare Brazil's independence?

B. Why was there a period known as the Regency?

C. How did Brazil change during the long reign of Pedro II?

D. What steps ended slavery in Brazil?

SKILLS CHECK

WRITING SKILL

Use the information in this lesson to make a time line with some facts about the rulers who are mentioned. Begin with the year 1808 and end with the year 1889.

The Brazilian Republic

THINK ABOUT WHAT YOU KNOW

When people want a change, it usually means that they are not happy with a situation that affects them. Why might some people have been dissatisfied with the situation in Brazil in 1888?

STUDY THE VOCABULARY

censor
foreign debt

FOCUS YOUR READING

What major political changes have taken place in Brazil since it became a republic?

A. The End of an Empire

Unrest Among Planters The empire ended suddenly. In 1888, Pedro II, who loved to travel, had journeyed to Europe.

He left his daughter, Princess Isabella, as his regent. It was Isabella, in fact, who approved the Golden Law, which ended slavery. Slavery's end troubled those sugar and coffee planters who had large numbers of slaves. The Golden Law did not make any provision for paying the planters for the freed slaves.

The Republic of Brazil Other Brazilians had complaints too. Many business people thought that the empire didn't understand their needs. They wanted new government policies to help Brazil become a more modern nation. Military leaders thought Pedro's government had not given them enough support. They, too, believed that Brazil needed to change. The empire had no place in the modern world. The military, with support from the various other people who wanted change, overthrew the empire in 1889. Brazil became a republic.

Pedro II was in command as emperor until the year after slavery ended in Brazil.
▶ How long was the reign of Pedro II?

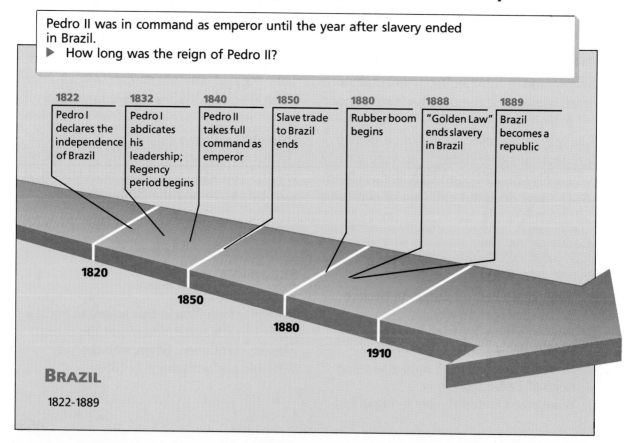

1822	1832	1840	1850	1880	1888	1889
Pedro I declares the independence of Brazil	Pedro I abdicates his leadership; Regency period begins	Pedro II takes full command as emperor	Slave trade to Brazil ends	Rubber boom begins	"Golden Law" ends slavery in Brazil	Brazil becomes a republic

1820

1850

1880

1910

BRAZIL

1822-1889

B. The Politics of Coffee

Brazil did not enjoy a happy beginning. A new constitution, adopted in 1891, made Brazil a federal republic, and the country's 20 provinces became states. The constitution gave the new states a great deal of independence. However, despite the constitution, Brazil went through a period in which rural violence and urban unrest occurred.

When Brazil became stable later in the 1890s, it was because of an arrangement between two of the countrys's most powerful states, São Paulo and Minas Gerais. They agreed to support each other's candidates for president, taking turns every four years. São Paulo and Minas Gerais, along with Rio de Janeiro, were the major coffee-producing states in Brazil.

The agreement gave Brazil a stable political system. However, the wealthy states, such as São Paulo, got most of the benefits. Once again, the republic seemed just as out of touch with the country's needs as the empire had been.

C. Getúlio Vargas

If you asked Brazilians to name the most important political figures in their country in the entire twentieth century, many of them would name Getúlio Vargas (zhuh TOO yoo VAR gus). Vargas came to power in a military coup in 1930. He ruled Brazil for the next 15 years and was important in Brazilian politics until his death in 1954.

Born in 1888, Vargas was the son of a wealthy cattle rancher in the southern Brazilian state of Rio Grande do Sul. As a young man, he attended military schools. Then, in 1907, he decided to become a law-

Getúlio Vargas, a popular leader of Brazil, is shown here.
▶ What in his background helped Vargas as he ruled Brazil?

yer. Vargas had a keen interest in politics. He quickly rose through the ranks of government in his home state and became governor in 1928.

When Vargas took over Brazil in 1930, he soon drew up important reforms. These included the writing of a new constitution, which gave more power to the central government. A new election law guaranteed a secret ballot and lowered the voting age from 21 to 18. It also gave women the right to vote.

D. From President to Dictator

In 1934, Vargas won election as Brazil's first president under the new constitution. That constitution did not allow a president to serve more than a single term. When Vargas reached the end of his term of office, he set up a coup to keep himself in power. From 1937 to 1945, the former president ruled as a dictator.

During this time, the central government gained even more power, and Vargas, as its head, began to reorganize Brazilian society. Workers gained the right to organize unions as well as a guaranteed minimum wage and retirement plans. Schools, highways, and other public works were built. Above all, Vargas encouraged industrial development. He took special pride in the building of the huge Volta Redonda steel plant. All of this was part of what Vargas called *O Estado Novo,* "the New State." Although this New State had many good programs, it was not democratic. Vargas jailed his opponents, took away the political rights of citizens, and **censored** the press so that he could not be criticized. To censor is to keep people from saying or printing anything that is thought to be harmful, usually to the government in power.

E. Democracy and the Military

Last Years for Vargas The New State ended in 1945, when the army forced Vargas from the presidency. Vargas stayed on in politics, serving as a senator. Then, in 1950, he ran for the presidency and won! However, this time he seemed to have lost his knack for solving problems. In 1954, the military ordered him to resign. Sadly, Vargas committed suicide.

Three Civilian Leaders After Vargas, three civilian presidents headed Brazil in a period of ten years. During that time, industry grew, and new roads penetrated the isolated interior of the country. During the administration of Juscelino Kubitschek (KOO buh chek), who became president in 1955, Brazil built a new national capital in the middle of the country. You will read about this amazing new capital, Brasília, in the next chapter.

The military again took over the country in 1964, and for the next 20 years, military governments ruled Brazil. The Brazilian economy began to grow at an enormous rate. Foreign companies helped the country become the biggest industrial power in Latin America. Commercial agriculture expanded, and cattle ranching grew. More new highways crossed the country, and hydroelectric plants began supplying the booming economy's ever-growing need for energy. Both at home and abroad, people spoke about the "Brazilian Miracle."

F. Problems That Needed Solutions

Another Side of the Miracle There were also victims of the miracle. Prices rose, but wages lagged behind. Social programs

Brazilian tanks roll through the city streets.
▶ What seems to be the attitude of the people on the sidewalks?

scarcely existed, and as the nation's population grew rapidly, Brazil seemed unable to meet the basic needs of its people. The military ruled harshly and censored those who spoke out for reforms. The governments controlled all information, including newspapers, magazines, television, and radio. When a popular Brazilian entertainer tried to sing a song he had written that seemed critical of the government, the police turned off the power in the auditorium. The governments often jailed, tortured, and even murdered their opponents.

Church leaders spoke out about the problems of the poor and the lack of freedom. Workers protested and organized demonstrations and strikes. Pressure on the military grew. Then the economy went into a tailspin. Inflation skyrocketed. Brazil's **foreign debt** also shot up. Foreign debt is money that a country owes to people and organizations located outside of the country. Brazil owes interest payments to international lenders, for example.

A Democratic Opening Military leaders began to speak about a "democratic opening," a slow return to democracy. In 1985, Brazilians elected a civilian to the presidency. He died before he could take office. His vice president-elect, José Sarnay (sahr NAY) then became president. In March of 1990, however, Fernando Collor

In 1992 Itamar Franco (right) assumed presidential powers in Brazil.
▶ Under what circumstance did Franco become president?

de Mello became the first popularly elected president of Brazil in 29 years.

On inauguration day, Collor de Mello promised social reforms and an end to inflation. He also told the Brazilian people, "My first commitment — inalterable — is to democracy." Thousands of people cheered and waved banners with words of hope: "A New Brazil."

Two years later, the people's hopes had been disappointed. Collor de Mello resigned in disgrace amid charges of corruption. The Brazilian Senate voted to remove him from office. His vice president, Itamar Franco, became the new president of Brazil.

LESSON **3** REVIEW

THINK AND WRITE
A. Why did the empire end?
B. What was the politics of coffee?
C. Who was Getúlio Vargas?
D. How did the New State change Brazil?
E. What important things happened in Brazil after Vargas died?
F. What was the "democratic opening"?

SKILLS CHECK

WRITING SKILL
Compare the problems that face Brazil with the problems that face Paraguay. In a paragraph or two, tell how they are similar or different.

The Brazilian Economy

THINK ABOUT WHAT YOU KNOW

Suppose the sixth-grade class at your school has successfully raised money for a special school activity for the last three years by selling candied apples. Can you think of some reasons why your class might decide to try raising money in a different way this year?

STUDY THE VOCABULARY

boom and bust
latex

FOCUS YOUR READING

What are some important features of the Brazilian economy?

A. Boom and Bust

"Every type of agriculture could be practiced here, for this land is blessed with great fertility, excellent climate, general wholesomeness, healthful air, and a thousand other virtues."

That description of Brazil was written in 1618. From earliest times, people have seen Brazil as a land of great natural riches. Brazilians have a long history of developing and making money from only one natural resource at a time. When the resource is used up or has lost its value, Brazilians turn their attention to another product. This approach to economic development has produced many periods of **boom and bust** in Brazil. A boom is a swift growth, often in the economy. It can result in a sudden collapse, sometimes called a bust in the economy.

The discovery of a new source of riches produces a boom as people rush to get a share of the wealth. As the resource is used up or its value goes down, the boom becomes a bust. Usually, little or nothing is done to find ways to make the resource last or to find better ways to produce the resource. When the boom turns into a bust, all that's left is disappointment.

B. The Amazon Rubber Boom

One of the best examples of this pattern of boom and bust is the story of the Brazilian rubber industry. Between 1880 and 1912, the world demand for rubber goods grew. Rubber trees grew wild in the Amazon rain forest. Brazilians rushed to extract the **latex** from those trees. Rubber

(Clockwise) A rubber tree is tapped, then the latex is treated. After that the latex is compressed into bales.
▶ Why can tapped trees still live?

is made from latex, the material found in rubber trees. Brazil had nearly all of the world's rubber trees. The Amazon rubber boom was in full swing.

Manaus (muh NOUS), a small Amazon village, suddenly became a major city. Its population soared. Wealthy rubber planters and merchants built fine mansions. The city even built a beautiful opera house that rivaled the best in Europe. Opera stars journeyed 1,000 miles (1,600 km) up the Amazon River from the coast to sing in the opera house at Manaus.

At the height of the boom, however, other nations were trying to end the Brazilian monopoly on rubber. In 1875, Brazilian rubber plants were secretly taken to London, England. The British eventually planted these trees in Asia. By 1913, the British plantations in Asia could produce rubber cheaper than the Brazilians could.

The Amazon rubber boom ended. The opera house shut down. Mansions were abandoned, and Manaus once more became a quiet river town.

C. A New Policy

Breaking the Old Pattern Gold, sugar, coffee, and rubber are just some of the resources that have boomed, then busted, at

The city of Manaus, with its opera house (in background), developed during the early rubber boom.
► What details do you notice?

one time or another in Brazil. Could this pattern ever be broken? In recent years Brazil certainly has tried very hard to do just that.

Industrial Growth Brazil's government has set out to make the country into a major industrial power. Much progress has been made. In fact, Brazil stands among the top ten nations of the world in GNP. The gross national product, you will recall, is a measure of the total value of a nation's economy. It includes all the goods and services that a nation produces. In 1990, Brazil had a $350 billion GNP.

Brazil is Latin America's largest producer of iron and steel. It is in fifth place among the world's major producers of hydroelectricity and of military equipment and weapons. Brazil manufactures automobiles, airplanes, computers, and other high-technology products as well as shoes and textiles. It has two communications satellites in space.

Agriculture and the Economy In addition to the emphasis on industry, Brazil continues to be an important producer of agricultural products. Coffee and sugar still produce large incomes for Brazil. Brazil is also a major producer of soybeans and beef. The Brazilian citrus industry is ex-panding rapidly. Much of the orange juice sold in the United States comes from Brazilian oranges.

Mineral Wealth Brazil is a treasure house of minerals. Gold and diamonds are plentiful. Less well known minerals have even greater importance in today's world. For example, you may not have heard of columbium, but it is critically important in the metals industry. The United States has no supply of this mineral. Brazil and Canada are the world's leading producers.

D. The Energy Problem

With all its natural wealth, however, Brazil does not have enough energy supplies. Coal fields in the southern state of Santa Catarina meet part of Brazil's demand for coal, but large amounts of coal must be imported as well. Also, Brazil's oil reserves are small.

Despite some offshore oil fields recently discovered in the Atlantic Ocean by Petrobras, the government-owned oil company, Brazil still produces only around one third of the oil it needs. Imports make up the rest. Therefore, although the drop in world oil prices in the 1980s hurt Venezuela and other Latin American producers, it helped Brazil.

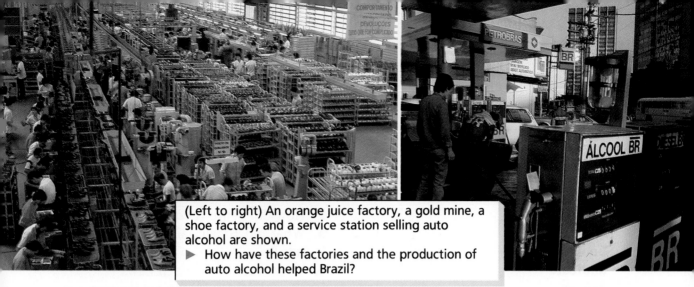

(Left to right) An orange juice factory, a gold mine, a shoe factory, and a service station selling auto alcohol are shown.

▶ How have these factories and the production of auto alcohol helped Brazil?

E. Three Energy Programs

Alcohol as Auto Fuel Automobiles jam the streets of most Brazilian cities. While there is nothing unusual about urban traffic jams, there is something different about Brazil's cars. They run on alcohol, made from sugarcane, manioc, and other crops that can be grown in large quantities, instead of on gasoline. Using alcohol is one of the three ways that Brazil is trying to meet its energy needs.

Hydroelectric Power Developing the great hydroelectric potential of Brazil is a second approach to this problem. You have already read about the joint project between Paraguay and Brazil. Right now, that project, the Itaipu (ee TYE poo) Dam, can produce just about as much electricity

as the famous Grand Coulee Dam in the United States. Itaipu will nearly double that output when it reaches full capacity.

Nuclear Power Where hydroelectric power is not practical, Brazil is building nuclear power plants. The country's first plant is now running, and one other plant is under construction. These plants make up the third energy program, one that is causing some concern both in Brazil and in the United States. Some Brazilians believe that safety factors have not received enough consideration. The United States worried that Brazil might soon be able to build nuclear weapons. However, in December 1990, Brazil signed a treaty with Argentina in which both nations agreed not to manufacture nuclear arms.

LESSON 4 REVIEW

THINK AND WRITE

A. What is meant by *boom and bust*?
B. Why did Brazil's rubber boom end?
C. How would you describe the economy that Brazil has today?
D. Why does Brazil have an energy problem?
E. Explain the three ways by which Brazil is trying to meet its energy needs.

SKILLS CHECK

MAP SKILL

Locate *Manaus* in the Gazetteer and find out what river it is on. Then use the physical map on page 597 to locate that river in Brazil.

18 *PUTTING IT ALL TOGETHER*

USING THE VOCABULARY

drought
sertão
araucaria
boom and bust
abdicate
censor
foreign debt
scrub
latex
regent

On a separate sheet of paper, write the number of the definition and the word from the list that matches the definition.

1. money owed to other countries
2. swift growth and then decline in the economy
3. person who rules in place of a king who is unable to rule or who is absent
4. pines with soft wood used for lumber
5. material found in rubber trees
6. give up a position of power
7. a place that is affected by very long, dry periods
8. to prevent people from talking against the government
9. a long period of dry weather
10. short, stubby trees

REMEMBERING WHAT YOU READ

1. Describe two of Brazil's climate areas.
2. How did Pedro II come to rule Brazil?
3. What did Brazil gain under Pedro II's rule?
4. What was the "Golden Law"?
5. When and why did Brazil become a republic?
6. List some reforms that Vargas made.
7. What problems arose during the twenty years (1964–1984) of military rule?
8. What is foreign debt?
9. Name some products that followed the pattern of "boom and bust."
10. How is Brazil trying to solve its energy problems?

TYING SCIENCE TO SOCIAL STUDIES

Find out about one of these sources of energy: solar power, wind power, hydroelectric power, or nuclear power. Read an article in a newspaper or magazine that discusses the advantages and disadvantages of one of these types of energy. Share your information with the class.

As an alternate assignment, find out how one of these sources of energy works. Share a report with your classmates. Use a diagram with your explanation, if you wish.

THINKING CRITICALLY

On a separate sheet of paper, answer the following questions in complete sentences.

1. Compare Vargas of Brazil with Perón of Argentina. What do they have in common as leaders of their countries?
2. Some dictators have been benevolent, or kind and generous, to their subjects. What are some dangers to people living under the rule of a benevolent dictator?
3. Why is Brazil called a major industrial power?
4. Automobiles in the United States could run on alcohol made from corn. Name some advantages to using this fuel.
5. Brazil has been building nuclear power plants. What are some dangers connected with nuclear power?

SUMMARIZING THE CHAPTER

On a separate sheet of paper, draw a graphic organizer like the one shown here. Copy the information from this graphic organizer on the one you have drawn. Under the main idea for each lesson, write details that support the main idea.

CHAPTER THEME
Brazil is a land rich in natural resources.
However, the country has had economic and political problems.

LESSON 1
Brazil is a very large and varied land in its physical features and its climates.

1. _____
2. _____
3. _____
4. _____
5. _____

LESSON 2
Brazil began as part of an empire and prospered as a monarchy.

1. _____
2. _____
3. _____

LESSON 3
Brazil became a republic, then a dictatorship, and now is a democracy.

1. _____
2. _____
3. _____
4. _____

LESSON 4
The Brazilian economy

1. boom or bust – _____
2. agriculture – _____
3. industry – _____
4. energy – _____

CHAPTER 19

BRAZIL TODAY

$\mathcal{I}$mportant cultural and economic differences mark off the five major regions of Brazil. Within these regions are unique cities, each with its own special flavor and attractions.

Many Brazils

THINK ABOUT WHAT YOU KNOW

A large country usually has various regions. With your classmates, discuss the various regions in the United States.

STUDY THE VOCABULARY

frontier   **vaquero**
flood plain

FOCUS YOUR READING

How do the regions of Brazil differ from one another?

A. Brazil's Regions

Five Regions Travel from one region of Brazil to another and you see lots of variety. Brazil has five regions—the North, the Central West, the Northeast, the Southeast, and the South. The map on this page shows these regions.

Size and Population As you can see, they differ in size. They also differ in population. For example, the North occupies almost 42 percent of Brazil's land but has only about 4.5 percent of the nation's population. That means the population density is low, and there are large areas of uninhabited land. The Southeast, with only 10 percent of Brazil's land, has nearly half of Brazil's people. Given these facts, what would you expect the population density to be in the Southeast?

Different Economies Brazil's several regions also differ in economy. Some, as you will learn, are wealthier than others. In the Southeast, for example, standards of living are generally high. The Northeast, however, is not so well off. To really know Brazil, you must learn about its regions.

B. The Vast North

Areas of Frontier Wilderness and **frontier**—that describes much of Brazil's North. A frontier is the edge of settlement. Throughout most of Brazil's history, centers of settlement lay along the Atlantic coast. The wealth of the country came from exporting products grown on coastal plantations. The North was far away from those early settled areas along the coast.

The Amazon Rain Forest The dense Amazon rain forest challenged all those who wanted to go to the north. Only occasional explorers and adventurers dared to meet that challenge. Settlers preferred less difficult conditions. On the other hand, many of Brazil's Indian peoples lived in the rain forest because they could live there

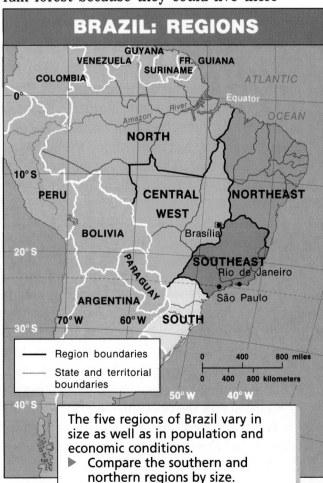

The five regions of Brazil vary in size as well as in population and economic conditions.
► Compare the southern and northern regions by size.

Brazil has made gains in developing road systems, such as this vast Transamazon Highway.
▶ Why are highways important today?

without too much interference from the Brazilian government. You will read more about the rain forest later in this chapter.

The Transamazon Highway Today, change has come to the North. The Brazilian government has built roads and settlements in the Northern region to encourage development. The best-known new road is the Transamazon Highway. It crosses the whole Amazon Basin, a distance of 3,350 miles (5,390 km). The Transamazon Highway connects the east coast with the Peruvian border.

Northern Flood Plains Development does not come easily in the North. The best farmland is on the **flood plains** of the many rivers. A flood plain is the level land near a river that may be covered with water when the river overflows its banks. Farmers on the flood plains plant crops of manioc, beans, and rice, using traditional ways of farming. The flood plains could produce large crops. However, little has

been done to teach the farmers in the North the modern, successful ways of farming on such lands.

Apart from the flood plains, most of the rest of the Amazon Basin has poor soil that loses its fertility quickly when the forest is cleared. Clearing the forest can actually make the land useless for agriculture.

C. The Central West

The area known as the Central West is another of Brazil's frontier areas. Study the map on page 471. You can see that, like the North, the Central West is also far away from the great cities of coastal Brazil. For example, a land distance of about 840 miles (1,352 km) separates Goiánia, the capital of the Central West state of Goiás, from Rio de Janeiro (REE oh day zhuh-NER oh). Goiánia is around 1,550 miles (2,494 km) from the Northeast's city of Salvador, which was Brazil's first capital.

Most of the Central West is a plateau covered with forest, vast stands of coconut trees, and campo cerrado. It also has fertile valleys, highlands, and an extensive river system. Jaguars, anteaters, and tapirs

This girl is selling a pirarucu, a large edible fish. Its scales are sold for nail files.
▶ What record might this fish hold?

roam the forests of this land, and countless fish swim in its rivers.

Despite its various resources, the Central West remained a land used mainly for grazing until recent years. The best grazing lands are in the extreme west, in a large tallgrass area around the Paraguay River. Here, during the rainy season, heavy rains swell the river and flood the land. During the dry season, the tallgrass feeds far more cattle per acre than does the campo cerrado.

In recent years, the Central West has started to grow rapidly. Cattle ranches have multiplied, and large farms, raising coffee and rice, occupy much of the land that formerly was used by Indians and small farmers. Plenty of unused space remains in the Central West. For example, the Central West states of Mato Grosso and Mato Grosso do Sul together have a population density of about 5 persons per square mile (2 persons per square kilometer).

D. Problems in the Northeast

The Decline of Plantations Once the richest part of Brazil, the Northeast today has become the poorest region of Brazil. Throughout most of the colonial period and the early years of independent Brazil, sugar from the plantations of the Northeast was the nation's major export. The great sugar planters, known as *fazendeiros* (fuh zen DER ohz), grew extremely wealthy, and the northeastern cities, such as Salvador and Recife, became the major urban centers of Brazil. Today, while other of Brazil's regions enjoy development, the Northeast is a place of too many people and too few resources.

Northeast Coast and Sertão The coast, however, is still an important agricultural area, producing cooking oil from African oil palms, sugar, cacao, tobacco, and cotton. Moving inland, the sertão, or dry interior backlands, once provided cattle, oxen, leather, and hides for the plantations of the coast. The sertão remains a cattle-raising area, but today's plantations have less use for its products.

The northeastern cowhand is called a **vaquero** (vah KER oh). The vaquero watches the cattle in return for a share of the new calves. Every fourth calf is given

Small farms and cattle ranches in the sertão area are often plagued by drought. Droughts have lasted for as long as five years.
▶ What problems does this present for farmers and for the cattle?

BRAZIL: CROPS AND NATURAL RESOURCES

COLOMBIA

VENEZUELA

GUYANA
SURINAME
FR. GUIANA

ATLANTIC OCEAN

Jari
Jarí Project

Amazon River

Belém

Equator

Fortaleza

Tucuruí Dam

Tocantins River

Recife

PERU

São Francisco R.

Salvador

10°

BOLIVIA

Brasília

São Francisco R.

Belo Horizonte

20°S

PARAGUAY

Itaipú Dam

Paraná River

Curitiba

Santos
São Paulo

Rio de Janeiro

Tropic of Capricorn

Paranaguá

ATLANTIC

ARGENTINA

Pôrto Alegre

OCEAN

URUGUAY

30°

70°W   60°W   50°W   40°W   30°W

Legend

Cattle	
Cotton	
Coffee	
Sugarcane	
Rice	
Wheat	
Tobacco	
Cacao	
Soybeans	
Iron	
Manganese	
Hydroelectric plants	
Oil	
Lumber	
Coal	
Cities	

0   200   400 miles

0   200   400 kilometers

Brazil is very rich in natural resources. Iron ore is Brazil's second leading export.

▶ Explain where deposits of iron ore are found in Brazil. Use something else on the map to explain each location.

to the vaquero. The vaquero wears heavy leather clothing — leggings, shin guards, gloves, a vest, and a hat — as protection against the thorny vegetation.

Droughts Cause Problems For centuries, droughts have plagued the sertão. From 1877 to 1879, for example, the Great Drought raged, causing the deaths of 200,000 people. It was one of the greatest natural disasters ever to occur in the Western Hemisphere. Whenever droughts come to the sertão, thousands of people — vaqueros and farmers — flee to the large cities of the Northeast. Others journey far to the south, to São Paulo or Rio de Janeiro, or they search for jobs on the Brazilian frontier.

Other Problems in the Northeast It would be easy to blame all the Northeast's troubles on the droughts. The true cause of the region's poverty is much more complicated than that.

The poor of the Northeast have a hard time improving their lives. They have little schooling. Many suffer from poor health caused by an inadequate diet. The government has tried to solve the problems of the Northeast through irrigation projects, industrial development, agricultural colonization, and education. These programs have only made slight changes in the lives of people in the Northeast.

E. Latin America's Industrial Center

A Manufacturing Center Join millions of Brazilians and head for the Southeast. There you'll find nearly all of the iron and steel plants, automobile factories, cement-making plants, and most of the rest of the industry in Brazil. In fact, the Southeast is the greatest manufacturing area in all of Latin America. Among the other products that come from the Southeast are textiles, light aircraft, food products, tires and other rubber goods, chemicals, machinery, and electrical products.

Important Southeast States The Southeast is Brazil's richest and most populous region. It includes such states as Rio de Janeiro and São Paulo, which have many large cities, factories, and corporations. Minas Gerais is another southeastern state. The name *Minas Gerais* is Portuguese for "general mines." That's because it's an area rich in minerals.

Even though it has many factories, the Southeast is also an important agricultural area. São Paulo State produces 40 percent of Brazil's coffee. The Southeast is also an important producer of rice, cotton, and soybeans. It now raises more sugarcane than the Northeast.

Both inside and outside this church in Minas Gerais are found the works of Aleijadinho, a famous sculptor.
▶ What might appear on the outside?

F. Brazil's Breadbasket

A Temperate Climate The South is temperate Brazil, and an area of good soil for farming. It produces wheat, potatoes, fruit, and even grapes—all crops that do not grow well in the tropical parts of Brazil.

A Region with Immigrants It is also a region with an important immigrant heritage. Germans were especially drawn to this area, and several important cities, including Blumenau (bloo muh NOU) and Joinville, were founded in the mid-nineteenth century by Germans. Italians also came in large numbers, and the majority of the people living today in Rio Grande do Sul and Santa Catarina, two of the states of the South, can trace their heritage to these two immigrant groups.

The third southern state, Paraná, also has an important immigrant heritage. It became home to people from Poland, Russia, and the Ukraine. It leads all other Brazilian states in the production of wheat, rye, potatoes, and black beans.

Cattle and Cowhands Usually, however, when people think of Brazil's South, they think of cattle. The Pampas extend into Rio Grande do Sul, and they make just as good grazing land there as they do in

The *churrasco*, a barbecue of steak and sausage, is often cooked on open grills and then served on long spits.
▶ Why is this a popular meal, especially in southern Brazil?

Argentina and Uruguay. The cowhands used to grill huge slabs of beef over open fires, and then, using enormous knives, would slice and eat the beef.

Today, you can enjoy this kind of meal in the many *churrascarias*, or barbecue restaurants, which are especially popular throughout southern and southeastern Brazil. Waiters bring a wide assortment of meats to the table. But they don't use platters. Instead, in imitation of the cowhands, they carry hunks of meat on large metal spits and use long, sharp knives to slice pieces of the meat onto dinner plates.

LESSON **1** *REVIEW*

THINK AND WRITE

A. What are the five regions of Brazil?
B. Why do so few people live in the North?
C. What are the major economic activities of the Central West?
D. In which ways has the Brazilian government tried to promote development in the Northeast?
E. Why is the Southeast important to Brazil?

F. How does the South differ from the rest of Brazil?

SKILLS CHECK

WRITING SKILL

The cities of Salvador and Recife were major urban centers in Brazil in the 1600s. Write a paragraph or two describing what these cities probably looked like at that time.

The Brazilian People

THINK ABOUT WHAT YOU KNOW
Brazil is often called "a young country." Think about that. In what ways might it be young?

STUDY THE VOCABULARY
multicultural

FOCUS YOUR READING
What is Brazil's population like, and what differences are there in the lives that people lead?

With a highway alongside it, this Rio coastline has sandy beaches that stretch for miles.
▶ What other natural features do you see in the photograph?

A. A Young Country

Recent Population Growth While touring a Brazilian city or visiting one of the country's many beautiful beaches, you would see many babies and young children. In 1970, Brazil had a population of about 90 million people. In 1980, it had grown to 120 million. Today's Brazil has about 148 million people. Study those numbers, and you should be able to figure out why Brazil today has so many children.

BRAZILIAN REGIONS: AREA AND POPULATION

Region	Area (In square miles)	Percent of Brazil's total area	Population (in millions)	Percent of Brazil's total population	Population density (per square mile)
North	1,380,000	42	5.9	5	4
Central West	723,000	22	7.5	6	10
Northeast	592,000	18	34.9	29	59
Southeast	361,000	11	51.7	44	143
South	230,000	7	19.0	16	83

One region of Brazil is not the largest in area in the nation, but it is the largest in population and in population density.
▶ Which region fits that description?

Needs of a Growing Population Brazil ranks sixth in the world in total population. This is a source of pride for many Brazilians. Brazil has vast empty spaces and an active frontier. It needs more people to settle those empty spaces and help the country develop. Other Brazilians worry about the country's growing population. More Brazilians means the country must provide more schools, housing, and health care. It also must provide more jobs. Brazil, however, has difficulty meeting the needs of its present population. Will Brazil manage to develop fast enough to take care of an even larger population in the future? How that question is answered will certainly have great importance in the years ahead.

B. Where the People Live

Brazil has a lower population density than the United States. Why, then, is it having trouble providing services for its people. Part of the answer has to do with the speed with which Brazil's population is growing. The faster the population grows, the less time there is to build new housing and train more teachers.

Part of the answer has to do with economics. Wealthy countries have more money to spend than developing countries do. As you know, Brazil has a large economy, but it is not so large when you take into account just how many Brazilians it needs to support.

There's another reason why Brazil has a population problem. Despite the nation's great size, most of its people are crowded into a few places. Most Brazilians live along the coast or in the eastern part of the Brazilian Highlands. About nine out of every ten Brazilians live within 300 miles (483 km) of the seacoast. If you think about Brazil's regions, you'll recall that the

Some Brazilians enjoy an afternoon in the park.
▶ What do many of them seem to be doing?

North and the Central West have very few people relative to their sizes. It is in the cities that population problems develop. You will read about Brazil's cities in the next lesson.

C. Many Peoples

Brazil, like the United States, is a **multicultural** country. The prefix *multi-* means "having many," and you know that *cultural* comes from the word *culture* and refers to different ethnic heritages. *Multicultural* means "having many different ethnic heritages." As you read earlier, many different groups of Native Americans lived in Brazil long before the Portuguese reached Brazil. Later, the African slave trade brought millions of blacks to Brazil. These three groups — Native Americans, Portuguese, and blacks — all mixed with one another.

Much of Brazil's Native American population, however, died because of diseases brought in by the Europeans. Those who remained fled to remote areas to be with other Indians who were already living in the Amazon rain forest, far removed from the areas of settlement on the coast. Colonists and Indians, then, were not in contact with each other for as long a time as they were in Mexico and the Andes. For that reason, Indian culture has had less influence in Brazil than in many other parts of Latin America.

Mixing between Portuguese colonists and Indians did give rise to a mestizo group, but the greatest mixing took place between blacks and Portuguese. In today's Brazil, official government figures say that 55 percent of the population is white, around 38 percent is mixed, and 6 percent is black. As happened in the neighboring countries of Argentina and Uruguay, many Italians, Spaniards, Portuguese, Germans, and other Europeans migrated to southern Brazil in the late 1800s and early 1900s.

Later in this century, many Japanese also migrated to Brazil. In fact, Brazil has the largest number of Japanese outside of Japan itself. People from Syria and Lebanon, two countries in the Middle East, have made their home in Brazil too. In general, the Southeast and South have received most of the immigration.

D. Different Worlds

Jangadas and Cargo Ships "Nothing this day created so much astonishment aboard our ship as the *jangadas*, sailing about in all directions. These are simply rafts of six logs, of a species of light timber, lashed or pinned together, a large sail, a paddle used as a rudder, and a seat for the steersman."

In Recife, fishers sail out on jangadas early in the morning and return in the afternoon.
▶ Describe the jangadas.

These photographs suggest a contrast between a homemaker living in a hut along the Amazon River and a homemaker living in São Paulo.
▶ How would you explain the differences?

You have just read a British traveler's account, written in 1809, of one of the sights in the harbor of the northeastern city of Recife. If you went to northeastern Brazil today, you could still see the jangadas setting out to sea. Of course, they don't sail out from major harbors any more because of the heavy traffic from the large cargo ships. However, along quieter shores, Brazilian fishers still use jangadas to earn their livelihood from the sea.

Cities and Rural Areas That's one of the ways in which there are really several Brazils. You have read that some parts of the country are richer and more developed than others. Where people live — in cities or in rural areas — makes a big difference in the kinds of lives they lead. Stroll the streets of major Brazilian cities, and you'd find just about any modern convenience available in the United States. Travel to smaller cities and towns, and the picture changes. There, instead of big supermarkets, you'd see people shopping at small stores. Many products that big-city dwellers use all the time are not available. Many of the smaller cities' streets are not paved.

If you were to journey to the countryside, the modern world would seem still farther away. Houses lack indoor plumbing. People get water from wells, streams, and public fountains. Development in Brazil is very uneven. While residents of big cities fight traffic jams, ride subways, and shop in air-conditioned stores, people who live in the countryside may ride horses or mules and wash their clothing on the banks of rivers.

LESSON 2 *REVIEW*

THINK AND WRITE

A. Why are there many young people in Brazil?
B. Where do most Brazilians live?
C. What different people make up Brazil's population?
D. How does life change from the urban to the rural areas in Brazil?

SKILLS CHECK

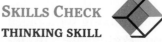

THINKING SKILL
Study the table on page 477 that compares the area and population of Brazil's five regions. Use the information in each of the five vertical columns to create five separate bar graphs.

Urban Brazil

THINK ABOUT WHAT YOU KNOW
You know that Washington, D.C., the capital of the United States, is near the East Coast. Think of reasons why some people might want to build a new capital closer to the center of the United States.

STUDY THE VOCABULARY
public services
favela

FOCUS YOUR READING
What are some features of Brazil's major cities?

A. Living in the Cities

Rapid Urban Growth   About three quarters of all Brazilians live in cities. Brazil's urban population is growing rapidly. That means that in the years ahead, the cities will be home to an even greater percentage of Brazilians.

Two Huge Cities   In Brazil you'll find two of the world's largest cities—São Paulo and Rio de Janeiro. São Paulo, with a metropolitan population of 18 million, ranks third in the world, after Mexico City and Tokyo. Rio de Janeiro's population of 11 million makes it the world's tenth largest city. Along with these giants, Brazil has several other cities with populations that exceed one million.

Challenges of Public Service   In part because the cities have been growing so rapidly, **public services** have had a difficult time keeping up. Public services are things that the government provides for its citizens. Like many other Latin American cities, most Brazilian cities cannot supply their citizens with enough clean drinking water. Storm sewers do not have enough capacity, so streets often flood during the heavy downpours of the rainy season.

Squatter Settlements   Housing, as you might expect, is a very serious problem. Many Brazilians live in squatter settlements, usually called **favelas** in Brazil. By now, you've learned a number of different names for squatter settlements. Unfortunately, all squatter settlements share similar problems.

Poor people have a difficult time getting enough to eat. They earn low wages. All members of the family have to work to help the family survive. Young boys, for example, may carry packages from the markets or keep an eye on people's cars while they are shopping. The small tips they receive for these services help to put food on the table.

The bustling city of São Paulo might be compared with New York or Los Angeles in the United States.
► How might they be alike?

481

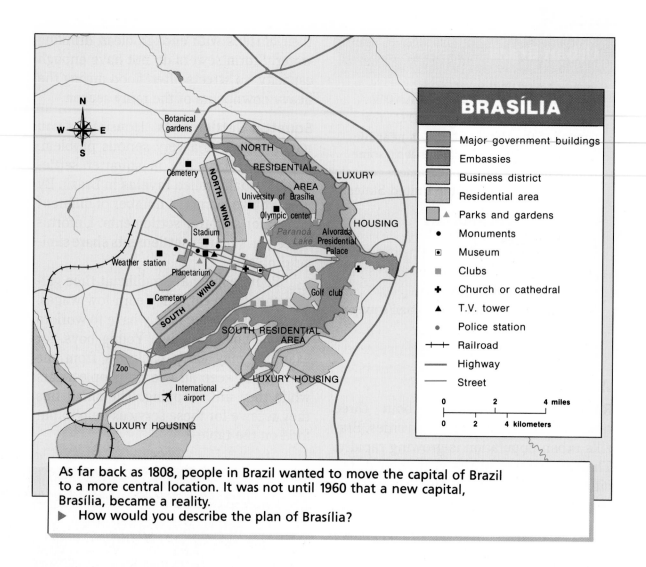

BRASÍLIA

- Major government buildings
- Embassies
- Business district
- Residential area
- ▲ Parks and gardens
- • Monuments
- ▣ Museum
- ■ Clubs
- ✝ Church or cathedral
- ▲ T.V. tower
- • Police station
- ┼┼┼ Railroad
- —— Highway
- —— Street

0   2   4 miles
0   2   4 kilometers

Botanical gardens
Cemetery
NORTH RESIDENTIAL AREA
LUXURY
NORTH WING
University of Brasília
Olympic center
HOUSING
Stadium
Paranoá Lake
Alvorada Presidential Palace
Weather station
Planetarium
SOUTH WING
Cemetery
Golf club
SOUTH RESIDENTIAL AREA
Zoo
LUXURY HOUSING
International airport
LUXURY HOUSING

As far back as 1808, people in Brazil wanted to move the capital of Brazil to a more central location. It was not until 1960 that a new capital, Brasília, became a reality.
▶ How would you describe the plan of Brasília?

Lifestyle of Wealthier People Wealthier people enjoy a different lifestyle. They often live in modern high-rise apartment buildings or in fine private houses. They can shop at elegant malls and dine in fine restaurants. Sometimes, these people have both city homes and places in the countryside or on the beach.

B. The New Capital

As seen from the sky, the city of Brasília (bruh ZIHL yuh) resembles a bent bow with an arrow notched through its center or perhaps the wings and body of some futuristic airplane. Look at the map on this page. The city itself has modern public buildings, massive blocks of apartment houses, and beautiful sculptures. Brasília is a special place. It's a totally planned city that was built to be Brazil's new capital. It officially became the capital in 1960, replacing Rio de Janeiro.

Why did the people of Brazil want to move their capital to an isolated spot in the Central West? The answer to that question is that Brazilians wanted to settle and develop the interior of the country. They hoped a new capital would draw people from the crowded coast to the empty and undeveloped interior.

Brasília's location and design were chosen to be an inspiration for the Brazilian people. In the words of Juscelino Kubitschek, who was president when Brasília was built, "Brasília is not only a project. It is an inheritance which we shall leave to those born here."

The city has large areas set aside for foreign embassies and for the homes of government officials and representatives of foreign governments. It has block after block of large apartment buildings for the thousands of middle-class government office workers. However, little thought was given to providing homes for the people who came to the city to work in the thousands of other jobs that keep a large city going. As a result, large favelas have sprung up in the Federal District around the city.

Over the years, these settlements have grown into towns. The population of the Federal District — that is, Brasília and the surrounding settlements — is almost 2 million.

Apart from the Federal District, the population of the Central West is still small, as you have read. Building Brasília did not lead to the growth of other cities nearby, and because of the poor soil, few farmers have come to the area.

Some people believe that the millions of dollars that were spent to build Brasília might have been better spent on projects to help areas where many poor people already live. Other people are pleased with Brasília. They see it as a demonstration of Brazilian skill in planning and as a symbol of Brazil's great future.

(Clockwise) Favela contrasts with the huge national cathedral, shown next in a close-up view. The cathedral is 108 feet (33 m) high and has concrete supporting the glass. The Brasília Theater is also shown.
▶ What other large buildings would you expect to see in Brasília?

BRAZIL: POLITICAL

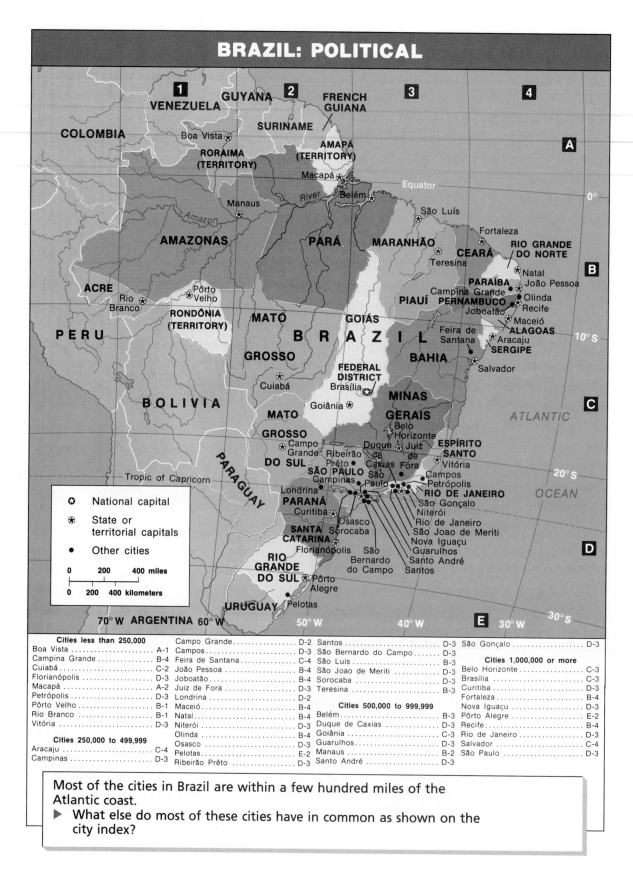

1 VENEZUELA GUYANA 2 FRENCH GUIANA 3 4

COLOMBIA SURINAME

Boa Vista ⊕

RORAIMA (TERRITORY) AMAPÁ (TERRITORY) A

Macapá ⊛ Equator 0°

Manaus ⊛ River Belém ⊛ São Luís

AMAZONAS PARÁ MARANHÃO Fortaleza

CEARÁ RIO GRANDE DO NORTE B

Teresina Natal

ACRE PARAÍBA João Pessoa

Rio Branco Campina Grande Olinda

Pôrto Velho PIAUÍ PERNAMBUCO Recife

RONDÔNIA (TERRITORY) Joboatão Maceió

PERU MATO GOIÁS Feira de Santana ALAGOAS Aracaju SERGIPE 10°S

GROSSO B R A Z I L BAHIA

BOLIVIA FEDERAL DISTRICT Salvador

Cuiabá ⊛ Brasília ⊛

Goiânia ⊛ MINAS

MATO GERAIS C

GROSSO Belo Horizonte ATLANTIC

Campo Grande ⊛ Juiz de Fora ESPÍRITO SANTO

DO SUL Ribeirão Prêto Duque de Caxias Vitória

PARAGUAY SÃO PAULO Campos

Campinas São Paulo Petrópolis 20°S

Londrina RIO DE JANEIRO OCEAN

PARANÁ São Gonçalo

Curitiba ⊛ Niterói

Osasco Rio de Janeiro

SANTA Sorocaba São Joao de Meriti

CATARINA Nova Iguaçu D

Florianópolis São Bernardo Guarulhos

RIO do Campo Santo André

GRANDE Santos

DO SUL Pôrto Alegre

URUGUAY Pelotas

70°W ARGENTINA 60°W 50°W 40°W E 30°W 30°S

⊕ National capital
⊛ State or territorial capitals
• Other cities

0   200   400 miles
0   200   400 kilometers

Tropic of Capricorn

Cities less than 250,000
Boa Vista A-1
Campina Grande B-4
Cuiabá C-2
Florianópolis D-3
Macapá A-2
Petrópolis D-3
Pôrto Velho B-1
Rio Branco B-1
Vitória D-3

Cities 250,000 to 499,999
Aracaju C-4
Campinas D-3

Campo Grande D-2
Campos D-3
Feira de Santana C-4
João Pessoa B-4
Joboatão B-4
Juiz de Fora D-3
Londrina D-2
Maceió B-4
Natal B-4
Niterói D-3
Olinda B-4
Osasco D-3
Pelotas E-2
Ribeirão Prêto D-3

Santos D-3
São Bernardo do Campo D-3
São Luís B-3
São Joao de Meriti D-3
Sorocaba D-3
Teresina B-3

Cities 500,000 to 999,999
Belém B-3
Duque de Caxias D-3
Goiânia C-3
Guarulhos D-3
Manaus B-2
Santo André D-3

São Gonçalo D-3

Cities 1,000,000 or more
Belo Horizonte C-3
Brasília C-3
Curitiba D-3
Fortaleza B-4
Nova Iguaçu D-3
Pôrto Alegre E-2
Recife B-4
Rio de Janeiro D-3
Salvador C-4
São Paulo D-3

Most of the cities in Brazil are within a few hundred miles of the Atlantic coast.

▶ What else do most of these cities have in common as shown on the city index?

484

C. São Paulo Never Stops

From a small city of about 26,000 people in 1872 to a giant metropolitan area in just over 100 years—that's the story of São Paulo. When coffee exports brought wealth to São Paulo during the late nineteenth century and early twentieth century, many planters put money into industry. The conditions for industry were very good. The many immigrants from Europe provided a supply of workers. The rivers near the city were dammed to make electricity to run factories. Although located in the Brazilian Highlands, São Paulo was close to the port of Santos. After the São Paulo railroad linked the two cities, goods could be shipped to and from São Paulo easily.

For those reasons, São Paulo has been the most rapidly growing city in Brazil for much of the twentieth century. It's residents, known as *Paulistanos*, are very proud of their city. Sometimes they boast that São Paulo is like a locomotive that is pulling the rest of the country along.

Paulistanos *do* have a lot to brag about. Their city is the largest industrial center in Latin America. It is home to three fifths of Brazil's largest businesses. It's also Brazil's commercial and financial center.

Block after block of skyscrapers pack the city's large downtown area. It looks something like New York City's downtown area, with its streets passing through deep "canyons" formed by the rows of tall buildings on either side.

Broad avenues lead to shopping centers and neighborhoods with beautiful homes. Around the city are suburbs, some of which have industrial centers of their own. Others are mainly places where people live and do their shopping. All of this growth has a price. São Paulo has serious air pollution problems. You should also keep in mind that between a quarter and a third of São Paulo's people live in favelas scattered around the city. Not everyone in São Paulo is rich. Of course, similar situations exist in and around most huge cities.

Many skyscrapers and residential areas can be found in São Paulo. This sprawling city covers 589 square miles (1526 sq km). Edificio Italia, the tallest building in South America, is in São Paulo.

▶ What impressions of the city do you have after viewing these two photographs?

Rio's Guanabara Bay and Sugar Loaf Mountain are pictured here.
▶ How is this setting described in the text material?

D. The Marvelous City of Rio

Perched beside Guanabara Bay at the foot of mountains, Rio de Janeiro has a stunning natural setting. Rio, as it is often called, is justly famed for the beauty of its beaches, parks, and buildings. Visitors from all over the world enjoy its many beaches, of which Copacabana (koh puh-kuh BAN uh) and Ipanema (ee puh NEE-muh) are the most famous. Visitors ride the cable car to the top of Sugar Loaf, the hill that is one of Rio's landmarks. They also marvel at the huge statue of Christ, set high atop another of the surrounding mountains. They delight, too, in the city's many restaurants and stores. With so much to see and do, it isn't surprising that Rio is Brazil's main tourist attraction.

The people themselves are also a main attraction of Rio. *Cariocas* is the nickname for Brazilians who live in Rio. Most Brazilians are warm and friendly people. Cariocas, however, have a special reputation for being friendly and for knowing how to enjoy themselves. In Rio there's an expression: "Paulistanos were made for work. Cariocas were made to enjoy life."

Despite the emphasis on play, Rio is also a hardworking city. It is a major port for Brazil and a center for commerce and industry. In fact, Rio's industry is second only to São Paulo's industry in Brazil.

LESSON **3** *REVIEW*

THINK AND WRITE

A. How is city life different for rich and poor Brazilians?

B. Why did Brazil build a new capital?

C. How would you describe the city of São Paulo?

D. Why do so many tourists visit Rio de Janeiro?

SKILLS CHECK

MAP SKILL

Locate *Brasília* and *Rio de Janeiro* on the map on page 484. Use the scales to estimate how far apart the two cities are in miles and kilometers.

486

USING THE VOCABULARY

frontier
flood plain
multicultural
vaquero
favela
public services

On a separate sheet of paper, write the best word to complete the sentence.

1. In the north, much farmland is on the _____, which are covered with water when the rivers overflow their banks.
2. A Brazilian name for a squatter settlement is a _____.
3. A cowhand in northeastern Brazil is called a _____.
4. Having many different ethnic heritages makes a country _____.
5. Schools, hospitals, clean water, and sewers are examples of _____ provided by a government.

REMEMBERING WHAT YOU READ

On a separate sheet of paper, answer the questions below in complete sentences.

1. Which region of Brazil has the lowest population density?
2. Describe the best-known new road in northern Brazil.
3. What is the poorest region of Brazil and why is it poor?
4. Which region is the most important manufacturing center in Latin America?

5. What problems does the rapidly increasing population of Brazil present?
6. Why does Brazil have overcrowding problems when it is so large?
7. Which two regions in Brazil have received the most immigration?
8. What fraction of Brazil's population live in cities?
9. Why was Brasília built far inland?
10. What is the most rapidly growing city in Brazil?

TYING LANGUAGE ARTS TO SOCIAL STUDIES

In Brazil, as in other Latin American countries, there are special names for some cities and the people who live in them. Similarly, in the United States there are nicknames for some cities and states and for the people who live in them.

Match the cities and states in the first column with the nicknames in the second column. Write on a separate sheet of paper.

1. Indiana	Show Me State
2. New York City	Windy City
3. Missouri	Big Easy
4. New Orleans	Bean Town
5. Los Angeles	Big Apple
6. Chicago	Angelinos
7. Boston	Hoosier

Add three more nicknames if you can.

8. _____
9. _____
10. _____

THINKING CRITICALLY

On a separate sheet of paper, answer the following questions.

1. Which region of Brazil would you choose to live in and why?
2. What might be the future effect of Brazil's rapid population growth?
3. Speculate on what life would be like in a favela.
4. Why, do you think, did so many people move into the large, crowded cities of Brazil?
5. In your opinion, do you think that moving the capital of Brazil to Brasília was a wise move? Explain why or why not.

SUMMARIZING THE CHAPTER

On a separate sheet of paper, draw a graphic organizer like the one shown here. Copy the information from this graphic organizer to the one you have drawn. Under the main idea for each lesson, write facts that support the main idea.

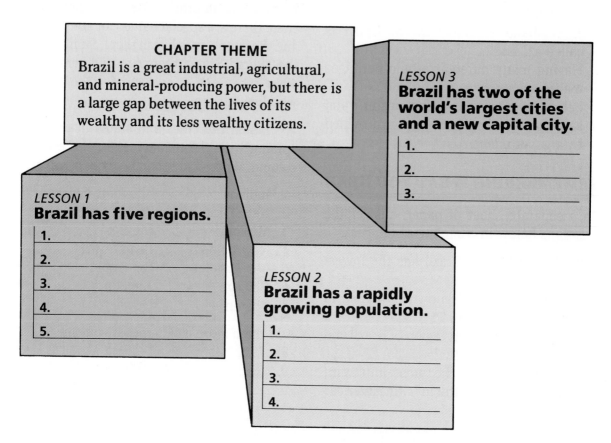

CHAPTER THEME
Brazil is a great industrial, agricultural, and mineral-producing power, but there is a large gap between the lives of its wealthy and its less wealthy citizens.

LESSON 3
Brazil has two of the world's largest cities and a new capital city.
1.
2.
3.

LESSON 1
Brazil has five regions.
1.
2.
3.
4.
5.

LESSON 2
Brazil has a rapidly growing population.
1.
2.
3.
4.

COOPERATIVE LEARNING

In Unit 5 you learned a great deal about South American countries. You read about each country's economy, government, culture, and geography.

It is sometimes difficult to comprehend this vast amount of information. A fun way to get to know your social studies material better is to create a game that includes challenging and interesting questions. For this unit, you can ask a variety of questions about each South American country.

PROJECT

In a group, discuss what kind of game you would like to design and produce. Think about games that you have played and enjoyed.

- For a social studies game, it is probably best to make up cards with questions for players to answer. Each correct answer will advance the player on a board.

- Your group can also decide what kind of board you want. Will there be bonus points on the board or will you create bonus cards? What type of markers will each player use? Will there be penalties for incorrect answers? As a group, discuss the format you would like to use.

- The game should include

challenging questions about each country's economy, government, or geography. You'll need to decide where the answers can be found.

- In your group, use your textbooks to make up questions for the game. Each member should contribute a few questions and answers.

- After you have created a variety of questions, you can design the game board. Each member should select one task to complete the design. One student should make up the question cards. Another should create the game pieces. Someone should draw a colorful, organized game board.

- When your board is completed, test the game. You can decide if you want to play against each other or compete as two groups.

PRESENTATION AND REVIEW

After your group has played the game, discuss the results. How could you improve the game? Are there any more questions you would like to add to it? When everyone in the group feels pleased with the results, present your game to the class. Then trade games with another group to see what else you can learn about the South American countries.

REMEMBER TO:
- Give your ideas.
- Listen to others' ideas.
- Plan your work with the group.
- Present your project.
- Discuss how your group worked.

A. WHY DO I NEED THIS SKILL?

Sometimes it is not easy to tell how things should be ordered, or put into a sequence. Sequencing is an important thinking skill because it helps you to organize information. In making an outline, for example, you need to know what information should come first, second, and so on, in order for the outline to be useful.

B. LEARNING THE SKILL

One way to learn how to organize information is to study the sequence used in producing an item, such as an agricultural product. You learned in this unit that South American countries produce and process a variety of agricultural products. One example is cloth that is produced from the cotton plant.

The diagram on the following page shows the sequence followed in the production of cotton fabric. As you can see from the diagram, the process begins with cotton plants that produce ripe and dry balls. The dry balls hold seeds that are attached to fluffy cotton fibers. After the cotton is har-

vested, it is taken to a cotton gin where the fibers are removed from the seeds and pressed into bales. The bales are then sent to a textile mill where the cotton is blended, cleaned, and combed. Then the cotton is spun into yarn or thread. Some yarns are dyed before they are finally woven into cloth.

C. PRACTICING THE SKILL

The following statements describe some of the steps in making cotton cloth. On a piece of paper, write the statements in the order in which they happen. Then write the letter of the picture that illustrates the statement.

1. The thread is either bleached or dyed.
2. The cotton fibers are separated from the seeds and baled.
3. Cotton grows on plants.
4. The cotton rope is spun into thread.
5. The fibers are blended, cleaned, combed, and then drawn into rope.
6. Thread is woven into cotton cloth.

D. APPLYING THE SKILL

Think of something that you have built or made. It could be an art project, a science project, or something you do for a hobby, such as building model airplanes. Write a sequence in which you describe how you made your "product." Be sure to put your steps in the correct order, numbering each one as you write it. Share your sequence with a partner. Have your partner write statements describing in correct order the steps you took in making your product.

A. WHY DO I NEED THIS SKILL?

Before you read a social studies lesson, you may sometimes wish to get a general idea of what the lesson is about. At other times, you may want to look only for a specific fact or idea. In these cases, you can skim or scan to get the information you want. Learning how to skim and scan will help you locate information more quickly and easily.

B. LEARNING THE SKILL

Skimming is reading something quickly to get an overview, general idea, or main idea of what a lesson is about. It is helpful to have an idea of a lesson's content before you read it carefully. The chart on the next page lists five steps to follow when you skim a selection for information.

Scanning is looking quickly over a lesson after you have read it in order to answer a question or find some specific information. The chart also lists four steps to follow when you scan for information.

C. PRACTICING THE SKILL

Skim Lesson 1 in Chapter 20, "Canadian Beginnings," to see if you can get a general idea of what it is about. Follow the five steps on the chart. Then write down a sentence or two that tells what you think the entire lesson will be about.

How well did you do? Did you write something like the following? *This section introduces the reader to major Native American groups who settled in various Canadian regions of North America.*

If you wrote something similar, you have done a good job skimming this lesson.

Skim Lesson 2 in Chapter 20 and write a short summary of what it is about. Compare your summary to a classmate's. Are they similar?

Now practice scanning by looking for answers to specific questions about information in Chapter 15, "Northern and Andean Countries Today." First, scan Lesson 1, pages 383 to 388, to find out what kinds of foods *quinoa* and *chuño* are. Follow the four steps on the chart and see how quickly you can find this information.

How well did you do? Did you find on page 386 that quinoa is a grain native to the Andes and that chuño is freeze-dried potatoes? Did the heading "Difficult Times for Subsistence Farmers" help you find the information more quickly? Did the pronunciation aid for each word help you scan for words?

Now scan Lesson 2 in Chapter 15, pages 389 to 394, to answer the following questions.

1. What does *Cerro Rico* mean, and why did the early Spaniards give this name to a mountain?
2. Why are so many fish found in the Peru Current?
3. Why did the demand for guano as an export drop after the 1870s?

SKIMMING AND SCANNING FOR INFORMATION			
What?	**When?**	**Why?**	**How?**
Skim	Usually **before** you read a selection	To get a general idea of what a selection is about	1. Read the lesson title and the FOCUS YOUR READING question. 2. Read the first paragraph of the lesson. 3. Quickly glance through the rest of the lesson. Read the first sentence in each paragraph. 4. Pay attention to boldfaced vocabulary terms, headings, and other key words in the lesson. 5. Read the last paragraph in the lesson and see if you can summarize the lesson in your own words.
Scan	Usually **after** you have read a selection	To look for specific information	1. Decide what question you have and what information you need to find. 2. Read through the section headings until you find a section related to information you need. 3. Move your eyes quickly through the section until you come to a key word related to your question. 4. Read the nearby text to try to find the answer to your question.

D. APPLYING THE SKILL

Use your skimming ability for help in previewing (reading before) lessons in your social studies textbook. This will prepare you to read it carefully so that you will understand and remember the important ideas.

Use your scanning ability for help in answering written questions about social studies lessons. Scan also to find answers to oral questions your teacher might ask during social studies class.

Unit **6**

CANADA

The east-to-west land area of Canada stretches 3,223 miles (5,186 km), and the country covers more than half of the North American continent. Canada's provinces have rich land and diverse histories.

▶ *Canadian artist Daphne Odjig portrays aspects of Native American culture in her paintings.*

*W*ith the arrival of the Europeans, Canada's Native Americans were now able to gain a livelihood by trading furs, but the effects of this arrival were not all positive.

The Granger Collection

Native Americans

THINK ABOUT WHAT YOU KNOW

Think about the Native American peoples of Latin America. What similarities and what differences would you expect to find between them and the Native Americans of Canada?

STUDY THE VOCABULARY

confederation	kayak
harpoon	igloo
edible	sod

FOCUS YOUR READING

What are some of the major Native American groups that lived in the land which became Canada?

A. Northeastern Woodland Indians

"These were the storybook Indians who skulked [moved in a sly manner] through dark forests, canoed blue waters, offered armloads of furs, and gave us the words *tomahawk, squaw, papoose, wigwam, squash,* and *powwow.*" The Native Americans spoken about in this excerpt from the story of the first Thanksgiving and those in James Fenimore Cooper's thrilling book *The Last of the Mohicans* lived in the woodlands.

In the forests surrounding the Great Lakes, around the St. Lawrence Valley, and all along the Atlantic coast from Newfoundland south to Virginia in the present-day United States lived many different groups of Native Americans. Native Americans from those areas were the people with whom the early French and British settlers in North America had the most contact. The term *red men* once was used to refer to Native Americans. It related to the people who lived in the northern woods. The people there once covered their bodies with bear grease that had been combined with a red dye. They did this to protect themselves against the cold.

The two major groups of Native Americans of the eastern woodlands are known as Algonquins (al GAHN kwihnz) and Iroquois (IHR uh kwoi). These names really refer to the languages that were spoken. Many different groups of Native Americans spoke a common or related language. For example, the Hurons, who lived on Lake Huron in southern Ontario, spoke Iroquois and so did the Mohawks of eastern New York State.

Descendants of Native Americans celebrate their heritage with special dances in Indian dress.
► What else might take place?

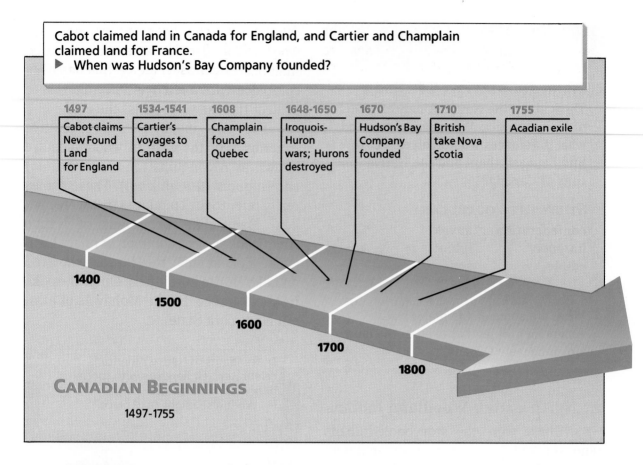

Cabot claimed land in Canada for England, and Cartier and Champlain claimed land for France.

▶ When was Hudson's Bay Company founded?

1497 Cabot claims New Found Land for England

1534-1541 Cartier's voyages to Canada

1608 Champlain founds Quebec

1648-1650 Iroquois-Huron wars; Hurons destroyed

1670 Hudson's Bay Company founded

1710 British take Nova Scotia

1755 Acadian exile

1400
1500
1600
1700
1800

CANADIAN BEGINNINGS
1497-1755

Both the Algonquins and the Iroquois farmed the land. Like the peoples of Mexico and Central America, they grew maize, beans, and squash. They also practiced shifting agriculture. The Algonquins, who lived farther to the north, lived more by hunting, fishing, and trapping. Because of the long cold winters of the northeast, they could not depend on the short growing season for their total subsistence.

The Iroquois are known for their palisaded villages. Along with six Indian groups — the Mohawks, Oneidas, Onondagas, Cayugas, Senecas, and Tuscaroras — they organized a **confederation**. A confederation is a group formed from independent groups for united action. The Iroquois confederation, known as the League of the Iroquois, was used as a model by the people of the newly independent United States when they wrote the Constitution. The Algonquins also joined confederations for protection from their enemies.

B. The Plains Indians

The Blackfeet and Crees are two Native American groups that roamed the Canadian plains. As you may recall from reading about Cortes, the Spaniards brought the first horses to the Western Hemisphere. The Blackfeet probably did not begin using horses until the middle of the eighteenth century.

Some of the Plains Indians were nomads, and others lived in villages. But apart from that, the Plains Indians in both Canada and the United States shared a common culture. Central to their way of life was the buffalo hunt. The tender summer grass brought thousands of buffaloes

498

to feed on the plains. Late in the fall, the buffaloes broke into herds and began to move off to areas where they could survive the winter's cold. The Plains Indians followed a pattern like that of the buffaloes. They, too, wintered in small bands in protected places. Then they came together in the summer to hunt buffaloes.

Since horses became very important for hunting, they had great value. Sometimes the Plains Indians would raid one another's settlements to seize horses. Young Blackfoot women often went with their husbands on these raids. In fact, a Blackfoot woman named Running Eagle gained fame as a leader of several such raids.

C. Northwestern Coast Indians

From southeastern Alaska south through British Columbia, many different Native American groups depended on the sea for food. They established villages in coves, or small bays, along the coast. The coastal Indians had canoes that they made from trees. Often they painted or carved designs on the canoes. The Indians used the canoes to go out into the open waters. These Indians travelled long distances over water in the canoes.

They used nets, lines, spears, and traps to bring in large catches of salmon and shellfish. They also used **harpoons** to hunt whales. A harpoon is like a spear, but its point has barbs that hook into the flesh of an animal.

The peoples of the coast made a wide range of tools from jade, obsidian, copper, and whalebone. With these tools, they made tall woodcarvings known as totem poles. The carvings represented important gods and spirits.

Fishers along the Pacific coast are shown using harpoons to catch fish.
▶ Describe the canoe they are in.

D. The Far North

As mentioned earlier, the Inuit, or Eskimos, lived in Canada's Far North, on the tundra along the shores of the Arctic Ocean and Hudson Bay. They were the only non-Indians who were in North America when the first European explorers arrived.

In the winter, snow and ice covered their land. The short summer brought a thaw, but even so the land could not be farmed. The Inuit were nomads. They moved from place to place, using spears to hunt for food. In the summer, they fished, hunted caribou, seals, and whales, and gathered the few **edible** plants that grew on the tundra. Edible plants are those that can be eaten. While hunting in summer, the Inuit lived in tents made of animal skins. In the seas along the coast, they paddled small skin-covered boats called **kayaks** (KYE aks), searching for seals and whales. They used harpoons to catch the animals. Ropes tied to the harpoons kept the hooked animals from escaping.

In order to hunt sea animals in the winter, the Inuit camped on the ice that formed over the sea. They hunted seals by waiting at holes in the ice where the animals came to breathe fresh air. When the seals came to the surface for air, they could be speared with harpoons. Seals were by far the most important source of food in winter. The Inuit used seal fat to make oil for lamps, and they used sealskins for clothing.

Sometimes, while they were hunting, the Inuit lived in **igloos**, which are small houses built with blocks of snow. Most of the time, however, the Inuit lived in **sod** or stone shelters. Sod is a thick mat made up of the upper layer of soil and the grass and plant roots that hold it together.

(Top) This painting shows a group of Inuit igloos from the outside.
(Bottom) Inuit and visitor keep warm inside an igloo.
▶ How do these people keep warm?

E. The Arrival of Europeans

Good and Bad Effects European exploration and settlement affected the Indian peoples of Canada in many ways. On the positive side, the woodland Indians gained a new source of livelihood by trading furs to the newcomers. However, as you will read, these Indians also became involved in battles between the European nations that had established colonies in North America. Many of the Indians were forced to move to the plains because of the Europeans. It was the pressure from European expansion that pushed them there.

Losses in Lives and Land As happened with the Native Americans of Latin America, the number of Native Americans in Canada rapidly declined because of diseases carried by the Europeans. The Indians saw their ways of life interfered with due to the actions of European traders and missionaries. Above all, the peoples continued to lose land because the growth of frontier colonies led to more European settlements. Indian peoples found refuge only in those areas remote from European settlements, on poor lands, often with climates that were not attractive to European settlers. All things considered, the coming of Europeans was a disaster for the Native Americans of Canada.

LESSON 1 REVIEW

THINK AND WRITE

A. What Indian groups lived in the forests of northeastern America?

B. Why were buffaloes and horses important to the Plains Indians?

C. How did the northwestern coast Indians get their food?

D. How did the Inuit survive in the Far North?

E. How did the Europeans change the lives of the Indians?

SKILLS CHECK

MAP SKILL

Look up *Lake Huron* in the Gazetteer to find information about its location and size. Then confirm the information by locating Lake Huron on the physical map of North America on page 596.

Early Explorations and Settlements

THINK ABOUT WHAT YOU KNOW

Imagine that you are an explorer or a missionary who has settled in a new region. What kinds of things would you record in a journal?

STUDY THE VOCABULARY

fishing bank **métis**
coureurs de bois **alliance**

FOCUS YOUR READING

What were some of the major steps in the exploring and settling of Canada?

A. Rich Fishing Grounds

An Early Viking Settlement In 1961, archaeologists found the remains of a Viking settlement in a tiny fishing village on the northern tip of the island of Newfoundland in Canada. Way back between the ninth and the eleventh centuries, the Vikings, explorers from Scandinavia—Denmark, Norway, and Sweden—had established colonies in Iceland and Greenland. They obviously established at least one small colony on Newfoundland too.

The Lure of Fishing Banks Other Europeans of courage and daring also sailed to the New World. Some established permanent settlements. For example, John Cabot's voyage in 1497 to Newfoundland, which you read about in Chapter 1, led the way for European fishers to come to North America to the **fishing banks** called the Grand Banks, about 75 miles (121 km) south of Newfoundland. Fishing banks are shallow parts of the ocean that offer fine fishing. The banks near Newfoundland are among the richest fishing grounds in the world. When Cabot sailed back to England, he told of the amazing numbers of fish he saw in his "New Found Land." The fish supplies of the Grand Banks drew people from France and Portugal as well as from England.

Fur-bearing Animals Between 1534 and 1542, Jacques Cartier made three voyages

The Granger Collec

When Cabot sailed home, he amazed people with tales of his "New Found Land" and the abundance of fish there.
▶ What was the result?

French North America. The king searched for someone who had the courage of an explorer and the management skills of a colonizer. Did any such man truly exist?

Samuel de Champlain The king chose well. He selected Samuel de Champlain (sham PLAYN), a man who would later be remembered as "the Father of Canada." Champlain sailed to North America in 1603 to find suitable sites for settlement. In 1605 he founded Port Royal (now Annapolis Royal, Nova Scotia), the first French settlement in North America. This was also the beginning of the colony of Acadia (uh KAY dee uh).

The Acadian Settlements Acadia was made up of settlements on the Atlantic coast and on the shores of the Gulf of the

Cartier stands before a map of land that he explored.
▶ How is the map different from maps in use today?

to northern North America. In 1538, Cartier established France's territorial claim to a part of Canada he called New France. In turn, Cartier's success caused still more people to travel to North America. From Cartier's report, for example, French traders learned that many fur-bearing animals, including beavers, roamed the forests of Canada. Since beaver hats were then very fashionable in Europe and could be sold for a high price, the traders became very interested in the new land.

B. Samuel de Champlain, Explorer and Colonizer

Henry IV's Idea In the early part of the seventeenth century, Henry IV, the king of France, became interested in settling

Samuel de Champlain devoted his life to the settlement of Canada in the 1600s.
▶ What does the drawing reveal about men's appearance at that time?

FIRST DAYS IN QUEBEC

You read that Samuel de Champlain kept a record of his travels and of day-to-day happenings in New France. Here is an excerpt from one of his journals. It tells about his first days in Quebec.

I searched for a place suitable for our settlement, but I could find none more convenient or better suited than the point of Quebec, so called by the Indians, which was covered with nut trees. I at once employed a portion of our workmen in cutting them down, so we might construct our habitation there. One I set to sawing boards, another to making a cellar and digging ditches. The first thing we made was the storehouse for our supplies.

I had the work on our quarters continued, which was composed of three buildings of two stories. Each one was three fathoms* long, and two and a half wide. The storehouse was six fathoms long and three wide, with a fine cellar. There were also ditches, fifteen feet [1.83 m] wide and six [1.83] deep. On the outer side of the ditches, I constructed several spurs, which enclosed a part of the dwelling, at the points where we placed our cannon. To the front of the habitation there is a place looking out on the river bank. Surrounding the habitation are very good gardens.

    * One fathom equals six feet(1.83 m). Today only the depth of water is measured in fathoms.

The Granger Collection

Understanding Source Material

1. Why did Champlain build a storehouse?
2. How can you tell that Champlain was concerned about an attack on the settlement?
3. Why, would you say, does it seem that Champlain chose a good site for the settlement?

A fur trader, in a council tepee, barters with the Indians.
▶ What did the Indians often get in trade for furs?

St. Lawrence. At first, Acadia included only the area that is now Nova Scotia. Later it also included parts that are now New Brunswick and eastern Maine.

Explorations Continue Champlain explored part of the land between the St. Lawrence Valley and the Great Lakes. He was probably the first European to see the land on which Ottawa, the present capital of Canada, now stands. He found Lake Huron and Lake Champlain and gave his name to the latter. Find Ottawa and Lake Huron on the map on page 570.

Champlain was more than just an able explorer and colonizer. He also kept careful records of everything he saw on his journeys. The records have been published in books that are important sources for the study of Canada's early history. Champlain had a talent for leadership. He devoted his life to the settlement of Canada.

C. Woodsmen and Missionaries

French Fur Traders In the mid sixteenth century, French fur traders arrived in Canada. Instead of trapping beavers themselves, they traded with the Indians for the beaver skins. It was a good exchange. The traders got the skins they wanted, and the Indians received metal tools and woven cloth from France.

The Métis Population Champlain understood the importance of being friends with the Indians. He sent men off to live among them and learn their ways. These men became the **coureurs de bois** (koo-rurz duh BWAH). *Coureurs de bois* is a French term used to mean "woodsmen" or "frontiersmen." The woodsmen lived in the forest with the Indians, trading for furs and exploring the land. Many of them married Indian women. This gave rise to a **métis** (may TEES) population. Métis are

505

Canadians of French and Indian parents. The métis carried on the work of the woodsmen from the early to the late nineteenth century.

Friendship with the Hurons Because of the fur trade, an **alliance,** or special union, developed between the French and Indians. This union of friendship lasted for more than a hundred years. The main allies, or supporters, of the French were the Huron Indians, for whom Lake Huron is named.

Friendship with the Indians allowed the French traders to move about freely. The system of rivers and lakes leading into the interior, or center, of North America made travel easy. There was money to be made from the fur trade. For these reasons, much of the continent west of the Appalachian Mountains was first explored by French traders.

Missionaries in Acadia Champlain also encouraged Catholic missionaries to come to New France. The first priests arrived in the colony of Acadia in 1611. Many other priests followed. They, like the coureurs de bois, lived among the Indians, but for a very different reason. The missionaries came to teach Christianity to the Hurons and other Native Americans. Both the woodsmen and the Catholic missionaries helped to make the Hurons and the French strong allies.

D. The Founding of Quebec

The real beginning of the colony of New France came in 1608, with the founding of Quebec. Quebec was the first permanent settlement in the St. Lawrence Valley. The choice of this site made good sense. The St. Lawrence River is like a great highway leading into the heart of North America. It is navigable as far as the rapids near Montreal, many miles from the sea. Beyond the rapids, the center of the continent could be reached by canoe on rivers and lakes.

Mother Marie de l'Incarnation and other Ursuline nuns arrive in Quebec in 1639.
▶ Why is this nun remembered today?

This drawing is an artist's idea of New France in 1608.
► How does it compare with Champlain's description?

In addition to the advantage of good transportation, the St. Lawrence Valley offered good weather. It lies in the southern part of Canada, where the winters are short and mild and the summers are a bit longer and warmer than in many other parts of the country. Also, the soil was better. In addition, there was less danger of Indian attack. You can see that the St. Lawrence Valley was a good place to start farms and build a colony.

E. Mother Marie's Convent

By the late 1600s, Quebec had become both the trade center for Canada and the home of the Roman Catholic Church in North America. Mother Marie de l'Incarnation was one of the people who helped Quebec grow. With three other nuns, Marie de l'Incarnation journeyed from France to Quebec in 1639. There she founded a convent and the first school for girls in Canada.

Mother Marie and the other nuns who came with her faced great hardship in establishing the convent. On the way from France, their ship was nearly sunk by a great iceberg. They spent their first winter in a small house near the river because there was no building for the convent. Through the long winter nights, in order to protect themselves from the bitter cold, they slept in chests, lined with wool cloth.

The sisters worked hard to create the convent and school, which still exist in Quebec today. Mother Marie was a skilled manager who organized the convent and school and ran them well. Also, she knew about farming, political matters, and law. She even learned the Huron and Algonquian languages. The citizens of Quebec, from the governor to the farmer and fur trader, asked Mother Marie for advice. She is remembered as a very important woman in Canadian history.

LESSON **2** REVIEW

THINK AND WRITE

A. Why did the voyages of Cabot and Cartier cause other Europeans to want to travel to North America?

B. Why is Champlain remembered as "the Father of Canada?"

C. How did their friendship with the Native Americans help the French?

D. What made the St. Lawrence Valley a good site for a settlement?

E. Why is Mother Marie remembered in Canadian history?

SKILLS CHECK

THINKING SKILL

Imagine that you are living in France in the 1600s. You have been hired by a land developer to encourage people to move to the St. Lawrence Valley in Canada. Prepare a persuasive talk about the area in and around Quebec.

LESSON 3

The Challenged French Colonies

THINK ABOUT WHAT YOU KNOW

You have read about European countries and their dealings with Native Americans in Latin America. You have also read about European countries and their rivalries with each other over land in Latin America. What do you predict will happen as the European rivals desire land in Canada?

STUDY THE VOCABULARY

Northwest   strategic point
  Passage
mutiny

FOCUS YOUR READING

How did other European nations interfere with France's North American territory?

A. Slow Growth

Daughters of the King Every year from 1635 to 1645, 40 young, unmarried women arrived in Quebec. In France they had lived in orphanages or with poor families. In New France they were to be brides for the many soldiers, fur traders, and other single men who lived in the colony. The colonists called these young women "daughters of the king," because the king of France paid the expense of sending them to Quebec.

Why was the king willing to spend money in this way? He did it to help the population of New France grow. When Champlain died in 1635, fewer than 250 settlers lived in New France. The king feared that raids by Indians or by English or Dutch colonists might completely wipe out the small colony of New France.

A Slow Growth About 160 other colonists were also sent each year, so after a while the colony did grow. Between 1635 and 1653, for example, the population of New France increased by ten times. Even with help from the French government, however, far fewer people lived in the French colonies than in the British colonies in North America.

What accounted for this difference? The harsh climate and little good farmland may have discouraged some settlers, but there were other problems as well. The economy of the colony was based on fur trading. However, few French people were needed in trading, since the

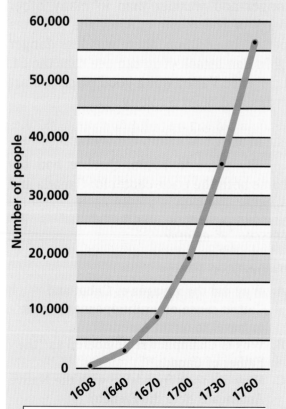

POPULATION OF NEW FRANCE: 1608-1760

The French government encouraged population growth in New France.
► In about which year did the population reach 5,000?

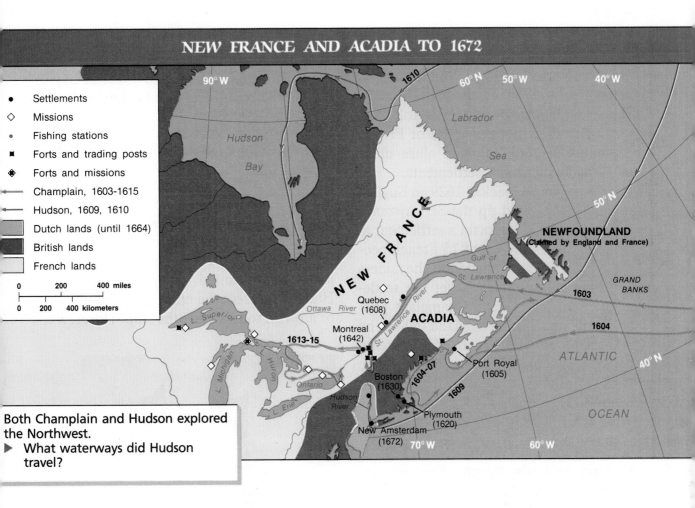

NEW FRANCE AND ACADIA TO 1672

Settlements
Missions
Fishing stations
Forts and trading posts
Forts and missions
Champlain, 1603-1615
Hudson, 1609, 1610
Dutch lands (until 1664)
British lands
French lands

0 200 400 miles
0 200 400 kilometers

Hudson Bay
Labrador
Sea
NEW FRANCE
NEWFOUNDLAND
(Claimed by England and France)
GRAND BANKS
Gulf of St. Lawrence
1603
1604
ATLANTIC
Quebec (1608)
Ottawa River
ACADIA
Montreal (1642)
1613-15
St. Lawrence River
L. Superior
L. Michigan
L. Huron
L. Ontario
L. Erie
Boston (1630)
1604-07
Port Royal (1605)
1609
Hudson River
Plymouth (1620)
New Amsterdam (1672)
OCEAN

Both Champlain and Hudson explored the Northwest.
▶ What waterways did Hudson travel?

Indians did the trapping and prepared the furs. Also, from the very beginning of settlement, New France was under constant threat of attack from the Iroquois and the English forces. Few people wanted to come to such a troubled colony.

B. Rivals for Empire

French and English Rivalry Why did the French colonies fear an attack from England? During the seventeenth and eighteenth centuries, France and England were rivals. They each tried to set up colonies and capture trade all around the world. The two countries fought wars in Europe. They also fought in places where they both had established colonies.

Many conflicts over land took place in North America. The colonies of France and England lay close together, and boundaries were poorly marked. While the French were settling Acadia and the St. Lawrence Valley, English colonists were settling farther south, along the Atlantic coast of North America. Colonies were started there in 1607 and later in places that eventually became part of the United States.

The English also had settlements along the coast north of the Gulf of St. Lawrence. British fishers still held the east coast of Newfoundland, as they had almost from the time of Cabot's voyage in 1497. Then, in the early 1600s, England made its claims to land in the Far North.

Each country wanted as much land as possible. The English and French fought each other in North America off and on from about 1614 to 1760, a period of nearly 150 years. Sometimes they fought full-scale wars. At other times, English or French adventurers or their Indian allies made small raids on forts or settlements.

For example, back in 1629 an English raiding party sailed up the St. Lawrence River to attack Champlain's settlement at Quebec. Since only about 75 French people lived in Quebec at that time, the raiders had little trouble taking over the settlement. The raiders took Champlain prisoner and sent him to England, where he was kept for four years. In 1632 a treaty between England and France gave Quebec back to France and allowed Champlain to return to New France.

C. Henry Hudson

Hudson and the Dutch England and France were not alone in their rivalry. The Netherlands grew in wealth and power in the sixteenth and seventeenth centuries. The Dutch, too, wanted a share of the New World. The man responsible for Dutch claims to North America was Henry Hudson. Hudson, an Englishman, was hired by a Dutch company in 1609 to sail to North America. On this voyage he discovered a river that would later be named for him, the Hudson River. Hudson claimed the lands around the river for the Dutch.

Hudson and the English Hudson returned to North America the next year, 1610, this time under the English flag. He, like so many before, was looking for the **Northwest Passage**, a sea route through North America to Asia by sailing northwest. Hudson sailed north along the coast,

passing through the strait that now bears his name and into the large bay that is also named for him. He claimed Hudson Bay and all the lands around it for England.

Hudson's Sad Fate Hudson met a sad fate on this trip. He reached Hudson Bay late in the year and his ship was trapped in the ice when the bay froze over. By the spring of 1611, when the ice broke up, Hudson was ready to continue the search.

The ship's crew, ill from lack of food and fearful of what lay ahead, had other ideas. They wanted to turn back. When Hudson refused, the crew held a **mutiny**, or a revolt to take over the ship. The crew

Hudson and his crew searched for the Northwest Passage from 1610–1611.
▶ What, do you think, were some of the hardships faced by them?

Warfare was important in the life of the Iroquois, and it was encouraged by Europeans who wanted territory and fur trade control.
▶ Whom did the Iroquois defeat?

set Hudson, his son, and some loyal crew members adrift on a southern part of Hudson Bay in a small boat without food. Hudson and the others were never seen again.

D. Hurons and Iroquois

Constant Raids and Battles You may remember that the French had made friends with the Hurons when they first colonized the valley of the St. Lawrence. The Hurons were bitter enemies of the Iroquois. The English, Dutch, and French took advantage of the hatred between the Hurons and Iroquois.

The French armed the Hurons and encouraged them to raid the English and Dutch settlements. The Dutch and English armed the Iroquois, who raided the French settlements. Encouraged by the Europeans, the Hurons and Iroquois battled back and forth during much of the first half of the seventeenth century.

The Triumph of the Iroquois By 1648 the Iroquois were strong enough to make a direct attack on the Hurons. They killed many of the Hurons, along with the French missionaries who were living with them. The following year the Iroquois attacked again, wiping out the survivors of the first raid. By 1650 the ranks of the Hurons had been greatly reduced in number. The few Hurons who were left alive after the Iroquois raids fled to the French settlements or into the forest.

The Hurons were a very important link in the fur trade. Their defeat was a terrible blow to the economy of New France. Another serious setback for the French soon followed. This time, however, two French coureurs de bois were the ones who caused the damage.

E. Hudson's Bay Company

In 1660, Médard Chouart des Groseilliers (groh ze yay) and Pierre Esprit Radisson (ra dee sohn) entered New France with a large load of furs. Like many of the traders, they had little respect for government rules. The two men had journeyed to the country west of Lake Superior, a place where no other Europeans had been. They had gone without first asking the governor of New France for permission to trade. When they returned, the governor fined them and took away their valuable furs. Groseilliers and Radisson appealed to the government back in France because they were angered by the governor's action. The French government refused to help them get their furs back.

Because of this, they turned to the English and urged them to trade for furs in Hudson Bay. They convinced Prince Rupert, the nephew of King Charles of England, that fortunes could be made along the shores of Hudson Bay. English businessmen agreed to put money into the idea, and with the permission of King Charles, they formed a trading company. This was the beginning of the famous Hudson's Bay Company.

At the urging of the Hudson's Bay Company, the English built several forts at **strategic points** around the bay. A strategic point is one that is militarily or economically important. The English could

A royal charter from England gave the needed financial support to begin the Hudson's Bay Company.
▶ How were the trading post forts built for protection?

The agents of the Hudson's Bay Company are shown distributing goods with the Indians.
▶ Where does the actual trade seem to take place?

now compete more with the French in the fur trade, and they had an important foothold north of the French colonies.

Des Groseilliers returned to New France sometime in the 1670s. He may have died on a final trip to Hudson Bay about 1683. Radisson, who lived much longer, was loyal neither to France nor to England. He worked for the country that paid him the most. He worked for Hudson's Bay Company for ten years. Then he left to work for France again. He even led raids against the English forts on Hudson Bay that he had earlier helped to build. In 1684 he went back to the English as a member of the Hudson's Bay Company. He lived out his old age in England and died there in 1710.

LESSON 3 REVIEW

THINK, AND WRITE

A. Why did the king of France pay to send settlers to North America?

B. In what areas did the English establish colonies?

C. What did Henry Hudson discover?

D. Why did Europeans encourage the Hurons and the Iroquois to fight with one another?

E. How did the Hudson's Bay Company hurt the French?

SKILLS CHECK

WRITING SKILL

Reread the last section in this lesson. Then write a short biographical sketch about Pierre Esprit Radisson.

USING THE VOCABULARY

Northwest Passage
alliance
harpoon
métis
coureurs de bois
strategic point
igloo
confederation
kayak
mutiny
sod
edible

On a separate sheet of paper, write the number of the definition and the word from the list that matches the definition.

1. A revolt in order to take over a ship
2. A group, such as the League of the Iroquois, formed from independent groups for united action
3. Canadians who are of French and Indian parentage
4. Thick mat made up of the upper layer of soil and the grass and plant roots that hold it together
5. Special union developed between the French and Indians
6. A place that is militarily or economically important
7. French term to mean "woodsmen" or "frontiersmen"
8. A sea route through North America to Asia
9. A spear for killing seals and whales
10. Eskimo boat

REMEMBERING WHAT YOU READ

On a separate sheet of paper, answer the questions in complete sentences.

1. What are some of the major Native American groups in Canada?
2. Why was the arrival of Europeans a disaster for the Native Americans of Canada?
3. The fish supplies of the Grand Banks drew people from which countries?
4. What were the results of Cartier's three expeditions to the northern part of North America?
5. Who was Samuel de Champlain?
6. Why was the location of Quebec, the first permanent settlement, a strategic one?
7. Why did the French colonies grow more slowly than the British colonies?
8. Why did the French fight with the British in North America?
9. For which countries did Hudson claim land?
10. Why was the Hudson's Bay Company important to England?

TYING LANGUAGE ARTS TO SOCIAL STUDIES

Write a letter back home as if you were on one of the expeditions mentioned in this chapter. Include your reactions to what you saw, the hardships you may have experienced, and how you feel about the new land.

THINKING CRITICALLY

On a separate sheet of paper, answer the following questions in complete sentences.

1. With which group of Indians would you have preferred to associate? Tell why.
2. Why, do you think, did the colonies established by the Vikings in Iceland and Greenland not last very long?
3. Why did the English and French use Indian allies to attack each other?
4. Some French colonists lived among the Indians and formed a strong friendship with them. Why was this a good policy?
5. Choose one person mentioned in this chapter. Tell why you admire him or her.

SUMMARIZING THE CHAPTER

On a separate sheet of paper, draw a graphic organizer like the one shown here. Copy the information from this graphic organizer on the one you have drawn. Under the main idea for each lesson, write facts that support the main idea.

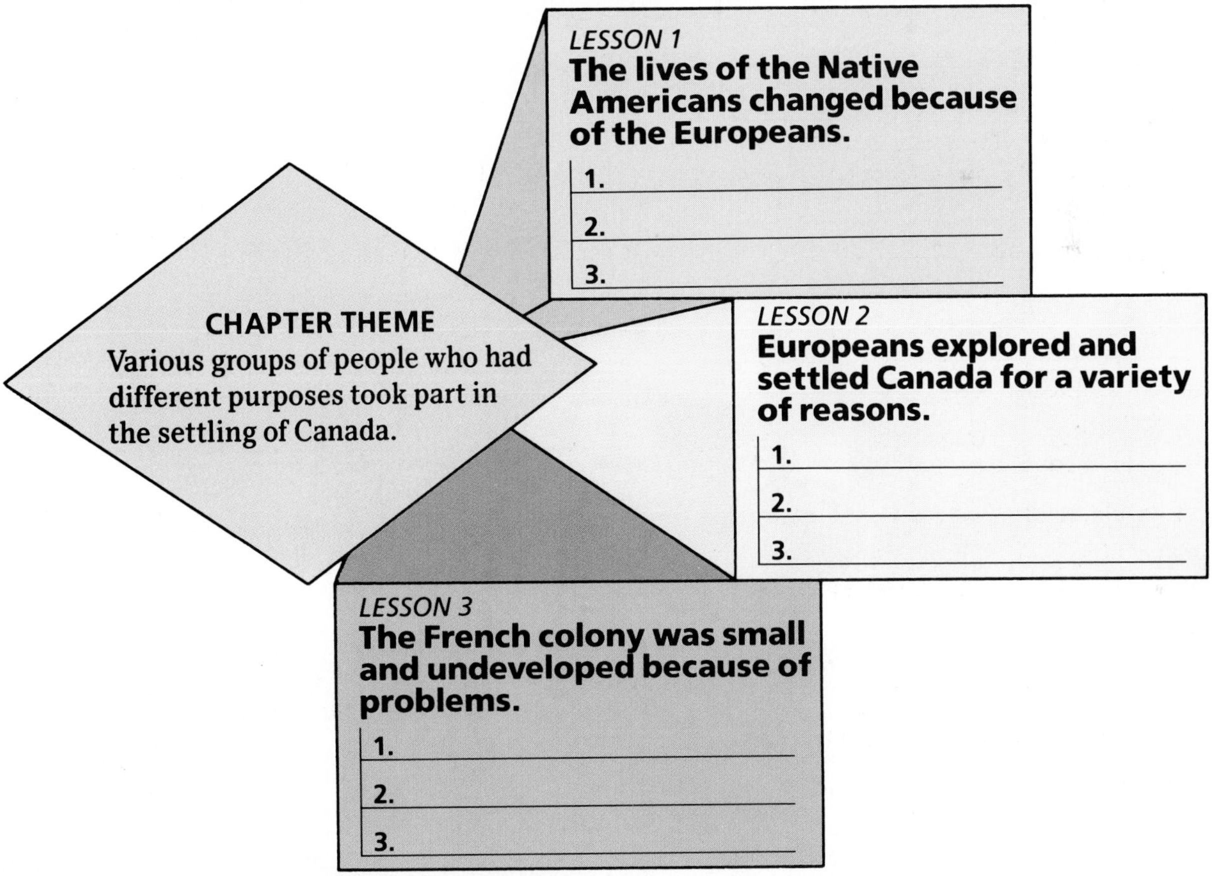

LESSON 1
The lives of the Native Americans changed because of the Europeans.
1. _____
2. _____
3. _____

CHAPTER THEME
Various groups of people who had different purposes took part in the settling of Canada.

LESSON 2
Europeans explored and settled Canada for a variety of reasons.
1. _____
2. _____
3. _____

LESSON 3
The French colony was small and undeveloped because of problems.
1. _____
2. _____
3. _____

21 CANADA FROM 1710 TO TODAY

Canada, first colonized by the French, had fallen to the British by 1763. To this day, Canada remains a nation of both French and British cultures.

A Great War Develops

THINK ABOUT WHAT YOU KNOW

Sometimes battles are won by strategy, and sometimes they are won by "a stroke of luck." With this in mind, have a discussion with your classmates. What might occur as the trouble between the British and the French continued in the eighteenth century?

STUDY THE VOCABULARY

neutral   sentry

artillery   Parliament

FOCUS YOUR READING

How did Canada become a British colony?

A. Trouble in Acadia

The British had captured Acadia from the French in 1710 and changed the colony's name to *Nova Scotia*. That's also when the name *Annapolis Royal* (honoring Britain's Queen Anne) replaced the name *Port Royal*.

Many of the French Acadians had stayed on after the British takeover. However, they had refused to swear allegiance to the British king because it would have meant taking up arms against French soldiers in case of war. The Acadians wanted to stay **neutral**, or avoid taking part in either side of the dispute.

The British rounded up all the Acadians and placed them on ships. They

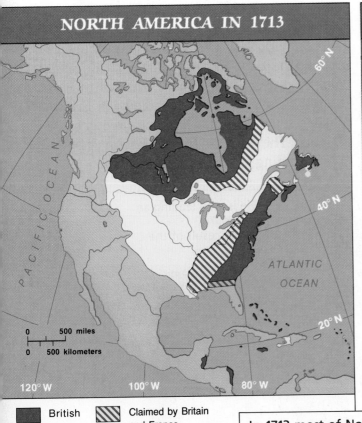

NORTH AMERICA IN 1713

NORTH AMERICA IN 1763

British

French

Spanish

Claimed by Britain and France

Claimed by England and Spain

British

French

Spanish

Russian

In 1713 most of North America was claimed by Great Britain, France, and Spain.
▶ Which two countries claimed most of North America in 1763?

A young Acadian woman comforts an older Acadian as others prepare to board the ships.
▶ Why is the soldier present?

planned to scatter the Acadians throughout the other British colonies in America. The little ships could not hold all the exiles and their belongings, so people had to give up even the small bags they tried to carry with them. Families became separated, some never to be reunited.

Some of the Acadians made their way to the French territory of Louisiana, where they settled. The Cajun (KAY jun) people of Louisiana are the descendants of these Acadian exiles. The Cajuns still speak a dialect of French among themselves.

B. The French and Indian War

The exile of the Acadians was only one chapter in the French and Indian War. In North America, this war between the British and French was called the French and Indian War because so many Indians joined the French in battle. The war in North America actually began in 1754. The fighting ended in 1760. When the peace treaty was signed in 1763, the French had lost all their land in North America except two tiny islands off Newfoundland and some islands in the Caribbean.

Two major battles in the French and Indian War were turning points of this long struggle. The first was the battle for the French fortress at Louisbourg on Cape Breton Island. Louisbourg guarded the entrance to the St. Lawrence River. It protected all the French settlements along the river. That made it a very important fort.

The French put most of their army at Louisbourg, knowing that it was a very strategic location. In 1758, British troops under the command of General James Wolfe landed and attacked the fort. British ships shelled the fort as Wolfe attacked on the ground. The battle lasted for nearly two months. Finally, the British proved too much for the French defenders. The French surrendered.

The British victory at Louisbourg opened the way for the next major battle of the war, the fight for Quebec. The destruction of Fort Louisbourg enabled the English to sail up the St. Lawrence directly to Quebec. They went up river the next year, 1759, landing in late June.

General Wolfe is seen leading an attack on Louisbourg.
▶ What was the result of the attack?

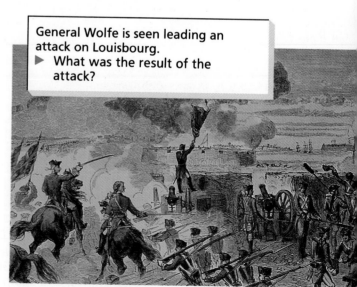

FROM:

Another Shore

By: Nancy Bond
Setting: Louisbourg, Nova Scotia,
1983 and 1744

The author, Nancy Bond, says of this novel: "In 1980 I visited Louisbourg National Historic Park on Cape Breton Island, Nova Scotia, for the first time, and my story found its home. . . . Many of the eighteenth-century people who appear in this story were real—their names are in the town records."

In the early part of this novel, Lyn, a seventeen-year-old girl from Belmont, Massachusetts, has taken a summer job as a waitress in the reconstructed fort of Louisbourg.

couldn't see—it knocked the breath out of her, she fell.

She had fainted. She knew it almost as soon as it happened, but she couldn't do anything about it.

Kneeling on the floor in front of Lyn was a young woman, her soft anxious face framed in white ruffles. The young woman blinked, and caught Lyn's hand between her two before Lyn could resist. "Elisabeth," she said, and then a lot more Lyn couldn't begin to follow. The vowel sounds and inflections were French, she was sure—if only she didn't feel so awful.

Everyone who worked in the fortress had to know something about its history and what life had been like in the colonial town in 1744, the year they had chosen to recreate. Even the waitresses wore costumes and were expected to answer questions—mainly about eighteenth-century food and eating habits, but everything else as well. It was like performing in an extemporaneous play: every morning Lyn assumed the character of Elisabeth Bernard, a girl her own age, who had actually lived in the town.

Ahead of her, in the rue Royale, Lyn could hear Kate's voice again, lecturing about colonial government. As she turned the corner, Lyn had the oddest sensation as if she was watching herself. She collided hard with something she

British ships unload troops under the cliffs of Quebec.
▶ How did the British manage a successful attack?

C. The Fight for Quebec

Quebec's Walled Fortress Quebec is on the north side of the St. Lawrence River. Part of the city lies along the river, but the main part rests on a high plain, separated from the river by cliffs. A cliff is a steep face of rock or earth that rises above the surrounding land or water. Most of the French army, which was led by General Louis Joseph de Montcalm, occupied a walled fortress in the upper part of the city. Many of the people lived along the river, below the fortress.

Destruction of Quebec City The British army, still under the command of General James Wolfe, set up its **artillery**, or large guns, on the southern bank of the river. From there the guns could shell the city. By September of 1759 the shelling had destroyed most of Lower Quebec, but the strong fortress on the cliffs remained unharmed.

Challenge of the Walled Fortress Time was growing short for the British because

THE BATTLE OF QUEBEC

St. Charles River

St. Lawrence River

Plains of Abraham

Quebec

ISLE OF ORLEANS

Wolfe's artillery

Path up the cliffs

St. Lawrence River

Notice both the location of Quebec and the site of Wolfe's artillery.
▶ What advantages and disadvantages did the site present for Wolfe's army?

the river would soon begin to freeze. Their ships would have to leave before that happened. Wolfe grew desperate. He wanted to attack the fort, but how could he safely move his army across the river and up the cliffs?

Luck for the British Then came a stroke of luck! On the evening of September 12, 1759, careless French **sentries**, the soldiers assigned to guard duty, let the British ships sail west up the river, past the city. Moving quickly, Wolfe's men made a surprise landing and overcame the few French soldiers guarding a steep and narrow path up the cliffs. All that night, small boats went back and forth, carrying Wolfe's men ashore. By the time the first light of day lit the cliff top, called the Plains of Abraham, 4,500 British soldiers had scaled the narrow path.

The French Surrender Roused from his sleep, General Montcalm quickly gathered his men, about 4,000 strong, and marched out to meet the invaders. A brief, but bloody, battle gave victory to the English. The French surrendered Quebec. Wolfe did not live to celebrate that triumph. He died on the battlefield. Montcalm was mortally wounded in the battle, and died later on.

The Treaty of Paris, 1763 The French and Indian War dragged on for one more year, but after the battle of Quebec, few French settlements remained. In 1763, the Treaty of Paris formally gave France's Canadian territory to England.

D. The Quebec Act

Differences in Heritage The victorious British decided to call New France by the name *Quebec*. Changing a colony's name is one thing. Changing the loyalty of its people is quite another. Quebec had a population of about 70,000 people, and most of them came from a French background. They spoke French, not English. They were Roman Catholics, and most of the British colonists were Protestants. They had lived under French laws and customs, which were very different from the laws and customs of the British. How could such a large group of French colonists be made to accept British rule?

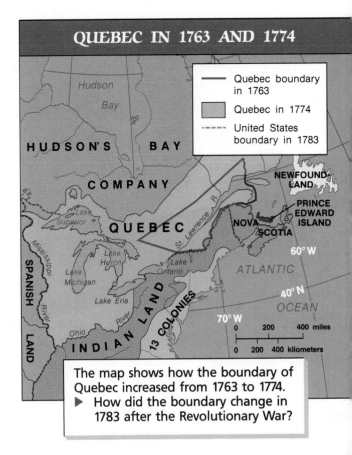

QUEBEC IN 1763 AND 1774

The map shows how the boundary of Quebec increased from 1763 to 1774.
▶ How did the boundary change in 1783 after the Revolutionary War?

The Quebec Act of 1774 Britain hoped that the Quebec Act, passed in 1774 by **Parliament**, the lawmaking body of Great Britain, would provide the answer. The Quebec Act guaranteed religious freedom for the Roman Catholics of Quebec. It preserved many French laws and kept the landowning system that had been started in Quebec under French rule. It also set up a council that was given power to pass laws to govern the people of Quebec. Members of the council were to be appointed by the British king or queen.

The Quebec Act also set the boundaries of the province of Quebec. The new boundaries took in all land east of the Mississippi River and north of the Ohio river. Today, Ohio, Indiana, Illinois, Michigan, Wisconsin, and part of Minnesota are located in that area.

The time line shows events and dates of Canada's history, beginning with the Quebec Act of 1774.
▶ On what date was another historic act signed?

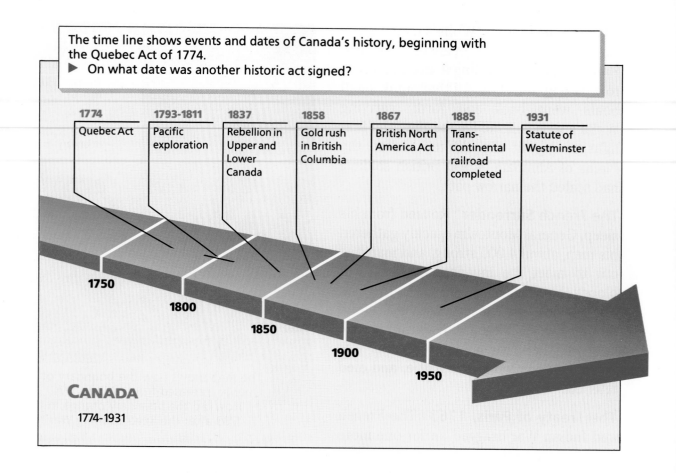

1774	1793-1811	1837	1858	1867	1885	1931
Quebec Act	Pacific exploration	Rebellion in Upper and Lower Canada	Gold rush in British Columbia	British North America Act	Trans-continental railroad completed	Statute of Westminster

1750
1800
1850
1900
1950

CANADA
1774-1931

This huge territory had been claimed by France before the French and Indian War. After that war, American colonists tried to claim it. The British, who ruled the colonies, ignored the Americans' claims.

By allowing the French Canadians to keep their religion, laws, language, and customs, the Quebec Act recognized and accepted the differences between French Canadians and Anglo-Canadians. Such *tolerance*, or acceptance of differences, was unusual for those days. It was a landmark in the history of understanding between peoples. However, as you will read, the Quebec Act had few supporters among the American colonists.

LESSON *1* REVIEW

THINK AND WRITE
A. Why did the British exile the Acadians?
B. What two battles turned the tide of the French and Indian War?
C. How did the British manage to defeat the French at the battle of Quebec?
D. What were the important points of the Quebec Act?

SKILLS CHECK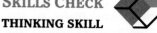
THINKING SKILL
Now that you have read the lesson, think about the victory of the British over the French. How much strategy and how much luck, would you say, were involved?

522

Reactions to the Quebec Act

THINK ABOUT WHAT YOU KNOW
Think about the word *loyalty* and its meaning. When might loyalty cause people problems?

STUDY THE VOCABULARY
representative   invade
Loyalist

FOCUS YOUR READING
How did the outcome of wars affect Canada?

A. A Divided North America

A Question of Fairness The Quebec Act may have pleased the French in Quebec, but it angered other North American colonists. The colonists said that Great Britain had granted rights to the French that had been denied to them. To make matters even worse, England had given western land claimed by the American colonists to Quebec. Why, the colonists wondered, was England treating a former enemy better than it treated them?

First Continental Congress In 1774, the American colonists held the meeting that is now called the First Continental Congress. They met to talk over their complaints about British rule, including the Quebec Act. The First Continental Congress was a major step on the road to the Revolutionary War, the war in which the 13 British colonies gained independence.

The organizers of the First Continental Congress invited Quebec and Nova Scotia to send **representatives**, or persons who act on behalf of others. Quebec

and Nova Scotia refused to attend. By this action, Quebec and Nova Scotia had begun to separate themselves from the other British colonies in North America. When the Revolutionary War broke out in 1776, Great Britain's northern colonies stayed loyal to Britain and eventually became Canada. The southern colonies broke away from Britain to become the United States of America.

B. The Impact of War

The Loyalists In the southern colonies, not all of the people there wanted to separate from Britain. Because these colonists were loyal to Britain, they were called **Loyalists**. Many Loyalists were forced to flee from their homes during the Revolutionary War. Others chose to leave after the war ended. Although some Loyalists went to Britain or to the British colonies in the Caribbean, most went to Canada.

The Granger Collection

After the American Revolution, some Loyalists made their way to Upper Canada.
▶ What were their means of travel?

523

Creation of Three Provinces In the 1800s, a British province was a land that was not actually a part of Britain but was governed by people appointed by the British king or queen. The Constitution Act of 1791, passed by the British Parliament, created the province of New Brunswick out of the western part of Nova Scotia.

The act also spurred the division of Quebec into two parts. By that time, some 130,000 people lived in Quebec. Of these, about 21,000 were English speaking. Two thirds of these people lived in the western portion of Quebec, which became known as Upper Canada. Eastern Quebec, where most of the French Catholics lived, soon became known as Lower Canada. Each province had its own laws, an elected assembly, and was largely self-governing. The Constitution Act promoted the separation of French and British Canada, which still exists. You will read more about this in Chapter 23.

C. New Boundaries

Canada Loses Land The American Revolutionary War also affected the boundaries of Canada. After the war, the United States demanded that the British give it all the lands east of the Mississippi River and south of the Great Lakes as far as Florida. These lands included the area that had been given to Quebec in the Quebec Act. Canada lost an area that would later become some of the world's most productive farmland. The boundary established by this agreement remains today.

The War of 1812 In 1812, the United States and Great Britain were again at war, and again the treaty affected Canadian boundaries. In the War of 1812, American

The mighty battleship *Constitution* (*"Old Ironsides"*) fires upon Britain's *Guerrière* in 1812.
▶ Which side surely won this battle?

McDonough led a bloody sea battle near Plattsburg, New York, on the Lake Champlain Waterway.
▶ Describe the scene shown.

armies **invaded** Canada and burned the city of Toronto. To invade is to enter the territory of another country, usually with the intention of conquering it.

The Convention of 1818 Since neither Britain nor the United States won a clear victory, the Convention of 1818 was held in London. This meeting led to an agreement on a boundary between the United States and Canada from the Great Lakes to the Rocky Mountains. The convention also set up committees to work out boundaries between the state of Maine and the province of New Brunswick.

LESSON 2 REVIEW

THINK AND WRITE

A. How did Britain's colonies in North America come to be divided into two parts?

B. How did the American Revolutionary War affect Canada?

C. How did wars between the United States and Great Britain change Canada's boundaries?

SKILLS CHECK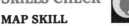

MAP SKILL

Locate *Nova Scotia* in the Gazetteer and find the names of the two bodies of water on which it is located. Then find Nova Scotia on the map on page 521.

Toward Union and Independence

THINK ABOUT WHAT YOU KNOW

Think about what it means to mature and to become more responsible. Do maturity and responsibility happen suddenly? How do you know that you are ready to act on your own?

STUDY THE VOCABULARY

legislative

FOCUS YOUR READING

What steps led to Canada's becoming an independent nation?

A. A Change Without a Revolution

Years of Small Changes   Canada gained independence in an unusual way. Instead of a sudden, revolutionary change or one great war for independence, Canada went through many small changes. These changes took place over a period of nearly 200 years. Canada's path to independence was a slow but steady process.

The Provinces in 1818   In 1818, a united country called Canada did not exist. Instead, there were six separate provinces, each with its own **legislative**, or lawmaking, body. Each province also had a governor appointed by Great Britain. The provinces were Cape Breton Island, Nova Scotia, Prince Edward Island, New Brunswick, Lower Canada, and Upper Canada. Cape Breton Island later became part of Nova Scotia. Lower Canada is now Quebec, and Upper Canada is now Ontario.

Besides the provinces, British North America had two territories—Newfoundland and Prince Rupert's Land, which was centered on Hudson Bay. Neither territory had its own government. The British directly ruled Newfoundland, and the Hudson's Bay Company controlled Prince Rupert's Land.

B. Lord Durham and His Report

Peaceful Times   For the most part, the four eastern provinces—Cape Breton Island, Nova Scotia, Prince Edward Island, and New Brunswick—enjoyed peaceful times in the years after the Convention of 1818. People in New Brunswick and Nova Scotia grew wealthy as they carried on trade with Britain. The population grew as many immigrants came to farm the land and to work at other trades.

Revolts in Upper and Lower Canada   In 1837, however, revolts broke out in the two large provinces of Upper and Lower Canada. A Scottish immigrant, William

Courtesy National Portrait Gallery, London

Lord Durham spent only five months in Canada. The report he made was significant.
▶ Find out what he recommended.

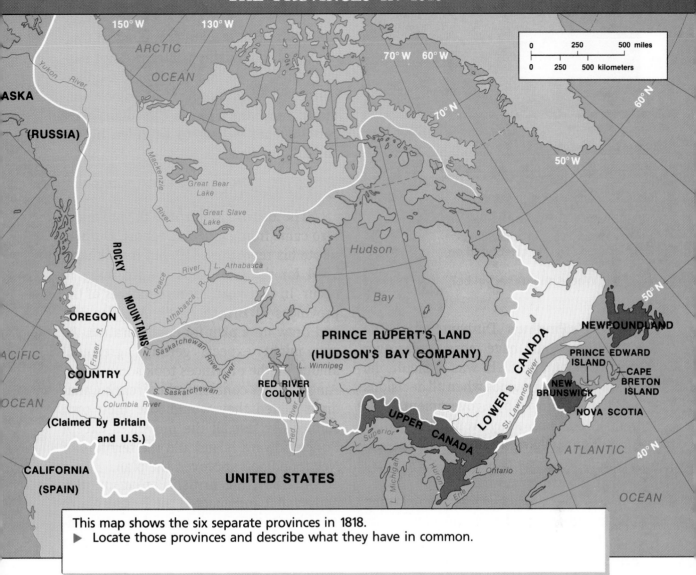

This map shows the six separate provinces in 1818.
▶ Locate those provinces and describe what they have in common.

Lyon Mackenzie, sparked the revolt in Upper Canada. A French politician, Louis Papineau (pah pee noh), led the rebellion in Lower Canada. Each of these men wanted to change the form of government to make it more like that of the United States.

The British quickly crushed both revolts. Still, those uprisings caused England to take a serious look at the governing of its Canadian provinces. In 1838, Britain's Queen Victoria sent Lord Durham, a respected political leader, to serve as governor general of all the provinces. The government wanted him to find a way to deal with the troubles in Upper and Lower Canada. After only five months in Canada, Durham resigned because of an argument with the British government and returned home.

In England, Durham prepared a report on conditions in Canada. Even though Durham had left office, the British government paid close attention to his report. So should you, because it helped to change the way Great Britain governed Canada.

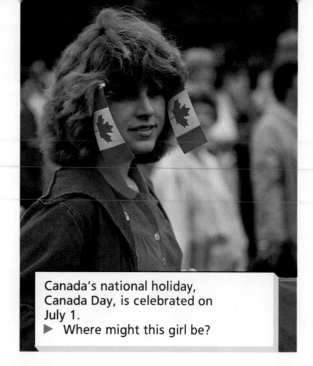

Canada's national holiday,
Canada Day, is celebrated on
July 1.
▶ Where might this girl be?

Durham's Findings Durham thought the provinces should have more power over their local matters. It was difficult, he wrote, to run a province when all decisions had to be approved by a government 3,000 miles (4,827 km) away. At first the British did not go along with this idea, but gradually the provinces did gain more control over their own government.

His report also suggested combining Upper and Lower Canada into one province. He thought that as more and more British people moved to Canada, the French Canadians would become a minority group and have less importance. Why, then, should the two provinces remain separate.

Although the two provinces were united for a time as the province of Canada, what Durham expected did not happen. In Quebec, the French Canadians continued to outnumber the Anglo-Canadians. Also, the French Canadians were certainly not willing to be ruled by the Anglo-Canadians.

C. The Dominion

The idea of a union of all the provinces also came from Durham's report. Durham wrote his report in 1839, but it took until 1864 for the first steps toward unity to occur. In that year, representatives of the provinces of British North America met and drew up a plan for confederation. As you might expect, getting agreement among all the provinces took some doing. Among other concerns, the French Canadians feared they would lose their own culture. At last all the provinces except Prince Edward Island and the territory of Newfoundland approved the plan.

In 1867, the British Parliament also approved it and enacted the British North America Act. This act created the Dominion of Canada. The new nation had four charter provinces: Ontario, Quebec, Nova Scotia, and New Brunswick. The act became law on July 1, 1867. As you may recall from Chapter 2, July 1 is Canada's national holiday, Canada Day.

LESSON **3** *REVIEW*

THINK AND WRITE

A. What is unusual about Canada's path to independence?
B. Why did rebellions break out in Upper and Lower Canada?
C. How did the British North America Act change Canada?

SKILLS CHECK

WRITING SKILL

Imagine that the year is 1860 and you live in Canada. You favor a confederation of provinces. Write a letter to Queen Victoria in which you present reasons why Canada should become a dominion.

The Canadian West

Imagine that you and your friends always went to the same place to hang out and talk. Think of some things that might cause you to go to a different place.

canyon
crest

How did the west become part of Canada?

A. The North West Company

The four provinces that approved the 1867 plan for confederation were all in the eastern portion of Canada. So were the two that wouldn't sign the agreement. What about the lands to the west? Why weren't they involved? To answer that question, you have to go back in time to the British takeover of Canada after the French and Indian War. When French rule ended, Anglo-Canadians wanted to enter the fur trade. Because the Hudson's Bay Company dominated the forests of the north, the Canadians had to look elsewhere for furs. A group of Canadian traders formed the North West Company in 1779. This company sought furs in the forests and mountains far to the west, beyond the area controlled by the Hudson's Bay Company.

B. On to the Pacific

Alexander Mackenzie, a young Scotsman, worked as one of the traders for the North West Company. Mackenzie wanted to find a river route to the Pacific coast so

Upon reaching the Pacific Ocean, Mackenzie inscribed something on a cliff.
▶ What exactly did he write?

Alex Mackenzie from Canada by land 22d July 1793

that the furs from western forests could be transported more easily to market in the east. He tried first in 1789, but the river he chose flowed north to the Arctic Ocean. This great river was later named for him. Find the Mackenzie River on the map at the right.

Mackenzie refused to be discouraged. He tried again in 1793 to find a route to the west. This time he crossed the Rocky Mountains and found a westward-flowing stream. When Mackenzie tried to follow it to the ocean, he came upon deep **canyons**, or valleys with steep sides, and wild rapids. That route certainly didn't look promising. Also, Mackenzie had heard rumors of hostile Native Americans nearby. He decided to try a safer route.

Finally, Mackenzie did reach the Pacific Ocean by land. He stayed on the coast only long enough to leave proof that he had been there. He wrote as proof on a cliff near the ocean: "Alex. Mackenzie, from Canada by land 22d [twenty-second] July 1793." He was the first explorer to travel all the way across the continent.

C. Competition for Furs

Fifteen years later, Simon Fraser, a partner in the North West Company, reached the west coast by river. Following the river that Mackenzie had abandoned, Fraser reached the ocean in 1808. The river he followed now bears his name. You can find the Fraser River on the map shown.

Other Canadian fur traders and explorers followed Mackenzie and Fraser. The North West Company set up trading posts at various places in the west. So did the Hudson's Bay Company. The two companies competed fiercely, often raiding one another's trading posts. Furs were stolen, and lives were lost.

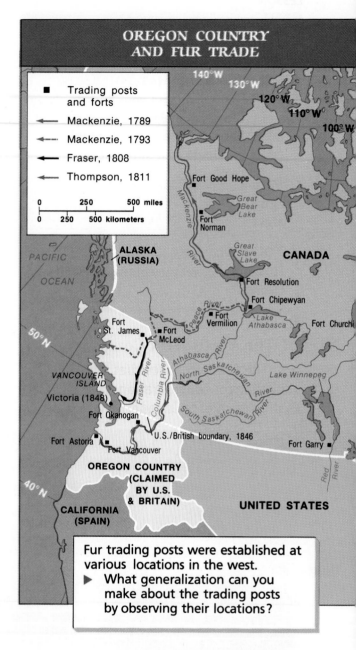

OREGON COUNTRY AND FUR TRADE

■ Trading posts and forts
← Mackenzie, 1789
←-- Mackenzie, 1793
← Fraser, 1808
← Thompson, 1811

Fur trading posts were established at various locations in the west.
▶ What generalization can you make about the trading posts by observing their locations?

In 1811, the North West Company wanted mapmaker and surveyor David Thompson to start up a trading post at the mouth of the Columbia River. Thompson reached it, but an American, John Jacob Astor, had already built a trading post there. This post gave the Americans an edge in the competition—at first for the furs in the area and later on for the land itself.

D. The Oregon Country

Both the United States and Great Britain claimed the land in the far west. As you may recall, the Convention of 1818 set the boundary between British North America and the United States only as far as the Rocky Mountains. Beyond the **crest**, or highest part, of the Rockies was the area called the Oregon Country. The Oregon Country stretched all the way to the Pacific Ocean. It reached as far south as California and as far north as Alaska.

At first, Native Americans and fur traders made up most of the population in the Oregon Country. By the 1840s, immigrants from the United States had started moving to Oregon. Very few British settlers lived there. The Americans demanded that the entire area be made part of the United States. They even threatened to go to war over the matter.

In 1846, Britain and the United States avoided a war by agreeing to set the boundary at 49° N latitude, just as it was east of the Rocky Mountains. The land to the south of this parallel became part of the United States. Today that area includes Oregon, Washington, and Idaho and parts of Montana and Wyoming. The land to the north went to Canada, and became the province of British Columbia.

E. Life in the Far West

A True Account Amelia Douglas was born in 1812. Her father was a French fur trader who worked for the Hudson's Bay Company. Her mother was the daughter of a Cree Indian chief. That meant Amelia was a métis. At the age of 16, she married a young fur trader named James Douglas. Amelia and James lived for a while at Fort St. James in the mountains of British Columbia. Then they spent 15 years at Fort Vancouver. This fort was on the Columbia River at the present day site of the city of Vancouver, Washington.

The Granger Collection

Astoria, at the mouth of the Columbia River, was part of the disputed Oregon Country.
▶ Find it on the map on page 530.

In 1849, they went to Victoria, now the capital of British Columbia. This trip was made by wagon and ship. That was a big improvement over the long, slow journeys by canoe that Amelia remembered from the earlier years when she had traveled with her fur-trading father.

Amelia and James had 13 children, but only 6 lived past childhood. There were no doctors or hospitals at the trading posts. Many children died as babies. Many of those who lived past infancy died of illnesses that now can be cured.

Governor James Douglas In 1858, while the Douglases were at Victoria, gold was discovered on the Fraser River. Word of this discovery set off a gold rush. Thousands of people, many of them Americans, went to the area hoping to make their fortunes. To keep the United States from claiming the land, the British government quickly created the colony of British Columbia and named James Douglas as its governor. James served as governor of British Columbia until 1864. Toward the end of his career, he was knighted for his services to Great Britain. The wife of a knight is called a lady, so Amelia became

The Granger Collection

Since gold is heavy, it sinks almost to the bottom of the gravel beds in streams.
► Describe panning for gold.

Lady Amelia Douglas. As the governor's wife, the métis from a frontier trading post had been the social leader of the growing city of Victoria. Now she had a title as well.

Amelia Douglas died in 1890, 13 years after her husband died. She had lived to see Victoria grow from a wilderness fort of 200 people to the capital of an important province in a growing nation.

LESSON **4** REVIEW

THINK AND WRITE

A. Why was the North West Company formed?

B. What did Alexander Mackenzie accomplish?

C. What did Thompson find when he reached the Columbia River?

D. How did England and the United States settle the issue of Oregon?

E. What lessons can be learned about frontier life from reading about Amelia Douglas?

SKILLS CHECK

MAP SKILL

Look up the *Fraser River* and the *Columbia River* in the Gazetteer and find two ways in which they are alike. Then locate each one on the physical map of Canada on page 545.

Building a Nation

THINK ABOUT WHAT YOU KNOW

By the late nineteenth century, Canada had become a vast land. With your classmates, discuss why many Canadians probably pushed to get better means of transportation across their country.

STUDY THE VOCABULARY

prime minister	transcontinental
negotiation	homesteaders

FOCUS YOUR READING

In what important ways did Canada change after it became a Dominion?

A. Canada's First Prime Minister

Sir John Macdonald A good part of the credit for the progress that Amelia Douglas saw during her life belongs to Canada's first **prime minister**, Sir John A. Macdonald. A prime minister is the head of a government that has a Parliament. You will read about Canada's government in the next chapter. Macdonald served in two separate periods, from 1867 to 1873 and again from 1878 until his death in 1891.

During Macdonald's years in office, three new provinces—Manitoba, British Columbia, and Prince Edward Island—joined the Dominion. Macdonald proved to be skilled at **negotiation**. Negotiation is the process of arriving at a solution acceptable to all parties. Macdonald peacefully put down a rebellion in the Northwest Territories. He also convinced the people of British Columbia to join Canada instead of the United States. By 1873, Canadian lands stretched from the Atlantic to the Pacific and from the shores of Lake Erie to the Arctic Ocean. With such a vast amount of land, many leading Canadians wanted a **transcontinental** railroad—a railroad across the continent, linking the Atlantic and the Pacific coasts. The Canadians wanted to connect goods and people on one shore with those on the other.

The Canadian Pacific Railroad Macdonald was one of the people who fought to get the railroad, but even with his efforts, it took a long time to build. It costs money to build a railroad, and money was in short supply then. Also, rugged land along much of the route made it difficult to lay the tracks. Finally, in 1885, the Canadian Pacific Railroad was completed, linking British Columbia and the Atlantic coast. It began regular service in 1886.

Sir John Macdonald tried hard to get a transcontinental railroad completed.
► What does the plaque say?

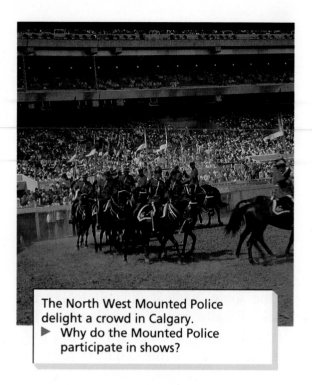

The North West Mounted Police delight a crowd in Calgary.
▶ Why do the Mounted Police participate in shows?

B. The Royal Canadian Mounted Police

The North West Mounted Police Sir John Macdonald also gets credit for Canada's very special police force, the famous North West Mounted Police.

The force began in 1873, just after the Northwest Territories joined the Dominion. The government wanted to bring law and order to this rough frontier area. It created the North West Mounted Police to carry out that mission.

Like many frontier areas, Canada's lightly settled west had some pretty tough customers. One problem needed immediate attention. Fur traders had built trading posts on the western frontier. In exchange for furs, traders gave the Indians whiskey. This resulted in so much drunkenness and trouble that the trading posts became known as whiskey forts.

The Mounted Police got the whiskey trade under control and made peace with the Indians of Canada's plains. The good relations between the police and the Indians is one reason why Canada did not have Indian wars like those that cost so many lives in the United States.

Royal Canadian Mounted Police Today the force is called the Royal Canadian Mounted Police, or RCMP, and the officers are nicknamed Mounties. The Mounties enforce all federal laws in Canada. They are the only police force in the Northwest Territories and in the Yukon Territory.

C. The Red River Rebellion

The Homesteaders' Concerns When the Hudson's Bay Company sold its land to the Canadian government in 1869, the métis and other **homesteaders** of the Northwest Territories became worried. Homesteaders are people who buy land in the wilderness for the purpose of building homes and farming. They feared that the new government, so far away in the east, would not understand or care about the needs or problems of the people who lived in the Red River Valley.

The Métis Speak Out After a métis rebellion failed in 1869, a group of the leading métis went to Ottawa, Canada's capital. There they met with government officials and explained their concerns. The government promised to give the métis the rights to educate their children in French and to hold the land they settled. As more and more non-French settlers filled the region, these promises proved hard to keep. Many of the métis lost their lands. Gradually, they moved west, onto the plains.

The plains also were changing. The new railroad helped businesspeople and travelers, but it brought trouble to the métis and the Indians. The buffalo became almost extinct, and the métis found that their homesteads were again in danger.

Louis Riel In 1885, another Red River rebellion was organized. Once more, the métis asked Louis Riel (ryel) to lead them. Riel, a well-educated métis, had led the earlier unsuccessful rebellion and then had gone into exile in the United States. Riel returned. Another rebellion failed. The government tried Riel for his part in the revolt. He was judged guilty and executed.

British Canadians thought of Riel as a rebel and a criminal. French Canadians, however, thought of him as a hero who died fighting for the rights of French-speaking Canadians. Riel's death widened the gap between British and French Canadians. It also caused the Conservative party to lose power to the Liberal party. The Liberals were led by Wilfrid Laurier (LAW ree ay). In the election of 1896, Laurier became the country's first French-Canadian prime minister.

D. Prosperity and Growth

Advances in the Early 1900s Prosperity marked the early 1900s in Canada. Agriculture, transportation, and industries grew. Two new transcontinental railroads — the Grand Trunk Pacific and the Canadian Northern — began service in the early 1900s. Fertile land, expanding industry, and a stable government made Canada a very attractive country. More than 2 million immigrants from Europe, with skills important to the growing nation, arrived in Canada between 1896 and 1911.

This courtroom scene shows Louis Riel on trial.
▶ How did French Canadians view Riel after the trial?

WHEN THEY JOINED THE DOMINION

Province/Territory	Year
New Brunswick	1867
Nova Scotia	1867
Ontario	1867
Manitoba	1870
Northwest Territories	1870
British Columbia	1871
Prince Edward Island	1873
Yukon Territory	1898
Saskatchewan	1905
Alberta	1905
Newfoundland	1949

After the British North America Act was passed, the Dominion grew.
► What happened in 1870?

Two New Provinces The creation in 1905 of two new provinces — Alberta and Saskatchewan — was another sign that Canada was rapidly maturing and moving toward total independence from Britain. Canada signed its first independent treaty with another nation in 1923. Until that time, Canadians had to get permission from the British to sign a treaty.

The Statute of Westminster Then, in 1931, the British Parliament passed the Statute of Westminster. By passing this law, Parliament made Canada and the other countries of the British Commonwealth of Nations equal partners with Great Britain. The Commonwealth had been set up in the early 1900s. It was a group of countries and territories that were ruled by Great Britain or that had once been ruled by Britain. The Statute of Westminster allowed those countries to choose whether they wanted to be members of the Commonwealth. It also stated that the British government could make laws only for Great Britain, not for any of the other Commonwealth countries.

In a way, then, 1931 marked a second independence for Canada. It is the year the country finally became self-governing. Canada still did not have a constitution, however. That took another 50 years. You will read about the Canadian constitution in Chapter 23.

As the twentieth century continued, Canada became an even wealthier and more important nation. Canadians played an important role in World War II, which lasted from 1939 until 1945. Over a million Canadians served in the armed forces, and 40,000 died in battles. At the same time, Canada's factories turned out many

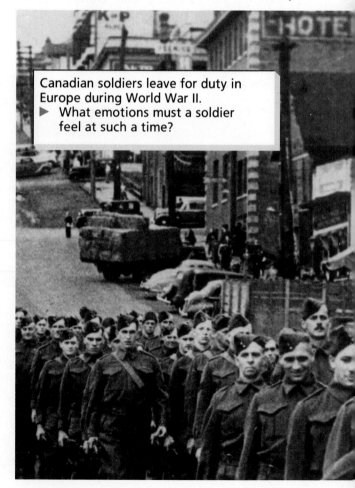

Canadian soldiers leave for duty in Europe during World War II.
► What emotions must a soldier feel at such a time?

The first Canadian soldiers arrive in Europe in December of 1939 at the start of World War II.
▶ In which countries might they have fought?

needed products, and the fertile lands provided food for the other nations that were its allies.

Canada and the United Nations Canada joined the United Nations as an original member after the war ended. The United Nations is an international organization, formed in 1945 in which nations can discuss their problems and concerns. Canada has played a major role in world affairs, helping to negotiate treaties and settle differences among other nations.

LESSON 5 REVIEW

THINK AND WRITE

A. What are some of the accomplishments of Sir John Macdonald?
B. Why did the new Canadian government create the RCMP?
C. Why did the métis rebel?
D. What is Canada's position in the world today?

SKILLS CHECK

THINKING SKILL

You read that good relations between the police and the Indians is one reason why Canada did not have Indian wars like those in the United States. What exactly, do you suppose, created that good relationship?

USING THE VOCABULARY

neutral	legislative
crest	artillery
sentries	canyon
Parliament	prime minister
representative	negotiation
Loyalists	transcontinental
invade	homesteaders

On a separate sheet of paper, write the word or words that best complete the sentences.

1. The _____ could shell the city with its large cannons.
2. Each _____ voted on behalf of the people he or she represented.
3. A _____ is the head of a country with a _____.
4. Many _____ bought and farmed land in the Canadian wilderness.
5. The _____ railroad linked the Atlantic and the Pacific coasts.
6. The _____ of a mountain is its highest point.
7. During the American Revolution, many _____ fled to Canada, where they could support Britain.
8. The _____ body makes the laws of a country.
9. Often, _____ countries will provide a place for warring countries to hold their meetings for peace.
10. The _____ kept watch at the fort for enemy soldiers.

REMEMBERING WHAT YOU READ

On a separate sheet of paper, write your answers in complete sentences.

1. Who are the Cajuns?
2. How did the Quebec Act help French Canadians?
3. Why did the British colonies of Quebec and Nova Scotia not send representatives to the First Continental Congress?
4. How did the wars between the United States and Great Britain in 1776 and 1812 affect Canada?
5. Why did Britain's Queen Victoria send Lord Durham to the Canadian provinces in 1838?
6. What was the British North America Act?
7. Who was the first Canadian explorer to reach the Pacific Ocean by land?
8. When the boundary to the west of the Rockies was set, what land did the United States get?
9. Name some of Sir John Macdonald's accomplishments as prime minister.
10. Whom did the metís consider to be their hero?

TYING ART TO SOCIAL STUDIES

Frontier life was exciting and dangerous for those who chose it in the 1800s. Amelia Douglas was born into that life and lived to see many changes in Canada. Create a poster or a mural with some classmates, depicting events in the life of Amelia Douglas. Use the information in this chapter or draw information from other sources so that your poster or mural will tell the story of her life.

THINKING CRITICALLY

On a separate sheet of paper, answer the following questions in complete sentences.

1. Why, do you think, was it difficult to make the people of Quebec be loyal to Britain?
2. Why was the First Continental Congress organized?
3. Is there a benefit to becoming independent slowly as Canada did? Explain.
4. Why were some provinces reluctant to become part of the union that was created by the British North America Act?
5. What effect did the Statute of Westminster have on the relationship between Canada and Great Britain?

SUMMARIZING THE CHAPTER

On a separate sheet of paper, draw a graphic organizer like the one shown here. Copy the information from this graphic organizer on the one you have drawn. Beside the main idea for each lesson, write details that support the main idea.

CHAPTER THEME
Canada, once French, becomes a British colony. It progresses to self-government within the British Commonwealth and becomes a world power.

LESSON 1
Canada becomes a British colony
1. _____ 2. _____ 3. _____

LESSON 2
Britain's wars with the United States affect Canada.
1. _____ 2. _____ 3. _____

LESSON 3
Canada moves slowly toward independence.
1. _____ 2. _____ 3. _____

LESSON 4
Canadians explore the west and set new boundaries.
1. _____ 2. _____ 3. _____

LESSON 5
Canada grows and prospers in the twentieth century.
1. _____ 2. _____ 3. _____ 4. _____

CHAPTER 22

THE RICH CANADIAN LAND

C anada's rugged interior is subject to long, cold winters, but its Pacific coast region is milder. Both regions are rich in natural resources.

Location and Climate

THINK ABOUT WHAT YOU KNOW

When people think about Latin America, images of sandy beaches and warm weather may come to mind. What kinds of land and weather come to mind when you think about Canada?

STUDY THE VOCABULARY

harbor	tree line
port	marine climate
deposit	continental climate
permafrost	coniferous

FOCUS YOUR READING

What types of location and climates does Canada have?

A. A Northern Land

When a Canadian who lives on the Atlantic coast sits down to dinner at 6:00 P.M., a Canadian who lives in the far northwest may not even have eaten lunch. That's because Canada's enormous east-to-west extent of some 3,223 miles (5,186 km) includes seven time zones.

Not only does Canada's size set it apart, but so does its location. On the political map of the world on pages 592 and 593 in the Atlas, you can see that only six other countries have land that lies north of the Arctic Circle. Canada's Ellesmere Island is nearly 1,200 miles (1,931 km) north of the Arctic Circle. In fact, Canada claims territory right up to the North Pole. Much of this land lies under the water and ice of the Arctic Ocean.

Even though Canada shares a land border with only one other country — the United States — it still has a strategic location. In some maps that you find in books or in classrooms, it is difficult to see why that is so. Those maps show the links between countries from east to west across the Atlantic and Pacific oceans. All you might notice is that Canada's closest neighbor across the Arctic Ocean is the former Soviet Union.

The map on the next page shows the world as if you were looking at it from just above the North Pole. On this kind of map, called a *polar projection*, you can see that the shortest routes from most parts of the United States and from southern Canada to many parts of Europe also cross Canada. If you wanted to fly from Washington, D.C., to Moscow, in the former Soviet Union, the shortest route would be across Canada and over the North Pole.

B. Ports and Harbors

Canada has **harbors** on three oceans —Atlantic, Pacific, and Arctic. A harbor is a place where ships can anchor protected from the wind and waves of the ocean. Canada's important **ports** are only on the Atlantic and Pacific coasts. A port is a place where products are loaded onto or taken off of ships. Most ports are built in harbors. Sometimes countries must build harbors for their ports because there are not enough natural harbors. Canada, however, has more harbors than it needs for ports.

Because much of the Arctic Ocean remains frozen all year long, shipping becomes possible in the Arctic only during the brief summer, when the ice has melted in the waters. Even so, because of the mineral **deposits** that are being found in the Far North, Canada's Arctic-coast harbors are gaining importance. A deposit is a large amount of a mineral found in a given place in the earth. Which minerals, do you think, might be found in the Far North?

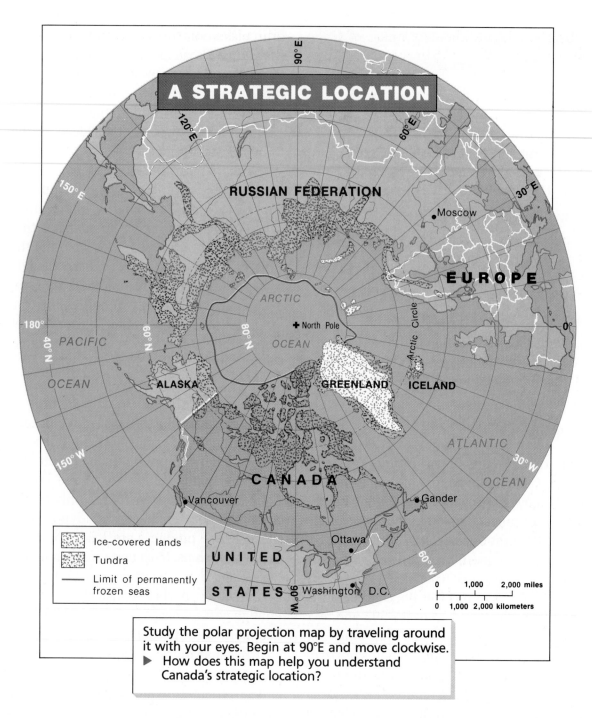

A STRATEGIC LOCATION

RUSSIAN FEDERATION

Moscow

EUROPE

ARCTIC

+ North Pole

OCEAN

Arctic Circle

ALASKA

GREENLAND   ICELAND

PACIFIC

OCEAN

ATLANTIC

OCEAN

C A N A D A

Vancouver

Gander

	Ice-covered lands
	Tundra
	Limit of permanently frozen seas

Ottawa

UNITED

STATES   Washington, D.C.

0   1,000   2,000 miles

0   1,000 2,000 kilometers

Study the polar projection map by traveling around it with your eyes. Begin at 90°E and move clockwise.
▶ How does this map help you understand Canada's strategic location?

From its Pacific and Atlantic coasts, it is easy for Canada to trade by sea with the countries of Asia and Europe. Sometimes, trading within its own country from one coast to the other is not as easy. The sea route through the Panama Canal from Canada's western port of Vancouver to its eastern port of Halifax is about 6,500 miles (10,459 km), about twice the distance from Halifax to Lisbon, Portugal.

C. A Land of Winter

The Tundra A Canadian poet once wrote, "My country is not a land, it's a winter." A subarctic climate blankets much of Canada's north, covering it with snow and ice for most of the year. This region is called the tundra. It is so far north that there is no real summer. The weather only gets warm enough to thaw out the top layer of frozen soil, about 1 to 4 feet (30 to 122 cm) thick. Beneath that, the soil is frozen all year long. This frozen soil of the tundra is called **permafrost**.

The Tree Line Not many plants can stand the extreme cold. Trees and other plants with deep roots cannot grow in this climate because their roots cannot penetrate the permafrost. The line beyond which trees cannot grow in northern regions is called the **tree line**. North of the tree line in the Arctic, there are only bushes and small, low growing plants, such as mosses. These types of plants grow quickly in the summer, when the ground is not frozen.

Difficulties in Travel During the summer, too, many swamps, marshes, and lakes form in the tundra because the permafrost keeps the water from seeping into the ground. This dampness makes the tundra difficult to travel over. It is easier to cross the tundra in winter, when the ground is frozen and hard. As you read more about the Canadian climates, refer to the two maps on this page.

D. Marine Climate

Other parts of Canada are much warmer, and it is in these warmer places that most Canadians live. Some parts of coastal Canada have a **marine climate.** A marine climate means that the temperature is affected by a nearby ocean. Canada's west coast enjoys a mild climate, mainly because of the winds from the Pacific Ocean. The ocean does not get as

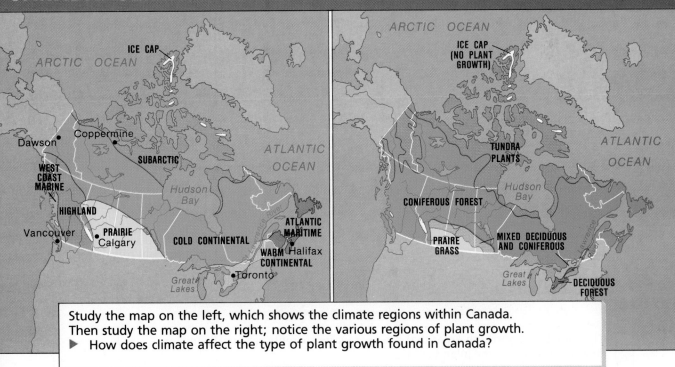

CANADA: CLIMATE REGIONS AND NATURAL PLANT GROWTH

Study the map on the left, which shows the climate regions within Canada.
Then study the map on the right; notice the various regions of plant growth.
▶ How does climate affect the type of plant growth found in Canada?

warm as land in summer nor as cold as land in winter. Winds blow across the ocean to the land. The cool ocean winds keep the coast from getting hot in summer, and they keep it from being extremely cold in winter.

The mountains near the coast also help to make the climate mild by blocking cold air from central Canada. The cold air rarely crosses the mountains to the coast. The Pacific coast of Canada is almost always warmer than other parts of Canada in the winter. The difference between summer and winter temperatures on the Pacific coast is small.

The ocean also affects precipitation. A warm ocean current, called the Alaskan Current, passes along the west coast of Canada. In Chapter 14, you read about a cold ocean current off the coast of Peru.

The Alaskan Current warms air that passes over it. The warmed air also picks up moisture from the ocean, since warm air can hold more moisture than cool air can. Then as the warm air passes inland from the coast, it begins to cool. Since cooler air can't hold as much moisture, clouds form, and some moisture falls as rain or snow. So the climate of the west coast of Canada is not only mild but also wet.

The Atlantic Ocean influences the marine climate of the provinces of New Brunswick, Nova Scotia, Prince Edward Island, and Newfoundland. These provinces are called the Maritime Provinces. They are near the sea, and the people living there have always made their living from the sea. *Maritime*, like the word *marine*, means "having to do with the sea." The Maritimes have a cooler climate than the west coast has in winter but a warmer climate than inland locations. Locate Halifax, Nova Scotia, on the map on page 543. Halifax has a marine climate.

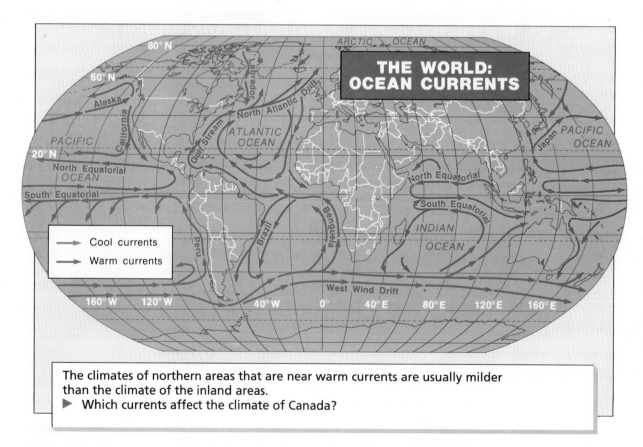

THE WORLD: OCEAN CURRENTS

The climates of northern areas that are near warm currents are usually milder than the climate of the inland areas.
▶ Which currents affect the climate of Canada?

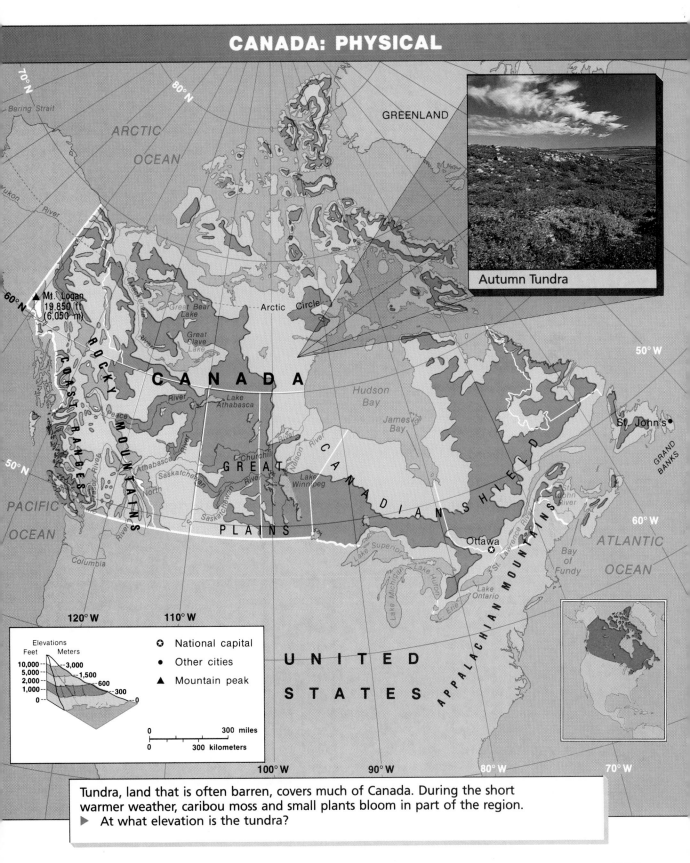

CANADA: PHYSICAL

GREENLAND

ARCTIC OCEAN

Bering Strait

70° N

80° N

Yukon River

60° N

▲ Mt. Logan
19,850 ft
(6,050 m)

Arctic Circle

Great Bear Lake

Great Slave Lake

ROCKY MOUNTAINS

COAST RANGES

PACIFIC OCEAN

50° N

CANADA

Peace River

Athabasca River

Lake Athabasca

Saskatchewan River

North

Saskatchewan

Columbia River

Fraser River

GREAT PLAINS

Churchill River

Nelson River

Lake Winnipeg

Hudson Bay

James Bay

CANADIAN SHIELD

50° W

St. John's •

GRAND BANKS

60° W

ATLANTIC OCEAN

Lake Superior

Lake Michigan

Lake Huron

Lake Ontario

Lake Erie

Ottawa ☆

St. Lawrence River

St. John River

APPALACHIAN MOUNTAINS

Bay of Fundy

Autumn Tundra

120° W   110° W

Elevations
Feet	Meters
10,000	3,000
5,000	1,500
2,000	600
1,000	300
0	0

✪ National capital
● Other cities
▲ Mountain peak

0   300 miles
0   300 kilometers

UNITED STATES

100° W   90° W   80° W   70° W

Tundra, land that is often barren, covers much of Canada. During the short warmer weather, caribou moss and small plants bloom in part of the region.
▶ At what elevation is the tundra?

Climograph:
CALGARY, ALBERTA

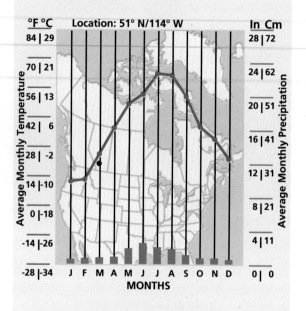

Location: 51° N/114° W

Climograph:
DAWSON, YUKON TERRITORY

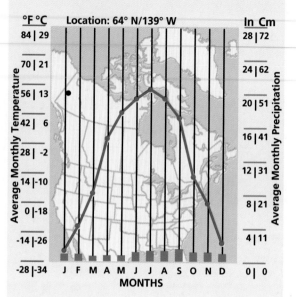

Location: 64° N/139° W

These climographs show the average monthly temperature and precipitation in different parts of Canada.

► Which two places have the most precipitation?

Climograph:
TORONTO, ONTARIO

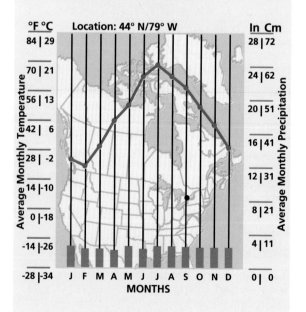

Location: 44° N/79° W

Climograph:
VANCOUVER, BRITISH COLUMBIA

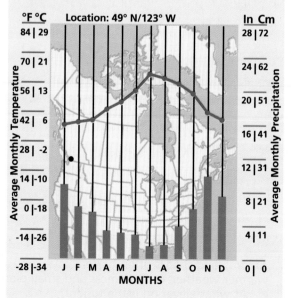

Location: 49° N/123° W

E. Continental Climates

A Dry Continental Climate Farther inland, away from the oceans, there are large differences between summer and winter temperatures. This type of climate is called a **continental climate**. The part of Canada east of the Rocky Mountains forms part of the Great Plains, the large plain in the middle of North America. Canadians call their southern portion of this plain the prairies. The Canadian prairies have long, cold winters, but the summers are warm. The prairies are too dry for most trees to grow, but grass grows well there.

The climograph for Calgary, Alberta, shows the climate of the Canadian prairies. Compare this climograph with the one for Vancouver. Calgary is drier than Vancouver. Winters in Calgary are colder and summers are warmer because Calgary is farther from the ocean than Vancouver is.

A Cold Continental Climate The middle part of Canada to the north of the prairies has a cold continental climate. This climate has the greatest difference between summer and winter temperatures of any Canadian climate. Dawson, in the Yukon Territory, has this type of climate. Compare the climographs for Dawson and Vancouver. You will notice that the winter temperatures in Dawson are much lower

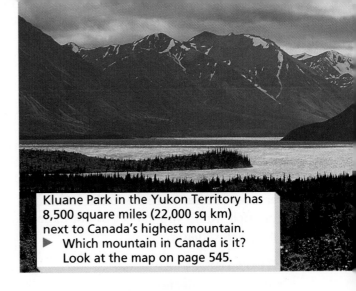

Kluane Park in the Yukon Territory has 8,500 square miles (22,000 sq km) next to Canada's highest mountain.
▶ Which mountain in Canada is it? Look at the map on page 545.

than they are in Vancouver. Lands with a cold continental climate have great forests of **coniferous**, or cone-bearing, trees. Coniferous trees have needles, and their seeds are carried in cones instead of in nuts or fruits.

A Warm Continental Climate A warm continental climate is found along the north shores of Lakes Erie and Ontario. This is the southernmost part of Canada. Summers in this part of Canada are long enough and warm enough for fruits and vegetables to grow. In summer the temperature may reach 90°F (32°C) or a little higher, but winters are long and cold. There is enough water from rain and snow for many different kinds of plant life to grow. The climograph for Toronto shows the climate of this area.

LESSON *1* REVIEW

THINK AND WRITE

A. Why is it correct to say that Canada has a strategic location?
B. Summarize the importance of Canada's ports and harbors.
C. Where is the coldest part of Canada?
D. What parts of Canada have a marine climate?

E. Summarize the three types of continental climates.

SKILLS CHECK

WRITING SKILL

Use the climographs on page 546 as models to make a climograph for your area for the next week. Include both precipitation and temperature.

Physical Features of Canada

You have read about the physical features of Latin America. What physical features similar to those found in Latin America would you expect or not expect to find in Canada?

STUDY THE VOCABULARY

pass	**glacier**
geologist	**barge**

FOCUS YOUR READING

What are some of Canada's major physical features?

A. Mountains

High Mountain Ranges Western Canada is a mountainous land. The Coast Ranges and the Rocky Mountains are very close together just north of the border with the United States. These two mountain ranges extend north all the way through Canada and into Alaska. They make up nearly 16 percent of Canada's territory. Find them on the map on page 545. The highest peak in the Canadian Rockies, Mount Robson in British Columbia, has an elevation of 12,972 feet (3,954 m). The highest point in all Canada is Mount Logan in the Coast Ranges. It rises to 19,850 feet (6,050 m). Valleys and **passes** cut these mountains. A pass is a narrow way through, especially through mountains.

The towering mountains make for spectacular scenery. That's one of the main attractions of Banff National Park in the Rockies in Alberta. Banff itself is 4,534 feet (1,382 m) above sea level, but you still have to look up at the peaks of the Rockies. Banff became Canada's first national park in 1885.

Low Mountain Ranges Eastern Canada has a much lower mountain range, the Appalachians. These mountains run from the southern United States to Newfoundland, the easternmost province of Canada. These are much older mountains than the Rockies, and over time they have become worn down. The highest Appalachian peak in Canada is Mount Jacques Cartier on the Gaspé Peninsula. It reaches a height of 4,160 feet (1,268 m).

B. The Canadian Shield

Geologists use the word *shield* to refer to large areas of very old, hard rock. Geologists are scientists who study the earth, including its rocks and fossils. You read a little about the Canadian Shield in Chapter 1. Curving around Hudson Bay,

Kirkland Lake, Ontario, was once a boom area for gold. Today, iron mining is more common.
▶ What might the miners be doing?

Niagara Falls lie between western New York State and southern Ontario. The Horseshoe Falls (shown) are on the Ontario side.
▶ How do travelers get from New York to Ontario?

the Canadian Shield covers about one half of Canada — all the land of eastern Canada from Lake Superior to the islands beyond the Arctic Circle in the Far North. Find the Canadian Shield on the map on page 545. The forested lands that stretch east from the city of Winnipeg are part of the Canadian Shield.

Glaciers, slow-moving bodies of ice, have scraped away most of the soft rock and soil that once covered the shield, leaving the old, hard rock exposed or very near the surface. As the glaciers melted, many lakes formed in low places. Lake Superior is the largest, but there are thousands of smaller lakes. Between the lakes are areas of low hills and marshes. Most of the Canadian Shield is hilly country.

Because of the poor soil and cold climate of the area, very few parts of the shield can be farmed. Not many people live there. Those who do generally work at mining or lumbering.

C. Niagara Falls

Two Sides to Niagara Falls The passengers wear raincoats to keep from getting wet. They have to shout to be heard above the nearly deafening roar of falling water. Those people are riding in *The Maid of the Mist*, a boat that gives tourists a close-up view of Niagara Falls. Every year, thousands of tourists flock to beautiful Niagara Falls on the Niagara River. The Niagara River flows between Lakes Erie and Ontario. It forms part of the border between the United States and Canada, so the falls have an American side, known as the American Falls, and a Canadian side, called Horseshoe Falls.

549

The height of the falls is not especially impressive. The American Falls are 182 feet (55 m) high, and the Horseshoe Falls are 173 feet (53 m) high. By comparison, the height of Angel Falls in Venezuela, as you have read, is 3,212 feet (979 m). However, Niagara Falls are the largest in North America in terms of the volume of water that spills over.

The Welland Ship Canal   The falls once blocked transportation between Lakes Erie and Ontario. Then in 1829 a **barge** canal was built on the Canadian side so that goods could be taken around the falls. A barge is a large, flat-bottomed boat that carries bulky loads. Over the years, the canal has been enlarged, and its route has been changed several times. Today the Welland Ship Canal connects the two lakes and carries large oceangoing ships.

The Welland Canal was opened in 1887 and later enlarged. The photograph shows a ship on the canal.
► What is very unusual here?

D. A Land of Water

Solution to a Problem   About 7 percent of Canada's area is made up of inland waterways. However, when you include coastal waters, such as the great Newfoundland fishing banks, as well as the immense northern waters of Foxe Basin, Hudson Bay, and James Bay, you can say that water makes up more than a quarter of the Canadian territory.

In Canada as in the United States, some important cities grew up on the shores of the Great Lakes. They include Toronto and Hamilton. The lakes provide good water transportation for trade. However, ships could not sail from the lakes all the way to the Atlantic Ocean. Canada and the United States cooperated to solve this problem.

The Great Lakes–St. Lawrence Waterway   Today, the Great Lakes, the St. Lawrence River, and several canals make up the Great Lakes — St. Lawrence Waterway. The Welland Canal is an important part of this waterway, which connects all the Great Lakes with the Atlantic Ocean.

The St. Lawrence Seaway   The canals near Montreal are known as the St. Lawrence Seaway. This seaway was completed in 1959 and is owned jointly by Canada and the United States. The seaway is about 450 miles (724 km) long. The seaway's canals have locks. As you may recall from the information about the Panama Canal, locks change the level of water so that ships can be raised and lowered. The seaway has canals at places where the river changes elevation. Once, ships could not pass the rapids near Montreal and sail on to Toronto. Now the ships can pass the rapids by going through the seaway.

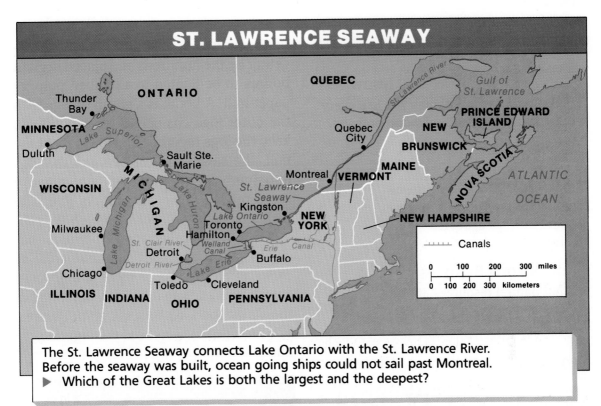

ST. LAWRENCE SEAWAY

The St. Lawrence Seaway connects Lake Ontario with the St. Lawrence River. Before the seaway was built, ocean going ships could not sail past Montreal.
▶ Which of the Great Lakes is both the largest and the deepest?

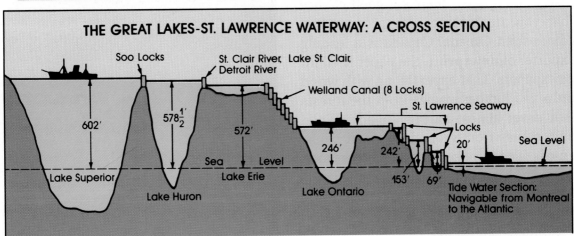

THE GREAT LAKES-ST. LAWRENCE WATERWAY: A CROSS SECTION

LESSON 2 REVIEW

THINK AND WRITE

A. How do the mountains on Canada's west coast compare with the mountains in eastern Canada?

B. What is the Canadian Shield?

C. Summarize the information given about Niagara Falls.

D. Why is the Great Lakes–St. Lawrence Waterway important?

SKILLS CHECK

MAP SKILL

Look up *Coast Ranges* and *Rocky Mountains* in the Gazetteer and compare ranges by their lengths.

551

Natural Resources

Make a list of some things you use every day that are made out of wood or wood products.

newsprint	water resource
wood pulp	management
boom	asbestos
inlet	

What natural resources are found in Canada, and how are they used?

A. Forests

Products from the Forests When you read a newspaper, there's a good chance that you are looking at a product that comes from Canada. Canada is a leading exporter of **newsprint**, the paper used for newspapers. That paper, along with **wood pulp** and lumber, comes from the forests that cover almost half of Canada. Wood pulp comes from ground-up wood chips. Pulp is used to make paper and other wood products. The making of pulp and paper is Canada's most important manufacturing industry.

Smaller trees, like those found in the Canadian Shield, are used to make wood pulp and paper. For lumber, however, large trees are best. British Columbia's giant Douglas fir trees near the coast as well as the spruce trees of the forests farther inland are ideal trees for lumber. British Columbia leads Canada in producing lumber and *plywood*. Plywood is board made of thin layers of wood glued and pressed together.

Moving Logs Loggers take the cut trees to a river, where the logs are gathered together by the hundreds and placed in giant **booms** to be floated to a lumber, pulp, or paper mill. A boom is a group of logs with the outer logs chained to one another to keep the logs together as they float. At the mill, the saws and grinders cut the logs into lumber or grind them up to make wood pulp. Some of the pulp is sold. The rest is made into paper.

There's another forest product that comes from Canada. It's not as useful as paper, but it sure tastes good. Maple syrup comes from the sugar maple trees found in the hardwood forests of southern Quebec. The province of Quebec is the biggest producer of maple syrup in North America.

Lumber booms are also used in British Columbia.
▶ Where might these booms be headed?

B. Food from Oceans

Fishing in Shallow Waters If you fish the oceans off Canada, it's best to stay near the coast. That's because most ocean fish live in shallow waters, which have rich food supplies for the fish. Most commercial fishing takes place near the coast or in other shallow waters, such as the Grand Banks. The two main fishing areas are the Atlantic fishery and the Pacific fishery. The Atlantic fishery accounts for about 60 percent of the total weight of fish taken in Canada. The catch includes cod, herring haddock, lobsters, and scallops. The fishing industry remains an important source of income. Over half of Canada's exports are to the United States.

Inshore Fisheries The Atlantic fishery of Canada is divided into inshore and offshore fisheries. Inshore fisheries are near the shore and in bays and **inlets**. An inlet is a narrow body of water that runs into the land. People who fish in inshore fisheries use small boats and light nets or lines. They go back and forth between the port and the sea each day.

Offshore Fisheries Offshore fisheries, such as the Grand Banks, are farther away from the coast. Offshore fishers use large boats called *trawlers*. These boats pull huge nets either through the water or along the bottom of the ocean. Fish get caught in the nets and are hauled on board the ship. Large trawlers may stay at sea for several weeks at a time.

Salmon and Herring In the Pacific fisheries, salmon and herring are the most important fish. Salmon leads both in the value of fish caught and in the weight. Salmon swim into freshwater streams to spawn, or to lay their eggs. The young

Inshore fishers catch cod near Twillingate, New World Island, Newfoundland.
▶ How are they catching the fish?

salmon live in the streams for up to two years after they are born. Then they swim out to sea. They may stay in the ocean for as long as ten years before returning to lay their eggs in the same streams where they were born.

Regulating the Waters Because of the importance of its maritime resources, Canada claims authority over waters up to 230 miles (370 km) from its coasts. In that way, it controls who fishes those waters. Regulating fishing activities and water quality is **water resource management.** Today, as concerns about pollution and the environment grow, water resource management has become more important.

MINERALS MINED IN CANADA

Mineral	Rank in world production	Use(s)	Mineral	Rank in world production	Use(s)
Asbestos	2	Insulation, shingles, brake linings	Natural gas	3	Fuel, fertilizer, chemicals
Coal	11	Fuel, chemicals	Nickel	2	Metal plating, alloy with other metals
Cobalt	4	Chemical industry, medicine, pigment (coloring)	Petroleum	10	Fuel, lubrication, plastics, synthetic fibers and fabrics
Copper	4	Electrical wire and equipment, coins, roofing, cooking ware	Platinum	3	Jewelry, laboratory equipment, electronic equipment
Gold	3	Jewelry, coins, dentistry, electronic equipment	Potash	2	Fertilizer
Iron	7	Metal products, construction, heavy equipment	Silver	5	Jewelry, silverware, coins, photographic materials
Lead	4	Storage batteries, solder, type, radiation shielding	Uranium	1	Nuclear power, military uses
Molybdenum	3	Alloy with other metals, spacecraft, high-temperature equipment	Zinc	1	Chemical industry, alloy with other metals, metal plating

Mining has caused economic growth in Canada. People have moved to remote regions of the country because of the mining industry.

► Different minerals can have common uses. Which three minerals mined in Canada does the jewelry industry depend upon?

C. Minerals and Metals

Canada ranks third, behind the United States and the former Soviet Union, among the world's mineral producers. In the export of minerals, however, Canada ranks number one. Canada has many rich mineral deposits, especially in the Canadian Shield and in the Rocky Mountains. The largest **asbestos** deposits in the Western Hemisphere are in eastern Quebec. Asbestos is a mineral found in long fibers which can be made into paper, cloth, or other products. Because asbestos will not burn, it is often used for making fireproof curtains, roofs, filters, and so on.

The table on this page shows some uses of potash, asbestos, coal, petroleum, and other minerals produced in Canada. Canada also leads the world in the production of nickel and zinc, and it is among the leaders in the mining of silver, gold, and platinum. It produces many other metals, too, such as copper, lead, and iron. Canadian resources also include large coal deposits in the southern Rockies of Alberta and British Columbia.

LESSON 3 REVIEW

THINK AND WRITE

A. What products come from the forests of Canada?
B. Why is fishing important in Canada?
C. What are some of the important minerals mined in Canada?

SKILLS CHECK

MAP SKILL

Look up *Nova Scotia* in the Gazetteer and find out what bodies of water border its shores. Then use the information to locate Nova Scotia on the map on page 545.

Abundant Energy

THINK ABOUT WHAT YOU KNOW

Think about ways that gas and electric energy are useful to you and your family. How important are such energies to any country?

STUDY THE VOCABULARY

potential
natural gas

FOCUS YOUR READING

What energy resources are there in Canada, and why are they important?

A. Oil

Tar Sands Have you ever walked on a sandy beach when your feet were wet? If so, you probably had a tough time brushing off all the sand that stuck to your feet. In central Alberta, there's no beach, but there are tar sands. These great beds of sand are saturated, or filled, with oil. Sand clings to the thick, sticky oil. To get the oil, the sand has to be dug up too. Then the oil and sand must be separated. The process used today removes only about 10 percent of the thick oil. It is an expensive way of getting oil.

The tar sands are a **potential**, or possible, resource. That is, although the oil is there and can be used, it is not being used. Until better ways are found to separate the oil from the sand, the tar sands will remain only a potential resource.

Oil-producing Regions Canada already benefits from major deposits of oil and of **natural gas** in Alberta, one of the Prairie Provinces. Natural gas is a mixture of gases, mostly methane, that is found naturally in the earth. It is taken out through pipes to be used as fuel. Alberta produces about 80 percent of the oil and natural gas

Laborers work on shifts to keep this Newfoundland rig operating constantly.
▶ From which angle is this photo taken—oblique or vertical?

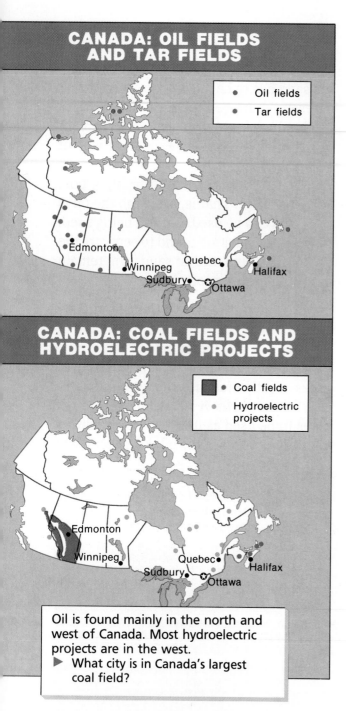

CANADA: OIL FIELDS AND TAR FIELDS

- Oil fields
- Tar fields

CANADA: COAL FIELDS AND HYDROELECTRIC PROJECTS

- Coal fields
- Hydroelectric projects

Oil is found mainly in the north and west of Canada. Most hydroelectric projects are in the west.
▶ What city is in Canada's largest coal field?

bernian Oil Project. It is the largest and most expensive oil project in Canada's history. As part of this project, which will be located about 180 miles (290 km) off the Newfoundland coast, workers will anchor a huge concrete platform to the ocean floor. This area lies near the Grand Banks. The project has caused some worry among those who earn their living from the sea.

Exports to the United States Canada exports large amounts of petroleum products and natural gas to the United States. The products include gasoline, refined oil, and many chemicals made from petroleum. Canada supplies about 13 percent of the petroleum products imported by the United States. No single country supplies more. Canada also supplies 4 percent of the natural gas used in the United States. Because of its location and rich energy resources, Canada is very important to the United States economy.

B. Generating Electricity

Hydroelectricity supplies about 70 percent of the energy used in Canada. Canada produces more hydroelectricity than any other country except the United States.

Canada's greatest potential sources of hydroelectricity, as well as its greatest actual sources, are the waters of the Canadian Shield. Dams and power plants could be built at many spots on the shield's hundreds of rivers and lakes. However, many rivers of the shield are far away from large cities, where the need for electric power is greatest. Until fairly recently, it was not possible to move electricity long distances. For that reason, the rivers of the Canadian Shield were not used to make electricity.

in Canada. Other oil-producing regions are in British Columbia, Saskatchewan, and the Northwest Territories. The Canadian government is also cooperating with the government of the province of Newfoundland and private oil companies on the Hi-

Today, new and better ways of moving electricity make it possible to send power from generators in the Canadian Shield to cities far to the south. A large hydroelectric plant has been built at Churchill Falls in the region of Labrador in Newfoundland. High-voltage wires carry electricity from Churchill Falls all the way to Quebec City and other cities in the St. Lawrence River valley. These cities are over 500 miles (805 km) away.

C. Giant Plants

Hydroelectric Plants A large hydroelectric plant in Quebec is on the Manicouagan (man uh KWAHG un) and Aux Outardes (oo TAHRD) rivers. It is part of a group of dams and generating plants that produces nearly one third of Quebec's hydroelectric power. This power is used in Quebec City, Montreal, and the northeastern United States. An even larger project is built on La Grande River, about 850 miles (1,368 km) north of Montreal. La Grande River flows into James Bay, at the south end of Hudson Bay. The project is named the James Bay Project.

The La Grande Complex The La Grande complex is the largest hydroelectric plant in North America. It is also one of the largest hydroelectric power projects in the world. It has many dams and four separate

Most all of British Columbia's electricity is generated by HEP.
▶ For what, do you think, does HEP stand?

power plants. One of them is the world's largest underground power plant. The James Bay Project alone produces about half the hydroelectricity used in Quebec.

James Bay Project: Phase 2 With the importance of energy in today's world, Canada wants to continue developing its hydroelectric resources. In 1988, Canada announced that it would begin Phase 2 of the James Bay Project. This will involve building three new dams to increase the output of hydroelectric energy by about 40 percent. Much of this power will be sold to New York State.

LESSON *4* REVIEW

THINK AND WRITE

A. Summarize why oil and gas are important to Canada.
B. What resource supplies most of Canada's energy needs?
C. What is the James Bay Project?

SKILL CHECK
WRITING SKILL

Look up *Quebec City* in the Gazetteer. Use the three important facts given to write a short definition of Quebec City.

LESSON 5

The Canadian Economy

THINK ABOUT WHAT YOU KNOW
You have read about Canada's wealth of natural resources. What predictions can you make about the income and standard of living for Canadians?

STUDY THE VOCABULARY
combine   diversified
mixed farm

FOCUS YOUR READING
What are Canada's major economic activities?

A. A Developed Country

In the Early 1900s At the beginning of the twentieth century, Canada's economy resembled the kind of economy that many Latin American nations have today. Most Canadians worked as farmers or miners, and Canada exported agricultural products and raw materials.

Growth of Manufacturing Over the years, however, there were many developments. Manufacturing grew. Much of this manufacturing involved the processing of Canada's rich natural resources. For example, Canada used its vast forests as the base for a wood and paper industry. Canada did not rely on just one type of product. Because of this change, Canada became a developed nation.

Needs and Surplus The powerful Canadian economy churns out an enormous amount of goods and services. Canada's gross national product (GNP) of about $400 billion exceeds that of every nation in the Western Hemisphere except the United States. The size of Canada's economy becomes even more impressive when you consider Canada's relatively small population of 27 million. If you divide that large amount of production among that small population, you see the average Canadian is very productive and lives well. This per capita income gives a clearer picture of the economy.

Study the chart on this page. Notice how much poorer Brazil appears when you divide its large GNP among 148 million Brazilians. Canada's relatively small population provides another advantage. After taking care of the needs of its own people, Canada still has surpluses to sell abroad.

In Canada, as in other countries in the Western Hemisphere, some people have enormous wealth, and others live in poverty. Also, as you will read, not all of the regions in Canada enjoy an equal level of development or standard of living. In general, developed countries can provide a decent standard of living for most of their people. Canadians today enjoy one of the highest standards of living in the world.

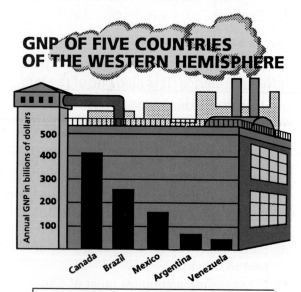

GNP OF FIVE COUNTRIES OF THE WESTERN HEMISPHERE

Annual GNP in billions of dollars

500 400 300 200 100

Canada   Brazil   Mexico   Argentina   Venezuela

The gross national products (GNP) for five nations are shown above.
▶ Compare Canada's GNP with the other nations' GNP's.

B. Farming the Land

Hard Wheat and Other Crops Only about 4 percent of its land can be farmed, but Canada still is one of the world's great agricultural countries. Remember, Canada is a huge country, so 4 percent of its total land area equals about 110 million acres (45 million ha) of land suited to farming.

Nearly four fifths of Canada's agricultural lands are in the Prairie Provinces of Alberta, Saskatchewan, and Manitoba. Saskatchewan alone has 40 percent of all the land cleared for farming in Canada. Although the farms of the prairies also grow barley, rye, and oats, their main crop is wheat. Canada is the world's second largest exporter of wheat. The United States is the largest. Much of the wheat grown in Canada is hard wheat. That's the best kind to use to make macaroni and spaghetti as well as bakery items, such as bread and cakes.

The farms of the prairies are the largest in Canada. The size of the average farm on the prairies is over 800 acres (324 ha) — big enough to hold more than 600 football fields! On such large farms, plowing and planting are done with huge tractors. Some of these tractors have tires that are taller than a person. Harvesting is done with **combines** (KAHM bynz). A combine is a large machine that can cut the plants and separate the grain from the stalks in one operation.

Canada has other agricultural areas too. For example, Quebec farmers grow apples, blueberries, raspberries, potatoes, beans, cabbage, carrots, peas, and other fruits and vegetables. These crops do not need very warm temperatures or a long growing season.

Along the shores of the Great Lakes and in the St. Lawrence Valley, the farms

In Manitoba a farmer harvests his wheat crop using a combine. This machine can cut and thresh grains of wheat in one operation.
▶ In which region is Manitoba located?

of both Quebec and Ontario supply fruits, vegetables, and dairy products. Often, several different crops are grown. A farm that grows a variety of crops is called a **mixed farm**.

About three quarters of Canada's farms raise livestock. There are many cattle ranches, sheep ranches, and hog farms in the Prairie Provinces. Most of those animals are raised for meat. Quebec has many dairy farms. Part of the milk is bottled for sale, but most of it is used to make dairy products, such as butter, cheese, and ice cream.

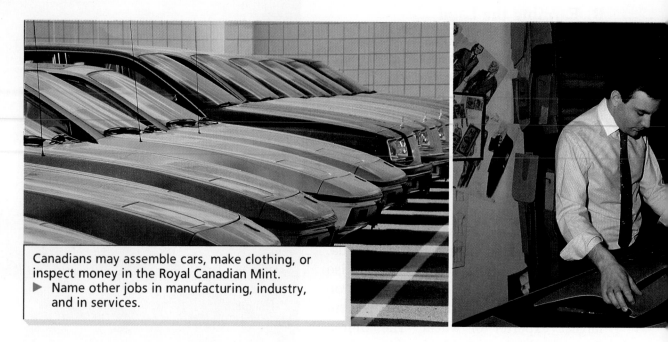

Canadians may assemble cars, make clothing, or inspect money in the Royal Canadian Mint.
▶ Name other jobs in manufacturing, industry, and in services.

C. Manufacturing

Leaders of the Nation Canadian factories turn out a wide variety of goods, from processed food and beverages to heavy machinery and aircraft equipment. Canada's leading industries are motor vehicles, wood pulp and paper, meat processing, oil refining, and iron and steel. Much of this manufacturing takes place in the province of Ontario. That's why it has the nickname "the workshop of the nation." Quebec is Canada's other major manufacturing area. These two provinces of Ontario and Quebec together account for about two thirds of all of Canada's manufacturing.

Ontario leads the nation in the production of iron and steel. The Ontario cities of Oshawa and Windsor are centers of automobile manufacturing. The "big three" automobile makers of the United States — Chrysler, Ford, and General Motors — have major operations in Canada.

Different Industries Canada's single largest center of manufacturing is metropolitan Toronto, in Ontario. This area has **diversified** industry. That means it has industries of many different kinds. Cloth, food, beverages, and farm equipment are important industries. Machinery and the steel to be used in buildings and for heavy equipment are other industries. Books and magazines, as well as many other things are made in and near Toronto.

Montreal, Quebec, is Canada's second largest manufacturing center. Montreal is a center for Canada's clothing industry. This industry produces clothes made from fur and cloth. Furs don't have the importance they used to have, but Canadians still trap beavers and muskrats in the forests of the Canadian Shield and Rocky Mountains. Ranches also raise animals, especially fox and mink, for furs. Other important industries in Montreal are food and beverage making and oil refining. Montreal's oil refineries produce about one third of Canada's gasoline. The factories of Montreal also make railroad locomotives and airplanes.

D. Services

Not everyone in Canada's labor force works in farms or factories. In fact, the single largest employment area is that of service industries. Workers in service industries represent people in court, teach school, sell various products, and type letters. In other words, they provide services, usually some type of information, instead of producing goods.

Today, nearly three out of every four Canadian workers are in service industries. In Canada, the United States, and other countries with advanced, or developed, economies, employment in service industries is growing faster than it is in manufacturing, farming, mining, or any other part of the economy.

The proportion of service jobs to manufacturing jobs in these countries will probably continue to grow. This is due to several things. First, manufacturing is moving to countries in Asia, Latin America, and Africa, where workers' wages are lower. Second, as more and better machinery is invented for factories, farms, and mines, fewer workers will be needed to produce the same amount of goods. At the same time, people want more information services from government and business.

LESSON 5 REVIEW

THINK AND WRITE

A. How has Canada's economy changed during the twentieth century?
B. What are some of Canada's important agricultural products?
C. What are Canada's leading industries?
D. Why is the importance of service industries growing in Canada?

SKILLS CHECK

THINKING SKILL

Select one service job, such as that of a librarian, lawyer, or banker. What type of information might that service work provide for other people? Share your ideas with some classmates.

561

22 PUTTING IT ALL TOGETHER

USING THE VOCABULARY

permafrost	water resource
asbestos	management
coniferous	marine climate
diversified	inlet
potential	combine
	glacier

On a separate sheet of paper, write the words that best match the definitions.

1. regulating fishing activities and water quality
   a. marine climate
   b. water resource management
2. many different kinds
   a. diversified
   b. combine
3. narrow body of water that runs into land
   a. inlet
   b. glacier
4. something that may be used in the future
   a. coniferous
   b. potential
5. frozen soil of the tundra
   a. permafrost
   b. asbestos

REMEMBERING WHAT YOU READ

1. Why are Canada's Arctic coast harbors gaining importance?
2. Name and briefly describe the two main types of climate — marine and continental — found in Canada.
3. Name the major mountain ranges in Canada. What makes them different?
4. What are the famous falls on the border of the United States and Canada?
5. Name some of the many products the United States depends on from Canada's forests.
6. What is the difference between an inshore fishery and an offshore fishery?
7. What energy source does the United States import from Canada?
8. What energy source does Canada depend on and use to produce a major part of its energy?
9. What caused Canada to change from a farming nation to an industrial one?
10. Why is Canada still a great agricultural country?

TYING SCIENCE TO SOCIAL STUDIES

Energy and the resources needed to supply it are important topics in every country. Likewise, scientists are constantly looking for ways to help governments meet energy needs while practicing conservation. Research the ways that Canada is meeting its energy needs. What projects are underway to better use the abundant supply of water in the country? Is the Far North being used more to find oil? Have any potential sources, like tar sands, been developed more? Use your findings to write a report or create some graphs to illustrate the information.

THINKING CRITICALLY

On a separate sheet of paper, write your answers in complete sentences.

1. Geographically speaking, why is Canada in a fortunate position?
2. Why is it important for the United States and Canada to cooperate in using the St. Lawrence Seaway?
3. Why are the Canadian people and their government concerned about pollution of Canada's waters? What must they do to protect the waters?
4. Why is Canada looking for better ways to produce hydroelectric power?
5. How will the people of Canada be affected as service industries become more important than manufacturing, mining, and farming?

SUMMARIZING THE CHAPTER

On a separate sheet of paper, draw a graphic organizer like the one shown here. Copy the information from this graphic organizer on the one you have drawn. Under each lesson heading, write three facts you have learned.

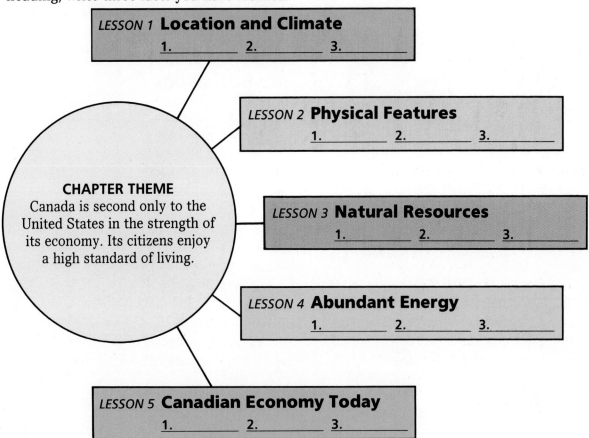

LESSON 1 **Location and Climate**
1._____ 2._____ 3._____

LESSON 2 **Physical Features**
1._____ 2._____ 3._____

CHAPTER THEME
Canada is second only to the United States in the strength of its economy. Its citizens enjoy a high standard of living.

LESSON 3 **Natural Resources**
1._____ 2._____ 3._____

LESSON 4 **Abundant Energy**
1._____ 2._____ 3._____

LESSON 5 **Canadian Economy Today**
1._____ 2._____ 3._____

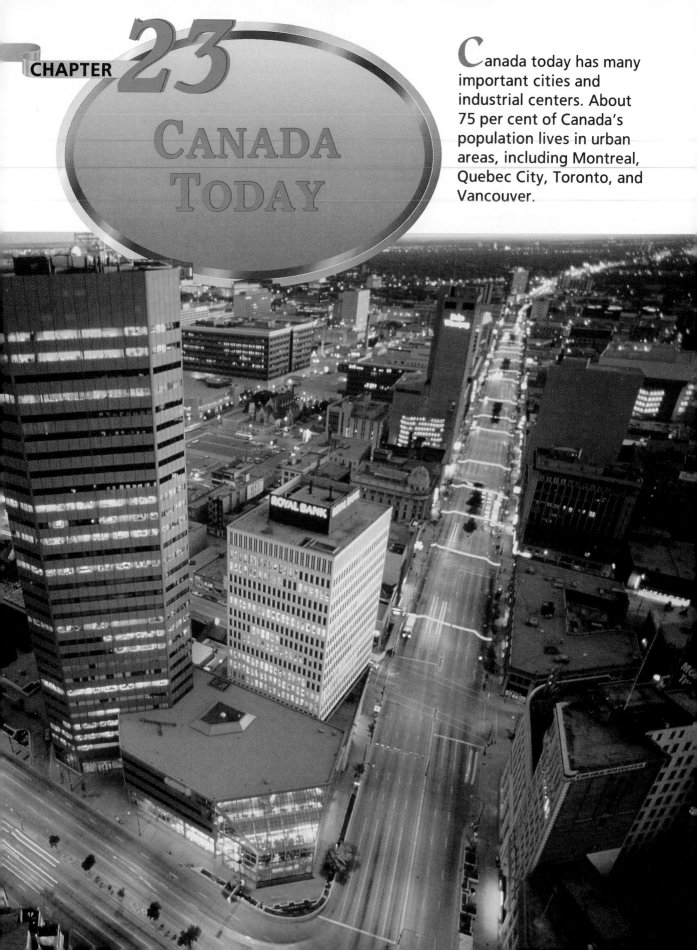

CHAPTER

23

CANADA TODAY

*C*anada today has many important cities and industrial centers. About 75 per cent of Canada's population lives in urban areas, including Montreal, Quebec City, Toronto, and Vancouver.

Canada's Regions

You have read elsewhere in this book about regions, areas that have common characteristics. Think about what you have learned about Canada. What parts of the country would you put together as regions?

urbanization
Pacific Rim

What are the different regions that make up Canada?

A. Land of Contrasts

After reading about Canada's climates and resources, you may be thinking about how very different the parts of Canada are from one another. That's because Canada, like many of the Western Hemisphere countries, is a land of many regions.

As you may recall, there are different ways to think about regions. Some people say that there are really two regions of Canada, one with a French heritage and the other with a British heritage. This is a way to think of Canada as two cultural regions. When other people speak about two Canadas, however, they are referring to the largely unpopulated northern area and the highly populated southern area bordering the United States. In addition to these distinctions between French and English and north and south, there are other ways to divide Canada into regions. In the rest of this lesson, you will read about another division of regions within Canada. The regions are the Yukon and the Northwest Territories, the Atlantic Provinces, Ontario, Quebec, the Prairie Provinces, and British Columbia.

B. The Territories and the Atlantic Provinces

The Territories The Yukon Territory and the Northwest Territories have similar characteristics. They both are far away from Canada's centers of population and are inhabited mostly by either Inuit or Native Americans. Neither is self-governing.

Atlantic Provinces The three Maritime Provinces — Prince Edward Island, Nova Scotia, and New Brunswick — along with Newfoundland and Labrador, make up the region known as the Atlantic Provinces. This region is the poorest region outside of the territories. It has 10 percent of Canada's population, but it provides only 5

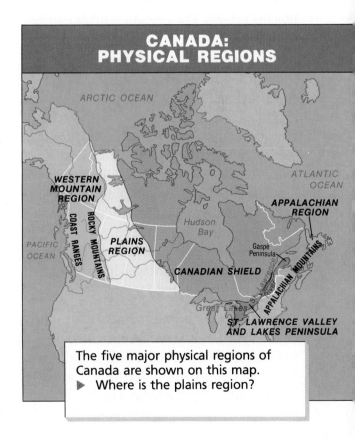

CANADA: PHYSICAL REGIONS

The five major physical regions of Canada are shown on this map.
▶ Where is the plains region?

percent of the nation's gross national product (GNP). The region of the Atlantic Provinces has less manufacturing than any part of Canada except the Yukon and the Northwest Territories. The major industries of this region are food processing, forest products, and textiles.

In a way, the Atlantic Provinces region is similar to the Brazilian Northeast. It once was the very heart of Canada, supplying much of the wealth and leadership for the nation. Today, however, many people leave the Atlantic Provinces for other parts of Canada to seek better economic opportunities.

C. Ontario and Quebec

Ontario If the region of the Atlantic Provinces is like Brazil's poorer Northeast, then Ontario is like the wealthy Southeast of Brazil. About 35 percent of all Canadians live in Ontario. They produce 40 percent of Canada's GNP and about 50 percent of all that Canada manufactures. Ontario is home to Canada's national capital, Ottawa, as well as to the country's largest metropolitan area, Toronto. In many ways, Ontario is the intellectual and cultural leader of English-speaking Canada.

Ontario enjoys a good climate and a favorable location for shipping. It has easy access to the Great Lakes trade and access to the Atlantic through the Great Lakes–St. Lawrence Waterway. This location also gives it advantages in trading with markets in the United States.

Quebec The one province that truly challenges Ontario is Quebec. About 28 percent of all Canadians call Quebec home. Many of them live in Montreal, Canada's largest city. After Ontario, Quebec is Canada's most urbanized province.

About 80 percent of Quebec's people speak French as their first language. However, many of the citizens here also speak English, the main language spoken in the other provinces. You will read more about Quebec's two languages in Lesson 4.

The St. Lawrence River flows through Quebec, so even before the building of the St. Lawrence Waterway, Quebec had a good location for trade. Quebec is a major manufacturing region. It is not a farming area. The rocky soil of the Canadian Shield makes agriculture difficult.

Although Quebec rivals Ontario in many areas, Quebec's people are far less wealthy. In fact, people who live in the

The Château Frontenac, a hotel, is a well-known landmark in Quebec City.
▶ Using the map on page 570, name the river on which Quebec is located.

A group of teenagers stop to sing in Old Montreal.
▶ Think of at least two reasons they might sing in public.

port of Thunder Bay, the most important Canadian port on Lake Superior. Thunder Bay was once the twin cities of Fort William and Port Arthur. The two cities joined in 1969 and took the name *Thunder Bay*.

The prairies also lead Canada in producing fuel, but until recently, not much manufacturing took place in the Prairie Provinces. Now a petrochemical industry has grown up. The increasing wealth of the prairies has also sparked **urbanization**. Urbanization is the condition of changing from rural to urban in character. Now that the prairies have gained economically, the people there have also begun to complain about eastern Canada's superior role.

portion of Quebec that is downstream from Quebec City have the lowest average income in all of Canada. The poverty of these French Canadians has often been an important political issue.

D. The Prairie Provinces

European Immigrants The Prairie Provinces were the last part of southern Canada to be settled. Beginning in the late nineteenth century, immigrants from many countries made their homes on the prairies. Most of these immigrants came from eastern Europe. That immigration continues today. There are towns on the prairies where nearly everyone is from Hungary or Germany or Ukraine, which was a part of the former Soviet Union. You can pick out a town with Ukrainians by its church with an onion-shaped dome atop it.

Economy in the Provinces The Prairie Provinces provide most of Canada's agricultural production, especially wheat. Most of the wheat produced on the Canadian prairies is shipped by railroad to the

In Saskatchewan, Ukrainian dancers participate in the Saskatoon Folk Festival.
▶ Where is Saskatchewan?

Vancouver is British Columbia's largest city.
▶ In what part of the city might this suspension bridge be?

E. British Columbia

British Influence Since British Columbia only has a little over 10 percent of Canada's population, you may wonder why this province should be considered separately. Part of the reason is that British Columbia really doesn't fit well with the other provinces of Canada. Unlike the eastern provinces, which, as you may recall, became provinces of Britain after the French and Indian War, British Columbia first came under British control in 1843. Most other western provinces had strong trade relations with eastern Canada. British Columbia, however, had most of its trade relations with Britain for many years.

Part of the Pacific Rim British Columbia's location on the Pacific Ocean also makes a difference. It is part of the **Pacific Rim**. The term *Pacific Rim* refers to countries and parts of countries in Asia and the Americas that border the Pacific Ocean. That region includes some of the fastest-growing economic powers in today's world. Japan and South Korea are Pacific Rim countries.

Throughout its history, British Columbia has looked to the Orient, especially Japan, for trade. Many Japanese people live in British Columbia's capital city, Vancouver. People from Hong Kong and Singapore are setting up businesses in Vancouver and buying property in British Columbia. Also, British Columbia carries on a lively trade with the Pacific Coast United States.

LESSON *1* REVIEW

THINK AND WRITE

A. What are some different ways of dividing Canada into regions?

B. How would you describe the region of the Atlantic Provinces?

C. Compare and contrast Ontario and Quebec.

D. What do the Prairie Provinces have in common?

E. Why can British Columbia be considered as a separate region?

SKILLS CHECK

WRITING SKILL

Think about life in the Yukon and the Northwest Territories. Write a persuasive advertisement to attract more people to live there.

LESSON 2

An Urban Nation

THINK ABOUT WHAT YOU KNOW

Make a list of some of the cities of Canada that you have read about, visited, or seen in documentary films on television. Pick a city of your choice and tell why you would like to visit it.

STUDY THE VOCABULARY

centennial
fjord

FOCUS YOUR READING

What are some important cities in Canada?

This photograph shows a view of the city of Winnipeg.
► What does it show that is also mentioned in the text?

A. A Nation of Cities

Population Patterns In 1945, only 58 percent of Canadians lived in towns or cities. Today, about 75 percent of Canada's people live in urban areas. Canada has 24 metropolitan areas. The size of a metropolitan area shows the importance of the area much better than the size of its main city.

In this lesson you will be reading about some major metropolitan areas in Canada. They are Winnipeg, Calgary, Ottawa, Montreal, Quebec City, Toronto, and Vancouver. Locate each of these cities on the map on page 570.

Winnipeg in Manitoba There really is not enough space to include information about every city in Canada. That's a shame, because so many of them are interesting places. For example, there's Winnipeg, the capital of the province of Manitoba and the largest city in central Canada. It is an important transportation and agricultural center. Winnipeg is also a city of beautiful parks.

Calgary in Alberta Then there's Calgary, a city in the Prairie Province of Alberta that some people call the Dallas of Canada. Calgary, like Dallas, began as a cattle-raising center. It still holds a famous rodeo, the Calgary Stampede, each summer. Today, Calgary is also an oil-and-gas-producing center. Over 400 oil and gas companies have offices there. Calgary received a big boost when it hosted the 1988 Winter Olympic Games.

Ottawa, Canada's Capital Ottawa is a lovely city, known for its beautiful parks and fine universities. Of course, it is also known for its important governmental buildings, such as those where Parliament meets.

B. Montreal

An Island City On an island in the St. Lawrence River, you'll find Canada's second largest city, Montreal. It's also the second largest French-speaking city in the

569

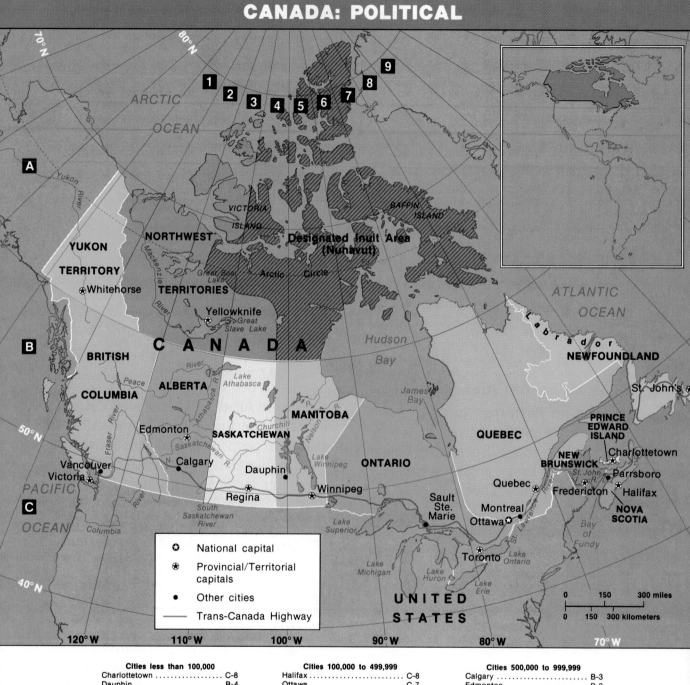

CANADA: POLITICAL

National capital ⬡
Provincial/Territorial capitals ✪
Other cities ●
Trans-Canada Highway ▬

Cities less than 100,000

Charlottetown	C-8
Dauphin	B-4
Fredericton	C-8
Parrsboro	C-8
St. John's	C-9
Sault Ste. Marie	C-6
Victoria	C-2
Whitehorse	A-1
Yellowknife	A-3

Cities 100,000 to 499,999

Halifax	C-8
Ottawa	C-7
Quebec	C-7
Regina	B-4
Vancouver	C-2

Cities 500,000 to 999,999

Calgary	B-3
Edmonton	B-3
Montreal	C-7
Toronto	C-7
Winnipeg	C-5

Canada, the world's second largest country, extends from Newfoundland on the Atlantic Coast to British Columbia on the Pacific Coast.
▶ Through which provinces does the Trans-Canada Highway pass?

In Montreal, some people travel by subway, using the Métro (bottom). Others cross the Jacques Cartier, the Victoria, or the Champlain bridge.
► Which same river do all the bridges span?

world. The only larger French-speaking city is Paris, the capital of France. Two thirds of Montreal's people are of French background. Most street signs and advertisements are in French. Both English and French plays and films appear in the theaters, and the stores sell books and newspapers in both languages.

Old Montreal The historical part of the city is called Old Montreal. Winding your way through narrow streets, you'll see many restored old buildings. Be sure to stop for a moment at the Place d'Armes, a central square like those you read about earlier in Latin American cities. In that square in 1644, the founders of Montreal had their first encounter with the Iroquois.

Modern Montreal Tall glass-and-steel skyscrapers can be seen in the newer sections of Montreal. You can take a ride on one of the world's most interesting subways. A different architect decorated each

of the subway stations in a special style. The city also has a large number of museums, parks, and recreational facilities.

Attractive to Tourists People from all over the world visit Montreal for pleasure or business. Many foreign visitors went to Montreal for Expo '67, the Canadian World's Fair. It was held in 1967 as part of Canada's **centennial**, or one hundredth anniversary, celebration. Expo '67 closed after one year, but the buildings that housed that 1967 World's Fair are still open. Each summer there are displays about different cultures of the world.

Winter sports are popular in the vicinity of Montreal. The Laurentian Mountains, near Montreal, are famous for their fine ski runs. People also enjoy sports activities during the other seasons. The Montreal Marathon, held every September, attracts thousands of runners and spectators from all over the world.

Events during Winter Carnival in Quebec include canoe races and snow sculpture contests.
▶ What other events might take place during Winter Carnival?

C. Quebec City

Have you ever seen pictures of old cities surrounded by great walls? There's only one such city left in all of North America. It's Quebec City, the capital of the province of Quebec. The part of the city inside the walls is called the Old City. It has many buildings that were built in the seventeenth and eighteenth centuries. These old stone buildings, like those of Old Montreal, have been restored. They show what Quebec City was like long ago. Beyond the walls, the city is modern, with shopping centers, skyscrapers, and so on.

The population of Quebec City is 95 percent French-speaking. Because the majority of the people are of French heritage, Quebec City has kept more of the traditional French-Canadian ways. For example, if you go to a restaurant in Quebec City, you can order some of the French-Canadian specialties, such as thick pea soup, tourtières (toor TYAIRZ), and lobster salad. The pea soup is made with yellow peas, not the green ones you may be used to. A tourtières is a pie made with meat. Spiced ground pork is a favorite filling, but any kind of meat can be used. For dessert you may want to order maple sugar pie with cream.

While you are in Quebec City, you will want to visit the Château Frontenac (sha-TOH FRAHNT uh nak). It is a large hotel, built in 1892 on the spot where Samuel de Champlain lived. The present building is in French style with steep, copper-covered roofs and thick stone walls. Looking out from the Château Frontenac, you'll have a fine view of the lower city and of the St. Lawrence River valley.

PROVINCES AND TERRITORIES OF CANADA

	CAPITAL CITY AND POPULATION	FLAG	TOTAL AREA	POPULATION AND DENSITY	MAIN PRODUCTS
ALBERTA	Edmonton 574,000		255,285 sq mi 661,190 sq km	2,340,600 9 per sq mi 4 per sq km	Oil
BRITISH COLUMBIA	Victoria 66,000		365,946 sq mi 947,800 sq km	2,800,500 8 per sq mi 3 per sq km	Lumber
MANITOBA	Winnipeg 595,000		250,946 sq mi 649,950 sq km	1,042,500 4 per sq mi 2 per sq km	Wheat
NEW BRUNSWICK	Fredericton 44,000		28,355 sq mi 73,440 sq km	706,300 25 per sq mi 10 per sq km	Potatoes
NEWFOUNDLAND	St. John's 96,000		156,648 sq mi 405,720 sq km	575,900 4 per sq mi 1 per sq km	Fish
NOVA SCOTIA	Halifax 114,000		21,425 sq mi 55,490 sq km	857,100 40 per sq mi 15 per sq km	Fish
ONTARIO	Toronto 612,000		412,579 sq mi 1,068,580 sq km	8,753,600 25 per sq mi 9 per sq km	Minerals
PRINCE EDWARD ISLAND	Charlottetown 16,000		2,185 sq mi 5,660 sq km	123,600 57 per sq mi 22 per sq km	Potatoes
QUEBEC	Quebec City 165,000		594,856 sq mi 1,540,680 sq km	6,477,800 11 per sq mi 4 per sq km	Pulp & Paper
SASKATCHEWAN	Regina 175,000		251,865 sq mi 652,330 sq km	991,000 4 per sq mi 2 per sq km	Wheat
NORTHWEST TERRITORIES	Yellowknife 12,000		1,322,902 sq mi 3,426,320 sq km	47,400 0.04 per sq mi 0.01 per sq km	Minerals
YUKON TERRITORY	Whitehorse 15,000		186,660 sq mi 483,450 sq km	23,200 0.1 per sq mi 0.05 per sq km	Minerals

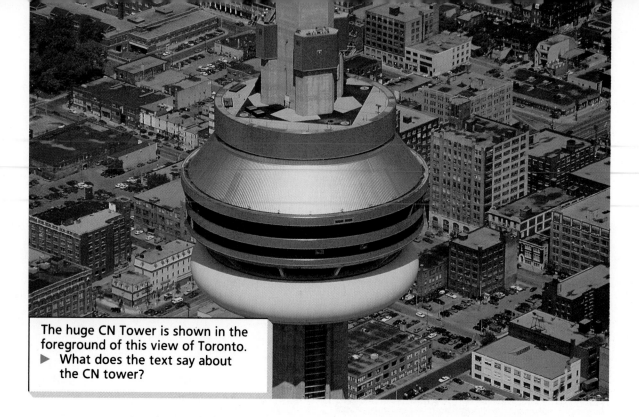

The huge CN Tower is shown in the foreground of this view of Toronto.
► What does the text say about the CN tower?

Every February, thousands of visitors travel to Quebec City to join in the festivities of the ten-day winter carnival. Parades, contests to make giant snow statues, and many other events all make for a good time. The winter carnivals began in the mid-1800s.

D. Toronto

The name *Toronto* comes from a Huron Indian word that means "meeting place." Toronto is Canada's largest metropolitan area. It is also the nation's business and transportation center. Many business-people and tourists visit the city.

To get a magnificent view of the city, you can visit the CN Tower. Owned by the Canadian National Railways, it is the tallest tower in the world! The tip of the television mast on top of the tower is 1,815 feet (553 m) above the ground. This is as tall as a 140-story building would be.

From the CN Tower you can see the ships in the port of Toronto on the shore of Lake Ontario. Although Toronto is about 1,300 miles (2,092 km) from the sea, it is one of the most important ports in Canada. As you have read, ships come up the St. Lawrence Waterway from the Atlantic Ocean. On the lakefront, there's a 96-acre (39 ha) waterfront community known as Harbourfront. There you can find art galleries, an antique market, a festival hall, and plenty of shops and restaurants.

Many people in Toronto shop at the Eaton Centre, a 300-store complex that sits under a glass-roofed arcade. They also attend the city's fine theaters.

E. Vancouver

A West Coast Port City Captain George Vancouver was sailing along the waters of the Pacific Ocean in search of the Northwest Passage in 1792. He landed on the shore of the Burrard Inlet, near the mouth of the Fraser River. Today, that's the site of Vancouver, the great western port city that is Canada's gateway to the Orient.

Burrard Inlet is a **fjord** (fyord), a deep channel carved into the coast long ago by glaciers. A glacier is like a river of ice. The ice moves very slowly, but it can dig up the land as it travels. When the ancient glaciers melted, seawater filled Burrard Inlet, creating a harbor. The Coast Ranges rise directly from the coast at Vancouver. The northern part of the city lies on the lower slopes of this range.

The Metropolitan Population With over a million people, the Vancouver metropolitan area is Canada's third largest. Vancouver has the largest port in Canada.

Vancouver is a modern city with shopping centers, tall office buildings, and highways. The population is largely of English heritage, but it also has a large number of other ethnic groups. They include Germans, French, Scandinavians, Dutch, Latin Americans, and Chinese.

Of course, there's plenty to see and do in a big city like Vancouver. One place you might like is Gastown, the earliest settlement in the city. It dates back to 1867. There you can see restored buildings from the time when Vancouver was a frontier town. Vancouver's Chinatown is also worth a visit. In addition to markets and

The Burrard Inlet is near the mouth of the Fraser River in Vancouver.
▶ Describe the inlet.

restaurants, it has the world's thinnest building.

An Island Capital Before leaving Vancouver, you should take the Skyride to the top of Grouse Mountain. From this 3,974-foot (1,211-m) peak in North Vancouver you can see Vancouver Island. Victoria, the capital of British Columbia, is on this large island. Vancouver Island is 24 miles (38 km) west of the city of Vancouver. It can be reached by taking a ferryboat across the Strait of Georgia. This strait separates Vancouver Island from the mainland.

LESSON 2 REVIEW

THINK AND WRITE

A. What are some of the major metropolitan areas in Canada?
B. Why is Montreal considered an important city?
C. What are some unique characteristics of Quebec City?
D. For what things is Toronto known?
E. Summarize the important facts that appeared in the section about Vancouver.

SKILLS CHECK

THINKING SKILL

Locate *Winnipeg* in the Gazetteer and find three important facts about its location and size. What two additional important facts did you learn about Winnipeg from reading the text?

ADVANTAGES AND DISADVANTAGES OF A MULTICULTURAL SOCIETY

Over 25 million people live in Canada. Except for about 370,000 Native Americans and 20,000 Inuit (Eskimos), the Canadian people came from all over the world. The two largest groups of Canadians are those with British and French backgrounds. About 47 percent of Canada's people are of British descent. Some 27 percent are of French descent.

The British and the French were among the first European immigrants to Canada. After the American Revolution began, thousands of settlers of British ancestry in the colonies that became the United States moved to the north. They were loyal to the British Empire and did not support the American revolution. They came to be known as the United Empire Loyalists.

The next large waves of immigration to Canada took place during the latter part of the nineteenth and early part of the twentieth centuries. Other large waves of immigration took place following World War II. Twenty-three percent of today's Canadians are descendants of these immigrants who came from such European countries as Germany, the Netherlands, Poland, Italy, Greece, the Scandinavian countries, Portugal, and some of the European republics of the Soviet Union.

Chinese, Japanese, and other Asians comprise about 3 percent of the Canadian people. In addition, there are about 35,000 people of African descent living in Canada.

As in the United States, the people of Canada live in a multicultural society. For the most part the various groups tolerate each other and live in peace. The various ethnic cultures flourish side by side and enrich each other. This is especially true in the large cities. In the countryside the communities tend to be more uniform. It is not uncommon to drive through the prairies of Canada and encounter entire communities made up of people from one nationality. These people think of themselves as Canadians, but they also want to preserve their heritage and do so through their language, customs, food, and music.

Because of its various cultures, Canada impresses visitors as a free and interesting society. As you learned in this unit, multiculturalism can also give rise to some problems. The two largest groups — the people of British and French heritages — could not agree, for example, on one language as the official language of the country. That is the language in which the government conducts its business and students are instructed in the schools. So, Canada ended up with two official languages. In Quebec, the official language is French. In New Brunswick, both English and French are official languages. English is the official language in all the other provinces.

Because of their difference in language and culture, over many years some French Canadians in Quebec have wanted their province to become a separate country. These people have become known as separatists. In 1980, the people of Quebec went to the polls to decide whether they wished to separate or remain as part of Canada. To the surprise of the separatists, nearly 60 percent of the people in Quebec voted to stay as part of Canada.

Thinking for Yourself

On a separate sheet of paper, write your answers in complete sentences.

1. In your opinion, what are the advantages of living in a multicultural society?
2. What are some of the problems Canada faces because it is multicultural?
3. Some Americans think that Spanish as well as English should be an official language in the United States. Do you agree or disagree? Tell why.

The Canadian Government

A. A British Model

Canada separated from Britain very slowly, so British influence has remained very strong, even in government. In fact, the king or queen of the United Kingdom of Great Britain and Northern Ireland is also the king or queen of Canada.

Canada's government, like that of Britain, is a **constitutional monarchy**. In such a government, the king or queen does not have total power. He or she must rule according to a constitution. Queen Elizabeth II, the present queen of the United Kingdom, cannot make laws. Her role is mostly ceremonial, especially in Canada. The queen visits Canada as well as other Commonwealth nations only on important occasions.

Because of this, the queen must have a representative in Canada. The queen's representative is called the governor general. Today, the governor general has many duties but no true power. His duties, too, are largely ceremonial.

B. Parliament's Two Houses

Parliament In Canada, as in Britain, the laws are passed by a governing body called Parliament. The Canadian Parliament is made up of two houses — the Senate and the House of Commons. The Congress of the United States also has two houses — the Senate and the House of Representatives, but there are important differences between Parliament and Congress.

In the United States, all members of Congress are elected. In Canada, the members of the Senate are appointed. They hold office until they reach the age of 75. Then they must retire.

The other house of Parliament is the House of Commons, whose members are elected. These elected officials are called Members of Parliament, or MP's. The House of Commons is the more powerful house in Canada's Parliament. It is the one through which the voice of the people is heard most directly.

In 1993 Kim Campbell becomes Canada's first female prime minister.
▶ What qualities do you think a person needs to be a successful leader?

A throng is gathered outside the Parliament building in Ottawa.
► Why might people be gathered here?

C. The Prime Minister

Electing a Prime Minister The most important official in Canada's government is the prime minister. The prime minister is a member of the House of Commons. Like other members, the prime minister is elected to office. He or she is the leader of the party that wins the most seats in the House of Commons.

The prime minister sets the goals for the government and chooses the other members of the Cabinet. Heads of the government agencies and ministries, or departments, make up the Cabinet.

The prime minister has to call an election at least once every five years. However, an election may occur anytime before the five years is up if the prime minister wishes. When an election is called, all 282 members of the House of Commons must run for election.

The prime minister may be voted out of office at any time if his or her party loses majority support in Parliament. When that happens, an election will usually be held.

Again, all the seats in the House of Commons must be filled.

Other Government Officials The governor general, who is the queen's representative, appoints senators, members of the Cabinet, and judges. However, the names of the people to be appointed come from a list made up by the prime minister and given to the governor general. In fact, the prime minister also appoints the governor general.

D. Governing the Provinces

Canada's ten provinces are somewhat like states in the United States. They have the power to make laws about local matters. Each province has a one-house parliament. A provincial parliament has a Legislative Assembly (called National Assembly in Quebec) but no Senate. Each provincial government is led by a premier. Each province also has a lieutenant governor. Like the governor general, the lieutenant governors represent the queen, and their positions are mostly ceremonial.

The national government directly governs the two territories of Canada—the Northwest Territories and the Yukon Territory. Each territory has an elected council that can pass certain laws. Over the years, the territories have gained more control over their own affairs.

E. Canada's Constitution

Why didn't Canada get its own constitution when the Statute of Westminster was passed? The provinces could not agree on a constitution, so they asked that the British North America Act remain in force. That meant the British government still had the power to change Canada's laws. However, the British never used this

Queen Elizabeth II (seated) signs the Constitution Act in Ottawa on April 17, 1982.
▶ What power did this transfer?

power. They only made changes in the British North America Act when the Canadian government requested it.

Many Canadians wanted to have a constitution that could be changed without a vote from the British Parliament. A constitution would be the last step on Canada's long road to full independence.

Except for one year, Pierre Trudeau (troo DOH) was Canada's prime minister from 1968 to 1984. Trudeau wanted very badly to have a Canadian constitution. He worked toward that goal throughout much of the 1970s, but the provinces still could not agree on a constitution.

Finally, in 1981, all of the provinces except Quebec had agreed to the proposed constitution. In spite of Quebec's objections, Canada sent the constitution to the British Parliament. The British Parliament approved the Canadian constitution. On April 7, 1982, Queen Elizabeth II went to Ottawa and signed the Constitution Act, which replaced the British North America Act. This bill made the constitution the law of the land.

LESSON 3 REVIEW

THINK AND WRITE

A. How are the governments of Canada and the United States alike, and how are they different?

B. Explain the difference between the two houses of Canada's Parliament.

C. What powers does the prime minister of Canada have?

D. What is the difference between a lieutenant governor and a premier in Canada?

E. When did Canada get its first constitution?

SKILLS CHECK

MAP SKILL

Find *Ottawa* on the map on page 570. Describe its location in relation to other Canadian cities in Ontario.

National Issues

THINK ABOUT WHAT YOU KNOW

Every day, things happen all over the world, but only some of them become important issues that many people talk about. With your classmates, discuss some of the issues that are important in your school and at home. Why do you care about them?

STUDY THE VOCABULARY

separatists	wage
veto	acid rain
referendum	contaminate

FOCUS YOUR READING

What political issues are important in today's Canada?

Montreal police stand by as several hundred separatists protest against the use of bilingual signs.
▶ Why do they object to such signs?

A. Separatists

You may have wondered why Quebec refused to approve Canada's constitution. Quebec's stand was another chapter in a long story of difficulties between English-speaking and French-speaking Canadians.

Some French Canadians believe they would be better off if they had their own country. They want to separate from Canada. These people are called **separatists**. Separatists believe that French-speaking Canadians are treated unfairly when they live or work in the English-speaking parts of the country. They also point out that unemployment is higher in Quebec than in Ontario and the western provinces.

Quebec had not approved the Canadian constitution, partly because the constitution was to make Canada a bilingual country. French and English were to be equal. In Quebec, however, the laws favored French.

Quebec was also unhappy because it would lose the power to **veto**, or refuse to approve, changes in the constitution. Quebec did have this right under the British North America Act.

Bill 101 In 1976, René Levesque (ruh NAY LUH VEK) became premier of the province of Quebec. Lévesque and his party wanted Quebec to become an independent French-Canadian country. The first step in this direction was a law called Bill 101, passed in 1977. It made French the official language of Quebec. All signs and advertising in the province of Quebec

581

were to be in French. French became the language of government and business in the province as well as the language in Quebec's schools.

Bill 101 strictly limits who can attend English-language schools. Because of this law, many Anglo-Canadians have left Quebec and moved to the English-speaking provinces.

The Referendum of 1980 Lévesque promised to hold a **referendum,** or an election to decide an issue, to find out how many people really wanted Quebec to become independent. In 1980, the people of Quebec went to the polls to vote on the referendum. To the surprise of the separatists, nearly 60 percent of the voters chose to keep Quebec as part of Canada.

The referendum in Quebec ended the threat of separation, at least for a time. However, many of the other problems that led to the calling of the election still remain. Many Quebecers, or people of Quebec, would still prefer some form of relationship with Canada that would give their province greater self-government and independence.

B. The Inuit

The DEW Line About 20,000 Inuit live in today's Canada. Beginning in the late 1950s, many changes came to Canada's north and affected the lives of the Inuit. At that time, the United States and Canada agreed to build the DEW line, a network of radar stations in the Arctic. *DEW* stands for Distant Early Warning. The purpose of the DEW line was to watch for a surprise air attack from the former Soviet Union. Many Inuit were hired to help build the DEW line stations. This was the first time that many of them had worked for **wages**, or a regular rate of pay.

About the same time, the Canadian government began to build schools and set up health clinics in the north. Villages were built to house the government agents and those Inuit who wanted to give up their nomadic way of life.

Now most of the Inuit live in villages all year long. Few Inuit hunt to live. If they can, they find jobs. The Canadian government gives some help to those who cannot find work.

C. A Giant Land Transfer

The Agreement in 1991 It could be called the biggest land transaction since the United States bought Alaska. In 1991 the Canadian government agreed to grant the Inuit over 770,000 square miles (1,994,300 sq km) of land in the eastern portion of the Northwest Territories. This vast area, known as Nunavut, is equal in size to a fifth of Canada. Find Nunavut on the map on page 570. You can see that Nunavut covers nearly two thirds of the Northwest Territories. In the language of the Inuit, the word *nunavut* means "our land."

The agreement in 1991 resulted from a 15-year-long struggle by the Inuit to secure rights to land that their ancestors had lived in long before the first European explorers and settlers came to Canada. "This agreement will make the Inuit of Nunavut the largest landowners in North America," said John Amagoalik, a leader of the Inuit delegation that negotiated the agreement with the Canadian government.

The new agreement grants the Inuit limited rights over mineral and other resource development in Nunavut. Some experts believe that this land holds valuable deposits of oil, gas, and precious metals.

An Inuit family travels across the snow-covered land.
▶ Look at the map on page 570. How is the Inuit area called *Nunavut* shown on the map?

A New Province? If everything in the agreement works out, the term *Northwest Territories* will disappear from the map of Canada, and *Nunavut* will take its place. For the agreement to become final, the Inuit and the Canadian government must iron out a number of details. One difficulty is the resistance to the agreement that comes from other native people, particularly those who live in the one third of the Northwest Territories that will not go to the Inuit. One big step toward the creation of Nunavut came in November 1992 when the Tungavik Federation, representing about 8,000 Inuit, voted to support the agreement.

D. Feelings Toward the United States

Sleeping Next to an Elephant Imagine that you were a mouse sleeping next to an elephant. Would you get nervous if the elephant became restless? According to Pierre Trudeau, that's the uncomfortable feeling that Canada has because it is so close to the United States. After all, no matter how careful the elephant is, when it moves, the mouse is bound to be shaken.

Some Canadians think the people of the United States take them for granted. They believe that people in the United States rarely think about Canada unless they want something or unless Canada does something the United States does not like. They also say that people in the United States do not know very much about Canada and that some people in the United States think of Canada almost as a part of the United States, not as a truly independent nation.

Canadians worry about the great effect the United States has on their country. Most Canadians live close to the border with the United States. They watch United States television and buy United States goods in stores. Citizens from the United States own many businesses in Canada.

Acid Rain Some things that occur in the United States can have a powerful effect on Canada. For example, pollution produced by industries in the United States results in **acid rain** in Canada. Acid rain is rain water or other form of precipitation that contains acid from industrial pollution. Sometimes the rain gets as acid as vinegar. When it falls, it damages crops and trees, and **contaminates**, or pollutes the drinking water. It can also kill fish living in freshwater lakes. Many of Quebec's sugar maple trees as well as various Canadian lakes and rivers have been damaged by acid rain. It is easy to see why Canadians at times might feel uneasy about their powerful neighbor.

E. A New Trade Agreement

Elimination of Tariffs Canada and the United States are the world's biggest trading partners. Each year, the two countries trade goods valued at over $130 billion. A recent agreement eliminated all tariffs on goods traded between the two countries. As you may recall from reading about the Central American Common Market, a tariff is a tax on trade. The new agreement made it easier for United States firms to invest in Canada and to establish industries there, such as service industries.

Mixed Opinions Brian Mulroney, the Canadian prime minister, stood firmly behind the trade agreement that he was negotiating with then United States President Ronald Reagan. Mulroney said the trade agreement would mean more economic growth for Canada. Other Canadians were uneasy. They worried that the influence of the United States, already very strong in Canada, would grow even more powerful. They feared that Canada would be overwhelmed by a new flood of United States goods and money.

In 1993 Canada's House of Commons supported extending this agreement to include Mexico. However, this North

The Peace Arch in Blaine, Washington, is at the Canadian border.
► What must it commemorate?

American Free Trade Agreement (NAFTA) still had strong critics in Canada. In fact, Mulroney lost his post as prime minister in part because of anger over NAFTA.

In the United States, President Bill Clinton, backed by former Presidents Bush, Reagan, Carter, and Ford, strongly favored the agreement. Others, however, including some environmentalists, labor unions, and farmers, opposed NAFTA. At the end of 1993, then, the future of this trade agreement was very much in doubt.

LESSON 4 REVIEW

THINK AND WRITE

A. What are Canadian separatists?

B. How has life changed for the Inuit since the late 1950s?

C. Why is landownership important to the Inuit and the Indians?

D. In your opinion, is the uneasiness of some Canadians about living so close to the United States justified? Explain your answer.

E. Contrast the views of Canadians who opposed the trade agreement between Canada and the United States with the views of those who supported it.

SKILLS CHECK

THINKING SKILL

What else do you know about Canadians and the nation of Canada through your own experience or through other sources of information? Share your information with your classmates.

584

USING THE VOCABULARY

Pacific Rim
centennial
fjord
separatists
contaminate
consitutional monarchy
veto
referendum
wage
acid rain

On a separate sheet of paper, write the word or words that best complete the sentences.

1. The _____ celebration marked a hundredth anniversary.
2. _____ is a direct result of industrial pollution.
3. The _____ was voted on to see how many Canadians wanted Quebec to be independent.
4. Many French-speaking Canadians are called _____ because they would like Quebec to be independent.
5. Glaciers carved a _____ into the coast.
6. Canadians hope that acid rain will not _____ their water.
7. The president can _____, or turn down, a bill.
8. Workers earn a _____ for doing their job.
9. Many _____ countries are economic powers in the world.
10. A king or queen must rule according to the constitution in a _____ .

REMEMBERING WHAT YOU READ

On a separate sheet of paper, write your answers in complete sentences.

1. In what different ways can Canada's regions be grouped?
2. What province is often considered the intellectual and cultural center of English-speaking Canada?
3. What makes British Columbia so different from the rest of Canada?
4. Name one interesting fact about the following cities: Winnipeg, Calgary, Ottawa.
5. Compare the cities of Toronto and Montreal.
6. What is the role of Britain's queen in Canada?
7. Describe Canada's governing body, the Parliament.
8. Which man worked to get a Canadian constitution, which was passed in 1982?
9. What were some of Quebec's reasons for not signing the constitution?
10. What happened in 1988 to ensure that Canada and the United States would continue to be the world's biggest trading partners?

TYING CREATIVE WRITING AND ART TO SOCIAL STUDIES

Pick one of the many cities mentioned in this chapter. Prepare a travel brochure highlighting the points of interest to a tourist. Decorate the folder with drawings appropriate to the city.

THINKING CRITICALLY

On a separate sheet of paper, write your answers in complete sentences.

1. Considering what you now know about Ontario and Quebec, in which province would you prefer to live?
2. As an English-speaking person, describe some difficulties you might have if you traveled to a French-speaking city.
3. Why has Canada stayed more closely tied to Britain than the United States did after it wrote its Constitution?
4. Since the late 1950s, many changes have come to the Inuit people of the north. What do you think the effects on the Inuit way of life have been?
5. Explain in your own words what the phrase "sleeping next to an elephant" (Lesson 4, Section D) means?

SUMMARIZING THE CHAPTER

On a separate sheet of paper, draw a graphic organizer like the one shown here. Copy the information from this graphic organizer on the one you have drawn. Beside the questions, fill in the blanks with answers from this chapter.

CHAPTER THEME

Canada today is an independent country with a constitution. It is a prosperous nation with many important cities. Today Canadians are debating some important issues about their future.

WHAT are Canada's six regions?	
WHICH cities are most important?	
HOW can the government be described?	
WHAT are the recent issues?	

UNIT 6 REVIEW

COOPERATIVE LEARNING

It is somewhat difficult to imagine what people said or did hundreds of years ago. However, historians have discovered information that can give you an understanding of many important historical events. These important events can form the basis of a *reenactment*. A reenactment is a play in which people perform an event from history as it is supposed to have happened. Except for important speeches, the dialogue used in a reenactment is often made up.

PROJECT

In Unit 6, you learned about many of the important events in Canadian history. With a small group of classmates, choose an event from Canadian history and re-enact it for your class. First decide upon the characters and create a script. You might divide the work among group members as follows: Assign two members to research the event. Another member should make a list of possible characters. The remaining members can work on writing the script.

Here is a list of possible events your group could reenact.

● The establishment of a settlement in Quebec by Samuel de Champlain

● The discovery of Hudson Bay and the mutiny on Henry Hudson's ship (Why were Henry Hudson's discoveries important? What may have caused the mutiny?)

● The fight for Quebec and the surrender of the French army under General Montcalm (Why was the battle of Quebec a turning point in the war? How did it lead to the Treaty of Paris in 1763?)

● The life of Amelia and James Douglas (What do you think life was like for a young fur trader and his wife? What qualities might James have had that won him the job of governor? How could it have been important for Canada that a *métis* became the governor's wife?)

Be sure to include a narrator in your script. The narrator will help the audience understand the action and make the transition from one scene to another easy to follow. The narrator can close the reenactment by telling how the events portrayed were important to Canada.

Make sure that everyone in your group has a part. Those who have short parts can take more than one role.

PRESENTATION AND REVIEW

Present your reenactment to your class. If time permits, you may want to use costumes and props for your reenactment.

After the reenactment, work as a group to answer questions from the class. Then meet as a group and review your performance. Was your reenactment successful?

REMEMBER TO:
● Give your ideas.
● Listen to others' ideas.
● Plan your work with the group.
● Present your project.
● Discuss how your group worked.

A. Why Do I Need This Skill?

The kinds of natural resources that countries have has much to do with what products those countries can make. Natural resources, then, are very important for the economies of nations. However, natural resources are not evenly distributed throughout the world. Countries that do not have certain natural resources have to gain them through trade with nations that do have those resources. This has a major effect on the way countries deal with one another. Resource maps show us the distribution of various natural resources in particular areas.

B. Learning the Skill

At right is a resource map showing areas of coal deposits and oil fields in the Americas. There are a number of colored dots within most of the countries. The green dots represent the areas where oil fields are located. The red dots represent coal deposits.

By looking at this map, you can see that most countries of the Americas have some oil fields. You can also see that most of the countries have at least some coal deposits. However, if you take a closer look at the map, you will learn a great deal of information. For example, some countries have many oil fields and only a few areas of coal deposits. Other countries have more areas of coal deposits and only a few oil fields. Some countries have no coal or oil at all.

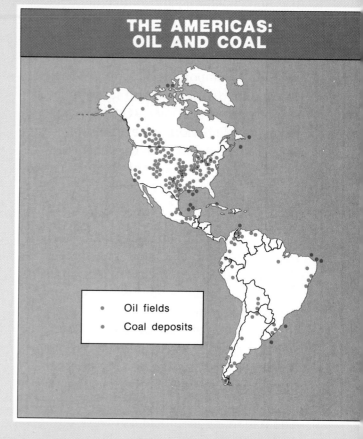

THE AMERICAS: OIL AND COAL

- Oil fields
- Coal deposits

In addition to showing the distribution of natural resources, resource maps help us figure out what industries a country or region may have. For example, a country with oil fields may have oil refineries. If that is true, then that country might also have a well-developed system for exporting oil. Countries with large coal deposits may rely on coal for fueling their industries. These nations might then have problems associated with air pollution.

C. PRACTICING THE SKILL

Answer the following questions by using the natural resource map on page 588 and the maps of North America and South America found on pages 592, 596, and 597.

1. Which continent, North America or South America, has more coal deposits?
2. List three countries of South America that have no coal deposits or oil fields.
3. Which country has the most coal deposits and oil fields?
4. Is most of Canada's coal and oil in western or eastern Canada?
5. What South American country has the most coal deposits?

Answer the following questions by using the natural resource map on this page and the maps of North America and South America mentioned above.

1. What is the major mineral that is mined around the Great Lakes?
2. Does Mexico mine more iron ore or other minerals?
3. What resource is abundant in Brazil?
4. What is the only resource mined in the country of Argentina?
5. Does the United States or Canada mine more iron ore?

D. APPLYING THE SKILL

Find information about the leading natural

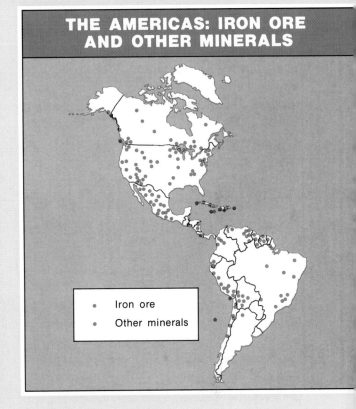

THE AMERICAS: IRON ORE AND OTHER MINERALS

- Iron ore
- Other minerals

resources in your state and where they are located. Next trace or draw a map of your state. Then choose at least two of your state's resources and make your own state resource map, using the map shown above and the one on page 588 as examples. Remember to add a title and a key box to the map. You can be creative by using different colors and symbols on your map. When you and the other members of your class have completed your maps, display them in the classroom.

Writing
SKILLBUILDER
a Summary

A. Why Do I Need This Skill?

Lessons in your social studies book contain a wealth of information, and it is impossible for you to remember all of it. It is important, therefore, for you to remember the writer's main points. One way to do this is to write a summary. A summary is a short way of telling, in your own words, the important ideas in a piece of writing.

B. Learning the Skill

The lessons in your social studies book are organized by main ideas. Lesson titles give you the themes of the lessons. Within the lessons, the sections beginning with the letters **A, B, C,** and so on, give the main ideas that support the lesson themes.

These main ideas can help you write a summary for a lesson. One kind of summary is a summary ladder, such as the one shown on the next page. Note that the chapter number and title and the lesson number and title appear beside the top of the ladder. Below the steps, or rungs, of the ladder are the section headings, which begin with capital letters. Between the rungs are the important details that tell about or explain the main ideas in the lesson.

C. Practicing the Skill

Construct a summary ladder for Lesson 1, "Location and Climate," in Chapter 22, "The Rich Canadian Land." Lesson 1 begins on page 541. On a sheet of paper, draw the summary ladder shown on page 591. To complete it, first reread each section of the lesson in turn, thinking about the main idea and details as you read. Then write the section heading and the important details from the section.

For example, for Section **A,** "A Northern Land," the important points told how wide Canada is, how many time zones it has, how far north much of it is, and that a polar projection map shows that the shortest routes between parts of the United States and Europe cross Canada. Ask yourself, "What is the section about?" as you look for important details. Write the details in your own words; don't copy sentences exactly from the book.

Complete the summary ladder by filling in the remaining headings and writing important details from Sections **B, C, D,** and **E** in Lesson 1 of Chapter 22.

D. Applying the Skill

Construct another summary ladder, this one for Lesson 2 in Chapter 23. You will need five rungs for this ladder also, since there are five sections in this lesson.

Summary ladders can be helpful as you prepare for tests in social studies. They can also be useful when you read and study textbooks in other subjects.

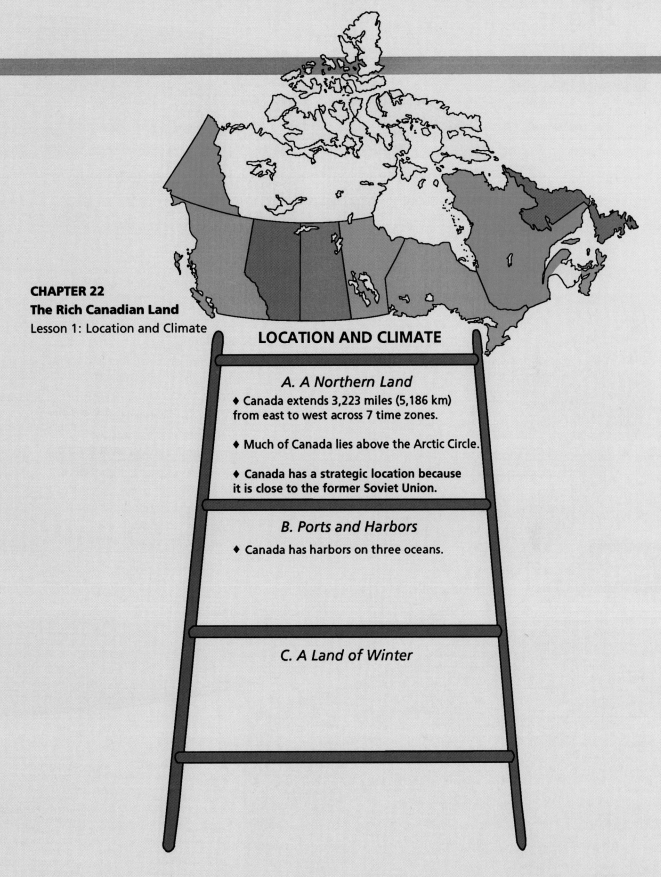

LOCATION AND CLIMATE

A. A Northern Land

♦ Canada extends 3,223 miles (5,186 km) from east to west across 7 time zones.

♦ Much of Canada lies above the Arctic Circle.

♦ Canada has a strategic location because it is close to the former Soviet Union.

B. Ports and Harbors

♦ Canada has harbors on three oceans.

C. A Land of Winter

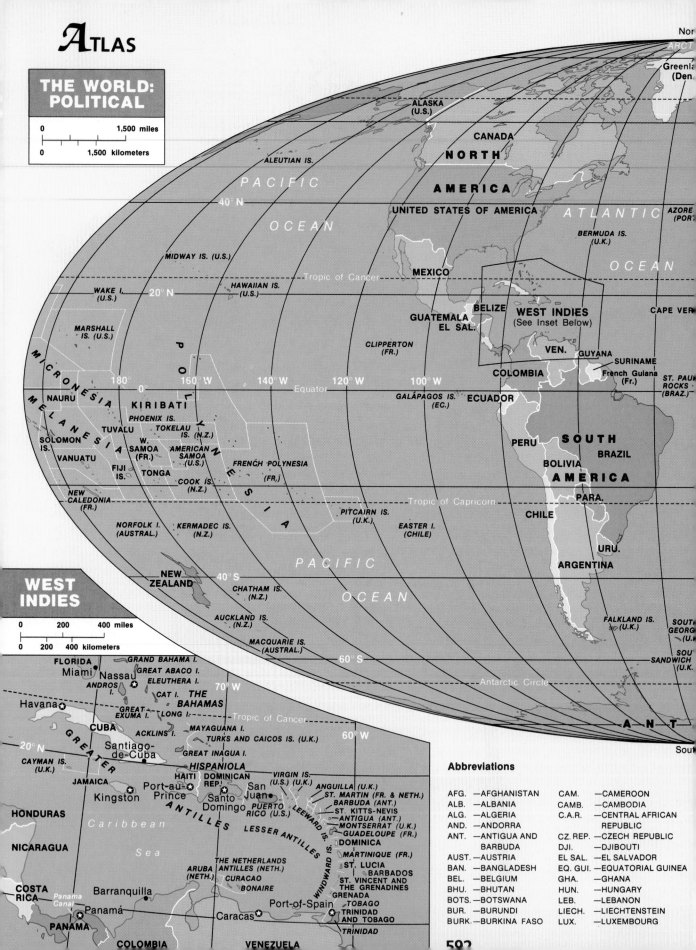

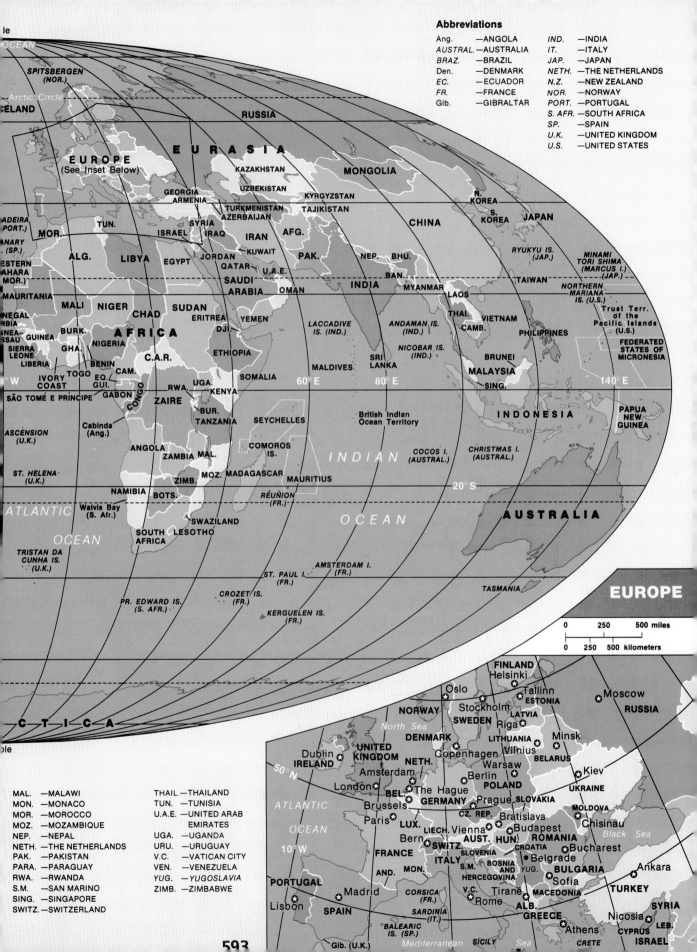

SPITSBERGEN
(NOR.)

Arctic Circle

CELAND

EUROPE
(See Inset Below)

RUSSIA

EURASIA

KAZAKHSTAN

MONGOLIA

N.
KOREA

S.
KOREA

JAPAN

GEORGIA
ARMENIA

UZBEKISTAN

KYRGYZSTAN

ADEIRA
PORT.)

TUN.

TURKMENISTAN

TAJIKISTAN

CHINA

ANARY
(SP.)

MOR.

SYRIA

AZERBAIJAN

ISRAEL

IRAQ

IRAN

AFG.

ESTERN
HARA
MOR.)

ALG.

LIBYA

EGYPT

JORDAN

KUWAIT

QATAR

U.A.E.

PAK.

NEP.

BHU.

RYUKYU IS.
(JAP.)

MINAMI
TORI SHIMA
(MARCUS I.)
(JAP.)

SAUDI
ARABIA

OMAN

BAN.

TAIWAN

NORTHERN
MARIANA
IS. (U.S.)

MAURITANIA

MALI

NIGER

CHAD

SUDAN

ERITREA

YEMEN

INDIA

MYANMAR

LAOS

VIETNAM

Trust Terr.
of the
Pacific Islands
(U.S.)

NEGAL
BIA

BURK.

AFRICA

DJI.

LACCADIVE
IS. (IND.)

ANDAMAN IS.
(IND.)

THAI.

CAMB.

FEDERATED
STATES OF
MICRONESIA

NEA-
SSAU
GUINEA

SIERRA
LEONE

GHA.

BENIN

NIGERIA

C.A.R.

ETHIOPIA

NICOBAR IS.
(IND.)

SRI
LANKA

BRUNEI

LIBERIA

W

IVORY
COAST

TOGO

EQ.
GUI.

CAM.

UGA.

KENYA

MALDIVES

60° E

80° E

MALAYSIA

PHILIPPINES

SING.

140° E

SÃO TOMÉ E PRÍNCIPE

GABON

CONGO

ZAIRE

RWA.

BUR.

TANZANIA

SEYCHELLES

British Indian
Ocean Territory

INDONESIA

PAPUA
NEW
GUINEA

ASCENSION
(U.K.)

Cabinda
(Ang.)

ANGOLA

ZAMBIA

MAL.

COMOROS
IS.

INDIAN

COCOS I.
(AUSTRAL.)

CHRISTMAS I.
(AUSTRAL.)

ST. HELENA
(U.K.)

MOZ.

ZIMB.

MADAGASCAR

MAURITIUS

NAMIBIA

BOTS.

20° S

ATLANTIC

Walvis Bay
(S. Afr.)

OCEAN

AUSTRALIA

OCEAN

SWAZILAND

RÉUNION
(FR.)

TRISTAN DA
CUNHA IS.
(U.K.)

SOUTH
AFRICA

LESOTHO

ST. PAUL I.
(FR.)

AMSTERDAM I.
(FR.)

PR. EDWARD IS.
(S. AFR.)

CROZET IS.
(FR.)

TASMANIA

KERGUELEN IS.
(FR.)

C T I C A

ple

Ang.	—ANGOLA	IND.	—INDIA
AUSTRAL.	—AUSTRALIA	IT.	—ITALY
BRAZ.	—BRAZIL	JAP.	—JAPAN
Den.	—DENMARK	NETH.	—THE NETHERLANDS
EC.	—ECUADOR	N.Z.	—NEW ZEALAND
FR.	—FRANCE	NOR.	—NORWAY
Gib.	—GIBRALTAR	PORT.	—PORTUGAL
		S. AFR.	—SOUTH AFRICA
		SP.	—SPAIN
		U.K.	—UNITED KINGDOM
		U.S.	—UNITED STATES

EUROPE

0	250	500 miles
0	250	500 kilometers

FINLAND
Helsinki

Oslo

Tallinn
ESTONIA

Moscow

RUSSIA

NORWAY

Stockholm

LATVIA

SWEDEN

Riga

Minsk

North Sea

DENMARK

Copenhagen

LITHUANIA

Vilnius

BELARUS

Dublin

UNITED
KINGDOM

IRELAND

NETH.

Amsterdam

Berlin

Warsaw

POLAND

Kiev

UKRAINE

London

The Hague

BEL.

GERMANY

Prague

SLOVAKIA

ATLANTIC

Brussels

CZ. REP.

Bratislava

MOLDOVA

Paris

LUX.

LIECH.

Vienna

Budapest

Chisinau

OCEAN

Bern

AUST.

HUN.

ROMANIA

Black Sea

10° W

SWITZ.

SLOVENIA

CROATIA

Belgrade

Bucharest

FRANCE

ITALY

S.M.

BOSNIA
AND
HERCEGOVINA

YUG.

BULGARIA

Ankara

AND.

MON.

Sofia

PORTUGAL

Madrid

CORSICA
(FR.)

V.C.

Tiranë

MACEDONIA

TURKEY

SYRIA

Lisbon

SPAIN

Rome

ALB.

GREECE

Nicosia

LEB.

SARDINIA
(IT.)

BALEARIC
IS. (SP.)

Athens

CYPRUS

ISRAEL

Gib. (U.K.)

SICILY

Mediterranean

CRETE

Sea

50° N

MAL.	—MALAWI
MON.	—MONACO
MOR.	—MOROCCO
MOZ.	—MOZAMBIQUE
NEP.	—NEPAL
NETH.	—THE NETHERLANDS
PAK.	—PAKISTAN
PARA.	—PARAGUAY
RWA.	—RWANDA
S.M.	—SAN MARINO
SING.	—SINGAPORE
SWITZ.	—SWITZERLAND
THAIL.	—THAILAND
TUN.	—TUNISIA
U.A.E.	—UNITED ARAB
	EMIRATES
UGA.	—UGANDA
URU.	—URUGUAY
V.C.	—VATICAN CITY
VEN.	—VENEZUELA
YUG.	—YUGOSLAVIA
ZIMB.	—ZIMBABWE

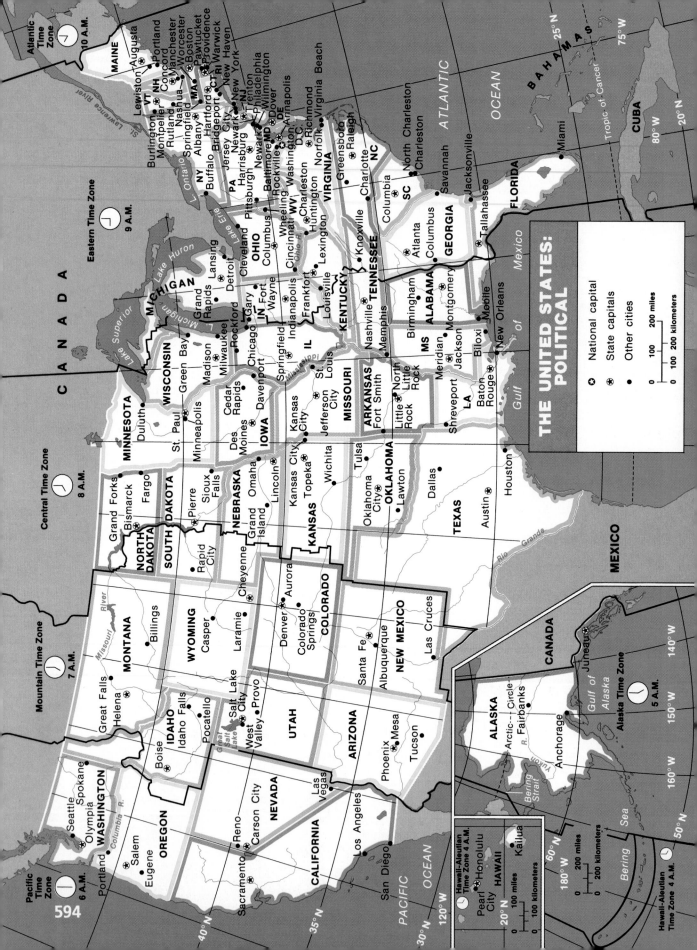

THE UNITED STATES: POLITICAL

Legend:
- ✪ National capital
- ✪ State capitals
- • Other cities

0   100   200 miles
0 100 200 kilometers

Time Zones:
- Atlantic Time Zone — 10 A.M.
- Eastern Time Zone — 9 A.M.
- Central Time Zone — 8 A.M.
- Mountain Time Zone — 7 A.M.
- Pacific Time Zone — 6 A.M.
- Alaska Time Zone — 5 A.M.
- Hawaii-Aleutian Time Zone 4 A.M.

States and cities:

CANADA

MAINE — Augusta, Lewiston, Portland
NH — Concord, Manchester, Nashua
VT — Montpelier, Burlington, Rutland
MA — Boston, Worcester, Springfield, Pittsfield
CT — Hartford, Bridgeport, New Haven
RI — Providence, Pawtucket, Warwick, Nantucket
NY — Albany, Buffalo, New York
NJ — Trenton, Jersey City, Newark
PA — Harrisburg, Philadelphia, Pittsburgh
DE — Dover, Wilmington
MD — Annapolis, Baltimore, Rockville
WASHINGTON, D.C.
VIRGINIA — Richmond, Norfolk, Virginia Beach, Charleston
WV — Wheeling, Huntington, Charleston
NC — Raleigh, Greensboro, Charlotte
SC — Columbia, North Charleston, Charleston

MICHIGAN — Lansing, Detroit, Grand Rapids
OHIO — Columbus, Cleveland, Cincinnati
KENTUCKY — Frankfort, Louisville, Lexington
TENNESSEE — Nashville, Knoxville, Memphis
IN — Indianapolis, Fort Wayne, Gary
IL — Springfield, Chicago, Rockford
GEORGIA — Atlanta, Columbus, Savannah
FLORIDA — Tallahassee, Jacksonville, Miami
ALABAMA — Montgomery, Birmingham, Mobile
MS — Jackson, Meridian, Biloxi
LA — Baton Rouge, Shreveport, New Orleans

WISCONSIN — Madison, Green Bay, Milwaukee
MINNESOTA — St. Paul, Duluth, Minneapolis
IOWA — Des Moines, Cedar Rapids, Davenport
MISSOURI — Jefferson City, Kansas City, St. Louis, Springfield
ARKANSAS — Little Rock, North Little Rock, Fort Smith

NORTH DAKOTA — Bismarck, Grand Forks, Fargo
SOUTH DAKOTA — Pierre, Rapid City, Sioux Falls
NEBRASKA — Lincoln, Grand Island, Omaha
KANSAS — Topeka, Wichita, Kansas City
OKLAHOMA — Oklahoma City, Tulsa, Lawton
TEXAS — Austin, Dallas, Houston

MONTANA — Helena, Great Falls, Billings
WYOMING — Cheyenne, Casper, Laramie
COLORADO — Denver, Colorado Springs, Aurora
NEW MEXICO — Santa Fe, Albuquerque, Las Cruces

IDAHO — Boise, Pocatello, Idaho Falls
UTAH — Salt Lake City, West Valley, Provo
ARIZONA — Phoenix, Mesa, Tucson
NEVADA — Carson City, Reno, Las Vegas

WASHINGTON — Olympia, Seattle, Spokane
OREGON — Salem, Portland, Eugene
CALIFORNIA — Sacramento, San Francisco, Los Angeles, San Diego

ALASKA — Juneau, Fairbanks, Anchorage
HAWAII — Honolulu, Pearl City, Kailua

MEXICO

CUBA

BAHAMAS

THE UNITED STATES: PHYSICAL

Abbreviations

Mt. —MOUNT
MTS. —MOUNTAINS
I. —ISLAND

Elevations

Feet	Meters
12,000	3,658
9,000	2,743
6,000	1,524
2,000	610
1,000	305
500	152
0	0

CANADA

St. Lawrence River

Cape Cod

ADIRONDACK MTS.

LONG ISLAND

Boston

Hudson R.

New York

Cape May

Philadelphia

Baltimore

Cape Charles

Chesapeake Bay

Washington, D.C.

Cape Hatteras

ATLANTIC OCEAN

APPALACHIAN MTS.

ALLEGHENY MTS.

BLUE RIDGE

Columbus

Ohio River

Mt. Mitchell
6,684 ft.
(2,037 m)

Cape Fear

Atlanta

Cape Canaveral

ATLANTIC COASTAL PLAIN

Cape Sable

FLORIDA KEYS

Tropic of Cancer

Straits of Florida

CUBA

L. Ontario

Lake Erie

Lake Huron

Lake Superior

Lake Michigan

Detroit

Milwaukee

Chicago

Indianapolis

Illinois River

Wabash River

Nashville

Memphis

Cumberland River

Tennessee River

Alabama River

Jacksonville

Gulf of Mexico

Cape San Blas

Mississippi Delta

New Orleans

GULF COASTAL PLAIN

Houston

Mississippi River

St. Louis

Kansas City

Missouri River

Platte River

G R E A T   P L A I N S

OZARK PLATEAU

Arkansas River

Red River

Brazos River

Oklahoma City

Canadian River

LLANO ESTACADO

Pecos R.

Rio Grande

MEXICO

BLACK HILLS

Cheyenne River

North Platte River

S. Platte R.

Longs Peak
14,256 ft.
(4,345 m)

Denver

Pikes Peak
14,110 ft.
(4,301 m)

Mt. Elbert
14,433 ft.
(4,399 m)

Blanca Peak
14,317 ft.
(4,364 m)

Albuquerque

CONTINENTAL DIVIDE

ROCKY MOUNTAINS

Yellowstone River

Green River

Colorado River

COLORADO PLATEAU

Phoenix

Grand Teton
13,766 ft.
(4,196 m)

Snake River

Salmon River

COLUMBIA PLATEAU

GREAT BASIN

Humboldt River

DEATH VALLEY

MOJAVE DESERT

Los Angeles

NEVADA

SIERRA

CENTRAL VALLEY

Sacramento River

San Joaquin River

Mt. Whitney
14,495 ft.
(4,418 m)

Point Conception

PACIFIC OCEAN

Cape Mendocino

Cape Blanco

COAST RANGES

CASCADE RANGE

Mt. Rainier
14,410 ft.
(4,392 m)

Portland

Seattle

Cape Flattery

CANADA

100 miles
200 miles
0

100 kilometers
200 kilometers
0

BROOKS RANGE

Barrow

Yukon River

ALASKA RANGE

Mt. McKinley
20,320 ft.
(6,194 m)

Anchorage

KODIAK I.

Gulf of Alaska

CANADA

ARCTIC OCEAN

RUSSIA

Bering Sea

0   200 miles

0   200 kilometers

KAUAI

OAHU

Honolulu

MOLOKAI

MAUI

HAWAII

0   100 miles

0   100 kilometers

595

45° N

40° N

35° N

30° N

25° N

20° N

120° W

80° W

75° W

180°

170° W

160° W

150° W

140° W

50° N

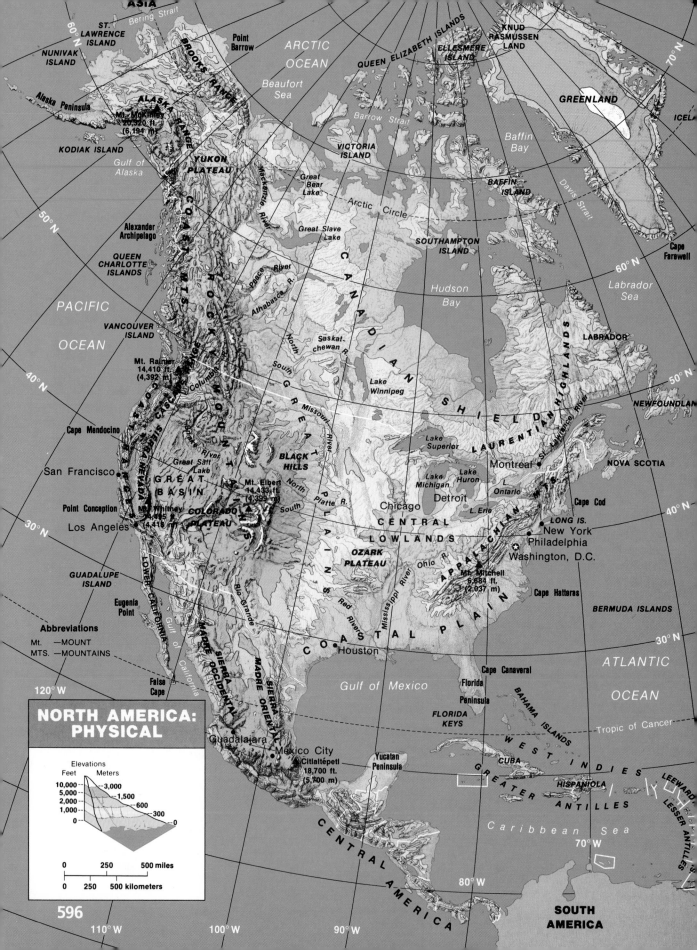

NORTH AMERICA: PHYSICAL

ASIA

ARCTIC OCEAN

Bering Strait

ST. LAWRENCE ISLAND

NUNIVAK ISLAND

Point Barrow

Beaufort Sea

QUEEN ELIZABETH ISLANDS

ELLESMERE ISLAND

KNUD RASMUSSEN LAND

GREENLAND

ICEL

Alaska Peninsula

BROOKS RANGE

ALASKA RANGE
Mt. McKinley
20,320 ft.
(6,194 m)

KODIAK ISLAND

YUKON PLATEAU

VICTORIA ISLAND

Barrow Strait

Baffin Bay

Cape Farewell

Gulf of Alaska

Mackenzie River

Great Bear Lake

Arctic Circle

BAFFIN ISLAND

Davis Strait

60° N

70°

Alexander Archipelago

Peace River

Great Slave Lake

SOUTHAMPTON ISLAND

Labrador Sea

QUEEN CHARLOTTE ISLANDS

Athabasca R.

C A N A D I A N   S H I E L D

LABRADOR

PACIFIC OCEAN

VANCOUVER ISLAND

North Saskat-chewan R.

Hudson Bay

50° N

Mt. Rainier
14,410 ft.
(4,392 m)

South Saskatchewan R.

Columbia

G R E A T

Lake Winnipeg

LAURENTIAN HIGHLANDS

St. Lawrence River

NEWFOUNDLAN

Cape Mendocino

Snake River

Missouri River

BLACK HILLS

Lake Superior

Montreal

NOVA SCOTIA

San Francisco

Great Salt Lake

GREAT BASIN

Mt. Elbert
14,433 ft.
(4,399 m)

North Platte R.

P L A I N S

Lake Michigan

Lake Huron

L. Ontario

Cape Cod

Point Conception

Mt. Whitney
14,495
(4,418 m)

COLORADO PLATEAU

South Platte

Chicago

Detroit

L. Erie

LONG IS.

New York

Philadelphia

40° N

Los Angeles

C E N T R A L   L O W L A N D S

APPALACHIAN MTS.

Washington, D.C.

GUADALUPE ISLAND

OZARK PLATEAU

Ohio R.

Mt. Mitchell
6,684 ft.
(2,037 m)

Cape Hatteras

Eugenia Point

LOWER CALIFORNIA

Rio Grande

Red River

Mississippi River

BERMUDA ISLANDS

30° N

Abbreviations

Mt. —MOUNT
MTS. —MOUNTAINS

Gulf of California

C O A S T A L   P L A I N

Houston

ATLANTIC OCEAN

120° W

False Cape

MADRE SIERRA

SIERRA MADRE ORIENTAL

Cape Canaveral

Florida Peninsula

BAHAMA ISLANDS

Tropic of Cancer

NORTH AMERICA: PHYSICAL

Guadalajara

Mexico City

FLORIDA KEYS

W E S T   I N D I E S

70° W

Elevations

Feet	Meters
10,000	3,000
5,000	1,500
2,000	600
1,000	300
0	0

Citlaltépetl
18,700 ft.
(5,700 m)

Yucatan Peninsula

CUBA

GREATER ANTILLES

HISPANIOLA

LEEWARD IS.

0   250   500 miles

0   250   500 kilometers

C E N T R A L   A M E R I C A

Caribbean Sea

LESSER ANTILLES

80° W

110° W

100° W

90° W

SOUTH AMERICA

Caribbean Sea

Guajira Pen.

MARGARITA I.

Caracas

Orinoco River Delta

L. Maracaibo

Orinoco R.

10° N

G. of Panama

LLANOS

GUIANA HIGHLANDS

Angel Falls

DEVILS I.

C. Orange

Abbreviations

ARCH. —ARCHIPELAGO
C. —CAPE
G. —GULF
Mt. —MOUNT
Pen. —PENINSULA
Pt. —POINT
U.K. —UNITED KINGDOM

Mt. Tolima
18,425 ft.
(5,616 m)

Bogotá

Meta R.

Orinoco R.

Rio

LPELO I.

Caqueta R.

Negro

Amazon River Delta

0°

AMAZON

MARAJÓ I.

Equator

Mt. Chimborazo
20,561 ft.
(6,267 m)

Japura

Amazon R.

C. São Roque

Gulf of Guayaquil

Marañón R.

BASIN

Tapalóz R.

Xingu

Tocantins R.

Parnaiba R.

Aguja Pt.

Juruá

R.

Purus

Madeira

R.

Araguaia

Tocantins

São

Francisco

Mt. Huascarán
22,205 ft.
(6,768 m)

Beni R.

Mamoré

10° S

Lima

Lake Titicaca

MATO

GROSSO

Brasília

BRAZILIAN

Mt. Ancohuma
20,958 ft.
(6,388 m)

R.

PLATEAU

HIGHLANDS

L. Poopó

ANDES

Paraguay R.

Mt. Bandeira
9,495 ft.
(2,894 m)

20° S

Tropic of Capricorn

ATACAMA DESERT

Pilcomayo

GRAN CHACO

Parana R.

São Paulo

C. Frio

Rio de Janeiro

SAN FELIX I.

SAN AMBROSIO I.

R.

R.

MOUNTAINS

Salado

R.

ATLANTIC

Mt. Aconcagua
22,834 ft.
(6,960 m)

Paraná

R.

R.

30° S

PACIFIC

Santiago

Uruguay

OCEAN

JUAN FERNÁNDEZ IS.

PAMPAS

Buenos Aires

Montevideo

Rio de la Plata

40° W

30° W

OCEAN

Colorado R.

Blanca Bay

SOUTH AMERICA: PHYSICAL

San Matías Gulf

40° S

CHILOÉ I.

Valdés Pen.

PATAGONIA

CHONOS ARCH.

Gulf of San Jorge

Elevations

Feet   Meters

10,000 —— 3,000

5,000 —— 1,500

2,000 —— 600

1,000 —— 300

0 —— 0

Taitao Pen.

C. Tres Puntas

90° W

80° W

FALKLAND IS. (U.K.)
(MALVINAS IS.)

50° S

Grande Bay

Strait of Magellan

60° W

Strait of Magellan

50° W

597

0   500 miles

0   500 kilometers

TIERRA DEL FUEGO

Cape Horn

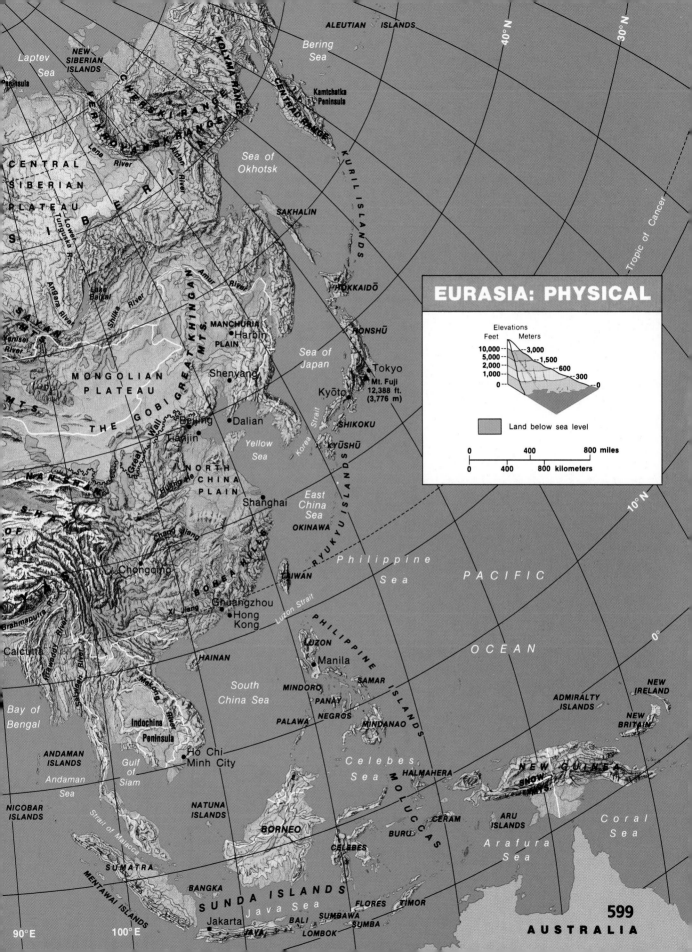

EURASIA: PHYSICAL

Elevations
Feet   Meters
10,000 — 3,000
5,000 — 1,500
2,000 — 600
1,000 — 300
0 — 0

Land below sea level

0   400   800 miles
0   400   800 kilometers

599
AUSTRALIA

Laptev Sea
NEW SIBERIAN ISLANDS
Peninsula
KOLYMA RANGE
Bering Sea
Aleutian Islands
40° N
30° N

CHERSKI RANGE
Kamchatka Peninsula
CENTRAL RANGE

CENTRAL SIBERIAN PLATEAU
Lena River
Aldan River
Sea of Okhotsk
KURIL ISLANDS
Tropic of Cancer

SIBERIA
Lower Tunguska R.
Angara River
Shilka River
Lake Baikal
Amur River
SAKHALIN
HOKKAIDO

SAYAN MTS.
Yenisei River
MONGOLIAN PLATEAU
MANCHURIA PLAIN
Harbin
HONSHŪ
Sea of Japan
Tokyo
Mt. Fuji 12,388 ft. (3,776 m)

THE GOBI
GREAT KHINGAN MTS.
Shenyang
Kyōto
SHIKOKU
Korea Strait
KYŪSHŪ

NAN SHAN MTS.
(Great Wall)
Beijing
Dalian
Tianjin
Yellow Sea
RYUKYU ISLANDS
10° N

SHAN
OF TET
NORTH CHINA PLAIN
Huang He
Shanghai
East China Sea
OKINAWA

HIMALAYAS
Chang Jiang
Chongqing
Philippine Sea
PACIFIC

Brahmaputra River
BORZA HILLS
TAIWAN
Luzon Strait

Calcutta
Xi Jiang
Guangzhou
Hong Kong
LUZON
OCEAN

Irrawaddy River
Salween River
HAINAN
Manila
PHILIPPINE ISLANDS
SAMAR
ADMIRALTY ISLANDS
NEW IRELAND

Bay of Bengal
Mekong River
South China Sea
MINDORO
PANAY
NEGROS
NEW BRITAIN

ANDAMAN ISLANDS
Indochina Peninsula
PALAWAN
MINDANAO

Andaman Sea
Gulf of Siam
Ho Chi Minh City
CELEBES Sea
HALMAHERA
NEW GUINEA
SNOW MTS.

NICOBAR ISLANDS
NATUNA ISLANDS
MOLUCCAS
CERAM
ARU ISLANDS
Coral Sea

Strait of Malacca
BORNEO
BURU
Arafura Sea

SUMATRA
CELEBES

MENTAWAI ISLANDS
BANGKA
SUNDA ISLANDS
FLORES
TIMOR

Jakarta
JAVA
Java Sea
BALI
LOMBOK
SUMBAWA
SUMBA

90° E
100° E
0°

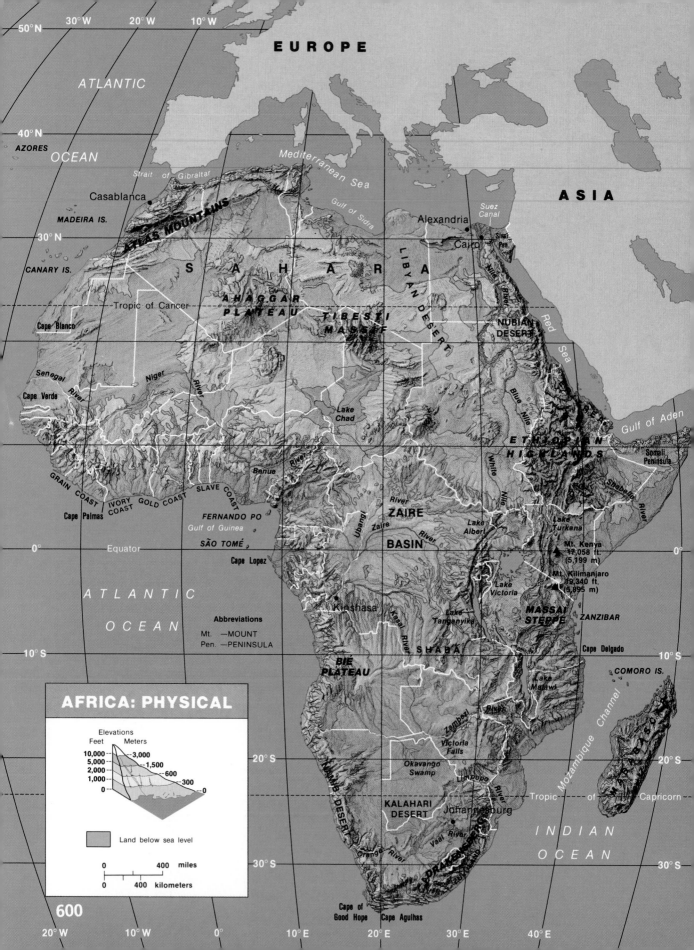

AFRICA: PHYSICAL

Elevations

Feet	Meters
10,000	3,000
5,000	1,500
2,000	600
1,000	300
0	0

Land below sea level

0   400   miles

0   400   kilometers

Abbreviations
Mt. —MOUNT
Pen. —PENINSULA

EUROPE

ASIA

ATLANTIC OCEAN

AZORES

MADEIRA IS.

CANARY IS.

Strait of Gibraltar

Mediterranean Sea

Gulf of Sidra

Casablanca

ATLAS MOUNTAINS

Alexandria

Suez Canal

Cairo

Sinai Pen.

S A H A R A

LIBYAN DESERT

Tropic of Cancer

AHAGGAR PLATEAU

TIBESTI MASSIF

NUBIAN DESERT

Cape Blanco

Red Sea

Senegal River

Niger River

Lake Chad

Blue Nile

Cape Verde

White Nile

Nile River

ETHIOPIAN HIGHLANDS

Gulf of Aden

Somali Peninsula

GRAIN COAST

IVORY COAST

GOLD COAST

SLAVE COAST

Benue

River

Cape Palmas

FERNANDO PO

Gulf of Guinea

SÃO TOMÉ

Ubangi

Zaire

ZAIRE BASIN

River

River

Nile

Lake Albert

Shabelle River

Equator

Cape Lopez

ATLANTIC OCEAN

Mt. Kenya
17,058 ft.
(5,199 m)

Lake Turkana

Kinshasa

Kasai River

Lake Victoria

Mt. Kilimanjaro
19,340 ft.
(5,895 m)

Lake Tanganyika

MASSAI STEPPE

ZANZIBAR

SHABA

Cape Delgado

COMORO IS.

BIÉ PLATEAU

Lake Malawi

Victoria Falls

Zambezi

River

Okavango Swamp

Limpopo River

Mozambique Channel

MADAGASCAR

Tropic of Capricorn

NAMIB DESERT

KALAHARI DESERT

Johannesburg

Vaal River

DRAKENSBERG

Orange River

INDIAN OCEAN

Cape of Good Hope   Cape Agulhas

600

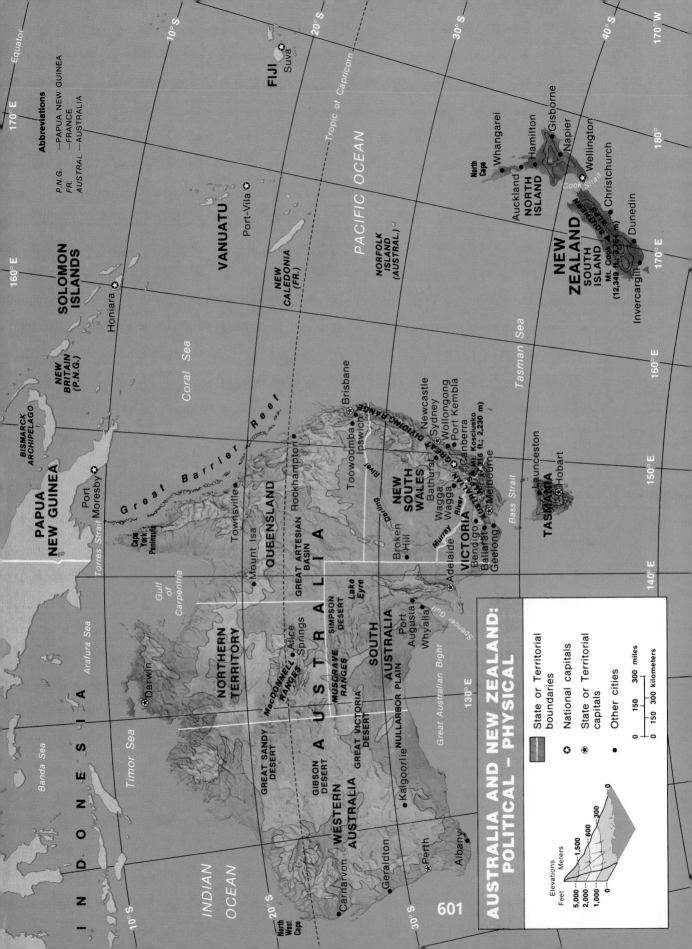

AUSTRALIA AND NEW ZEALAND: POLITICAL – PHYSICAL

State or Territorial boundaries

✪ National capitals

✪ State or Territorial capitals

• Other cities

Elevations	
Feet	Meters
5,000	1,500
2,000	600
1,000	300
0	0

0   150   300 miles
0   150   300 kilometers

Abbreviations

P.N.G. — PAPUA NEW GUINEA
FR. — FRANCE
AUSTRAL. — AUSTRALIA

INDONESIA

Banda Sea

Arafura Sea

Timor Sea

PAPUA NEW GUINEA

BISMARCK ARCHIPELAGO

NEW BRITAIN (P.N.G.)

Port Moresby ✪

Torres Strait

SOLOMON ISLANDS

Honiara ✪

VANUATU

Port-Vila ✪

NEW CALEDONIA (FR.)

FIJI

Suva ✪

Coral Sea

Great Barrier Reef

Cape York Peninsula

Gulf of Carpentria

Darwin ✪

NORTHERN TERRITORY

GREAT SANDY DESERT

GIBSON DESERT

WESTERN AUSTRALIA

GREAT VICTORIA DESERT

MacDONNELL RANGES

Alice Springs •

MUSGRAVE RANGES

SIMPSON DESERT

Lake Eyre

A U S T R A L I A

Carnarvon •

Geraldton •

Perth ✪

Kalgoorlie •

Albany •

North West Cape

NULLARBOR PLAIN

Great Australian Bight

SOUTH AUSTRALIA

GREAT ARTESIAN BASIN

QUEENSLAND

Mount Isa •

Townsville •

Rockhampton •

Toowoomba •
Ipswich •

Brisbane ✪

Whyalla •
Port Augusta •

Spencer Gulf

Adelaide ✪

Broken Hill •

NEW SOUTH WALES

Darling River

Murray River

Bathurst •
Wagga Wagga •

Newcastle •

Sydney ✪
Wollongong •
Port Kembla •

GREAT DIVIDING RANGE

Canberra ✪

Mt. Kosciusko (7,316 ft; 2,230 m)

VICTORIA

Bendigo •
Ballarat •
Geelong •

Melbourne ✪

Bass Strait

TASMANIA

Launceston •

Hobart ✪

Tasman Sea

NEW ZEALAND

North Cape

Whangarei •

Auckland •

NORTH ISLAND

Hamilton •

Gisborne •

Napier •

Wellington ✪

Cook Strait

SOUTH ISLAND

SOUTHERN ALPS

Mt. Cook (12,349 ft; 3,764 m)

Christchurch •

Dunedin •

Invercargill •

INDIAN OCEAN

PACIFIC OCEAN

Tropic of Capricorn

Equator

NORFOLK ISLAND (AUSTRAL.)

601

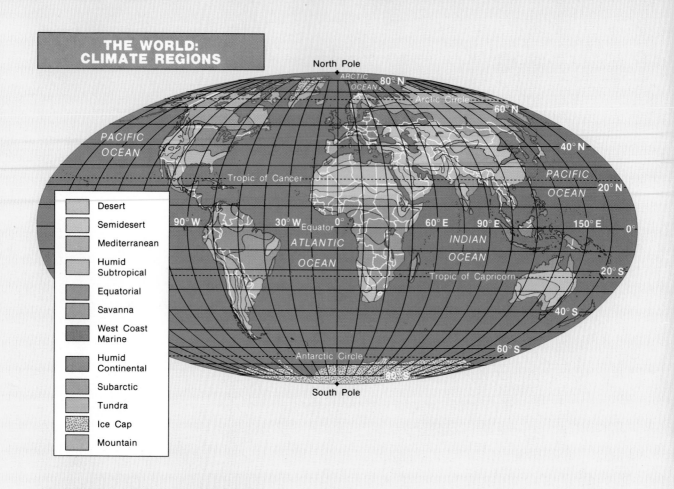

THE WORLD: CLIMATE REGIONS

Legend:
- Desert
- Semidesert
- Mediterranean
- Humid Subtropical
- Equatorial
- Savanna
- West Coast Marine
- Humid Continental
- Subarctic
- Tundra
- Ice Cap
- Mountain

North Pole
ARCTIC OCEAN
80° N
Arctic Circle
60° N
40° N
PACIFIC OCEAN
Tropic of Cancer
20° N
PACIFIC OCEAN
90° W
30° W
Equator
0°
60° E
90° E
150° E
0°
ATLANTIC OCEAN
INDIAN OCEAN
Tropic of Capricorn
20° S
40° S
60° S
Antarctic Circle
80° S
South Pole

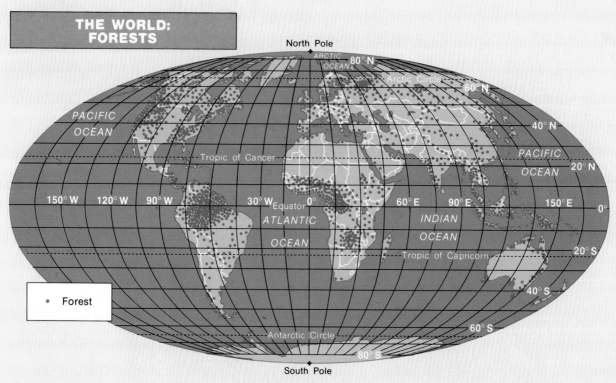

THE WORLD: FORESTS

- Forest

North Pole
ARCTIC OCEAN
80° N
Arctic Circle
60° N
40° N
PACIFIC OCEAN
Tropic of Cancer
20° N
PACIFIC OCEAN
150° W
120° W
90° W
30° W
Equator
0°
60° E
90° E
150° E
0°
ATLANTIC OCEAN
INDIAN OCEAN
Tropic of Capricorn
20° S
40° S
60° S
Antarctic Circle
80° S
South Pole

The Gazetteer is a geographical dictionary. It shows latitude and longitude for cities and certain other places. Latitude and longitude are shown in this form: 36°N/84°W. This means "36 degress north latitude and 84 degrees west longitude." The page reference tells where the entry may be found on a map.

PRONUNCIATION KEY

Some words in this book may be new to you or difficult to pronounce. Those words have been spelled phonetically in parentheses. The syllable that receives stress in a word is shown in small capital letters.

For example: **Chicago** (shuh KAH goh)

Most phonetic spellings are easy to read. In the following Pronunciation Key, you can see how letters are used to show different sounds.

a	after	(AF tur)	oh	flow	(floh)	ch	chicken	(CHIHK un)
ah	father	(FAH thhur)	oi	boy	(boi)	g	game	(gaym)
ai	care	(kair)	oo	rule	(rool)	ing	coming	(KUM ing)
aw	dog	(dawg)	or	horse	(hors)	j	job	(jahb)
ay	paper	(PAY pur)	ou	cow	(kou)	k	came	(kaym)
						ng	long	(lawng)
e	letter	(LET ur)	yoo	few	(fyoo)	s	city	(SIHT ee)
ee	eat	(eet)	u	taken	(TAYK un)	sh	ship	(shihp)
				matter	(MAT ur)	th	thin	(thihn)
ih	trip	(trihp)	uh	ago	(uh GOH)	thh	feather	(FETHH ur)
eye	idea	(eye DEE uh)				y	yard	(yahrd)
y	hide	(hyd)				z	size	(syz)
ye	lie	(lye)				zh	division	(duh VIHZH un)

A

Acadia (uh KAY dee uh). A region of early French settlement on the Atlantic coast of North America. Later, under the English, it became Nova Scotia. p. 509.

Acapulco (ah kuh POOL koh). A seaport and resort city on the Pacific coast of Mexico. (17°N/100°W) p. 11.

Aconcagua (ah kawn KAH gwuh). A mountain in Argentina near the boundary with Chile. It is the highest peak in the Andes and in the Western Hemisphere. Its elevation is 22,834 ft (6,960 m). (33°S/70°W) p. 53.

Alaska Current (uh LAS kuh KUR unt). A warm ocean current that moves north off the Pacific coast of Canada. p. 544.

Alberta (al BURT uh). A province of Canada that is located between British Columbia and Saskatchewan. p. 19.

Altiplano (al tih PLAH noh). A large, high basin in the Andes in Peru and Bolivia. Its elevation is about 12,500 ft (3,810 m) and higher. p. 360.

Amazon Basin (AM uh zahn BAYS un). The area in South America that is drained by the Amazon River and its tributaries. p. 53.

Amazon River (AM uh zahn RIHV ur). The largest river in the world in amount of water. Its tributaries rise in the Andes and Guiana Highlands. It flows across northern Brazil and into the Atlantic Ocean at the Equator. p. 17.

Andes (AN deez). High mountains that stretch north to south along the western side of South America. The highest peak, with an elevation of 22,834 ft (6,960 m), is Aconcagua. p. 53.

Angel Falls (AYN jul fawlz). A waterfall in the Guiana Highlands in southern Venezuela. It is the world's highest waterfall. (6°N/63°W) p. 360.

Anglo-America (ANG gloh uh MER uh kuh). A region made up of Canada and the United States. p. 51.

Antarctic Circle (ant AHRK tihk SUR kul). A line of latitude located at 66½° south latitude. p. 5.

Antofagasta (ahn taw fuh GAHS tuh). A city on the northern coast of Chile. It is a port for exporting nitrates. (24°S/70°W) p. 437.

Appalachian Mountains (ap uh LAY chun MOUNT unz). A chain of mountains stretching from Newfoundland and the Maritime Provinces in Canada to Alabama. p. 19.

Arctic Circle (AHRK tihk SUR kul). A line of latitude located at 66½ north latitude. p. 5.

Arctic Ocean (AHRK tihk OH shun). A large body of water north of the Arctic Circle. p. 9.

Asuncíon (ah soon SYOHN). The capital of Paraguay. It is located on the Paraguay River. (25°S/58°W) p. 165.

Atacama Desert (ah tah KAH muh DEZ urt). A dry area in northern Chile. This area is a major source of nitrates. p. 406.

Ayacucho (ah yah KOO choh). A town in southern Peru. At this place Sucre's army defeated the Spaniards in 1824. (13°S/74°W) p. 204.

B

Bahama Islands (buh HAH muh EYE lundz) or *Bahamas* (buh HAH muhz). A group of islands in the West Indies. They are southeast of Florida and north of Cuba. p. 50.

Bahia (buh HEE uh). A state in northeastern Brazil. p. 484.

Bahia (buh HEE uh). A city on the coast of Brazil. Bahia was the capital of Brazil until 1763. It is now called Salvador. (13°S/38°W) p. 183.

Baja California (BAH hah kal uh FOR nyuh). A peninsula that separates the Pacific Ocean and the Gulf of California. It is also called Lower California. p. 220.

Barranquilla (bah rahn KEE yah). A seaport city on the Magdalena River, near where it flows into the Caribbean Sea in northern Colombia. (11°N/75°W) p. 17.

Bayovar (bah YOH vahr). A new port city on the northwest coast of Peru. (6°S/81°W) p. 397.

Belmopan (bel moh PAN). Capital of Belize. (17°N/89°W) p. 262.

Belo Horizonte (BAY loh hawr uh ZAHN tee). The capital of the state of Minas Gerais in Brazil. This city is an industrial center. (20°S/44°W) p. 17.

Bering Strait (BER ing strayt). A narrow body of water that connects the Arctic Ocean and the Bering Sea. It separates Asia from North America. p. 100.

Blumenau (bloo muh NOU). A town on the Itajaí River in southeastern Brazil. (27°S/49°W)

Bogotá (boh guh TAH). The capital of Colombia. This city is located in the Eastern Cordillera of the Andes. (5°N/74°W) p. 17.

Bonaire (buh NAR). An island off the coast of Venezuela. Part of the Netherlands Antilles. (12°N/68°W). p. 592.

Boyacá (boi yuh KAH). A town in central Colombia. At this place Bolivar's army defeated the Spaniards in 1819. p. 204.

Brasília (bruh ZIHL yuh). The capital of Brazil since 1960. It is located in the plateau country about 600 mi (965 km) northwest of Rio de Janeiro. (16°S/48°W) p. 17.

Brazilian Highlands (bruh ZIHL yun HYE lundz). A highland area that is located in southeastern Brazil. p. 450.

British Columbia (BRIHT ihsh kuh LUM bee uh). The province of Canada that borders the Pacific Ocean. p. 19.

Buenos Aires (BWAY nus ER eez). The capital and most populated city of Argentina. It is located on the Río de la Plata. (35°S/58°W) p. 17.

C

Cajamarca (kah huh MAHR kuh). An Inca town in the Andes of Peru. (7°S/79°W) p. 134.

Calgary (KAL guh ree). A city in Alberta, Canada. It is an oil-industry center. (51°N/114°W) p. 570.

Cali (KAH lee). A city in western Colombia. It is located in the Cauca Valley (3°N/77°W) p. 17.

Canadian Shield (kuh NAY dee un sheeld). An upland region that extends in a horseshoe shape from the Labrador coast to the Arctic Ocean west of Victoria Island. p. 19.

Canal Zone (kuh NAL zohn). A strip of land in which the Panama Canal is located. It was controlled by the United States until 1979, but it is now under Panama's control. p. 277.

Canary Islands (kuh NER ee EYE lundz). A group of Spanish islands off the northwest coast of Africa. p. 151.

Cape Breton Island (kayp BRET un EYE lund). The northeastern part of Nova Scotia, Canada. p. 527.

Caracas (kuh RAHK us). The capital and most populated city of Venezuela. (11°N/67°W) p. 17.

Caribbean Islands. See West Indies.

Caribbean Sea (kar uh BEE un see). A part of the Atlantic Ocean, bounded by South America on the south, Central America on the west, and Cuba, Puerto Rico, and other islands on the north and east. p. 22.

Caroní River (kahr un NEE RIHV ur). A river that is located in southeast Venezuela and that flows north into the Orinoco River near its mouth. p. 360.

Cartagena (kahr tuh HAY nuh). A seaport on the north coast of Colombia, on the Caribbean Sea. Cartagena was a center of Spanish colonial trade. (10°N/76°W) p. 165.

Cauca River (KOU kah RIHV ur). A river that is located in western Colombia and that flows north into the Magdalena River.

Cayenne (kye EN). The capital of French Guiana. (5°N/52°W) p. 17.

Central America (SEN trul uh MER ih kuh). The southern mainland of North America that is south of Mexico. It includes Guatemala, Belize, El Salvador, Honduras, Nicaragua, Costa Rica, and Panama. p. 55.

Chaco. See Gran Chaco.

Champerico (chahm puh REE koh). A seaport on the Pacific Ocean in southwest Guatemala. (14°N/92°W)

Charlottetown (SHAHR lut toun). The capital of Prince Edward Island, Canada. (46°N/63°W) p. 568.

Chichén Itzá (chee CHEN eet SAH). A village in Yucatán state, Mexico. It is the site of extensive Mayan ruins. (21°N/89°W)

Choco (chuh KOH). A section of northwest Colombia, on the Pacific Ocean, known for its heavy rainfall. p. 360.

Cholula (chuh LOO luh). A town in central Mexico. (19°N/98°W) p. 164.

Ciudad Guayana (syoo DAHD gye AN uh). A new industrial city in eastern Venezuela. It is located where the Caroní River joins the Orinoco River. (8°N/63°W) p. 397.

Ciudad Juárez (syoo DAHD HWAH res). A city on the northern border of Mexico, across the Rio Grande from El Paso, Texas. (32°N/106°W) p. 11.

Coast Ranges (kohst RAYNJ uz). Mountains along the Pacific coast of North America. They stretch from Alaska to California. p. 19.

Cochabamba (koh chuh BAHM buh). A city in central Bolivia that is the center of a commercial farming area. (17°S/66°W) p. 397.

Colón (kuh LOHN). City in north-central Panama at the entrance to the Panama Canal. (10°N/80°W) p. 277.

Columbia River (kuh LUM bee uh RIHV ur). A river that rises in the Rocky Mountains in Canada and flows into the Pacific Ocean. It forms part of the Washington-Oregon boundary. p. 527.

Concepción (kun sep see OHN). A city near the coast of central Chile. It is a manufacturing center. (37°S/73°W) p. 437.

Córdoba (KOR duh buh). A large city in central Argentina. (31°S/64°W) p. 17.

Cotopaxi (koh tuh PAK see). An active volcano in the Andes of central Ecuador. Its elevation is 19,347 ft (5,897 m). (1°S/78°W) p. 360.

Cuernavaca (kwer nuh VAH kuh). A resort city in the manufacturing area of Mexico. (19°N/99°W) p. 11.

Cuzco (KOOS koh). A city in the Andes of Peru. It was the capital of the Inca civilization. (14°S/72°W) p. 22.

D

Dolores (duh LOHR us). Town in Argentina, 125 miles southeast of Buenos Aires. (36°S/57°W)

E

Edmonton (ED mun tun). The capital of Alberta, Canada. It is located on the North Saskatchewan River. (54°N/113°W) p. 570.

El Petén (el pe TEN). A forest-covered lowland in northern Guatemala and northern Belize. p. 262.

F

Falkland Islands (FAWK lund EYE lundz) or **Islas Malvinas** (EEZ lahs mal VEE nus). Islands located in the South Atlantic Ocean, east of the southern tip of South America. p. 17.

Federation of the West Indies (fed ur AY shun uv thhuh west IHN deez). A union of British colonies that lasted from 1958 to 1962. p. 312.

Fort Vancouver (fort van KOO vur). A trading post on the Columbia River. Now it is the site of Vancouver, Washington. (46°N/123°W) p. 530.

Fortaleza (for tuh LAY zuh). A port city in northeastern Brazil. (4°S/39°W) p. 17.

Fraser River (FRAY zur RIHV ur). A river that rises in the Canadian Rockies and flows into the Pacific Ocean near Vancouver, British Columbia. p. 19.

Fredericton (FRED uh rik tun). The capital of New Brunswick, Canada. (46°N/67°W) p. 570.

Fuego (FWAY goh). A volcano in Guatemala that erupted in 1974. Its elevation is 12,346 ft (3,763 m). (14°N/91°W) p. 262.

G

Gatun Lake (gah TOON layk). A lake in Panama that forms part of the Panama Canal waterway. p. 277.

Georgetown (JORJ toun). The capital and chief port of Guyana. (7°N/58°W) p. 17.

Gran Chaco (grahn CHAH koh). A lowland region in southern Bolivia, western Paraguay, and northern Argentina. It is mostly grassland and scrub forest and is used for cattle raising. p. 360.

Grand Banks (grand bangks). A rich fishing area in the Atlantic Ocean south of Newfoundland. p. 545.

Great Lakes (grayt layks). A chain of five large lakes in central North America. Except for Lake Michigan, the lakes are on the Canada–United States boundary. p. 53.

Greater Antilles (GRAYT ur an TIHL eez). A group of islands in the West Indies, including the islands of Cuba, Jamaica, Puerto Rico, and Hispaniola. p. 50.

Greenland (GREEN lund). A large island belonging to Denmark, off the coast of northeast North America. It is the largest island in the world with the exception of the continent of Australia. p. 25.

Guadalajara (gwah dul uh HAHR uh). The second most populated city in Mexico. (21°N/103°W) p. 11.

Guajira Peninsula (gwah HIHR uh puh NIHN suh luh). The most northern part of Colombia. The peninsula extends into the Caribbean Sea. p. 597.

Guatemala City (gwah tuh MAH luh SIHT ee). The capital of Guatemala. This city is located in a volcanic region. (15°N/91°W) p. 262.

Guayaquil (gwye ah KEEL). A seaport on the southwest coast of Ecuador. (2°S/80°W) p. 16.

Guiana Highlands (gee AN uh HYE lundz). The highlands in northern South America that extend from Venezuela through northern Brazil and the Guianas. p. 360.

Gulf Coastal Plain (gulf KOHST ul playn). A lowland in eastern Mexico that borders the Gulf of Mexico and includes the Yucatán Peninsula. p. 220.

Gulf of California (gulf uv kal uh FOR nyuh). The bay of the Pacific Ocean east of the peninsula of Baja California in northwest Mexico. In Mexico it is called the Sea of Cortés. p. 220.

Gulf of Mexico (gulf uv MEK sih koh). A large bay of the Atlantic Ocean that is bounded by Mexico on the west and south, Cuba on the east, and the United States on the north. p. 11.

H

Halifax (HAL uh faks). Capital of Nova Scotia, Canada, located on the Atlantic Ocean. (45°N/64°W) p. 570.

Hamilton (HAM ul tun). An industrial city in Ontario, Canada. (43°N/80°W) p. 551.

Havana (huh VAN uh). The capital of Cuba and the most populated city in the West Indies. (23°N/82°W) p. 332.

Hispaniola (hihs pun YOH luh). The second largest island in the West Indies. It is divided between Haiti and the Dominican Republic. p. 164.

Hudson Bay (HUD sun bay). A large body of water in Canada that is connected with the Atlantic Ocean by the Hudson Strait. p. 19.

I

Iberian Peninsula (eye BIHR ee un puh NIHN suh luh). European peninsula southwest of the Pyrenees. Spain and Portugal are on this peninsula. p. 598.

Iceland (EYE slund). An island between the Atlantic and Arctic oceans and between Norway and Greenland. p. 542.

International Date Line (inn tur NASH uh nul dayt lyn). A line mostly on the 180° longitude line, which was agreed on as the place where each calendar day begins. p. 32.

Iquitos (ee KEE tohs). A city on the upper Amazon River in northeastern Peru. (4°S/73°W) p. 397.

Irazú (ihr uh ZOO). A volcano in central Costa Rica that erupted in 1963. Its elevation is 11,260 ft (3,432 m). (10°N/84°W) p. 262.

Isthmus of Tehuantepec (IHS mus uv tuh WAHNT uh pek). A narrow region of southern Mexico between the Gulf of Mexico on the north and the Pacific Ocean on the south. p. 220.

Ixtacihuatl (ees tah SEE waht ul). A volcano in central Mexico. Its elevation is 17,343 ft (5,286 m). (19°N/99°W) p. 220.

J

James Bay (jaymz bay). The southern extension of Hudson Bay, Canada, between Ontario and Quebec. (52°N/80°W) p. 570.

Jari River (zhuh REE RIHV ur). A river located in northeastern Brazil. It flows into the Amazon River near its mouth. p. 450.

Joinvile (zhoin VEE lee). A city in southeastern Brazil. (26°S/49°W)

K

Kingston (KINGZ tun). The capital and chief seaport of Jamaica. (18°N/77°W) p. 308.

L

Labrador (LAB ruh dor). The mainland part of the province of Newfoundland, Canada. It borders the Atlantic Ocean. p. 596.

La Guaira (luh GWYE ruh). A seaport town on the Caribbean coast of Venezuela. It is the port for Caracas. (11°N/67°W) p. 360.

Lake Atitlán (layk aht ih TLAHN). A lake in the mountains of southwestern Guatemala.

Lake Erie (layk IHR ee). One of the Great Lakes. It is located on the Canada–United States boundary. p. 19.

Lake Huron (layk HYOOR ahn). The second largest of the Great Lakes. It is located on the Canada–United States boundary. p. 19

Lake Maracaibo (layk mar uh KYE boh). An extension of the Caribbean Sea. It is located in northwestern Venezuela and surrounded by rich oil fields. p. 360.

Lake Nicaragua (layk nihk uh RAH gwuh). A large lake in southern Nicaragua. It is the largest lake in Central America. p. 262.

Lake Ontario (layk ahn TER ee oh). One of the Great Lakes. It is located on the Canada–United States boundary. p. 19.

Lake Superior (layk suh PIHR ee ur). The largest of the Great Lakes. It is located on the Canada–United States boundary. p. 19.

Lake Texcoco (layk tay SKOH koh). The lake where the Aztec city of Tenochtitlán was built in Mexico. It is now dry. p. 122.

Lake Titicaca (layk tiht ih KAH kuh). A large lake in the Altiplano of the Andes in Peru and Bolivia. Its elevation is 12,500 ft (3,810 m). p. 17.

Lakes Peninsula (layks puh NIHN suh luh). A peninsula that borders on Lake Ontario, Lake Erie, and Lake Huron in Ontario, Canada. p. 565.

La Paz (luh pahz). The administrative capital and most populated city of Bolivia. It is the highest capital in the world, having an elevation 12,000 ft (3,658 m). (17°S/68°W) p. 17.

La Paz (luh pahz). A town near the southern end of Baja California, Mexico, on the Gulf of California. (24°N/110°W) p. 220.

La Plata (lah PLAHT uh). A seaport on the Río de la Plata, southeast of Buenos Aires, Argentina. (35°S/58°W). p. 437.

Latin America (LAT un uh MER ih kuh). All the lands of North America that are south of the United States and all of South America. p. 51.

Leeward Islands (LEE wurd EYE lundz). The northern chain of islands in the Lesser Antilles, in the West Indies. p. 308.

León (le OHN). A city in the manufacturing area of Mexico. (21°N/102°W) p. 11.

Lesser Antilles (LES ur an TIHL eez). A group of islands in the West Indies. Included in this island group are the Virgin Islands, Leeward Islands, and Windward Islands. p. 50.

Lima (LEE muh). The capital and most populated city of Peru. It is located near the coast. (12°S/77°W) p. 17.

Lisbon (LIHZ bun). The capital of Portugal and mainland Europe's westernmost port city. (39°N/9°W) p. 151.

Llanos (LAH nohz). The large plain in northern South America. It is drained by the Orinoco River. p. 360.

Louisbourg (LOO ihs burg). A French town and fortress on Cape Breton Island. It guarded the entrance to the

Gulf of St. Lawrence. (46°N/60°W)

Lower Canada (LOH ur KAN uh duh). The area in Canada that became the province of Quebec. p. 527.

M

Mackenzie River (muh KEN zee RIHV ur). A river located in Northwest Territories, Canada. It flows from the Great Slave Lake to the Arctic Ocean. p. 19.

Madrid (muh DRIHD). The national capital of Spain. It is also the second most populated city in Europe. (40°N/4°W) p. 593.

Magdalena River (mahg dah LE nah RIHV ur). A river located in central Colombia that is an important transportation route. It flows north into the Caribbean Sea. p. 397.

Managua (mah NAH gwah). The capital and most populated city of Nicaragua. It is located on Lake Managua. (12°N/86°W) p. 262.

Manaus (mah NOUS). A city in the rain forest of Brazil. It is located on the Río Negro, a branch of the Amazon River. (3°S/60°W) p. 17.

Manila (muh NIHL uh). The capital and most populated city of the Philippines. It is located on Manila Bay on the island of Luzon. (15°N/121°E) p. 599.

Manitoba (man uh TOH buh). A province of Canada. It is located between Saskatchewan and Ontario. p. 19.

Maracaibo (mar uh KYE boh). A city and an oil-industry center in northwestern Venezuela. It is located on the channel between Lake Maracaibo and the Caribbean Sea. (11°N/72°W) p. 17.

Mato Grosso (MAHT OO GROH SOO) The state in western Brazil that borders Bolivia and Paraguay. p. 484.

Mayapán (mah yah PAHN). An archaeological site in Mexico. It is located about 25 mi (40 km) southeast of Mérida, Yucatán. (21°N/89°W)

Medellín (may day YEEN). The second largest city in Colombia. (6°N/76°W) p. 17.

Mendoza (men DOH zuh). A city in western Argentina, a center of grape culture. (33°S/69°W) p. 437.

Mérida (ME ree dah). The capital of the state of Yucatán, Mexico. (21°N/90°W) p. 164.

Mexican plateau (MEKS ih kun pla TOH). A high region in northern and central Mexico, between the Sierra Madre Occidental and the Sierra Madre Oriental. p. 53.

Mexico City (MEKS ih koh SIHT ee). The capital of Mexico and the most populated city in Latin America. It was built on the site of the Aztec city of Tenochtitlán. (19°N/99°W) p. 11.

Middle America (MIHD ul uh MER ih kuh). Southern North America, including Mexico, Central America, and the islands of the Caribbean Sea (West Indies). p. 53.

Minas Gerais (MEE nus zhuh RYS). The region in southeastern Brazil where there was a gold rush in the 1700s. It is now a state of Brazil. p. 484

Mississippi River (mihs uh SIHP ee RIHV ur). The second longest river in the United States. It rises in northern Minnesota and flows into the Gulf of Mexico near New Orleans, Louisiana. p. 50.

Montego Bay (mahn TEE goh bay). A seaport in northwestern Jamaica. Formerly the site of a large Arawak Indian village. (18°N/76°W)

Monterrey (mahn tuh RAY). An industrial city in northern Mexico. (26°N/100°W) p. 11.

Montevideo (mahnt uh vuh DAY oh). The capital and most populated city of Uruguay. It is located on the Río de la Plata. (35°S/56°W) p. 17.

Montreal (mahn tree AWL). Most populated city of Canada. It is located on an island in the St. Lawrence River. (45°N/73°W) p. 570.

N

New Brunswick (noo BRUNZ wihk). A province of Canada. It is located between Nova Scotia and Quebec. p. 19.

Newfoundland (NOO fund lund). An island in the Atlantic Ocean, off the east coast of Canada. Together with Labrador it forms a province of Canada. p. 19.

New France (noo frans). The possessions of France in North America from 1534 to the end of the French and Indian War in 1763. p. 509.

New Spain (noo spayn). A former Spanish vice royalty in North America. It included all Spanish lands north of Panama. p. 169.

North Pole (north pohl). The most northern place on the earth. p. 5.

Northwest Territories (north WEST TER uh tor eez). A large area in northern Canada that extends to the Arctic Ocean. p. 19.

Nova Scotia (NOH vuh SKOH shuh). A province of Canada. It is located on the Atlantic Ocean and the Gulf of St. Lawrence. p. 19.

O

Oaxaca (wah HAH kah). A city in southern Mexico. It is the capital of the state of Oaxaca. (17°N/97°W) p. 246.

Ohio River (oh HYE oh RIHV ur). The river formed at Pittsburgh, Pennsylvania, by the joining of the Allegheny and Monongahela rivers. It flows into the Mississippi River at Cairo, Illinois. p. 521.

Olinda (oh LIHN duh). A city on the northeast coast of Brazil near Recife. (8°S/35°W) p. 183.

Ontario (ahn TER ee oh). A province of Canada. It is located between Quebec and Manitoba. p. 570.

Oregon Country (OR ih gun KUN tree). The land between the Rocky Mountains and the Pacific Ocean and between Alaska and California. p. 527

Orinoco River (or uh NOH koh RIHV ur). A river located in Venezuela. It rises in the Guiana Highlands and flows into the Atlantic Ocean near Trinidad and Tobago. p. 17.

Orizaba (aw ree SAH bah) or **Citlaltépetl** (see tlahl TAY pet ul). A volcano in central Mexico. It is the highest mountain in Mexico, having an elevation of 18,700 ft (5,700 m). (19°N/97°W) p. 220

Oruro (aw ROOR oh). A city in central Bolivia. It is the center of a mining area. (18°S/67°W) p. 397.

Oshawa (AHSH uh wuh). An industrial city in Ontario, Canada. (44°N/79°W)

Ottawa (AHT uh wuh). The capital of Canada. It is located in southeastern Ontario. (45°N/76°W) p. 570.

Ouro Prêto (oh roo PRAY too). A town in the state of Minas Gerais, Brazil. It was a center of gold mining in the 1700s. (20°S/44°W)

P

Palos (PAH lohs). The town in southwestern Spain from which Columbus started his first voyage to the Americas. (37°N/7°W) p. 151.

Pampas (PAHM puz). The fertile agricultural plains that are located in Argentina and Uruguay. The area is noted for wheat farming and cattle grazing. p. 406.

Panama Canal (PAN uh mah kuh NAL). The ship canal that crosses the Isthmus of Panama. The canal is about 40 mi (64 km) long. It connects the Caribbean Sea and the Pacific Ocean. p. 277.

Panama City (pan uh mah SIHT ee). The capital of Panama. It is located on the Pacific Ocean near the Panama Canal. (9°N/80°W) p. 262.

Pan-American Highway (pan uh MER ih kun HYE way). The international highway system that extends from the United States–Canada border to Santiago, Chile. p. 277.

Paraguay River (PAR uh gway RIHV ur). The river that rises in Brazil and flows across Paraguay and into the Paraná River at the southwestern corner of Paraguay. p. 406.

Paramaribo (par uh MAR ih boh). The seaport city and capital of Suriname. (6°N/55°W) p. 17.

Paraná (par rah NAH). A state in southern Brazil. p. 484.

Paraná River (pah rah NAH RIHV ur). A river that rises in Brazil and flows through eastern Argentina into the Río de la Plata. p. 17.

Paranaguá (pah rah nah GWAH). A seaport city in southern Brazil, in the state of Paraná. (25°S/49°W) p. 474.

Patagonia (pat uh GOH nee uh). A cool, dry, plateau region in southern Argentina. The region is used for raising sheep. p. 406.

Peru (puh ROO). A country in South America. Also, the former Spanish viceroyalty in South America and Panama. Its northern and southern parts became New Granada and La Plata. p. 17.

Peru Current (puh ROO KER unt). A cold ocean current that moves north off the Pacific coast of Chile and Peru. p. 544.

Pico Duarte (PEE koh DWAHRT ee). A mountain in central Dominican Republic. Its elevation is 10,414 ft (3,174 m). p. 308.

Ponce (POHN se). A seaport city on the south coast of Puerto Rico. (18°N/67°W) p. 332.

Popayán (paw pah YAHN). City in southwestern Colombia. (2°/77°W)

Popocatépetl (poh poh kah TE pet ul). A volcano in central Mexico. Its elevation is 17,887 ft (5,452 m). (19°N/99°W) p. 220.

Port Royal (port ROI ul). The first French settlement in North America. It was founded by Champlain in 1605 in what is now Nova Scotia, Canada. (45°N/66°W) p. 509.

Pôrto Alegre (POR too ah LE gruh). A seaport city in southern Brazil on an inlet of the Atlantic Ocean. (30°S/51°W) p. 17.

Portobelo (pohrt uh BEL oh). A village on the Caribbean coast of Panama. It was a center of Spanish colonial trade. (10°N/80°W) p. 165.

Port-of-Spain (port uv spayn). The capital of Tobago and Trinidad. Located on the island of Trinidad. (11°N/62°W) p. 332.

Potosí (poh toh SEE). A city in southern Bolivia. It is noted as a center of mining, first for silver and later for tin. (20°S/66°W) p. 397.

Prime Meridian (prym muh RIHD ee un). The line of longitude that passes through Greenwich, England, and is labeled 0°. It divides the earth into the Eastern and Western Hemispheres. p. 7.

Prince Edward Island (prihns ED wurd EYE lund). A province of Canada. It is located in the Gulf of St. Lawrence. p. 19.

Puebla (PWE blah). A city in the manufacturing area of Mexico. (19°N/98°W) p. 11.

Q

Quebec (kwee BEK). A province of Canada. Also, a British province after the French and Indian War. It was formerly the colony of New France. (47°N/71°W) p. 19.

Quebec City (kwee BEK SIHT ee). A city in Canada and the capital of the province of Quebec, located on the north side of the St. Lawrence River. It was founded in 1608 by Samuel de Champlain. (47°N/71°W) p. 551.

Querétaro (ke RE tah roh). A city in the manufacturing area of Mexico. (21°N/100°W) p. 246.

Quezaltenango (ke sahl te NAHN goh). A city in the mountains of western Guatemala. (15°N/92°W) p. 262.

Quito (KEE toh). The capital of Ecuador. (0°lat./79°W) p. 16.

R

Recife (ruh SEE fuh). A seaport city located on the Atlantic coast of Brazil, on the eastern bulge. (8°S/35°W). p. 17.

Red River (red RIHV ur). A river in Manitoba, Canada. It flows north from the United States to Lake Winnipeg. p. 527.

Regina (rih JYE nuh). The capital of Saskatchewan, Canada. (50°N/105°W) p. 570.

Retalhuleu (ret uh loo LE oo). A town in southwestern Guatemala. It is in a farming region near the Pacific coast. (15°N/92°W)

Rio de Janeiro (REE oh day zhuh NER oh). The second most populated city in South America. It is a major port of Brazil and is located on the Atlantic coast. It was the capital of Brazil from 1763 to 1960. (23°S/43°W) p. 17.

Río de la Plata (REE oh de lah PLAH tah). The bay that begins where the Paraná and Uruguay rivers flow into the Atlantic Ocean near Buenos Aires. (35°S/57°W) p. 17.

Rio Grande (REE oh grand). A river that rises in the Rocky Mountains in Colorado. It empties into the Gulf of Mexico near Brownsville, Texas. It forms part of the boundary between Texas and Mexico. p. 227.

Rio Grande do Sul (REE oh GRAND ee duh SOOL). A state in southern Brazil. p. 484.

Rio Negro (REE oh NAY groh). A river in Colombia, Venezuela, and northwestern Brazil. It flows into the Amazon River near Manaus. p. 406.

Rocky Mountains (RAHK ee MOUNT unz). The longest mountain chain in Canada and the United States. It stretches from Alaska to Mexico. The highest peak of the Rockies in Canada is Mount Robson, British Columbia, having an elevation of 12,972 ft (3,954 m). p. 53.

Rosario (roh ZAHR ee oh). A city in Argentina. It is located on the Paraná River. (33°S/61°W) p. 17.

S

St. Johns (saynt jahnz). The capital of Antigua, in the West Indies. (17°N/62°W) p. 308.

St. John's (saynt jahnz). The capital of Newfoundland, Canada. It is located on the southeast coast of the island of Newfoundland. (48°N/53°W) p. 570.

St. Lawrence River (saynt LOR uns RIHV ur). A river that forms part of the boundary between Canada and the United States. It flows northeast from Lake Ontario to the Atlantic Ocean at the Gulf of St. Lawrence. p. 19.

St. Lawrence Seaway (saynt LOR uns SEE way). A waterway for ocean ships that includes the St. Lawrence River, canals, and the Great Lakes. p. 551.

Salvador (SAL vuh dor). A city on the coast of Brazil. Formerly called Bahia, it was the capital of Brazil until 1763. (13°S/39°W) p. 17.

San Antonio (san un TOH nee oh). A large city in Texas. It is located on the San Antonio River and is the site of the Alamo. (29°N/99°W) p. 227.

San Jacinto River (san juh SIHN toh RIHV ur). A river located in southeastern Texas. It flows into the Gulf of Mexico and is the site of a battle between Texans and Mexicans. p. 227.

San José (sahn hoh SE). The capital of Costa Rica. It is a center of coffee production. (10°N/84°W) p. 262.

San Juan (san hwahn). The capital and most populated city of Puerto Rico. (18°N/66°W) p. 12.

San Pedro Sula (san PE droh SOO lah). A city in northwestern Honduras. It is a commercial center. (15°N/88°W) p. 262.

San Salvador (san SAL vuh dor). A small island in the Bahama Islands, where Columbus landed on October 12, 1492. (24°N/75°W). p. 151.

San Salvador (san SAL vuh dor). The capital and commercial and industrial center of El Salvador, in Central America. (14°N/89°W) p. 262.

Santa Catarina (SAHN tah kah tuh REE nuh). A state in southern Brazil. p. 484.

Santa Cruz (SAN tuh krooz). A city in the eastern lowlands of Bolivia. (18°S/63°W) p. 397.

Santa Fe (SAN tuh FAY). A Spanish settlement started in 1609. Today it is the capital of New Mexico. (36°N/106°W) p. 227.

Santa María (SANT uh muh REE uh). A volcano in western Guatemala, near Quezaltenango. Its elevation is 12,375 ft (3,772 m). (15°N/92°W) p. 262.

Santiago (san tee AH goh). The capital and most populated city of Chile. (33°S/71°W) p. 17.

Santo Domingo (SAN toh doh MING goh). The capital and chief seaport of the Dominican Republic. It was founded by Columbus in 1496. (19°N/70°W) p. 164.

Santos (SAHN toos). A seaport in southeastern Brazil. It is the port for São Paulo and is the largest coffee-exporting port in the world. (24°S/46°W) p. 474.

São Paulo (soun POU loo). A state in southeastern Brazil. p. 484.

São Paulo (soun POU loo). The most populated city in South America. It is located in southeastern Brazil, in the state of São Paulo. (24°S/47°W) p. 17.

São Vicente (soun vee SAYN tuh). A city on the coast of Brazil, near Santos. It was the first permanent settlement in Brazil, founded in 1532. (24°S/46°W) p. 183.

Saskatchewan (sas KACH uh wahn). A province of Canada, located between Alberta and Manitoba. p. 19.

Sea of Cortés (see uv kor TEZ). See Gulf of California.

Seville (suh VIHL). A city in southwestern Spain, the center of Spanish colonial trade. (37°N/6°W) p. 174.

Sierra Madre Occidental (see ER uh MAH dray ahk suh DENT ul). The mountain range in western Mexico that runs north and south. p. 220.

Sierra Madre Oriental (see ER uh MAH dray or ee ENT ul). The mountain range in eastern Mexico that runs north and south. p. 220.

South Pole (south pohl). The most southern place on the earth. p. 5.

Strait of Magellan (strayt uv muh JEL un). The winding strait near the southern end of South America, between the mainland and Tierra del Fuego. It connects the Atlantic and Pacific oceans. p. 17.

Sucre (SOO kray). The constitutional capital of Bolivia. It is located in the Andes about 260 mi (418 km) southeast of La Paz. (19°S/65°W) p. 17.

Sudbury (SUD ber ee). A nickel-mining city in Ontario, Canada. The world's largest supply of nickel is in the area. (47°N/81°W) p. 556.

T

Tajumulco (tah hoo MOOL koh). A volcano in western Guatemala. With an elevation of 13,845 ft (4,220 m), it is the highest point in Central America. (15°N/92°W) p. 262.

Tegucigalpa (tuh goo suh GAL puh) The capital of Honduras. (14°N/87°W) p. 262.

Tenochtitlán (te nawch tee TLAHN). A city in Mexico that was first built by the Aztecs. The city no longer exists; Mexico City has been built on its ruins. (19°N/99°W) p. 122.

Thunder Bay (THUN dur bay). A port city on Lake Superior in Ontario, Canada. (48°N/89°W) p. 551.

Tierra del Fuego (tee ER uh del FWAY goh). A group of islands south of the Strait of Magellan in southern South America. p. 406.

Tikal (tih KAHL). A city in northern Guatemala. Site of ancient Maya ruins. It is located within Tikal National Park. (18°N/90°W)

Tlaxcala (tlahs KAH lah). A town in central Mexico. (19°N/98°W). p. 164.

Tobago (toh BAY goh). A small island north of Trinidad in the West Indies. It joined with Trinidad to form the country of Trinidad and Tobago. p. 50.

Toluca (tuh LOO kuh). A city in the manufacturing area of Mexico. (19°N/100°W) p. 246.

Toronto (tuh RAHNT oh). The capital of Ontario, Canada. It is located on the northwest end of Lake Ontario. (44°N/79°W) p. 570.

Trinidad (TRIHN uh dad). An island off the coast of Venezuela. It is one of the continental islands of the West Indies. It forms part of the country of Trinidad and Tobago. p. 50.

Tropic of Cancer (TRAHP ihk uv KAN sur). A line of latitude located at 23½° north latitude. p. 5.

Tropic of Capricorn (TRAHP ihk uv KAP rih korn). A line of latitude located at 23½° south latitude. p. 5.

Trujillo (troo HEE yoh). A city near the coast of northwestern Peru. (8°S/79°W) p. 397.

Tucumán (too koo MAHN). A city in northwestern Argentina. It is a center of the sugar industry. (27°S/65°W)

Tumbes (TOOM bays). Town in northwestern Peru, near the border of Ecuador. (4°S/80°W) p. 165.

U

Upper Canada (UP ur KAN uh duh). The area that later became the province of Ontario, Canada. p. 527.

V

Valley of Mexico (VAL ee uv MEKS ih koh). A broad, flat valley in central Mexico, where Mexico City is located. It is part of the Mexican plateau. p. 220.

Valparaíso (val puh RAY zoh). A major seaport of Chile. (33°S/72°W) p. 437.

Vancouver (van KOO vur). A city in British Columbia, Canada. It is located on an inlet of the Pacific Ocean and is Canada's most important Pacific seaport. (49°N/123°W) p. 570.

Vancouver Island (van KOO vur EYE lund). A large island in the Pacific Ocean in southern British Columbia, Canada. Its chief city is Victoria. p. 530.

Veracruz (ver uh KROOZ). A seaport on the east coast of Mexico, on the Gulf of Mexico. It was a center of Spanish colonial trade. (19°N/96°W) p. 164.

Victoria (vihk TOR ee uh). The capital of British Columbia, Canada. It is located on Vancouver Island. (48°N/123°W) p. 570.

W

West Indies (west IHN deez). The group of islands that stretch about 2,500 miles (4,022 km) from near Florida to near Venezuela, in the northern and eastern parts of the Caribbean Sea. The West Indies are also called the Caribbean islands. p. 312.

Western Cordillera (WES turn kor dihl YER uz). One of three mountain ranges of the Andes in Colombia. p. 360.

Windsor (WIHN zur). An industrial city in Ontario, Canada. (42°N/83°W)

Windward Islands (WIHND wurd EYE lundz). The southern chain of islands in the Lesser Antilles, in the West Indies. p. 308.

Winnipeg (WIHN uh peg). The capital of Manitoba, Canada, located on the Red River. (50°N/97°W) p. 570.

Y

Yucatán Peninsula (yoo kah TAHN puh NIHN suh luh). The coastal plain in southeastern Mexico and in northern Guatemala and Belize. It separates the Gulf of Mexico and the Caribbean Sea. p. 220.

Yukon Territory (YOO kahn TER uh tor ee). The territory in northwestern Canada bounded by the Northwest Territories, British Columbia, and Alaska. p. 570.

Yungay (yung GYE). A former city in northwestern Peru, west of Mount Huascarán. It was destroyed by earthquake and landslide in 1970. p. 360.

GLOSSARY

The page references tell where each entry
first appears in the text.

A

abdicate (AB dih kayt). To give up a position of power, such as a kingship. p. 457.

acid rain (AS ihd rayn) Precipitation that contains acid from industrial pollution. p. 583.

agrarian reform (uh GRER ee un rih FORM). Land and farming improvements. p. 416.

alliance (uh LYE uns). A close connection or friendship, sometimes made formal by written agreement. p. 506.

ally (AL eye). One who is closely connected with another, either by friendship or by formal written agreement. p. 156.

alpaca (al PAK uh). An animal of the camel family used in the Andes as a source of wool. p. 369.

A.M. The abbreviation for the Latin phrase *ante meridiem,* which means "before noon." It is used for time from midnight up to but not including noon. p. 30.

amnesty (AM nus tee). A pardon for acts committed against the government. p. 443.

ancestor (AN ses tur). A person on one's family tree, such as a great-grandparent or great-great-grandparent. p. 78.

Altiplano (al tih PLAH noh). The high plateau near the border between Peru and Bolivia. p. 368.

Anglo-America (an gloh un MER ih kuh). A cultural region made up of Canada and the United States. p. 49.

araucaria (ar aw KER ee uh). A South American tree whose soft wood is good for lumber. It is also called Paraná pine. p. 453.

archaeologist (ahr kee AHL uh jihst). A person who studies prehistory by examining the remains of animals and of people and the things they left behind. p. 97.

armada (ahr MAH duh). A Spanish word for a fleet of armed ships. p. 177.

artifact (AHRT uh fakt). Anything, such as a bit of pottery or a knife or the remains of a building, that people leave behind after they have lived somewhere. p. 97.

artillery (ahr TIHL ur ee). Large guns that are mounted on a carriage and fired by a crew of soldiers. p. 520.

artisan (AHRT uh zun). A craftworker, or a person who is skilled at making things by hand. p. 250.

asbestos (as BES tus). A mineral found in long fibers that can be made into paper, cloth, or other products. p. 554.

B

bandeirantes (bahn day ee RAHN tes). Brazilians who explored the interior of South America, looking for wealth. p. 186.

barge (bahrj). A large, flat-bottomed boat that carries bulky loads. p. 550.

barrio (BAHR ee oh). A name given to a squatter settlement. p. 399.

basin (BAYS un). A broad, flat valley. p. 55.

bauxite (BAWKS yt). The raw material from which aluminum is obtained. p. 391.

bilingual (bye LING qwel). Having or speaking two languages. p. 396.

boom (boom). A raft made up of hundreds of logs roped together to be floated downriver to a pulp or paper mill. p. 552.

boom and bust (boom un bust). A period of swift economic growth followed by a sudden collapse. p. 464.

buccaneer (buk uh NIHR). A pirate. A robber upon the sea, especially one who preyed upon early Spanish ships and settlements. p. 175.

byproduct (BYE prahd ukt). Something produced in the course of processing a desired product. p. 336.

C

cacao (kuh KAY oh). The seeds from which chocolate is made. Also, the tree that produces these seeds. p. 385.

callampa (kah YAHM pah). The name given to any of the squatter settlements in Chile. p. 438.

canyon (KAN yun). A valley with steep sides cut into the earth's surface by the moving water of a river. p. 530.

capital (KAP ut ul). The accumulated wealth of an individual, a business, or a country. p. 148.

captaincy (KAP tun see). A large land grant in Brazil given to people who agreed to develop the land and send settlers there. p. 183.

cartographer (kahr TAHG ruh fur). A mapmaker. p. 15.

causeway ● culture

causeway (KAWZ way). A bridge made over water or marshy ground by building up earth in narrow strips until it is above the water. p. 122.

censor (SEN sur). To keep people from saying or printing anything that is thought to be harmful. p. 462.

centennial (sen TEN ee ul). A one-hundredth anniversary; the celebration of a one-hundredth anniversary. p. 571.

chinampa (chih NAHM pah). An island built by the Aztecs of layers of reeds, other plants, and mud and planted with crops. p. 123.

chuño (CHOO nyoh). A food made by freezing and drying potatoes. p. 386.

circumnavigate (sur kum NAV uh gayt). To sail around, such as to circumnavigate the world. p. 152.

civil rights (SIHV ul ryts). The rights of a citizen to life, freedom, owning property, voting, and equal treatment under the law. p. 268.

civil war (SIHV ul wor). A war fought between groups of citizens of the same country. p. 161.

civilization (sihv uh luh ZAY shun). The state of a human society in which the arts, sciences, religion, government, cities, trade, and other ways of living are highly developed and fairly complex. p. 108.

cliff (klihfl). A very steep face of rock or earth that rises above the surrounding land. p. 520.

climate (KLYE mut). The normal pattern of weather in an area over a period of many years. p. 60.

colonization (kahl uh nye ZAY shun). The founding or establishing of a settlement in a land distant from that of the government. p. 165.

colony (KAHL uh nee). A place that is settled at a distance from the country that governs it. p. 69.

combine (KAHM byn). A machine that cuts grain plants and separates the grain from the stalk in one operation. p. 559.

commerce (KAHM urs). The buying and selling of goods and services. p. 173.

commercial farm (kuh MUR shul fahrm). A farm on which crops are raised for sale rather than for home use. p. 242.

common market (KAHM un MAHR kiht). An organization each of whose members agrees to lower tariffs on products imported from the other member countries. p. 291.

commonwealth (KAHM un welth). A political unit somewhat like a state. p. 321.

communist (KAHM yoo nihst). Having to do with communism, a political system in which the government owns or controls all property and industry. Also, a person who believes in communism. p. 318.

compass rose (KUM pus rohz). A drawing used to show orientation on maps that do not have a grid system. p. 7.

confederation (kun fed ur AY shun). The act of uniting, or joining together. Also, the group formed by such joining together. p. 498.

coniferous (koh NIHF ur us). Cone-bearing. p. 547.

conquistador (kan KWIHS tuh dor). Conqueror. A leader in the Spanish conquest of America and especially of Mexico and Peru. p. 159.

constitutional monarchy (kahn stuh TOO shuh nul MAHN ur kee). A kind of government in which the monarch's powers are limited by a constitution. p. 578.

contaminate (kun TAM uh nayt). To make dirty, impure, or infected; to pollute. p. 583.

continental climate (kahn tun NENT ul KLYE mut). A climate in which there is a great difference between summer and winter temperatures because the ocean is far away. p. 547.

continental island (kahn tuh NENT ul EYE lund). An island that is part of the same kind of rock formation that makes up the mainland of a continent. p. 307.

contour lines (KAHN toor linz). Any of the lines that are used to show elevation on a topographical map. p. 12.

cooperative (koh AHP ur uh tihv). A plantation or other business that is owned by the people who work on it. p. 388.

cordillera (koh dihl YER uh). A system of mountain ranges, often of parallel ranges. p. 361.

coup (koo). The sudden overthrow of a government by force. p. 224.

coureur de bois (koo rur duh BWAH). One of the French woodsmen of North America who lived in the forest, trading with the Indians for furs and exploring the land. p. 505.

Creole (KREE ohl). A person in the Spanish colonies who was of Spanish ancestry but who was born in the colonies. p. 181.

crest (krest). The highest point. p. 531.

culture (KUL chur). Customs or way of life. p. 67.

D

debt peonage (det PEE uh nihj). A system in which workers are held for service until they can pay off their debts. p. 180.

democracy (dih MAHK ruh see). Government of, for, and by the people. p. 231.

department (dee PAHRT munt). A division of France that is somewhat like a state in the United States. p. 312.

depose (dih POHZ). To remove from office or from a position of authority. p. 191.

deposit (dee PAHZ iht). A large amount of a mineral found in a given place in the earth. p. 541.

deputy (DEP yoo tee). In Mexico, a person elected by the people of a state to represent them in the Mexican Congress. p. 253.

dialect (DYE uh lekt). A form of a language that is used in a certain area or by a certain people. p. 325.

dictator (DIHK tayt ur). A leader with complete control, who rules a country with little regard for its laws or for people's rights. p. 224.

diplomat (DIHP luh mat). One who represents his or her government in important dealings with other nations. p. 204.

distortion (dih STOR shun). The changing of the form of something. Special mirrors at carnivals and sideshows *distort* your face. p. 23.

diversified (duh VUR suh fyd). Having a variety of, having many different kinds. p. 560.

domesticate (doh MES tih kayt). To change plants by selecting qualities that make them more useful for people; to tame an animal. p. 107.

dominion (duh MIHN yun). A self-governing, or nearly self-governing, nation that has close ties with England and that regards the British ruler as its own ruler, although the ruler has very little real power. p. 69.

drought (drout). A long period of dry weather, with little or no precipitation. p. 452.

E

economy (ih KAHN uh mee). The production and management of a country's resources. p. 185.

edible (ED uh bul). Fit to be eaten, eatable. p. 500.

ejido (ay HEE doh). Land given to a village to provide farms for the people of the village. p. 234.

elevation (el uh VAY shun). The height of the land. Usually given as the height above sea level, which is considered to be 0 elevation. p. 10.

emigrate (EM ih grayt). To leave one country to settle in another. p. 339.

empire (EM pyr). The territories and peoples under the control of a powerful nation. p. 120.

encomendero (en koh men DAY roh). Spanish colonist placed in charge of an encomienda. p. 171.

encomienda (en koh mee EN dah). A group of Indians placed in the care of a Spanish colonist called an encomendero. p. 171.

epidemic (ep uh DEM ihk). The rapid spread of disease among a large number of people. p. 83.

erosion (ee ROH zhun). The wearing away of the earth's surface by wind, ice, running water, or waves. p. 241.

estancia (es TAHN syah). A large South American ranch. p. 434.

estuary (ES tyoo er ee). The wide mouth of a river into which the tide flows. p. 440.

exile (EG zyl). The removal by force from one's homeland; a person so removed. p. 224.

expedition (eks puh DIHSH un). A journey undertaken for a specific purpose, such as exploration. p. 78.

export (eks PORT). To ship products to another country, usually to sell them. p. 73.

expropriate (eks PROH pree ayt). To take over the property of another. p. 235.

extinct (ek STINGKT). No longer living. Usually used in speaking of a whole group of plants or animals rather than one individual. p. 101.

F

fault (fawlt). A break in the solid rock layer of the earth formed when pressure inside the earth causes the rock to break and move. p. 262.

favela (fuh VE luh). The name given to a squatter settlement in Brazil. p. 481.

fazenda (fuh ZEN duh). The name given a large estate, such as a coffee farm of Brazil. p. 186.

federation (fed ur AY shun). A union of colonies or nations under one government. p. 313.

fishing banks (FIHSH ing bangks). A part of an ocean that is shallow because of the height of the undersea land and that has large supplies of fish. p. 502.

fjord (fyord). A deep and narrow channel carved into a coast by glaciers. p. 575.

flood plain (flud playn). The level land near a river that may be covered with water when the river overflows its banks. p. 472.

foot plow ● *International Date Line*

foot plow (foot plou). A plow used by the Indians of Bolivia. It has one curved end, which is the handle. A stone or metal blade, which is attached to the straight end, is driven into the ground by the force of the farmer's foot against the footrest near the blade. p. 385.

foreign debt (FOR ihn det). Money that a country owes to people and organizations located outside the country. p. 463.

frigid zones (FRIHJ ihd zohnz). The areas in the high latitudes that have long, cold winters and cool summers, usually considered to be between 66½°S and 90°S and between 66½°N and 90°N. p. 61.

frontier (frun TIHR). The edge of settlement. p. 471.

G

gaucho (GOU choh). A cowboy of the Pampas. p. 410.

generator (JEN ur ayt ur). A machine that produces (generates) electricity. p. 557.

geographic coordinates (jee uh GRAF ihk koh OR duh nihts). The numbers in the geographic grid system; the numbers that give the latitude and longitude of a place. p. 7.

geologist (jee AHL uh jihst). Scientist who studies the earth, including its rocks and fossils. p. 548.

glacier (GLAY shur). A slow-moving body of ice. p. 549.

glyph (glihf). A Maya writing symbol such as a pictograph or other character or sign. p. 129.

gross national product (GNP) (grohs NASH uh nul PRAHD ukt). The total value of a nation's goods and services produced and sold in a single year. p. 240.

guano (GWAH noh). Bird droppings. p. 393.

guerrilla (guh RIHL uh). A fighter who is fighting on his or her own, rather than as a part of a country's regular army. Guerrillas usually form small groups that make quick hit-and-run attacks or ambushes, rather than fighting long battles. p. 198.

H

hacienda (hah see EN duh). A large estate, such as a ranch or plantation, especially in a Spanish-speaking country. p. 179.

harbor (HAHR bur). A place where a ship at anchor is protected from the wind and waves of the ocean. p. 541.

harpoon (hahr POON). A spear-like hunting tool with barbs that hook into the flesh of the animal being hunted. p. 499.

hemisphere (HEM ih sfihr). One half of the earth. p. 6.

heritage (HER ih tihj). Something passed on by people who have gone before. All the ideas, laws, customs, and feelings passed on by one's ancestors. p. 51.

homesteader (HOHM sted ur). A person who buys land in a wilderness area and builds a home and starts a farm on that land. To encourage the settlement of an unsettled area, a government often provides cheap or even free land to homesteaders. p. 534.

human rights (HYOO mun ryts). Basic freedoms, such as freedom of speech, religion, and the press. p. 299.

hurricane (HUR ih kayn). A tropical storm with strong winds and heavy rains. p. 175.

hydroelectric (hye droh ee LEK trihk). Electricity made from waterpower, which is the force of flowing water. p. 432.

I

igloo (IHG loo). A small house built with blocks of snow. p. 500.

immigration (ihm uh GRAY shun). The coming into a country or region to live there. p. 72.

import (ihm PORT). To bring in products from one country into another country, usually to sell the products. p. 73.

industrial complex (ihn DUS tree ul kahm PLEKS). A group of factories, refineries, and other plants. p. 392.

industry (IHN dus tree). The making and sale of goods or services; any area of trade, business, manufacturing, or agriculture, such as the steel *industry* or the tobacco *industry*. p. 71.

inflation (ihn FLAY shun). An economic condition in which the value of money goes down and prices go up. p. 377.

inlet (IHN let). A small bay. p. 553.

interdependent (ihn tur dee PEN dunt). Relying or depending on one another. p. 70.

interest (IHN trihst). A percentage charged by a lender for the use of money. p. 255.

International Date Line (ihn tur NASH uh nul dayt lyn). The line at roughly 180° longitude that marks the place where each calendar day begins. p. 34.

invade (ihn VAYD). To enter to conquer. p. 525.

invest (ihn VEST). To use money to build businesses or factories or to develop resources, in order to make more money. p. 230.

irrigation (ihr uh GAY shun). The bringing of water to crops. p. 108.

isthmus (IHS mus). A narrow strip of land joining two larger bodies of land. p. 159.

J

junta (HOON tuh). A group of people who rule as a committee and who have usually used force to gain control of a country. p. 326.

K

kayak (KYE ak). A small skin-covered boat used by the Inuit. p. 500.

key (kee). The part of a map that explains the symbols used on the map. p. 7.

L

labor (LAY bur). Work. p. 171.

land bridge (land brihj). A piece of land that connects two larger bodies of land. p. 99.

landforms (land formz). The earth's surface features, such as mountains, valleys, and plains. p. 18.

land grant (land grant). Land given to a colonist by a government. p. 179.

landmass (land mas). A very large area of land, such as a continent. p. 153.

landlocked (land lahkt). Being shut in on all sides or nearly all sides by land. p. 74.

latex (LAY teks). The material found in rubber trees from which rubber is made. p. 464.

Latin America (LAT un uh MER ih kuh). A cultural region made up of all of South America and the lands of North America that are south of the United States. p. 51.

latitude (LAT uh tood). Distances north or south of the Equator. p. 5.

lava (LAH vuh). The melted rock that comes out of a volcano. p. 222.

leaching (LEECH ing). Leaching is the carrying off by rainwater of much of the soil's minerals, which crops need for growth. p. 114.

leeward (lee ward). Facing away from the wind. p. 310.

legislative (LEJ ihs layt ihv). Lawmaking. p. 526.

liberate (LIHB ur ayt). To set free. p. 200.

light industry (lyt IHN dus tree). An industry that uses small machines and few raw materials to produce goods. p. 347.

limestone island (LYM stohn EYE lund). An island formed from a kind of rock that often forms at the bottom of seas and oceans. p. 309.

literacy (LIHT ur uh see). The ability to read and write. p. 319.

literacy rate (LIHT ur uh see rayt). The percentage of people in an area who can read and write. p. 270.

llama (LAH muh). An animal of the camel family that is used in the Andes as a pack animal and as a source of wool. p. 113.

llanero (lyah NAY roh). A cowhand from the llanos. p. 200.

llano (LAH noh). Any large, grassy plain of South America. p. 200.

lock (lahk). The part of a canal where ships are raised or lowered. p. 277.

longitude (LAHN juh tood). Distance east or west of the Prime Meridian. p. 6.

Loyalist (LOI ul ihst). Any of the people who disapproved of the American Revolution and who remained loyal to Great Britain. p. 523.

M

mainland (MAYN land). The main part of a country or continent. p. 46.

manioc (MAN ee ahk). A tropical plant similar to the potato. p. 107.

manufacturing (man yoo FAK chur ing). Making goods, especially by machinery, on a large scale. p. 239.

marine climate (muh REEN KLYE mut). A climate, such as the mild, wet climate of Canada's Pacific coast, that is affected by a nearby ocean. p. 543.

maritime (MAR ih tym). Having to do with shipping or sailing. p. 148.

Marxist (MAHRKS ihst). A follower of Karl Marx, who believed in socialism. p. 416.

mechanize (MEK uh nyz). To replace human and animal labor with machines. p. 383.

meridian (muh RIHD ee un). A line of longitude; any of the north-south lines drawn on maps and globes. p. 6.

mesa (MAY suh). A flat-topped mountain. p. 363.

mestizo ● per capita income

mestizo (mes TEE zoh). A person of mixed European and American Indian ancestry. p. 79.

métis (may TEES). Canadians of mixed French and Indian parentage. p. 505.

metropolis (muh TRAHP ul ihs). The main city of a state, country, or region. p. 436.

metropolitan area (me troh PAHL ih tun ER ee uh). An area made up of a large city or several large cities and the towns and other communities around it. p. 84.

migrant (MYE grunt). A person who leaves one place to live in another. p. 245.

migration (mye GRAY shun). The act of moving from one land to another. Usually used to refer to groups, rather than individuals. p. 99.

mita (MEE tuh). A system of forced labor. p. 134.

mixed farm (mihkst fahrm). A farm on which a variety of crops are raised. p. 559.

monarchy (MAHN ur kee). A country ruled by a king or a queen. p. 148.

monopoly (muh NAHP uh lee). Sole control of an entire industry. p. 173.

mulatto (muh LAHT oh). A person of mixed black and white ancestry. p. 79.

multicultural (mul tih KUL chur ul). Having many different ethnic heritages. p. 479.

mutiny (MYOOT un ee). The taking over of a ship and its captain by the ship's crew. p. 510.

N

nationalism (NASH uh nul ihz um). Devotion to one's country. p. 148.

natural gas (NACH ur ul gas). A mixture of gases, mostly methane, that is found naturally in the earth. p. 555.

natural increase (NACH ur ul IHN krees). Change in population that comes from differences in the number of births and deaths. p. 83.

negotiation (nih goh shee AY shun). The process of arriving at a solution acceptable to all parties. p. 533.

neutral (NOO trul). Not taking sides; supporting neither one nor the other. p. 517.

newsprint (NOOZ prihnt). The kind of paper on which newspapers are printed. p. 552.

nomad (NOH mad). A person with no permanent home who travels from place to place. p. 100.

Northwest Passage (north WEST PAS ihj). A sea route through North America to Asia by sailing northwest. p. 510.

nuclear America (NOO klee ur uh MER ih kuh). Term used by archaeologists and anthropologists that refers to the areas of the great Indian civilizations. p. 119.

O

observatory (ub ZURV uh tor ee). A place for studying the sky. p. 128.

ocean current (OH shun KUR unt). A regular movement of the surface water of an ocean or a river, caused mostly by winds and differences in water temperature. p. 367.

opposition (ahp uh ZIHSH un). The group of people who disagree with the group in power. p. 192.

orientation (or ee en TAY shun). The location of directions on maps. p. 5.

overseer (OH vur see ur). A person who managed a plantation. p. 336.

P

Pacific Rim (puh SIHF ihk rihm). Countries and parts of countries that border the Pacific Ocean. p. 568.

palisade (pal uh SAYD). A fence made of large, pointed stakes, set firmly in the ground as a defense against attack. p. 115.

pampero (pahm PAY roh). One of the cold winds from the west or southwest that blows across the Pampas in winter. p. 408.

parallel (PAHR uh lel). A line of latitude; any of the east-west lines drawn on maps and globes. p. 5.

Parliament (PAHR luh munt). The lawmaking body of Britain, of Canada, or certain other countries. p. 521.

pass (pas). A place in the mountains that is low enough for people to pass over. p. 548.

patois (PA twah). A local dialect. p. 331.

peninsula (puh NIHN suh luh). A piece of land that reaches out into the sea from a larger body of land. p. 51.

peninsulars (puh NIHN suh lurz). People in the Spanish colonies who were not born in the colonies but who came from Spain. p. 181.

peon (PEE un). A person who lived and worked on a hacienda. p. 234.

per capita income (pur KAP ih tuh IHN kum). The average amount of money earned in a year by each person in a nation. Found by dividing the total amount of money earned by the total number of people. p. 347.

permafrost (PUR muh frawst). The layer of soil that is frozen all year long in Arctic regions. p. 543.

personalismo (payr soh nah LEES moh). A Spanish word meaning "leadership by personality," used to refer to dictators like Castro of Cuba who rule on the strength of their own personality rather than with the support of a strong political party. p. 319.

perspective (pur SPEK tihv). The point from which a map is drawn. p. 18.

petrochemical (pe troh KEM ih kul). A chemical or synthetic material manufactured from petroleum. p. 394.

plain (playn). Flat lands that usually are low in elevation. p. 54.

plateau (pla TOH). A large, high, rather level area that is raised above the surrounding land. p. 55.

plebiscite (PLEB uh syt). A vote that shows how people feel about a question or problem. Action does not have to be taken as a result of the voting. p. 348.

P.M. The abbreviation for the Latin phrase *post meridiem*, which means "after noon." Used for time from noon up to but not including midnight. p. 30.

pochteca (pohch TAY kahs). An Aztec trader who also acted as a spy when visiting other Indian cities. p. 126.

police state (puh LEES stayt). A type of government that uses police, especially secret national police, to keep political opposition down. p. 418.

policy (PAHL uh see). A plan of action. p. 317.

population density (pahp yoo LAY shun DEN suh tee). The average number of people per given unit of area. p. 82.

port (port). A place where products are loaded on to or taken off of ships. p. 541.

potential (poh TEN shul). Possible; available for use but not yet in use. p. 555.

prairie (PRER ee). A flat, grass-covered plain. p. 54.

precipitation (pree sihp uh TAY shun). The moisture that falls from the air; such as rain, snow, sleet, or hail. p. 60.

pre-Columbian (pree kuh LUM bee un). Having to do with time before Columbus reached the Americas. p. 97.

prehistoric (pree hihs TOR ihk). The time before the written word was available. p. 97.

primate city (PRYE mayt SIHT ee). A city that is 2½ times the size of the next largest city. It stands out above the other cities in a nation in terms of its businesses, industries, cultural and educational institutions, government offices, and transportation facilities. p. 85.

prime minister (prym MIHN ihs tur). A head of government in a parliamentary system. The prime minister's duties are similar to those of the President of the United States. p. 533.

privateer (prye vuh TIHR). A pirate with a privately owned, armed ship and the government's permission to attack enemy ships. p. 177.

profile (PROH fyl). A map or diagram drawn as if the land had been cut away so that the earth can be viewed from the side. p. 18.

profit (PRAHF iht). Gain. p. 284.

projection (proh JEK shun). The representation on a map of the earth's surface or a part of it. p. 24.

province (PRAHV ihns). **1.** (Of Britain) A land that was not actually a part of England, but was governed by England. **2.** A part of Canada somewhat like a state in the United States. p. 526.

provision grounds (proh VIHZH un groundz). Areas in which the slaves of Haiti and Jamaica were allowed to grow their own food. p. 336.

public housing (PUB lihk HOU zing). Houses or, more frequently, apartments built by a government for citizens who cannot afford to own or rent their own homes or apartments. p. 400.

public services (PUB lihk SUR vihs ihz). Things the government provides for its citizens. p. 481.

Q

quebracho (kay BRAH choh). A tree of the Gran Chaco whose very hard wood has many uses and which yields the chemical called tannin. p. 408.

quipu (KEE poo). A series of strings knotted at particular places to indicate quantity. p. 135.

R

rain shadow (rayn SHAD oh). The condition of dryness that occurs on the leeward side of high coastal mountains. p. 409.

ratify (RAT uh fye). To give formal approval. p. 276.

ration (RASH un). To limit the amount of scarce items, such as gasoline and meat, that each person can buy. p. 299.

rebellion (rih BEL yun). An armed fight against the government. p. 228.

617

redistribution ● strike

redistribution (ree dihs trih BYOO shun). The dividing of large land holdings into smaller parcels so that more people can own land. p. 327.

referendum (ref uh REN dum). An election to decide an issue. A referendum allows the people to vote on a law. p. 582.

refinery (rih FYN ur ee). A plant in which a raw material is purified. p. 338.

reform (rih FORM). A change that stops something that is wrong or unfair. p. 415.

regent (REE junt). A person appointed to rule for a king or queen who is too young or too ill to rule. p. 457.

region (REE jun). An area that has some common characteristic, such as plains. p. 49.

regionalism (REE jun ul ihz um). Loyalty to a region above loyalty to a country. p. 375.

relief (rih LEEF). Differences in elevation of the land. p. 18.

representative (rep ruh ZEN tuh tihv). Someone who speaks and acts for another person or for a state, nation, colony, or other group. p. 523.

republic (rih PUB lihk). A country that has a president or similar leader rather than a king or queen. p. 253.

reserve (rih ZURV). Supply, such as oil, that is available in the ground. p. 241.

resort (rih ZORT). A place that appeals to people for a vacation. p. 342.

revolt (rih VOHLT). An act of rising up or rebelling against the government. p. 191.

revolution (rev uh LOO shun). A sudden, complete change. p. 191.

revolutionist (rev uh LOO shun ihst). Someone who is in favor of or takes part in a revolt. p. 192.

Royal Fifth (ROI ul fihfth). The part of any wealth gained by a Spanish conquistador on his expeditions that had to be set aside for the Spanish crown. p. 154.

rural area (ROOR ul ER ee uh). Countryside. p. 86.

rurales (roo RAH lays). The much-feared rural police force set up by Díaz to control the bandits who roamed the Mexican countryside. p. 230.

S

savanna (suh VAN uh). A tropical grassland. p. 363.

scale (skayl). The relationship between distance on a map and actual distance on the earth. p. 10.

scrub (skrub). Trees that do not grow very high because of the conditions of the land in which they grow. p. 452.

selva (SEL vuh). A tropical forest, especially of South America. p. 361.

semiarid (sem ee AR ihd). Dry, but not as dry as a desert. p. 222.

sentry (SEN tree). A soldier assigned to guard duty. p. 520.

Separatist (SEP ur uh tihst). A person who would like Quebec to become an independent nation, separate from Canada. p. 581.

sertão (ser TOUN). The Brazilian word for the dry interior lands of northeastern Brazil. p. 452.

settlement (SET ul munt). A place where people live gathered together, such as a village or town. p. 163.

shifting agriculture (SHIHFT ing AG rih kul chur). Clearing and burning of the forest to clear the ground for planting. Also called slash-and-burn agriculture. p. 108.

social class (SOH shul klas). A person's rank in society based on birth, wealth, or the type of work the person does. p. 181.

socialism (SOH shul ihz um). A system of government in which land and industries are controlled by the government rather than by individuals or private companies. p. 272.

sod (sahd). A thick mat made up of the upper layer of the soil and the grass and plant roots that hold it together. p. 500.

sorghum (SOR gum). A grain that can be used to feed cattle and other livestock. p. 292.

specialization (spesh ul eye ZAY shun). The limiting to one thing or crop. p. 108.

spherical (SFER ih kul). Ball-shaped. p. 23.

squatter settlement (SKWAHT ur SET ul munt). A community of migrant families who live in shacks built of scraps of lumber, tin, and cardboard on unused land at the edges of a city. p. 247.

standard time zone (STAN durd tym zohn). One of the 24 divisions of the earth in which the clock time is the same. p. 32

strait (strayt). A narrow body of water that connects two larger bodies of water. p. 47.

strategic point (struh TEE jihk point). Of great importance, militarily or economically. p. 512.

strike (stryk). The refusal of workers to go to work. p. 422.

subsistence (sub SIHS tuns). The way a person or group supports itself. p. 106.

subsistence farm (sub SIHS tuns FAHRM). A farm on which crops are grown chiefly for home use and whose crops are needed for the farm family's survival. p. 241.

subtropical (sub TRAHP ih kul). Near the tropics. p. 407.

summit (SUM iht). The top of a mountain; a peak. p. 221.

surplus (SUR plus). An extra amount, more than necessary. p. 109.

T

tariff (TAR ihf). A tax placed on imported goods. p. 291.

temperate zones (TEM pur iht zohnz). The areas in the middle latitudes on either side of the tropics that have warm summers and cold winters; usually considered to be between 23½°S and 66½°S and between 23½°N and 66½°N. p. 61.

temperature (TEM pur uh chur). The amount of heat in something such as the air. p. 60.

tenant (TEN unt). A person who rents land or housing. p. 434.

territory (TER uh tor ee). An area of land. p. 46.

terrorist (TER ur ihst). A person who uses fear to force others to do what he or she wants them to do. p. 269.

thatch (thach). Grass, straw, rushes, palm leaves, and other materials matted together to make a roof or walls for a house. p. 114.

time line (tym lyn). A line, representing a period of time, on which dates and the order of events are shown. p. 35.

tone language (tohn LANG qwihj). A language in which a word's meaning changes according to how the word is sounded. p. 331.

trade winds (trayd windz). Steady winds that blow almost constantly in one direction. p. 310.

tradition (truh DIHSH un). Something that people have done for years and years. Hanging mistletoe is a Christmas *tradition.* p. 293.

transcontinental (trans kahn tuh NENT ul). Stretching across a continent. p. 533.

treason (TREE zun). The betraying of one's country by waging war against it or by giving away secrets to the country's enemies. p. 162.

tree line (tree lyn). The line in northern regions beyond which trees cannot grow. p. 543.

tributary (TRIHB yoo ter ee). A stream or river that flows into a larger stream or river. p. 114.

tropics (TRAHP ihks). The area of warm climates in the low latitudes north and south of the Equator, usually considered to be between 23½°S and 23½°N. p. 60.

tundra (TUN druh). A treeless plain found in Arctic regions. p. 53.

U

urban (UR bun). Having to do with the city rather than the countryside. p. 245.

urbanization (ur bun ih ZAY shun). Condition of changing from rural to urban in character. p. 567.

V

vaquero (vah KER oh). The Brazilian word for "cowboy." p. 473.

vertical exaggeration (VUR tih kul eg zaj ur AY shun). The showing of elevation at a scale larger than the scale used for distance. p. 20.

veto (VEE toh) To refuse to approve. p. 581.

viceroy (VYS roi). A leader appointed by the Spanish crown to rule in the Spanish colonies. p. 170.

viceroyalty (vys ROI ul tee). An area ruled by a viceroy. p. 170.

volcanic island (vahl KAN ihk eye lund). An island that is the top of a volcano that extends above the surface of the sea. p. 309.

volcano (vahl KAY noh). An opening in the earth, usually at the top of a cone-shaped hill, out of which gases, rock, ashes, and or lava may pour from time to time. Also, the hill around such an opening. p. 55.

W

wage (wayj). The money a person earns for the work he or she does. p. 582.

water resource management (WAWT ur REE sors MAN ihj munt). Regulation of fishing and water quality in order to control pollution and preserve the marine environment. p. 553.

weather (WETHH ur). The condition of the air at a given time and place. p. 60.

windward (WIND wurd). Facing the wind. p. 310.

wood pulp (wood pulp). A wet, soggy mass of ground-up wood chips, which is used to make paper, cardboard, and other products. p. 552.

INDEX

A

Acadia, colony of, 503, 505, 506, 509, 517–518
Anchoveta, 393
Acid rain, 74, 583
Aconcagua (mountain), 55, 407
Aerial photographs, 15
Africa and Africans, 22, 56, 78, 152, 180–181, 183–187, 334, 336, 561. *See also* Blacks.
African languages, 325, 331
Afro-Indian populations, 287
Agrarian reform, 416
Agricultural products in Latin America, 241–242, 383–387, 464–465, 466
Agriculture industry, 242. *See also* Farming.
Alamo, the, 225
Alaska, 33, 34, 61, 100, 499, 531, 546
Alaska Current, 544
Alaska Standard Time Zone, 33–34
Alberdi, Juan, 434
Alberta, Canada, 536, 546, 547, 548, 554, 555, 559, 569
Alcohol, as fuel, 467
Alessandri, Arturo, 415
Aleutian Islands, 34
Alfonsín, Raúl, 443
Algonquin Indians, 497–498, 507
Allende, Salvador, 416–418
Alliance and allies, 318, 506, 584
Almagro, Diego de, 159–160, 162
Alpacas, 113, 369
Altiplano, 368–369, 400
Altitude sickness, 205
Alto Peru, 206
Aluminum, 391
A.M. (ante meridiem), 28–29
Amazon Basin, 55, 114, 115, 361, 366, 369, 370, 375, 392, 451, 452, 472
Amazon River, 55–56, 57, 114, 115, 165, 451, 465
America, naming of, 45, 47–48
American Falls, 549
American Popular Revolutionary Alliance (APRA), 377–378
American Revolution, 192, 336, 523, 524
Americans, 52
Andes, the, 55, 57, 78, 80, 108, 119, 120, 131, 134, 160, 161, 201, 205, 309, 359, 361, 366–370, 375, 383,

386, 389, 392, 394, 395, 397, 398, 400, 406, 407, 409, 432, 433, 438, 479. *See also* Bolivia; Ecuador; Peru.
Andes highlands, 362
Angel Falls, 57, 363, 550
Anglo-America, 49-52, 54, 82, 83, 86, 242
Animals, great extinction of, 101–103
Annapolis Royal, Nova Scotia, 503, 517
Ante Meridiem (A.M.), 28–30
Anthropologists, 119
Antigua, 332
Antilles, 346
Antofagasta, Chile, 405
Antonio López, Carlos, 419–420
Appalachian Mountains, 506, 548
Araucanian Indians, 113–114, 433
Araucaria, 453
Arawak Indians, 110–111
Arbenz Guzmán, Jacobo, 268–269
Archaeologists, 97–101, 103, 119, 120, 128, 133, 134
Arctic Circle, 53, 541, 543, 549
Arctic Ocean, 53, 500, 530, 533, 541, 583
Arévalo, Juan José, 268
Argentina, 55, 67, 112, 120, 134, 165, 392, 419, 422, 476, 479
area covered by, 405
cities of, 84–86, 436, 438, 441
climate of, 113, 408–409
culture of, 67, 71, 433–435
economy of, 412–413, 441
energy resources of, 432, 451
farm products from, 73, 427–430
landforms of, 408–409, 449, 453
Pampas of, 57, 408, 427–428
as part of "Contadora Support Group," 300
people of, 433–435
political problems in, 410–413, 442–443, 444
population patterns in, 436
rebellion in, 204
regions of, 370
as United Provinces of La Plata, 204
and war with Britain, 442–443
and War of the Triple Alliance, 420–421
Árias Peace Plan, 301

Árias Sánchez, Oscar, 301
Aristide, Jean-Bertrand, 326
Arizona, 225, 227
Armada, Spanish, 177
Artifacts, 97–98, 100, 102–103
Artigas, José, 440
Artisans, 250
Aruba, 331, 394
Asbestos, 554
Asia, 5, 22, 34, 45, 46, 55, 78, 79, 99, 100, 102, 183, 186, 261, 337, 465, 510, 561
Astor, John Jacob, 530
Asunción, Paraguay, 165, 436, 438
Atacama Desert, 407, 431
Atahualpa, 161–162
Atarazana, La, 333
Atitlán, Lake, 263
Atlantic Ocean, 45, 46, 53, 56, 57, 150, 152–153, 165, 275, 307, 334, 405, 435, 442, 449, 451, 466, 497, 503, 509, 533, 541, 544, 550, 553, 565–566, 574
Atlantic Provinces, 565–566
Aurora borealis, 56, 57
Australia, 22
Austria, 229
Aux Outardes River, 557
Avenida Juárez, 249
Avenue of the Volcanoes, 367
Ayacucho, Battle of (1824), 206
Aymara language, 396
Aztecs, 119–126, 128, 134, 135, 154–158, 159, 197, 221, 234, 240, 241, 248, 257, 290

B

Bahamas, 307, 309, 313–314, 332
Bahia, (Salvador), Brazil, 184
Baja California, 219, 222
Balaguer, Joaquín, 326–327
Balboa, Vasco Núñez de, 159, 275
Ballet Folklórico de México, 249
Banana republic, 267
Bananas, 73, 267, 286, 287, 288–289, 292, 385
Bandeirantes, 186
Banff National Park, Alberta, 548
Barbados, 287, 313–314, 331
Barbuda, 332
Barge canal, 550
Bar graph, 81–82
Barranquilla, Colombia, 398
Barrios, 399
Barrios Chamorro, Violeta de. *See* **Chamorro, Violeta**

de Barrios.
Baseball, 71
Basin, 55
Batista, Fulgencio, 318
Batlle y Ordóñez, José, 422
Bauxite, 340, 391
Beef, 68, 73, 288, 428, 430, 438, 466. *See also* **Cattle industry.**
Belaúnde Terry, Fernando, 377
Belize, 119, 127, 219, 261, 265, 267, 283, 287, 297
Belize City, 297
Belmopan, Belize, 297
Benalcázar, Sebastián de, 164
Bering Strait, 99–100
Betancourt, Rómulo, 372
Bible, the, 171
Bilingual nations, 396, 581
Bill, 101, 581
Blackfeet Indians, 498
Blacks
in Andean countries, 396
in Brazil, 79, 185–187, 479
in Colombia and Venezuela, 395–396
in Costa Rica, 287
in Latin America, 79–80, 180–181, 193–194, 283, 286–287, 323–324, 395–396
in Nicaragua, 287
in Panama, 277, 287
in St. Domingue, 323–324
in Santo Domingo, 323
in the United States, 72
in West Indies, 79, 180–181, 193–194, 323–324
Blanco, Salvador Jorge, 327
Blumenau, Brazil, 476
Bogota, Colombia, 112, 170, 201, 396, 397, 398
Bolas, 107
Bolívar, Símon, 200–203, 206–207, 267, 371, 398, 401
Bolivia, 204, 359
and Chaco War, 376, 420
cities of, 397, 400
climate of, 368–370
earning a living in, 385–386
landforms of, 366, 368–370
land reform in, 386–387
as landlocked country, 366, 375–376
natural resources in, 389–390, 392
political problems in, 375–377, 378
population patterns in, 368–370, 386
regions of, 366, 369–370
Bonaire, 331
Bonaparte, Joseph, 191–192

Borja Cevallos, Rodrigo, 379
Bourbons, 178
Boyacá, Battle of (1819), 201
Braceros, 243
Brasília, Brazil, 462, 482–483
Brazil, 362, 420, 422, 432, 566
 area covered by, 81–82, 449
 boom-and-bust in, 464–466
 climates of, 451–453
 crops of, 334, 464–465, 466
 culture of, 68, 71, 479–480
 discovery of, 151–152, 183
 economy of, 462, 463, 464–
  467, 479
 emigration to, 434
 from empire to republic,
  460–463
 gold rush in, 186
 people of, 79–80, 81–82,
  83, 86, 477–480
 population patterns in, 471,
  477–480
 Portuguese colony of, 169,
  183–187, 208
 regions of, 471–476
 and War of the Triple
  Alliance, 420–421
Brazilian Highlands, 449,
 451, 452, 479, 485
Brazilwood, 184–185
Bristol, England, 46
Britain and British, 178. *See
 also* **England.**
British colonies. *See* **Belize;
 Canada; United States.**
British Columbia, 499,
 531–532, 533, 552, 554,
 556, 565, 568, 575
**British Commonwealth of
 Nations,** 536
British Guiana, 391
British heritage, 51
British Honduras. *See*
 Belize.
**British North America Act
 (1867),** 69, 528, 579–580, 581
British West Indies, 180–181,
 313–314, 336, 339
Brooklyn, New York, 277
Buccaneers. *See* **Pirates.**
Buenos Aires, Argentina, 67,
 84–86, 165, 170, 204, 205,
 411–412, 433, 434, 436,
 438, 440, 441
Buffalo, 498–499, 534
Burnett, David, 225
Burrard Inlet, 574–575
Bush, George, 299
Byproduct, 336

C

Cabot, John, 46, 99, 502, 509
Cabral, Pedro Álvares, 152, 183

Cacao, 385, 473
Cádiz, 174
Cajamarca (Inca city),
 161–162
Cajun people, 325, 518
Calendars, 59, 126, 129–130,
 156
Calgary, Alberta, 547, 569
Calgary Stampede, 569
Cali, Colombia, 164, 397
California, 72, 225, 227, 531
Callampas, 438
Campbell, Kim, 578
Campos cerrados, 452, 472, 473
Canada, 18, 20, 52, 73, 107, 290
 area and population of, 81–86
 border between United
  States and, 54, 85, 523,
  525, 541, 549, 583
 cities of, 571–575
 climate of, 60, 61, 501, 507,
  509, 542–545, 566
 as colony of Britain, 69, 523
 constitution of, 579–580
 and Convention of 1818,
  525, 526, 531
 culture of, 565 571, 572–575
 discovery of, 46–47
 Dominion of, 69, 528, 533,
  534
 exchanging ideas with, 71
 farming in, 427, 559
 and French Canadians, 80,
  522, 523–525, 528, 534–
  535, 565, 567, 573, 581–
  582
 French-English rivalry in,
  68, 509–513, 519–522, 524
 frontier life in, 507, 534
 government of, 51, 533,
  578–580
 immigration to, 434, 526, 535
 immigration to United
  States from, 72
 imports to United States
  from, 70, 73–74, 556,
  557, 570
 independence of, 69, 526–
  528, 536, 580
 on Mercator projection, 26
 mining in, 549, 554
 manufacturing in, 560
 name of, 47
 natural resources in, 70, 73,
  466, 549, 552–557, 558–
  561
 as part of Anglo–America,
  49–51, 80
 physical features of, 53–54,
  56, 548–550
 population patterns in, 82,
  84–85, 524, 528, 571
 ports and harbors of, 541–542

 provinces in 1818, 526
 Quebec Act in, 521–522,
  523–525
 regions of, 565–570
 service industries in, 561
 settlement of, 434, 502–513
 in twentieth century, 536–
  537
 Viking settlement in, 502
 women in, 505, 507, 531–532
Canada Day, 69, 528
Canadian National Railways,
 574
**Canadian Northern
 Railroad,** 535
Canadian Pacific Railroad,
 79, 533
Canadian Shield, 53–54,
 548, 552, 554, 556–557,
 560, 566
Canals, 275–279, 550
Canal Zone, 278–279
Canning, 429–430
Cape Breton Island, 518, 526
Captaincies of Brazil, 183–184
Carabobo, Battle of (1821), 201
Caracas, Venezuela, 199,
 200, 372, 396, 398–399
Cárdenas, Cuauhtemoc, 257
Cárdenas, Lázaro, 235, 241,
 257
Caribbean islands. *See* **West
 Indies.**
Caribbean National Forest,
 311
Caribbean Sea, 154, 159, 174,
 175, 177, 180, 261, 263,
 265, 275, 285, 287,
 307–309, 344, 359, 395
Carib Indians, 110–111
Carlos Galan, Luis, 374
Carranza, Venustiano, 233
Cartagena, Colombia, 174
Carter, Jimmy, 278, 299
Cartier, Jacques, 46, 502–503
Cartographer, 15, 24, 47, 48.
 See also **Maps, making.**
Casa Rosada, 438
Castro, Fidel, 318–319
Cattle, 71, 180, 186, 242, 288,
 292, 362, 370, 378, 385,
 393, 428, 430, 433, 434,
 452, 453, 461, 473, 476,
 559. *See also* **Beef.**
Cauca River, 361
Caudillos, 326, 371, 410–412
Cayuga Indians, 498
Celsius, 8, 222
Central America, 51, 108,
 119, 498
 cities of, 292–297
 climates in, 264–265
 countries of, 261, 266–267

 economies in, 288–291, 299
 farming in, 288–291
 highlands of, 261, 265, 286,
  290
 independence of, 266, 267
 isthmus of, 159, 283
 life in, 292–297
 lowlands of, 261–262, 264–
  265, 290
 and Panama Canal, 275–279
 physical features of, 55, 57,
  261–265
 political unrest in, 266–
  274, 278–279, 298–301
 products of, 288–291
 population of, 80, 85–86,
  283–287
 United States influence on, 71
**Central American Common
 Market,** 291
Central Andes. *See* **Bolivia;
 Ecuador; Peru.**
Central Cordillera, 361
Central Standard Time Zone,
 33–34
Cerro Rico, 389
Chaco War (1932–1935), 376,
 421
**Chamorro, Violeta de
 Barrios,** 299
Champerico, Guatemala, 292
Champlain, Samuel de, 503–
 505, 510, 573
Chapeton, 432
**Chapultepec Castle, Mexico
 City,** 250
**Chapultepec Park, Mexico
 City,** 249–250
Charles of England, King, 512
**Charlotte Amalie, St.
 Thomas,** 314
Château Frontenac, 572
Chibcha Indians, 111–112, 113
Chichén Itzá, Mexico, 59, 128
Chile, 112, 113, 120, 131, 134,
 164, 361, 366, 434, 435
 area covered by, 405
 cities of, 164, 436, 438, 441
 climate of, 406–407
 democracy fails in, 418, 443
 economy, 414–416, 441
 farming in, 430
 independence of, 205
 landforms of, 406–407
 natural resources of, 430–
  431, 432, 441
Chimborazo, Mount, 62
Chinampas, 123
China and the Chinese, 5,
 79, 135, 396, 575
Chocó, 365
Choropleths, 20
Christian religion, 154, 171,

184, 185, 435, 506
Chrysler Corporation, 560
Chuño, 396
Chuquicamata, 432–433
**Churchill Falls,
Newfoundland,** 557
Circum-Caribbeans, 110–111
Citaltépetl, 221
Cities, primate, 85, 245, 294, 436
Citizenship, 314, 320, 322, 375
City maps, 22
Ciudad Guayana, Venezuela, 391
Ciudad Juárez, Mexico, 220
Ciudad Netzahualacóyotl, Mexico, 247
Civilizations, 59, 108, 115, 119–121, 126, 130
Civil rights, 268, 418
Class, social. *See* **Social classes.**
Classic Period, 120
Climate, 1, 15, 20
of Brazil, 63, 451–453
of Canada, 61, 501, 507, 508, 542–544, 547, 566
in Central America, 264–265, 290
continental, 547
marine, 543–544
of Mexico, 60, 222–223
semiarid, 222
of southern-cone countries, 405–409
tropical, 264–265
of West Indies, 310–311
Climographs, 222–223, 543, 544, 545
Clocks, 28–34
CN Tower, 574
Coal, 389, 432, 441, 446, 554
Coast Ranges, 548, 575
Cocaine, 374
Cochabamba, Bolivia, 385
Coffee, 70, 73, 242, 270, 293, 383, 385, 394, 458, 460, 465, 466, 473, 475, 485
Collor de Mello, Fernando, 463
Colombia, 135
cities of, 164, 174, 361, 398
climate of, 363–364
culture of, 359
farming in, 70, 383
highlands of, 361
independence of, 200–203, 267, 371
Indians in, 111–112, 120, 134
loss of Panama, 276
lowlands of, 361
natural resources of, 389

part of Contadora group, 300–301
political parties in, 372–373
political problems in, 371–374
population pattern in, 395–397
Colón, Panama, 287
Colonies
of Britain in North America, 69, 509, 510–513, 518–522, 523
of France in North America, 503–513
in Latin America, 78–79, 169–187, 191–208, 378
Portuguese, 183–187
Colonization, land reform through, 387, 475
Colorado, 225
Columbia River, 530, 531
Columbium, 466
Columbus, Bartholomew, 333
Columbus, Christopher, 45, 78, 97, 99, 101, 108, 110, 147, 148, 150–151, 153, 165, 169, 183, 333, 334, 346
Columbus, Diego, 333
Comarcas, 286
Combines, 559
Commercial farming, 242, 263, 270, 339, 340, 383, 385, 387, 462
Common market, 291
Commonwealth, 321, 348
Commonwealth of Nations, British, 536, 578
Communication system, Inca, 134–135
Communism and Communists, 298, 318, 319
Comonfort, Ignaciao, 228
Compasses, 4–5, 25
Compass rose, 7
Computers, 54
Concepción, Chile, 431, 441
Condado, 345
Congress, United States, 322, 578
Conquistador, 159, 169, 270
Constitution
of Argentina, 412
of Brazil, 461
of Canada, 536, 579–580
of Dominican Republic, 326
of Mexico, 228, 233
of United States, 320, 498
Constitution Act
of 1791, 524
of 1982, 580
Constitutional monarchy, 578

Contadora Group, 300–301
Continental climate, 547
Continental islands, 307–309
Contour plowing, 241
Contours, 12
Contras in Nicaragua, 272–274, 298, 299
Conucos, 386
Convention of 1818, 525, 526, 531
Cooper, James Fenimore, 497
Cooperatives, 388
Coordinates, geographic, 7
Copacabana Beach, 486
Copper, 240, 390, 391, 416, 430–431, 499
Copper Canyon, 220
Coppermine, Northwest Territories, 543
Cordilleras, 361
Córdoba, Argentina, 85, 441
Corn, 106, 107, 123, 241, 292, 293, 427
Corpus Posadas, 432
Cortés Hernando, 154–158, 159, 160, 169, 172, 179, 219, 334, 498
Cortés, Sea of, 219, 220
Costa Rica, 225, 261, 265, 266, 269–270, 274, 287, 288, 291, 295, 301
Cotopaxi, Mount, 62, 367, 449
Cotton production, 186, 242, 288, 292, 293, 430, 473, 475
Coup, 224, 271, 326, 418, 421, 444, 461
Coureurs de bois, 505–506, 512–513
Cowhands, 57, 70–71, 410, 428, 473
Crafts, 111–112
Cree Indians, 498, 531
Creoles, 181, 192, 193, 195, 197, 198, 200, 206, 325
Cristiani, Alfredo, 298
Crops
tropical, 62
shown by maps, 15, 20
See also individual crops.
Cross section, 18
Cry of Dolores. *See* **Grito de Dolores.**
Cuauhtémoc, 158, 197
Cuba and Cubans, 72, 154, 159, 174, 175, 181, 191, 219, 274, 296, 307, 315–319, 325, 332, 333, 340
Cuernaveca, Mexico, 239
Culture, 49, 59, 67–69, 75, 108, 109–110, 187, 323, 325, 341, 359, 361, 395, 479, 498, 572

Cuna Indians, 285–286
Curaçao, 331, 341
Cuyo, Argentina, 205
Cuzco, Peru, 131, 133, 134, 162, 368, 399

D

Da Gama, Vasco, 151, 183
Darién, Panama, 159
"Daughters of the King," 508
Dawson, Yukon Territory, 546
Declaration of the Rights of Man and of the Citizen, 192–193
Degree (latitude or longitude), 5–6
Degree (temperature), 8
Democracy and democratic politics, 231, 270, 271, 299, 321, 326, 327, 372, 412, 418, 444, 463
in Anglo-America, 51
Denmark, 314, 502
Deserts, 57, 179, 222, 367, 376
DEW line, 582
Dialect, 325
Diamonds, 391
Díaz, Porfirio, 224, 229–231, 326, 371
Dictators and dictatorship, 224, 228, 229–231, 268, 271, 273, 274, 319, 326, 371–372, 391, 410–412, 419–421, 444, 461–462
Dirty war, 413, 443
Diseases, 83, 157, 194, 275, 287, 296, 367, 412, 438, 479, 501
Distant Early Warning (DEW) line, 582
Distortion on maps, 18, 20, 23–24
Distribution maps, 20–21
Dolores, Mexico, 195–196
Domestication, 107, 109, 113
Dominica, 331, 332
Dominican Republic, 308, 323, 325–327, 333, 340, 342
Dominion of Canada, 69, 528, 533, 534
Dominion Day, 69
Doña Marina, 154–155
Douglas, Amelia, 531–532
Drake, Sir Francis, 177
Droughts, 452, 475
Drugs, 374, 377
Dry season, 63
Duarte, José Napoléon, 298
Duque, Carlos, 299
Durham, Lord, 527–528
Dutch (language), 331
Dutch (people), 79, 80, 180,

183, 184–185, 186, 277,
508, 509, 510, 511, 575. *See
also* Netherlands.
Duvalier, François, 326
Duvalier, Jean-Claude, 326

E
Earth
distortion in flat maps of, 24
rotation of, 34
Earthquakes, 272, 294–295,
361, 368, 392, 438
Eastern Cordillera, 361, 362,
389, 398
Eastern Hemisphere, 7, 49
Eastern Sierra Madre. *See*
Sierra Madre Oriental.
**Eastern Standard Time
Zone,** 33–34
Eaton Centre, 574
Economy, 422, 423
of Argentina, 412–413, 442
of Bolivia, 376
of Brazil, 462, 463,
464–467, 471
of Canada, 535, 558–561, 567
of Central America, 266,
288–291
of Cuba, 318
defined, 185
of Mexico, 230, 231,
239–243, 253, 254–255
of New France, 512
of Nicaragua, 274
of Peru, 377
of Puerto Rico, 321, 347
Ecuador, 16, 62, 131, 135,
160, 201, 359, 395
cities of, 164, 378–379,
397, 400–401
coastal areas of, 367
earning a living in, 385–386
landforms of, 366–370
land reform in, 386–387
natural resources in, 392, 393
political problems in, 371,
375, 378–379
population patterns in,
367–370, 378, 386
regions of, 366–370
Education, 244
Egyptians, 28
Ejido, 234, 235
El Angel, 249
El Caracol, 128
El Castillo, 59
El Dorado, land of, 163
Elevation, 10–12, 16, 18,
61–63, 265
Elizabeth I, Queen, 177
Elizabeth II, Queen, 578, 580
Ellesmere Island, Canada, 541
El Morro (fort), 344

El Salvador (country), 119,
127, 261, 265, 266, 267,
268, 283, 286, 288, 290,
291, 294–295, 298, 300, 301
El Salvador (mine), 431
El Teniente, 431
El Yunque, 311
Emeralds, 389
Encomendero, 171, 179
Encomiendas, 171–172, 179
Endara, Guillermo, 299
England and the English, 6,
79, 199, 200, 204, 271, 287,
332, 339, 394, 411, 428,
430, 442, 458, 465, 480,
497, 532
and claim to Newfoundland,
46
and colonies in North
America, 192, 509–513,
517–522
and independence of
Canada, 526–528,
579–580
and independence of West
Indies, 313
English (language), 51, 277,
287, 325, 331, 377, 566,
581–582
Environment, 553
Equal-area projection, 26–27
Equator, 5–6, 26, 49, 58, 60,
62, 63
plane of the, 59
Ercilla y Zúñiga, Alonso de,
113–114
Erie, Lake, 533, 547, 549,
550
Erosion, 241
Eskimos. *See* Inuit.
Esmeraldas, Ecuador, 393
Estancias, 434
Ethnic groups, 283
Europe, 22, 45, 242, 334,
341, 460, 567
use of 24-hour clock in, 30
Europeans. *See* names of
specific countries.
Exchanges
cultural, 75
students, 67, 75
Exile of Acadians, 517–518
Explorers, 45 147, 163. *See
also* individual explorers.
**Expo '67 (Canadian World's
Fair),** 571
Expropriation
of land, 269, 388
of mines, 431
of oil industry in Mexico,
235, 240
Extinction of animals,
101–103

F
Fahrenheit, 8, 9, 222
Falkland Islands, 442
Fall, 58
Far East, 5
Farabundo Martí, Augustin,
298
Farabundo Martí, Augustín,
298
**Farabundo Martí National
Liberation Front,** 298
Far North, 71, 107, 500, 509,
541, 549
Faults, 262–263, 295
**Federation of the West
Indies,** 313–314
Ferdinand VII, 191, 204
Fertilizers, 376, 391, 393,
394, 431
Finlay, Carlos, 203, 296
First Continental Congress,
523
Fish and fishing, 73, 107,
111, 114, 115, 286, 393, 394,
498–500, 553
Fishing banks, 502, 553
Fjord, 575
Flemish (people), 48
Flood plains, 472
Florence, Italy, 147
Florida, 72, 107, 163, 174,
175, 272, 299, 309, 315,
318, 332, 343, 524
**Florida (street in Buenos
Aires),** 438
Foot plows, 385
Ford Motors, 560
Foreign debt, 463
Fortaleza, Brazil, 452
Foxe Basin, 550
Francia, José de, 419
Francis I, King of France,
177
Franklin, Benjamin, 192,
204
Fraser River, 530, 532, 574
Fraser, Simon, 530
Frei, Eduardo, 416, 418
French and Indian War,
518–522, 529, 568
French Canada,
503–513, 517–522,
523–524
French Guiana, 359, 361,
362–363
French (language),
68, 325, 331, 505,
535, 566, 571,
581–582
French Revolution, 192–193,
200
Frigid climate, 61
Frigid zones, 61

G
Gadsden, James, 227
Gadsden Purchase, 227
García, Alán, 378
García, Richard, 84
Gas, natural. *See* Oil.
Gaspé Peninsula, 548
**"Gaucho Martín Fierro,
The,"** 428
Gauchos, 410, 428
Geographers, 49
Geographic coordinates, 7
Georgia, Strait of,
575
Germans and Germany, 47,
80, 287, 288, 435, 444, 479,
567, 575
Globe, 24
Glyphs, 129
**Goethals, George
Washington,** 277
Goiánia, 472
Goiás, Brazil, 472
Gold, 135, 149, 160, 162, 170,
171, 173, 186, 187, 208, 240,
389, 391, 465, 466
Gómez, Álvaro, 374
Gómez, Juan Vicente,
371–372
Good Neighbor Policy, 317–
318
government
See under specific
countries, government of,
or political problems in.
Governor general of Canada,
578–579
Gran Chaco, 370, 375, 376,
408, 427
Gran Colombia, 207, 371
Grand Banks, 502, 553, 556
Grand Coulee Dam, 467
**Grand Trunk Pacific
Railroad,** 535
Gran Minería mines, 431
Graphs, 81–82
Great Britain. *See* England.
Great Drought, the, 475
Greater Antilles, 178, 307
Great Lakes, 54, 497, 505,
524, 525, 559, 566
**Great Lakes–St. Lawrence
Waterway,** 550
Great Plains, 545
Greenland, 26, 502
Greenwich, England, 6
Grenada, 340
Grid system, 5–7, 22
Grito de Dolores, 195–196
**Groseilliers, Médart Chouart
des,** 512–513
Gross National Product, 240,
466, 558, 566

Grouse Mountain, 575
Guadalajara, Mexico, 220, 239, 250
Guadalupe Hidalgo, Treaty of (1848), 227
Guadeloupe, West Indies, 312
Guanabara Bay, 486
Guano, 393–394
Guaraní Indians, 435
Guaraní language, 435
Guatemala, 78, 119, 127, 219, 225, 261, 263, 264, 265, 266, 268–269, 270, 283–286, 288, 290, 291, 292–293, 294, 301
Guatemala City, 294
Guayaquil, Ecuador, 206, 378–379, 392, 401
Guayas River, 401
Guerrillas, 198, 269, 271, 272, 298, 373, 378, 423, 442
Guiana Highlands, the, 362–363, 391, 449
Guianas, the, 110, 359, 361, 363–363, 449. *See also* Guyana; Suriname; French Guiana.
Gulf Coast. *See* Mexico, Gulf of.
Gulf Coastal Plain, 219, 222, 223
Guyana, 79, 359, 361, 362–363
Guzmán, Antonio, 327
Guzmán Blanco, Antonio, 371

H
Haiti, 68, 178, 193–194, 308, 323–326, 336, 337, 340
Halifax, Nova Scotia, 542, 544
Hamilton, Ontario, 550
Harpoons, 499
Havana, Cuba, 174, 317, 333
Haya de la Torre, Víctor Raúl, 377
Hawaii, 33, 34
Hawaii-Aleutian Standard Time Zone, 34
Health, public, 83, 319
Hemispheres, 6, 49
Henry IV of France, King, 503
Hernández, José, 428
Hibernian Oil Project, 556
Hidalgo, Miguel, 195–198, 199, 232
Highways, 2, 462. *See also* Roads.
Hiram Bithorn Baseball Stadium, Puerto Rico, 345
Hispaniola, 110, 154, 159, 169, 178, 183, 193–194, 308, 323–327, 334. *See also* Dominican Republic; Haiti.
Historical maps, 21–22

Holidays, 69
Homesteaders, 534
Honduras, 73, 119, 127, 225, 261, 265, 266, 267–268, 271, 272, 283, 286, 290, 291, 295, 301, 307
Hong Kong, 570
Horseshoe Falls, 549
House of Commons, Canadian, 579–580
Hudson Bay, 500, 510–511, 512–513, 526, 548, 550, 557
Hudson, Henry, 510–511
Hudson River, 510
Hudson's Bay Company, 512–513, 526, 529–531, 534
Huerta, Victoriano, 233
Huilliche Indians, 113–114
Human rights, 299, 443
Hungary, 567
Hunting, 106–107, 113, 498–501. *See also* Fur trade and traders.
Huron, Lake, 497, 505, 506
Huron Indians, 497, 506, 507, 511–512, 574
Hurricanes, 175
Hydroelectricity, 432, 462, 466, 467, 556–557

I
Iberian heritage, 51
Iberian Peninsula, 51, 181
Igloos, 500
Immigration and immigrants, 72, 243, 287, 323, 396, 433, 458, 479, 535, 567
Incas, 119–121, 131–136, 159–162, 199, 396, 401
Independence
of Canada, 69, 526–528, 536
of Cuba, 315–318, 319
holidays celebrating, 69, 195, 204, 456
of West Indies, 312–314, 337
India, 79, 152, 184, 186
Indiana, 521
Indians, 147, 148, 163
in Andean countries, 78, 367, 375, 376, 377, 386, 387, 396, 401
Araucanian, 113–114, 164, 433
in Argentina, 112–113, 428, 433
Aztec, 119–126, 128, 134, 135, 154–158, 159, 197, 221, 234, 240, 241, 248, 290
in Brazil, 115, 185, 186, 471–472, 473, 479
in Canada, 47, 71, 80, 497–501, 508, 509, 510, 511–

512, 530, 531, 534, 565, 571, 583
in Caribbean, 110–111
in Central America, 266, 268, 269, 283–287, 290, 293
Chibcha, 111–112, 113
of Colombia and Venezuela, 111–112, 395
farming, hunting, and fishing by, 106–109, 111–115, 367, 385–386, 498–501
fur traders and, 497, 501, 506, 511–512
Guarani, 435
in Guatemala, 78, 283–285
Inca, 119–121, 131–136, 159–162, 394, 396, 401
influence on other cultures, 78, 497
in Latin American colonies, 78–79, 171–172, 179, 181, 428, 435
knowledge of, 59, 106–109, 120, 127–130
Mayan, 59–60, 119–121, 127–130, 135, 283–284, 290
Indies, 151, 153, 183
Indonesia, 79
Industrial complexes, 392
Industry. *See* names of specific industries.
Industry, light, 347
Inflation, 377, 390, 463
Institutional Revolutionary Party (PRI), 253–255, 257
Interdependent neighbors, 70–75
Interest, 255
International Date Line, 34
Interrupted projection, 27
Inuit, 71, 100, 107, 500, 565, 582–583
Ipanema, 486
Ipiranga River, 456
Iquitos, Peru, 57
Iron ore, 391, 441
Iroquois Indians, 497–498, 509, 511, 573
Irrigation, 108, 111, 363, 367, 385, 387, 409, 452, 475
Isabella, Princess, 460
Isabella of Spain, Queen, 148, 150
Islands, kinds of, 307–309
Isla Verde, 345
Isthmus of Panama, 159, 174, 219
Itaipú Dam, 467
Italians, 45, 46, 80, 434, 458, 479

Iturbide, Augustin de, 198, 224
Ixtacihuatl, 221

J
Jacques Cartier, Mount, 548
Jamaica, 71, 178, 287, 308, 313–314, 331, 333, 336–337, 340, 341, 342
James Bay, 550, 557
James Bay Project, 557
Jangadas, 479–480
Japanese (people), in Brazil, 479
Jefferson, Thomas, 192
Jesuits, 435
John III of Portugal, King, 183–184
John VI of Portugal, King, 456
Joinvile, Brazil, 476
José de Urquiza, Justo, 411
Juan, Jorge, 176
Juárez, Benito, 224, 228–229, 230, 232, 249
Juntas, 326, 418

K
Kakfwi, Stephen, 583
Kayaks, 500
Key to map, 7, 9, 16, 18, 21, 22
Kingston, Jamaica, 333
Kubitschek, Juscelino, 462, 483

L
Labor unions, 233
Labrador, 557, 565–566
La Brea tar pits, 101–102
La Grande River, 557
La Malinche, 154–155
Land bridge, 99–102, 261
Land grants, 179, 183–184
Landlocked country, 366, 375
Language
body, 68
differences, 67–68, 325, 331
tone, 331
La Paz, Bolivia, 400
La Paz, Mexico, 222–223
La Perla Theatre, 346
La Plata, Argentina, 441
La Plata, viceroyalty of, 170, 204, 410
La Reforma, 228, 232
La Reforma (avenue in Guatemala City), 294
La Serena, Chile, 431
Last of the Mohicans, The, 497
Latex, 464–465
Latin America, 293, 300,

318, 391, 399, 420, 427, 432, 456, 558, 561, 573, 575
area covered by, 81–82
cities of, 247, 248–252, 294–297, 343–345, 395–401, 436–441, 481–486
climates of, 60–63, 222, 363–365, 367, 369–370, 405–409, 451–453
on Mercator projection, 27
name of, 51
physical features of, 54–57, 219–223, 261–265, 307–311, 359–365, 405–409, 449–453
political systems in, 51, 224, 371–379, 442–445, 460–463
population of, 78–80, 81–86, 244–247, 283–287, 331–333, 395–401, 477–480
United States and, 72
use of 24-hour clock in, 30
Latin language, 5, 51, 111
Latitude, 5, 7, 9, 16, 60–63, 85, 152, 222, 405
Laurentian Mountains, 571
Laurier, Wilfred, 535
Lava, 55, 222. *See also* Volcanoes.
Laws, 51, 186, 224, 243, 521, 522, 524, 581
League of the Iroquois, 498, 499
Lebanon, 479
Leeward coast, 310
Leeward Islands, 313–314
Legend, *see* Key.
Le Lo Lai, 345
Leningrad, Soviet Union, 25
León, Mexico, 239
Lesser Antilles, 110, 177, 309, 314, 336, 342
Lévesque, René, 581–582
Light industries, 347
Lima, Peru, 54, 170, 174, 182, 206, 367, 397, 399–400
Limestone island, 309
Lincoln, Abraham, 226
Line graph, 82–83
Lisbon, Portugal, 208, 542
Literacy, 270, 319, 420
Llamas, 113, 114, 135, 369
Llaneros, 200–201
Llanos, 200, 361, 362, 365, 370
Locator map, 16
Locks, ship, 277
Logan, Mount, 548
London, England, 199, 436, 465
Longitude, 6, 7, 9, 16, 32
Los Angeles, California, 398

Louisbourg, battle of (1758), 518
Louisiana, exiles from Acadia in, 518
Lower Canada, 524, 526–528
Loyalists, migration to Canada of, 523
Lumber and lumbering, 363, 549, 552
Luna, Marina, 390
Luque, Fernado de, 159–160
Luquillo Mountains, 311

M

M-19, 374
Macdonald, Sir John A., 533–534
Mackenzie, Alexander, 529–530
Mackenzie River, 530
Mackenzie, William Lyon, 526–527
MacLeish, Archibald, 436
Madero, Francisco, 231–233
Magdalena River, 361, 398
Magellan, Ferdinand, 34, 152–153, 159
Magellan, Strait of, 153
Maine, (battleship), 315–317
Maize, 241, 242, 284, 290
Malvinas, 442
Mama Ocllo, 133, 135
Managua, Lake, 295
Managua, Nicaragua, 272, 295
Manaus, Brazil, 63, 465
Manco Capac, 133, 135
Manicouagan River, 557
Manioc, 107, 111, 290, 337, 467, 472
Manitoba, Canada, 533, 559, 571
Manufacturing, 239, 251, 347, 560
Maple syrup, 552
Mapocho River, 438
Maps
in atlases, 7, 22
distortion in, 18, 20, 23–24
elements of, 5–22, 24
grid system in, 5–6
kinds of, 16–22
making, 15, 23–27, 45–47
orientation of, 4, 5, 7
orienteering with, 4–5
perspective of, 18
projections of, 23–27
scale of, 10, 18, 20, 24
symbols and keys to, 7, 9, 12, 16–22
uses of, 2, 4–5, 16–22

Mapuches Indians, 113–114
Maracaibo, Lake, 362, 391, 399
Maracaibo lowland, 362
Maracaibo, Venezuela, 396, 399
Maracana, 81
Marie de l'Incarnation, Mother, 507
Marijuana, 374
Marine climate, 543–544
Maritime Provinces of Canada, 544, 565–566
Martí, José, 315
Martinique, 312, 341
Marxism, 416
Marx, Karl, 416–417
Massachusetts, 336
Maté, 427
Mato Grosso, Brazil, 473
Mato Grosso do Sul, Brazil, 473
Matthew (ship), 46
Maximilian, Emperor, 229
Maya, 59–60, 119–121, 127–130, 135, 264, 283–284, 290
Mayagüez, Puerto Rico, 346
Maya language, 129, 155
Mayapán, 130
Mechanization, 383
Medellín, Colombia, 397
Mediterranean climate, 407
Mediterranean Sea, 149
Members of Parliament (MP's), 578
Menchu, Rigoberta, 285
Mendoza, Argentina, 427, 441
Mendoza, Pedro de, 165
Menem, Carlos, 443
Mercado Libertad, 250
Mercator, Gerardus, 25, 48
Mercator projection, 25–27, 48
Mérida, Mexico, 59, 223
Meridians, 6–7, 25, 32
Mesas, 363
Mestizos, 79–80, 181, 195–198, 230, 231, 283, 286–287, 395, 396, 428, 435, 479
Métis, 505, 531, 534–535
Methane, 555
Metric system of measurement, 8
Metropolitan area, 84
Mexica. *See* Aztecs.
Mexican plateau, 55, 221, 239, 242
Mexican Revolution, 229, 232–233, 241
Mexico, 10, 51, 71, 107, 108, 119, 120, 122, 127, 163, 172, 174, 290, 326, 371, 387, 438, 479, 498
cities of, 239, 248–252
climate of, 60, 222–223
conquest of, 154–158, 234

consitutions of, 228, 233
culture of, 69, 248–252
farming in, 241–242
government of, 253–257
immigration to United States from, 72, 242–243
imports to United States from, 71, 73
independence of, 194, 195–198, 199, 224, 225, 249, 266
landforms of, 219–223
as part of Contadora Group, 300–301
people of, 80, 244–247
physical features of, 55, 57, 219–223
political parties of, 253–257
population patterns in, 82–86, 244–247
Revolution of 1910 in, 232–233, 253
Mexico City, 10, 84, 119, 163, 170, 172, 182, 198, 221, 225, 227, 228, 229, 239, 247, 248–250, 481
Mexico, Gulf, of, 163–164, 219, 221, 240, 244, 307, 309
Mexico, University of, 195
Mexico, Valley of, 221
Miami, Florida, 72
Middle America, 55, 119, 124
Middle East, 149, 334, 479
Midnight, 30
Migrants, 245–246, 268
Milan, Italy, 147
Millenium, 35
Minas Gerais, Brazil, 186, 461, 475
Minerals, mines, and mining, 233, 240, 376, 377, 389–391, 416, 430–431, 466, 475, 541, 554, 561. *See also* specific natural resources
Minorities, American, 72
Miranda, Francisco de, 199–200
Miskito Indians, 285–287
Missionaries, 506
Mississippi River, 521, 524
Mita, 134
Moctezuma, 155–157
Mohawk Indians, 497, 498
Molasses, 336
Monarchy, constitutional, 578
Monopoly, Spanish, 173–178
Montcalm, General Louis Joseph, 520–521
Monte Alban ruins, 252
Monte Caseros, Battle of (1852), 411
Montego Bay, Jamaica, 342
Monterrey, Mexico, 251

Montevideo, Uruguay, 423, 436, 440, 443

Montreal, Quebec, 84, 506, 550, 557, 560, 566, 571–572

Montreal Marathon, 571

Morelos, José María, 197, 198

Moreno, Mariano, 204, 438

Morgan, Henry, 296

Moscow, Soviet Union, 541

Mountain Standard Time Zone, 33–34

Mounties, Canadian. *See* Royal Canadian Mounted Police.

Mulattoes, 79–80, 181, 325

Mulroney, Brian, 584

Muñoz Marín, Luis, 321, 347, 348

Muñoz Rivera, Luis, 348

Museums, 112, 135, 248, 346

Music, Latin American influences in, 71

Muslims, 334

N

Nahuatl language, 155

Nambuco, Joaquim, 459

Napoleon Bonaparte, 191–192, 194, 200, 204, 208, 456

Narváez, Pánfilo de, 163

National Action Party (PAN), 257

National Agrarian Institute, 372

National Democratic Front, 257

National Guard (Nicaraguan), 271, 272

Nationalism, 148

National Museum of History, Mexico City, 250

National Opera, Mexico City, 249

National Palace, Mexico City, 248

Native Americans. *See* Indians.

Navigation, 25, 48

Netherland Antilles, 331, 394

Netherlands, 79, 177, 185, 510. *See also* Dutch.

Nevada, 225

Nevado del Ruiz (volcano), 361

Nevis, 331

New Brunswick, Canada, 505, 524, 525, 526, 528, 544, 565–566

New England, colonies of, 336

Newfoundland, 46–47, 497, 502, 509, 518, 526, 528, 544, 548, 550, 556, 557, 565–566

New France, 47, 503–513, 521

New Granada, viceroyalty of, 170, 200–201, 267

New Hampshire, 72, 333

New Mexico, 225, 227

New Orleans, Louisiana, 325

New Spain, viceroyalty of, 170, 266

Newsprint, 552

New World, 45, 48, 147, 150–151, 153, 159, 169, 170, 177, 178, 183, 334, 336, 344, 502, 510

New York (state), 72, 497, 557

New York City, New York, 34, 85, 485

Niagara Falls, 549

Niagara River, 549

Nicaragua, 72, 225, 261, 265, 268, 269, 271–274, 283, 285, 286, 287, 288, 291, 298–299, 300, 301, 326

Nicaragua, Lake, 263

Niña (ship), 150

Nitrates, 376, 431

Nobel Peace Prize, 285, 301

Noche Triste, La, 157

Nomadic people, 100, 106, 112–113, 498, 500

Noon, 29

Noriega, Manuel Antonio, 299

Norse people. *See* Vikings.

North America, 22, 45, 51, 54, 55, 99–101, 103, 107, 219, 261, 341, 501, 503, 506, 507, 509, 510, 518, 545, 552
British, 46
climate of, 61, 406, 542–545
first use of term, 48
on Mercator projection, 26, 48
See also Canada; United States.

North American Free Trade Agreement (NAFTA), 257, 584

North Americans, 52, 341

Northern Hemisphere, 6, 49, 58, 61

Northern lights. *See* Aurora borealis.

North Pole, 6, 26, 27, 53, 60, 61

North West Company, 529–530

North West Mounted Police, 534

Northwest Passage, 510, 574

Northwest territories of Canada, 533, 534, 556, 565–566, 582

Norway, 25, 502

Nova Scotia, Canada, 517, 523, 526, 528, 544, 565–566. *See also* Acadia, colony of.

Nuclear America, 119–120

Nuclear Power, 467

Nunavut, Canada, 570, 582–583

O

Oaxaca, Mexico, 172, 228, 251

Obregón, Álvaro, 233

Ocean current, 367

Ochos Rios, Jamaica, 342

O'Higgins, Bernardo, 205

Oil
in Brazil, 466
in Bolivia, 392
in Canada, 73, 554, 560
in Colombia, 389
in Ecuador, 392–393
in Mexico, 73, 233, 235, 240–241
in Peru, 392
reserves, 241, 392
in southern cone, 432, 441
in Venezuela, 73, 362, 372, 391, 394, 399
in Trinidad, 340

Oklahoma, 225

Old San Juan, 344

Olympic Games, 571

Onas Indians, 113

Oneida Indians, 498

Onondaga Indians, 498

Ontario, Canada, 497, 526, 528, 559, 560, 565, 566, 574, 581

Ontario, Lake, 545, 549, 550

Operation Bootstrap, 321, 347

Oranges, 73, 385, 466

Oregón (battleship), 275

Oregon Country, 531

Oregon (state), 531

Orellana, Francisco de, 165

Organization of American States (OAS), 75, 300–301, 327, 440

Orient, 5, 149, 173, 568, 574

Oriental, 395

Oriente, 392

Orientation, 5, 7

Orienteering, 4, 5

Orinoco River, 361, 362, 391

Orizaba, 221

Orozco, José Clemente, 235

Ortega, Daniel, 299

Oruro, Bolivia, 390

Oshawa, Ontario, 560

Oslo, Norway, 25

Ottawa, Ontario, 505, 534, 566, 569

P

Pacific Ocean, 7, 34, 45, 153, 159, 244, 275, 393, 405, 530, 543, 544, 568

Pacific Rim, 568

Pacific Standard Time Zone, 33–34

Páez, José Antonio, 200, 371

Pampas, the, 57, 408, 427–428, 430, 433, 434, 453

Pamperos, 408

Panama, 159–160, 162, 170, 174, 177, 261, 265, 267, 275–279, 285, 286, 287, 299, 301, 359, 365

Panama Canal, 275–279, 287, 307, 542, 550

Panama City, 275, 287, 296, 299

Panama, Isthmus of, 159, 274

Panamanian Defense Forces, 299

Pan-American Highway, 365

Papermaking industry, 552, 558, 560

Papiamento, 331

Papineau, Louis Joseph, 517

Paraguay, 112, 204, 370, 376, 405, 407–408, 411, 412, 419–421, 430, 432, 436, 438, 440, 444–445, 449, 451, 467

Paraguay River, 165, 407–408, 438, 443, 451, 473

Parallels, 5, 25, 26

Paraná pines, 453

Paraná Plateau, 449

Paraná River, 165, 432, 451

Paraná (state), Brazil, 476

Paricutín (volcano), 221–222

Paris, France, 436, 573

Paris, Treaty of (1763), 521

Parliament, Canadian, 578–579

Parque Central, 398

Pascal-Trouillot, Ertha, 326

Paseo de la Reforma, 249

Passport, 322

Patagonia, 57, 409, 432

Patois, 331

Patrias chicas, 245, 284–285, 375

Pau brasil. *See* Brazilwood.

Paulo Afonso Falls, 451

Paz Estenssoro, Víctor, 376–377, 390

Paz Zamora, Jaime, 377, 390

Pedro I, 208, 456–457

Pedro II, 457–458, 460

Peninsulars, 181, 192

Pennsylvania, 307

Peons and peonage, 180, 234, 241, 420

Per capita income, 347, 558

Pérez Jiménez, Marcos, 372, 391

Permafrost, 543

Pernambuco, Brazil, 184

Perón, Eva Duarte de (Evita), 412
Perón, Isabel, 413, 442
Perón, Juan Domingo, 412–413
Personalismo, 319
Peru, 79, 134, 135, 160, 164, 165, 174, 175, 359, 472
  cities of, 397, 399–400
  climate of, 367, 369–370
  coast of, 367, 544
  earning a living in, 385–386
  farming in, 385–386
  Incas of, 119–121, 131–136
  independence of, 205–206
  landforms in, 366–370
  land reform in, 388
  natural resources in, 391, 392, 393–394
Peru Current, 367, 544
Petén, the, 264
Petrobras, 466
Petrochemicals, 336, 394
Petroleum. *See* Oil.
Philip II of Spain, King, 184
Philippine Islands, 170, 317
Phosphates, 391
Photographs, aerial, 15
Physical maps, 18, 20
Pico da Neblina, 449
Pico Duarte, 308
Picunche Indians, 113
Pie graph, 81
Pinochet, Augusto, 418, 444
Pinta (ship), 150
Pirates, 175, 177, 296
Pizarro, Francisco, 22, 159–162, 399
Pizarro, Hernando, 162
Place d'Armes, 571
Plains of Abraham, 521
Plains Indians, 498
Plan de Iguala, 198
Plantations, 180–181, 267, 269, 270, 284–285, 287, 289, 293, 336, 337, 339, 385, 449, 458, 465, 473
Plateau, 55
Platt Amendment, 317–318
Plaza de Armas, 399
Plaza Constitución, 440
Plaza de Francia, 296
Plaza de Mayo, 436, 438
Plaza Independencia, 440
Plaza Las Américas, 345
Plaza San Martín, 399
Plebiscite, 348, 444
Plows, foot, 385
P.M. (post meridiem), 28–30
Pochtecas, 126
Poland, 476
Polar regions, 61
Police state, 418
Political maps, 16

Polk, James K., 226
Pollution, 74, 485, 553, 583
Ponce, Puerto Rico, 310, 345–346
Ponce de León, Juan, 343
Ponce Museum of Art, 346
Popayán, Colombia, 164
Popocatépetl, 221
Population
  density, 82
  growth, rate of, 83
  See also under specific countries.
Population density maps, 22
Portales, Diego, 414
Port Arthur, 567
Portobelo, Panama, 174, 176, 275
Port Royal, Acadia, 503, 517
Ports
  in Canada, 541–542
  in West Indies, 174–175
Portugal and the Portuguese, 51, 78, 151–152, 169, 177, 183–186, 191, 208, 336, 456, 457, 475, 479, 502
Portuguese America. *See* Brazil.
Portuguese language, 51, 68, 186
Post meridiem (P.M.), 28–29
Postclassic Period, 120–121
Potash, 554
Potatoes, 68, 106, 107, 114, 386, 476, 559
Potosí, Bolivia, 389–390, 409
Prairie Provinces of Canada, 555, 559, 565, 567, 569
  See also Alberta, Canada; Manitoba, Canada; Saskatchewan, Canada.
Precipitation, 60, 63, 222–223, 264–265, 363, 365
Pre-Columbian times, 97–103, 106–115
Primate cities, 85, 245, 294, 436
Prime Meridian, 7, 32, 49
Prime minister of Canada, 579–580
Prince Edward Island, 47, 526, 528, 533, 544, 565–566
Prince Rupert's Land, 526
Privateers in Caribbean, 177, 181
Profile, 18, 20
Projections, map, 23–27
Provincial government in Canada, 579
Provision grounds, 337
Public housing, 400
Public services, 244, 481

Puebla, Mexico, 239
Puerto Plata, Dominican Republic, 342
Puerto Rico, 191, 308, 310, 311, 314, 315, 317, 320–322, 325, 342, 343–348
Punta del Este, 440
Pyramid, 59, 120, 127–128, 130

Q
Quebec, Canada, 508, 518, 520–522, 523, 524, 526, 528, 554, 557, 559, 560, 565, 566–567, 572, 580–582
  English action against, 510, 518–522
  farming in, 552
  founding of, 507
Quebec Act, 521–522, 523–525
Quebec City, Quebec, 557, 567, 572, 574
Quebracho trees, 408, 427
Quechua language, 131, 134, 396
Querétaro, Mexico, 239
Quetzalcóatl, 155
Quezaltenango, Guatemala, 292–294
Quiche, 285
Quinoa, 386
Quipu, 135
Quito, Ecuador, 7, 164, 378–379, 400–401

R
Racism, 319
Radisson, Pierre Esprit, 512–513
Rae, Fort, 583
Railroads, 229, 230, 275, 287, 340, 369, 428, 434, 458, 485, 533, 535
Rain forest, 55, 63, 114, 130, 179, 264, 311, 471–472, 479
Rain shadow, 409
Rainy season, 63
Ranching, 57, 242, 290, 362, 428, 430, 452, 453, 559, 560. *See also* cattle.
Rancho La Brea, California, 101–102
Reagan, Ronald, 584
Recife, Brazil, 185, 451, 473, 480
Redistribution, land, 253, 372, 387
Red River, 535
Red River Rebellion, 534–535
Red River Valley, 534
Referendum of 1980, 582
Refineries, 338, 340, 392

Reform, land, 228, 253, 347, 372, 386–387, 416
Reform, the (1855), 228, 232, 249
Refrigeration, 430
Regents, 457, 460
Regionalism, problem of, 375, 378–379
Regions, 1, 15, 20, 49, 60, 63, 375, 471
Relief, 18
Religion, 110, 111, 115, 122, 123, 124, 126, 128, 135, 155, 187, 234, 522
  Christian, 154, 171, 184, 185, 435
  Jewish, 148
  Islamic, 148
  missionaries and, 171
  Protestant, 148, 185, 521
  Roman Catholic, 148, 185, 198, 325, 373, 506, 507, 521, 524
Reserves, oil, 241, 392
Retalhuleu, Guatemala, 292
Rhode Island, 314, 332
Rice, 242, 290, 427, 472, 473, 475
Riel, Louis, 535
Rímac River, 367
Rio de Janeiro, Brazil (city), 86, 186, 208, 456, 461, 475, 481, 482, 486
Rio de Janeiro, Brazil (state), 461, 475
Rio de la Plata, 408, 440
Rio Grande, 219
Rio Grande do Sul, Brazil, 461, 476
Rio Piedras, Puerto Rico, 345
Rivera, Diego, 124, 195, 216–217, 235
Road maps, 22
Roads, 229, 325, 326, 340, 363, 371, 420, 462, 472
Robson, Mount, 548
Roca, Julio, 433
Rocky Mountains, 33, 54, 525, 530, 531, 545, 548, 554, 560
Rodríguez Andres, 421, 444–445
Roman Catholic Church. *See* Religion, Roman Catholic.
Romans, 5, 28–29
Roosevelt, Franklin Delano, 317–318
Rosas, Juan Manuel de, 411–412
Rotation of earth, 34
Royal Canadian Mounted Police (RCMP), 534
Royal Fifth, 154

Royal Greenwich Observatory, 6
Rubber production, 464–465
Running Eagle, 499
Rupert, Prince, 512
Rurales, 230
Rural population in Latin America, 86. *See also* Farming.
Russia, 476

S

Sagas, Viking, 87
St. Christopher-Nevis, 81, 331
St. Croix, Virgin Islands, 314
St. Domingue, 178, 193–194, 323. *See also* Haiti.
St. James, Fort, 531
St. John, Virgin Islands, 314
St. John's, Newfoundland, 85
St. Johns, Virgin Islands, 332
St. Kitts, 331
St. Lawrence, Gulf of, 503–504, 509
St. Lawrence River, 47, 506, 510, 518, 520, 550, 557, 566, 569
St. Lawrence Seaway, 550
St. Lawrence Valley, 497, 505, 506, 507, 509, 511, 557, 559, 573
St. Lawrence Waterway, 550, 566, 574
St. Lucia, 81
St. Thomas, Virgin Islands, 314
Salinas de Gortari, Carlos, 255
Salmon, fishing for, 553
Salvador, Brazil, 184, 451, 472, 473
San Antonio, Texas, 225, 251
San Cristóbal (fort), 344
Sandinista, 272–273, 299
Sandista Liberation Front, 272
Sandino, Augusto César, 217
Sanguinetti, Julio María, 423
San Jacinto River, 225–226
San José, Costa Rica, 295–296
San Juan, Puerto Rico, 310, 333, 342, 343–345, 346
San Juan Parangaricutiro, Mexico, 222
San Martín, José de, 204–206, 401, 438
San Salvador, El Salvador, 294–295
Santa Anna, Antonio López de, 224–227
Santa Catarina, Brazil, 476
Santa Cruz, Bolivia, 392
Santa María, Cathedral of, 333
Santa Maria (ship), 150
Santa María, (volcano), 292–293

Santiago, Chile, 131, 164, 205, 431, 436, 438, 441
Santo Domingo, 323–324. *See also* Dominican Republic.
Santo Domingo (city), Dominican Republic, 327, 333
Santo Domingo, Church of, 252
Santos, Brazil, 184, 405, 458, 485
São Francisco River, 451
São Paulo, Brazil (city), 84, 186, 436, 458, 475, 481, 485, 486
São Paulo, Brazil (state), 453, 461, 475
São Vincente, Brazil, 183, 184
Sarney, José, 463
Saskatchewan, Canada, 536, 556, 559
Saudi Arabia, 241
Savannas, 363, 365, 366, 395, 452
Scale
    of maps, 10, 18, 20, 22, 24
    of time lines, 35
Scandinavia, 80, 502, 575
Scottish people, 526, 529
Scouts, 5
Seasons, 28, 58, 59, 61–63, 112
    reversed in Northern and Southern hemispheres, 58
Selva, 361, 363, 365, 392, 452
Semiarid climate, 222
Senate in Canadian Parliament, 578
Seneca Indians, 498
Separatists, 581–582
Serapes, 252
Sertão region, Brazil, 473, 475
Service industries, 561
Seville, Spain, 174
Sheep, 57, 180, 242, 369, 430, 559
Shifting agriculture, 108, 111, 114, 498
Shining Path, 378
Sierra de Perijá, 362
Sierra Madre Occidental, 220, 251
Sierra Madre Oriental, 220, 221, 251
Sierra Nevada de Mérida, 362
Silva compasses, 4–5
Silver, 135, 149, 160, 162, 170, 171, 173, 177, 389, 390, 391, 554
Singapore, 568
Siqueiros, David Alfaro, 235
Slash-and-burn agriculture. *See* Shifting agriculture.

Slaves and slavery, 78, 171, 180–181, 185, 186–187, 193, 226, 287, 323, 336–337, 375, 378, 395–396, 458–459
Sleet, 60
Smallpox, 157
Snow, 60, 61
Social classes, 108, 126, 181, 247, 270
Socialism, 272, 299, 417, 418
Sod, 500
Solar year, 130
Solano López, Francisco, 420
Somoza, Anastasio, 271–272, 326
Somoza, Luis, 272, 326
Sousa, Tomé de, 184
South America, 16, 20, 22, 45, 49, 51, 55, 101, 107, 108, 110, 119, 131, 176, 261, 275, 290, 372, 391, 392, 395, 400, 405, 449, 458
    climates of, 60–63, 363–365, 405–409, 451–453
    conquest of, 159–162, 164–165
    first use of term, 48
    highland areas of, 359–365, 366–370, 449
    independence for, 191–208, 438
    lowland areas of, 55, 359–365, 366–370, 449, 451
    on Mercator projection, 26, 48
    physical features of, 55–57, 359–363, 405–409, 449–453
    population patterns in, 81–86, 360, 362, 363, 365, 433–435, 477–480, 481
    southern cone of, 405–423, 427–445
South Brazil, 480–482
Southern cone, 405–423, 427–445, 435
Southern Hemisphere, 6, 51, 58, 61, 406, 436
South Korea, 570
South Pole, 6, 27, 60, 61
Soviet Union, 25, 34, 274, 298, 300, 318, 541, 554, 567
Spain and the Spanish, 34, 51, 77, 135, 150–152, 154, 158, 179, 183, 184, 196–198, 367, 368, 394, 400, 410, 412, 428, 433, 435, 479
    colonies of, 154, 169–187, 185, 186, 191–206, 296, 315–317, 344, 359, 399
    Napoleon's control of, 191–192

Treaty of Tordesillas, 152
War between United States and, 275, 315, 317
Spanish-American War, 275, 315, 317
Spanish armada, 177
Spanish language, 51, 62, 68, 153, 171, 193, 244, 245, 272, 285, 287, 325, 331, 373, 375, 377, 396, 435
Special—interest maps, 21
Spring, 58
Squatter settlements, 247
Standard Fruit Company, 267
Standard Time System, 34
Standard time zones, 32–34
Statute of Westminster, 536, 579
Strait, 47
Strait of Belle Isle, 47
Strategic location, 518
    of Canada, 541
    of West Indies, 307
Strategic points, 512
Stroessner, Alfredo, 421, 444–445
Suárez, Inés de, 164
Subsistence farming, 106, 241, 284, 385–386
Subtropical climate, 407
Sucre, José de, 206
Sucre, Bolivia, 390, 400
Sugar and sugarcane, 73, 180–181, 184–186, 242, 293, 312, 318, 323, 326, 333, 334–338, 340, 378, 385, 449, 458, 460, 465, 466, 467, 473, 475
Sugar Loaf (mountain), 486
Summer, 58, 61–63
    length of days in, 28
    temperatures, 56
Sun, direct rays of, 58
Superior, Lake, 512, 549
Suriname, 79, 359–361, 363, 391
Surpluses, 109
Sweden, 5, 502
Syria, 479

T

Taiwan, 5
Tannin, 409
Tariffs, 291, 584
Tarija, Bolivia, 385
Tar sands, 555
Tegucigalpa, Honduras, 295
Tehuantepec, Isthmus of, 219
Temperate climate, 61–62
Temperate zones, 61–62, 405

Tenochtitlán, 120, 122–123, 125, 127, 156–158, 163, 197
Terrorists, 269
Texcoco, Lake, 122, 123, 156–158
Thompson, David, 530
Thunder Bay, Canada, 567
Tibes Indian Ceremonial Center, 346
Tierra caliente, 62, 222, 265
Tierra del Fuego, 432, 441
Tierra fria, 62, 222, 265, 293
Tierra templada, 62, 265, 288, 293, 383
Tikal, 127–128, 264
Time, 28–34
  clock, 34
  daylight, 28
  keeping, 30, 32
  lines, 35
  units of, 28
  zones, 32–34
Tin, 376, 390
Titicaca, Lake, 133, 368–369
Tlaxcala, Mexico, 156–158
Tobago, 313–314
Tokyo, Japan, 481
Toluca, Mexico, 239
Tone languages, 331
Tordesillas, Treaty of, 152
Toronto, Ontario, 84, 525, 545, 550, 560, 566, 574
Torre, Raúl Haya de la. *See* Haya de la Torre, Victor Raúl
Torrijos, Omar, 278
Tourism, 73, 240, 333, 341–342
Toussaint L'Ouverture, Pierre Dominque, 193–194
Trade winds, 310
Transamazon Highway, 472
Trancontinental railroad, 533
Transportation, 240, 291, 507, 535, 511. *See also* Railroads; Roads.
Travel. *See* Tourism.
Treason, 162
Tree line, 543
Trinidad, 79, 307, 309, 313–314, 339, 340
Tropic of Cancer, 58, 222
Tropic of Capricorn, 58, 405
Tropics, 60, 62, 63, 108, 363, 406, 452
Trudeau, Pierre, 580, 583
Trujillo, Peru, 377
Trujillo, Rafael, 326
Tucumán, Argentina, 441
Tumbes, Peru 160
Tundra, 53, 56, 57, 543

Tupi language, 115
Tupinamba Indians, 115

U
Ulloa, Antonio de, 176
Union of Soviet Socialist Republics, *see* Soviet Union.
Unitarios, 411
United Fruit Company, 267, 269, 288–289
United National Opposition (UNO), 299
United Nations, 537
United Provinces of Central America, 266
United Provinces of La Plata, 204, 410–412
United States
  area covered by, 81
  Atlantic coast, of, 33, 509
  border between Canada and, 54, 85, 524–525, 549
  border between Mexico and, 219
United States Army Corps of Engineers, 277
United States Marines, 271, 325–326, 327
United States National Forest System, 311
United States of Mexico. *See* Mexico.
Upper Canada, 524, 526–528
Urban areas, 245
Urbanization, 567
Uruguay, 112, 204, 300, 405, 408, 411, 420, 430, 434–435, 436, 440, 443, 444, 453, 476, 479
Uspallata Pass, 205
Utah, 225

V
Vaca, Cabeza de, 163–164
Vaccination, 83
Valdivia, Pedro de, 164
Valparaíso, Chile, 414, 441
Vancouver, British Columbia, 85, 546, 574–575
Vancouver, Captain George, 574
Vancouver, Fort, 531
Vancouver Island, 575
Vaquero, 473
Vargas, Getúlio, 461–462
Vegetation, 22
Vegetation maps, 22
Velázquez, Diego, 154

Venezuela, 466, 550
  cities of, 396, 398–399
  farming in, 362, 386
  independence movement in, 199–201
  land reform in, 387
  mountains and lowland of, 55, 362
  as part of Contadora Group, 300–301
  political problems in, 371–372
  population patterns in, 362, 395–397
  Spanish colonization of, 86
Venice, Italy, 147
Venus, (planet), 129
Vera Cruz, Ilha de, 152
Veracruz, Mexico, 155, 156, 174, 219, 229, 239
Vermont, 72, 333
Vertical exaggeration, 20
Vespucci, Amerigo, 45, 47–48
Veto, 581
Viceroys and viceroyalties, 170–173, 410
Victoria, British Columbia, 532
Victoria, Queen, 527
Vieira, Father António, 187
Vikings, 502
Villa, Pancho, 232–233
Violencia, La, 373, 374
Virginia, 497
Virgin Islands, 309, 313–314, 341
Volcanic islands, 309
Volcanoes, 55, 221–222, 261, 263, 292–293, 294, 309, 367
Volta Redonda, 462

W
Waldseemüller, Martin, 47–48
Walker, William, 271
War of 1812, 524–525
War of the Pacific (1879–1884), 376, 431
War of the Thousand Days (1899–1902), 372
War of the Triple Alliance, 420–421
Washington, George, 194
Water resource management, 553
Weather, 60, 61. *See also* Climate.
Welland Ship Canal, 550
Western Cordillera, 361
Western Hemisphere, 7, 49,

51, 55, 70, 73–74, 417, 427, 434, 475, 498, 554, 558, 565
Western Sierra Madre. *See* Sierra Madra Occidental.
West Indies, 51, 55, 71, 79, 80, 81, 108, 110, 170, 181, 185, 277, 287, 307–327, 336
  British, 180, 313–314, 331, 336, 339, 458
  cities of, 310, 314, 333
  climate of, 310–311
  crops and natural resources of, 180, 186, 290, 312, 334–338, 339–341
  culture of, 68, 71, 331, 361
  earning a living in, 339–342
  Federation of the, 313–314
  French, Dutch, or United States Islands of, 79, 180, 308, 309, 311, 314, 331, 458, 518
  landforms in, 307–309
  kinds of islands in, 307–308
Wheat, 242, 284, 290, 427, 430, 433, 476, 567
Whiskey trade, 534
White, Jon Manchip, 158
Whites, 395–396, 479
Winds, trade, 310
Windsor, Ontario, 560
Windward coast, 310
Windward Islands, 313–314
Winnipeg, Manitoba, 549, 571
Winter, length of days in, 28
Wisconsin, 521
Wolfe, James, 518–521
Women, 326, 422, 461, 499
  in Canada, 505, 507, 531–532
  in Cuba, 319
  in Sandinista army, 274
Wood pulp, 552
World War II, 536
Wyoming, 225

Y
Year, length of, 130
Yerba maté, 427
Yucatán Peninsula, 58–60, 119, 219, 223, 245, 264, 309
Yukon Territory, 534, 546, 565–566
Yungay, Peru, 368

Z
Zapata, Emiliano, 232–233
Zapotec Indians, 228
Zócalo, Mexico City, 248–249

CREDITS